International Law

Classic and Contemporary Readings

edited by

Charlotte Ku & Paul F. Diehl

LYNNE
RIENNER
PUBLISHERS

BOULDER
LONDON

Published in the United States of America in 1998 by
Lynne Rienner Publishers, Inc.
1800 30th Street, Boulder, Colorado 80301

and in the United Kingdom by
Lynne Rienner Publishers, Inc.
3 Henrietta Street, Covent Garden, London WC2E 8LU

Library of Congress Cataloging-in-Publication Data
International law : classic and contemporary readings / edited by
    Charlotte Ku and Paul F. Diehl.
    Includes index.
    ISBN 1-55587-765-6 (pbk. : alk. paper)
    ISBN 1-55587-760-5 (hbk. : alk. paper)
    1. International law. I. Ku, Charlotte, 1950– . II. Diehl,
    Paul F. (Paul Francis)
    KZ1242.I583 1998
    341—dc21   98-5999
                                                                  CIP

British Cataloguing in Publication Data
A Cataloguing in Publication record for this book
is available from the British Library.

Printed and bound in the United States of America

          The paper used in this publication meets the requirements
  ∞   of the American National Standard for Permanence of
          Paper for Printed Library Materials Z39.48-1984.

     5 4 3 2 1

WITHDRAWN

International Law

WITHDRAWN

International Law

Contents

Part 4
The Future of International Law

PART 1

Introduction:
International Law and Politics

1

International Law as Operating and Normative Systems: An Overview

Charlotte Ku and Paul F. Diehl

The end of the Cold War in 1989 heralded the advent of a new international order including a renewed emphasis on and concern with international law. U.S. president George Bush and others identified international relations "governed by the rule of law" as the defining feature of the emerging world order. Yet acts of genocide in Bosnia and Rwanda, together with the failure of the United Nations to meet renewed expectations, have left us with a world in which rules and norms are not always clearly defined nor carefully observed.

In this collection, we consider international law from a fresh perspective, seeking to move beyond esoteric descriptions of the law prevalent in scholarly legal treatments, by examining international law's influence on political behavior, something largely ignored in standard analyses of international relations. There are several unique features of this effort. First, the book is perhaps the only collection that focuses on the politics of international law and does so by covering the main topics of the subject (e.g., sources, participants, courts, dispute settlement, jurisdiction, and sovereignty). Second, the book is contemporary, reflecting the major changes in international relations after the Cold War and covering emerging topics in the subject such as human rights and the environment. Third, this book attempts to draw a bridge between the purely legal and purely political consideration of public international law. Finally, the book offers a new organizational scheme for considering international law, drawing the distinction between elements of international law that function as an operating system for international relations (e.g., courts, jurisdiction, etc.) and those that present a normative system that seeks to direct behavior in the international system (e.g., human rights, environmental prescriptions).

We begin by addressing the most basic of questions: what is international law? We then move to develop our conceptions of international law as a dual system for regulating interactions, both generally and within specific areas.

3

What Is International Law?

The question, "What is international law?" is straightforward enough. It would also seem simple enough to answer. After all, we have a general image of what "law" is, and the word "international" seems self-evident. Yet, when we put the two words together, we find ourselves faced with other questions—questions that stem from our understanding of the two key words. "Law" in Western democracies immediately conjures up images of legislatures, police, and courts that create law, enforce it, and punish those who violate it. "International" brings up images not only of the United Nations, but of wide ranging global differences—economic, cultural, and political. How can these two sets of images come together? How can one imagine a structured and developed legal system functioning in a political environment that is diffuse, disparate, and unregulated—and conventionally described as anarchic?

The basic question of "What is international law?" embodies several other questions that need to be answered in order to understand what we are examining: (1) What does international law do? (2) How does it work? (3) Is it effective in what it does? and ultimately, (4) What can we expect from it?

The first three questions necessarily deal with the diffusion and lack of regulation that exist in a political system consisting of multiple sovereign actors. As the principal possessors of coercive means in international relations, states seem to have their own exclusive recourse to the resolution of disputes. How can states be restrained? What can possibly modify their behavior? Yet, behavior is restrained, and anarchy is not always the dominant mode of international politics. States also do not have a monopoly on international intercourse. International organizations, non-governmental organizations, multinational corporations, and even private individuals have come to play an increasing role in international relations, and accordingly international legal rules have evolved to engage these new actors.

This leads to the last of the four questions. If international law is a factor in state behavior, what can we expect it to do? First and foremost, we expect it to facilitate and support the daily business of international relations and politics. It does so principally by allocating decisionmaking power within the international system, thereby providing an alternative to unregulated competition. The structure and process of international law prevent the pursuit of multiple national or private interests from dissolving into anarchy. They also allow for the coexistence of multiple political units and their interaction. They provide a framework for the international system to *operate* effectively. Second, international law advances particular values—the regulation of the use of force, the protection of individual rights, and the management of the commons are prominent examples of such values. In this area, international law promotes the creation of a *nor-mative* consensus on international behavior.

State behavior over the centuries provides evidence of widespread acceptance of a general operating system within which to conduct international relations. But when changes are sought in the operating system or in the pursuit of particular values, differences sharpen and the politics become more intense. Questions are raised as to whose agenda is being pursued, at what cost to others in the international system, and why. In this, international law does not differ from more hierarchical and structured domestic legal systems. In both international and domestic law, one begins at a point of general agreement that there should be a basic operating system. In a domestic legal system, this is often set out in a constitution that establishes various institutions and details the relative functions and powers of the units within the system. In international law, the players in international politics create and maintain the operating system themselves.

The first section of this book includes two articles that discuss the political component of international law, noting how international law is the product of political decision-making and explicating its place in international relations. Louis Henkin provides a brief survey of the reasons why states choose to use international law (or effectively choose *not* to do so) and the processes under which that law is made. This goes beyond the traditional listing of the different sources of international law to a consideration of how law is part of the international political process.

As with any legal system, politics is the dynamic and catalytic force in international law. Similar to domestic law, international law provides the framework within which competition and interests are pursued. Politics are the expression of this competition. The tension between law and politics seems more acute at the international level because the politics are less regulated by elaborated institutions. John Fried describes this through a series of images of international law, reflecting commonly held criticisms of international law as irrelevant or wholly subordinate to the political process:

The Orphan Theory. International law is so weak and defenseless, so unable to assert itself, that it can be, and is, consistently disregarded, or at best that only dreamers would put any reliance on it.

The Harlot Theory. International law is so vague and inchoate that, with some juggling and legalistic gymnastics it can be made to serve virtually every policy.

The Jailer Theory. The central quality of every legal system is the threat of punishment. As long as no machinery exists to enforce that law, that is, to punish violators, international law lacks the essential characteristic of law.

The Never-Never Theory. Until international law is "universally binding" and "universally enforceable," there can be little reliance on international law "lest others take unfair advantage of your credulity."

Examples from international politics for each of Fried's "theories" are plentiful and he concludes that "all these criticisms combine underestimation with overexpectation." Fried does not so much reject these critiques for a vision of the law that is a polar opposite, but rather puts those critiques in perspective so that the reader has a balanced and more realistic view (somewhere between the rejectionist and optimist positions) about the current state and potential of international law.

The view that law should be kept apart from politics is misguided. Law and politics are different; yet law is a product of politics, and law is used to channel politics. The most frequent criticism of international law is that it expects potential violators to police themselves. For the skeptic, this seems an operational impossibility. This criticism assumes that law is a dichotomy of order *versus* the uncontrolled pursuit of interest. But the creation and maintenance of any legal system requires a significant amount of self-policing by the subjects of that law. Moreover, every legal system is based on limits to the pursuit of individual interests in order to safeguard the opportunity for ongoing competition by others. International law lacks the hierarchy of a domestic legal system that establishes under what circumstances force or some noncoercive means will be used to enforce the law; but it shares with all legal systems a need to redefine constantly which norms are fundamental to effective operation of the system and how they will be upheld. Leo Gross points out that international law's lack of hierarchy was a conscious choice made by the powers that shaped our present international system. They might have chosen to place international law above the sovereign states, but opted instead for a legal system which operated "*between* rather than above states [emphasis added]." That choice remains largely in place today.

The Dual Character of International Law

International law provides both an operating system and a normative system for international relations. Conceptualizing international law as an operating system considers, in a broad sense, how it sets the general procedures and institutions for the conduct of international relations. As an operating system, international law provides the framework for establishing rules and norms, outlines the parameters of interaction, and provides the procedures and forums for resolving disputes among those taking part in these interactions. In contrast, international law as a normative system provides direction for international relations by identifying the substantive values and goals to be pursued. If the operating system designates the "structures" (in a loose sense) that help channel international politics, then the normative element gives form to the aspirations and values of the participants of the system. As a normative system, law is a product of the structures and processes that make up the operating system. The operating system is based on state consensus as expressed through widespread practice over time; the normative system must build a base of support for each of its undertakings. As an operating system, international law functions much as a constitution does in a domestic legal system by setting out the consensus of its constituent actors (states) on distribution of authority, responsibilities in governing, and the units that will carry out specific functions. As a normative system, international law takes on a principally legislative character, by mandating particular values and directing specific changes in state behavior.

International Law as Operating System

International law as an operating system fulfils its constituent function—to support the business of state relations—in several ways.

1. It serves as a *means for communication* by providing a widely understood language through which a single unit or group of units can make known what is expected of its (their) fellow units in the international arena. It can also make known potential penalties for not fulfilling those expectations. Vehicles for communication include the exchange of diplomats, membership in intergovernmental organizations, and the negotiation and acceptance of treaty obligations, which set out terms and ranges of behavior in specific areas.

2. It serves as a *gatekeeper* to ensure that changes and pressures do not impede the basic functioning of the operating system. It does so by "testing" aspiring state and non-state participants as to their ability to function within the overall system. It also assesses the implications of according legal status to entities that might challenge the authority of the state (the major unit in the international system), for example, transnational corporations or groups. To the extent that these tests do not permanently impede the will and direction of the system's constituent elements, these measures allow for incremental changes to the operating system. In this way, international law provides a flexible and dynamic, but settled, operating system.

Because international law lacks the institutional trappings and hierarchical character of domestic law, its organizing principles and how they work are important to identify. These are the elements of the operating system. First, one must know where to find international law. Because the international legal system has no single legislative body, it can be difficult to know where to start. One begins with state behavior, and examines the sources of international law to interpret state behavior and to identify when such behavior takes on an obligatory character. The sources of international law further provide guidance on how to find the substance of international law by highlighting key moments in the law-making process. Sources help us to locate the products of the law-making process by identifying its form. For example, international agreements are generally to be found in written texts. Law created by custom, however, will require locating patterns of state behavior over time and assessing whether this behavior is compelled by any sense of legal obligation. *Ext or custom*

John Gamble adds a dynamic dimension to the topic of sources by examining the interplay among the sources, particularly between the two most widely recognized sources of international law—treaty and custom. Treaty-based practice may become customary law if, for example, the treaty is not in force or important parties fail to accept the treaty formally. Prior to its entry into force in 1994, the Third United Nations Law of the Sea Convention was of this character. In contrast, practices that are accepted as customary law may become codified in treaty form. The Vienna Convention on Diplomatic and Consular Immunities is such an example.

At the same time, to understand fully how international law can affect the behavior of states, it is essential to understand why states sometimes choose not to depend on what has become the most prominent source of international law in the last thirty years: treaties. Charles Lipson traces the political and other reasons why many international agreements are never formalized, but why states still bind themselves to perform a series of actions in a legal or quasi-legal fashion. Lipson concludes that despite the shortfalls of informal agreements, they can be important in fostering international cooperation and modifying state behavior by making available specially designed modes of achieving a common objective by the relevant (and interested) parties.

A second element of the international law operating system is the participants in the process who create the law and are the subjects of its precepts. This is central because international law is a system that relies on self-regulation by the system's units. The number of participants will affect the character of the political process of law creation by determining the number of interests that need to be taken into account, the available resources, and modes of implementation. The substance of international law will reflect the interests and capacities of the participants in the international system. How, where, and with what effect the law is implemented depend on the economic, political, and other circumstances of those participants.

It is in the steady increase in both the number and type of participants in the international legal process that we see some of the most tangible changes in international law. This increase is a critical change because who is included and who is allowed a voice in the process affects both how the law operates and determines the content of the law. This is amply demonstrated in the intricate political and doctrinal interplay described in the chapters on making the law that today serves as the basis for international protection of the environment, management of the commons, and regulation of economic activity.

The increase in participants began with the end of the Thirty Years War in 1648 and the acceptance of participation by Protestant princes within the same system as Catholic princes in Europe. The next increase resulted from the dissolution of the European empires, which brought non-European states into the legal process. Most recently, the move has been to bring individuals and non-governmental organizations, including multinational corporations, into the process. Each addition of participants increases the complexity of the law-making process. At the same time, many of the issues in international law today require multiple layers of cooperative and coordinated activity crossing public and private sectors for effective regulation and implementation. Complexity, therefore, cannot be avoided, and indeed, may now be required for the effective operation of international law.

Despite this trend toward adding new participants, states remain key to the creation and operation of international law. But how do states become part of the international legal process and under what terms? Oscar Schachter describes the interaction between law and politics as reflected in the practice on state succession, which determines each new state's initial legal obligations. This is an especially important concern in the post–Cold War era with the breakup of states in Eastern Europe and other possible changes on the horizon on various continents. Schachter reviews past practice on state succession and reflects on the emerging law in this area; this will become critical as the need increases to sort out the status of various obligations as states continue to implode or separate.

If the addition of states and governments to the system is not a routine matter, the difficulty of adding a different category of participant should be apparent. This is particularly so in the area of individuals, when according them legal status might result in individuals challenging the authority of states. This is also the heart of the issue in Patrick Thornberry's analysis of the rights that groups (especially ethnic groups) might have under international law, including whether special rights to form their own state exist or whether special international protections might be accorded their treatment by the dominant group within states. The developing rights of groups are one of the most sensitive areas for international law as it tries to reconcile potentially inconsistent values. The inconsistency stems from most states' dilemma in balancing the goal of national unity with a tolerance of ethnic heterogeneity. Yet how to recognize the existence of various groups within a common set of borders without compromising the ability of the state to govern its population is emerging as one of the sharpest problems of the post–Cold War world.

As the network of international economic activity expands, transnational enterprises are growing in importance as international participants. As Donna Arzt and Igor Lukashuk note, many of these enterprises are more powerful than all but the largest states, yet they mostly lack their own international legal personality. And this is unlikely to change as long as substantial portions of the international community oppose such a status. There has been a major shift, however, in the twentieth century with individuals in more active rather than passive interactions with international law. And, it appears that this trend is only beginning.

A third element of the international law operating system is the process under which law is implemented and actors comply (or fail to do so) with international law. Although the number of international agreements has increased and the requirements are more elaborated, surprisingly little is known about what induces compliance with international obligations. Harold Jacobson and Edith Brown Weiss note that "international accords are only as effective as the respective parties make them." In their study examining compliance with international environmental accords, Jacobson and Weiss identify four sets of factors relevant to assessing compliance with and implementation of international accords. Preliminary findings of this systematic study of compliance with five environmental treaties "underscore[d] the importance of the underlying strength and health of national political-economic systems for efforts to protect the global environment." This points to the reliance of the international legal system on domestic political and legal processes and institutions to carry out international obligations.

Another aspect of creating an effective international law operating system is determining how remedies for wrongful acts or grievances will work. This requires an understanding of what the wrongful act or grievance is, who the aggrieved party is, who might be responsible for the act, and the applicable law for the situation. The applicable law will then determine the relevant forum or procedure for examining the grievance and identify available remedies. D. W. Bowett provides a comprehensive review of the bases of jurisdiction and the operational consequences of each, including the complicated interplay of conflicting or concurring jurisdictions. Although the discussion of how jurisdiction is established may appear arcane, the exercise has a very practical objective—to provide the basis for a legal solution to a problem.

Responding to the impression that one of international law's weaknesses as a legal system is its lack of institutions, much effort has been put toward setting up such institutions. The expectation was that the availability of international legal institutions, particularly judicial institutions, would foster greater use of international law as an alternative to the use of force for settling disputes. Thus, a final element of the international law operating system is its formal legal structures. One of the most significant developments in international legal institution building is the establishment of an International Court of Justice—a permanent tribunal with judges elected to serve in their individual capacities to settle disputes between states. Nevertheless, the nearly 80 years of the operation of the Permanent Court of International Justice and its successor the International Court of Justice demonstrate that the existence of a standing court has neither replaced the use of force nor other non-judicial methods to resolve international disputes. Richard Bilder observes that there are many ways to organize an effective legal system and that many disputes are settled in ways other than by court decisions. From the standpoint of international law, the settlement of disputes is the major objective. Whether this is better achieved through the use of a standing court or an array of methods is a different issue. Bilder offers an overview of international adjudication and, more specifically, assesses the advantages and disadvantages of adjudication from the perspective of states. His analysis helps us to understand when and under what conditions states may seek to have their disputes heard before the International Court of Justice; special attention is given to U.S. reluctance to accept the compulsory jurisdiction of that court.

A key element of the General Agreement on Tariffs and Trade treaty (GATT) concluded in April 1994 was the establishment of a World Trade Organization (WTO) that has legal authority to monitor and adjudicate trade disputes between states. Steven Croley and John Jackson provide a review of those procedures and analyze the role of the WTO vis-à-vis the responsibilities left to national governments. The story of the institutionalization of WTO dispute settlement shows the great care that international procedures and organizations have to take in order to gain acceptance and to earn credibility in the international system.

The need for variety in international legal structures is further highlighted by Christopher Blakesley, who points to some of the practical obstacles faced by those seeking to create a permanent war crimes tribunal. In light of the genocide in Bosnia and Rwanda, ad hoc war crimes tribunals under United Nations auspices have been created, and various proposals to insure the ongoing protection of lives include a permanent judicial structure for international accountability of war criminals. Blakesley identifies the impediments to overcome before such proposals can become a reality. The problems are varied and include the lack of resources and authority available to such tribunals to pursue criminals wherever and whenever crimes occur. The complexities involved in the selection of a credible prosecutor and the ways in which evidence is collected and presented are daunting, yet the symbolic value of holding individuals accountable for atrocities committed has been a compelling reason to continue the effort to establish such tribunals.

The materials presented in this section demonstrate that while key elements of the operating system are settled, they do not remain static. Pressures for change are ongoing and will succeed when changes are required to keep the operating system appropriate and effective in supporting contemporary international politics. The elements of the operating system must continuously pass a test of functionality—if they fail to perform, the elements will be replaced by others that serve the broad and general interest of allocating power and of ensuring reasonable order in the conduct of international relations. Competing demands and interests among the operating elements help to identify areas in which adjustments are needed so that when the political circumstances dictate change, international law is ready to respond.

International Law as a Normative System

The second and less settled role of international law is as a normative system. Prominent activity under this facet of international law has been in the regulation of the use of force, the protection of human rights, the protection of the environment, the management of the commons, and the regulation of economic activity. In shaping these specific bodies of law, the participants in the international legal process engage in a political and legislative exercise that defines the substance and scope of the law and creates the institutions and mechanisms necessary for its implementation. Throughout the exercise, there can be disagreements about specific issues, their scope, the approach to them, and the relative responsibilities among parties. These debates are ongoing in any major domestic legislative action, as they are in international law, and the complexity and intensity of legislative politics is present in both cases. Yet legislating with over 180 states from a variety of cultural traditions, historical backgrounds, and economic circumstances means that the international legislative process will be slower and more difficult.

In each of the five normative areas we have selected, the political bases of international law can be seen as states struggle to ensure the goals of peace, justice, and prosperity while not fully negating the rights accorded to them under national sovereignty. We find that many of these areas require the balancing or reconciling of inconsistencies as international law searches for generally applicable standards against a background of economic disparity and historic exploitation that stemmed from political and technological weakness.

The oldest segment of the international normative system concerns the use of force. Paradoxically, it is at the same time the most developed, but also the least restrictive on state behavior. Oscar Schachter's discussion of self-defense captures this inconsistency as the unilateral use of violence has been outlawed by the United Nations Charter while militarized defense—including unilateral defense—against such use of violence is allowed. At the same time, Schachter points out the considerable incentives to induce states to comply with the restraints placed on the use of force. Although these incentives have not eliminated force, they have conditioned its use through the undertaking of specific obligations and through the creation of procedures and institutions to assess its use. Anthony Arend and Robert Beck provide a historical perspective and analyze whether the legal "paradigm" has shifted from one based on self-help to a more restrictive principle.

The piercing of the shell of state sovereignty is perhaps most dramatic in the area of human rights, where states no longer have full reign over actions within their borders. Philip Alston provides a review of the work of the United Nations in the development and implementation of human rights standards. It is worth noting that the United Nations is an institution created by states, and is yet largely responsible for the body of human rights law in existence today. Another example of the changing character of state sovereignty today is in the argument put forward by Thomas Weiss and Jarat Chopra for an emerging right of humanitarian intervention. This further limits the notion of state sovereignty in favor of a system that would permit greater use of military force, but for humanitarian ends. Although international law seems to have moved away from pursuing the overall elimination of the use of force as a goal, it struggles with the issue of when to use force, and above all, by whom.

Environmental protection is relatively new on the international legal agenda. Yet over the past two decades, states have increasingly regulated their own behavior by signing agreements establishing strict environmental standards and controls. The Rio summit of 1992 is only a recent example of how prominent the environmental issue has become in international relations. Alexandre Kiss reviews the stages of development in efforts to protect the environment through law. Catherine Tinker adds a post-Rio note to Kiss's overview in the area of protection of biological diversity. The environmental area challenges international law to address changing situations that render regulation through specific legal standards and obligations difficult. This has moved law-making into creating frameworks for cooperation and coordination in addition to creating specific legal obligations.

Closely related to international environmental efforts are normative constraints to preserve the benefits and riches of the global commons for all. Global commons are defined as areas or resources that are the collective property of mankind and not under the sovereignty of any one state (e.g., portions of the oceans and outer space). The most developed effort to protect the global commons has been with respect to the law of the sea. Christopher Joyner and Elizabeth Martell look at the Third United Nations

Law of the Sea Conference (UNCLOS III) for insights on not only how the law of the sea has developed, but also to derive lessons for international law as it turns to other parts of the global commons. In particular, Martell and Joyner examine the differences between the viewpoints of the North and the South and the implications of a belief that the present global economic order is so discriminatory and so flawed that there is no way to redress this issue other than to challenge it directly. We will encounter this view again in the economic sphere in the context of the New International Economic Order. The difficulty of closing this gap is demonstrated in the story of the negotiation and bringing into force of a comprehensive law of the sea. Given the long negotiation phase (9 years) and the subsequent long hiatus between signature and entry into force (12 years, and then only after adoption of a special modification to include U.S. concerns), the experience of UNCLOS III raises questions about the effectiveness of the package-deal approach as a legislative device. Katherine Gorove and Elena Kamenetskaya review the critical legal issues that arise in setting rules for the exploitation of a more distant part of the commons: outer space. With the development of space stations and the proliferation of private satellite operations, this area of international law is expected to increase in prominence in the coming decades.

The final normative topic we take up is that of the international regulation of economic activity. John Jackson, who helped to define much of the field, gives a brief overview of what international economic law is. In contrast to environmental law, we find in this area a move from less formal to more institutionalized and formal arrangements. Using law effectively and purposively to address economic phenomena and behavior is at the crux of this topic. Burns Weston's article discusses the regulation of foreign investment, expropriation, compensation, and related issues that have been at the centerpiece of the North-South debate in international organizations and other diplomatic forums. Whereas the law of the sea highlighted the notion of *res communis,* in which there is common ownership and common stewardship, the law dealing with investment and natural resources highlights the use of *res nullius,* in which if a resource is not being used, anyone who is able to use it can claim it. The issue at the center of the New International Economic Order (NIEO) is how states can reclaim the resources that they were not able to exploit and on what basis they can do so. Weston focuses specifically on the Third World sponsored charter calling for a New International Economic Order and closely examines the implications and viability of the position whereby states declare their permanent sovereignty "over all its wealth, natural resources and economic activities." Until global wealth is more evenly distributed than at present, these issues will remain part of the international legal and political agenda.

We conclude the book with a look into the future by Louis Henkin, who sees law-making shifting from a focus on state values to a focus on human values. Henkin predicts that state values—those that safeguard the independence and freedom of states as political units in the international system—will be maintained and will remain powerful. Nevertheless, he also sees growing attention to human values and that "the right of a state 'to be left alone' subsumes the rights of its inhabitants to be let alone." He further notes that the ability of states to maintain their state values of independence and freedom may well depend on their ability to meet the emerging needs of human values—in the protection of the environment, economic prosperity, and security from violence.

Henkin's vision accepts a shift to the normative as the point of focus for international law replacing its historic concentration on elements of the operating system. Although a shift, perhaps this vision also signals a maturing of the international legal system whereby enduring and emerging issues that may not have ready legal solutions can be addressed without fear of threatening the viability of the basic operating system. Of course, it can also be argued that the legal system has little choice but to address the issues of force, the commons, the environment, and economic relations because these are the activities and concerns of contemporary international life. If international law cannot find ways of addressing the questions raised and challenges posed by these existing conditions, then it will fall into disuse. We can therefore expect that more time and resources in the future will be devoted to the pursuit of elements of the normative system.

To address these effectively will require adjustments to the operating system. Like much else in contemporary life, international law will be expected to make more complicated adjustments more rapidly and more frequently than at any other period of its development. This makes the study of this subject at the dawn of the twenty-first century a richly rewarding exercise. It makes the practice of international law a daunting but richly creative exercise as new legal ground is broken to address changing circumstances. It further affirms the symbiotic relationship between the operating system and the normative system in which the capacity to sustain the operating system will increasingly depend on how well the international community can address its normative concerns.

2

The Politics of Law-Making

Louis Henkin

Why Nations Make Law

Much international law was there "from the beginning." From "natural law," from widespread influences of Roman and Canon law, from laws common to all "civilized" countries and legal systems reaching back before history, early relations between communities reflected notions of property, contract, and tort that are basic to international as to domestic law. Even notions of territorial and ethnic identity, and an individual's links to a territory or a "people," long antedated the modern nation-state and the concepts of territorial sovereignty and nationality in modern international law. The use of "ambassadors" and the practice of granting them extraordinary respect also have ancient roots and came nearly full-blown into modern international law.

Some principles of customary international law are centuries old, among them the principle that international agreements shall be observed. On entering international society, new nations find these obligations (and corresponding rights) upon them, and few purport to reject them or even to seek jurisprudential answers as to why they are subject to them. Especially at times of great flux, like those that have followed the Second World War and the proliferation of states resulting from the end of colonialism, new nations (and some old ones) may find a common interest to challenge a particular norm or standard, e.g., the obligation to compensate for nationalized alien properties. But there has not been a major challenge to the system of international law as a whole, to the bulk of its content, to its major norms. Nations old and new also accept or help to develop new law and enter into new international agreements.

Every nation derives some benefits from international law and international agreements. Law keeps international society running, contributes to order and stability, provides a basis and a framework for common enterprise and mutual intercourse. Because it limits the actions of other governments, law enhances each nation's independence and security; in other ways, too, by general law or particular agreement, one nation gets others to behave as it desires. General law establishes common standards where they seem desirable. Both general law and particular agreement avoid the need for negotiating anew in every new instance; both create justified expectation and warrant confidence as to how others will behave.

All these advantages of law and agreement have their price. Law limits freedom of action: nations are "bound" to do (or not to do) other than they might like when the time to act comes. Political arrangements legitimized by law are more difficult to undo or modify. Stability and order mean that a particular nation is not free to be disorderly or readily to promote external change. To promote its own independence and security and the inviolability of its territory, to control the behavior of other governments, a nation may have to accept corresponding limitations on its own behavior. For the confidence bred by law, one pays the price of not being free to frustrate the expectations of others.

More or less consciously, more or less willingly, all governments give up some autonomy and freedom and accept international law in principle as the price of "membership" in international society and of having relations with other nations. For that reason, too, they accept basic traditional international law, undertaking to do (or not to do) unto others what they would have done (or not done) unto them. Since much of its foreign policy is reflected in international agreements, bilateral or multilateral, every nation accepts the legal principle that agreements shall be observed. For the rest, whether a nation desires more law or less and whether it will desire some new law or agreement are also questions of foreign policy, and nations accept or refuse new law—universal, multilateral, or bilateral—in terms of their national interest, as they see it. Nations may have "attitudes" in regard to the desirability of extending the domain of law. At different times they see greater or less interest in self-limitation and cooperation than in the freedom of "no law" and the flexibility of negotiation and improvisation. Nations differ in regard to how much "freedom" they are prepared to sacrifice for some common enterprise or to some supranational institution. They differ too as to how much confidence they have in law as a means to achieve peace, security, order, justice, welfare. The amount and kind of law which international society will achieve will depend, of course, on the degree of homogeneity of the political system and the degree of common or reciprocal interest.

Periodically—particularly after major disorder, like a world war—nations dedicate themselves anew to increased order, make an extraordinary sacrifice of their freedom, and accept law in the common interest (e.g., the United Nations Charter). At any time a nation's foreign policy may include a desire for some particular law: a revised definition of the coastal states' jurisdiction out to sea, a treaty against proliferation of nuclear weapons, a prohibition against racial discrimination, or a new regime for international trade. While willingness to accept a law or agreement will depend on what it provides, powerful nations often see less interest in curtailing their own freedom. Even the rich and the mighty, however, cannot commonly obtain what they want by force or dictation and must be prepared to pay the price of reciprocal or compensating obligation. Even they, moreover, seek legitimacy and acceptance for their policies, desire order and dependability in their relations and the conservative influence of law. Sometimes, even, they seek protection in the law from the will of majorities and the "tyranny of the weak." And they may agree to limit themselves in order to achieve corresponding limitations on competing powerful nations, as, for example, in the Nuclear Test-Ban Treaty of 1963, or the later Strategic Arms Limitations Talks (SALT).

Other nations, too, see advantage in law. They adhere to old law as a mark of their acceptance in international society; or because they approve of its objectives; or because they desire its advantages; or because they would assert their adherence to laudable principles. In new law they may seek codification or clarification to eliminate uncertainties. Governments feel freer, of course, to accept law which may in fact not hinder them seriously, in order to see such law accepted by others (e.g., the non-proliferation treaty, for states that can have little hope of becoming nuclear powers), perhaps also to satisfy world or domestic opinion (e.g., international human rights covenants).

A foreign-policy decision whether to accept new law involves considerations very different from those which determine whether a nation will observe existing law. Refusal to accept new law does not usually bring "sanctions" or other undesirable consequences.[1] Nations which are reluctant to undertake new obligations may be scrupulous about honoring those which they accepted. In fact, a nation particularly concerned to observe law may be more hesitant about accepting new law in the first instance. Occasionally, however, a government will agree to a law with little intention of observing it, in order to gain some kudos and perhaps the advantage of observance by others, especially if it believes that its violations night not be detected. Hitler accepted the Munich Pact, probably without intention to observe it, perhaps to lull the Allies into a false sense of security; the United States has feared that the Soviet Union might enter into disarmament agreements it had no intention to keep, unless its compliance could be verified. Some believe that a number of states have adhered to international covenants on human rights because it is "the thing to do," because there are pressures to do so, without seriously expecting to honor them fully. But these are exceptional cases in exceptional situations for exceptional kinds of international law. Generally, nations seek law they wish others to observe and are prepared to observe it themselves.

How Law Is Made

The character, shape, and content of international law—as of national law—are determined by prevailing political forces within the political system,[2] as refracted through the way law is made.

The core of traditional international law and its principal assumptions and foundations have been unwritten "customary law," made over time by widespread practice of governments acting from a sense of legal obligation. Increasingly, however, customary law is being codified and modified and new universal and regional law is also made by formal international agreement negotiated at international conferences. In some measure, law is made also by resolutions or declarations of international organizations, notably the U.N. General Assembly, and some, too, by the actions of such organizations interpreting existing law.

International law has been built on the "principle of unanimity": no state is bound by any proposed norm or regulation without its consent, though consent once given is binding and cannot be withdrawn at will. The principle of unanimity has been justified on the ground of the sovereign equality of states.[3] But the equality of states in constitutional theory does not imply that all states are equal in their influence in the making of law. While the law that emerges, moreover, may apply equally to all, it will often not be even-handed in fact: a norm requiring "justice" for aliens and their property, for example, applies equally everywhere; but, obviously, it has favored states that export people and capital, and has been an obstacle to governments seeking to divest foreign holdings as a basis for social revolution.

Emerging law will depend on the interest of influential states to espouse it, a common interest in developing it, and the inability, or lack of interest, of others to resist it. Political influence in law-making, however, does not lie exclusively, or even primarily, where it is commonly assumed to be—that is, with militarily or economically powerful states. Even when war and threats of force were not unlawful, military power did not necessarily determine the law, for force could not be used or threatened lightly or frequently for less-than-compelling purposes.[4] Economic pressure or persuasion, too, was not always available and effective to obtain the consent of a resisting state. In our day, "power" (i.e., influence, both in law-making and elsewhere in international relations) belongs also to small developing states, joined in blocs, adroit at exploiting the competition of the powerful, and armed with ideas claiming their time has come.

Because the process of making customary law is informal, haphazard, not deliberate, even partly unintentional and fortuitous, the resulting law may also suffer these qualities. While influence in the formation of customary law is of the same stuff as elsewhere, here it is not readily focused. Some principle, norm, or standard may result from the fortuitous initiative of a statesman, the coincidence of need and opportunity, and acquiescence or lack of care by others. Consent or acquiescence can be "bought," or compelled by political pressure from other states, or by the press of circumstances; it may go on in one corner while others are unaware, unconcerned, or not mobilized to act.

The process being unstructured and slow, there is opportunity for modifying the law and adjusting to it. Over centuries, of course, customary norms have responded to changed circumstances and interests and new configurations of influence. Whether in the same or in a modified form, moreover, norms that are originally imposed or one-sided, may become widely acceptable. For example, one can surmise that some particular powerful prince early asserted sovereign or diplomatic immunity, and his lawyers provided conceptual underpinning for it. But the example and precedent thus provided doubtless prompted similar claims even by the less-powerful. In time the norms of immunity found appeal with officials of all governments as being important to effective and smooth international relations. Similarly, that freedom of the sea for navigation became the governing principle reflected the prevailing balance of naval power and the inability of any one nation to assert and maintain hegemony over the large seas against all others during the years when the law was being formed. In fact, freedom of the seas proved generally acceptable in time of peace as the basis of intercourse, and of competition in discovery and commerce. The growth of an exception to freedom of the seas in a narrow band of "territorial sea" reflected a common concern of coastal states for their security against military enemies, marauders, or smugglers. Powerful maritime states, while chafing at such limitations on their freedom, did not challenge the authority even of weaker coastal states, or were unwilling to bear the cost of challenging it by force. In time the maritime states, themselves also coastal states and concerned to protect their coasts, came to appreciate the "territorial sea" and were generally content with the "trade-off."

The politics of law-making is less disorderly and more comprehensible when general law is made by formal multilateral agreement,[5] the dominant method of law-making in our time. Negotiated at a particular time, with virtually all states participating, any emerging treaty will reflect what the participants perceived as their interests as regards the matter at issue, in the context of the system at large. But with ever more governments participating, with their interests often varied and complex, the process is confused and the result often not only impossible to predict but even difficult to explain when it appears. It may help to perceive both process and result with mathematical analogy or metaphor: when vectors of different magnitude and direction are brought to bear at one point, a vector of particular force and direction results. To be sure, political influence cannot be measured, and neither its magnitude nor direction is firm; both respond to other forces, to the bargaining situation, to conference procedures, strategy, personalities, to other issues in negotiation, to political interests and forces beyond the conference and the subject. In the large, however, the law that comes out of a conference can be seen as the result of the various directions in which different participants pulled and the magnitude of the influence they were able to bring to bear in support of their preferences.

The emphasis on international law-making as a process of interaction among national policies of particular influence, as well as the metaphor that sees them as forces producing a resultant vector, both risk giving the impression that every nation's policy on law-making is monolithic, firm, and straightforward. The process of developing national policy itself, in fact, often brings to bear a complex of forces with the resultant policy also inviting the vector metaphor.

A government's policy as to whether some activity of international interest should remain unregulated, or what form regulation should take, is a political decision like others made by policy-makers in the light of national interest as they see it. But national interest is not a single or simp!e thing; and often various national interests are implicated, and policy-makers must attempt to balance, compromise, or choose among them.

The process of deciding, and the difficulty of decision, will be different for different governments on different issues. For the United States, for example, a single issue may involve competing political, military, economic, and other public interests, as well as the interests of particular citizens or national companies. The process of developing policy will often reflect the size and complexity of the executive branch; the constitutional dependence of the executive on the Senate for consent to treaties, and on Congress as a whole for implementing them; the influence of private interests and public opinion on the executive branch and on Congress; and, inevitably, the bureaucratic and personal interests of a host of individual participants. Smaller, oligarchic governments can decide more simply, but they too will often suffer internal differences, as well as the difficulty of deciding what their national interest requires, and which of competing national interests they should prefer or how these should be accommodated.

Failures to Make Law

An international political system of sovereign states is inherently "laissez-faire," resisting regulation by law. Surely, norms curtailing national autonomy in any important respect are not likely to be adopted unless the need for them is commonly seen as compelling and the result promises compensating advantage. Often, the absence of control by international law is purposeful, and many would say desirable: for states, too, there is an area of "privacy," i.e., autonomy, that's not the law's business. Even law commonly seen as desirable, however, is prevented or delayed by the diffuse law-making process.

No doubt, law-making in the international system is seriously hampered by "the principle of unanimity," which prevents a majority from making law binding on dissenters. Efforts to circumvent that principle, particularly in international organizations which use majority vote for other purposes, occasionally have small successes, as majorities devise means to make law in other guises while pretending not to. But surely in a world of unequal and diverse states, law-making by majority vote will not be accepted by the big and the powerful, and indeed is usually resisted even by the small and the weak. Law-making will have to be by agreed compromise or by various forms of consensus, or will be limited to those who can agree:[6] nothing prevents the like-minded from making law for themselves when less-than-universal agreements serve some purpose.

Notes

1. There are exceptions in special cases: the founding nations were determined that all nations had to abide by the law of the United Nations Charter outlawing the use of force [Article 2(6)1]; the foreign relations of France have suffered because it failed to honor the limitations of the nuclear test ban of 1963; there would be sharp reaction if wealthy nations refuse to contribute to development and other assistance programs; the Federal Republic of Germany would not dream of abstaining from the Genocide Convention.

2. The scope and the content of international law are commonly credited to (or blamed upon) lawyers. That is an error. For international as for national law, law-making is a political act, the work of politicians; lawyers, *qua lawyers,* contribute to that process only peripherally and interstitially—when they advise and provide technical assistance to policy-makers engaged in law-making, when they interpret and apply the law, in advising political actors, or in handling claims between their government and others.

International judges get few opportunities to make law by adjudication, and on those infrequent occasions they tend to be restrained. Even national judges with "activist" traditions (e.g., those of the United States) are restrained in developing international law by its international character and by deference to the political branches of their government. Compare *Banco Nacional de Cuba v. Sabbatino,* 376 U.S. 398 (1964).

"Publicists" made important contributions to customary international law in past centuries and are still recognized as a "subsidiary means for the determination of rules of law." Statute of the Inrernational Court of Justice, Article 38(1)d. Their influence in law-making has decreased, especially as new law is increasingly made and customary law is being codified and developed by treaty, but they contribute indirectly through the codification and development activities of the International Law Commission and other bodies.

3. In domestic societies, even where the principle of the equality of individuals was accepted, it did not lead to the principle of unanimity, but to equal vote and majority rule—perhaps from the ancient lineage of majority vote, perhaps because the individual did not acquire the aura and trappings of "sovereignry," perhaps from the practical difficulty of governing growing numbers by unanimity, or of allowing dissenters not to participate.

Unanimity does not imply veto, the ability to prevent others from taking a decision. The consenting states can make law for themselves, but it is not binding on the dissenters.

4. Traditional international law did not question a state's consent on the ground that it was coerced, and for special reasons international law accepted even the wholly fictitious consent of a state to a peace treaty imposed on it upon defeat in war and unconditional surrender.

5. A treaty between two states also makes law, for the parties, and will be the result of what each desires from the other, and their comparative bargaining power; it will not be impervious to other interests of the parties, or to their relations with other nations. A traditional treaty of friendship, commerce and navigation may be reciprocal in form, granting each other the same privileges; in fact, of course, a provision, say, in a treaty between the United States and a small undeveloped country that guarantees the investment of each against expropriation by the other is only speciously reciprocal. But even a powerful state cannot impose its will, at will, in peaceful negotiation: it cannot take all and give little; it cannot lightly discriminate in its relations with different states; it cannot disregard standards that prevail between other states.

6. The international system, of course, is not alone in failing to achieve desirable results. Even the most enlightened society, surely democratic societies, suffer the difficulties of law-making due to conflicting interests, disagreements about the desirability of regulation by law, or about what law is desirable, failures of will, perception and understanding, or inadequate legislative process. Indeed, even the most totalitarian of societies, governed effectively by a single powerful legislator, is often hampered in law-making by competing values and inrerests, by the need to accommodate conflicting "constituencies," and by external pressures.

3

International Law—
Neither Orphan Nor Harlot,
Neither Jailer Nor Never-Never Land

John H. E. Fried

When we ask "how efficient is international law?" we ask, in essence, how efficient are the rules and tools of international statecraft? By "tools" are meant, first, the *concepts* and *constructs* which are the brick and mortar of the edifice of international law—"independent state," "recognition," "treaty," "reprisal," etc.; but "tools" also include, as part and parcel of that edifice, the *institutions* of the world community—international and regional organizations, agencies, courts, peace-keeping forces, etc. Like every legal system, international law is in constant flux; and its adequacy, merits and defects, like those of every legal system, depend in large measure on the foresight and imaginativeness that go into the creation, adaptation and perfection of the rules and institutions on all levels, and especially on the constitutional or organic level.[1]

Evidently, there is a close interplay between "rules" and "tools." The law creates, or consists of, both, as the case may be. The legislature passes a rent control act, which establishes a rent control commission endowed with certain legal prerogatives; and the U.N. Charter creates a Trusteeship system, pursuant to which Visiting Missions are endowed with certain prerogatives.

Just as the term "domestic legal system" describes the sum total of substantive and procedural norms-constitution, statute books, etc.—as well as the institutions, from the cabinet to the regulatory commissions, the bureaucracy, the judiciary, the tax collector, and so on—so does the term "international law" describe the whole panorama of its norms and institutions. In view of their sheer number and, above all, ever-increasing concrete role and significance, the question which, oddly enough, is still sometimes posed, namely, whether there is such a thing as international law, can be dismissed from the outset.

It must be added that the growth of international law and institutions has resulted in increased intertwining of international and national law and institutions. When Maitland spoke of the evolution from "status to contract," we can speak of the evolution from (relatively few) ad hoc conferences and treaties to permanent organization and, in many cases, to international operation.

It is not unnecessary to point at the sequence, or cause-and-effect relation. It is because of the growth in the number and significance of international matters that we witness the growth of international organizations and arrangements. The objective realities require states to set up, or to widen the functions of international organizations and arrangements, for sheer self-interest.[2] It is not the other way around; namely, that the growth of those institutions and arrangements increasingly "infringes" upon the individual state. If this were more generally appreciated, especially by the man in the street, much misunderstanding and bewilderment would be avoided. For example, matters of importance to individual states are frequently discussed at and influenced by the United Nations. Just as, at a certain stage of development, matters formerly determined on the village or county level have to be decided on a provincial or nation-wide level, so must, for example, the United Nations be considered not as "intruder" or "outsider" but as an organ or instrumentality of the individual member states where issues transcending local significance are dealt with.[3]

Criticism of International Law

If the above diagnosis is correct, it follows inescapably that the proper functioning and further development of international law is of gravest concern for the well-being and possibly the survival of mankind.[4]

It is therefore disquieting to note how much is being said about the weaknesses and imperfections of international law. Even among high-level decision-makers, the attitude toward international law covers the entire spectrum from disregard, to allegations about the miracles it could perform at some undisclosed future time or under imaginary conditions.

Exaggerating somewhat for bolder emphasis, we can say that most criticisms of international law fall under one of the following four categories; or constitute some combinations of them:

1) International law is so weak and defenseless, so unable to assert itself that it can be, and is, constantly disregarded, or at best that only dreamers would put any reliance on it. This can be called the "orphan" theory of international law.

2) International law is so vague and inchoate that, with some juggling and legalistic gymnastics it can be made to serve virtually every policy. It is

full of loopholes; it can be bent to serve and *
power politics. This can be called the "harlo'
   3) International law, on the contrar'
body of norms which, indeed, are or sh'
is the absence, or virtual absence, of a rel..
ment machinery. The central quality of every
punishment. As long as no machinery exists to en..
punish violators, and as long as that machinery is n..
independent from even the strongest potential violator, h..
(such critics may even say, so-called international law) lacks ..
characteristic of law. This can be called the "jailer" theory of inteh..
law.
   4) International law is unfortunately still in its infancy. All states must
so change their character that they will bow to a central Legislature which
will pass laws universally binding as well as universally enforceable; and
all states must pledge to submit their controversies to judicial settlement.[5]
Until that happy time will come, not too much reliance can unfortunately
be bestowed on international law, lest others will take unfair advantage of
your credulity. This can be called the "magician" theory, or the "never-
never" theory of international law.

   Evidently, these criticisms partly contradict each other and partly can-
cel each other out. For example, the complaint that international law "has
no teeth," that it can be broken with impunity, because it "cannot be
enforced" contradicts the complaint that it does not provide clear rules (for
if it is overly vague, it can hardly be "broken"), and is partly invalidated by
the other complaint, namely, that enforcement too often lies in the hands of
the wronged party itself.
   All these criticisms combine underestimation with over-expectation.
They single out the international legal order to accuse it of shortcomings
which, however, are to some extent inherent in every legal order. They ask
for performances which the law cannot perform, and simultaneously show
altogether too little appreciation for what it does perform, and in what
direction it is developing. They thereby stunt the potentialities for its
growth.
   To begin with the extreme position (implied in different variations of
the "harlot" theory), even the most hard-boiled adherent of power politics
has only two alternatives with regard to international law: (a) to claim that
the rules can be so manipulated and stretched as to appear to justify his
behavior; or (b) to make an open challenge, that is, to disregard the rules in
a specific case, and to boast that his interests will thus be better served, so
that the gain is well worth the price of not bothering about "legalisms."
   In either case, the existence of international rules is thereby admitted.
Indeed, experience shows that the most flagrant breaches of the rules will

e accompanied by particularly self-righteous professions of adher-
them. This, of course, is no triumph for international law. If we
.g., at Hitler's record, we see that he went to extremes in legal gym-
cs, in assuming the first alternative.[6]

However, this self-permissiveness will regularly be accompanied by a
osture of scrupulousness regarding the behavior of others: as far as other
nations are concerned, they are not permitted the slightest improprieties.
The law-breaker will constantly invoke the sacredness of treaties if his
opponents' obedience to them will be to his advantage. In fact, his aim
must be to paralyze his prospective victims to such an extent that they will
be unable to make use of the possibilities which international law offers
them to forestall his scheme. If he is skillful, he will use to the hilt the
respect which international law enjoys.

To give two random examples: Hitler's extremely adroit utilization of
the principle of the sovereign equality of states, in order to obtain consent
for rearmament (which, as he knew best, was for the illegal purpose of
preparing aggressions), and his insistence on the principle of national self-
determination, to justify machinations in neighboring countries which were
for the same illegal purposes. "That practis'd falsehood under saintly shew,
Deep malice to conceal, couch'd with revenge" (Milton, *Paradise Lost*, Bk.
iv).

The schemer will always have to include in his own calculations the
validity and, indeed, the functioning of the very law he is intent upon
breaking. These are among the objective data for the planning and execution of his own improper actions. Hence, he himself will violate or
"stretch" *certain* norms of that legal system but obey, probably punctilious-
ly, other norms because he expects the rest of the international community
to obey all rules, and especially those in his favor. He will do everything to
blunt the severity and avoid the watchfulness of the law. It is a bungling
bank-robber who speeds through the red traffic light on his way to the
bank. By the same token, he will shout "hold the thief" after the robbery.

The selectiveness of the would-be law-breaker may pose specific problems for the legal system, on the municipal as well as international level.
On all levels, the legal system must bend every effort to create norms and
institutions which will with high probability frustrate the intent of the
selective violator by providing maximum risks for him and minimum risk
for itself.

But what if legally improper power politics are pursued not under the
visor of hypocritical homage to international law, but, as said above, in outright challenge to it. The dictum, "the sword is more powerful than the
law" postulates, not that there is no international law, but that that law permits revolutionary unilateral creation of new law: whereas the sword was
used for purposes unlawful under the then existing law, its success abro-
gates that law and creates new law in its stead. Why, then, is the doctrine

"the sword is more powerful than the law" or, briefly, "might makes right"[7] untenable? The answer is: because international law does not recognize this form of abrogation and creation of norms.

We are not concerned here with a situation where an international norm is generally and for a considerable period of time consistently disregarded and thus ceases to be valid (dissuetude). We are merely stating that if a certain type of behavior is prohibited, this prohibition continues to be valid if it is broken by an individual state or even by a group of states.

*   *   *

The different varieties of the "harlot theory" are not put forth by true friends of international law. However, other criticisms of international law are often proffered with genuine sorrow, or are accompanied by demands for far-reaching changes which, in the best of cases, would require a long time to materialize. They usually center around the problem of enforcement, and of auto-interpretation. Characteristically, they take domestic law as the model. They all imply "that international law lags far behind the municipal legal order of developed countries; that the latter has overcome those weaknesses; and that international law will become stronger and more reliable, as it will more closely approximate that model.

The Problem of Enforcement

Leo Gross has pointed out, not only that "states by and large obey international law" but that this fact of fairly general obedience "is *commonly accepted.*"[8] Such consensus of the experts is probably surprising to the deprecators of international law, and goes rather far in refuting the "orphan theory."

The point which has created so much difficulty for the theory of international law and which, of course, is of paramount importance, especially in the nuclear age, is, what happens if states do *not* obey the law—"in cases of breaches of international law or, one ought to say more properly, perhaps, of *alleged* breaches of international law"? Since many of them, as Gross says between quotation marks "remain unpunished," "it is arguable . . . that the international legal order is not efficacious."[9] At this point, Gross introduces his theory of auto-interpretation. In his view, the frequency of auto-interpretation by states, that is, of autonomy (instead of heteronomy which allegedly predominates or, indeed, reigns supreme in domestic law), does not necessarily justify the pessimistic conclusions which are sometimes drawn; he shows that, not so infrequently, disputes are, in fact, solved, not unilaterally but by the parties concerned, or with the help of a heteronomous agency; and that, i.a., the further "development of [international] institutions [is] a desirable and indeed a feasible method to make international law an effective order without sacrificing its character as a law regulating the conduct of states on the basis of equality."[10]

Gross' carefully reasoned argument could, thus, put to rest some of the standard criticisms of international law. However, the problem of enforceability has been so frequently invoked that some further observations are to be made here.

The term "violation" of the law conjures up connotations of doing violence to somebody or something, or at least to the law. When a state charges another with violating some obligation toward it, emotions ranging from noble patriotism to dangerous self-righteousness to outright self-deception or hypocrisy are often aroused. There is, psychologically, a small step from violation of law, to violation of any country; and the anger of individuals and masses at being "wronged" in the symbolic figure of their country or government, or in the collective image of their country's power or integrity, may create reactions altogether disproportionate to the facts.

The term "enforcement" carries analogous, opposite overtones of force, of doing harm. Especially if strong collective emotions are involved, it will often be forgotten that by no means all enforcement is meant to do any serious harm, to say nothing of physical harm. Delay in paying a debt usually carries only the "penalty" of an obligation to pay interest. If the carpenter fails to deliver a pre-paid piece of furniture as promised, the wronged party may purchase the piece elsewhere, and charge the price to the carpenter. It is the hallmark of a mature legal system not to use the connotation of violence and punishment indiscriminately, but to distinguish carefully between civil and criminal law; and within the latter, again between, for example, misdemeanor and more serious types of offenses, between objective wrong and subjective culpability; between different degrees of *mens rea;* etc. To imprison a non-felonious debtor has long since been considered an improper penalty.

"The enforcement of law is a troublesome matter. Even in well-developed countries like the United States the number of thefts that go unpunished, or the breaches of contract that bring no recompense to the wronged parties, make shocking figures. In the world community it must be admitted that no international sheriff or marshal is available to handcuff and haul either states or individuals before an international bar of justice."[11]

This comparison between the municipal and the international legal order is more tempered than others, because it distinguishes between civil and criminal law in the former, and does not claim perfection for either on the domestic scene. But the reference to the handcuffing and hauling before the bar of justice uses the typical approach, of comparing the administration of justice in every-day life (yes, involving ordinary criminals) with the assertion of the law in matters of state.

The hauling before the bar of international justice in the Nuremberg and Tokyo trials constituted unique events. But the handcuffing and hauling of organs of large collectives and, above all, of organs exercising the imperium or authority of the state, is equally rare in the annals of individual states.[12]

The legal model or hypothetical judgment, "If someone steals, he ought to be punished," applies, also in domestic law, hardly to all norm-addressees. Altogether, it is, in this absolute formulation, incomplete and therefore incorrect. It bestows upon municipal (criminal) law a definitiveness and "reliability" which the latter does not possess. It thus stacks the cards for the comparison with the allegedly so much less reliable international law. To be correct, the model would have to be qualified by a long tail of modifications, restrictions, conditions and provisos—indeed, a large part of the country's entire legal and political system.

One fact alone destroys the implied generality of the model: the suspected thief (and even to call him thus entitles him to sue you for libel) ought not to be tried, to say nothing of being punished, unless he be indicted. Now, the decision to indict will in most countries lie in the discretion of a political (not a judicial) organ or of a judicial organ bound by instructions of a political organ. For example, no grand jury can indict unless the public prosecutor presents the case to it; and whether he does so, may depend on many extra-legal considerations. Hence, the situation is the same as in the Security Council which may decide not to pursue a matter which it would be legally authorized to pursue. Even old Rome was very reluctant to allow an *actio popularis* ("indictment by the people") and virtually every advanced municipal legal order shows the same reluctance. Again, the internal legal situation is identical with the international; Foreign Offices and other political organs wish to control the decision whether or not to invoke a treaty provision against another country.

The "thieves ought to be punished" model suffers from another deficiency. It leaves out the vaster part of all advanced legal systems, namely, non-criminal law. To be sure, such law provides for unpleasant consequences, including ultimate coercion in the event of disobedience to definitive court decisions. However, those consequences are conditioned upon the discretion of the allegedly wronged party. Since so much of domestic law is not criminal law, the "thieves ought to be punished" model could only be relied upon if it could be widened by the addition *"and every tenant who does not pay his rent ought to be evicted."* Evidently, the model cannot be so widened. For, in non-criminal law the locus of the norm-creating power is enormously diluted: at least, one would have to add "but it is up to each of millions of landlords even to take the first step toward this possibility, and furthermore each landlord may behave differently toward different defaulting tenants." Yet, the "thieves ought to be punished" model *alone* is represented as the paradigm of domestic law, *and the only desirable goal* and the *essential sign of perfection* of international law. It thus fortifies the dangerous popular notion that *all* improper international behavior is somehow *criminal*. It hides from the man in the street the fact that also under his own country's law, however furious he may be at his unpunctual debtor, criminal sanctions are not available, and if the debtor has no money, *the law cannot help him.*

The central point is that *domestic law insofar as it applies to petty everyday affairs cannot suitably be compared with international law.* In its most important aspects, international law regulates the behavior of states, that is, of large collectives; it deals with highly complex matters involving interests of macro-organisms. Hence, it should be compared, not with domestic law pertaining to minor issues, as implied in the statement "If someone steals he ought to be punished"; but with that part of domestic law which deals with analogous matters of great import and regulating the behavior of large collectives, namely, *constitutional law.*

If comparison is made on that level, some difficulties disappear. For example, the image, frequently used, of the policeman regulating automobile traffic as the desirable goal for a truly "working" system of world law, is mis-leading and, indeed, absurd. Even within a nation, large collectives (such as provinces) or major agents (such as the legislature or the cabinet) are *not* regulated by traffic cops. They are under the law, but they themselves make the law; the proposition that nations will ever be subjected to the orders of traffic cops, and perhaps be arrested by them, conjures up wrong connotations. On the top level, *even within the domestic legal system,* no cop gives orders, and hardly ever will a cop be (legally or factually) in a position to arrest the top organs.

Even in everyday "ordinary" criminality, sanctions present a paradox: in order to *protect* certain community values such as "life, liberty, dignity, and property," and whether they be designed to punish, restrain, reform, or deter, they constitute a *deprivation* of "life, liberty, dignity, and property."

This dilemma is as old as criminal law itself. Essentially, there exist three ways of handling it: by increasing refinement and flexibility of the substantive and procedural rules regarding the "retribution"—a process which was started when the killing of a man could be avenged by means other than killing the killer; by "de-criminalizing" certain behavior which, in essence, is tantamount to the widening of individual and group autonomy or auto-interpretation or self-determination; and by social engineering (which, of course, always expresses itself in the society's legal order) aimed at prevention rather than retribution, and which includes the build-up of distributive, as distinguished from retributive, justice. *Fiat justifia, pereat mundus* was a cry of despair; at best, of zealots; and when coined, nobody knew that one day in the nuclear age, it could indeed mean the destruction of the world.

In the last analysis, the principle is also a confession of the *defeat* of justice. Confronted by very big issues (or, if to be applied against powerful opposition), or, worst, because of the clumsiness of the sanction apparatus, the law is faced with the dilemma of either being "brazenly violated"; or, if applied, defeating its own purpose—namely, to be a rational means of maintaining and re-establishing *order.*

Altogether, one of the essential aspects of penology is to look beyond penology—acknowledging that punishment is but one of the methods to protect society against offenders and to prevent offenses.

As Hans Aufricht pointed out, to consider as properly belonging to the legal system only those laws which are coupled with a sanction, tends to distort the empirically experienced reality of the law; for, such definition excludes all those legal relationships which do not provide sanctions.[13] The distortion becomes even greater if, as the "jailer theory" insists, only criminal sanctions (punishment, use of force) are *true* sanctions.

For example, in case of misconduct of a public official, the consequences may range from informal warning, to a variety of disciplinary actions, to criminal prosecution. The decision to put into motion the machinery which could lead to any of these measures may hinge on political considerations. If the pertinent law permits wide discretion, as it often does, the exercise of such discretion is legally correct. Furthermore, in many a country the allegedly aggrieved citizen is legally or realistically unable to put that machinery in motion. He then is in a worse position than the wronged state is in international relations. This is particularly true in regard to elected public officials with regard to whom the problem of sanctions is one of particular delicacy.

The fact that domestic law may be unenforced or unenforceable has been mentioned, e.g., by Quincy Wright: This may occur especially "where the society has within it political subgroups which rival in power. In such circumstances, the force at the disposal of the central organs to enforce law is frequently faced by opposition which cannot be dealt with by normal methods of law enforcement, such as police action, judicial administration, and execution of judgments. . . . History discloses many instances of the difficulty of law enforcement in a state, within which are powerful feudal barons, ecclesiastical organizations, chartered municipalities, cultural minorities, historic states which were once sovereign, monopolistic corporations, or wealthy trade unions."[14]

Is, then, law enforcement in the sense of "punishment" always and unconditionally desirable? The answer depends on several considerations, including at least: the social importance of the rule; the severity of the violation; the severity of the "sanctions"; the social costs of the application of the sanctions. Even criminal law, and all the more civil law, therefore, leaves a great deal of leeway to the law-applying organs ("the penalty may range from a $25 fine to 10 years' imprisonment"); and in civil law, the very decision as to whether the wheels of justice are to be put in motion, rests with the allegedly aggrieved party. Furthermore, the dividing line between criminal and civil law is neither obvious nor constant: firstly, it is frequently very controversial as to whether certain *types* of behavior should, or should not, be considered "criminal"—from violations of the building code, to the sale of liquor to minors; secondly, there is often great uncertainty whether a specific case constitutes a permissible "sharp deal" or violated civil law or overstepped the threshold into criminality.

In general, it cannot be stated unqualifiedly that strict—so-to-speak "automatic"—application of penalties will always be conducive to achievement of the very goal for which the sanction was instituted. Illustrations abound. To take a random example, would the student population or the community be better served if all rules regarding school discipline were rigidly applied? If every student's infraction were reported and followed up?

In spite of all efforts to rationalize the law and its applications, the aim of making a society's answer to a violation of a legal norm commensurate to the violation is often not achieved. For, setting into motion the wheels of justice is like throwing a stone into the water; how many rings it will form depends on many factors unconnected with the shape of the stone. For the truck driver who after years of unemployment finally lands a job, but on the first day receives a police summons for speeding and thereupon is dismissed, the "sanction" is not a $5 fine, but the prospect of years of additional unemployment; his eviction from his apartment because of his inability to pay the rent; etc.

Even if the administration of justice were as perfect as humanly possible, the discrepancy between what the law intends, and what the law's application in the concrete case may realistically lead to, cannot be altogether avoided. It is an aspect of a seemingly cosmic fact, namely, of the frequent *incongruity of cause and effect*. . . . The laws of physics ordained that a specific bullet killed President Kennedy. We are not reviving here the "nose of Cleopatra" controversy of the metaphysicians and philosophers of history. We are simply stating that law (which is a device to bring about foreseeable and rationally manageable effects) is by its nature interested in avoiding incongruous and unplanned repercussions, because such repercussions contradict the very definition of the law, and can negate its social usefulness. Social institutions of which the law is one, must in fact be considered as being engaged in a constant—and never fully successful—combat against the incongruity of cause and effect.

Again, even in countries proud of their impartial administration of justice, the severity of punishment for the *same* wrongs may fluctuate very considerably. On occasion, judges find it proper to state openly that they impose a particularly severe penalty in view of an especially grave analogous but unconnected case or "to establish an example."

All of this militates against the concept of the *automaticity* of the application of domestic law. Amnesties, reprieves, and the like, must be mentioned in this connection.

International organizations may play a role in changes of attitudes. For example, on the very recommendation of the International Monetary Fund, exchange transactions in country X, yesterday punishable as black market operations, become today permissible and are, in fact, encouraged under a new financial policy. Above all, a vitally important part of the efforts of the United Nations, including its convention-making efforts, are directed at inducing *changes* in the municipal legal systems, be it the abolition of institutions akin to slavery, or the widening of the political rights of women, or prohibiting certain types of forced labor, or the sale of addiction-producing drugs, or racial discrimination, and so on.

It is therefore said without cynicism that the goddess of justice can be only conditionally blind; perhaps she must see, and very perceptively. To be able to see, she must wear eyeglasses; the opticians prescribing them are the legislators and other decision-makers. Can we really overlook the frequent fact that even while the revolutionary is awaiting execution, the government may be deliberating whether to offer him a post in a coalition regime? Can we overlook the fact that the teacher who just imposed the grave sanction of expulsion from school on a pupil, may on the same day at a legislative hearing advocate altogether different treatment of similar cases?

Decriminalization is not identical with "softness"; and of course does not prevent occasional tightening of the sanctions. Furthermore, *prevention* of socially undesirable behavior and (if prevention fails) *rehabilitation* of the offenders are essential demands of modern penology. The attitude is not based on false sentimentality but on advanced notions of social engineering. The more successful policy will consist in *cooperation* of the agency which, if offense were to occur, would have to impose a sanction, with the subjects (norm-addressees) who by virtue of such cooperation will hopefully not commit the offense; and in creating and developing institutions which will make the offense less probable.

Like the maturation of domestic law, the maturation of international law can be measured by the diversification of "sanction" and "enforcement" and by the variability and sheer number, the flexibility, and the gradation of severity of "sanctions." Lord Palmerston was not too strongly contradicted when in 1848 he enunciated the doctrine that a state, in order to protect a subject creditor of another state, may even resort to military intervention against a defaulting debtor state. When, later on, the practice met with increasing opposition, the Drago doctrine superseded it but had to be couched as a virtual corollary to the Monroe doctrine.[15] The Hague Convention for Limiting the Employment of Force to the Recovery of Contract Debts still conditionally permitted resort to armed force if the "delinquent" state refused to accept arbitration or to submit to an arbitral award. There followed the Good Neighbor policy, and the inter-American treaties; and e.g., the rules of the International Monetary Fund make ante-diluvian the bombing of towns for default on foreign debts.

The crudity or refinement of any legal system is expressed in the paucity or variety and flexibility of the answers it provides for violations of rules: and in the refinement of methods to establish, in the first place, whether a violation has taken place. The evolution can be further measured by the increasing emphasis on proportionality between wrongs and reme-dies; i.e., by an increasing awareness of the hierarchy of values the legal system is to defend.

Hence, characteristically, the emphasis may shift from the eye-for-an-eye principle; and from the "punishment" of disturbances, to their preven-tion.[16] This means, also, that, as the evolution of U.N. methods shows, emphasis has shifted from "sanctions" to "peacekeeping."

Even in cases where one could argue convincingly that there was aggression or a breach of the peace, the injured state itself may rather endeavor to obtain help for a constructive and conciliatory solution, such as a U.N. presence. This trend is greatly enhanced by the fact, as Leo Gross pointed out, that since the creation of the League of Nations and the U.N., the search for constructive solutions has become the concern (or, legally expressed, the right or function) of outside states and of international organs.

The making of international rules is part of the political and diplomatic process. They reflect political realities, just as does the domestic statute or agreement that emerges from the efforts to strike a compromise between the demands of powerful interior groups in municipal lawmaking.

Often, then, the rules will not contain "sanctions" in the sense of threatened rigid adverse consequences; rather, procedures and devices will be incorporated which will leave or put the removal of the difficulty in the hands of the parties, including the alleged wrongdoer.

In some cases, such caution is certainly regrettable, and the law should have more "teeth." But if the history of municipal law enforcement against powerful groups is any indication, enforcement in the sense of "punishing" or even "hauling before the bars of justice," will hardly become the rule. Figures of speech are sometimes unexpectedly revealing if we pause to look at them; the somewhat hackneyed simile of the "teeth" of the law is no exception. Only some wild beasts rely altogether on their fangs as tool and death-bringing weapon. Enforcement is not identical with implementation. If enforcement is not always possible, or commensurate with the very pur-poses of the law, then the law is not truly helped if it is endowed with it on paper, or if one maintains the pretense of its complete reliance on enforce-ment. Rather, additional other legislative and institutional, preventive and remedial methods have to be fashioned, to implement the goals of the law. . . .

The Problem of Auto-interpretation

We come now to another standard accusation against international law (or the handling of "international matters"): namely, that states are the judges of their own lawful behavior, and, as it is sometimes formulated, are prosecutors, judges and executioners regarding the behavior of other states which they consider unlawful.

In the words of two learned authors,[17] "The 'absence of an authority [that is, a disinterested third-party authority] to declare what the law is at any given time, how it applies to a given situation or dispute, and what the appropriate sanction may be' is commonly regarded as a most basic defect in international law. 'In the absence of such an authority, and failing agreement between the states at variance on these points,' writes Professor Leo Gross in full fidelity to tradition, 'each state has a right to interpret the law, the right of auto-interpretation, as it might be called.'"

We must agree with their observation that the right of auto-interpretation carries a "potentiality of many conflicting interpretations." This is true. If running wild, auto-interpretation would make the world a jungle, and the law a harlot.

Hence, it is indispensable to *limit* that right; and as Leo Gross has pointed out, the tendency has been in this direction. This tendency must by all means be strengthened. The basic philosophy of the United Nations system is to bring about *mutually acceptable* solutions in case of controversy, also by fostering various forms of third-party participation; and, simultaneously, to erect strict barriers against excesses of auto-interpretation in cases where no commonly acceptable solution is found.

However, the proposition, frequently made or implied, that auto-interpretation is a particular weakness of the international legal order, and somehow unthinkable in a mature domestic system, is unfounded. It denies a most basic fact, namely, that every law creates a framework for various sorts of behavior. No legal system could function unless the vast majority of cases were determined by autonomously acting persons or collectives. The business man makes his contracts; the employer hires and fires employees. *Everybody engages daily in auto-interpretation of the law.* Thus, everybody continuously creates specific law, as delegated to him by the legal order.

Auto-interpretation of course implies choice and discretion, and the weighing of mutually contradictory self-interests, remote consequences, etc. The law, if so trivial a comparison is permitted, is like a travel agency:

it offers many different trips to many different destinations; the client has to choose among them; or can decide against all, and stay home. Not every employer always makes use of his right to dismiss; not every betrayed husband tries to obtain a divorce. The rules cannot play the game, but the players do. In fact, it is often proper and desirable for them to *change* the very rules, or to *forfeit* a possibility legally available. The world of the law bristles with paradoxes, but only because the realities it has to cope with are so often paradoxical.

No Unbridgeable Abyss between "Political" and "Legal"

Misunderstandings which go far beyond terminology are caused by the threefold meaning of the term "legal." The term sometimes denotes "proper" pursuant to the law: In country A the law permits the hunting of a bird species, hence there such hunting is "legal"; in country B, the law forbids it, and it is therefore "illegal." It should be obvious that in this sense, any "political" act permissible under the law is, indeed, "legal."

The term "legal" is also used to mean "regulated in detail" by the law. This can lead to conclusion that whenever the law does not regulate a matter in detail, the law has abdicated (the matter is "extra-legal").[18] The conclusion is wrong because in the absence of a detailed rule, the wider rule applies. For example, in domestic law, wage controversies are usually not decided by "the law." The law usually does not say whether an 8-cent increase or 5-cent decrease in the hourly wage is proper. But the law defines what steps (e.g., strikes) may, and what steps (e.g., killing the employers) may not be taken in the context. The same is true in international law. It does not say whether a specific contested border area should change hands; but prohibits war over it. "International law is then never formally or intrinsically incapable of giving a decision, or the basis of law, as to the rights of the parties of any dispute."[19]

Finally, exaggerated emphasis on judicial decision-making sometimes leads to the conclusion, which must also be rejected, that in order to be "legal," a question must be at least amenable to decision by a court of law, and that non-justiciable disputes are not questions of law, but of power. The fact is that international law can as little overlook the existence of differences of power, as the law of contracts can overlook the existence of money or differences in wealth. The very aim of law, on any subject, is to regulate, not to deny, realities. But it is evidently as erroneous to assert that in the international arena the parties are exempt from the law whenever their dispute is not solved or solvable by the World Court, as it is erroneous to assert that governments and legislators are free to violate their respective constitutions in all countries where the constitutionality of their acts is not subject to judicial review.

Since international law is largely addressed to organs engaged in politics—since, in other words, most of its very subject matter is political—it is only logical that decisions made within its framework will be governed by "political" considerations: just as, within the framework of the pertinent law, merchants will make commercial decisions, bankers financial decisions, and sea captains maritime decisions. We are again back at auto-interpretation. All such political, commercial, financial, and maritime decisions are, however (as long as they stay within the respective norms), "legal" in two ways: they enjoy the approval and protection of the norms which they "apply"; and they are themselves concretizations of those norms, and thus possess a legal character; they lay down the law for the specific situation. No marital law can determine whether Joe should or should not marry Joan; but once they do, their marriage is a concretization of those general norms and creates a new specific legal institution or situation, from which flow further legal consequences *that had not existed before.*

Unless so much were made of the allegedly basic difference between "legal" as contrasted to "political" settlements, it would be pedantic to point out that whenever states do seek a "political" solution through negotiation and other pacific means, they are *of course fulfilling the prescription of the law.* Hammarskjold rightly insisted that the full use of those devices is, indeed, a *legal obligation,* to which the members of the U.N. "must give a new serious consideration."[20]

However we look at it, there is no watertight differentiation between "political" and "legal." Proper flexibility is an asset of wise law because it allows varying interpretation and proper adaptability; a law which too slavishly intends to nail down a particular constellation for "all future," will either become a handicap, or a dead letter—hence, in either case, invites its own violation or abrogation.[21]

Nor is there an abyss, contrast or antinomy between judicial procedure on the one hand, and negotiation, adjustment and "amicable settlement" on the other. Every lawyer and every judge knows that. Long lists of statutes could be quoted which show the law-giver's preference or ready permission for the latter method of settlement—whether we look at the 1964 U. S. civil rights legislation, or at the handling of litigious civil law in Japan,[22] or at the innumerable Court-encouraged settlements "out of Court" occurring everywhere in the world.

Municipal law without exception approves of this interplay between settlement by third-party (judicial) decision and by compromise among the parties; this is best proven by the fact that even after court litigation has led to a definite decision, the parties are still free to agree *not* to abide by it but to settle the *res judicata* differently.[23] Even in some types of criminal cases, the law often permits some forms of negotiated adjustment, or a quid-pro-quo arrangement between the public authority and persons gravely suspected, if not actually convicted, of criminal acts.

Basically the same approach, namely, the weighing of advantages and disadvantages for the community as a whole (here, the world community), is expressed in the substantive and procedural rules of international law.

It could be objected that in a truly well-developed state, there will be a differentiation of functions, and different organs will watch over each other. Yet, if the prerogatives of those agencies are examined, it will be found that discretion to stop or alter their action—to say nothing of imposing sanctions—will often lie in the hands of the decision-making individuals or bodies themselves. In particular, in the conduct of "foreign affairs," many crucial decisions affecting *other* states are altogether exempted from any scrutiny on the domestic level.

In fact, many an improper action of individual governments has been subjected to scrutiny and opposition in the United Nations, which has gone uncriticized, to say nothing of having led to "sanctions," within the respective countries' municipal legal systems.

It is strongly urged that a public censure in the solemn form of a U.N. General Assembly resolution should be acknowledged as a "sanction"—that is, the imposition of a negative response by a properly constituted outside organ. From a positivistic viewpoint, this should create no difficulty: since "sanction" is *any* consequence which the legal order permits or demands, and since censure by the General Assembly is exactly one of those sanctions, the definition is fulfilled. But the argument also stands if considered from a political or socio-psychological viewpoint. A sanction is any measure which expresses disapproval and condemnation; it furthermore may aim at preventing the repetition of the wrong, by instilling fear of similar condemnation; and by no means can it, by the nature of things, always or often brief about the actual undoing of the wrong. Once the victim of the careless driver is dead, no punishment can make him alive again. But, as said above, the comparison should not be made with that level of law enforcement. Whenever a national community wishes to express disapproval of actions of powerful groups, the true sanction will often consist in adverse publicity; and "shaming" the wrongdoer is the essence of punitive sanction. Why does a corporation fight for years a legal action to avoid being sentenced under Anti-Trust laws to a fine amounting to a fraction of the cost of the law-suit? Because it wishes to defend its image, good name and reputation.[24] Similarly, if a censure by the General Assembly were really insignificant, why then do they engender impassioned debate, and the long caucuses, and the stir and heat?

It is undeniable that such condemnation (and other relatively mild sanctions) may prove inefficacious. This, to be sure, is a cause of deep regret for the friend of international order, but should not cause too much glee to its detractors. First of all, the situation is not different from that under domestic law. Secondly, the analogy between the behavior of an individual and that of large collectives, such as states, should not be carried too far. The latter's "life span" and hence, "sense of time" is different from that of individuals. Condemnation may "work" as a corroding influence, and the effects may be more slow in coming, than they can be within an individual's life. Finally, whereas the system of sanctions available under present international law is far from perfect, its arsenal contains measures of graded severity, and the sparing use of the more severe measures may often be in the true interest of the world community.

Scarcity of Judicial Review of Constitutionality, Comparable to Scarcity of Use of World Court

It is regrettable that countries make scarce use of the judicial process for the settlement of disputes. Yet, on this point again, the situation is not unique to the international scene.

Mutatis mutandis, the reluctance of governments to go before the World Court can be compared to the reluctance of constitution-makers even to offer the *possibility* for the highest State organs to submit to judicial review by a *domestic* court.

Judicial review of the constitutionality of acts of State organs remains a rare exception: only a very few nations have seen fit to adopt it either in their constitutions or, like the U.S.A., as accepted practice. Even the handful of constitutions providing for judicial review do so with great restraint. . . .

Judicial review may be particularly desirable in a federal system. However, for example, the Swiss Federal Court does not have the power to review constitutionality of "acts of a duly elected (federal) legislature." Its power of judicial review is confined to cantonal laws and to actions by cantonal and sometimes federal executives.[25]

In the United States the Supreme Court also has its political aspects. To begin with, political considerations cannot and properly need not be absent in the very appointment of the Supreme Court judges.[26] Nor can the Court's policy-making function be denied; or the fact that individual Court decisions have been vehemently attacked by critics of the policy "made" by the Court, while other critics have with equal vehemence attacked other rulings of the Court for failure to make policy.

Furthermore, on the domestic scene, political decisions guide or bind the judiciary in cases admittedly justiciable. For example, even in the United States where separation of powers between the branches of government is a basic constitutional principle, the Courts are widely guided by executive suggestions in matters involving international disputes. Professor

Michael H. Cardoz, in an article descriptively titled, "Judicial Deference to State Department Suggestions: Recognition [by the Courts] of [Executive] Prerogative or Abdication to Usurper," states:

> In no cases do the courts of this country defer to executive suggestions as often and as fully as in those having international ramifications; while occasionally accepted as a wise 'accommodation by abdication' this deference periodically provokes charges that the courts are abdicating their responsibility and that the Department of State is usurping the judiciary's role. Those are serious charges in our domestic affairs but internationally the consequences of a rejection of executive suggestions in such cases can be grave in a world where friendly relations often rest on very thin ice.[27]

Constitutional Law Faces at Least the Same Difficulties of Enforcement as Does International Law

Much of the constitutional law of individual countries wrestles with the same problem as does much of international law: *viz.,* how to regulate the behavior of large collectives. This is a persuasive argument for comparing these two types of law. If we do that, we find that *constitutions face even greater difficulties* in being enforced, than does international law.

Whereas the reliability of the policeman's arresting the thief is so often held up as a reproach to international law, the actual frailty and frequent unenforceability of the highest level of domestic law, namely, constitutional law, is hardly ever mentioned in this connection.

Many countries offer the frequent spectacle of their constitutions being overthrown—the supreme expression of unenforceability. Even in countries with long traditions of constitutional "sanctity" *and judicial review*, examples of non-enforcement are not difficult to find.

Culminating more than a century of sporadic efforts to end racial segregation through court action, the U.S. Supreme Court in *Brown v. Topeka* (1954) stated unequivocally that racially separate public school facilities are a violation "of equal protection of the law as guaranteed by the Fourteenth Amendment and thus violate the Constitution." But the Court granted a great deal of discretion or auto-interpretation to administrative and other organs, in stating that "the courts will require . . . a *prompt and reasonable start* toward full compliance with our . . . ruling," requesting "all deliberate speed."

Subsequent Supreme Court decisions clarifying the meaning of "all deliberate speed" tended to define the permissible discretion. Yet, ten years after the Supreme Court decision, the authoritative periodical, *Southern School News* (published by the Southern Education Reporting Service in Nashville, Tenn.) pointed out that during the decade, legislators of Southern States "adopted almost 450 laws and regulations dealing with desegregation—most of them designed to delay or limit the admission of Negroes to schools with whites"[28] Various courses of action were open to the U.S. Government, under the Constitution, to enforce federal court decisions; but the U.S. Government, using its discretion or auto-interpretation—chose not to use them, or to use them very sparingly.

Furthermore, even casual inspection reveals that many a constitution is very vague on fundamentals. One would assume that, the more vital a matter is for the community, the more precise and iron-clad will be the respective rules. This is not so. . . .

Unenforceability or deliberate non-enforcement, as well as vagueness and lacunae in constitutions, may be disturbing not only for the people living under that basic law, but of grave concern for outside countries and the community of nations as a whole. If the *essentials* of domestic legal systems were reliable and stable, the international scene would throughout history have been incomparably calmer than it has been. Diplomats would have had fewer worries; and the peace would have been less often disturbed. How many military alliances have been made and broken, and how many wars fought, for example, in view of the uncertainty whether the rules of dynastic succession would be obeyed or because after the monarch's death they were disobeyed!

. . . If international issues are intertwined with constitutional issues, the close connection between international and constitutional law is of course particularly obvious. This was, for example, seen in the long stalemate regarding Austria after World War II, and in the solution of the Austrian question in 1955; or in the repercussions of the Cyprus crisis. During the attempted secession of Katanga from the Congo (Leopoldville), the whole world had to hold its breath; and the outcome of the U.N. Operations there evidently depended upon—and influenced—the outcome of that constitutional controversy; which controversy, in turn, was considerably influenced, also, by international policies of outside countries.[29]

International difficulties are often caused by disobedience to ("non-enforcement" or unenforceability of) domestic constitutional law, namely, by the governments themselves. This fact has received much too little attention. According to the constitutions of many countries, violation of a treaty violates the respective country's constitution. This is, at least, true under constitutions which consider treaties, as the U.S. Constitution puts it, "the law of the land." The legislatures of countries whose constitutions do not permit abrogation or amendment of treaty obligations by simple statute, violate the constitution by adopting a statute violative of treaty obligations. By the same token, all governmental organs (heads of state, foreign ministers, military leaders, etc.) bound by constitutions or other rules to "administer the laws" and be faithful to the constitution, violate that legal duty, if by their actions they violate a treaty to which their country is committed. The U.N. Charter itself is such a treaty. It forbids certain behavior, e.g., the threat or use of force. In violating the Charter, these governmental organs violate their own country's law and/or constitution, as the case may be.

Hence, in many cases, the very need for international enforcement only arises because enforcement of domestic law is not forthcoming. It follows that one way of strengthening *inter*national law is to strengthen, or more fully to respect, the provisions of *domestic* law which safeguard the implementation of international obligations.

It is exactly when constitutions are being broken, when governments are being overthrown, when rebellions erupt, when secession movements start—it is exactly in those situations that international problems arise. These "internal" events (and the fears and hopes that they may occur) are the stuff of which *"international"* complications are largely made. Hence, often, the reality is the very converse of the cliche that international law is impotent while domestic law is reliably "enforced." Rather, it is in situations where constitutional law breaks down, that international law and international organizations may have to come to the rescue.

In this era of frequent changes of constitutions, of frequent revolutions and domestic turmoil, it becomes particularly clear that the rules of international law form a stabilizing element within the whirlwind. "Permanency" or longevity or stability of constitutions and governments can often not be relied upon. In such cases, the only higher law on which reliance can be put, is international law. Whether or not the new government is legitimate according to the respective nation's constitution, whether or not a domestic authority is an usurper according to that country's legal order—international law will still be binding upon such governments and authorities (and, insofar as international rules are binding upon individuals, also on the latter). Violations of international obligations in such cases also occur; and the interpretations of what is and is not permissible under international law may differ widely. Nonetheless, it is actually less frequent to see an international obligation blatantly disregarded than a constitutional or other domestic law.

Stating it very simply: If we look at the realities of the world scene, we notice that insurgents run *smaller* risks of untoward repercussions if they are successful in overthrowing their own government than if they violate international obligations. Once the *coup* or revolution is victorious, there is nobody to uphold or enforce the violated constitution. But if international obligations are violated, various untoward repercussions (non-recognition, break-off of diplomatic relations, suspension of treaties, reprisals, etc.) may ensue. This follows logically from the fact that the previous *domestic* order has caused to be valid, or at least has no longer any defender—whereas the previous *international* order continues to be valid and has not been deprived of defenders.

International law has had to take cognizance of the vulnerability of municipal law in order to avoid or attenuate the undesirable consequences which may otherwise appear for the community of nations. Hence, it has tended to evolve rules regarding such questions as to when a new state or a new government comes into existence (however illegally); what consequences this may have on obligations entered into by the former state or government; and the like. The fact that it takes cognizance of those changes (which are illegal from the *domestic* viewpoint), cannot be blamed on international law--as little as sickness or congenital deformities can be blamed on the art of medicine. Those conditions are the raw material for international law, and the latter has to make the best of it, namely, safeguard the international order, minimizing as much as possible disturbances caused by the members of the family of nations.[30] . . .

We thus arrive at a remarkable superiority of international over domestic law: *the basic tenets of international law are more stable and reliable, more resilient and less destructible than are the allegedly firm, but actually often fragile, basic laws or constitutions of nations.* To put it differently: governments and constitutions can be overthrown. Once broken and replaced by another constitution, the old one can, like Humpty Dumpty, not be put together again. International law, to be sure, can be violated but can by its own logic never be "overthrown." The supremacy of international law is not a fine point of legal theory. Its continued validity in time of turmoil, civil war, dictatorial omnipotence and other situations when constitutions and domestic laws are disregarded, is the last protection of citizens and foreigners alike.

Closer inspection also shows that international law can exercise a highly salutary restraining influence on the application of constitutions which are *not* disregarded; that the evolution of international law can heal or mitigate shortcomings of domestic legal systems. International and constitutional law depend on each other. They influence and mirror each other. The most impressive illustration is the nuclear armaments race. The peoples of the world can rightly complain—and should complain more—about the imperfection of an international order which has so far failed to alleviate their fears of nuclear disaster. But is it not equally disquieting that pursuant to the respective internal law of the nuclear states a very few individuals may pass an ultimate death sentence of unforeseeable dimensions? No human being should possess such power but they can exercise it without formally violating any law of their country, acting as accuser, jury, court and executioner. More than that: pursuant to rules which are remarkably nebulous and often secret, the prerogative to "push the button" can be delegated to an undisclosed number of other individuals. Nor do constitutions of countries not yet in possession of nuclear armor prevent its acquisition and, thereafter, the exercise of the same awe-inspiring power by some individuals. Hence, the world is exposed to potentially ever greater dangers because of the inadequacies (auto-interpretation) of an ever larger number of national legal systems.

To be sure, any treaty which will eventually remove these dangers can only be made pursuant to the constitutions of the countries concerned (and the constitutional characteristics of as yet non-nuclear nations should give a strong impetus to the nuclear powers to conclude a treaty which also prevents proliferation). The point here emphasized, is that only an *inter*national treaty or treaties can be a safeguard against the vastness of power possessed by a few individuals under their national law, to unleash the disaster.

*   *   *

In this essay, not all aspects of what we dubbed the "orphan," the "harlot" and the "jailer" theories of international law can be discussed. One central point is to de-emphasize the "cop-at-the-corner" model, and to stop using the cliche of the policeman regulating traffic, or arresting a thief (or supposed to arrest the thief), as *the* paradigm for the world legal order. Instead, the rules and legal institutions for *international* statecraft must be compared with those for *national* statecraft, especially constitutional and other municipal law governing the relations of large collectives. Only comparisons between *them* does justice to their respective performances, weaknesses, strengths, and possibilities of development. Neither juridically nor sociologically is the conduct of the major affairs of the domestic community—e.g., the struggle over and settlement of a major wage dispute between powerful management and labor organizations, or the making of crucial decisions by Chiefs of Staff—described by the "cop-arrest-the-violator" model.

Furthermore, it must finally be admitted that if international law were as insistently broken, or unenforceable, or unenforced, or inadequate as traffic law seems to be—considering the traffic casualty statistics, the frequency of non-punishment of hit-and-run drivers, the loopholes in the rules regarding compulsory insurance, etc.—the world would be worse off than it is.

The most that can be said in favor of the traffic cop comparison is that on the traffic cop level, international law functions remarkably well. If a customs official violates a trade agreement, or a foreign diplomat is molested, remedies are easily found. Also on matters of very much greater import, the world legal order functions rather well, and is provided with a whole arsenal of responses and devices to deal with infractions. It is true that, when it comes to ultimate clashes between States, enforcement by force may so imperil the very fabric of the community it is to protect, as to make it legally or factually questionable. The same dilemma exists on the domestic scene, whenever major collectives clash. Hence, both national and international law follow the wise rule, *principiis obsta*—nip potentially major dangers in the bud. Secret societies and unauthorized sales of weapons are forbidden, long before any insurgency can start. The entire United Nations system is devised to check untoward developments and to settle or at least "defuse" conflicts, before an eruption occurs.

*   *   *

The question, "How efficient is international law?" can then be answered, "It is at least as efficient as is domestic law."

Now, the fact that domestic law, from the constitutional to the lowest level, is not perfect either, and that it is probably less reliably enforced or enforceable than is international law, is not offered as "consolation." Rather, some significant conclusions can be drawn from it.

1. Since much of the criticism of international law is based on the double assumption that (a) it is constantly being broken, and (b) with impunity, and since both assumptions are incorrect on the pragmatic test of efficiency, these criticisms lose much of their weight. The world legal order is not a helpless orphan, even if not always accompanied by a jailer ready to clamp on the hand-cuffs.

2. This also refutes many of the conclusions drawn from the asserted helplessness, first of all the proposition that if only more *force* (which, in a world of states, can only mean more *bombings,* more *war* as enforcement) were available, things would be better—nay, that only in that direction lies salvation. Further specific means to prevent digression against the international order are certainly required. But overemphasis on "crude force" is analogous to the assumption, generally denied, that armament races increase the security of the nations engaged in them. This overemphasis focuses attention on the unattainable, and distracts it from the attainable.

3. Since many international conflicts and complications are due to inadequacies or inadequate observance of domestic law, it is evidently hypocritical to decry the frailty of international law, while overlooking the problems which these factors create for the international community. There is reason to suspect that those who consider international law little better than a harlot, do not always hold their own country's law in much greater respect. Since the international and the domestic legal orders are intertwined, the former can be greatly strengthened by proper respect for the latter.

4. Altogether, the major harm which exaggerated criticisms, even if proffered in good faith, render to the growth of the international order is that, however unintentionally, they engender a corroding scepticism and cynicism which cannot but undermine *respect* for international law. For, as indeed every cop knows, no law can prosper unless held in respect. After all is said and done, respect for law is the best and foremost prerequisite for its efficiency, if not its validity. No army of policemen nor multitude of jails can prevail against disrespect of the law,—i.a., because disrespect is bound to infect the guardians of the law (as, for example, the fate of the

Prohibition Amendment to the U.S. Constitution proved). Since the proper functioning of the international order is as indispensable for the well-being of states and individuals as is that of the domestic order, both deserve the same respect, in spite of deficiencies of both, and the same constant and devoted efforts toward improvement.

By the same token, international law must be shielded from excessive expectations. It is not only starry-eyed but dangerous to expect from it, and from the institutions built under it, results which it cannot bring. By itself, it can never "abolish" famine and conflict, poverty and revolutions--just as thousands of years of domestic law have not "abolished" theft and murder.

The fight against the ills of mankind is the task of many disciplines and endeavors--political science and chemistry, biology and psychology, medicine and economics, etc. International law and the institutions based on it are, however, as Cordell Hull said, "an incalculably powerful force for human progress,"[31] because they create the ever more indispensable framework for such endeavors. The world is only really starting on this road toward cooperation, or of the internationalization of the beneficial effects of constructive endeavors.

The arsenal of methods and devices to cope with international problems has been greatly increased. The evolution of these institutions constitutes the progress of international law; and indicates the constructive trends to be followed.

Notes

1. In view of the ever-broadening scope of international law and organization, it is advisable for theoretical and practical reasons to be aware of the different subdivisions or areas of international law, just as is done in domestic law. Louis Sohn, for example, emphasized the distinctions, all within international law, between "constitutional law," administrative law, law of torts (responsibility of states), law of contracts (law of treaties), and so on"; and in another categorization, between "'public law' areas" and "'private law' areas" of international law ("The Many Faces of International Law" in 57 *A.J.I.L.* 4 (Oct. 1963), 869.)

2. "The truest safeguard of sovereignty in an interdependent world is ... an effective international law. The strengthening of international law is consequently in the long-term interest of states, even though it might occasionally conflict with short-time interests. Since the life of states is measured in centuries and their activities are manifold, statesmen have every reason to take a long-range objective view. Though disorder may profit their states today in one case, it may hurt them in another tomorrow, and in the long run is bound to work them harm." (Dag Hammarskjold, "Liberty and Law in International Life." Lecture at the annual convention of the American Bar Association, 1955. Reprinted in *International Law in A Changing World,* 1963, pp. 24–25.)

3. If governments and peoples would accept the fact that, e.g., the United Nations is in that sense an organ of their own country, they might also be less reluc-

tant to contribute financially to the Organization. Even the terminology, "contributing to the U.N.," would then be seen to be inexact insofar as it connotes almost a *subsidy* for an *outsider*. National budgets do not "contribute" to their countries' Foreign Offices; by the same token, since at the United Nations functions are fulfilled which otherwise would have to be done through diplomatic channels or ad hoc conferences, some of the "costs" of the United Nations are, in fact, costs for the conduct of the Members' international affairs. Furthermore, if for example the U.N. decides on a peace-keeping operation, this will save individual countries the effort and expense of their own military intervention, or of increased preparedness measures, etc. For all of these reasons, seen realistically, "the United Nations costs nothing." See John G. Stoessinger and Associates (including the present author), *Financing the United Nations System,* 1964.

4. Throughout this paper, the term "international law" is to include, of course, its most important part, namely, international consitutional law, that is, the norms establishing international organizations and institutions and setting forth their respective functions, prerogatives and obligations.

5. This is not meant to include some of the more realistic, gradualist schools advocating increased prerogatives for carefully specified purposes, of international agendas; whether these proposals advocate some form of "world government" or on the contrary deliberately avoid such name, is a question of terminology and of highly legitimate concern in view of deep-rooted socio-psychological factors.

6. Characteristically, this was also true of his techniques during his "fight for power" *within* Germany: his final ascent to power was officially represented as *both* a revolution (i.e., breach of municipal law) and as the culmination of policies which were *formally legal,* by stretching and undermining the law of the Weimar Republic. In other words, he treated his own country's constitution as much like a harlot as he subsequently treated international law.

7. Pursuing the logic of the argumentation, these two formulas are more sophisticated than is the formula, "right or wrong my country." The latter implies a half-hearted attempt to defend the undefendable position that my country is right when it is wrong, and hence actually admits that in those cases it is wrong.

8. Leo Gross, "States as Organs of International Law and the Problems of Auto-interpretation," in, G. A. Lipsky, ed., *Law and Politics in the World Community,* 1963, p. 64. (Italics added.)

The same has been pointed out by other authors, e.g., Larson, *When Nations Disagree; Briefly, The Law of Nations* (5th ed., p. 72): "It is a *common mistake* that . . . the most conspicuous [defect of international law] is the frequency of its violations." (Italics added.)

9. Gross, ibid., p. 64 (ital. added).

10. Gross, l.c., passim, and p. 88 (ital. added).

11. Mangone, *The Elements of International Law,* 1963, p. 4.

12. Professor Mangone agrees that "the existence of law cannot be bound to the single criterion of enforcement. 'The true gauge of the law,' said Supreme Court Justice William O. Douglas, 'is not command, but conduct'" *(l.c.).*

13. Hans Aufricht, "Der Rechtssatz als Gegenstand der vergleichenden Rechtswissenschaft," 1961 *Zeitschrift für Rechtsvergleichung,* p. 164. As he explains, the theory of law which he (and the present paper) subscribes to, denies, not that sanctions constitute legal consequence (Rechtsfolgen) but that sanctions are the only legally consequence, because this view would deprive highly significant parts of the legal system of its character as law.

14. In G. A. Lipsky, ed., *Law and Politics in the World Community,* l.c., p. 6; p. 320, n. 10. See also Quincy Wright, *Problems of Stability and Progress in International Relations,* 1959, 267.

15. At present, it sounds quaint that public debts of Central and South American States must not "occasion armed intervention nor *even* [sic] the *actual occupation* of the territory of the American nations by a *European power.*" (See J. G. Starke, *An Introduction to International Law,* 5th ed., London: Butterworth, 1967. p. 252.)

16. The positivist school, claiming as it does disinterest in or unconcern with the actual character of the sanction (as long as any sanction is provided for) is not, of course, intrinsically blood-thirsty. However, some formulations of positivists have obscured this point, and thus unwittingly fostered the wide-spread notion that the majesty of the law is best served if it is most forceful."

17. Myres S. McDougal and F. P. Feliciano, *Law and Minimum World Order,* 1961, p. 365.

18. Depending on the argumentation in a specific case, this implies any of the four views of international law mentioned above—as orphan, as harlot, as jailer, or as never-never promise; or any combination of them.

19. Brierly, l.c., p. 367.

20. In: *International Law in a Changing World,* p. 29.

21. The International Court of Justice, in its majority; advisory definition on *Conditions of Membership in the United Nations,* declared that the five Conditions for membership enumerated in Art. 4, par. 1 of the Charter, are exhaustive; but that this exhaustive character "does not forbid the taking into account of any factor which it is possible reasonably and in good faith to connect with the condition . . . *no relevant political factor is excluded.*" (I.C.J. Reports, 1948, pp. 57, 62); whereas the four of the six dissenting judges who filed a joint dissenting opinion, pointed out that a Member, in voting for or against the admission of a state, "is participating in a *political decision* and is *therefore legally entitled* to make its consent to the admission dependent on any political considerations which seem to it to be relevant . . . (having) regard to the principle of good faith . . ." (ibid., p. 91). Leo Gross pointed out that these two opinions "on at least one or two points are perhaps not so far apart as they may appear. It is common ground that Members are bound to act in good faith but are not bound to state the reasons for their vote or veto." His analysis shows that not only the eligibility is covered by the law (Art. 4,1) but also the political decision, to admit or not to admit an eligible state, is covered by the law (Art. 4,2). It may be respectfully noted that the formulation of Judge Alvarez is conceivably open to misunderstanding: "cases may arise . . . [where] even if the conditions for admission are fulfilled by an applicant, admission may be refused. In such cases, the question is *no longer a legal one,* it *becomes a political one* and must be regarded as such." (Leo Gross, "Election of States to United Nations Membership" in 1954 *Proceedings of the American Society of International Law,* pp. 40, 41, 44, 45.) The meaning is that, since the law permits political discretion, the exercise of such discretion is "legal" and beyond judicial critique. (Italics added.)

22. In Japan there "are frequent and informal discussions among judges and counsel. In a sense, the trial proceeds like an incessant pre-trial conference in the U.S." (*The Japanese Judicial System under the New Constitution*, Tokyo, Supreme Court of Japan, 1947, quoted A. W. Burke, *The Government of Japan,* 1961, p. 171.)

23. Similarly, "the use which the successful party makes of the judgment [of the International Court of Justice] is a matter which lies on the political and not on the judicial plane." (Case of the *Cameroons v. The United Kingdom,* Judgment of Dec. 2, 1963 [1963] I.C.J. Report, p. 37.) For Leo Gross' comments on this judgment, see 58 *A.J.I.L.* (1964), pp. 415-431.

24. Censure by an international organ may be compared to the penalty of rep-

rimand envisaged in various domestic legislations (see, e.g., Jerome Han, *General Principles of Criminal Law,* 1960, note 1 on pp. 611-612). A strong censure by an international organ may be compared to the penalty of (temporary) demotion of the censured nation in its international reputation. This is a time-honored and often efficacious way of asserting the law and imposing "retribution." Former ages endowed such sanctions with deliberately impressive ritual and ceremony: characteristically, in military organizations, which have kept some of the flavor of feudal times, demotion is accompanied by vivid formalities, and considered one of the worst punishments. The same is true of demotions in other old institutions, for example, certain religious hierarchies.

25. G. A. Codding, Jr., *The Federal Government of Switzerland,* 1961, pp. 33, 106.

26. The limitations to the political nature of the appointments according to national mores became apparent in the opposition to President Roosevelt's "court packing" plan.

27. Therefore, after careful analysis, he concludes that: "Courts are also part of the government. The voices of the judges, when they pass over the edge [of the country's boundaries] must harmonize with the executive's. The exercise of judicial deference is then recognition of the executive's prerogative, not abdication of judicial responsibility." (48 *Cornell Law Quarterly* (1963), 461, 498.)

28. Jim Leeson, "Fewer than One in Ten Negroes Attending School with Whites," in *Southern School News,* l.c., p. 1; ital. added.

29. According to Secretary General U Thant, "The elements of international law applied in the Congo crisis were not mere technicalities, but represented the long-range aspirations and ideals which the great majority of states share, and on the basis of which they look to the U.N. as the main protector of their common interests." (U.N. Doc. A/4390, Add. 1, p. 7.)

30. A very large portion of the international legal order applies also between states and governments which do not recognize each other or are otherwise not on speaking terms; and this is a very wise rule of international law.

31. "The Spirit of International Law. Address before the Bar Association of Tennessee, June 3, 1938." Dept. of State Publ. 1190, p. 13, 7–8.

PART 2.1

International Law as
Operating System:
Meeting the Requirements
of the International System

4

The Peace of Westphalia, 1648–1948

Leo Gross

The acceptance of the United Nations Charter by the overwhelming majority of the members of the family of nations brings to mind the first great European or world charter, the Peace of Westphalia. To it is traditionally attributed the importance and dignity of being the best of several attempts to establish something resembling world unity on the basis of states exercising untrammeled sovereignty over certain territories and subordinated to no earthly authority.

The next attempt, the settlement of Vienna of 1815 and the Congress of Aix-la Chapelle of 1818, which in a sense completed the former, gave birth to that loose system of consultation between the Great Powers known as the Concert of Europe. Born of the cataclysm of the Napoleonic Wars and anchored in the Protocol of the Aix-la-Chapelle of November 15, 1818, the Concert provided some sort of a self-appointed directing board for the maintenance and manipulation of that balance of power on which the European peace precariously reposed for about a hundred years. Uncertain in its foundations, devoid of much organization or continuity, it was characterized as much by the devotion of the Great Powers which composed it to the policy of a free hand as it was, in consequence, by the absence of definite commitments. Consultation and conference on problems of mutual interest was a frequent practice but no obligation of the Great Powers. It was precisely this flexibility, frequently regarded and praised as the chief virtue of the concert system, which ultimately brought about its ruin at a moment when it was most desperately needed. The policy of free hands reaped a large harvest in World War I.

Faced with the devastating results of World War I and the bankruptcy of the Concert, the Paris Settlement of 1919, without essentially departing

Reproduced with permission from 42 *AJIL* 20 (1948), © The American Society of International Law.

from the Peace of Westphalia, attempted a novel solution, drawing for its inspiration on the Concert, the Hague Peace Conferences, the experience of the nineteenth and twentieth centuries in non-political international collaboration, and the wartime collaboration between the allied and associated Powers. It produced the League of Nations, in which the member states assumed certain commitments to cooperate in various fields and, above all, without abolishing the right of war, *jus ad bellum,* to establish "the undertakings of international law as the actual rule of conduct among governments." It is a moot question whether the failure of the League should be attributed to a defective legal technique in organizing international security or to a kind of fatal and gradual relapse of the Great Powers into the traditional methods of consultation untrammeled by and frequently in open disregard of their obligations under the Covenant. The climax in this process of degeneration was reached in 1939 when alliances were hurriedly tossed around and when Poland, though attacked by Germany on September 1, 1939, found it convenient to manifest its contempt of the League of Nations by not even appealing to it under article 10 of the Covenant, and when Great Britain and France went to the assistance of Poland not because they were legally bound to do so by the Covenant but because they felt in honor bound to fulfill their obligations as allies in Poland. Thus World War II started in the customary way, even as if the League were non-existent; as a consequence the League was doomed.

Critics of the United Nations Charter point out that it includes some of the elements of the League organization and that it relies even more heavily than did the League on the notion of consultation, on limited obligations in the political, and the method of voluntary cooperation in the non-political, field. The charter proclaims that the organization is based on the sovereign equality of all the members only in order the firmer to establish the hegemony of a group of Great Powers. On the other hand, in articles 24 and 25, the principal framers of the Charter almost obtained what the Concert never succeeded in obtaining, namely, the recognition by the lesser nations of the preeminent position of the Great Powers as the guardians of international peace and security. In spite of this and other important indications of a new approach to the problem of international security and relations, the Charter at first glance would seem to have left essentially unchanged the framework of the state system and of international law resulting from the Peace of Westphalia.

Thus the Peace of Westphalia may be said to continue its sway over political man's mind as the *ratio scripta* that it was held to be of yore. What is the explanation of this curious phenomenon? In view of this continued influence of the Peace of Westphalia, it may not be amiss to discuss briefly its character, background and implications.

It should be clear from the outset that the actual provisions of the Treaties of Osnabrück between the Empire and Sweden, and of Münster between the Empire and France and their respective confederates and allies, have undergone more than one substantial change in the course of time. The political map of Europe as outlined in these Treaties is no longer. It should be noted, however, that the chief political idea underlying the Franco-German settlement of 1648 has undergone relatively little change. Then the axiom of French politics was that the best guarantee of French security lies in a divided and impotent Germany, and that this division and impotence must be secured by appropriate provisions such as those which gave France a right to intervene when necessary in order to vindicate the principle of the sanctity of treaties.

The Thirty Years' War had its origin, at any rate partially, in a religious conflict or, as one might say, in religious intolerance. The Peace of Westphalia consecrated the principle of toleration by establishing the equality between Protestant and Catholic states and by providing some safeguards for religious minorities. To be sure, the principle of liberty of conscience was applied only incompletely and without reciprocity. The religious Peace of Augsburg of 1555 and the rule *cujus regio ejus religio* were confirmed. With a view to alleviating the lot of religious minorities, however, the Treaty of Osnabrück provided that

> subjects who in 1627 had been debarred from the free exercise of their religion, other than that of their ruler, were by the Peace granted the right of conducting private worship, and of educating their children, at home or abroad, in conformity with their own faith; they were not to suffer in any civil capacity nor to be denied religious burial, but were to be at liberty to emigrate, selling their estates or leaving them to be managed by others.[1]

Moreover, in an effort to assure equality between Catholic and Protestant members of the German Diet, the Treaty of Osnabrück laid down the important rule that in matters pertaining to religion

> a majority of votes should no longer be held decisive at the Diet; but that such questions should be settled by an amicable 'composition' between its two parts or *corpora*. . . . In the same spirit of parity it was agreed that when possible there should be equality of consulting and voting power between the two religions on all commissions of the Diet, including those *Deputationstage* which had come to exercise an authority nearly equalling that of the Diets themselves.[2]

The principle of religious equality was placed as part of the peace under an international guarantee. The Peace of Westphalia thereby established a precedent of far-reaching importance. One or two illustrations may be in order. The Constitution of the Germanic Confederation of June 8, 1815, which forms part of the Final Act of the Congress of Vienna of June 9, 1815, stipulates in article XVI that the difference between the Christian religions should cause no difference in the enjoyment by their adherents of civil and political rights, and, furthermore, that the German Diet should consider the grant of civil rights to Jews on condition that they assume all civic duties incumbent on other citizens. By the time the Congress of Berlin convened the principle of religious tolerance had become so firmly established that the delegate of France, M. Waddington, could make the following statement:

> Mr. Waddington believes that it is important to take advantage of this solemn opportunity to cause the principles of religious liberty to be affirmed by the representatives of Europe. His Excellency adds that Serbia, who claims to enter the European family on the same basis as other states, must previously recognize the principles which are the basis of social organization in all states of Europe and accept them as a necessary condition of the favor which she asks for.[3]

The representatives of Great Britain, Germany, Italy, Austria-Hungary, and of the Ottoman Empire concurred in the view propounded by M. Waddington and the Congress acted accordingly in the case of Serbia, Montenegro, and Rumania.

This precedent was relied upon by the Principal Allied and Associated Powers in submitting to Poland the Treaty of June 28, 1919, concerning the protection of minorities. In his covering letter to M. Paderewski, the President of the Paris Peace Conference stated that "This treaty does not constitute any fresh departure," and continued as follows:

> It has for long been the established procedure of the public law of Europe that when a state is created, or even when large accessions of territory are made to an established state, the joint and formal recognition by the Great Powers should be accompanied by the requirement that such State should, in the form of a binding international convention, undertake to comply with certain principles of government.[4]

The latest step in this long line of evolution is represented by the United Nations Charter, the Preamble of which declares that the peoples of the United Nations are determined "to reaffirm faith in fundamental human rights, in the dignity and worth of the human person, in the equal rights of men and women, and of nations, large and small," and, "to practice tolerance and live together in peace with one-another as good neighbors." It is one of the basic purposes of the United Nations to achieve international cooperation "in promoting and encouraging respect for human rights and for fundamental freedoms for all without distinction as to race, sex, language, or religion." If the efforts of the United Nations are crowned with success by the adoption of an international bill of the fundamental rights of man, they will have accomplished the task which originated in the religious schism of Europe and which had found its first, albeit an inadequate, solution on an international basis in the Peace of Westphalia.

Another aspect of the Peace of Westphalia which exercised considerable influence on future developments relates to the guarantee of the peace
itself. Both treaties declare that the peace concluded shall remain in force
and that all parties to it "shall be obliged to defend and protect all and every
article of this peace against anyone, without distinction of religion."[5] This
was by no means a new departure. . . . Nevertheless this guarantee of the
observance and the execution of an agreed international transaction, including as it did clauses of a constitutional character, as far as the Empire was
concerned, came to assume in the following decades an overriding significance. It was pointed out that "no guarantee was more important or has
been more often referred to than that included in the treaties of
Westphalia."

> These treaties contain clauses by which Sweden and France not only make
> peace with the Emperor on certain terms, but pledge themselves to their
> allies, the subordinate German Princes, that they will ensure that the privi-
> leges and immunities conferred on the Princes and free cities of (Germany
> in the treaty shall be upheld and maintained. This is constantly referred to
> in these treaties as the guarantee for the execution of the terms of the
> treaty and, as Sir Ernest Satow has pointed out, it continued to be re-
> garded as valid almost down to the outbreak of the French Revolution.
> Here, again, the fate of the guarantee was of the highest importance in en-
> suring that the treaties should be observed and that they should continue
> to hold their place as part of the general European System.[6]

For the first time Europe thus received "what may fairly be described as an
international constitution, which gave to all its adherents the right of intervention to enforce its engagements."[7] That this attempt to guarantee effectively a peace so laboriously achieved was not wholly successful needs
hardly to be emphasized. In this respect the Settlement of Westphalia is in
good company with many other international instruments of historical
importance.

In addition to the guarantee, the Settlement of Westphalia formulated
certain extremely interesting rules for the peaceful settlement of disputes
and collective sanctions against aggressors. Thus the Treaty of Münster, in
Articles CXIII and CXXIV stipulates that

> if it happens that any point should be violated, the Offended shall before
> all things exhort the Offender not to come to any Hostility, submitting the
> Cause to a friendly Composition, or the ordinary Proceedings of Justice.
> Nevertheless, if for the space of three years the Difference cannot be ter-
> minated, by any of those means, all and every one of those concerned in
> this Transaction shall be obliged to join the injured Party, and assist him
> with Counsel and Force to repel the Injury, being first advertised by the
> injured that gentle Means and Justice prevailed nothing; but without prej-
> udice, nevertheless, to every one's Jurisdiction, and the Administration of
> Justice conformable to the Laws of each Prince and State; and it shall not

be permitted to any State of the Empire to pursue his Right by Force and arms; but if any difference has happened or happens for the future (between the states of the Empire), every one shall try the means of ordinary Justice, and the Contravener shall be regarded as an Infringer of the Peace. That which has been determined (between the States of the Empire) by Sentence of the Judge, shall be put in execution, without distinction of Condition, as the Laws of the Empire enjoin touching the Execution of arrests and Sentences.

This was a "novel feature" in international treaty and peacemaking. The provisions for a moratorium of war, the settlement of disputes by peaceful means, and for individual and collective sanctions against the aggressor, after a delay of three years, although proclaimed primarily for the Empire, the members of which had been given their sovereign rights to conclude treaties of alliance, have nevertheless served as a model for numerous subsequent treaties. They constitute, in a sense, an early precedent for Articles 10, 12, and 16, of the Covenant of the League of Nations.

The grave dislocations in the social and economic life of Europe caused by the long war prompted the delegates to the Congress of Westphalia to discuss means designed to facilitate reconstruction. For this purpose two clauses were inserted in the Treaties of Münster and Osnabrück. One aimed at restoring freedom of commerce by abolishing barriers to trade which had developed in the course of the war, and the other intended to provide a measure of free navigation on the Rhine. In this respect, as in many others, there is apparent the particular character of the Westphalian peace which distinguishes it sharply from routine peace treaties and which points out its kinship with the great peace settlements of 1815 and 1919.

As the above rapid survey of some of the salient features of the Peace Settlement of 1648 discloses, the actual terms of the settlement, interesting and novel as they may be, would hardly suffice to account for the outstanding place attributed to it in the evolution of international relations. In order to find a more adequate explanation it would seem appropriate to search not so much in the text of the treaties themselves as in their implications, in the broad conceptions on which they rest and the developments to which they provided impetus.

In this order of ideas it has been affirmed that the Peace of Westphalia was the starting point for the development of modern international law. It has also been contended that it constituted "the first faint beginning of an international constitutional law" and the first instance "of deliberate enactment of common regulations by concerted action."[8] In this connection the special merits of the work of Grotius have been stressed. On the one hand it has been argued that "Grotius adapted the (old) Law of Nature to fill the vacuum created by the extinction of the supreme authority of Emperor and Pope."[9] On the other hand it has been affirmed that Grotius developed a system of international law which would equally appeal to, and be approved by, the believers and the atheists, and which would apply to all states irrespective of the character and dignity of their rulers. It can hardly be denied that the Peace of Westphalia marked an epoch in the evolution of international law. It undoubtedly promoted the laicization of international law by divorcing it from any particular religious background, and the extension of its scope so as to include, on a footing of equality, republican and monarchical states. Indeed these two by-products of the Peace of 1648 would seem significant enough for students of international law and relations to regard it as an event of outstanding and lasting value. It would seem hazardous, however, to regard the Settlement of Westphalia and the work of Grotius as more than states in the gradual, though by no means uniform, process which antedates and continues beyond the year 1648. As to the contention that Grotius filled the vacuum created by the deposition of Pope and Emperor, more will be said about this in a different context.

Closely related with the stimulus to international law is the impetus said to have been given by the Peace of Westphalia to the theory and practice of the balance of power. Indeed, the existence of a political equilibrium has frequently been regarded as a necessary condition for the existence of the Law of Nations. It has also become virtually axiomatic that the maintenance of the state system depends upon the preservation of a balance of power between its component and independent parts. There is substantial evidence for the fact that while the principle of the balance of power had been evolved prior to 1648, the Peace of Westphalia first illustrates its application on a grand scale. The operation of the maxim *partager pour équilibrer* can be traced in the territorial clauses of the Treaties of Münster and Osnabrück. This is notably the case in those referring to the aggrandizement of France and Sweden, to the independence of the United Provinces, of the Swiss Confederation, and to the consolidation of about nine hundred units of the Empire into about three hundred. Henceforth, in the organization of Europe resulting from the Peace, *tout repose sur la convenance de balancer les forces et de garantir les situations acquises par l'éstablissement de contrepoids.*[10] It is interesting to note that the advocacy of a political equilibrium in the literature of the Renaissance has been interpreted as having the character of a protest against the rival principle of a universal monarchy. It was argued, in effect, that the freedom of all states would be brought about as a result of the establishment of a political equilibrium. In this sense the balance of power doctrine forms an important part of that body of political thought which came to fruition in the Peace of Westphalia. It assumed, thereby, increased significance and prestige.

Of even greater importance than any of these particular aspects of developments of the Treaties of Osnabrück and Münster were the general political ideas, the triumph of which they apparently consecrated in the mind of man. The Peace of Westphalia, for better or worse, marks the end of an epoch and the opening of another. It represents the majestic portal which leads from the old into the new world. The old world, we are told, lived in the idea of a Christian commonwealth, of a world harmoniously ordered and governed in the spiritual and temporal realms by the Pope and Emperor. This medieval world was characterized by a hierarchical conception of the relationship between the existing political entities on the one hand, and the Emperor on the other. For a long time preceding the Peace of 1648, however, powerful intellectual, political, and social forces were at work which opposed and, by opposing them, undermined, both the aspirations and the remaining realities of the unified control of Pope and Emperor. In particular the Reformation and the Renaissance, and, expressive of the rising urge of individualism in politics, nationalism, each in its own field, attacked the supreme authority claimed by the Pope and the Emperor. The combined impact of these centrifugal forces could not, in the long run, be resisted solely by the writings of the defenders of their authority. To maintain the claims it would have been necessary to display a real overpowering authority. Neither the Pope nor the Emperor, however, was at that time in the position to restrain effectively the centrifugal tendencies. The latter was ultimately forced to abandon all pretenses on the field of battle and the former's protest against the Peace of Westphalia, the Bull *Zel Domus* of November 26, 1648, failed to restrain the course of history. In the spiritual field the Treaty of Westphalia was said to be "a public act of disregard of the international authority of the Papacy."[11] In the political field it marked man's abandonment of the idea of a hierarchical structure of society and his option for a new system characterized by the coexistence of a multiplicity of states, each sovereign within its territory, equal to one another, and free from any external earthly authority. The idea of an authority or organization above the sovereign states is no longer. What takes its place is the notion that all states form a worldwide political system or that, at any rate, the states of Western Europe form a single political system. This new system rests on international law and the balance of power, a law operating between rather than above states and a power operating between rather than above states.

It is true that the powers assembled at the Congress of Westphalia paid homage to the old conception of world unity by proclaiming in the preamble of the Treaty of Münster that it was made *ad Christianae Reipublicae salutem* and in that of the Treaty of Osnabrück *au salut de la Republique Chrestienne*. Nevertheless, there is a notable lack of consensus in the appreciation of the major implications of the Peace of Westphalia. According to one view the old system was simply superseded by a modern, the present political, state system, a world-wide system.[12] On the other hand the view is also held that the Peace of Westphalia marks a decisive date in the history of the disorganization of the public law of Europe. In this order of ideas it was argued that the system inaugurated by the Peace, while it may be new, was "as utterly remote as possible from a juridical order founded on a common respect for law";[13] and that in spite of all the appearances of the birth of a new international society of nations "even the germ of such a society was likely to be absent under a system in direct opposition to any impingement upon the sovereign independence of each individual state."[14] Which of these conflicting views is accurate? The answer is difficult in the extreme for the materials regarding the basic problems of the origin of our state system lack coordination and clarity and all the necessary sources are not readily available. For these reasons the following remarks are necessarily tentative and intended to indicate rather than to solve the problems connected with the rise of the modern state system and the particular role of the Peace of Westphalia in this vital process.

The imperial authority, the gradual weakening of which is sometimes said to have set in as early as the Treaty of Verdun of 843, probably received a serious blow in the course and as a result of the Great Interregnum (1254–73) on the one hand, and the rise of independent or quasi-independent communities in Italy and of national states in England, Spain, and France, on the other. The discovery of the New World and the extension of intercourse between the Western Christian and Eastern non-Christian world provided those opposing the claim of the Emperor to universal dominion with arguments of considerable persuasiveness. The Great Schism in the Church (1378–1417) and the rise of sects and eventually of the Reformation weakened correspondingly the authority of the Pope. These developments in the secular and spiritual fields which finally culminated in the Thirty Years' War and the Peace of Westphalia, were reflected in and stimulated by contemporaneous political thought.

One of the early opponents of the Emperor was Bartolus of Sassoferrato who drew a fine distinction between the *de jure* overlordship of the Emperor and the *de facto* existence of *civitates superiorem non recognoscentes*. The formula, said to be of French origin, was later cast by Baldus in a sharper form: *Rex in regno suo est Imperator regni sui*. In that sentence, observed Professor Barker, "we may hear the cracking of the Middle Ages."[15] Bartolus, however, in spite of his insistence on the *de facto* independence of Italian city states, still recognized the Empire and the Emperor as the Lord of the world albeit on an idealistic or spiritualistic plane. In France a similar movement against the universalistic claims of both Emperor and Pope was on foot. The development of the theory of sovereignty by Bodin may be regarded as marking the end, on the doctrinal level, of the efforts to throw off the overlordship of the Emperor and vindicate the independence of states. This movement was not unopposed. Imperialist writers continued to defend and support the claims of the Emperor. Their argument was, broadly, that being of divine origin, the rights of the Emperor existed irrespective of their actual exercise. No voluntary abandonment, not even an express grant, was susceptible of impairing them. As late as the seventeenth century, imperialist lawyers repeated the claim that the King of France, like other princes, was of right, and must forever remain, subject to the Roman Emperor.

While some of the jurists of the sixteenth century questioned with increasing boldness the claim of any single potentate to be *totius orbis dominus* others combined their opposition with the exposition of a new positive doctrine, that of an international community of states. This doctrine is admittedly of ancient origin. The conception of the entire human race forming a single society goes back to the Stoa and the teachings of the early church fathers. It experienced a revival in the works of some of the early writers of international law, notably those of Victoria, Suarez, and Gentili. They denied, on the one hand, the claim of the Emperor to exercise temporal jurisdiction over princes, and affirmed, on the other, the existence of an international community governed by international law.

Victoria, in a famous passage arguing the binding force of laws made by a king upon the king himself, irrespective of his will, and of pacts entered into by the free will of the contracting parties upon them, declares:

> From all that has been said, a corollary may be inferred, namely: that international law has not only the force of a pact and agreement among men, but also the force of a law; for the world as a whole, being in a way one single State, has the power to create laws that are just and fitting for all persons, as are the rules of international law. Consequently, it is clear that they who violate these international rules, whether in peace or in war, commit a mortal sin; moreover, in the gravest matters, such as the inviolability of ambassadors, it is not permissible for one country to refuse to be bound by international law, the latter having been established by the authority of the whole world.[16]

Gentili referred with approval to the teachings of the Stoics that

> the whole world formed one state, and that all men were fellow citizens and fellow townsmen, like a single herd feeding in a common pasture. All this universe which you see, in which things divine and human are included, is one, and we are members of a great body. And, in truth, the world is one body.[17]

And again, he declared:

> Now what Plato and those expounders of the law say of private citizens we feel justified in applying to sovereigns and nations, since the rule which governs a private citizen in his own state ought to govern a public citizen, that is to say a sovereign or a sovereign people, in this public and universal state formed by the world. As a private citizen conducts himself with reference to another private citizen, so ought it to be between one sovereign and another, says Baldus.[18]

Suarez' conception of the international society is expounded in the following "perhaps the most memorable passage of the 'Law of Nations.'"

The rational basis . . . of this phase of law consists in the fact that the human race howsoever many the various peoples and kingdoms into which it may be divided, always preserves a certain unity . . . enjoined the natural precept of mutual love and mercy; a precept which applies to all, even to strangers of every nation.

Therefore, although a given sovereign state, commonwealth, or kingdom, may constitute a perfect community in itself, consisting of its own members, nevertheless, each one of these states is also, in a certain sense, and viewed in relation to the human race, a member of that universal society; for these states when standing alone are never so self-sufficient that they do not require some mutual assistance, association, and intercourse, at times for their own greater welfare and advantage, but at other times because also of some moral necessity or need. This fact is made manifest by actual usage.

Consequently, such communities have need of some system of law whereby they may be directed and properly ordered with regard to this kind of intercourse and association; and although that guidance is in large measure provided by natural reason, it is not provided in sufficient measure and in a direct manner with respect to all matters; therefore, it was possible for certain special rules of law to be introduced through the practice of these same nations. For just as in one state or province law is introduced by custom, so among the human race as a whole it was possible for laws to be introduced by the habitual conduct of nations. This was the more feasible because the matters comprised within the law in questioned few, very closely related to natural law and most easily deduced therefrom in a manner so advantageous and so in harmony with nature itself that, while this derivation (of the law of nations from the natural law) may not be self-evident that is, not essentially and absolutely required for moral rectitude is nevertheless quite in accord with nature, and universally acceptable for its own sake.[19]

It is this conception of an international society embracing, on a footing of equality, the entire human race irrespective of religion and form of government which is usually said to have triumphed in the seventeenth century over the medieval conception of a more restricted Christian society organized hierarchically, that is, on the basis of inequality, as the dominating political position of the Roman Emperor had gradually but decidedly declined in the centuries and decades preceding the Peace of Westphalia, it is probably correct to say that the Peace merely finally sealed an existing state of affairs. Lord Bryce said that the Peace of Westphalia "did no more than legalize a condition of things already in existence, but which, by being legalized, acquired new importance."[20] It is probably also true, in a broad sense, that with the Congress of Westphalia the various states entered into the legal concept of a *societas gentium* which had long before been established by the science of natural law. It is equally correct that the so-called Grotian Law of Nature school continued to expound the concept of a society of states. Christian Wolfe's ides of a *civitas gentium maxima* is a noteworthy and well-known example. A sideline of this type of thinking and writing is represented by the writers who in one form or another, on a restricted or universal basis, advocate the establishment of a more definite society of states than in their view appeared to be actually in existence. One might mention as representatives of this school of thought Dante, Pierre Dubois, George of Podebrad, Erasmus, Emeric Cruce, Sully, William Penn, the Abbé de Saint-Pierre, Rousseau, Jeremy Bentham, Immanuel Kant, William Ladd, William Jay, Elihu Burritt, Saint-Simon, Jean de Bloch, A. H. Fried, J. Novicov, and others. To some extent their writings should have served as evidence that the *pluriversum* which emerged in the sixteenth and seventeenth centuries was not quite an international community and that the states did not always behave as members of one body politic.

Be that as it may, it would seem not altogether unjustified to observe that the development of international law, a determining factor of any conception of an international community, did not come to a standstill with the Peace of Westphalia. It would seem possible to distinguish at least three trends of thought on the subject of the binding force of international law prior to 1648. In Victoria one might discern the attempt to base international law or an objective foundation irrespective of the will of the states and to conceive international law as a law above states. In Suarez the objective foundation is at least overshadowed if not replaced by a subjective foundation in the will of the states. Suarez presented the *jus gentium* as a law between states. In Gentili, of whom it has been said that he had taken the first step towards making international law what it is, namely, almost exclusively positive, international law still appears to be based on natural reason and derived from a law of nature superior to the nations. Gentili's doctrine "marked progress because it affirmed the existence of an autonomous system of rules of law distinct from the precepts of religion and ethics and directed at regulating international relations according to abstract principles justice."[21] But what, precisely, we may ask, was the nature of that autonomy? An indication of its meaning may perhaps be gleaned from Gentili's doctrine of the just war. One of the essential conditions of a just war is that it must be waged for a just cause. Gentili affirms that war may be waged with justice on both sides. He is said to come close to Machiavelli's opinion that all necessary wars are justified. But who decides whether there is a just cause, whether the necessity is of such a nature as to justify war? The answer to this question must obviously be of decisive importance for the understanding not only of Gentili's doctrine of just war but equally for his conception of international law. Now it is extremely interesting to note that the decision "concerning the lawfulness of war is on the whole left to each belligerent."[22] If this is an accurate interpretation of Gentili's doctrine, then the autonomy of international law would seem to assume s deeper meaning. It would indicate not merely the independence of international law from the precepts of civil law, religion, and ethics. It would also seem to indicate that the contents of international law as well as the existence or non-existence of international law depends upon the insight of the states concerned, or, to use a modern phrase, upon the will of the states.

Grotius and several subsequent writers still maintain natural or divine law alongside of customary law as a source of international law. It would seem, however, that with Grotius the accent begins to be transferred from the Law of Nature or divine law to that branch of human law which "has received its obligatory force from the will of nations, or of many nations."[23] Zouche, the "second founder of the Law of Nations," rather than Grotius, is called the father of positivism for the emphasis given by him to customary international law. Without any attempt to trace the development of the doctrine of the will of states as the basis of international law, it may be useful to conclude this brief survey with a few remarks about Vattel. Vattel, regarded as a Grotian, still maintains the distinction between different types of branches of the Law of Nations. Within the positive law of nations, based on the agreement of nations, he differentiates three divisions: the voluntary, the conventional, and the customary law. The voluntary law proceeds from their presumed consent, the conventional law from their express consent, and the customary law from their tacit consent. Positive international law is distinguished from the natural or necessary law of nations which Vattel undertakes to treat separately. In order to understand the respective functions of natural and positive international law Vattel draws the following distinction:

> But after having established on each point what the necessary law prescribes, we shall then explain how and by these precepts must be modified by the voluntary law; or, to put it in another way, we shall show how, by reason of the liberty of nations and the rules of their natural society, the external law which they must observe towards one another differs on certain points from the principles of the internal law, which, however, are always binding upon the conscience.[24]

With these nice distinctions in mind one may ask legitimately what precisely is the role of these branches of the law of nations with respect to the conduct of states in relation to one another. Vattel leaves no doubt about it, for he declares that while the necessary law is at all times obligatory upon the conscience, and that a nation must never lose sight of it when deliberating on the course it must pursue in order to fulfill its duty, it must consult the voluntary law "when there is question of what it can demand from other states."[25] It may not be unreasonable to conclude that according to Vattel only those rules of the law of nations which proceed from and are based on the consent of states are enforceable in international relations. This rather significant feature of Vattel's doctrine, it is believed, may not have entirely escaped the attention of diplomats to whom it was addressed, and it may, therefore, account at least partially for his immense popularity. But Vattel's international law is no longer above but beside the diplomat.

Although he does not rank as a strict positivist, Vattel prepared the ground for the era of uninhibited positivism. He helped to establish, precisely because of his popularity, perhaps more than any of his predecessors or successors, the consensus character of international law and to reduce natural law from the function of supplying an objective basis for the validity, the binding force, of the law of nations to the function of supplying rules for filling gaps in positive international law. This distinction between the dual function of natural law in relation to the law of nations is not always observed and yet it would seem to deserve close attention.

The development of international law along the lines indicated above, was bound to influence the concept of an international society of states. In the course of time it became purely formal. *Ubi ius, ibi societas.* Those who argued the existence of a law of nations accepted the use, though rarely more, of the phrase, "Family of Nations." In the period following the Peace of Westphalia the development of international relations would seem to have followed decidedly not the conception of an objectively founded international law and community of Victoria but that indicated in the teachings of Suarez, if indeed it be accurate to assume an essential difference between their doctrines. From the 18th century and, in particular, from Vattel onward, however, there can be no doubt as to the trend of the development. It was predominately positivist and consensual. The will of states seems to explain both the contents and the binding force of international law. The concept of the Family of Nations recedes in the background. To have paved the way for this development by liquidating, with a degree of apparent finality, the idea of the Middle Ages of an objective order of things personified by the Emperor in the secular realm, would seem to be one of the more vital aspects of the consequences of the Peace of Westphalia and of its place in the evolution of international relations. Viewed in this light the answer to the question formulated above cannot be doubtful. Instead of heralding the era of a genuine international community of nations subordinated to the role of the law of nations, it led to the era of absolutist states, jealous of their territorial sovereignty to a point where the idea of an international community became an almost empty phrase and where international law came to depend upon the will of states more concerned with the preservation and expansion of their power than with the establishment of a rule of law. In the period immediately following the Peace, of the objective validity of international law there may be some doubt. Of the subjective character of much of modern international law there can hardly be any doubt.

It may be said, by way of summary, that on the threshold of the modern era of international relations there were two doctrines with respect to the binding force of international law and the existence of an international community of states. The doctrine of Victoria is characterized by an objective approach to the problem of the binding force of international law and by an organic conception of the international community of states. The other doctrine, characterized by the voluntaristic conception of the binding force of international law, is adumbrated in the work of Suarez. It is developed in the writings of Gentili, Grotius and Zouche, and it breaks to the fore in the work of Vattel who, emphasizing the independence rather than the interdependence of states, wrote the international law of political liberty. The growth of the voluntaristic conception of international law is accompanied by a weakening of the notion that all states form and are part of an international community. It is still very strong in the writings of Suarez and Gentili, although it seems to have assumed a character different from that attributed to it by Victoria. The test of the strength of the community doctrine may be said to have come in the seventeenth century. The liquidation of the universalistic claims of the Empire and the recognition of a multiplicity of states wielding the same powers as those hitherto reserved for the Emperor should have created a political and juridical condition favorable for the establishment of a genuine society of states. The opportunity which may have existed at the end of the Thirty Years' War for substituting a new order based on the impersonal supremacy of international law for the old order based on the personal supremacy of the Empire, was not, however, utilized. Instead of creating a society of states, the Peace of Westphalia, while paying lip service to the idea of a Christian commonwealth, merely ushers in the era of sovereign absolutist states which recognized no superior authority. In this era the liberty of states becomes increasingly incompatible with the concept of the international community, governed by international law independent of the will of states. On the contrary this era may be said to be characterized by the reign of positivism in international law. This positivism could not admit the existence of a society of states for the simple reason that it was unable to find a treaty or custom, proceeding from the will of states, which could be interpreted as the legal foundation of a community of states. In the nineteenth century, after the Napoleonic wars, there may be discerned in the Congress and Concert system the beginning of a conscious effort to establish a community of states based on the will of all states or at least on the will of the Great Powers. The Hague Peace Conferences, the League of Nations and, we may confidently assert, the United Nations are further stages in this development cognizable by positive international law.

This reaction against the unrestrained liberty of states, recognized as self-destructive in its ultimate implications was accentuated by a reaction against the prevailing voluntaristic conception of international law. The attempts to provide international law with an objective foundation, without, however, abandoning altogether the will of states doctrine, are illustrated by Bergbohm's and Triepel's theory of the *Vereinbarung*. A radical departure from the consensual view of international law is characteristic of Kelsen's theory of the initial hypothesis, and of the recent revival of natural law thinking in the field of international law. Other writers follow this trend away from the purely consensual nature of international law by emphasizing the role of *pacta sunt servanda* as the fundamental norm in international law. Others still suggested that international law is based on the maxim *voluntas civitatis maximae est servanda*. The sociological interpretations of the binding force of international law should not be forgotten in this connection. It is common to all these schools of thought that they strive to vindicate for international law a binding force, independent of the will of the states and to substitute for the doctrine that international law is a law of coordination, the old-new doctrine, that international law is, and, if it is to be law, must be, a law of subordination, that is, a law above states.

An international law thus conceived could be interpreted as a law of an international community constituting a legal order for the existing states. It would seem doubtful, however, whether this result can be achieved without the creation of some new institutions or the strengthening of existing institutions. It was pointed out that the efforts to establish the binding force of international law independent of the will of states are bound to cause international lawyers to advocate the creation of an international legislature or, as a very minimum, of an international tribunal endowed with compulsory jurisdiction over disputes between states. While the creation of an international legislature would be concomitant with the formation of a super-state "the objective ascertainment of rights by courts is one (manifestation of the legal nature of international law) which could be effected within the frame of the existing practice and doctrine of international law."[26] The absence of an international court of justice with compulsory jurisdiction over disputes between states does not merely strain the legal character of international law to the breaking point. In truth, it would seem to jeopardize altogether the conception of international law as a body of rules governing the conduct of states.

The history of the past three hundred years tends to show that international law, increasingly separated from its roots in right reason and natural law and deprived of its sources of objective and heteronomous validity, could but inadequately perform the task which evolved upon it following the disappearance of the secular rule of the Empire and its aspiration to be the Universal Monarchy envisioned by Dante. Such an international law, rugged individualism of territorial and heterogeneous states, balance of power, equality of states, and toleration—these are among the legacies of the Settlement of Westphalia. That rugged individualism of states ill accommodates itself to an international rule of law reenforced by necessary institutions. It would seem that the national will to self-control which after a prolonged struggle first threw off the external shackles of Pope and Emperor is the same which *mutatis mutandis* persists today in declining any far-reaching subordination to external international controls. It was one of the essential characteristics of the League of Nations and it is one of the chief weaknesses of the United Nations.

The tercentenary of the Peace of Westphalia would seem to invite a thorough reexamination of the foundations of international law and organization, and of the political, economic, ideological and other factors which have determined their development. It may not be unreasonable to believe that such a broad inquiry, strong with important insights into the forces which have shaped in the past and which shape at present the course of international law and organization, might also yield some precise data regarding the ways and means of harmonizing the will of major states to self-control with the exigencies of an international society which by and large yearns for order under law.

Notes

1. Sir A.W. Ward, *The Peace of Westphalia,* The Cambridge Modern History, Vol. IV, 1934, p. 412.

2. Ibid., p. 414.

3. Protocol of June 28, 1878. 69 *British and Foreign State Papers, 1877–1878,* p. 960.

4. See letter quoted in the preceding note.

5. Text from Article CXIII of the Treaty of Münster, in *A General Collection of Treatys,* vol. I 1710, p. 36.

6. Sir James Headlam-Moreley, *Studies in Diplomatic Hisotry,* 1930, p. 108.

7. David Jayne Hill, *A History of Diplomacy in the International Development of Europe,* Vol. II, 1925, p. 602.

8. F.S. Dunn, "International Legislation," 42 *Political Science Quarterly* (1927), p. 577.

9. P.H. Winfield, *The Foundations and the Future of International Law,* 1941, p. 20.

10. Charles Dupuis, *Le Principe d'Equilibre et le Concert Européen,* 1909, p. 22.

11. John Eppstein, *The Catholic Tradition of the Law of Nations,* 1935, p. 192; see also p. 325.

12. Van Vollenhoven, *The Law of Peace,* p. 81.

13. de la Briere, *La Société des Nations?,* 1918, p. 53.

14. Van Vollenhoven, *The Law of Peace,* p. 93.

15. Ernest Barker, *Church, State, and Study,* 1930, p. 65.

16. Reflection of the Reverend Father, Brother Faranciscus de Victoria, Concerning Civil Power, a translation by Gladys L. Williams. In James Brown Scott, *The Spanish Origin of International Law,* 1934. Appendix C. p. xc.

17. Alberico Gentili, *De Iure Belli Libri Tres,* translation of the edition of 1612 by John C. Rolfe, *The Classics of International Law,* edited by James Brown Scott, 1933, p. 67.

18. Gentili, work cited, p. 68.

19. James Brown Scott, *The Spanish Conception of International Law and of Sanctions,* 1934, p. 90. The English translation of the above quotation from Suarez,

De Legibus, Book II, Ch. XIX, paragraph 9, as taken from Scott, *The Law, the State, and the International Community,* Vol. II, p. 257.

20. James Bryce, *The Holy Roman Empire,* 1866, p. 372.

21. A.P. Sereni, *The Italian Conception of International Law,* 1943, p. 107.

22. Ibid., p. 109.

23. Grotius, *De Jure Belli Ac Pacis,* translated by Francis W. Kelsey, *The Classics of International Law,* edited by James Brown Scott, Vol. II, 1925, Book I. Ch. I, paragraph 14. Phillipson's *Introduction,* p. 22a.

24. E. Vattel, *The Law of Nations,* translated by Charles G. Fenwick, *The Classics of International Law,* edited by James Brown Scott, Vol. II, 1916, p. 9.

25. Ibid.

26. H. Lauterpacht, *The Function of Law in the International Community,* 1933, p. 426.

PART 2.2

International Law as
Operating System:
Sources of International Law

5

The Treaty/Custom Dichotomy

John King Gamble, Jr.

Introduction

M ost of us who learned international law in the last thirty years took a
basic course or two in the subject and then specialized in one or a
couple of the major subfields. This quick specialization may be to blame
for the lack of a rich theoretical literature in contemporary international
law. Specialization often reduces the broad field of vision that evokes genuinely theoretical questions. This rapid transformation from novice to spe-
cialist means that few of us paid much attention to the sources of international law as a subject unto itself. All of us are aware of the "shopping list"
of sources contained in the statutes of the Permanent Court of International
Justice and the International Court of Justice (ICJ).[1] But academics seldom
think seriously about what the two principal sources, treaty and custom,
mean, how they relate to each other, and how they may have clouded or
distorted our view of the field.

I have the distinct impression that the following inconsistency exists.
While few of us are concerned about the topic of sources of international
law for its own sake, the hierarchy of sources, with treaty and custom clearly at the top, helps to grind the lens through which we view, myopically
perhaps, international law. This can, of course, have deleterious consequences, rather like failing to learn good grammar as a child then trying
to speak and write intelligently in later life.

At the most basic level, one might ask whether a doctrine of sources
has any meaning outside of theoretical discussion of the sources of international law. It seems to me that a tacit assumption made in most international legal literature is that sources do have a wider significance. Others, such
as Professor Koers, feel that "source" is an artificial construct that loses all

Reprinted with permission from the *Texas International Law Journal.*

meaning aside from largely academic discussion of the sources of international law.[2] The idea here is not so much that the concept of "source" is useless, but rather that reality is not as neat as the short list of sources given in the textbooks. Cursory discussions of sources create an impression of mutual exclusivity that may be inapplicable to most real world situations. If one accepts the "hardline" point of view expressed by Professor Koers, then further academic energy should not be devoted to sources.

Instead, the approach taken here will look carefully at the theory and use of sources and at how the two principal sources, treaty and custom, interrelate. Many of the misconceptions about sources of international law may derive from the false simplicity arising from Article 38 of the ICJ Statute. It is not, of course, that Article 38 is patently deficient; in fact, it was probably not intended to be interpreted as it has been. Some of the academic literature contributes to the confusion. For example, Waldock wrote:

> The view of most international lawyers is that customary law is not a form of tacit treaty but an independent form of law and, that when a custom satisfying the definition in Article 38 is established, it constitutes a general rule of international law which, subject to one reservation, applies to every state.[3]

Technically Waldock is correct, but his points are subject to varying interpretations, some of which imply an isolation of treaty from custom that is unrealistic. The listing provided in Article 38 tends to suggest this exclusivity, as if treaty and custom were two parallel lines in Euclidian geometry:

Article 38

1. The Court, whose function is to decide in accordance with international law such disputes as are submitted to it shall apply:
   (a) international conventions, whether general or particular, establishing rules expressly recognized by the contesting States;
   (b) international custom, as evidence of a general practice accepted as law;
   (c) the general principles of law recognized by civilised nations;
   (d) subject to the provisions of Article 59, judicial decisions and the teachings of the most highly qualified publicists of the various nations, as subsidiary means for the determination of rules of law.
2. This provision shall not prejudice the power of the Court to decide a case *ex aequo et bono,* if the parties agree thereto.[4]

The point to be emphasized is that the structure of Article 38 implies that treaty and custom *can be* different sources leading to different international law. The statute obscures the fact that these two principal sources interrelate. In fact, the structure of Article 38 probably discourages investigation into how these sources influence each other. The balance of this paper will be organized as follows. First, a precise definition of "source" will be sought. The term is often used loosely with legal and everyday meanings intermixed. Next, possible interrelationships between treaty and custom as sources will be examined. Finally, the case for a resurgence of custom will be discussed.

Toward Precision in Defining Sources

Academic approaches to sources of international law display great variety. Some experts find the term so clear that it is self-defining. Others expend great effort explaining vagaries in the usage of the concept. Still others are totally unconcerned in their own use of "source," vacillating between precise legal and colloquial meanings. Most eloquent in their pleas for care and precision are Hans Kelsen and Maarten Bos. Professor Kelsen wrote:

> "Sources" of law is a figurative and highly ambiguous expression. It is used not only to designate the different methods of creating law but also to characterize the reason for the validity of law, and especially the ultimate reason. But, in a wider sense, every legal norm is a source of that other norm the creation of which it regulates. It is a characteristic element of the law in general, and hence also of international law, that it regulates its own creation.[5]

Subsequently, Kelsen seemed to prefer the term "creation" to "source," concluding: "The ambiguity of the term "source" of law seems to render the term rather useless. Instead of a misleading figurative expression, one ought to introduce an expression that clearly and directly describes the phenomenon one has in mind."[6]

One of the preeminent experts on sources is Professor Maarten Bos of the University of Utrecht. Bos agreed with Kelsen about the imprecise use of the term "source."

> In law . . . one cannot escape the impression that the term "source" has been, and still is being, used to indicate all and sundry of these very divergent factors behind the real source, and even more than that. In order to avoid this confusion, the very first thing to be done is to limit the use of "source" to what corresponds to the geological concept, *ie.,* to those places where law "comes to light." But confusion being so avoided, the term, as will be shown below, for other reasons yet should be thrown out altogether to be replaced by the expression "recognized manifestation of law."[7]

Werner Levi, in what is typical of many modern approaches, avoids the term "source" altogether, opting instead for "creation of international law."[8] Levi amplified his approach in this way: "All laws are derived from the character of men as conditioned by social reality and consciousness of the environment. The substance of the norms is largely determined by the necessities of the society as shaped by the principles of the society's culture."[9] Somewhat ironic is the imprecise use of the term "source" by no less of an authority than Quincy Wright. Professor Wright, in describing "widening sources of international,"[10] uses the term loosely, with little of the precision advocated by Professors Kelsen and Bos.

Gerhard von Glahn equated sources of international law, with nothing more than how rules of international law are determined.[11] Whitaker, on the other hand, was concerned with where rules are found.[12] This variance raises an important question, to wit, whether sources are concerned with how rules are determined, where they are found, or both. The answer to this question may hinge upon the specific source one is discussing. It is not surprising that Whitaker's formulation, older and more traditional, is more appropriate to custom, whereas von Glahn's is somewhat more applicable to conventions.

Any definition that is synthesized here obviously must accommodate both treaty and custom since they will be the focus of the rest of this discussion. Given this goal, Bos' formulation seems to be the most appropriate. In effect, it subsumes the definitions offered by Kelsen, von Glahn and Whitaker. Therefore "source" of international law will be understood to mean "recognized manifestation" of international law.

Relationships Between Treaty and Custom

An important aspect of the treaty/custom dichotomy is the exact relationship between the two. The relationship might be approached in several ways. For example, it would be interesting to see what custom implies about treaties. However, this is a virtually impossible task because custom is such a broad concept. It would be like trying to define "being" or using an optical microscope to view atomic particles. The opposite approach is easier, namely, inquiry into what various treaties have to say about custom, specifically, about the relationship between their substance and custom on the same subject. An exhaustive examination of all treaties to discern trends in textual references to custom is not yet possible. The most thorough collection of treaty data does not include such information.[13]

Reference to Custom in Treaties

In approaching almost any aspect of the law of treaties, it is instructive to look at the treaty on treaties, the 1969 Vienna Convention on the Law of Treaties.[14] This treaty, which only recently entered into force, could be expected to incorporate many aspects of customary international law into its provisions. Particularly noteworthy in this regard are the sections on *pacta sunt servanda*,[15] coercion,[16] and *jus cogens*.[17] But there are only two places where the convention explicitly addresses custom. Interestingly, the treaty takes a rather conservative stance, asserting only that treaties are of "ever-increasing importance" as a source of international law.[18] Given the length of time the convention took to garner the needed thirty-five parties, one would expect the relative importance of treaties to have increased further. The Vienna Convention took this approach on the matter of custom: "*Affirming* that the rules of customary international law will continue to govern questions not regulated by the provisions of the present convention."[19] This suggests several categories into which treaties can be placed according to their stance on custom:

1. treaties that say nothing about the subject (most treaties fall into this category);
2. treaties that follow the model of the Vienna Convention by stating that those areas not covered in the treaty are assumed to continue to operate according to relevant customary rules;
3. treaties that purport to codify customary international law; and
4. treaties that deliberately create new law different and/or in conflict with customary international law.

Most treaties say nothing about the subject precisely because most are so trivial that such matters are irrelevant. It is interesting to speculate why the second type is needed at all. Any student of international law should understand that this follows automatically; it seems almost tautological. The third type is not as innocent as it appears at first blush. Such a formulation is of enormous interest because it equates treaty and custom. Treaties purporting to codify custom are not self-verifying on that point. It seems likely that this kind of provision may be used to develop new law under the guise of codifying custom. The fourth type has little potential for articulated links with custom. Given the gentle nature of diplomats, explicit condemnations of customary international law are not likely to be frequent. On the contrary, such provisions will be subtle and often tacit. Many would argue that this approach amounts more to creation of new law, than to denunciation of older customary international law.

It must be emphasized that it is uncertain how many treaties fall into each of these categories, except that the first type is the most prevalent. It may be instructive to give one more example of each of the other three types. The Vienna Convention on Diplomatic Relations[20] emplifies the second type: "*Affirming* that the rules of customary international law should continue to govern questions not expressly regulated by the provisions of the present Convention."[21] It is interesting to speculate about the important difference resulting from this formulation, "should continue," and that of the Convention on the Law of Treaties, "will continue." Perhaps it is due both to different negotiating procedures and different subject matter.[22]

One of the best examples of the third type is the 1958 Geneva Convention on the High Seas.[23] The treaty begins: "Desiring to codify the rules of international law relating to the high seas. . . ."[24] This provision has an increased impact because the other three Geneva conventions, negotiated and signed at the same time, make no statements about custom. This clearly indicates an unusual kind of treaty, one that is on firm customary ground, and illustrates the great care exercised by states in bringing treaty provisions under the umbrella of custom.

A good example of the fourth type is the Convention on the Elimination of All Forms of Discrimination against Women.[25] This treaty deals with an area where customary international law is either lacking or conflicts with the principles espoused in the treaty. With typical diplomatic politeness, custom is not even mentioned. The convention does, however, address other methods of achieving its goals stating:

> Nothing in this Convention shall affect any provisions that are more conducive to the achievement of equality between men and women which may be contained:
> (a) in the legislation of a State Party; or
> (b) in any other international convention, treaty, or agreement in force for that State.[26]

The lack of any reference to custom suggests that the drafters of the convention felt that it was the failure of customary international law that necessitated the treaty in the first place.

Now that some of the "raw material" of the relationship between treaty and custom has been examined, it is desirable to look at expert opinion on the issue. A few writers see a fundamental difference between treaty and custom. Bos placed great importance in whether the source is written or unwritten:

> Written and unwritten manifestations all have their own *raison d'étre* and character. Their character, it is submitted, largely depends on the measure of induction or deduction they represent. A maximum degree of induction is made possible in the handling of written manifestations, though deductions even then will not be absent. Deduction increases with custom, still more with general principles of law recognized by civilized nations.[27]

Hans Kelsen made an analogous point, although couched in different terms: "Legislation is conscious and deliberate law-making . . . custom is unconscious and unintentional law-making. In establishing a custom, men do not necessarily know that they create by their conduct a rule of law, nor do they necessarily intend to create law."[28] These are important distinctions that get to the heart of the relation between treaty and custom.

Conventions Creating Customary International Law

An important and oft repeated point in the literature is that a rule of international law may be conventional for some states and customary for others. Sørensen thought the situation to be widespread:

> Some rules of international law then are of a mixed sort: conventional as regards states parties to treaties in which they are laid down, and customary as regards others. This is far from unusual. It is a situation which constantly arises in connection with codification, as also where a practice originally based on particular treaties acquires those characteristics of generality and continuity which the process of creation of customary rules demand.[29]

Bos also addressed the subject:

> Meanwhile, it should be clear that a rule of customary international law may be prevailing between more than two States and is codified only between a restricted number of them. The rule then continues to exist between the State or States not consenting to the codification and the others until it is replaced or terminated.[30]

It should also be borne in mind that such ideas are not necessarily part of a new theory of sources. Over thirty years ago, the International Law Commission was aware of the issue and its implications:

> Perhaps the differentiation between conventional international law and customary international law ought not to be too rigidly insisted upon, however. A principle or rule of customary international law may be embodied in a bipartite or multipartite agreement so as to have, within the stated limits, conventional force for the States parties to the agreement so long as the agreement is in force; yet it would continue to be binding as a principle or rule of customary international law for other States.[31]

These are important findings because they cast treaty and custom in a realistic light, as intertwined threads in the fabric of international law. This approach implies an entirely different kind of legal system from the one envisioned if treaty and custom are viewed as largely independent sources.

Another important point made in the literature is that treaties, if repeated often enough, can form the basis of customary international law. This is the opposite sequence from that found when multilateral treaties assert themselves to be the codification of customary international law. Professor Baxter surveyed many different situations where this has occurred; such situations are not limited to the post–World War II period.[32] Kopelmanas offered a good explanation, though he may have overstated the frequency of this occurrence:

International practice in legal matters readily admits that the repetition of the same rules in a certain number of treaties confers on those rules a legal value even beyond the legal systems of signatory states. Frequent examples are to be found in cases before both the Permanent Court of Arbitration and the Permanent Court of International Justice.[33]

An excellent study that not only discusses this situation in theory but gives an example of its operation is Jordan's article on status of forces agreements. Jordan points out that this sequence is not at all new; it was recognized as far back as Cornelius van Bynkershoek.[34] Jordan illustrates how United States status of forces treaties evolved into a rule of customary international law on the subject by repeating the same provisions in many different bilateral treaties.[35] The universality of this rule was confirmed by an acid test when the Soviet Union used the United States scheme as a model,[36] lending further weight to the proposition that the process of establishing customary international law by way of treaty is underway.

If this discussion does nothing else, it should serve to emphasize the profound interrelationship between treaty and custom. This is not to say that differences, relative strengths and weaknesses, do not exist. They surely do. One interesting way to view the advantages of each was given by D'Amato: "Article 38 of the ICJ statute indicates another reason for the central importance of custom. The statute directs the Court to apply treaties that establish rules 'expressly recognized by the contesting states,' but no limit of express recognition attaches to the requirement that the Court apply 'international custom.'"[37] The extreme judicial flexibility seen here is no doubt part of the reason why the Soviet Union has been leery of custom and has repeatedly displayed a strong disposition in favor of treaty law.[38]

It is also clear from this discussion that there is little reason to limit oneself to the sequence that forms part of the mind set of international law students, namely, customary law develops slowly, after which it may be codified in treaty form. There are strong arguments for the existence of another process through which repetition of treaties dealing with the same subject creates a rule of customary international law. The important point is that treaty and custom ought not be viewed in isolation. Usually both are simultaneously relevant as evidence of the international law relative to a certain subject. In the next section, the issue of the resurgence of custom will be viewed. An interesting issue is whether treaty, custom and their interaction resemble a zero-sum game of sources of international law—if law is not being made by treaty then does custom "swing into place and take up the slack?"

Is There a Resurgence of Custom?

It is one thing to assert that custom as a source of international law is still active in some spheres; it is quite another to maintain that custom is experiencing a resurgence. It must be acknowledged at the outset that there are few effective ways to test this proposition. No rigorous empirical tests exist to measure the relative importance of treaty and custom. There are, however, several strategies that might help to resolve the issue. For example, it might be instructive to survey the cases heard by the International Court of Justice during its thirty-five year history to see if there are trends in the reliance on certain sources. This research strategy is risky because it assumes that the work of the ICJ is representative of the whole fabric of international law, an assumption that is problematical.

Given the limitations on researching this issue thoroughly, I shall suggest several reasons why it is reasonable to believe that a resurgence of custom may now be underway. First, there is the possibility that treaty, custom and their interaction constitute a zero-sum game. If so, then proof that treaties are decreasing in importance implies that custom will be increasing. Second, a common observation about international law is that newly independent states that participate little in the development of customary international law tend to be suspicious of law thus derived. It is possible that many of these new states, since they have now begun to participate more meaningfully in all phases of international relations, will feel more comfortable with custom as a source of international law. There are certain reasons to believe that treaties have reached their maximum relative importance. Most things that are amenable to treaty regulation may have already been dealt with. The principal focus then will shift to the implementation and interpretation of those treaties, a process squarely within the realm of customary international law.

The idea that treaty and custom, as the two principal sources of international law, relate in a zero-sum game situation deserves thorough examination. If one takes the position that international law is constantly developing, then treaty and custom may be a constant-sum game: "The most fully developed game theory is the two-person zero-sum game, in which one player's loss is equal to the other player's gain. This is a special case of a constant sum game, in which the players' gain or loss is a constant."[39] In fact, if one is hopeful about the overall progression of international law, treaty and custom may be a positive-sum game.[40]

The exact type of game is not critical. The issue is whether it is a tenable hypothesis that the role relinquished by treaty will be assumed by custom and vice versa. Impinging on this hypothesis is the question whether the other sources of international law are sufficiently significant to assume increased importance if the role of either treaty or custom decreases. Since the subsidiary sources are applied so seldom, it is unlikely they would refute the hypothesis. This is not to say that the other sources are not cited; they are, but virtually always in support of the primary sources, treaty and custom.

It seems then that it is reasonable to expect that if treaties are playing less of a role as sources, custom will play a more important role. It is possible to document a reduced role for treaties, especially in the last decade or so. The present interpretation must assume that the aggregate corpus of international law is growing; otherwise it is possible that both sources are receding in importance as the range of behaviors regulated by international law declines. Such a contingency is remote enough that it will not constitute a major obstacle.

There is wide agreement that one of the reasons for the post–World War II preeminence of treaty over custom as a source of international law has been the growing group of newly independent states that were suspicious of the substantive outcome of the customary process. The influx of these new states has had both quantitative and qualitative effects on treaty and custom.[41] There is ample reason to believe that the two and one-half fold increase occurring since World War II can never be repeated.[42] Additionally, it is probable that many new states, now more socialized into the international system, will be more willing to give custom a chance as a source of international law. Added support for this argument develops when treaty patterns are examined. If it can be shown that treaty activity peaked in the late 1960s or 1970s, then custom's resurgence can be inferred.

One way to draw some conclusions about the amount of treaty activity is to analyze data available from the Treaty Research Center at the University of Washington. That data, organized according to four five-year time intervals, show treaty frequencies as follows:

Number of Treaties Entering into Force

	1946–50	1951–55	1956–60	1961–65
All States[43]	4460	5582	6921	6886
W. Europe[44]	1754	2018	2133	1934
African[45]	12	51	175	737

These data strongly suggest that maximum treaty activity has already been reached. Of course, developing states continue to show increases, but it is reasonable to infer that by the 1980s they, too, will have begun to decline.

It is also desirable to examine multilateral treaties. One study has dealt with all multilateral treaties entering into force between 1919 and 1971.[46] The nature of multilateral treaties means that it is perhaps a decade after entry into force before patterns become clear.[47] For each period, except the war years which obviously are incomparable, it is possible to compute the number of multilateral treaties entering into force. It is also instructive to know how many treaties entered into force in comparison to the number of independent states in the world. These are the results:[48]

Time Period	Number of Multilateral Treaties Entering into Force	Number of Multilateral Treaties/Number of States
1919–23	53	.68
1924–28	120	1.51
1929–33	124	1.51
1934–338	108	1.30
1947–51	105	1.14
1952–56	145	1.48
1957–61	141	1.26
1962–66	148	1.08
1967–71	170	1.10

These results confirm some diminution of the importance of treaties.

These data can be viewed in another way. Since many multilateral treaties create an institution having a lasting significance, their effect is really cumulative. It has been shown that about eighty percent of multilateral treaties create continuing obligations with an average duration of twenty-five years.[49] This raises an interesting question. Suppose a treaty creates an institution that continues to operate for a considerable period of time. Does the work of that institution contribute to international law within the realm of custom or the realm of treaty? The answer is not clear. But it is perfectly reasonable to view treaties as creating contexts within which customary law operates.

Summary and Conclusions

This paper was motivated in part by the fact that some international law experts have gone too far in asserting the dominance of treaty over custom as a source of international law. Even the most ambitious efforts at codifying international law demonstrate that an important role remains for custom. The definition of "source" adopted here—*recognized manifestation of law*—includes both treaty and custom. More importantly, it suggests a constant interplay between treaty and custom. It seems that many international law teachers and practitioners view treaty and custom in the unrealistic way illustrated in Figure 5.1.

The misconceptions which Figure 5.1 illustrates were created in part by the statutes of the World Courts. Two important inaccuracies are illustrated. First, treaty and custom include too small a portion of international law. Second, treaty and custom are mutually exclusive for the most part. Neither of these representations is realistic. Figure 5.2 corresponds more closely to reality. Here one sees that treaty and custom overlap significantly, illustrating the fact that in most instances both are recognized manifestations of the same legal rules. There are some instances where they lead

Figure 5.1 Traditional View

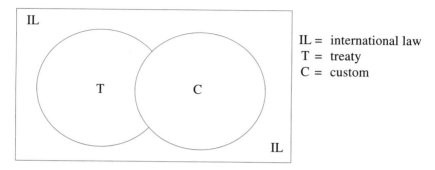

IL = international law
T = treaty
C = custom

Figure 5.2 Suggested View

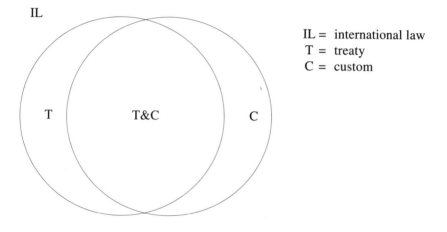

IL = international law
T = treaty
C = custom

toward different law, but these are the exceptions. The other important difference is that treaty and custom together encompass most of international law. Other sources, in combination, are relatively insignificant.

Another point worthy of reiteration is that treaty and custom interrelate in more than one sequence. The dominant impression is that custom as the older source of international law usually evolves to a point at which the developing law may be codified. This does occur. But there are many instances where repetition of identical treaties on the same subject will generate a rule of customary international law. There are other cases where treaty and custom simultaneously influence each other. In some instances, there is a long causal chain with custom and treaty alternately assuming principal roles. The modern history of the international law of the continental shelf is a good example. The Truman Proclamation and its sequels (customary process) led to a treaty (the 1958 Geneva Convention) which, in turn, produced customary law responses. At present it is unclear whether the next stage in the development of this important area of international law will be led by custom or treaty.

There can be no doubt that a thorough understanding of international law is possible only with attention both to treaty and custom so that each receives its due. The late Judge Baxter stated it well:

> Treaties will continue to exercise a most important impact on the content of general international law. Even if all States should expressly assume the obligations of codification treaties, regard will still have to be paid to customary international law in the interpretations of those instruments, and the treaties will in turn generate new customary international law growing out the application of the agreements.... The interesting point to be watched in the future is how these sources or evidence of internaional law ... will interact, vie for position, and influence one another.[50]

Notes

1. *I.C.J. Stat.* art. 38, reprinted in I. Brownlie, *Basic Documents in International Law* 276 (2d ed. 1972). The language of Article 38 is reproduced at text accompanying note 4 *infra.*

2. Professor Albert W. Koers, Dean of the Faculty of Law of the University of Utrecht, expresses this view in *State Practice in Zones of Special Jurisdiction,* (T. Clingon, ed., 1981).

3. Waldock, General Course on Public International Law, 106 *Recueil des Cours* 49 (1962).

4. *I.C.J. Stat.* art. 38, supra note 1. Article 59 ICJ statute provides: "The decision of the Court has no binding force except between the parties and in respect of that particular case." There is a disagreement about whether the predecessor of Article 38 in the Statute of the Permanent Court of International Justice established an implied hierarchy of sources.

5. H. Kelsen, *Principles of International Law* 437 (2d ed. R. Tucker 1966).

6. Ibid. at 438.

7. Bos, *The Recognized Manifestations of International Law: A New Theory of Sources,* (1977) *Ger Y.B. Int'l L.* 10.

8. W. Levi, *Contemporary International Law: A Concise Introduction* 33 (1979).

9. Ibid. at 34.

10. Q. Wright, *Contemporary International Law: A Balance Sheet* 26 (1955).

11. G. Von Glahn, *Law Among Nations* 16 (4th ed. 1981).

12. U. Whitaker, *Politics and Power: A Text in International Law* 57 (1964).

13. In response to my inquiry, the Treaty Research Center, stated that such information had not been tabulated.

14. Reprinted in 8 *Intl. Leg. Mat'ls.* 679 (1969) & 63 *Am. J. Intl. L.* 875 (1960–1969) The Vienna convention entered into force on Jan. 27, 1980, but the United States has yet to become a party.

15. Ibid. art. 26.

16. Ibid. arts. 51, 52.

17. Ibid. art. 53.

18. Ibid. at preamble.

19. Ibid.

20. *Vienna Convention on Diplomatic Relations,* done April 18, 1961, 23 U.S. T. 3227, T.I. A. S.No. 7502, 500 U.N/T. S. 95 (entered into force April 24. 1964, ratified by the United States Sept. 1965).

21. Ibid at preamble 23 U.S. T. at 3230, 500 U.N.TS. at 96.

22. S. Rosenne, The Law of Treaties: A Guide to the Legislative History of the Vienna Convention 96-101 (1970).

23. Geneva Convention on the High Seas, *done* Apr. 29, 1958, 13 U.S.T. 2312, T.I.A.S. No. 5200, 450 U.N.T.S. 11 (*entered into force* Sept. 30, 1962).

24. Ibid. at introduction, 31 U.S.T. at 2314, 450 U.N.T.S. at 82.

25. *Convention on the Elimination of All Forems of Discrimination Against Women,* opened for signature March 1, 1980, U.N. Doc. A/RES.34/180, reprinted in 19 *Intl. Lg. Matls.* 33 (1980)

26. Ibid. art. 23, at 44.

27. Bos, supra note 7 a, at 76 (footnote omitted).

28. H. Kelsen, supra note 5, at 441.

29. M. Søreson, *Manual of Public International Law* 129 (1968) (citations omitted).

30. Bos, supra note 7, at 74.

31. Report of the International Law Commission to the General Assembly, [1950] *Y.B. Intl. l. Comm'n* 368 (United Nations), U.N. Doc. A/CN. 4/SER. A/Add.1 (1950).

32. See Baxter, *Multilateral Treaties as Evidence of Customary International Law,* [1965–1966] *Brit. Y.B. Int'l L.* 275, 275–80 (1968).

33. Kopelmanas, *Custom as a Means of the Creation of International Law,* [1937] *Brit. Y.B. Int'l L.* 136.

34. Jordan, *Creation of Customary International Law by Way of Treaty,* 9 A.F. JAG L. Rev. 43 (1967).

35. Ibid at 45-48.

36. Ibid. at 48.

37. D'Amato, *Wanted: A Comprehensive Theory of Custom in International Law,* 4 *Tex. Int'l L.F.* 28 (1967).

38. See J. Triska & R. Slusser, *The Theory, Law and Policy of Soviet Treaties* 11 2(1962)

39. W. Sher & R. Pinola, *Microeconomic Theory* 483 (1981).

40. See ibid. at 488–89.

41. See Miles, *Intangible and Non-ocean Elements to be Negotiated,* in *The Law of the Sea: A New Geneva Conference* 125 (L. Alexander ed. 1972).

42. See generally E. Plishcke, *Microstates in World Affairs* (1977).

43. P. Rohn, *Treaty Profiles* 57 (1976).

44. Ibid. at 55.

45. Ibid. at 49.

46. See Gamble, *Reservations to Mulilateral Treaties: A Macroscopic View of State Practice,* 74 *Am. J. Intl. L.* 372 (1980).

47. See ibid. at 376–78.

48. Ibid. at 377.

49. See Gamble, *Multilateral Treaties: The Significacnce of the Name of the Instrument,* 10 *Cal. W. int'l L.J. 1,* 16–17 (1980).

50. Baxter, *Treaties and Custom,* 129 *Recueil des Cours* 103–04 (1970) (footnotes omitted).

6

Why Are Some International Agreements Informal?

Charles Lipson

"V erbal contracts," Samuel Goldwyn once said, "aren't worth the paper they're written on." Yet informal agreements and oral bargains suffuse international affairs. They are the form that international cooperation takes in a wide range of issues, from exchange rates to nuclear weapons. Take monetary affairs, for instance. Except for the regional European Monetary System, there have been no formal, comprehensive agreements on exchange rates since the downfall of the Bretton Woods system in 1971. A prolonged effort to resurrect the pegged-rate system failed, although new treaties were drawn up and duly signed. Private financial markets simply overwhelmed these official efforts, and central bankers eventually conceded the point. The one comprehensive agreement since then, concluded in 1976 in Jamaica, merely ratified a system of floating rates that had emerged unplanned. For the past fifteen years, monetary arrangements have been a succession of informal agreements of indefinite duration, most recently the Plaza Communiqué and the Louvre Accord, designed to cope with volatile currency movements. The Bretton Woods system itself depended on such agreements in its declining years. It was held together by the tacit agreement of European central banks not to convert their major dollar holdings into gold. The system fell apart when Germany and France abandoned that commitment. They did so because they believed that the United States had abandoned its own (tacit) commitment to restrain inflation and to avoid large current account deficits. Put another way, the U.S. formal pledge to convert dollars into gold at $35 per ounce—the very heart of the Bretton Woods system—was sustained only by silent agreements that America would not be called upon to do so.

Such informal agreements are vital in security relationships as well.

Charles Lipson, "Why Are Some International Agreements Informal?" *International Organization* 45, 4 (Autumn 1991), pp. 495–538 © 1991 by the World Peace Foundation and the Massachusetts Institute of Technology.

America's relations with the Soviet Union have relied heavily on unspoken understandings. These tacit relationships are crucial for two reasons. First, the Americans and Soviets have made very few direct treaty commitments, and fewer still in key areas of national security. Second, for much of the postwar period, each side was openly hostile to the other and outspoken in denying the value and even the legitimacy of cooperation. The rhetoric went much further at times, challenging the adversary's right to govern at home, its basic security interests abroad, and its trustworthiness in diplomatic dealings. For all that, the United States and Soviet Union have generally framed their basic security policies in more prudent and cautious terms. The U.S. decision to pursue containment rather than "rollback," even at the height of Cold War tensions, was a tacit acknowledgment of the Soviet sphere of influence in Eastern Europe. When popular uprisings broke out during the 1950s, the United States did nothing—nothing to aid resistance movements in Germany, Poland, and Hungary and nothing to deter their forcible suppression. In a related area of unspoken agreement, each side has been careful to avoid any direct engagement of military forces, despite the frequent involvement of Soviets and Americans in limited wars around the world. Paul Keal has termed such policies the "unspoken rules" of superpower diplomacy.[1]

Unspoken rules are not the only kinds of informal arrangements between the superpowers. In the case of strategic arms limitations, both the Americans and the Soviets publicly announced that they would continue to observe the first SALT treaty after it expired in October 1977. The principal aim was to sustain a climate of cooperation while SALT II was being negotiated. Leonid Brezhnev and Jimmy Carter signed an interim SALT II agreement in 1979, but the treaty itself was never ratified by the Senate. It was finally withdrawn in 1981. Even so, the Americans and Soviets avoided undercutting the agreement and tacitly observed its key provisions until the late 1980s. This cooperation is remarkable because the Reagan administration had come to power strenuously opposing ratification of the SALT II agreement, helped prevent its passage in the Senate, and held fast to its declared opposition. In dealing with the Soviets, however, the administration was more accommodating. In the early days of the Reagan administration, the State Department announced that the United States "would not undercut" the agreement. The President himself made a similar statement in 1982 and largely kept to the bargain. The unratified treaty was observed informally even during the Reagan administration's major arms buildup. Both sides restricted specific categories of long-range nuclear weapons to meet SALT II limitations, despite the absence of any formal agreement to do so.

The Reagan administration always claimed that its nuclear policies were unilateral and voluntary. Yet it devoted considerable attention to possible Soviet "violations" of what was, after all, a nonexistent treaty. These violations were important because President Reagan always stated that U.S. arms restraints depended on Soviet reciprocity and progress toward a new arms treaty. Reagan repeatedly criticized the Soviets on both counts but in practice continued to observe SALT limits until well after the expiration date of the proposed treaty. The agreement was tacit, but no less an agreement for that.

Informal accords among states and transnational actors are not exceptional. The scale and the diversity of such accords indicate that they are an important feature of world politics, not rare and peripheral. The very informality of so many agreements illuminates basic features of international politics. It highlights the continuing search for international cooperation, the profusion of forms it takes, and the serious obstacles to more durable commitments.

All international agreements, whether formal or informal, are promises about future national behavior. To be considered genuine agreements, they must entail some reciprocal promises or actions, implying future commitments. Agreements may be considered informal, to a greater or lesser degree, if they lack the state's fullest and most authoritative imprimatur, which is given most clearly in treaty ratification.

The informality of agreements varies by degrees, along two principal dimensions. The first is the government level at which the agreement is made. A commitment made by the head of state (an executive agreement) is the most visible and credible sign of policy intentions short of a ratified treaty. In important matters, commitments by lower-level bureaucracies are less effective in binding national policy. They are simply less constraining on heads of state, senior political leaders, and other branches of government, partly because they lack a visible impact on national reputation. The second dimension is the form, or means, by which an agreement is expressed. It may be outlined in an elaborate written document, or it may involve a less formal exchange of notes, a joint communiqué, an oral bargain, or even a tacit bargain.[2] Written agreements allow greater attention to detail and more explicit consideration of the contingencies that might arise. They permit the parties to set the boundaries of their promises, to control them more precisely, or to create deliberate ambiguity and omissions on controversial matters. At the other end of the spectrum—most informal of all—are oral and tacit agreements. Their promises are generally more ambiguous and less clearly delimited, and the very authority to make and execute them may be in doubt. If disputes later arise, it is often difficult to specify what was intended *ex ante*. Indeed, it may be difficult to show that there *was* an agreement.[3]

The interpretive problems are even more acute with tacit understandings and implicit rules that are not well articulated between the parties. Are these arrangements cooperative agreements at all? That depends. They are *not* if they simply involve each actor's best strategic choice, given others' independent choices. This Nash equilibrium may produce order and predictability—that is, regular behavior and stable expectations—without cooperation. Genuine tacit cooperation involves something more. It is based on shared expectations that each party can improve its own outcome if its strategic choices are modified in expectation of reciprocal changes by others. Shared "understandings" can arise in either case. They are not a unique marker of cooperative agreements. What distinguishes cooperation, whether tacit or explicit, are the subtle forms of mutual reliance and the possibilities of betrayal and regret.

The central point here is not taxonomic, presenting definitions of tacit arrangements and other informal bargains simply to classify them. The goal is to understand how different kinds of agreements can be used to order international relationships. The means of international cooperation are frequently informal, and it is important to explore their rationale, uses, and limitations. At the same time, we should not mistake all shared understandings for voluntary, informal bargains.

Informality is best understood as a device for minimizing the impediments to cooperation, at both the domestic and international levels. What are the impediments? And what are the advantages of informal agreements in addressing them? First, informal bargains are more flexible than treaties. They are willows, not oaks. They can be adapted to meet uncertain conditions and unpredictable shocks. "One of the greatest advantages of an informal instrument," according to a legal counselor in Britain's Foreign Office, "is the ease with which it can be amended."[4] Although treaties often contain clauses permitting renegotiation, the process is slow and cumbersome and is nearly always impractical. This point can be put in another, less obvious way: informal agreements make fewer informational demands on the parties. Negotiators need not try to predict all future states and comprehensively contract for them. Second, because informal arrangements do not require elaborate ratification, they can be concluded and implemented quickly if need be. In complex, rapidly changing environments, speed is a particular advantage.

Finally, informal agreements are generally less public and prominent, even when they are not secret. This lower profile has important consequences for democratic oversight, bureaucratic control, and diplomatic precedent. Informal agreements can escape the public controversies of a ratification debate. They can avoid the disclosures, unilateral "understandings," and amendments that sometimes arise in that open process. Because of their lower profile, they are also more tightly controlled by the government bureaucracies that negotiate and implement the agreements and less exposed to intrusion by other agencies. Agencies dealing with specific international issues, such as environmental pollution or foreign intelligence, can use informal agreements to seal quiet bargains with their foreign counterparts, avoiding close scrutiny and active involvement by other government agencies with different agendas.

The lower profile and the absence of formal national commitment also mean that informal agreements are less constraining as diplomatic precedents. They do not stand as visible and general policy commitments, as treaties so often do. In all these ways, the most sensitive and embarrassing implications of an agreement can remain nebulous or unstated for both domestic and international audiences, or even hidden from them.

Yet all of these diplomatic benefits come at a price, and sometimes a very high one. The flexibility of informal agreements also means that they are more easily abandoned. Avoiding public debates conceals the depth of national support for an agreement. Ratification debates can also serve to mobilize and integrate the multiple constituencies interested in an agreement. These policy networks of public officials (executive, legislative, and bureaucratic) and private actors sustain agreements during the implementation stage. Joint communiqués and executive agreements sidestep these basic democratic processes. This evasion typically means that the final agreements are less reliable for all participants.

These costs and benefits suggest the basic reasons for agreements:

(1) the desire to avoid formal and visible pledges,
(2) the desire to avoid ratification,
(3) the ability to renegotiate or modify as circumstances change, or
(4) the need to reach agreements quickly.

Because speed, simplicity, flexibility, and privacy are all common diplomatic requirements, we would expect to find informal agreements used frequently. Because the associated costs and benefits vary in different circumstances, we would also expect to find a distinct pattern of formal and informal agreements. Finally, we would expect to find various types of informal agreements used to meet particular needs.

This article examines the strengths and weaknesses of informal agreements. It is an inquiry into the neglected institutional constraints on international cooperation—and the imperfect devices to overcome them. It considers the basic choices between treaties and informal instruments, as well as the choices among different kinds of informal arrangements, all of which can be used to express cooperation among states. Finally, it asks what these varied forms of cooperation can tell us about the more general impediments to international agreement. The aim here is to use the *choice of forms of agreement* to explore some problems of rational cooperation in international affairs and particularly their contextual and institutional dimensions.

Self-Help and the Limits of International Agreement

When states cooperate, they can choose from a wide variety of forms to express their commitments, obligations, and expectations. The most formal are bilateral and multilateral treaties, in which states acknowledge their promises as binding commitments with full international legal status. At the other extreme are tacit agreements, in which obligations and commitments are implied or inferred but not openly declared, and oral agreements, in which bargains are expressly stated but not documented. In between lie a variety of written instruments to express national obligations with greater precision and openness than tacit or oral agreements but without the full ratification and national pledges that accompany formal treaties. These informal arrangements range from executive agreements and nonbinding treaties to joint declarations, final communiqués, agreed minutes, memoranda of understanding, and agreements pursuant to legislation. Unlike treaties, these informal agreements generally come into effect without ratification and do not require international publication or registration.

Although these agreements differ in form and political intent, legal scholars rarely distinguish among them. The dominant view is that international agreements, whatever their title, are legally binding upon the signatories, unless clearly stated otherwise. Thus, informal agreements, if they contain explicit promises, are conflated with treaties. They are rarely studied directly, except for the curiosity of "nonbinding" agreements such as the Helsinki Final Act.

This distinction between agreements that legally bind and agreements that do not is a traditional one. It is central to the technical definition of treaties codified in the Vienna Convention on the Law of Treaties. Article 26 states that treaties are "binding upon the parties" and "must be performed by them in good faith." Similarly, texts on international law emphasize the binding nature of treaties and, indeed, a wide range of other international agreements.[5]

The implicit claim is that international agreements have a status similar to domestic contracts, which are binding and enforceable. This claim is seriously misleading. It is a faulty and legalistic characterization of international agreements in practice and is also a poor guide to why states sometimes use treaties and other times use informal means to express agreements. Although international agreements are contracted commitments, any simple analogy to domestic contracts is mistaken for several reasons. First, in domestic legal systems, binding agreements are adjudicated and enforced by courts, backed by the instruments of state power. This judicial power is wide-ranging. It includes, among other things, the right to interpret the parties' intentions at the time the bargain was initially made, the right to decide whether an agreement exists legally or is impermissible because it is procedurally flawed or violates public policy, and the right to interpose missing contract clauses to deal with unforeseen conditions. Most fundamentally, the courts can hold parties responsible for their promises, whether those promises were originally intended as contracts or not, and can settle their meaning. When parties discuss compliance after agreements have been signed, they bargain in the shadow of law and judicial enforcement.

Individuals and corporations can appeal to the courts to determine whether an ostensible promise, perhaps one given orally or without full documentation, is actually binding, with specific obligations. The courts can thus transmute informal or incomplete agreements into formal obligations. There is simply no equivalent at the international level.[6] The legal battle between Texaco and Pennzoil illustrates this judicial power. Their case hinged on the meaning of Pennzoil's "agreement in principle" to buy Getty Oil. Was their agreement binding even though the final contract was never signed? The question arose because, soon after the agreement had been reached, another company, Texaco, mounted a higher bid for Getty. Texaco indemnified Getty and its largest shareholders against any lawsuits and completed the purchase. Pennzoil then sued Texaco. The size of the companies meant that the stakes were unusually high: the jury awarded Pennzoil over $10 billion and the final out-of-court settlement was for $3 billion. But the stakes were high for another reason as well. The case raised significant questions about the legal status of "agreements in principle," which are commonly used in business as precursors to formal contracts. The size of Pennzoil's victory was unprecedented. But there was nothing unprecedented about the power of the courts to settle contractual disputes such as this, to determine whether a contract even exists, to infer its terms, and to ensure compliance with any damage awards, however large.

The definitive settlement of such conflicts is the routine province of domestic legal systems. Courts are empowered to decide rights and obligations in specific disputes. They can sort out the inevitable mistakes, negligence, and outright fraud that bedevil agreements. They can set a price to be paid for nonperformance. In unusual cases, they can order a party to perform its contractual obligations, as the courts interpret them ("specific performance"). We need not concern ourselves here with this body of law in any detail or with important cross-national differences. But we should recognize the fundamental impact of judicial authority on exchange relationships.

Whether the issue involves simple promises or complicated commercial transactions, the availability of effective, compulsory arbitration by courts supports and facilitates agreements. It does so, in the last resort, by compelling adherence to promises privately made or, more commonly, by requiring compensatory payment for promises broken. Moreover, the prospect of such enforcement colors out-of-court bargaining.

There is no debate over the propriety of these judicial functions. They are crucial in complex capitalist economies in which independent agents work together by voluntary agreement. What legal scholars debate is not the propriety of enforcement power but its substantive content and the underlying principles that should govern damage awards when promises are broken. At the very least, it is argued, recipients should receive the costs they incurred by relying on a broken promise. The majority view, in both legal scholarship and common law courts, requires something more. It demands that the recipients of promises receive the benefits they might reasonably have expected had the promises been kept.

Whatever the standard for damages, it is clear that the courts offer political backing for the exchange of promises and, indeed, for the institution of promising in all its facets. Their role provides an important measure of protection to those who receive promises. It diminishes the tasks of self-protection, lowers the costs of transactions, and thereby promotes contractual agreements and exchange in general.

To lower the burdens of self-protection is not to eliminate them entirely. Using local courts to sustain agreements is often costly or impractical. The enforcement of contractual rights and obligations is imperfect. These costs and uncertainties raise the possibility that breaches of contract will go uncompensated or undercompensated. Knowing that, the parties must look to themselves for some protection against opportunism. It is also true that domestic courts do not become involved in contract disputes through their own independent initiatives. They are called upon by parties to the dispute—at the parties' own initiative, at their own cost, and at their own risk. In that sense, access to the courts may be seen as an adjunct to other forms of self-help. Like these other forms, it is costly and the results uncertain.

But the fact that self-help is common to all agreements does not eradicate the fundamental differences between domestic and international bargains. Hanging over domestic bargains is the prospect of judicial interpretation and enforcement, whether the disputes are settled in court or not. There is simply no analogue for these functions in international agreements. Of course, the parties to an interstate dispute may, by mutual consent, seek judicial rulings or private arbitration. In multilateral treaties, states may also agree in advance to use procedures for dispute resolution. These procedures may have teeth. They can raise the diplomatic costs of violations and ease the burdens of retaliation. But the punishments are also highly circumscribed. For the most part, they simply define and justify certain limited acts of self-enforcement or retaliation. At most, they may force a violator to withdraw from an agreement or a multilateral organization, giving up the benefits of participation. That can be punishment, to be sure, but it falls far short of the legal sanctions for violating domestic contracts. There, the rights of withdrawal are accompanied by external enforcement of damages, usually based on disappointed expectations of profit. The fact that all agreements contain some elements of self-protection and some institutions for private governance should not obscure these basic differences between domestic and international bargains.

Domestic legal systems not only aid in enforcing contracts but also set effective boundaries on the scope and nature of private agreements. Statutes and court rulings limit the private, voluntary ordering of relationships. A significant portion of criminal law, for example, is devoted specifically to punishing certain categories of private agreements, from prostitution and gambling to the sale of illicit drugs. The rationale is that larger public purposes should override the immediate parties' own desires: their bargains should be barred or constrained. Civil laws governing rent control, usury, insider trading, cartel price-fixing, homosexual marriage, and indentured servitude are all directed at preventing private bargains, for better or for worse. Such restrictions and the rules governing them are central elements of domestic legal systems.

Similarly, the law can restrict the *form* of agreements. One clear-cut and prominent example is the U.S. Statute of Frauds, which requires that certain agreements be put in writing. According to the statute, if a contract is larger than $500, and if neither party has made payment or performed its obligations, then the courts will only enforce *written* agreements. Although there are exceptions to this straightforward rule, it does underscore the capacity of domestic law to channel agreements, by requiring particular documentation, for example, or witnesses or specific language.[8]

Again, there are simply no equivalent restrictions on either the form or substance of international agreements. The domain of *permissible* international agreements is simply the domain of *possible* agreements.[9] This absence of restraint is not due simply to the lack of an international legislature and executive (though surely they are absent). It is due equally to the absence of an effective system of adjudication. One major limitation on prohibited domestic bargains, aside from any direct penalties, is that illicit bargains are not enforced by courts. This restricts such bargains by making them more costly to execute. To implement illegal contracts requires special precautions and sometimes entails the establishment of a broader set of institutional arrangements: a criminal enterprise.

These high costs of self-enforcement and the dangers of opportunism are important obstacles to extralegal agreements. Indeed, the costs may be prohibitive if they leave unsolved such basic problems as moral hazard and time inconsistency. The same obstacles are inherent features of interstate bargaining and must be resolved if agreements are to be concluded and carried out. Resolving them depends on the parties' preference orderings, the transparency of their preferences and choices (asymmetrical information), and the private institutional mechanisms set up to secure their bargains. It has little to do, however, with whether an international agreement is considered "legally binding" or not. In domestic affairs, on the other hand, these legal boundaries make an enormous difference—the difference between selling contraband whiskey in Al Capone's Chicago and selling the same product legally ten years later.

In international affairs, then, the term "binding agreement" is a misleading hyperbole. To enforce their bargains, states must act for themselves. This limitation is crucial: it is a recognition that international politics is a realm of contesting sovereign powers. For that reason, it is misleading to understand treaties (as international lawyers typically do) in purely formal, legal terms, as instruments that somehow bind states to their promises. It is quite true that treaties incorporate the language of formal obligation, chiefly phrases such as "we shall" and "we undertake," together with specific commitments. Such conventional diplomatic language is a defining feature of modern treaties. But that language cannot accomplish its ambitious task of binding states to their promises. This inability is an inherent limitation on bargaining for international cooperation. It means that treaties, like all international agreements, must be enforced endogenously.

What Do Treaties Do?

If treaties do not truly bind, why do states use that language? Why frame agreements in that form? The chief reason, I think, is that states wish to signal their intentions with special intensity and gravity and are using a well-understood form to do so. The decision to encode a bargain in treaty form is primarily a decision to highlight the importance of the agreement and, even more, to underscore the durability and significance of the underlying promises. The language of "binding commitments," in other words, is a diplomatic communication aimed at other signatories and, often, at third parties. In the absence of international institutions that permit effective self-binding or offer external guarantees for promises, treaties use conventional forms to signify a seriousness of commitment. By making that commitment both solemn and public, the parties indicate their intention, at least, to adhere to a particular bargain.

The effect of treaties, then, is to raise the political costs of noncompliance. That cost is raised not only for others but also for oneself. The more formal and public the agreement, the higher the reputational costs of noncompliance. The costs are highest when the agreement contains specific written promises, made publicly by senior officials with the state's fullest imprimatur. States deliberately choose to impose these costs on themselves in order to benefit from the counterpromises (or actions) of others. Given the inherent constraints of international institutions, these formal pledges are as close as states can come to precommitment—to a contractual exchange of promises. In short, one crucial element of treaties is that they visibly stake the parties' reputations to their pledges. The loss of credibility (because of deliberate violations) is a real loss, although it is certainly *not* always a decisive one, in terms of policy calculus. Informal agreements are generally less reliable and convincing precisely because they involve less of a reputational stake.[10] The stakes are diminished either because the agreements are less public (the audience is narrower and more specialized) or because high-level officials are less directly involved.

In a world of imperfect information, where others' current and future preferences cannot be known with certainty, reputation has value. As a result, it can be used as a "hostage" or bond to support contracts. Because breaking a contract or even appearing to do so degrades reputation, it produces a loss of reputational capital. The threat of such loss promotes compliance, although it cannot guarantee it. Whether it succeeds depends on (1) the immediate gains from breaking an agreement, (2) the lost stream of future benefits and the rate of discount applied to that stream, and (3) the expected costs to reputation from specific violations.

Not all violations discredit equally. First, not all are witnessed. Some that are seen may be considered justifiable or excusable, perhaps because others have already violated the agreement, because circumstances have changed significantly, because compliance is no longer feasible, or because the contracted terms appear ambiguous. Thus, memory, inference, and context—social learning and constructed meaning—all matter. Second, not all actors have a reputation worth preserving. Some simply do not have much to lose, whether their violations are visible or not. Moreover, they may not choose to invest in reputation, presumably because the costs of building a good name outweigh the incremental stream of rewards. Sovereign debtors, for example, value their reputation least when they do not expect to borrow again. Alternatively, actors with poor reputations (or little track record) may choose to invest in them precisely to create expectations about future performance. If these expectations can produce a stream of rewards and if the future is highly valued, it may be rational to make such investments. Thus, the value of reputation lost depends on the visibility and clarity of both promises and performance, on the value of an actor's prior reputation, and on the perceived usefulness of reputation in supporting other agreements.

Compliance with treaties, as I have noted, is specifically designed to be a salient issue, supported by reputation. Unfortunately, the hostage of reputation is not always strong support. Some states foresee little gain from enhanced reputation, either because the immediate costs are too high or the ongoing rewards are too little, too late. They may sign treaties cynically, knowing that they can violate them cheaply. Others may sign treaties in good faith but simply abandon them if their calculations about future rewards change. Finally, some states may invest heavily to demonstrate the credibility of their promises, to show that they are reliable partners, unswayed by short-term gains from defection. The general importance of reputation, in other words, does not eliminate the problem of multiple equilibria. Just as there can be economic markets with some sellers of high-quality goods and some sellers of shoddy goods, both of them rational, there can be diplomatic environments in which some states are reliable treaty partners and some are not.

Reputation, then, can contribute to treaty self-enforcement if not ensure it. Self-enforcement simply means that an agreement remains in force because, at any given moment, each party believes it gains more by sustaining the agreement than by terminating it. That calculation includes all future benefits and costs, appropriately discounted to give their present value. Enhancing a reputation for reliability is one such benefit. It is of particular value to governments engaged in a range of international transactions requiring trust and mutual reliance. Of course, other costs and benefits may outweigh these reputational issues.[11] The key point, however, is that reputation can be used to support international cooperation and has important implications for its form. The choice of a formal, visible document such as a treaty magnifies the reputational effects of adherence and buttresses self-enforcement.

Nations still can and do break even their most formal and solemn commitments to other states. Indeed, the unscrupulous may use treaty commitments as a way of deceiving unwary partners, deliberately creating false expectations or simply cheating when the opportunity arises. (Informal agreements are less susceptible to these dangers. They raise expectations less than treaties and so are less likely to dupe the naive.) But states pay a serious price for acting in bad faith and, more generally, for renouncing their commitments. This price comes not so much from adverse judicial decisions at The Hague but from the decline in national reputation as a reliable partner, which impedes future agreements. Indeed, opinions of the World Court gain much of their significance by reinforcing these costs to national reputation.

Put simply, *treaties are a conventional way of raising the credibility of promises by staking national reputation on adherence.* The price of noncompliance takes several forms. First, there is loss of reputation as a reliable partner. A reputation for reliability is important in reaching other cooperative agreements where there is some uncertainty about compliance. Second, the violation or perceived violation of a treaty may give rise to specific, costly retaliation, ranging from simple withdrawal of cooperation in one area to broader forms of noncooperation and specific sanctions. Some formal agreements, such as the General Agreement on Tariffs and Trade (GATT), even establish a limited set of permissible responses to violations, although most treaties do not. Finally, treaty violations may recast national reputation in a still broader and more dramatic way, depicting a nation that is not only untrustworthy but is also a deceitful enemy, one that makes promises in order to deceive.

This logic also suggests circumstances in which treaties—and, indeed, *all* international agreements—ought to be most vulnerable. An actor's reputation for reliability has a value over time. The present value of that reputation is the discounted stream of these current and future benefits. When time horizons are long, even distant benefits are considered valuable now. When horizons are short, these future benefits are worth little, while the gains from breaking an agreement are likely to be more immediate and tangible. Thus, under pressing circumstances, such as the looming prospect of war or economic crisis, the long-term value of a reputation for reliability will be sharply discounted. As a consequence, adherence to agreements must be considered less profitable and therefore less reliable. This points to a striking paradox of treaties: they are often used to seal partnerships for vital actions, such as war, but they are weakest at precisely that moment because the present looms larger and the future is more heavily discounted.

This weakness is sometimes recognized, though rarely emphasized, in studies of international law. It has no place at all, however, in the law of treaties. All treaties are treated equally, as legally binding commitments, and typically lumped together with a wide range of informal bargains. Treaties that declare alliances, establish neutral territories, or announce broad policy guidelines are not classified separately. Their legal status is the same as that of any other treaty. Yet it is also understood, by diplomats and jurists alike, that these three types of treaty are especially vulnerable to violation or renunciation. For this reason, Richard Baxter has characterized them as "soft" or "weak" law, noting that "if a State refuses to come to the aid of another under the terms of an alliance, nothing can force it to. It was never expected that the treaty would be 'enforced.'"[12]

According to Baxter, treaties announcing alliances or broad policy guidelines are sustained only by perceptions of mutual advantage.[13] He calls them "political treaties" and emphasizes their fragility: "They . . . are merely joint statements of policy which will remain alive only so long as the States concerned see it to be in their mutual interest to concert their policies. One simply cannot think of 'violations' of such instruments."[14]

What Baxter shrinks from are the full implications of position: it applies quite generally to all kinds of international agreements. Baxter admits, in effect, that international law is marginal to the major political projects of states. He admits, too, that treaties are sometimes concluded with no expectation of effective enforcement. He limits his judgment to what he terms "political treaties." But are *any* treaties really founded on this expectation of external enforcement, as opposed to self-interested adherence and self-generated sanctions? If treaties of alliance are weak because they lack such enforcement mechanisms, so are most international bargains. (The salient exception is when local courts can be used to enforce international obligations. That, however, is less an exception than a confirmation of the weakness of international enforcement.) If "political treaties" are sustained solely by perceptions of mutual advantage, so are all international bargains. There is simply no institutional infrastructure to do more.

The real point is to understand how these perceptions of mutual advantage can support various kinds of international cooperation and how different legal forms, such as treaties, fit into this essentially political dynamic. The environment of contesting sovereign powers does not mean, as realist theories of international politics would have it, that cooperation is largely irrelevant or limited to common cause against military foes. Nor does it mean that conflict and the resources for it are always dominant in international affairs. It does mean, however, that the bases for cooperation are decentralized and often fragile. Unfortunately, neither the language of treaties nor their putative legal status can transcend these limitations.

Rationales For Informal Agreements

Speed and Obscurity

What we have concentrated on thus far are the fundamental problems of international agreements. Treaties, like less formal instruments, are plagued by difficulties of noncompliance and self-enforcement. These potential problems limit agreements when monitoring is difficult, enforcement is costly, and expected gains from noncompliance are immediate and significant. The traditional legal view that treaties are valuable because they are binding is inadequate precisely because it fails to comprehend these basic and recurrent problems.

To understand the choice between treaties and informal agreements, however, we need to move beyond the generic problems of monitoring, betrayal, and self-enforcement. Imperfect information and incentives to defect apply to all kinds of international bargains; they do not explain why some are framed as joint declarations and some as treaties. We therefore need to consider more specific properties of informal and formal agreements, along with their particular advantages and limitations.

To begin with, treaties are the most serious and deliberate form of international agreement and are often the most detailed. As such, they are the slowest to complete. After the diplomats have finally left the table, the agreement must still win final approval from the signatories. That usually means a slow passage through the full domestic process of ratification. The process naturally differs from country to country, but in complex governments, and especially in democracies with some shared powers, gaining assent can be time-consuming. If the executive lacks a secure governing majority or if the legislature has significant powers of oversight, it can take months. It also opens the agreement and the silent calculus behind it to public scrutiny and time-consuming debate.

For controversial treaties, such as the ones ceding U.S. control over the Panama Canal, ratification can be very slow and painful indeed. The canal treaties had virtually universal support among foreign policy professionals dealing with Central and South America. But they also faced heated opposition within the U.S. Senate, mainly from conservative Republicans, who charged that America was giving away a valuable strategic asset and getting nothing tangible in return. When the treaties were presented for ratification, the 1978 midterm elections were approaching, and polling data showed that some proponents were vulnerable on this issue. After exhaustive hearings, the Senate Foreign Relations Committee reported the bill favorably. The treaty debate on the Senate floor was the second longest in American history; repetitive arguments dragged on through February, March, and April 1978. Opponents had a clear incentive to prolong the debate, not only to defeat the treaty or weaken it with unfriendly amendments but also to punish treaty supporters in particular and the Democratic party in general on election day.

Even when agreements are much less contentious, the machinery of ratification can grind slowly, as in the case of the relatively straightforward treaty covering criminal extradition between the United States and Turkey. Extradition treaties are commonplace. They use standardized language, make standard exceptions (refusing, for example, to extradite suspects for political crimes), and leave room for both policy discretion and ordinary court procedures. There was nothing unusual about the U.S. treaty with Turkey, nor was there any special domestic opposition to it. It was signed on 7 June 1979. From there, ratification proceeded at a stately pace. The President transmitted it to the Senate in early August. The Senate Foreign Relations Committee acted quickly, as such matters go, and reported favorably on 20 November 1979. The full Senate gave its consent eight days later. Turkey did not complete its ratification for another year, in late November 1980. The formal exchange of ratifications between the governments took place two weeks later. At the end of December, the U.S. President proclaimed the treaty, and it entered into force the next day, 1 January 1981, some eighteen months after the initial documents had been signed.

It is little wonder, then, that governments prefer simpler, more convenient instruments. It is plain, too, that executives prefer instruments that they can control unambiguously, without legislative advice or consent. But there are important domestic constraints, some rooted in constitutional prerogatives, some in legal precedent, and some in the shifting balance of domestic power. To cede control of the Panama Canal, for instance, the President had no choice but to use a treaty. His authority to conduct foreign affairs is broad, but not broad enough to hand over the canal and surrounding territory to Panama without Senate approval.[15] Similarly, criminal extradition between the United States and Turkey needed a treaty, at least on the U.S. side. American courts, following common law precedent, simply will not extradite defendants without this formal instrument. Informal extradition, done at the discretion of political authorities, is permitted in some countries with judicial systems based on Roman civil law. But the United States, Britain, and most other common law countries require explicit, reciprocal treaty arrangements.

Aside from extradition, which bears directly on the civil rights of accused criminals, the courts rarely affect the form of international agreements. That is true even for U.S. courts, which are normally quite willing to review political decisions. They try to avoid direct involvement in foreign policy issues and hold to this narrow line even when larger constitutional questions arise. They have done little, for instance, to restrict the widespread use of executive agreements, which evade the Senate's constitutional right to give "advice and consent" on formal treaties.

Despite the courts' reluctance to rule on these issues, informal agreements do raise important questions about the organization of state authority for the conduct of foreign affairs. Informal agreements shift power toward the executive and away from the legislature. In recent decades, the U.S. Congress responded by publicly challenging the President's right to make serious international commitments without at least notifying the Senate. It also disputed the President's control over undeclared foreign conflicts by passing the War Powers Resolution.

During the final years of the Vietnam War, when the President's authority over foreign affairs was most bitterly contested, a congressional committee investigated the use of informal agreements and discovered a "vast mass of agreements, commitments, and correspondence ... in which undertakings of one sort or another [were] made."[16] Another congressional committee found that "there [had] been numerous agreements contracted with foreign governments in recent years, particularly agreements of a military nature, which remain[ed] wholly unknown to Congress and to the people."[17] The result was a law—the Case Act—which promoted congressional oversight of informal agreements. It required that the State Department transmit to Congress *all* agreements. It required that the State Department transmit international agreements, including written versions of oral agreements, within two months of their conclusion. This law fell short of equating informal agreements with treaties, since it did not require congressional approval for all informal bargains, as is constitutionally required for treaties. But it did serve notice that informal agreements had proliferated unacceptably and had assumed important implications for policymaking. The Case Act tentatively bid to open these back channels to legislative supervision and broader debate.

To summarize, then, informal agreements are often chosen because they allow governments to act quickly and quietly. These two rationales are often intertwined, but each is important in its own right, and each is sufficient for choosing informal means of international cooperation.

Uncertainty and Renegotiation

Informal agreements may also be favored for an entirely different reason: they are more easily renegotiated and less costly to abandon than treaties. This flexibility is useful if there is considerable uncertainty about the distribution of future benefits under a particular agreement. In economic issues, this uncertainty may arise because of a shift in production functions or demand schedules, the use of new raw materials or substitute products, or a fluctuation in macroeconomic conditions or exchange rates. These changes could sabotage national interests in particular international agreements. The consequences might involve an unacceptable surge in imports under existing trade pacts, for example, or the collapse of producer cartels. In security affairs, nations might be uncertain about the rate of technological progress or the potential for new weapons systems. By restricting these innovations, existing arms treaties may create unexpected future costs for one side. Such developments can produce unexpected winners and losers, in either absolute or relative terms, and change the value of existing contractual relations. Put another way, institutional arrangements (including agreements) can magnify or diminish the distributional impact of exogenous shocks or unexpected changes.

States are naturally reluctant to make long-term, inflexible bargains behind this veil of ignorance. Even if one state is committed to upholding an agreement despite possible windfall gains or losses, there is no guarantee that others will do the same. The crucial point is that an agreement might not be self-sustaining if there is an unexpected asymmetry in benefits. Such uncertainties about future benefits, together with the difficulties of self-enforcement; pose serious threats to treaty reliability under conditions of rapid technological change, market volatility, or changing strategic vulnerabilities. The presence of such uncertainties and the dangers they pose for breach of treaty obligations foster the pursuit of substitute arrangements with greater flexibility.

States use several basic techniques to capture the potential gains from cooperation despite the uncertainties. First, they craft agreements (formal or informal) of limited duration so that all participants can calculate their risks and benefits under the agreement with some confidence. Strategic arms treaties of several years' duration are a good example. Second, they include provisions that permit legitimate withdrawal from commitments under specified terms and conditions. In practice, states can *always* abandon their international commitments, since enforcement is so costly and problematic. The real point of such treaty terms, then, is to lower the general reputational costs of withdrawal and thereby encourage states to cooperate initially despite the risks and uncertainties. Third, they incorporate provisions that permit partial withdrawal, covering either a temporary period or a limited set of obligations. GATT escape clauses, which permit post hoc protection of endangered industries, are a well-known example. Finally, states sometimes frame their agreements in purely informal terms to permit their frequent adjustment. The quota agreements of the Organization of Petroleum Exporting Countries (OPEC) do exactly that. While the OPEC agreements are critically important to the participants and are central to their economic performance, they are framed informally to permit rapid shifts in response to changing market conditions. Once again, the form of agreements is *not* dictated by their substantive significance.

OPEC's primary goal is to enhance national revenues by managing the world oil market. It is a producer cartel, or at least it hopes to be. Its basic strategy is to achieve price targets through quotas for individual members. That entails frequent meetings on an irregular schedule, at least twice a year and sometimes more if conditions warrant. After all, energy demand is hard to forecast, and OPEC does not entirely control the supply. Its control is incomplete because there are important non-OPEC producers, because there are alternatives to petroleum, and because OPEC members cheat on their quotas. This cheating is another reason for frequent OPEC meetings: they provide the opportunity to direct collective pressure and individual threats at cheaters.

To facilitate these negotiations, there is a small formal organization, headquartered in Vienna. But OPEC's reasons for existence—its price targeting and production quotas—are set out in informal agreements and conference communiqués, approved by participating oil ministers. These agreements are designed to last for only a few months, at most. The oil output quotas reached in June 1989, for example, covered only the second half of the year. As soon as the bargain was sealed, the ministers agreed to meet again in three months to review market conditions and quotas. OPEC's formal, institutional framework can facilitate negotiations, but it does not transcend or transform the immediate purposes of the member states. What really matters is not the formal organization but the nexus of informal agreements on crude oil production and the members' (uneven) compliance.

At the other end of the spectrum, in terms of formality, lie arms control treaties with detailed limitations on specific weapons systems for relatively long periods. They, too, must confront some important uncertainties. They do so principally by restricting the agreement to verifiable terms and a time frame that essentially excludes new weapons systems. The institutional arrangements are thus tailored to the environment they regulate.

Modern weapons systems require long lead times to build and deploy. As a result, military capacity and technological advantages shift slowly within specific weapons categories. With modern surveillance techniques, these new weapons programs and shifting technological capacities are not opaque to adversaries. The military environment to be regulated is relatively stable, then, so the costs and benefits of treaty restraints can be projected with some confidence over the medium term.

Given these conditions, treaties offer some clear advantages in arms control. They represent detailed public commitments, duly ratified by national political authorities. Although an aggrieved party would still need to identify and punish any alleged breach, the use of treaties raises the political costs of flagrant or deliberate violations (or, for that matter, unprovoked punishment). It does so by making disputes more salient and accessible and by underscoring the gravity of promises. Moreover, at least in nuclear weaponry, both sides feel that they could cope with major treaty violations, if necessary, by withdrawing from the treaty and pursuing their own weapons programs at an accelerated pace. Strong treaty commitments, in other words, would not expose them to the possibility of a devastating surprise defection. Both sides are confident that their satellites and human intelligence can detect major violations in time to produce and deploy countervailing weapons.

Following this logic, most arms control agreements have been set out in treaty form. Whether the subject is nuclear or conventional forces, test bans or weapons ceilings, American and Soviet negotiators have always aimed at formal documents with full ratification. Discussions during a summit meeting or a walk in the woods may lay the essential groundwork for an arms agreement, but they are *not* agreements in themselves.[18]

Over the history of superpower arms control, only the tacit observance of SALT II could be classified as a major informal agreement. Of course, the SALT negotiators had actually produced a formal agreement, filled with contractual details and the language of binding commitments. It had majority support in the U.S. Senate, but a final vote was never held because it lacked the necessary two-thirds majority.

After ratification foundered, the treaty lived a twilight existence. Members of the Reagan administration publicly debated the matter with no guidance from above. The hawkish secretary of the navy, John Lehman, announced that the United States should not comply with either SALT I or SALT II. The State Department, on the other hand, announced that the United States would "take no action that would undercut existing agreements so long as the Soviet Union exercises the same restraint.[19] This language is actually a diplomatic code: it is the standard way to acknowledge legal obligations while a treaty is pending ratification. For well over a year, however, the President himself refused to make a similar acknowledgment. He finally did so in May 1982, but at the same time he continued to criticize SALT and actually stated that the United States would observe only those portions of the agreement dealing "with the monitoring of each other's weaponry."[20] In practice, the United States did not exceed the treaty's limitations on specific weapons for some years. Still, the scope of official commitments was always informal and ambiguous. Perhaps these tacit arrangements and encoded signals were the most that could be salvaged from the failed treaty.

SALT II, in its informal guise, actually survived beyond the expiration date of the proposed treaty. Like most arms control agreements, it had been written with a limited life span so that it applied in predictable ways to existing weaponry, not to new and unforeseen developments. Time limits like these are used to manage risks in a wide range of international agreements. They are especially important in cases of superpower arms control, in which the desirability of specific agreements is related both to particular weaponry and to the overall strategic balance. As the military setting changes, existing commitments become more or less desirable. Arms control agreements must cope with these fluctuating benefits over the life of the agreement.

The idea is to forge agreements that provide sufficient benefits to each side, when evaluated at each point during the life of the agreement, so that each will choose to comply out of self-interest in order to perpetuate the treaty. This self-generated compliance is crucial in superpower arms control. Given the relative equality of power, U.S.–Soviet military agreements are not so much enforced as observed voluntarily. What sustains them is each participant's perception that they are valuable and that cheating would prove too costly if it were matched by the other side or if it caused the agreement to collapse altogether. To ensure that treaties remain valuable over their entire life span, negotiators typically try to restrict them to known weaponry and stock piles. That translates into fixed expiration dates.

When agreements stretch beyond this finite horizon, signatories may be tempted to defect as they develop new and unforeseen advantages or become more vulnerable to surprise defection, issues that were not fully anticipated when the agreement was made. The preference orderings that once supported cooperation may no longer hold. That has been one of the dilemmas surrounding the antiballistic missile (ABM) treaty in recent years.

The ABM treaty established strict, permanent limits on U.S. and Soviet missile defenses. Since its ratification in 1972, however, the possibilities of missile defense have advanced considerably. The United States, with its more advanced economy, has widened its lead in the relevant new technologies of microelectronics, software, and lasers. The Reagan administration relied on this superiority to develop the strategic defense initiative (SDI) and urged a reinterpretation of the ABM treaty in order to test some of its weaponry. The dispute over how to interpret the ABM treaty is thus grounded in the consequences of these new technologies and in the slow, cumulative shift in national advantages they have produced. The debate illustrates, once again, the difficulties of using rigid, formal instruments, which lack external enforcement, to regulate a shifting and unpredictable international environment.

All of these issues refer to the detailed regulation of slow-changing strategic environments. Although the issues are crucial to national defense, they are not so sensitive diplomatically that the agreement itself must be hidden from view. Cooperative arrangements in such issues, according to the arguments presented here, are likely to be in treaty form.

Hidden Agreements

When security issues must be resolved quickly or quietly to avoid serious conflict, then less formal instruments will be chosen. If the terms are especially sensitive, perhaps because they would humiliate one party or convey unacceptable precedents, then the agreement itself may be hidden from view.[21] The most dangerous crisis of the nuclear era, the Cuban missile crisis, was settled by the most informal and secret exchanges between the superpowers. The overriding aim was to defuse the immediate threat. That meant rapid agreement on a few crucial issues, with implementation to follow quickly. These informal exchanges were not the prelude to agreement, as in SALT or ABM negotiations; they *were* the agreement.

The deal to remove missiles from Cuba was crafted through an exchange of letters, supplemented by secret oral promises. During the crisis, the Soviets had put forward a number of inconsistent proposals for settlement. President Kennedy responded to the most conciliatory: Premier Khrushchev's letter of 26 October 1962. The next day, Kennedy accepted its basic terms and set a quick deadline for Soviet counter acceptance. The essence of the bargain was that the Soviets would remove all missiles from Cuba in return for America's pledge not to invade the island. The terms were a clear U.S. victory. They completely overturned the Soviet policy of putting nuclear missiles in the Western Hemisphere. The Soviets got nothing publicly. They were humiliated.

U.S. acceptance of the bargain was set out in diplomatic messages sent directly to Khrushchev. President Kennedy also sent his brother Robert to speak with Soviet Ambassador Anatoly Dobrynin, to convey U.S. acceptance and to add several points that were too sensitive to include in any documentation, however informal. Years later, the substance of their conversation became public. Dobrynin had asked if the United States would also remove its older missiles from Turkey (and perhaps Italy) as part of the deal. The Soviets had pressed this point before. Their aim was to salvage some thread of victory from the diplomatic confrontation. The Turkish missiles were no longer strategically important, and for some time the United States had been considering withdrawing them unilaterally. But now any agreement to remove them would acquire a markedly different meaning. That is exactly what the Soviets wanted: a visible quid pro quo. The Soviets could then claim some symmetry in the outcome of the Cuban missile crisis. Each side would have gotten its adversary to remove some threatening missiles based near its territory. The United States, bargaining from a position of overwhelming nuclear superiority, refused this direct, visible linkage. Robert Kennedy informed Dobrynin that the United States would not unilaterally withdraw missiles that had been stationed there by an allied decision made by the North Atlantic Treaty Organization (NATO). A concession on the Turkish missiles simply could not be part of the Cuban missile agreement. Having said this, the President's brother then stated that the United States "expected" the Turkish missiles to "be gone" soon after the crisis. Both sides understood this as a firm pledge, but one that must remain invisible, lest it signal any U.S. weakness. While framed as a unilateral choice, its timing and its immediate disclosure to the Soviets were clearly designed to help settle the Cuban missile crisis.

The Soviets continued to press for some written assurances, not because they doubted that the missiles would be removed but because they wanted some credit for their removal. Dobrynin took an unsigned letter from Khrushchev to Robert Kennedy on 29 October 1962, again seeking some direct, written commitment on the Turkish and Italian missiles. "Robert Kennedy called Dobrynin back the next day," according to Raymond Garthoff, "returned the draft Khrushchev letter, and categorically rejected any such written exchange. He informed Dobrynin that if the Soviet Union published anything claiming that there *was* such a deal, the U.S. intentions with respect to the Jupiter missiles would change, and it would negatively reflect on the U.S.-Soviet relations. The Soviets dropped the matter."[22] This part of the deal remained secret and deniable. The Soviets said nothing publicly, and NATO quietly removed its aging missiles from Turkey and Italy within six months.

The bargains that ended the Cuban missile crisis were all informal, but their motives and their degree of informality differed. The key decisions to remove missiles from Cuba in exchange for a pledge of noninvasion were informal because of time pressure. They were embodied in an exchange of messages, rather than in a single signed document, but at least the key points were in writing. The removal of outdated Turkish and Italian missiles was also part of the overall bargain—an essential part, according to some participants—but it was couched in even more informal terms because of political sensitivity. The sensitivity in this case was America's concern with its image as a great power and, to a lesser extent, with its role in NATO. This kind of concern with external images is one reason why informal agreements are used for politically sensitive bargains: they can be hidden.

Once again, there are costs to be considered. If a hidden agreement is exposed, its presence could well suggest deception—to the public, to allies, and to other government agencies. Even if the agreement does stay hidden, its secrecy imperils its reliability. Hidden agreements carry little information about the depth of the signatories' commitments, poorly bind successor governments, and fail to signal intentions to third parties. These costs are clearly exemplified in the secret treaties between Britain and France before World War I. They could do nothing to deter Germany, which did not know about them. Moreover, they permitted the signatories to develop markedly different conceptions about their implied commitments as allies.

Hidden agreements carry another potential cost. They may not be well understood inside a signatory's own government. On the one hand, this low profile may be a valuable tool of bureaucratic or executive control, excluding other agencies from direct participation in making or implementing international agreements. On the other hand, the ignorance of the excluded actors may well prove costly if their actions must later be coordinated as part of the agreement. When that happens, hidden agreements can become a comedy of errors.

One example is the postwar American effort to restrict exports to the Soviet bloc. To succeed, the embargo needed European support. With considerable reluctance, West European governments finally agreed to help, but they demanded secrecy because the embargo was so unpopular at home. As a result, the U.S. Congress never knew that the Europeans were actually cooperating with the American effort. In confused belligerence, the Congress actually passed a law to cut off foreign aid to Europe if the allies did not aid in the embargo.

This weak signaling function has another significant implication: it limits the value of informal agreements as diplomatic precedents, even if the agreements themselves are public. This limitation has two sources. First, informal agreements are generally less visible and prominent, and so they are less readily available as models. Second, treaties are considered better evidence of deliberate state practice, according to diplomatic convention and international law. Public, formal agreements are conventionally understood as contributing to diplomatic precedent. Precisely for that reason informal agreements are less useful as precedents and more useful when states want to limit any broader, adverse implications of specific bargains. They frame an agreement in more circumscribed ways than a treaty. Discussions between long-time adversaries, for instance, usually begin on an informal, low-level basis to avoid any implicit recognition of wider claims. Trade relations may also be conducted indirectly, using third-party entrepots, to avoid any formal contract relationships between estranged governments.

Relations between the People's Republic of China and Taiwan have been conducted informally for these very reasons. The point is not so much to keep the dealings secret (they are, in fact, sometimes announced) but to limit linkage to any larger issues. Both sides, for example, can profit from commercial exchange, but neither wants to prejudice its claim to be the sole legitimate government of China. The result is a proliferation of informal contacts and agreements, often using overseas Chinese as middlemen. Hong Kong and Singapore, with their large populations of ethnic Chinese, have frequently served as intermediaries.

Hong Kong [was] particularly well located to facilitate indirect trade and investment between Taiwan and the mainland. Singapore, which has cultivated political ties to both countries, now occupies "a unique position of advantage in the conduct of informal relations" between them, according to Michael Leifer and Michael Yahuda. In April 1989, Singapore served as the conduit for the first known criminal extradition from the mainland to the island. Three mainland police flew to Singapore with their prisoner and transferred him to Taiwanese officers for return to the island. A more formal, regularized procedure, like the extradition treaty between the United States and Turkey, would present insurmountable problems. It would require documentation that named the two signatories and was ratified by them. Would the document refer to the Republic of China or to the province of Taiwan? Either reference would concede a much larger issue: diplomatic recognition. In this case and in many others, informal agreements are useful because they facilitate cooperation on specific issues while constraining any wider implications regarding other issues or third parties. They permit bounded cooperation.

The Status of Tacit Agreements

We have concentrated, until now, on informal bargains that are openly expressed, at least among the participants themselves. The form may be written or oral, detailed or general, but there is some kind of explicit bargain.

Tacit agreements, on the other hand, are not explicit. They are implied, understood, or inferred rather than directly stated. Such implicit arrangements extend the scope of informal cooperation. They go beyond the secrecy of oral agreements and, at times, may be the only way to avoid serious conflict on sensitive issues. Such bargains, however, are all too often mirages, carrying the superficial appearance of agreement but not its substance.

The unspoken "rules" of the Cold War are sometimes considered tacit agreements. The superpowers staked out their respective spheres of influence and did not directly engage each other's forces. Yet they made no explicit agreements on either point. In the early years of the Cold War, the United States quietly conceded de facto control over Eastern Europe to the Soviets. The policies that laid the basis for NATO were designed to contain the Soviet Union, both diplomatically and militarily, but nothing more. They made no effort to roll back the Soviet army's wartime gains, which had been converted into harsh political dominion in the late 1940s. America's restraint amounted to a spheres-of-influence policy without actually acknowledging Moscow's regional security interests. This silence only confirmed the Soviets' worst fears and contributed to bipolar hostilities.

In the bitter climate of the early Cold War period, however, no U.S. official was prepared to concede the Soviets' dominance in Eastern Europe. Earlier conferences at Yalta and Potsdam had seemed to do so, but now these concessions were pushed aside, at least rhetorically. While Democrats reinterpreted these agreements or considered them irrelevant because of Soviet violations, Republicans denounced them as immoral or even treasonous. Backed by these domestic sentiments, U.S. foreign policy was couched in the language of universal freedoms, conceding nothing to the Soviets in Eastern Europe. In practice, however, the United States tacitly accepted Soviet control up to the borders of West Germany.

How does tacit acceptance of this kind compare with the informal but explicit bargains we have been considering? They are quite different in principle, I think. The most fundamental problem in analyzing so-called tacit bargains lies in determining whether any real agreement exists. More broadly, is there some kind of mutual policy adjustment that is (implicitly) contingent on reciprocity? If so, what are the parties' commitments, as they understand them? Often, what pass for tacit bargains are actually policies that have been chosen unilaterally and independently, in light of the unilateral policies of others. There may be an "understanding" of other parties' policies but no implicit agreements to adjust these policies on a mutual or contingent basis. Each party is simply maximizing its own values, subject to the independent choices made or expected to be made by others. What looks like a silent bargain may simply be a Nash equilibrium.

This is not to say that tacit bargains are always a chimera. Each party can adjust its policies on a provisional basis, awaiting some conforming adjustment by others. Thomas Schelling has consistently argued that this is the most fruitful approach to superpower arms control.[25] Robert Axelrod has used experimental games to analyze the possibilities and robustness of such tacit bargains. In Axelrod's games, there can be no explicit bargains, however informal, because direct communication is prohibited. After all, the prisoners' dilemma is no dilemma at all if players can openly contract around it. Still, some players may effectively offer tacit agreements. They confront new partners by making an initial "generous" move.[26] That move is sensible only if some respond with generosity themselves, rather than aggressively playing them for a sucker. The whole point of a tit-for-tat strategy is to communicate the possibility of a tacit bargain: a willingness to play cooperatively if, and only if, the other side will do so as well. The problem, as George Downs and David Rocke have shown, is that states may not always know when others are cooperating or defecting and may not know what their intentions are.[27] One state may then punish others for noncompliance or defections that are more apparent than real and thus begin a downward spiral of retaliation. Such imperfect knowledge does not prevent tacit cooperation, but it does suggest serious impediments and risks to tacit bargaining, the need for more "fault tolerant" strategies, and the potential gains from more explicit communication and greater transparency.

In ongoing diplomatic interactions in which each side continually responds to the other's policies and initiatives, it may also be difficult to distinguish between tacit bargains and unilateral acts. One side may consider its own restraint part of an implicit bargain, while the other considers it nothing more than prudent self-interest. In the early Cold War, for instance, the United States could do nothing to reverse Soviet control in Eastern Europe without waging war. There was little to be gained by providing substantial aid to local resistance movements. Their chances for success were slim, and the dangers of escalation were significant. Any U.S. efforts to destabilize Soviet control in Eastern Europe would have markedly increased international tensions and raised the dangers of U.S.-Soviet conflict in central Europe. Under the circumstances, American policy was restrained. More aggressive action in Eastern Europe was deterred by the risks and poor chances of success, not by the implied promise of some reciprocal restraint by the Soviets. There was a learning process but no tacit bargain.

In any case, most tacit bargains are hard to identify with confidence. By their very nature, implicit agreements leave little trace. Moreover, what may appear to be implicit agreements are often explicable as outcomes of more narrowly self-interested unilateral policies. Given these difficulties, one valuable approach to uncovering tacit bargains is to examine the reactions and discourse surrounding possible "violations." Tacit bargains, like their more explicit counterparts, are based on the reciprocal exchange of benefits. Breaking the terms of that exchange is likely to be given voice. There will be talk of betrayal and recriminations, words of regret at having extended generous but uncompensated concessions. There ought to be some distinctive recognition that reasonable expectations and inferences, built up during the course of joint interactions, have been breached. Thus, there is regret and not merely surprise.

Consider the differences in America's reaction to expanded Soviet influence in two cases: Cuba in 1959–60 and Afghanistan in 1979–80. After the Cuban revolution, the Soviets managed to develop a de facto ally in the Western Hemisphere. The United States was shocked by a challenge so close to its own territory. It was shocked because the Soviet–Cuban alliance challenged America's unique power in the Western Hemisphere and posed significant new strategic problems, not because it broke some silent understanding with the Soviets over respective spheres of influence. What had been violated was America's unchallenged position as the great power in its own region. America's assertion of that unique position had been the beginning of its rise to global power in the late nineteenth century. Since then, it had taken all challenges to its regional hegemony very seriously indeed. There was no claim, however, that the Soviets had violated some general understanding with the United States or had somehow failed to reciprocate America's restrained policies near the Soviet border. On the basis of America's pronouncements and reactive policies, there was simply no evidence that a tacit bargain had been broken.

Compare that with America's reaction to the Soviet invasion of Afghanistan. The Carter administration, which had been pursuing a policy of increased trade and normalized relations with the Soviets, clearly considered the invasion a direct attack on the broad, implicit agreement underlying detente. For the first time, Soviet troops had been used for aggressive purposes outside Eastern Europe. President Carter's own sense of shock, outrage, and betrayal were widely shared in America and, to a lesser extent, among the Western allies. It was this deep sense of violation, and not just the potential military threat to the Persian Gulf, that ended a decade of closer ties between the superpowers.

The Soviets, of course, saw matters differently. They viewed detente in more restrictive terms, related principally to the nuclear balance, European diplomacy, and trade flows, detached from the invasion of Afghanistan or support for guerrilla factions in the Horn of Africa, Angola, Mozambique, or Central America.

These different understandings, which have been so well documented,[28] are important to raise here because they illustrate a common defect in tacit understandings: they are often vague and ambiguous, sometimes disastrously so. They may give rise to radically different interpretations, which go unnoticed at the time. There is, unfortunately, no way to identify and reconcile such differing views except retroactively, when disputes arise over nonperformance. By then, the prospects of future cooperation may already be destroyed by recriminations over "bad faith."

The dangers of misunderstanding are certainly not unique to tacit agreements. They lurk in all contracts, even the most formal and detailed. But the process of negotiating written agreements does offer a chance to clarify understandings, to agree on joint interpretations, to draft detailed, restrictive language, and to establish mechanisms for ongoing consultation, such as the U.S.-Soviet Standing Consultative Commission. Tacit agreements, by definition, lack these procedures, lack this detail, and lack any explicit understandings.

These limitations in tacit agreements are not always a drawback. If the agreement covers only a few basic points, if the parties clearly understand the provisions in the same way, and if there are no individual incentives to betray or distort the terms, then some key defects of tacit bargains are irrelevant. Some coordination problems fit this description. They involve tacit agreement among multiple participants who cannot communicate directly with one another.

Unfortunately, the hard issues of international politics are different. They involve complicated questions without salient solutions, where national interests are less than congruent. Any commitments to cooperate need to be specified in some detail.[29] The agreements themselves are not so simply self-sustaining. If cooperation is to be achieved, the terms must be crafted deliberately to minimize the risks of misunderstanding and noncompliance.

Choosing Between Treaties and Informal Agreements

Because tacit bargains are so limited, states are reluctant to depend on them when undertaking important projects. They want some clear, written signal that an agreement has been reached and includes specific terms. When a state's choice of policies is contingent on the choices of others, it will prefer to spell out these respective choices and the commitments they entail and will want to improve information flows among interdependent actors. These requirements can be met by either a formal treaty or an informal agreement, each with its own generic strengths and weaknesses. Each is more or less suited to resolving specific kinds of international bargaining problems.

These differences mean that actors must choose between them for specific agreements. However, they may also complement each other as elements of more inclusive bargains. The treaty commitments that define NATO, for instance, are given their military and diplomatic significance by a stream of informal summit declarations that address contemporary alliance issues such as weapons modernization, arms control, and Soviet policy initiatives.

Informal agreements, as I have noted, are themselves quite varied, ranging from simple oral commitments to joint summit declarations to elaborate letters of intent, such as stabilization agreements with the International Monetary Fund (IMF). Some of the most elaborate are quite similar to treaties but with two crucial exceptions. The diplomatic status of the promises is less clear-cut, and the agreements typically do not require elaborate ratification procedures. They lack, to a greater or lesser extent, the state's fullest and most authoritative imprimatur. The effects on reputation are thus constrained, but so is the dependability of the agreement.

States equivocate, in principle, on their adherence to these informal bargains. They are often unwilling to grant them the status of legally binding agreements. But what does that mean in practice, given that *no* international agreements can bind their signatories like domestic contracts can?

The argument presented here is that treaties send a conventional signal to other signatories and to third parties concerning the *gravity* and *irreversibility* of a state's commitments. By putting reputation at stake, they add to the costs of breaking agreements or, rather, they do so if a signatory values reputation. Informal agreements are typically more elusive on these counts.

These escape hatches are the common denominators of informal agreements, from the most elaborate written documents to the sketchiest oral agreements. The Helsinki Final Act, with its prominent commitments on human rights, is otherwise virtually identical to a treaty. It includes sixty pages of detailed provisions, only to declare that it should not be considered a treaty with binding commitments. At the other extreme are oral bargains, which are the most secret, the most malleable, and the quickest to conclude. Like their more elaborate counterparts, they are a kind of moral and legal oxymoron: an equivocal promise.

The speed and simplicity of oral bargains make them particularly suited for clandestine deals and crisis resolution. But for obvious reasons, states are reluctant to depend on them more generally. Oral agreements can encompass only a few major points of agreement; they cannot set out complicated obligations in any detail. They are unreliable in several distinct ways. First, it is difficult to tell whether they have been officially authorized and whether the government as a whole is committed to them. Second, they usually lack the visibility and public commitment that support compliance. Third, to ensure implementation in complex bureaucratic states, oral agreements must be translated into written directives at some point. Sincere mistakes, omissions, and misunderstandings may creep in during this translation process with no opportunity to correct them before an interstate dispute emerges. Last, but most important of all, it is easier to disclaim oral bargains or to recast them on favorable terms. Nobody ever lost an argument in the retelling, and oral bargains have many of the same properties. Perhaps this is what Sam Goldwyn had in mind when he said that verbal contracts were not worth the paper they were written on.

Putting informal agreements into writing avoids most of these problems. It generally produces evidence of an intended bargain. What it still lacks is the depth of national commitment associated with treaties. That is the irreducible price of maintaining policy flexibility.

Informal agreements are also less public than treaties, in two ways. First, because states do not acknowledge them as fundamental, self-binding commitments, they are less convincing evidence of recognized state practices. They are thus less significant as precedents. For example, informal agreements on trade or extradition are no proof of implicit diplomatic recognition, as a formal treaty would be. These limitations mean that informal agreements are more easily restricted to a particular issue. They have fewer ramifications for collateral issues or third parties. They permit cooperation to be circumscribed. Second, informal agreements are more easily kept secret, if need be. There is no requirement to ratify them or to enact them into domestic law, and there is no need to register them with international organizations for publication. For highly sensitive bargains, such as the use of noncombatants' territory in guerrilla wars, that is a crucial attribute.

Treaties, too, can be kept secret. There is no inherent reason why they must be made public. Indeed, secret treaties were a central instrument of balance-of-power diplomacy in the eighteenth and nineteenth centuries. But there are powerful reasons why secret treaties are rare today. The first and most fundamental is the rise of democratic states with principles of public accountability and some powers of legislative oversight. Secret treaties are difficult to reconcile with these democratic procedures. The second reason is that ever since the United States entered World War I, it has opposed secret agreements as a matter of basic principle and has enshrined its position in the peace settlements of both world wars.

The decline of centralized foreign policy institutions, which worked closely with a handful of political leaders, sharply limits the uses of secret treaties. Foreign ministries no longer hold the same powers to commit states to alliances, to shift those alliances, to divide conquered territory, and to hide such critical commitments from public view. The discretionary powers of a Bismarck or Metternich have no equivalent in modern Western states. Instead, democratic leaders rely on informal instruments to strike international bargains in spite of domestic institutional restraints. That is precisely the objection raised by the U.S. Congress regarding war powers and executive agreements.

When leaders are freed from such institutional restraints, they can hide their bargains without making them informal. They can simply use secret treaties and protocols, as Stalin and Hitler did in August 1939 when they carved up Eastern Europe. The Soviets accurately informed the Germans that "ratification . . . was merely a formality" and would be completed immediately by the Presidium of the Supreme Soviet.[30] The actual Treaty of Non-Aggression was made public. What was kept secret was the attached protocol that partitioned Poland and the Baltic into spheres of influence. The following month, the Nazis and Soviets added two more secret protocols, declaring Latvia, Estonia, and Lithuania part of the Soviet sphere. Within a year, the Baltic states had been forcibly incorporated into the Soviet Union. For the next fifty years, including the first four years of *glasnost,* the Soviets refused to acknowledge these secret protocols. They scorned the Baltic nationalists (who knew about the deal) and ignored the inconvenient fact that the Allies had copies of the German documents. The old Soviet-Nazi protocols remain sensitive because they undermine the legitimacy of Soviet territorial expansion. They directly impugn the sources of Soviet dominance of a multinational state. There is ample reason, then, why the agreement was made secretly and why the Soviets long tried to keep it that way.

Aside from these protocols, secret pacts have rarely been used for important interstate projects since World War I. That partly reflects the war experience itself and partly reflects America's rise to global prominence. While the war was still being fought, Leon Trotsky had published the czarist government's secret treaties. They showed how Italy had been enticed into the war (through the London treaty) and revealed that Russia had been promised control of Constantinople. The Allies were embarrassed by the publication of these self-seeking agreements and were forced to proclaim the larger principles for which their citizens were fighting and dying.

Woodrow Wilson had always wanted such a statement of intent. He argued that this was a war about big issues and grand ideals, not about narrow self-interest or territorial aggrandizement. He dissociated the United States from the Allies' earlier secret commitments and sought to abolish them forever once the war had been won. At the Versailles peace conference, where Wilson stated his Fourteen Points to guide the negotiations, he began with a commitment to "open covenants ... openly arrived at." He would simply eliminate "private international understandings of any kind [so that] diplomacy shall proceed always frankly and in the public view.[31]

These Wilsonian ideals were embodied in Article 18 of the League of Nations Covenant and later in Article 102 of the United Nations (UN) Charter. They provided a means for registering international agreements and, in the case of the UN, an incentive to do so. Only registered agreements could be accorded legal status before any UN affiliate, including the International Court of Justice. This mixture of legalism and idealism could never abolish private understandings, but it did virtually eliminate secret treaties among democratic states. Informal agreements live on as their closest modern substitutes.

Conclusion: International Cooperation by Informal Agreement

The varied uses of informal agreements illuminate the possibilities of international cooperation and some recurrent limitations. They underscore the fact that cooperation is often circumscribed and that its very limits may be fundamental to the participants. Their aim is often to restrict the scope and duration of agreements and to avoid any generalization of their implications. The ends are often particularistic, the means ad hoc. Informal bargains are delimited from the outset. More often than not, there is no intention (and no realistic possibility) of extending them to wider issues. Other actors, longer time periods, or more formal obligations. They are simply not the beginning of a more inclusive process of cooperation or a more durable one.

These constraints shape the form that agreements can take. Interstate bargains are frequently designed to be hidden from domestic constituencies, to avoid legislative ratification, to escape the attention of other states, or to be renegotiated. They may well be conceived with no view and no aspirations about the longer term. They are simply transitory arrangements, valuable now but ready to be abandoned or reordered as circumstances change. The diplomatic consequences and reputational effects are minimized by using informal agreements rather than treaties. Informal agreements may also be chosen because of time pressures. To resolve a crisis, the agreement may have to be struck quickly and definitively, with no time for elaborate documents.

Because informal agreements can accommodate these restrictions, they are common tools for international cooperation. States use them, and use them frequently, to pursue national goals by international agreement. They are flexible, and they are commonplace. They constitute, as Judge Richard Baxter once remarked, a "vast substructure of inter-governmental paper."[32] Their presence testifies to the perennial efforts to achieve international cooperation and to its institutional variety. Their form testifies silently to its limits.

Notes

1. See Paul Keal, *Unspoken Rules and Superpower Dominance* (London: Macmillan, 1983). Some diplomatic efforts were made to articulate the rules, but they did little in themselves to clarify expectations. In 1972, as the strategic arms limitation talks (SALT I) were concluded, Nixon and Brezhnev signed the Basic Principles Agreement. It sought to specify some key elements of the superpowers' relationship and thereby facilitate the development of detente. The product was vague and ambiguous. Worse, it seemed to indicate—wrongly—U.S. agreement with the Soviet position on peaceful coexistence and competition in other regions. Alexander George calls these elements "a pseudoagreement." For the text of the agreement, see *Department of State Bulletin,* 26 June 1972, pp. 898–99. For an analysis, see Alexander George, "The Basic Principles Agreement of 1972," in Alexander L. George, ed., *Managing U.S.–Soviet Rivalry: Problems of Crisis Prevention* (Boulder, Colo.: Westview Press, 1982), pp. 107–18.

2. It is worth noting that all of these distinctions are ignored in international law. Virtually all international commitments, whether oral or written, whether made by the head of state or a lower-level bureaucracy, are treated as "binding international commitments." What is missing is not only the political dimension of these agreements, including their status as domestic policy, but also any insight into why states choose more or less formal means for their international agreements.

3. Recognizing these limitations on oral bargains, domestic courts refuse to recognize such bargains in many cases, thereby creating a powerful incentive for

written contracts. There is no such incentive to avoid oral bargains in interstate agreements.

4. Anthony Aust, "The Theory and Practice of Informal International Instruments," *International and Comparative Law Quarterly* 35 (October 1986), p. 791.

5. See, for example, Lord McNair, *The Law of Treaties* (Oxford: Clarendon Press, 1961); and Taslim Eliase, *The Modern Law of Treaties* (Dobbs Ferry, N.Y.: Oceana Publications, 1974).

6. Incomplete domestic agreements can be filled in by court decisions. Incomplete international agreements remain incomplete. They are beyond the reach of international court decisions, much less enforcement.

7. Fried and Atiyah represent opposite poles in this debate. Fried argues that the common law of contracts is based on the moral institution of promising, rather than on commercial exchange. To sustain this institution, the recipients of broken promises should be awarded their expectations of profit. Atiyah argues that court decisions have moved away from this strict emphasis, which arose in the nineteenth century, and returned to an older notion of commercial practice, which limits awards to the costs incurred in relying on broken promises. See Charles Fried, *Contract as Promise: A Theory of Contractual Obligation* (Cambridge, Mass.: Harvard University Press, 1981); Patrick S. Atiyah, *From Principles to Pragmatism* (Oxford: Clarendon Press, 1978); and Patrick S. Atiyah, *The Rise and Fall of Freedom of Contract* (Oxford: Clarendon Press, 1979).

8. Three standard reasons are given for the legal requirement that contracts be put in writing. First, it should impart caution before an agreement is completed. Second, it should make clear to the parties that they have undertaken specific obligations. Third, if disagreements later arise, it should provide better evidence for courts. See the classic analysis by Lon L. Fuller: "Consideration and Form," *Columbia Law Review,* vol. 41, 1941, pp. 799–824; and *Anatomy of Law* (New York: Praeger, 1968), pp. 36–37.

9. There is one restriction worth noting on the legal form of international agreements. The World Court will only consider agreements that have been formally registered with the United Nations. If the World Court were a powerful enforcement body, this restriction would influence the form of major agreements.

10. In this sense, secret treaties are similar to informal agreements.

11. Thus, a single agreement can be self-enforcing, even if it is divorced from any reputational concerns. Conversely, even when reputational issues are salient, a treaty may break down if other costs are more important.

12. See Richard Baxter, "International Law in 'Her Infinite Variety,'" *International and Comparative Law Quarterly* 29 (October 1980), p. 550. See also Ignaz Seidl-Hohenfeldern, "International Economic Soft Law," *Recueil de cours* (Collected Courses of the Hague Academy of International Law), vol. 163, 1979, pp. 169–246.

13. See Baxter, "International Law in 'Her Infinite Variety,'" p. 551. Baxter refers to alliances and statements of broad political intent (such as the Yalta Agreement) as "political treaties." He does not define the term further or distinguish it from other kinds of treaties.

14. Ibid.

15. Just what agreements must be submitted as treaties remains ambiguous. It is a constitutional question, or course, but also a question of the political balance of power between the Congress and the President. At one point, President Carter's chief of staff, Hamilton Jordan, announced that Carter would decide whether the Panama Canal agreements were treaties or not. He "could present [the accords] to the Congress as a treaty, or as an agreement, and at the proper time he'll make that

decision." Interview on "Face the Nation," CBS News, cited by Loch K. Johnson in *The Making of International Agreements: Congress Confronts the Executive* (New York: New York University Press, 1984), p. 141.

16. See Baxter, "International Law in 'Her Infinite Variety,'" pp. 554–55.

17. U.S. Congress, Senate Committee on Foreign Relations, *Transmittal of Executive Agreements to Congress,* Senate Report no. 92-591, 92d Congress, 2d sess.l, 1972, pp. 3–4.

18. Note, however, that if the discussions pertained to domestic bargains, a court might interpret these "agreements in principle" as contractually binding, depending on the level of detail and the promissory language. Once again, the absence of effective international courts matters.

19. Public statement issued by U.S. Department of State on 4 March 1981.

20. Presidential response to a question on 13 May 1982, quoted in *Weekly Compilation of Presidential Documents,* vol. 18, no. 19, 17 May 1982, p. 635.

21. In modern international politics, these hidden agreements are informal because ratification is public and the treaties are registered with the United Nations. In earlier international systems, however, neither condition applied and secret treaties were possible.

22. Raymond L. Garthoff, *Reflections on the Cuban Missile Crisis,* revised ed. (Washington, D.C.: Brookings Institution, 1989), p. 95n.

23. Michael Leifer and Michael Yahuda, "Third Party China?" working paper, London School of Economics, 1989, p. 1.

24. Because informal extradition arrangements are ad hoc, they are easily severed. That is a mixed blessing. It means that extradition issues are directly implicated in the larger issues of bilateral diplomacy. They cannot be treated as distinct, technical issues covered by their own treaty rules. For example, the bloody suppression of popular uprisings in 1989 in the People's Republic of China blocked prisoner exchanges and made trade and investment ties politically riskier.

25. See Thomas C. Schelling, "Reciprocal Measures for Arms Stabilization," *Daedalus* 89 (Fall 1960), pp. 892–914; Thomas C. Schelling, "What Went Wrong with Arms Control?" *Foreign Affairs* 64 (Winter 1985–86), pp. 219–33; and Thomas C. Schelling and Morton H. Halperin, *Strategy and Arms Control,* 2d ed. (Washington, D.C.: Pergamon-Brassey, 1985), pp. 77–90. Schelling's point is strongly endorsed by Adelman in "Arms Control With and Without Agreements."

26. Robert Axelrod, *The Evolution of Cooperation* (New York: Basic Books, 1984).

27. See George W. Downs and David M. Rocke, *Tacit Bargaining Arms Races, and Arms Control* (Ann Arbor: University of Michigan Press, 1990).

28. See Mike Bowker and Phil Williams, *Superpower Detente: A Reappraisal* (London: Sage, 1988).

29. This does not rule out deliberate vagueness on some issues as part of a larger, more detailed settlement. Cooperation is not comprehensive, and some issues have to be finessed if any agreement is to be reached.

30. See "Telegram, Most Urgent, [from] the Ambassador in the Soviet Union to the [German] Foreign Ministry, August 30, 1939, Signed by Schulenburg," document no. 447.

31. Wilson's war aims were stated to a joint session of Congress on 8 January 1918. When European leaders later challenged this commitment to open covenants, Wilson announced that he would never compromise the "essentially American terms in the program," including Point One. See Edward M. House, *The Intimate Papers of Colonel House,* vol. 4, 3d. by Charles Seymour (London: Ernest Benn, 1928), pp. 182–83.

32. Baxter, "International Law in 'Her Infinite Variety,'" p. 549.

PART 2.3

International Law as Operating System: Participants in the International Legal Process

7

State Succession:
The Once and Future Law

Oscar Schachter

This [article] responds to the dramatic and unforeseen dissolution of states in Eastern Europe - the U.S.S.R., Yugoslavia and Czechoslovakia. It focuses on the legal category of "succession," a somewhat imprecise term that deals with the transmission or extinction of rights and obligations of a state that no longer exists or has lost part of its territory. State succession is one of the oldest subjects of international law. Even Aristotle speculated in his *Politics* on the problem of continuity when "the state is no longer the same."[1] Grotius and the other founding fathers of international law proposed distinctions on grounds of reason and natural justice.[2] State practice, as usual in international law, was largely determined by perceived political interests influenced in some degree by conceptions, analogies and metaphors derived from juristic commentary. Underlying the legal discourse we can discern the human dramas: the break-up of age-old empires and the emergence of new identities, new voices, new frontiers separating peoples or uniting them, deeply affecting their personal lives. These events are not only the stuff of history; they foreshadow the future. We can be quite sure, as we look around us today, that some states will split, others will be absorbed, frontiers will be moved, and new generations will question old alliances and commitments. The problem that concerned Aristotle in the fourth century B.C., of the stability of legal obligation when political identities change, will persist on both the international as well as the domestic level.

[We are reminded] that international law is in motion and that old formulas may not meet current needs. The prevailing legal view in the nineteenth and much of the twentieth century accepted two basic principles relating to succession. One was the critical difference between succession of states and changes in government. The principle of succession was

---

relevant only where one state was replaced by another in the responsibility for the international relations of a territory. The legal problem of succession did not arise when government—that is, internal political regimes—changed, no matter how profound or revolutionary a change. This principle, traced by scholars to Grotius, has been generally accepted by scholars, courts and foreign ministries. It was challenged, as Detlev Vagts points out, by the Soviet regime in its early effort to repudiate obligations of the Czarist government, an effort that did not succeed in changing doctrine or practice. It is evident that in sharply differentiating between "sovereignty" and "government," the law weighs heavily on the side of continuity of obligations when major political changes occur within sovereign states.

This basic differentiation between changes in government and changes in sovereignty is rarely questioned but, as pointed out by Daniel O'Connell (an eminent authority), the distinction "in some instances wears thin to the point of disappearance" and may be "quite arbitrary."[3] In his words, "[t]o permit the solution of complex political and economic problems to depend on this arbitrary cataloguing is to divorce the law from the actualities of international life."[4] Although O'Connell did not abandon the conceptual distinction, his skeptical comment is a reminder that the formal categories (which he attributes to hegelian notions of state "personality") are not as important as considering the practical consequences of political change in particular context. This pragmatic approach suggests that radical transformations of regimes may in some cases result in breaking the continuity of obligations, by applying the principle of *rebus sic stantibus* (or by treaty interpretation) rather than under the doctrine of state succession. [We are] more concerned with the practical consequences of continuity or disruption of sovereign obligations than with the formal structure of succession law. This does not mean that the traditional structure of the law of state succession will be quickly jettisoned, but we can be quite sure that it will change in response to political developments.

The Law of Succession—Then and Now

A few words about the doctrinal history may be appropriate here. In its origin, the law of succession on the international level drew a basic distinction between obligations that were "personal" (as were the sovereigns) and obligations that were "dispositive" because they were linked to the "land" (or "real"). Only the latter survived the extinction of the personality. This personal-dispositive dichotomy seemed to provide a simple solution. Political treaties, treaties of alliances, and at least some debts not linked to territorial benefits ("odious" debts) did not survive. (When the United States took over Cuba in 1898 and when the British annexed South Africa, neither successor paid the debts of the predecessor states.[5]) With regard to treaties, McNair introduced the metaphor of "clean slate" in the following much-quoted passage:

> [N]ewly established States which do not result from a political dismemberment and cannot fairly be said to involve political continuity with any predecessor, start with a clean slate . . . except as regards the purely local or 'real' obligations of the State formerly exercising sovereignty over the territory of the new State.[6]

Local or "real" obligations included, most importantly, the preexisting boundaries whether or not included in a treaty instrument. As Rein Mullerson points out in this symposium, *uti possidetis juris* is now recognized as a customary law principle that establishes continuity of borders. This was noted by the Arbitration Commission of the European Community in regard to the frontiers of the newly recognized states resulting from the break-up of the former Socialist Federated Republic of Yugoslavia.[7]

One effect of the prevailing "personal-real" dichotomy was that delictual responsibility of an extinct state was not transferred to a successor state. Wrongful acts and obligations flowing from such acts were generally treated as "personal" by tribunals in claims cases and by most writers.[8] Some acts of the communist states of Eastern Europe must have involved violations of international law for which those states would have been responsible internationally. The old view that such responsibility should not be transferable to successors is by no means self-evident and persuasive arguments based on general principles of law (including unjust enrichment) can be made to support succession of liability in some situations.[9]

In the 1960's, state succession was placed high on the agenda of international lawyers in many countries as a result of the wave of decolonization and the efforts of the U.N. International Law Commission to codify the law of succession in relation to treaties and, separately, in regard to debts, state property and state archives. In the 1960's and 1970's, this gave rise to considerable controversy centered mainly on the applicability of the clean slate principle to the newly independent states resulting from decolonization. Many members of the International Law Commission and the majority of states concluded that new states should not be bound by agreements made by former colonial rulers. Self-determination was often cited in support of this principle. It was included in the convention on treaty succession proposed by the International Law Commission and adopted by majority of states at the Vienna Plenipotentiary Conference in 1978.[10] That Vienna Convention did not, however, apply the clean slate principle to new states that arose from separation rather than decolonization.[11] Unlike colonies, those new states presumably had a voice in making and accepting the treaty. As Professor Vagts observes, this differentiation was rejected by the Restatement (Third) of the Foreign Relations Law of the United States ("Restatement"), which favored giving all newly independent states freedom to start afresh. The Vienna Convention went a step beyond the clean slate rule by giving the ex-colonial state a right to become a party to a multilateral agreement to which its predecessor state had adhered unless the new state's adherence would radically change the conditions for the operation of the treaty or if the consent of all treaty parties is expressly or impliedly required.[12] Thus, ex-colonial states not only had a right to escape the obligations of the predecessor state in this respect; they also could choose to become a party to a multilateral treaty in many cases irrespective of the consent of other parties. Although the Vienna Convention has not come into force, it has not been without influence. For example, the State Department Legal Adviser expressed the opinion in 1980 that the rules of the Vienna Convention were "generally regarded as declarative of existing customary law by the United States."[13]

Now that decolonization has come to an end, questions still remain whether states that have separated (*i.e.,* seceded) will be able to claim the right to pick and choose (as the Restatement would allow) or whether they would be bound by the principle of the Vienna Convention (but as a customary law rule) that a separated state which was not a colony is presumed to succeed to the treaty obligations and rights of the predecessor state unless this result would be incompatible with the object of the treaty.[14] The experience thus far with respect to the cases of the former Soviet Union and the former Yugoslavia supports a general presumption of continuity. That presumption would not, however, apply to membership in the United Nations or other general international organizations that provide for the election of new members. Nor would the separated states continue to have the rights of the predecessor where this would be contrary to the object of a treaty. A good example of the latter point, brought out in the article by Bunn and Rhinelander, relates to the important Nuclear Non-Proliferation Treaty ("NPT") of 1968, a general multilateral treaty open to all states.[15] Under that treaty, the U.S.S.R. was designated as a nuclear power. After the dissolution, Russia was recognized as the successor in this respect to the former U.S.S.R. However, to recognize some or all of the other republics as successors to the U.S.S.R. with the right to have nuclear weapons would undoubtedly be incompatible with the main objective of the NPT, which was to limit nuclear weapons to the five states that were nuclear powers prior to January 1, 1967. Obviously, a presumption of continuity that would give nuclear rights to the new states could not be acceptable.

The Future Law of Succession

Although state succession has been a subject of great controversy in the last fifty years, [there is] a good indication of the tendencies likely to shape future state practice and legal doctrine.

First, it seems probable that a general presumption of continuity of the obligations of a predecessor state will be accepted for new states that have come into being by secession or by dissolution of existing states. This is in accord with the position of the United States described by Williamson and Osborn in their authoritative article on recent U.S. practice. Most other countries may be expected to follow. Thus it is unlikely that the Restatement's rule of a clean slate for all new states will prevail in practice or theory.[16] We might recall, as James Crawford has pointed out, that "[t]he process of evolution towards a general regime of treaty continuity . . . was, remarkably, completed at the Second Session of the Vienna Conference."[17]

A presumption of continuity does not mean a categorical black-letter rule of succession. It is important to recognize that the particular circumstances may call for non-succession. This would apply to all successions whether of treaty, debt or delictual liability. As noted earlier, the symposium contributors all give examples of the need for exceptions to a continuity presumption. I suggest that the exceptions should not, of course, swallow the rule.

As a matter of policy, the case for presuming continuity makes sense today when the state system is increasingly fluid. Nation-states no longer appear immortal. Many seem likely to split or to be absorbed by others. Autonomous regions are likely to increase, central governments may even disappear for a time (as in Somalia or Cambodia), and mergers and integration will probably occur.

In this predictably pluralist world of kaleidoscopic change, stability in expectations will matter; it becomes more important than would be the case in a more settled period. The responses to the fragmentation of the Eastern European regimes revealed the concerns over the disruption of treaty relations. At the same time, the diversity and the particularities call for avoiding rigidities and for taking account of context in specific cases. Contextual solutions may be facilitated by relying on treaty rules, such as *rebus sic stantibus* or on equitable principles applicable to state debts or liability.

An especially strong case for continuity can be made in respect of multilateral treaties of a so-called "universal" character that are open to all states. Such treaties include the codification conventions like those on the law of treaties and on diplomatic and consular relations. In addition, there is good reason to include in this category other law-making treaties that have been widely accepted, even though they fall in the category of "development" of new law rather than codification of preexisting law. Mullerson supports this view, mentioning especially the U.N. human rights treaties which, while not codificatory, have been adhered to by the majority of states. He notes that Croatia and Slovenia declared themselves to be successor states to the former Yugoslavia in regard to human rights treaties which had been in force for Yugoslavia. While Mullerson is cautious in asserting a legal rule in this connection, I am inclined to predict that most such treaties of a general "legislative" character will be treated in the future as automatically binding on new states on the basis of adherence by their respective predecessor states. Support for this conclusion can even be found in earlier writings of European jurists.[18] The increase in such universal conventions expressing norms adopted at international assemblies by near-unanimity on the part of states from all regions of the world is indicative of a trend that should support succession by new states as a matter of course.

Mullerson also brings a helpful reminder that many treaties create acquired rights on the part of individuals. In this connection he refers to the decision of the Permanent Court of International Justice in the case of the German settlers which declared that acquired rights of individuals do not cease on a change of sovereignty.[19] Mullerson's suggestion that individual human rights should also be treated like acquired property rights entitled to respect in successor states is likely to be a much-cited legal contention on behalf of individuals in new states.

Still another reason to expect that a presumption of continuity will be widely accepted by new states is that it is helpful to the administration of treaties and other international legal relations of new states. International lawyers in the United States probably do not realize how difficult it is for new states to cope with the hundreds, even thousands, of treaties to which their predecessor states were parties. Lacking adequate documentation, severely limited in legally trained personnel and administrative resources, they cannot examine most treaties afresh and pick or choose among them. If these states are not considered presumptive successors to the treaties, they may not become parties because of their own administrative and technical deficiencies. A presumption of continuity would enable them to maintain rights and obligations generally. In the absence of that presumption, they may forego their rights and be heedless of obligations that call for action. For this reason, among others, it makes good sense for states to accept *prima facie* continuity as a basic premise, leaving for adjustment or exceptions when they appear necessary or desirable in a particular case.

In sum, my speculation about the future law of state succession rests on what appear to be the political trends relating to changes and turbulence in the nation-state system. It also gives weight to the practical aspects of administering the complicated effects of transfers of sovereignty and the need to avoid rigidity and doctrinaire solutions.

This approach, as some scholars may note, is far removed from the learned discourse of the renowned international legal authorities who discussed state succession largely in terms of philosophical theories of the state and justice. Enticing as these works may be to students of legal and political philosophy, they offer little guidance to the solution of actual problems. Our hope for a more orderly and equitable adjustment to political change lies in practical wisdom rather than in abstract theory.

Notes

1. Aristotle, The Politics, bk. III, ch. 3 (Stephen Everson ed., Cambridge University Press 1988).

2. Hugo Grotius, De Jure Belli ac Pacis Libri Tres, bk II, ch. IX at 310–19 (Carnegie Endowment trans. 1925 (1646)). For a comprehensive bibliography, see 1 D.P. O'Connell, State Succession in Municipal Law and international Law 543–62 (1967).

3. 1 O'Connell, supra note 2, at vi.

4. Ibid. Cf. Krystyna Marek, Identity and Continuity of State in Public International Law 31 (1954) ("The rule that revolution does not affect State identity and continuity has been fully adhered to in State practice for an impressively long period of time.")

5. See Ernst H. Feilchenfeld, Public Debts and State Succession 287–88, 294–96, 329–33 (1931).

6. Arnold D. McNair, The Law of Treaties 601 (1961).

7. Conference on Yugoslavia Arbitration Commission, Opinion No. 3, Jan. 11, 1992, reprinted in 31 I.L. M. 1499 (1992).

8. See Wladyslaw Czaplinski, Sate Succession and State Responsibility, 1990 Can. Y.B. Int'l L. 339, 353–54.

9. See Michael J. Volkovitsch, Note, Righting Wrongs: Towards a New Theory of State Succession to Responsibility for International Delicts, 92 Colum L. Rev. 2162 (1992).

10. Vienna Convention on Succession of State in Respect of Treaties, art. 16 17 IIL. M. on August 23, 19878, but has not yet received the required number of ratification or accessions to enter into force.

11. Ibid. art.34.

12. Treaty Succession Convention, supra note 10, arts. 17, 18. See 1 Restatement, supra note 5, para 210.

13. 1980 Digest of United States Practice in International Law 1041 n.43 (quoting memorandum of Roberts Owen, U.S. State Department Legal Adviser).

14. Treaty Succession Convention, supra note 10, art. 34.

15. Treaty on the Non-Proliferation of Nuclear Weapons, July 1, 1968, 21 U.S.T. 483, 729 U.N.T.S. 161.

16. 1 Restatement, supra note 5, para 210. Brownlie has supported the principle that all new states should have a clean slate on the basis of their sovereign rights. Ian Brownlie, Principles of Public International Law 668 (4th ed. 1990).

17. James Crawford, The Contribution of Professor D.P. O'Connell to the Discipline of International Law, 1980 Brit. Y.B. Int'L 1. 40.

18. See, for example, Charles De Visscher, Theory and Reality in Public International Law 179 (P.E. Corbett trans., rev. ed. 1968), who wrote that "the growing part played by multilateral treaties in the development of international law should count in favor of transmission rather than disappearance of obligations."

19. Advisory Opinion No. 6, 1923 P.C.I.J. (ser. B) No. 6, at 36.

8

Self-Determination, Minorities, Human Rights: A Review of International Instruments

Patrick Thornberry

Some Preliminary Questions

Self-determination and the rights of minorities are two sides of the same coin. When a colony or subject people accedes to independence in the name of self-determination, political unity and integral statehood will rarely be matched by national unity and ethnic homogeneity.[1] The new State will frequently be dominated by a particular ethnic group in a majority, and there will be ethnic minorities. The consequences for the smaller groups of the transition from Empire to statehood may be severe; inter-ethnic solidarity in the face of a common alien oppressor may be ruptured and replaced by a more intimate, local and knowing oppression. This applies both when the new State is "national" in the sense of having a developed national character at the inception of statehood, and when the new State is born of a territorial concept, and nationality is still to be forged, if necessary by the plundering of small groups to achieve assimilation.[2]

Accession to independence and defence of that independence parade under the banner of self-determination, a concept enshrined in the United Nations Charter, the International Covenants on Human Rights and other international instruments. The legal implications of this concept for minorities are, therefore, a matter of considerable moment. Self-determination is a concept of liberation. Its inscription in legal texts has coincided with an astounding transformation of political geography. States have replaced Empires. The age of colonialism becomes a historical *datum*, even if its long-term effects are profound. But the facts of ethnic diversity and diverging political and moral ambitions within States require that questions be

This article is reproduced from (1989) 30 I.C.L.Q. 867–869 with permission from the publishers, The British Institute of International and Comparative Law, 17 Russell Square, London WC1B 5DR.

asked of self-determination. Does it liberate ethnic groups within States or even concern them? Has the phrase "All peoples have the right of self-determination" in the International Covenants on Human Rights a real function as a principle of human rights? What are "peoples"? Are minorities justified in appropriating self-determination to state their claims and aspirations? Are they wise to do so?

The connection between minorities and self-determination has been discussed in the legal literature, though the volume of writings is limited and minorities are frequently not the main focus of enquiry. Minorities appropriate the vocabulary of self-determination whether governments or scholars approve or not. Conflicts between State and minority demonstrate a quality of endurance. Contemporary State-minority disputes of high topicality include those involving the Basques, Corsicans, Eritreans, Kurds, Sikhs, the protagonists in the civil strife in the Sudan, and the Tamils of Sri Lanka—there are many others. Minorities have utilised the notion of secession, where a group would form its own State. The Biafrans wanted to secede from Nigeria; the Bengalis achieved secession from Pakistan and statehood in Bangladesh. Even if the demands of minorities are not so "extreme," self-determination is part of their vocabulary.

Most recently, indigenous peoples have begun to articulate their grievances through the medium of self-determination. A document of the Four Directions Council "Declares that indigenous populations are 'peoples' within the meaning of the International Covenants of Human Rights . . ."[3] Principles drafted by the World Council of Indigenous Peoples paraphrase international instruments: "1. All indigenous peoples have the right of self-determination. By virtue of that right they may freely determine their political status and freely pursue their economic, social, religious and cultural development"[4] Indigenous groups are mostly within the international law governing minorities, but see themselves as "more than" minorities and entitled to the rights of peoples. This conveys a sentiment that self-determination is not "for" or "about" minorities—a proposition assented to by the governments of many States. Some minorities are nonetheless convinced that self-determination is the only concept that penetrates to the heart of their claims. This implies that the potential of self-determination is not yet exhausted, that it is not "passé."[5]

Towards the United Nations Charter

The United Nations Charter gave expression to a doctrine which had been maturing in international relations certainly since the American and French revolutions. These demonstrated two aspects of self-determination: casting off alien rule, and putting forward the people as the ultimate authority within the State—"external" and "internal" self-determination, respectively.

Self-determination and the right of minorities were linked in the legal arrangements accompanying nineteenth-century examples of nations becoming States. The doctrine of the nation-State shaped these arrangements: the ideal State is the State of single nationality. Mazzini's conception of Italy included its ethnic and cultural uniformity, even if this meant denationalising "foreign" populations. Slavs, Greeks and Romanians gave expression to similar views. Political theory stressed the benefits to democracy of ethnic homogeneity.[6] International law reflected a colder view. Statesmen foresaw the disruptive potential of nationalist fervour carried to excess. Legal constraints, usually in treaty form, were deployed to protect ethnic and religious minorities threatened by self-determination.[7]

The reciprocity of self-determination and safeguarding treaty was maintained throughout the nineteenth century. The "pattern" was flawed and betokened the existence of first- and second-class States: those which could be trusted to extend the benefits of democracy to all citizens and those which could not. The powers at the Paris Peace Conference following the First World War organised and expanded the "system" of independence coupled with a minorities guarantee into a determinate form. There was no "universal" arrangement. The powers did not threaten their own empires with self-determination. Nor were they subjected to minorities treaties. President Wilson's exhortations in favour of general acceptance of self-determination and obligations towards minorities were to little avail. While the mandate system inscribed in the Covenant promised ultimate self-government for ex-enemy colonies, minorities were not accorded any special position therein, but were dealt with through treaties and declarations applying to specific groups, under the supervision of the League. States under this regime were obliged to grant to all their inhabitants basic human rights. Special minorities provisions were designed to ensure that nationals belonging to minorities would enjoy the same treatment in law and in fact as other nationals. Autonomy rights were granted to certain groups.

The basic premises of the system was summed up by the Permanent Court of International Justice. It was:

> . . . to secure for certain elements incorporated in a State, the population of which differs from them in race, language or religion, the possibility of living peaceably alongside that population and co-operating amicably with it, while at the same time preserving the characteristics which distinguish them from the majority, and satisfying the ensuing special needs.[9]

But the promises of "peaceful living" and "amicable co-operation" were not realised. Some States treated their minorities badly; some minorities were "disloyal" to their States. Beyond pragmatic reconciliation of States and minorities, the ultimate purposes of the League regime were unclear. Latin American views implied that the regime was a staging post on the way to a complete national unity; the ideal State was a melting-pot of races and cultures, a cauldron of assimilation.[10] The rights of minorities under the League system fell far short of self-determination.

The United Nations Charter

Despite its invocation in the inter-war years, self-determination was not part of positive international law. The "principle" is expressly mentioned in the United Nations Charter, in Articles 1(2) and 55. Article 1(2) places the principle among the purposes of the United Nations. Article 55 provides: "With a view to the creation of conditions of stability and well-being which are necessary for peaceful and friendly relations among nations based on respect for the principle of equal rights and self-determination of peoples, the United Nations shall promote . . . "—there follows a list of important political, social and economic goals. By Article 56, UN members pledge themselves to support the purposes in Article 55.

Notwithstanding initial equivocation, it can now be seen that real obligations were created, if imperfectly expressed, in the Charter. Self-determination in the Charter attaches to "peoples." The meaning of "peoples" occasioned inconclusive discussion at the San Francisco Conference. The terms "State," "nation" and "people" are all used in the Charter. The UN Secretariat examined the terms: "The word 'nation' is broad . . . enough to include colonies, mandates, protectorates and quasi-States as well as States"; and, " . . . 'nations' is used in the sense of all political entities, States and non-States, whereas 'peoples' refers to groups of human beings who may, or may not, comprise States or nations."[11] The broad interpretation provoked a French delegate to say that the Charter appeared to sanction secession.[12] But the opinions of statesmen at the San Francisco Conference towards minorities were largely negative in character. Despite the high level of interest in human rights, proposals for the protection of minorities were lacking. Claude doubts whether the Charter carries any view of the minorities issue: "The United Nations Charter . . . was drafted without recognition of the minority problem as a significant item on the agenda of international relations."[13] It may be argued, however, that the Charter does have a view: the future of the "problem of minorities" merges into universal human rights. There is no lacuna: when the details of the new system of human rights were expounded, a rule for minorities would emerge. This is some distance from attributing self-determination to minorities.

The references to self-determination in Articles 1(2) and 55 are complemented by Chapters XI and XII on non-self-governing territories, and the international trusteeship system. Bowett states that it is permissible "to regard the entirety of Chapters XI and XII of the . . . Charter as reflections on the basic idea of self-determination."[14] Neither Chapter contains an express reference to self-determination, but the principle is established indirectly. Article 73 in Chapter XI describes the development of self-government in non-self-governing territories as a "sacred trust." Article 76 on the international trusteeship system refers to progressive development in the Trust Territories towards "self-government or independence." A key issue was the distinction between "self-government" and "independence." The colonial powers were unhappy about referring to "independence" in the generally applicable Article 73. In the view of the United States, however,"self-government" did not rule out "independence" in appropriate cases.[15] The Philippines interpreted Article 73 to imply eventual independence for dependent territories.[16]

Chapter XI of the Charter gave a tremendous impetus to the development of self-determination with a real possibility of implementation. Subsequent practice has hardened the meaning of Charter terms, but the result has been unfavourable to minorities. Chapter XI is a declaration on "Non-Self-Governing Territories." The territorial aspect is vital: the Chapter refers to "*territories* whose peoples have not attained a full measure of self-government"; the sacred trust is to promote "the well-being of the inhabitants of these *territories*." A territorial concept of self-determination appears to rule out minorities without a specific territorial base. Further, concentration on territory, in the light of the reality of mixed and inextricable populations, languages and religions, weighs heavily towards taking political demarcations as they stand, and making these the focal point of political change.

The Belgian Thesis

Article 73 of the Charter was utilised by the General Assembly in the promotion of self-determination through the requirement of reports on the progress made by States administering territories towards the objectives set by the Article. The main thrust of the Assembly's effort was in the direction of the colonial empires. The Belgian representatives pointed out that the Charter does not single out "colonialism," but non-self-governing territories. Belgium stated that:

> . . . a number of States were administering within their own frontiers territories which were not governed by the ordinary law; territories with well-defined limits, inhabited by homogeneous peoples differing from the rest of the population in race, language and culture. These populations were disenfranchised; they took no part in national life; they did not enjoy self-government in any sense of the word.[17]

It was not clear how such groups were excluded from the terms of Chapter XI. Groups in respect of which Chapter XI applied would include Indian tribes of Venezuela, the Nagas of India, indigenous African tribes in Liberia, Somalis in Ethiopia, tribals of the Philippines, Dyaks of Borneo, etc. The generality of the Belgian concerns was expressed in the delegate's remark that: "Similar problems [to colonialism] existed wherever there were underdeveloped groups."[18] The thesis radicalises self-determination by insisting that it can apply to indigenous groups and minorities.

The thesis did not prevail. Latin American States and their allies did not agree that their situation could be assimilated to that of the colonies. The problems of the indigenous groups were economic rather than colonial.[19] In the view of Iraq, the Belgian argument was based on "anger at the criticism directed against conditions in the non-self-governing territories by less advanced States."[20] One of the authors of the thesis, Dr. Van Langenhove, effectively admitted to the thesis as a Belgian tactic.

The United Nations built a consensus on self-determination in response to the Belgian thesis to bring order to the inevitable historical movement of decolonisation. The delegate of Iraq to the Fourth Committee of the General Assembly offered the opinion that: "In the long run, colonialism must give way to self-government . . ."[21] The thesis was rejected in favour of the theory of "salt-water" colonialism, summed up in General Assembly Resolution 1541(XV). Principle IV states that: "Prima facie there is an obligation . . . to transmit information in respect of a territory which is geographically separate and is distinct ethnically and/or culturally from the country administering it."[22] The coupling of geography and the ethnic factor is important; without geography, the designation of non-colonial territories as entitled to self-determination was a possibility, though even with this factor, the definition is not perfect if the intention is to exclude all minority groups.

The restrictive view of the non-applicability of self-determination to minority groups is strengthened by a consideration of General Assembly Resolution 1514—the Colonial declaration—passed on the day before Resolution 1541. The holder of the right of self-determination is, once more, declared to be the people. The meaning of the term "people" is conditioned by repeated references to colonialism. Paragraph 6 of the Resolution states that: "Any attempt aimed at the partial or total disruption of the national unity and the territorial integrity of a country is incompatible with the Purposes and Principles of the Charter of the United Nations." The effect is that colonial boundaries function as the boundaries of the emerging States. Minorities, therefore, may not secede from States—at least, international law gives them no *right* to do so. The logic of the resolution is relatively simple: peoples hold the right of self-determination; a people is the whole people of a territory; a people exercises its right through the achievement of independence.

General Assembly
Resolution 2625(XXV) and Minorities

Resolution 2625(XXV) appears, on one reading, to construct a link between self-determination and minorities.[23] The text deals with the most important principles of international law,[24] each principle to be construed in the light of the others.[25] Three preambular paragraphs of the Declaration refer to self-determination—the third reference reiterates the prohibition on disruption of the national unity and territorial integrity of a country, etc. The principle is set out at some length in the operative part of the Declaration. There is not the same emphasis on colonialism as in Resolution 1514(XV). The preferred modes of implementing self-determination reflect more flexible options set out in Resolution 1541(XV): independence, free association or integration with an independent State, "or the emergence into any other political status freely determined by a people."

Writers have given attention to the penultimate paragraph on self-determination:

> Nothing in the foregoing paragraphs shall be construed as authorising or encouraging any action which would dismember or impair, totally or in part, the territorial integrity or political unity of sovereign and independent States conducting themselves in compliance with the principle of [self-determination] and thus possessed of a government representing the whole people belonging to the territory without distinction as to race, creed or colour.[26]

This is followed by the obligatory clause on territorial integrity.

The reference to representative government has been picked out as innovative by Rosenstock: ". . . a close examination of its text will reward the reader with an affirmation of the applicability of the principle to peoples within existing States and the necessity for governments to represent the governed."[27] Thus, if "peoples within existing States" are treated in a grossly discriminatory fashion by an unrepresentative government, they can claim self-determination and not be defeated by arguments about territorial integrity. The guarantee of integrity is contingent upon the existence of representative government. There are, however, reasons to caution against this kind of claim, and Cassese doubts if the Declaration can be pressed too far.[28] In his view, the paragraph could apply only to a few peoples living under racist regimes. He emphasises the negative wording as forbidding self-determination where there is representative government and in particular where this government is non-racist.

The drafts support the more cautious views. A proposal of the United States made the "internal" aspect of self-determination much clearer:

> The existence of a sovereign and independent State possessing a representative government, effectively functioning as such to all distinct peoples

within its territory, is presumed to satisfy the principle of equal rights and, self-determination as regards those peoples.[29]

A text proposed by Czechoslovakia and others made a similar point.[30] The crucial difference between the United States draft and the final version is that, in the former, the key phrase is "all distinct peoples," whereas the final wording is "the whole people." The gaze of the international community is deflected from detailed "internal" scrutiny of most States and the conduct of governments towards the "peoples" within their territories: only pariah States like South Africa, which oppressed its majority on racial grounds, are likely to be affected. Whether one discusses "internal" or "external" self-determination, the point is that "whole" territories or peoples are the focus of rights, rather than ethnic groups, Cassese's analyses of "internal" self-determination should not be taken to fragment the meaning of "people."

The Covenant on Civil and Political Rights

Articles 1 and 27

The juxtaposition of self-determination in Article 1 of the Covenant on Civil and Political Rights and the rights of minorities in Article 27 provides an opportunity to compare closely what international law offers to peoples and minorities, respectively. Neither Article is particularly expansive, but there is an implementation framework, and a reasonable drafting record. Article 1 of both UN Human Rights Covenants commences with "All peoples have the right of self-determination." The other paragraphs refer to economic self-determination (paragraph 2); and to the duty of States parties to the Covenants to promote self-determination (paragraph 3). Article 27, which still stands as the only whole and general statement of the treaty rights of minorities in modern international law provides:

> In those States in which ethnic, religious or linguistic minorities exist, persons belonging to such minorities shall not be denied the right, in community with the other members of their group, to enjoy their own culture, to profess and practise their own religion, or to use their own language.

Neither Article ventures into further definition. The Special Rapporteur of the UN Sub-Commission on the Prevention of Discrimination and Protection of Minorities, Professor Capotorti, offered this definition for the purposes of Article 27: a minority is

> a group numerically inferior to the rest of the population of a State, in a non-dominant position, whose members—being nationals of the State—

possess ethnic, religious or linguistic characteristics differing from those of the rest of the population and show, if only implicitly, a sense of solidarity, directed towards preserving their culture, traditions, religion or language.[31]

A similar definition proposed to the Sub-Commission by the Canadian member in 1985 was forwarded to the UN Human Rights Commission, which is working on a draft declaration on minority rights.[32] The Capotorti definition is not part of any UN instrument but it is doubtful if a subsequent definition would diverge greatly from it. Article 27 and the Capotorti definition may be taken as a basis for comparing self-determination and minority rights in the Covenant.

The right of self-determination in the Covenants is universal. The text and *travaux* support the view that the Covenants reach beyond the colonial situation,[33] though there are indications of narrower views.[34] Some interest in this respect attaches to the declaration made by India on Article 1: " . . . the Government of the Republic of India declares that the words 'the right of self-determination' . . . apply only to the peoples under foreign domination and that these words do not apply to sovereign independent States or to a section of the people or nation—which is the essence of national integrity." Other States have objected to the declaration, which clearly curtails the scope of the Article. The Netherlands objection reads, in part: "Any attempt to limit the scope of [the] ... right or to attach conditions ... would undermine the concept of self-determination itself and would... seriously weaken its universally acceptable character."[35] The position of India has, however, been marked by inconsistency. Its delegate had earlier stated in the General Assembly's Third Committee that, "although there were good reasons to make special reference to the peoples of non-self-governing territories, it must be recognised that the field of application of the principle of self-determination was wider than that."[36] There is little reason to doubt the view that the Covenants mean what they say: that Article 1 applies to all peoples, and is not confined to colonial territories.

The "broad" view of the applicability of Article 1 is a fundamental assumption underlying the "General Comment" issued by the Human Rights Committee: " . . . it imposes specific obligations on States Parties, not only in relation to their own peoples but vis-a-vis all peoples which have not been able to exercise or have been deprived of the possibility of their right to self-determination."[37] This makes it clear that the right is universal, as can be expected in a document of human rights. The promotion of self-determination must be consistent with other provisions of international law: "in particular, States must refrain from interfering in the internal affairs of other States and thereby adversely affecting the exercise of the right." Self-determination in the Covenants includes internal self-determination. The Comment alludes to this: "With regard to paragraph 1 of Article

1, States Parties should describe the constitutional and political processes which in practice allow the exercise of [self-determination]." The Committee complains that many States in their reports "completely ignore Article 1, provide inadequate information in relation to it or confine themselves to a reference to election laws." The comment makes no contribution to the elucidation of any people/minority distinction. The assumption appears to be that minorities are covered by Article 27. The Committee has been unable to formulate a comment on the latter Article.[38]

The tension between "people" and "minority" is apparent at various stages in the drafting. Afghanistan and Saudi Arabia, authors of a draft resolution on self-determination, at one time deleted the term "peoples" from their draft. This was at the suggestion of delegations who feared that the term "might encourage minorities within a State to ask for the right to self-determination."[39] On the other hand, India argued that the problem of minorities should not be raised in the context of self-determination.[40] China declared that the issue "was that of national majorities and not of minorities."[41] The reference to "majorities" reflected the views of many in the debates; it may be taken as an infelicitous expression of the conviction that the right of self-determination is one for whole peoples, and not for sections of them. This view of self-determination dominates the *travaux,* despite occasional hesitations.

Sections of the people—minorities—enjoy more limited rights than the people itself. The Capotorti definition refers to "non-dominant" groups in a State and Article 27 is a statement of rights essential to the defence of minority identity in the face of assimilationist pressures: it encapsulates their "right to an identity" ("dominant" minorities, such as the whites of South Africa, have no need of such rights). There is a qualitative difference between the two categories: the right of self-determination means full rights in the cultural, economic and political spheres. The essence is political control, accompanied by other forms of control. The rights of minorities are enumerated and finite, and do not include political control. Article 27 does not even grant the minority an unequivocal collective right: it is "persons belonging to such minorities" who are accorded rights. The collective aspect of minority rights bedevils the elaboration of a more detailed instrument on minority rights—States are reluctant to concede rights to collectivities which may come to rival the State itself." The opening phrase of the Article, "In those States in which . . . minorities exist . . . ," almost invites States to deny that they exist, and many States have responded to the "invitation." Such denials of the presence of minority groups on State territory should not be allowed to function as an escape for States, most of which are obviously multi-ethnic: the absence of a final definition of minority has not inhibited the Human Rights Committee in its questioning of States on treatment of their minorities.

Finally, Article 27 appears to impose only a duty of toleration on

States, a duty of non-interference with the cultural and religious practices of the groups. But it can also be read to impose positive duties upon the State, based on the argument that, in order to function, the Article must go beyond the rule of non-discrimination and equality in law towards equality in fact, so that the continued existence of the minority group is not placed in jeopardy in a situation in which it is inherently the weaker party. Tenuous as these rights are, they are vital for minority groups and represent a minimum from which there should be no derogation.

Positive and Negative Interpretation

In the light of the limitations of Article 27, it appears ambitious to argue for a connection between minorities and self-determination. There are, however, at least two possibilities of "positive" interpretation implying a connection: (a) minorities are peoples within the meaning of Article 1—a view which is not supported by the *travaux;* (b) attribution of rights to whole peoples benefits minorities *indirectly* through "internal" self-determination. There is also a negative possibility: (c) self-determination is best understood as external, and internal self-determination is supererogatory.

In relation to (a), the practice of the Human Rights Committee is equivocal, but may be taken to buttress the view that minorities are not peoples. Questions on individual groups in a State which might imply that they are covered by Article 1 are often "fielded" by that State under Article 27. In the "communication" to the Committee by the Grand Captain of the Mikmaq Tribal Society, the applicant focused on Article 1 rather than Article 27. The communication was rejected at the admissibility stage because the author had "not proven that he is authorised to act as a representative . . . of the Mikmaq tribal society. In addition, the author has failed to advance any pertinent facts supporting his claim that he is personally a victim of any rights contained in the Covenant."[42] The impediments to his claim may have been procedural or substantive: the Committee's statement is not clear. This statement is hardly a basis for broad claims on the applicability of Article 1.

On the other hand, another communication involving Canadian Indians, that of Sandra Lovelace, has produced an unequivocal response from the Committee on the applicability of Article 27.[43] This case demonstrates that Article 27 applies to individuals belonging to Indian groups as members of minorities; the case involved the loss by an Indian woman of the right to live on a reservation following marriage to a non-Indian. The Committee did not, in fact, trouble to discuss the application of the term "minority" to the Indian band to which Sandra Lovelace belonged, but appears to have assumed the correctness of the attribution. The applicability of Article 27 was so clear to the Committee that it considered it unnecessary to examine the case under the other articles of the Covenant. The case contrasts vividly with the uncertainty engendered by the Mikmaq case. Whatever the self-descriptive terms employed by indigenous groups, the text of the Covenant accommodates them better under Article 27 than under Article 1.

If minorities are not the "peoples" of the Covenants, this does not mean that self-determination has no relevance to them. Minorities are protected by international law through such instruments as the Genocide Convention 1948 and the International Convention on the Elimination of all Forms of Racial Discrimination 1966, even though the protection is indirect. Similarly in the present context: the "internal" aspect of self-determination may have some incidence upon ethnic groups, even though the formal subject of a right is the "whole people." Internal self-determination has been much favoured as a concept by Western States, reflecting their notions of democracy. President Wilson's early use of the term depended very much on American constitutional tradition. From a socialist point of view, Lenin wrote that "the recognition of the right of all nations to self-determination implies the maximum of democracy and the minimum of nationalism."[44] For the States of the Third World, concerned with ridding themselves of Western domination, self-determination is externally orientated, and, in so far as it has an internal aspect, this is to do with majority rule (rule of the "whole people") and the avoidance of rule by minorities, especially white minorities. The question is, to what extent may any of these conceptions be taken to govern the Covenants? The comment of the Human Rights Committee is neither optimistic nor very illuminating. States do not find much use for Article 1 "internally." But the Committee's comment also incorporates a view about self-determination "underlying" human rights: "The right of self-determination is of particular importance because its realisation is an essential condition for the effective guarantee and observance of individual human rights." This could be read together with the reference to "political and constitutional processes" to signify that States must organise these processes to support the programme of human rights contained in the Covenants. The application of internal self-determination is to be gauged with reference to human rights, and not to ideologies beyond it. Violations of self-determination are violations of human rights. The "democracy" of the Covenants can be none other than the implementation of their provisions.

Such an interpretation appears to do little more than reiterate existing rights. It does, however, direct attention to the organisation of the State as a whole and how that organisation favours or disfavours human values to the benefit of all within the State, minorities included. It is probably in advance of the opinions of most States parties, which leads to possibility (c): perhaps the truth is that self-determination has little to do with human rights. The implementation of the covenant has not succeeded in showing how self-determination can be effective "internally." Frequently, the questions of the Human Rights Committee are directed to divining the attitude of States to apartheid, Namibia and Palestine, rather than to their own peoples, who should be the primary focus of interest.

Other Instruments

While this article does not attempt to present a full picture of minority rights in international law, it may be noted that minorities are guaranteed a basic "right of existence" through the Genocide Convention.[45] Further, the rule of non-discrimination in the enjoyment of human rights makes constant reference to race, colour, religion and language as impermissible grounds of distinction in human rights. Indigenous groups are given a measure of protection by the International Labour Organisation's Convention No.107 on Indigenous and Tribal populations, as well as being entitled to whatever rights accrue to minorities, since they are mostly minorities in the States they inhabit. The Convention (Article 1(i)) applies to:

> members of tribal or semi-tribal populations in independent countries whose social and economic conditions are at a less advanced stage than . . . other sections of the national community, and whose status is regulated wholly or partially by their own customs or traditions or by special laws or regulations . . . [and members of populations] regarded as indigenous on account of their descent from the populations which inhabited the country... at the time of conquest or colonisation, and which . . . live more in conformity with the . . . institutions of that time than with the institutions of the nation to which they belong.

The preferred term in the Convention, it may be noted, is not "peoples" but "populations": connotations of self-determination are thus avoided. The rights granted to indigenous groups under this Convention encompass the protection of their way of life and range through civil and political rights to recognition of rights to land traditionally occupied, and economic, social and cultural rights.

Unfortunately, the Convention lay heavy stress on "integration" of the populations to the benefit of States rather than the populations as such: it is a Convention on "the protection and integration" of indigenous populations. Indigenous groups see the Convention as little more than a licence for States to assimilate and eradicate them under the guise of humanitarianism and have demanded its revision. In no sense does the Convention incorporate a right of self-determination: Article 2(1) provides that "*Governments* shall have the primary responsibility for developing coordinated and systematic action for the protection of the populations concerned and their progressive integration into the life of their respective countries" (author's emphasis). Provisions for consultation with the indigenous groups are minimal: in the application of the Convention, governments shall, according to Article 5, "seek the collaboration of these populations and their representatives"—seek, but not necessarily find. Revision of the Convention will require less stress on integration and more on the wishes of the populations concerned, though it is doubtful if self-determination by that name will figure on the agenda.[46]

Other instruments maintain the dichotomy between minority rights and self-determination. The Helsinki Final Act is a case in point. Principle VII of the "Declaration on Principles" deals with human rights, and includes the following paragraph:

> The participating States on whose territories national minorities exist will respect the right of persons belonging to such minorities to equality before the law, will afford them the full opportunity for the actual enjoyment of Human Rights and fundamental freedoms and will, in this manner, protect their legitimate interests in this sphere.

This endorsement of minority rights is more limited than Article 27 of the Covenant on Civil and Political Rights. There is the same question of the "existence" of minorities; the different minorities are narrowed down to "national" minorities, implying a limitation of scope; there is no consideration of a "right to identity," only to equality before the law; and the Article describes "interests," which represent a lower logical category than "rights." This contrasts strongly with statements on self-determination in Principle VIII, which includes:

> By virtue of the principle of equal rights and self-determination of peoples, all peoples always have the right, in full freedom, to determine, when and as they wish, their internal and external political status, without external political interference, and to pursue as they wish their political, economic, social and cultural development.

As Cassese points out, the chief innovations here are the bold phrases on internal self-determination and the commitment to a continuing role for the principle of self-determination: peoples *always* have the right of self-determination, and in *full freedom*. He regards as "incontrovertible" the fact that "the Helsinki Declaration, when it discusses the principle of self-determination, extends the right only to groups identifying with sovereign States (for example, Italian, French and Soviet citizens)". The *travaux*, while rather sketchy, support his propositions.[47] Another commentator notes that "States with militant minorities, such as Canada and Yugoslavia, felt the need . . . for a limit to the application . . . [of self-determination] . . . to national minorities in order to avoid any implication that . . . [it] could be used to bring about the dissolution of federated States comprised of peoples of different nationalities or other minorities."[48] Rights of minorities in the Final Act are clearly of a lower order than the rights of peoples.

The African Charter on Human and Peoples' Rights 1981 offers even less to minorities: this is unsurprising, and reflects the view of many African States that the minorities "problem" is essentially European. The "peoples" of the Charter are not defined, but they have important rights. Article 19 reads: "All peoples shall be equal; they shall enjoy the same respect and shall have the same rights. Nothing shall justify the domination of a people by another." Article 20(1) reads: "All peoples shall have the right to existence. They shall have the unquestionable and inalienable right to self-determination." The rights of peoples are buttressed by the duties of individuals, which include the duty to "preserve and strengthen the national independence and the territorial integrity of . . . [their] country."[49] There is no explicit reference to "minorities," though Article 2 and the Preamble refer to discrimination based on "ethnic group," as well as "race, colour . . . language, religion . . . national and social origin." The Charter lays tremendous stress on its "African" character throughout. This includes the African views on self-determination which stress the integrity of the State, even in cases of severe oppression of minorities. There is little to suggest that "peoples" are other than the "whole peoples" of the States, and not ethnic or other groups. This conclusion is strongly supported by discussions at the Nairobi Conference convened by the International Commission of Jurists in December 1985, and is likely to represent the future practice of the African Commission of Human Rights.

Conclusion

Minorities use the vocabulary of self-determination and States deny its relevance to them. International law gives little support to minorities in their endeavours. The right of self-determination is a right of peoples, with strict limits on application. The international system is not immutable, and States are regularly subjected to challenge by minorities, occasionally to the point of dismemberment. It may come to pass that the legal texts will more clearly associate minorities with a right of self-determination, in terms of meaningful approaches to internal self-determination, and in cases of severe mistreatment.[50] On the other hand, existing norms on the rights of minorities are limited and inadequate to the task of ensuring that minorities do not have assimilation or integration forced upon them as a threat to their existence and identity.

Instead of starting from the collective right of self-determination, it may, therefore, be more productive to start from the rules of basic human rights. Minority protection could also be taken to require autonomy in certain instances. Many States accord a high level of self-management to ethnic groups in their constitutional law, though autonomy is not widely perceived as an obligation in general international law. These remarks also apply to indigenous populations—though there is a stronger international movement in their favour than for minorities in general. The International Labour Organisation's Convention on Indigenous and Tribal Populations is on the brink of revision, and the UN Working Group on Indigenous Populations is drafting a set of principles. A key concept in process of elaboration is that of "ethnodevelopment": the development of ethnic groups within the larger society as a compromise between ethnic self-determination and the nation-State.[51]

For both categories, there is need to strengthen implementation procedures, to amplify and specify norms, and to press for just treatment of groups. The humane regime should attempt to convince States that maltreatment of their minorities is a primary cause of internal and international strife. There is need also to bring to fruition the efforts of the United Nations to draft a minorities' instrument, and further to advance work on the rights of indigenous groups.[52] To achieve this would be to build rather than dream the future, starting from what is, rather than what might be.

Notes

1. The present author is compiling "profiles" of 50 States for the UN University which examine their legal arrangements relating to minorities, and include review of population composition. Some results of this Study are reviewed in Minorities and Human Rights Law, Minority Rights Group Report No. 73. (1987).

2. Definitions of assimilation, integration, etc., are essayed in the UN Special Study on Racial Discrimination in the Political, Economic, Social and Cultural Spheres, UN Sales No. 71./ XIV.2.

3. UNDOC E/CN. 4/Sub.2/AC.4/1983/CRP.1, annex.

4. UNDOC E?CN.4/Sub.2/AC.4/1985/WP.5

5. S. Prakash Sinha, "Is Self-Determination Passé?" (1973) 12 Col. J. Trans. L. 260.

6. ". . . . it is in general a necessary condition of free institutions that the boundaries of governments should coincide . . . with those of nationalities." Mill, "Considerations on Representative Government," in *John Stuart Mill, Three Essays* (1975), pp. 382 and 384. Some of the hierarchical assumptions which may lie under the surface of arguments in favor of assimilation of cultures are well expressed by Mill: "Experience proves, that it is possible for one nationality to merge and be absorbed in another: and when it was originally an inferior and more backward portion of the human race, the absorption is greatly to its advantage,: idem, p. 385.

7. Claude, *National Minorities. An International Problem* (1065); Fouques-Duparc, La Protection des Minorités de Race, de Langue et de Religion (1922); Laponce, *The Protection of Minorities* (1960); Macartney, *National States and National Minorities* (1934).

8. For a list of the States affected by the system, and its results, see De

Azcárate, *The League of Nations and National Minorities* (1945); Robinson et al., *Were the Minorities Treaties a Failure?* (1943); Thornberry, "Is There a Phoenix in the Ashes?, *International Law and Minority Rights:* (1980) 15 *Texas Int. L.J.*

9. "In order to attain this object, two things were regarded as particularly necessary . . . The first is to ensure that nationals belonging to racial, religious or linguistic minorities shall be placed in every respect on a footing of perfect equality with the other national of the State. The second is to ensure for the minority . . . suitable means for the preservation of their . . . peculiarities, their traditions and their national characteristics," *Minority Schools in Albania* (1935), *PCIJ Ser.A/B.* No. 64, p. 17.

10. Yepes, "Les Problèmes Fondamentaux du Droit des Gens en Amérique" (1934) 30(I) *Rec. des Cours* 14.

11. UNCIO DOCS, Vol. XVIII, pp. 657-658.

12. UNCIO DOCS, Vol. XVII, P. 142; Cassese, in Buergenthal and Hall (eds.), *Human Rights, International Law and the Helsinki Accord* (1977), pp. 95 et seq.; Russell and Muther, *A History of the United National Charter, The Role of the United States 1940-1945* (1958).

13. Claude, *op. cit. supra* n. 7 st p.113.

14. "Problems of Self-Determination and Political Rights Developing Countries" *Procs A.S.I.L.* (1966), p. 134.

15. Generally, Russell and Muther, *op. cit. supra* n. 12, at pp. 813 et seq.

16. Ibid.

17. Van Langenhove, "Le Problème de la Protection des Populations Aborigenes aux Nations Unites: (1956) 89 Rec. des Cours 3211, and The Question of Aborigines Before the United Nations: The Belgian Thesis (1954); Toussaint, "The Colonial Controversy in the United Nations" (1956) Y.B. World Affairs 177; Bennett, Aboriginal Rights in International Law, Occasional Paper of the Royal Anthropological Institute of Great Britain and Ireland (1978); UNDOC A/Ac. 67/2, p. 3–31.

18. UNDOC A/C.4/SR.419, paras. 14 et seq. The delegate also noted that the indigenous were still recognised as having problems akin to colonialism by the I.L.O.: see infra on I.L.O. convention 107.

19. Delegate of Peru to the Fourth Committee, UNDOC A/C.4/SR.420, para.40.

20. UNDOC A/C.4/SR.257, para.11.

21. UNDOC A/C.4/SR.257, paras. 11-14. The reference of the delegate is to Chap.XI; this need not be taken to rule out a post-colonial future for self-determination as such.

22. GAOR, 15th session, supp. 16. p. 29.

23. Rosenstock, "The Declaration of Principles of International Law, etc.: (1971) 65 *A.J.I.L.* 713.

24. See Arangio-Ruiz, "The Normative Role of the General Assembly of the United Nations and the Declaration of Principles on Friendly Relations" (1972) 137 *Rec. des Cours* 528.

25. The Declaration states: "In their interpretation and application the above principles are interrelated and each principle should be construed in the context of the other principles . . . Nothing in this Declaration shall be construed as prejudicing in any manner the provisions of the Charter or the rights and duties of Member States under the Charter or the rights of peoples under the Charter taking into account the elaboration of these rights in this Declaration: (authors' emphasis). This means that the self-determination principle must fit consistently with such principles as that of non-intervention in the domestic affairs of other States, the principle

of the sovereign equality of States, and the principle of the non-use of force. The text of the Declaration contains a number of references to territorial integrity and political independence of States. Under the heading of "The Principle of Sovereign Equality of States," we may note: "(d) The territorial integrity and political independence of the State are inviolable; (e) Each State has the right freely to choose and develop its political, social, economic and cultural systems." These principles clearly impinge on self-determination. The last would be just as appropriate in the context of the paragraphs on self-determination in that it states an important aspect of that concept. It may also, by implication, hint at the effective transformation of the right-holder into the State itself.

26. As in Res. 1514(XV). India expressed satisfaction that Res. 26256(XXV) retained this element, UNDOC A/8018.

27. Rosenstock, *op. cit. supra.* n. 23, at 732.

28. Cassese, in Buergenthal and Hall (eds.), *Human Rights, International Law and the Helsinki Accord* (1977), pp. 88-92.

29. UNDOC A/AC.125/L.32.

30. UNDOC A/AC.125/L. 74.

31. Capotorti, *Study of the Rights of Persons Belonging to Ethnic, Religious and Linguistic Minorities* (1979), Chap. 1.

32. Professor Deschenes defines a minority as a "group of citizens of a State, constituting a numerical minority and in a non-dominant position in that State, endowed with ethnic, religious or linguistic characteristics which differ from those of the majority of the population, having a sense of solidarity with one another, motivated, if only implicitly, by a collective will to survive and whose aim is to achieve equality with the majority in fact and in law," UNDOC E/CN.4/Sub.2/1985/31, p. 30.

33. Art.1(3): "The States Parties to the present Covenant, *including those having responsibility for . . . Non-Self-Governing and Trust territories,* shall promote the realisation of the right of self-determination . . ." (author's emphasis). The post-colonial future of self-determination was matter of relative unconcern to many States, though Western States insisted on a continuing function. Among other States, we may note the forthright statement of Afghanistan that self-determination "will have to be proclaimed even in a world from which colonial territories have vanished," UNDOC A/C.3/SR.644, para. 10.

34. Europe "had reached the ultimate goal where self-determination was concerned; now that European Powers were denying the right of self-determination to Asian and African peoples, there could be no doubt that the question of the inclusion of Article 1 of the Covenants was a *purely colonial issue"* (author's emphasis), UNDOC A/C.3/SR.648, para. 8 (Syria). Many States expressed the view that the colonies would be the first beneficiaries of self-determination. This does not rule out later beneficiaries.

35. UNDOC ST/HR/4/Rev. 4. p. 64.

36. UNDOC A/C.3/SR.399, para. 4.

37. There is a useful collection of these comments by the Human Rights Committee in 9 E.H.R.R. 169. The comment on self-determination was adopted by the Committee on 12 Apr. 1984.

38. The Human Rights Committee, in its report of 1986, stated that the draft of Art. 27 would be suspended pending "information gathering.," and promised that particular attention would be devoted to this article in the future, UNDOC A/41/40, para. 412.

39. A/C.3/SR.310, para.3.

40. A/C.3/SR.399, paras.5–6.

41. A/C.3/SR.369, para 13.

42. UNDOC A/39/40 (1984), p. 200, at p. 203; Communication No. 78.1980.

43. UNDOC A/36/40 (1981), p. 166; Communication No. R6/24; Selected Decisions under the Optional Protocol, 2nd-16th Sessions (New York, 1983), pp. 10, 37 and 83, UNDOC CCPR/C/OP/1.

44. *The Right of Nations to Self-Determination* (Eng. ed., Moscow, 1947), p. 45.

45. 78 U.N.T.S. 277. The Convention prohibits a range of grave attacks on the existence of national, ethnic, racial or religious groups, including the killing of their members. Minorities are natural victims of genocide, and any new instrument on minority rights must be concerned, *de minimis,* with securing existence at this basic level.

46. The revision of ILO Convention 107 will, in all probability, adopt the term "peoples" instead of "populations." However, a number of States contributing to the revision process have made it clear that the inclusion of "peoples" should not function as a base for an expanded range of claims by indigenous groups, International Labour Conference, 75th Session 1988, Report VI(2), Partial Revision of the Indigenous and Tribal Populations Convention, 1957 (No. 107), p. 13.

47. For a "reconstruction" of the *travaux,* see Ferraris (ed.), *Report on Negotiation, Helsinki-Geneva-Helsinki 1972–75* (1979).

48. Russell, "The Helsinki Declaration: Brobdingnag or Lilliput?" (1976) 70 A.J.I.L. 242, 269-270.

49. Art. 29.

50. See Kuper, *Genocide, Its Political Use in the Twentieth Century* (1981), and *The Prevention of Genocide* (1985).

51. For the proposed text for the International Labour Conference 1989, see *Report IV(2), Partial Revisions of the Indigenous and Tribunal Populations Conventions 1957,* No. 107.

52. *Editors' Note.* Developments since publication of this article in 1989 include: The Council of Europe Framework Convention for the Protection of National Minorities, done at Strasbourg, February 1, 1995, 1 at 34 I.L.M. 351 (1995); the CSCE Document of the Copenhagen Meeting of the Conference on the Human Dimension, June 19, 1990 at 20 I.L.M. 1305 (1990); and UN General Assembly Resolution 47/135, December 18, 1992 adopting the Declaration on the Rights of Persons Belonging to National or Ethnic, Religious and Linguistic Minorities at 32 I.L.M. 911 (1993).

9

Participants in International Legal Relations

Donna E. Arzt and Igor I. Lukashuk

T he classical theories of international law in both the United States and the former Soviet Union took for granted that states were and would continue to be the principal subjects of international legal relations. This traditional "Westphalian" conception[1] is reflected in the systematic treatises expounding international law in the two countries and in their respective textbooks used for teaching international law.[2] The conception is also reflected in the limitation on the contentious jurisdiction of the International Court of Justice, and before it the Permanent Court of International Justice, to cases in which the parties are states.

The traditional doctrine came under challenge years ago. It has long been understood that parties other than states can and do exert a great deal of influence on the international legal system. Gradually at least one category of these other parties came to be accepted as a full participant in international legal relations. By the middle of the twentieth century, international organizations came to be treated as subjects of international law for most purposes. It is no longer controversial that international organizations enjoy rights and exercise duties under international law and can enter into treaties with states and with other international organizations.[3]

Areas of controversy remain, nevertheless. Some of these have been framed in the literature as disputes in which the legal community in the former Soviet Union and the socialist bloc supposedly clung to the traditional state-centered view, while many U.S. and other Western scholars advocated a more inclusive perspective. The characterization of the controversy along U.S.-Soviet lines is undoubtedly too simplistic, however, because there was never a monolithic position on either side.[4] In fact, some in the United

States did not differ significantly from the approaches shared by the preponderance of the Soviet legal community, and likewise some Soviet scholars advocated positions that diverged considerably from traditional doctrine.[5] By the end of the 1980s it seemed that the gap, if there had in fact been one, was narrowing. Nevertheless, by the beginning of the 1990s, the question of a hypothetical U.S.-Soviet doctrinal split was overshadowed by new challenges to the international legal system, stemming from the disintegration of the USSR and related developments.

Neither interstate relations nor international law can avoid exposure to the wide range of influences that are today a part of global affairs. Ethnic groups and liberation movements, supranational economic communities and political parties, businesses, social and advocacy organizations, communications networks, and many other entities exert influence not only on relations within their own spheres but also on relations between states. As the international system becomes more democratic, the impact of these non-state actors can be expected to increase. This is not to say that states themselves must necessarily play a diminished role. The growing power of transnational corporations, for example, which was widely noted by many authors during the 1970s,[6] did not at that time lead to a decrease in the regulatory role of states. Indeed, it could be argued that over the same time frame, many states took on expanded regulatory powers, both within national economies and with respect to international transactions.[7] Nonetheless, the democratization of international life and the decentralization of political and economic authority are trends which must be taken into account.

In this chapter, we pose the question: Should there be expansion or stability among the participants in international legal relations? Should state domination continue, or should a trend be encouraged toward greater pluralism or, if you will, "privatization," in the international legal order? Rather than concentrating on the formal problem of what is a "subject" of international law, or who should enjoy "international legal personality," we ask more functional questions: Who should— and who, in effect, already does—enjoy rights and obligations under international law? Who should— and does—actually participate in the process of creating, making claims under, and enforcing international law?[8]

In particular, we focus on two of the currently more controversial participants in international legal relations: individuals and transnational enterprises. While these do not exhaust the areas of debate among and between the different legal schools (we could also have considered, for example, issues concerning federations, supra-national organizations, or dependent peoples with national liberation movements), these two categories have had special significance and are also especially relevant to the current period of transition to a new international legal order.

Individuals

Schools of Thought

The status of the individual is one of the most important yet difficult questions or modern international law. On the one hand, individuals occupy the central position in social life. The ancient Greeks developed the notion that the human being is the measure of all things. People unite in tribes, societies, nations, governments, and states in order to satisfy their spiritual and material needs. The missions of each of these unions is to serve humanity. On the other hand, as history testifies, the abuse of power by societies and states has been a constant occurrence. Government serves as an instrument not only for the defense of human rights but for their violation as well. Accordingly, determining the optimal relations between the rights of society and the rights of individuals is the central problem of any normative system, moral or juridical, national or international.

For most of its history, international law has dealt solely with states, completely ignoring the individual. Not until the end of the nineteenth century did it even begin to address problems such as slavery and injury during wartime. Only with the adoption of the U.N. Charter did it truly begin to be concerned with relations between states and their citizens, calling for "international cooperation . . . in promoting and encouraging respect for human rights and for fundamental freedoms for all without distinction as to race, sex, language or religion."[9] Contemporary international law is now firmly related to the rights of the person, one of which is the right to a social and international order in which human rights and freedoms can be fully realized.[10] Today, the individual is with ever greater frequency an active rather than a passive participant in international affairs, in ever closer contact with international law. From the Universal Declaration of Human Rights (1948) to the Vienna, Copenhagen, and Moscow final documents of the Conference on Security and Cooperation in Europe (1989, 1990, and 1991, respectively),[11] it is recognized that people have the right to contribute actively, either individually or in association with others, in the promotion and protection of their rights and freedoms. Moreover, international human rights norms play a crucial role in evaluating a regime's legitimacy and level of civilization.

Do these developments mean the collapse of the Westphalian conception of the international legal order—the "de-étatization" of international law? It is perhaps too soon for a definitive answer to this question. Two schools of thought can be identified, however, which begin to suggest an answer by addressing the status of the individual in international legal relations. One school, while supporting developments in the field of human rights, firmly believes that only states and international organizations can be subjects of international law. Another school maintains that to the extent that international law now contains norms on the rights of the individual, the latter is increasingly a subject of it. (A third school would consider the individual not as a subject but as a "beneficiary" of international law. This is really but a subsidiary of the first school.)

The first school of thought emphasizes that although international law requires respect for individual freedom and dignity, it is through states that this respect is to be implemented. In this view, in giving effect to the "international cooperation" called for under the U.N. Charter, states accept obligations to accord to the individual various rights, and also to create international procedures for the defense of those rights. Individuals enjoy the fruits of this cooperation. Although customary international law and global public opinion reduce the degree to which states, even by mutual agreement, can introduce limitations on these rights and procedures, states do retain the collective power to change or even to abolish them. Sovereign states still remain the source of the commanding energy of international law—energy without which international law could not function. By virtue of their sovereignty, states create international legal norms, give them obligatory force, and put into effect the mechanisms for their realization. This school sees individuals, at best, as having a derivative legal personality, as their connection with international law is mediated through another governing political-legal institution, the state.

It was through the legal writings of socialist scholars in the pre-Gorbachev era that this first school of thought was most cogently articulated. However, this view is also reflected in many aspects of the official United States approach to international law. It is among Western scholars (including in this group some former Soviets), as opposed to Western governments, that the second school finds its strongest adherents. These scholars believe that international law is departing from a state-centered orientation—that it must be a law created by human beings for human beings. This school rejects the notion that there is anything fixed or immutable in the lack of access of individuals to the International Court of Justice or to world-wide law-making bodies. As one of its advocates has posed the question: "Is the international community still composed of the "governors" only, or are the "governed" allowed to have a say?"[12]

The tension between these two schools of thought reflects the crossroads at which international law finds itself today. In what follows in this chapter, traces of this tension will be detectable. We now review prior doctrine concerning individuals in international relations, describe the current practice of individual access to human rights and other international tribunals, and then discuss emerging trends and issues.[13]

Prior Doctrine

In the late eighteenth and early nineteenth centuries, Blackstone and other Western jurists believed that individuals as well as states were bound by international law and were thereby liable for offenses against the law of nations, such as piracy and assault on diplomats. But this view lost its sway during the positivist era of state sovereignty, when the doctrine became entrenched that states alone have rights and duties and can make claims under international law. Publicists such as Oppenheim could then write that "since the Law of Nations is a law between States only and exclusively, States only and exclusively are subjects of the Law of Nations," individuals being only its objects. In the 1920s the Permanent Court of International Justice stated that while international agreements could adopt individual rights and duties enforceable in national courts, they do not create "direct" international rights and obligations for private individuals.[14] It also held that when a dispute between a private person and a state is taken up by the individual's government through diplomatic action or international judicial proceedings, "a State is in reality asserting its own rights—its right to ensure, in the person of its [nationals], respect for the rules of international law.[15]

The Court was reflecting the then-prevailing theory that treaties, at most, might impose the duty on states to incorporate individual rights into their municipal laws and that states, in their discretion, might diplomatically "espouse" the claims of their nationals, but that individual rights existed, at best, as rights of the state. This "espousal process," which has been called "a legal fiction,"[16] requires the national a) to convince its government to espouse the claim, b) to risk politicization of the claim, and c) to depend on its uncertain enforcement. All in all, this is a less than satisfactory posture. The U.S. State Department has long supported the "discretionary espousal" approach, maintaining that U.S. nationals have no automatic right to diplomatic intervention and no right to object to the amount of compensation negotiated on their behalf for injuries inflicted by other states. However, it recognizes that international human rights, at least, apply to individuals against violations by their own governments.

Beginning with the period after World War II, and occasionally even earlier, some Western publicists began to reassert the pre-nineteenth century position that individuals do have rights and duties under international law, even if their capacities "may be different from and less in number and substance than the capacities of states."[17] Thus in Lauterpacht's revision of Oppenheim's treatise, the word "primarily" is inserted in the original, "Since the Law of Nations is . . . a law between States . . .," and the author acknowledges developments which tend "to extend recognition, by means of international supervision and enforcement, to the elementary rights of at least some sections of the population of the state."[18] These developments include the International Military Tribunal at Nuremberg, treaties articulating standards of humanitarian law, and the human rights conventions of the United Nations system. However, these are all changes brought about by treaty or by an international authority deriving its power from states, thus indicating that if international rules protect or bind individuals, it is still only through the will of states.

Some U.S. courts have recently conferred jurisdiction over individuals for alleged violations of customary international law, regardless of the nationality of the victim,[19] but these are apparently minority positions, both within American and international jurisprudence. In cases involving human rights, such a construction is necessary because other than the Genocide and Torture conventions, and only recently the International Covenant on Civil and Political Rights, the U.S. has not ratified many of the other major human rights treaties.

Until the Gorbachev era, the Soviet view had concurred with the prevailing positivistic conception. "The Soviet science of international law has proved that individuals are under State jurisdiction and are legal persons in relations inside the State. They have no independent legal status and are not capable of the independent accomplishment of international rights and duties. Therefore, they are not international persons.[20] . . . Although these views reflected the traditional doctrine, the USSR had also rejected the traditional rule that a state is responsible under international law for injuries resulting from the taking of property of the national of another state, on the theory that an alien acquires property in and enters the territory of another state subject wholly to local law.

Soviet representatives argued in U.N. forums against the recognition of individuals because it would restrict the sovereignty of states over their own citizens and offer opportunities for interference with the internal affairs of states. F.I. Kozhevnikov, for instance, stated to the International Law Commission in 1953 that "the rights of the individual lay outside the direct scope of international law, and, it was only by virtue of the legal bond which existed between the individual and the State that his right could be protected."[21] Although in 1973 the USSR ratified the International Covenant on Civil and Political Rights—but not until July 1991 the Optional Protocol—it originally opposed the creation of the Human Rights Committee on the grounds that it would violate the U.N. Charter, the principle of national sovereignty, and the rule that individuals are not subjects of international law.

Even before the dissolution of the country, this orthodox Soviet view appears to have changed. Before speculating on the implications of such change, as well as evolving Western views, we will survey the international and regional tribunals in which individuals are held accountable or are able to seek their remedies.

Tribunal Practice

Although no international criminal court or penal tribunal has yet been established on a permanent basis, various humanitarian and other conventions require states to bring to punishment individuals, both officials and private citizens, who have violated the laws of war,[22] engaged in genocide,[23] or committed international terrorist acts.[24] Indeed, since 1815, over three hundred multilateral agreements have been reached which provide for over twenty categories of international crimes.[25] But until 1993 (when a special tribunal was created for crimes committed in the former Yugoslavia) there had been only two ad hoc international tribunals, at Nuremberg and Tokyo, that were created to try individuals for international crimes.

In his opening statement at the Nuremberg Trial of the Major War Criminals, the U.S. Chief Prosecutor, Justice Robert Jackson, declared, "Crimes against international law are committed by men, not by abstract entities, and only by punishing individuals who commit such crimes can the provisions of international law be enforced."[26] This Nuremberg principle of individual responsibility, originally proclaimed in the Charter entered into by the U.S., the USSR, France, and the U.K., has been reaffirmed unanimously by the United Nations and by numerous jurists as forming an authoritative part of contemporary international law. However, Nuremberg alone cannot establish the international legal personality of individuals, for it applied only to individuals acting under color of state law, not individuals acting on a purely private basis, and it did not provide for claims brought by individual victims.

In a limited number of international and regional fora, most predominantly in the area of human rights, individuals may bring claims against states for violations of international obligations; however, in each such forum, jurisdiction over individual claims has been specifically agreed to by the respondent state.[27] Conditions under which the claims are heard are, accordingly, quite restrictive and hardly favorable to individual litigants. Under Resolution 1503 of the U.N. Economic and Social Council, for instance, although a broad range of persons and groups is empowered to communicate directly with the U.N. Sub-Commission on Prevention of Discrimination and Protection of Minorities, petitioners must remain silent about the communication until the Sub-Commission makes a recommendation, and single individuals can assert claims only if their claim is an expression of a "consistent pattern of gross and reliably attested violations of human rights and fundamental freedoms." Given the confidentiality requirements and the fact that states which offer to cooperate can usually avoid public condemnation while continuing to violate human rights, many observers have concluded that this procedure "operates to protect rather than to expose countries responsible for systematic and gross violations of human rights."[28]

Under the Optional Protocol to the International Covenant on Civil and Political Rights, by contrast, individuals can petition the U.N.'s Human Rights Committee concerning just a single violation of the underlying Covenant. However, the claimant must normally be a personally affected victim or a duly appointed, closely connected representative. Over sixty states have ratified or acceded to the Optional Protocol, but that is only about half of all the state parties to the Covenant. A procedure for hearing individual communications is also established by the International

Convention on the Elimination of All Forms of Racial Discrimination and by the Torture Convention, but like the International Covenant procedure, such communications will not be received if the state complained about has not consented to the procedure.

Individual claimants are afforded somewhat less obstructed access in the European and Inter-American human rights systems; in fact, many more individual petitions have been adjudicated by the European Commission on Human Rights than by the U.N.'s Human Rights Committee under the Optional Protocol. While the Protocol speaks of "individuals," the European Convention for the Protection of Human Rights and Fundamental Freedoms permits "any person, non-governmental organization or group of individuals" claiming to be victimized by a member state's violation to lodge an application with the European Commission, provided that the respondent state "has declared that it recognizes the competence of the Commission to receive such petitions."[29] This is a narrower standard than the Convention's inter-state procedure, by which "any alleged breach of the provisions of the Convention by another High Contracting Party" may be referred to the Commission.[30] Nevertheless, realizing that "the Convention and its institutions were set up to protect the individual," the European Court of Human Rights has ruled that procedures must "be applied in a manner which serves to make the system of individual applications efficacious."[31] Thus, while the *actio popularis* is excluded, individuals may claim to be victims of a violation occasioned by the mere existence of legislation providing (for instance) for secret surveillance or, in the absence of an actual measure of implementation of a law, if they "run the risk of being directly affected by it."

According to Merrills, the European Court of Human Rights "sees itself as much more than a provider of remedies for isolated complaints. In the interests of the effectiveness of the Convention as a whole it is prepared to use individual applications as an opportunity to make points which it considers need to be made and interprets the concept of 'victim' accordingly."[32] Although individuals cannot institute proceedings directly in the European Court, under a recently revised rule, in cases that have been referred by the Commission or one of the concerned states, the individual "may present his own case" to the Court, either directly or through an advocate.

Individual access in the Inter-American human rights system is similar to the European, in that only states and the Commission can submit cases to the Court. However, an individual can petition the Commission concerning any state that has ratified the American Convention on Human Rights and may be a spouse, relative, friend, or even a person unknown to the aggrieved party. While the Inter-American system is newer than the European and far fewer cases have been adjudicated, its bar on individual standing before the Court has been criticized as weakening the Court's ability to effect fully its mandate to promote the observance of individual rights.

Outside the context of human rights, a small number of fora receive or were envisioned to receive individual claims. Within the U.N. system, individual inhabitants of trust territories have the theoretical right to petition the Trusteeship Council, while employees of the Organization have often attained legal recourse in the Administrative Tribunal. In addition, when it is established, the International Tribunal for the Law of the Sea will be open "to entities other than States Parties" in any case submitted pursuant to "an agreement conferring jurisdiction on the Tribunal which is accepted by all the parties to that case."[33]

By far the longest experience with individual access is in the Court of Justice of the European Communities, to which private persons may, in some limited circumstances, bring claims against the main organs of the EC, though not against Member States or other individuals. (Jurisdiction over some individual suits has been transferred to the EC's new Court of First Instance.) Individual standing in the European Court of Justice has been said to serve the important functions of checking the political power of Community institutions, circumventing possible efforts of the national judiciaries to rob the Court of its powers, and filling the void created by political barriers to Member State challenges, "thus preserving the smooth functioning and goodwill of the economic union."[34] But recognition that individuals are subjects of European Community law has more than a utilitarian purpose. As the Court has stated: "[T]he community constitutes a new legal order of international law for the benefit of which the States have limited their sovereign rights, albeit within limited fields, and the subjects of which comprise not only Member States but also their nationals independently of the legislation of Member States."[35]

Finally, mention should be made of The Iran–United States Tribunal, which is accessible to natural and juridical persons, as well as to the two states. Because most of the non-state litigants are corporations, the Tribunal is described in the "transnational enterprises" section of this chapter, below.

Emerging Trends and Issues

The preceding review of prior doctrine and tribunal practice reveals that at the present time, individuals have a precarious and uncertain status in international law. To the extent that they have international obligations, those are not enforced in any extant, permanent forum. The procedural right to initiate proceedings before an international body is meager and often rudimentary, limited to forwarding a complaint, without necessarily the opportunity to make a personal appearance. Even worse, the procedural right is granted only by treaty, so that it exists only in regard to selective, discrete matters, and often only in regard to states that have consented to individual claims. These ratifications, moreover, can be withdrawn at the state's discretion. Finally, the concomitant remedy to these procedural rights is often a mild, unenforceable report. The exceptions to this general set of restrictive conditions are further limited by region, respondent, or even time.

Despite these serious limitations, the current status of individuals in international law illustrates some remarkable developments. First, when individuals have an international procedural right, it is granted without regard to nationality. They can thereby complain against their own states or other states, irrespective of whether their own state agrees to represent their claim. Second, although the voluntary relinquishing of some sovereign prerogatives has not been easy, states have come to respect the tribunals which have adjudicated individual claims against them. Third, there is a growing emphasis on codification of individual responsibilities, in addition to rights, as illustrated by the Convention on the Rights of the Child (1989), which imposes on parents as well as states the affirmative duty to act on behalf of their children. These may seem like minor triumphs, but not when measured against what had been, at least until recently, the ostensibly absolute intractability of the Westphalian conception of public international law. Added together, the myriad of discrete tribunal procedures receiving individual claims, along with the influence of non-governmental organizations representing the interests of individuals, constitute a de facto, if not de jure, international personality for individuals. . . .

In the *Reparations* case, the World Court defined an international person as "capable of possessing international rights and duties ... and [having the] capacity to maintain its rights by bringing international claims."[36] It further stated that in any legal system, the subjects of law are not necessarily identical in nature or extent of their rights, "and their nature depends upon the needs of the community."[37] Although the Court was considering, in 1949, the international personality of an intergovernmental organization, the United Nations, this same test can be applied to individuals today. As already indicated, individuals do already possess international rights and duties, albeit limited in scope. But as with organizations, the rights and duties of individuals need not be identical to that of states. Whether individuals are capable of asserting rights by means of international demands is a function of what states are willing to allow. If not, this part of the I.C.J. definition is tautological: individuals are not capable of asserting international demands, because they are not recognized international subjects. International personality must mean more than merely the availability of a remedy, but how much more, and how much need be independent of the will of states?

An advocate of the traditional school of thought criticized in 1972 those Western jurists who drew "the conclusion that the existing subjects of international law are absolutely free to transform any object into a subject of international law. In order to achieve this, the presence of their wish is [according to them] the only necessary requirement needed."[38] He insisted at that time on two other prerequisites to international recognition: participation in the creation of international norms and the application and implementation of such norms. It was then and continues now to be unrealistic to expect individuals to create international law, although the prospect of a world legislature representing private persons seems less illusory today than only twenty years ago. . . .

The regional rudiments of such a body now exist in the European Parliament, in which members represent transnational political groups such as Socialists, Communists, Greens, and Christian Democrats. A world parliament of individuals might include representatives of transnational groups such as indigenous peoples, women, and scientists.

Individuals will fully be able to apply and to implement international norms only when they are held accountable for them in an international penal tribunal—the creation of which, again, depends on the will of states. This realization turns back to the I.C.J.'s formula that the nature of an international subject's rights "depends upon the needs of the community." Or as one of us articulated it in 1972, "the need . . . for the development of international cooperation based on the generally accepted principles of international law. Such a proposition testifies that international legal personality cannot exist without a social basis. The range of subjects of law, their types, and their nature are determined by social needs.[39]

The most important development of the recent period is that the world community is closer to agreeing on its common social needs. If both East and West (and, perhaps, North and South) can agree that cooperation through peaceful coexistence and the pursuit of common human values is wiser than world-wide class struggle, then surely they can cooperate in the recognition of an expanded legal status for individuals. Sovereign prerogatives are less imperative in a collaborative world than in an antagonistic one. The instrumental benefits of individual personality have already been demonstrated in the European Community, and even antagonists as polarized as the U.S. and Iran have experienced the gains, if not willingly or intentionally.

If states have heretofore been reluctant to grant legal personality to individuals, it was because they feared, quite accurately, that individual claims would be directed at them. But individuals with greater international status would not make demands on states alone. They are likely to direct them increasingly at international organizations. Or as Anthony D'Amato has speculated:

> [I]f the nineteenth century was characterized by State v. State, and the twentieth by Individual v. State, the twenty-first century might see international law becoming addressed to the claims of Individual v. Individual. Transboundary international legal claims involving individuals only, but

invoking public international law, might be the direction in which we are headed.[40]

Moreover, if states can collectively recognize that with the end of the Cold War, the greatest threats to world peace now come from drug trafficking and terrorism, torture and genocide, global warming and water contamination—acts committed not only by states but by individuals—then they can agree that an urgent need of the world community is the establishment of a world criminal court, to try individuals as well as states. The arguments to this effect of numerous individuals and organizations in both the United States and the former Soviet Union deserve wider attention.

International legal personality for individuals should not only result in a forum for enforcing international duties. It should also lead to wider ratification of human rights treaties, as well as to liberalization of the standing requirements in the existing tribunals that enforce international rights. As the World Court held in the *Barcelona Traction* case, obligations to the international community as a whole derive in contemporary international law from

> the outlawing of acts of aggression, and of genocide, as also from the principles and rules concerning the basic rights of the human person, including protection from slavery and racial discrimination. . . . In view of the importance of the rights involved, all States can be held to have a legal interest in their protection; they are obligations *erga omnes.*[41]

If all states are deemed injured by breaches of human rights, then surely are all individuals.

We now turn to perhaps an even more controversial topic, the status of transnational enterprises.

Transnational Enterprises

The Status of Transationals

Whether labeled "Transational" or "multinational corporations," "global enterprises" or variations thereof, the entities which we will call "transnational enterprises"[42] generally consist of economic organizations performing manufacturing, financial, technological or similar functions, headquartered in industrialized countries and pursuing business activities abroad, often in developing countries. They frequently operate through affiliates linked by common managerial and financial control, which share information, resources, and responsibilities and pursue integrated policies and strategies. Some are economically more powerful than all but the largest states. . . .

Despite their size and influence, transnational enterprises such as ITT, GM, Toyota, Royal Dutch/Shell, and Unilever have no formal international rights or duties. While they may participate in international proceedings with states, agree that public international law may govern their transactions with states, or otherwise exert influence on national and international policies, transnational enterprises have heretofore been treated within the international legal order as nationals of a given state, lacking their own international legal personality.

Admittedly, transnational enterprises are not totally without legal status in international tribunals. Private business ventures have legal standing in the European Economic Community and the European Coal and Steel Community. The Convention on the Settlement of Investment Disputes Between States and Nationals of Other States provides international methods of settlement for some such disputes. However, a provision in a contract between a transnational and a state stipulating that the governing law is international or general principles of law does not make the contract a treaty. Breach by the state does not normally permit the transnational to seek enforcement in an international forum.

One significant exception to this rule is the Iran-United States Claims Tribunal, established pursuant to the Algiers Declaration in 1981 to resolve claims against Iran by U.S. nationals, primarily corporations, claims against the U.S. by Iranian nationals, including corporations, and interstate claims. Although subject to a wide range of interpretations as to whether its law is private, public, national, "a-national," or international, the Tribunal was established to be a legal process, not a mediation or negotiation. Therefore, its practice regarding non-state litigants is more significant than that of regular commercial arbitration, and it clearly reflects an advance beyond the old "espousal doctrine," described above, in which claims of nationals were resolved intergovernmentally by lump sum settlement.

Although under typical commercial arbitration the capacity to agree to arbitration depends on the parties' own national law, because the Tribunal was created by international agreement, not private contract, it can be argued that the law of the Tribunal is public international law and that the corporate claimants are subjects thereof. Indeed, the Tribunal has rarely relied on national systems of law as the source of controlling rules, a process fundamental to arbitration under the auspices of the International Chamber of Commerce, the rules of the U.N. Commission for International Trade Law (UNCITRAL), and other typical approaches. Instead, it has regularly applied principles derived from the parties contracts, general principles of law, and public international law. Moreover, despite the positions taken by Iran and the U.S., respectively, that non-state claims in the Tribunal are in actuality diplomatically espoused interstate claims or that they are akin to commercial arbitration under the law of the forum state, the Netherlands, the Tribunal itself has uniformly rejected both of these views and has indicated that the claims belong to the private party and not to the state. Not only are awards made directly to corporate and individual litigants and claims captioned in litigants' private names, but the private parties themselves can argue their own claims and decide whether to accept settlement.

Whether or not the Iran-U.S. Claims Tribunal will have a lasting jurisprudential effect will depend on whether in later years it is viewed as a watershed or as merely *sui generis*. The U.N. Claims Commission established as part of the Gulf War ceasefire accepts consolidated claims submitted by governments on behalf of their nationals—pursuant to the traditional "espousal" doctrine—though, in an innovation, the Commission will hear claims by stateless or unrepresented parties, such as Palestinians. Unlike the Iran-U.S. Claims Tribunal, which largely ignored the losses of individual claimants, the U.N. Compensation Commission has put corporate claimants on hold, giving priority to individuals.

As regards transnational enterprises generally, states have almost universally agreed that their status should not be upgraded. Through the 1980s it could be said:

> Socialist countries are politically opposed to them and the majority of developing States are suspicious of their power; both groups would never allow them to play an autonomous role in international affairs. Even Western countries are reluctant to grant them international standing; they prefer to keep them under their control—of course, to the extent that this is possible.[43]

Moreover, the directors of transnationals "appear to agree with many national governments that [transnationals] ought not to participate directly in the international legal system—evidenced by the fact that [they] have not overtly sought broad international legal personality."[44] In the 1990s, the question of what to do about transnational enterprises may emerge as the centerpiece for restructuring the inequities in global economic relations. For no groups—including possibly the transnationals themselves—are happy with their current status. As the United Nations Group of Eminent Persons reported on these enterprises in 1974:

> Home countries are concerned about the undesirable effects that foreign investment by multinational corporations may have on domestic employment and the balance of payments, and about the capacity of such corporations to alter the normal play of competition. Host countries are concerned about the ownership and control of key economic sectors by foreign enterprises, the excessive cost to the domestic economy which their operations entail, the extent to which they may encroach upon political sovereignty and their possible adverse influence on sociocultural values. Labour interests are concerned about the impact of multinational corporations on employment and workers' welfare and on the bargaining

strength of trade unions. Consumer interests are concerned about the appropriateness, quality and price of the goods produced by multinational corporations. The multinational corporations themselves are concerned about the possible nationalization or expropriation of their assets without adequate compensation and about restrictive, unclear and frequently changing government policies.[45]

To these concerns a more contemporary report would add the problems of product dumping, destruction of the environment and modification of the climate in the course of states couraged development, and collaboration in the bolstering of unlawful *apartheid* regimes. Just as most states have concurred that transnationals are not subjects of international law, "[a]lmost all nations agree on the desirability, if not the necessity, of some form of international regulation of TNC's."[46] The problem is that they cannot agree on a form. Even if they could, because of the limitations of contemporary jurisprudence, regulation might not be effective.

In the remaining sections of this chapter, we will briefly review the efforts to assert international regulatory control over transnational enterprises. We will then speculate on future directions and discuss some current problems, including two reciprocal questions: how can the international claims of transnationals be presented, and how can international claims be presented against them?

Regulatory Efforts

The earliest regulation of transnationals took the form of bilateral investment, promotion, and protection treaties between "home" (state of incorporation) and "host" (state of operation) countries. Intended to protect foreign investors by dealing, most prominently, with questions of nationalization and compensation, these have traditionally been favored by industrialized states. Developing countries prefer newer forms of regulation by intergovernmental and nongovernmental organizations. Some categories and examples of these include: sectoral strategies by producers' associations, such as the Organization of Petroleum Exporting Countries or the inter-state Union of Banana Exporting Countries; harmonized policies and institutional arrangements at the subregional and regional levels, such as by the European Community, Latin American Free Trade Association and the Andean Common Market; guidelines issued by the inter-regional group of industrialized countries, the Organization for Economic Cooperation and Development; and international efforts within the U.N. system, which have commonly consisted of codes—both specialized ones by the Economic and Social Council (ECOSOC), the U.N. Conference on Trade and Development, the International Labour Organisation, the Food and Agriculture Organization and other agencies, and the more general Draft U.N. Code of Conduct on Transnational Corporations, prepared by the Commission and

Centre on Transnational Corporations on the recommendation of the Group of Eminent Persons. A common objective of all the codes, supported even by transnationals themselves, is harmonization of what are now unpredictable national laws and regulations through the formulation of internationally accepted models. The Draft U.N. Code of Conduct, lacking a preamble and list of objectives and containing some alternative provisions, is addressed to both transnationals and states. Its provisions include both standards for corporate conduct and principles for the treatment of transnationals by states. A major substantive dispute that is unresolved is the "host-state treatment" conflict. Industrialized countries insist on "national treatment" no less favorable than that given to the host state's domestic corporations. Developing countries support "qualified national treatment" which would allow them to refer to national objectives and priorities rather than international law or "established" development plans, as sought by developed countries.

Socialist countries, at least through the 1980s, believed that transnationals should enjoy a less privileged status than national corporations, denying, for instance, the former the investment incentives granted to the latter. On many issues related to transnationals, socialist states generally supported the position of developing countries, while simultaneously promoting their own ideological positions. The "host state treatment" conflict may be resolved depending on the position taken, and the influence asserted, by the formerly socialist states.

Among other legal issues remaining to be resolved are the relevance of customary international law to the norms established under the Code, questions concerning choice of law and the jurisdiction of national courts, and, most significantly for our purposes, the legal nature of the Code. ECOSOC originally called for a code that is "effective, comprehensive, generally accepted and universally adopted," without reference to its legal status.[47] During the drafting period, developing and socialist countries argue for a mandatory, legally binding code in the form of a treaty, believing that adopting states would then be obliged to observe not only those provisions addressed to them but also to enforce the sections relating to transnational conduct through national legislation and national enforcement machinery. A binding treaty would also entail effective international institutions not only to assess developments under the Code but also to reinforce national action. Industrialized countries and business interests, in contrast, rejected the notion of a binding code, urging instead the adoption of a voluntary code relying on moral suasion and without enforcement mechanisms. Although initially in favor of a binding code, since the Ford Administration the U.S. has supported a voluntary one and has also taken the position that code responsibilities must be balanced between governments and transnationals and must apply to state-owned enterprises as well, regardless of whether they are profitmaking.

From the look of the most recent draft of the Code, it is a typical compromise: more of its provisions apply to transnationals than to states, while the question of whether it applies to public corporations is left unresolved. However, it is expected to turn out to be a voluntary instrument. Nevertheless, merely reaching an agreement to put transnationals on a relatively equal footing with states in the Code has been a major concession of sovereignty by the drafters.

Given the current status of transnational enterprises in international law, both binding and non-binding codes are problematic. Some of these and other enforcement issues are taken up in the next section.

Current Problems and Proposals

Non-binding codes, with their guage and reliance on moral suasion, do not constitute international law, although one author has argued that voluntary codes may become recognized as such as a result of wide endorsement, national practice and intergovernmental monitoring. A possible virtue of voluntary codes is that, paradoxically, drafters may be willing to adopt stronger language and stricter standards in them than in enforceable codes. However, experience with the Sullivan Principles, a voluntary code of fair labor practices for U.S. firms operating in South Africa, indicates that even mild, progressively-structured yet optional standards would fail to meet ECOSOC's "effectiveness" test. After six years in existence, the Sullivan program had only 120 participants out of 400 eligible firms, and only two of the seven companies employing over 5000 workers. Moreover, host states as well as transnationals are legally free to disregard voluntary codes when enacting national laws, thus undermining the harmonization and predictability objectives of the code-drafting process.

Despite the uproar that it would cause in Western circles, a mandatory code would be binding only on states, which along with international organizations are the only entities that can enter into international conventions. Code provisions concerning standards of corporate conduct would then be implemented and enforced on the national level, without a real guarantee of state-to-state uniformity, either substantively or procedurally.

Only if transnationals themselves could become parties to the mandatory codes would all perspectives—industrialized and developing states, plus transnationals and non-corporate, private interests—be assured of protection for what is a mutual interest: equal access to fair tribunals, whether international or national, in which all claims concerning transnational enterprises can be heard.

The current system's failure to provide this kind of access extends beyond the problem of code enforcement to other sorts of legal claims. This is illustrated by the following all too real problem:[48]

Transnational enterprise ABC, incorporated in the United States and doing business in South American country XYZ, intends to construct oil and gas pipelines and processing plants in a tropical rainforest that is ecologically crucial to the survival of numerous plant and animal species and an indigenous tribal population, as well as the planet as a whole, as recent scientific studies have reported. Country XYZ supports and has approved permits for the construction.

Assuming current law, including the non-existence of a Code of Conduct, either binding or not, in what forum could relief be sought that would prevent this construction? In theory, there are three possibilities, but none is terribly viable. The first is the International Court of Justice, as no other relevant international forum exists. (A complaint which emphasized human rights rather than environmental issues might be presented before the Inter-American Commission on Human Rights, but this would seemingly require a stretch of the American Convention on Human Rights.) In the World Court, only state XYZ could be a respondent (naming the U.S. would be frivolous) and only another state could be a petitioner. Assuming that another state could be persuaded to espouse the ecological interests (an unlikely possibility), despite the probable *erga omnes* character of obligations to protect the environment, no obvious provisions of international law have been violated by XYZ in its approval of a permit for ABC to develop within XYZ. While a second avenue is litigation by the indigenous tribe or by environmentalists against ABC within the national courts of XYZ, it is unlikely that any national laws would prohibit the construction. Moreover, political considerations might make it unlikely that a suit concerning government-supported development would be taken seriously in XYZ's courts.

That essentially leaves litigation in the federal courts of the state of incorporation, the United States, under the Alien Tort Claims Act. Members of the tribe, backed by environmentalists, might sue both transnational ABC and state XYZ. However, claims against XYZ would almost certainly fail under sovereign immunity principles, and, unless bribery or other corruption was alleged, the act of state doctrine. That would leave ABC as a defendant, but it is not apparent that either laws of the U.S. or any international laws, conventional or customary, are applicable. Even if the U.N. Code of Conduct had been adopted as a binding agreement, its environmental provisions are weak and vaguely drafted. Unless transnational corporations are made parties to it, the Code would be binding only on state XYZ, which would have been dismissed from the suit. However, if the Code were binding on transnationals, ABC could be held accountable in U.S. courts (assuming either that the U.S. was a signatory or that it reflected customary international law[49]) or in an international tribunal with jurisdiction over transnationals that might be set up under such a Code system.

Transnationals also suffer from their inability to bring legal claims in their own name. In the *Barcelona Traction* case, involving expropriation of property of a transnational by Spain after the Spanish Civil War, the World Court faced the question whether Belgium could exercise diplomatic protection for shareholders, the overwhelming majority of whom were its nationals, but where the company was incorporated not in Belgium but in Canada. The Court held that only the state of incorporation could espouse the claim. This rule has left transnational enterprises and their shareholders subject to the whims of the "espousal doctrine," meaning the unappealable, unpredictable vagaries of government policy, a predicament shared by individuals. Where the place of incorporation becomes more and more a technicality, unrelated to the locus of corporate management or ownership, this rule is especially unrealistic.

It has already been suggested that an international companies law be created which would grant international charters to transnational enterprises. Such a law would also establish an intergovernmental agency to enforce standards such as share dispersal. In the European Community, a European Company Statute has already been proposed that would permit large corporations to achieve supranational incorporation under a law applicable in all EC jurisdictions. The proposal would obviate the need to harmonize the existing laws in the twelve member states without supplanting national securities and disclosure laws or local administrative and judicial supervision. Throughout the world, as the environmental impact of transnationals becomes more urgent—and more transborder—it should become even clearer that only through international status, supervised by international agencies and international tribunals, can the problems of transnationals be adequately addressed.

The main obstacle is that, so far, almost all relevant parties have opposed international personality for transnational enterprises. While international legal status for individuals is threatening enough to state sovereignty, most states, developing countries in particular, are likely to view such a development as over-empowering the very entities, corporations, that are already overly powerful. Perhaps the present gridlock can be broken by the formerly socialist states, which are in the process of reexamining their own relationships to transnationals, given their need and desire for development, as well as their growing awareness of the fragility of their own environments. . . .

Notes

[Editors' Note: Upon the entry into force of Protocol No. 11 to the Convention for the Protection of Human Rights and Fundamental Freedom on November 1, 1998, individuals will have the right to submit applications directly to the European Court of Human Rights once local remedies are exhausted. (Until entry into force of Protocol No. 11, this was an optional clause of the Convention.)]

1. The phrase is derived from the Peace of Westphalia (1648), which ended

the Thirty Years War and led to the era of the nation-state. See Falk, *The Interplay of Westphalia and Charter Conceptions of International Legal Order,* in The Future of the International Legal Order 43 (R. Falk & C. Black, eds, 1969.)

2. In the United States, the traditional treatment is followed in, inter alia, Restatement (Third) of the Foreign Relations Law of the United States, para.201-223 (1987) [hereinafter Restatement]; and in leading textbooks for use in law schools, including International Law: Cases and Materials 241-243 (L. Henkin et al. eds, 3rd, ed. 1993).

3. See Advisory Opinion on the United Nations, 1949 I.C.J. 174 [hereinafter the Reparations Case]; Convention on the Law of Treaties Between States and International Organizations or Between International Organizations, March 20, 1986, 25 I.L.M. 543.

4. See M.V. Zakharova, The Individual as a Subject of International Law, 1989 Soviet State and Law, No. 11, at 118; J. Quigley, Law for a World Community, 16 Syracuse J. int'l L. & Com. 1 (1989); R.A. Mullerson, Human Rights and the Individual as Subject of International Law: A Soviet View, 1 Eur. J. Int'l. L. 33, 35 (1990); R.A. Mullerson, Human Rights: Ideas, Norms, Reality (Moscow, 1991).

5. Id. See also V.S. Vereshchetin & R.A. Mullerson, The Primacy of International Law in World Politics, 1989 Soviet St. & L., No. 7, at 10.

6. Robert Gilpin wrote that the nation-state is "losing control over economic affairs to transnational actors like multinational corporations. It cannot retain its traditional independence and sovereignty and simultaneously meet the expanding economic needs and desires of its people." R. Gilpin, Three Models of the Future, 29 Int'l Organizations, No. 1, at 41 (1975).

7. See N.V. Mironov, Eternal Relations of Ministries, Unions, and Enterprises (Jurid. Lit. 1986).

8. "[I]t is not particularly helpful, either intellectually or operationally, to rely on the subject-object dichotomy that runs through so much of the writings. It is more helpful and closer to perceived reality to return to the policy-science view of international law as a particular decision-making process.... In this model, there are no subjects or objects, but only participants." Higgins, Conceptual Thinking About the Individual in International Law, 24 N.Y.L. Sch. L. Rev. 11, 15-16 (1978), citing D.P. O'Connell, International Law 117 (1965); McDougal, Some Basic Theoretical Concepts About International Law, 4 J. Conflict Resol. 337 (1960); McDougal et al., The World Constitutive Process of Authoritative Decision, 29 J. Legal Educ.253(1967).

9. U.N. Charter art. 1, para. 3. See also id., art. 55, 56.

10. Universal Declaration of Human Rights, G.A. Res. 217, art. 28 (1948).

11. See Final Document of the Vienna Meeting of the Conference on the Human Dimension of the Conference on Security and Cooperation in Europe, Principles 13.5 and 26, reprinted in 28 I.L.M. 527 (1989); Final Document of the Copenhagen Meeting of the Conference on the Human Dimension of the CSCE, Principles 10.3 and 11.3, reprinted in 29 I.L.M. 1305 (1990); and Final Document of the Moscow Meeting of the Conference on the Human Dimension of the CSCE, reprinted in 30 I.L.M. 1670 (1991). See also Final Act, Conference on Security and Cooperation in Europe, Basket III, reprinted in 14 I.L.M. 1292 (1975).

12. A. Cassese, International Law in a Divided World 4 (1986).

13. For an earlier review of many of the doctrines, tribunals, and trends discussed in this section of the chapter, see Brownlie, The Place of the Individual in International Law, 50 Va. L. Rev. 435 (1964).

14. Danzig Railway Officials (Jurisdiction), 1928 P.C.I.J. (ser. B) No. 15, at 17–18. Because it recognized the possibility of treaties creating individual rights and obligations, this decision has been said to have "dealt a decisive blow to the

dogma of the impenetrable barrier separating individuals from international law." H. Lauterpacht, International Law and Human Right 28 (1968).

15. Mavrommatis Palestine Concessions (Jurisdiction), 1924 P.C.I.J. (ser.A) No. 2, at 11–12. *See also* Panevezys-Saldutiskis Railway Case (Estonia v. Lithuania), 1939 P.C.I.J. (ser. A/B) No. 76, at 16.

16. In on view, espousal is a legal fiction, as the national has no real claim. The state is asserting its own claim. A. D'Amato, International Law: Process and Prospect 194-198 (1987).

17. O'Connell, International Law 108 (2nd ed. 1970).

18. Lauterpacht, Revision of Oppenheim (1955), excerpted in the Human Rights Reader, 167, 169 (W. Laqueur & B. Rubin Eds. 1973).

19. Most notably, Filartiga v. Pena-Irla, 630 F.2d 876 (2nd Cir. 1980).

20. Feldman, International Personality, 2 R.C.A.D.I. 359 (1986), citing International Law 82 (G. Tunkin ed. 1982). See Restatement, supra note 2, para. 712, reporter's note 1.

21. 1 Y.B. Int'l L. Comm'n 173 (1953), cited in Przetacnik, The Socialist Concept of Human Rights: Its Philosophical Background and Political Justification, 13 Review Belge de Droit Int'l 238, 249 (1977).

22. See Geneva Convention Relative to the Protection of Civilian Persons in Time of War, 75 U.N.T.S. 287 (1949); Geneva Convention Relative to the Treatment of Prisoners of War, 75 U.N.T.S. 135 (1949), each ratified by both the U.S. and U.S.S.R.

23. The Convention on the Prevention and Punishment of the Crime of Genocide, 78 U.N.T.S. 277 (1948), ratified by the U.S.S.R. in 1954 and the U.S. in 1988, provides in Article VI that "Persons charged with genocide . . . shall be tried by a competent tribunal of the State in the territory of which the act was committed, or by such international penal tribunal as may have jurisdiction."

24. See e.g., Tokyo Convention on Offenses and Certain Other Acts Committed on Board Aircraft, 704 U.N.T.S. 219 (1963); Hague Convention of the Suppression of Unlawful Seizure of Aircraft, 22 U.S.T. 1641, T.I.A.S. No. 7192 (1970); Montreal Convention for Suppression of Unlawful Acts Against the Safety of Civilian Aviation, 24 U.S.T. 565, T.I.A.S. No. 7570 (1971); International Convention Against the Taking of Hostages, U.N. Doc. A/Res/34/146 (1979).

25. See M. C. Bassiouni, International Crimes (1985).

26. Trial of the Major War Criminals Before the International Military Tribunal, Proceedings 34 (1947) [hereinafter Proceedings]. See also Trial of Japanese War Criminals, Documents 40 (1946).

27. Excluded from this discussion are human rights related petition procedures in specialized agencies of the U.N. such as the ILO and UNESCO. See, able, Valticos, The International Labour Organization and Saba, in The International Dimensions of Human Rights 363, 401 (K. Vasak & P. Alston eds. 1982). See generally United Nations Actions in the Field of Human Rights, U.N. Doc. ST/HR/2 Rev.1 (1983).

28. UN Commission on Human Rights—consideration of Gross Violations, 30 Review of the International Commission of Jurists 31, 34 (1983).

29. 213 U.N.T.S. 221 (1950), art. 25.

30. Id., art. 24.

31. Klass Case, 28 Eur. Ct. H.R. (ser A) at 18 (1978).

32. J. Merrills, The Development of International Law by the European Court of Human Rights 50 (1988).

33. United Nations Convention on the Law of the Sea, U.N. Doc. A/Conf.62/122 (1982) Annex VI, art. 20.

34. Parkinson, Admissibility of Direct Actions by Natural or Legal Persons in

the European Court of Justice, 24 Tex. Int'l L., 456, 457, 460 (1989). See generally A. Arnull, The General Principles of EEC Law and the Individual (1990).

35. Van Gend and Loos Case, 1963 O.J. 1, at 23.

36. Advisory Opinion on Reparations for Injuries Suffered in the Service of the United Nations, 1949 I.C.J. 174 (1949).

37. Id. at 178.

38. Lukashuk citing G. Schwarzenberger, A Manual of International Law 40 (1960) as one such dreamer.

39. Lukashuk, Parties to Treaties: The Right of Participation, in Academie de Droit International, 1 Recueil Des Cours 1972 (1973), at 240. See the Reparations Case, supra note 3.

40. D'Amato, supra note 16, at 199. A pre-tribunal screening mechanism, functioning much like the European Commission on Human Rights, would be needed to screen out frivolous claims. See Higgins, supra note 8.

41. Case Concerning the Barcelona Traction Light and Power Co. (Belgium v. Spain)(Second Phase), 1970 I.C.J. 3, at 32 [hereinafter Barcelona Case].

42. We will use "transnational enterprise," as "multinational: wrongly implies ownership and control by investors in several states, whereas most such entities consist of parent companies based in industrialized states with affiliates or subsidiaries in developing countries. Moreover, "corporations" is too narrow, as some are co-operatives or partnerships, or state-owned or mixed-ownership entities.

43. Cassese, supra note 12. at 103.

44. Charney, Transnational Corporations and Developing Public International Law, 1983, Duke L.J., at 766.

45. Report of the Group of Eminent Persons, The Impact of Multinational Corporations on Development and on International Relations, U.N. Doc. E/5500/Add 1 (1974), at 9-10.

46. Rubin, Transnational Corporations and international Codes of Conduct: A Study of the Relationship Between International Legal Cooperation and Economic Development, 30 Am. U.L. Rev. 903, 914 (1981). Note that the Declaration on the Establishment of a New International Economic Order, G.A. Res. 3201 (S-VI), May 1, 1974, 13 I.L.M. 715, states in para. 4 that the new economic order shall be founded on full respect for, inter alia, "(g) Regulation and supervision of the activities of transnational corporation by taking full measures in the interest of the national economics of the countries where such transnational corporation operate on the basis of the full sovereignty of those countries."

47. Draft Res. II, Progress Made Towards the Establishment of the New International Economic Order, Obstacles that Impede It and the Role of Transnational Corporations, ECOSOC Res. 1980/60, para 6(a).

48. The problem is based on a proposal for litigation by Huraorani Indians against DuPont's subsidiary, Conoco Ecuador. In June 1990, the Sierra Club Legal Defense Fund and CONFENIAE, an NGO representing indigenous peoples in Ecuadoran Amozon, petitioned the Inter-American Commission on Human Rights, arguing that an oil-pipeline service road to be built by Conoco and state-owned Petroecuado through 100 miles of rainforest would breach international human rights law. A proposal to sue in U.S. federal district court was considered but dropped.

49. Unless it received almost universal ratification, it would be unlikely that the Code would be said to reflect customary law. It is hard to make a case that, under current jurisprudence, transitional corporations are already bound by customary international law. At any rate, developing countries have already taken the position that customary international law should not be used to amplify or interpret the Code.

PART 2.4

International Law as
Operating System:
Implementation and
Compliance with
International Law

10

Strengthening Compliance with International Environmental Accords: Preliminary Observations from a Collaborative Project

Harold K. Jacobson and Edith Brown Weiss

In June 1992, heads of government gathered in Rio de Janeiro at the United Nations Conference on Environment and Development (UNCED) to launch a major international effort to achieve environmentally sustainable development. International environmental accords or binding legal instruments are an important part of this strategy. Twenty years earlier, when the United Nations Conference on the Human Environment was held in Stockholm, there were only a few dozen multilateral treaties dealing with environmental issues. By 1992, there were more than nine hundred international legal instruments (mostly binding) that either were fully directed to environmental protection or had more than one important provision addressing the issue.[1] In the early 1990s, about a dozen important multilateral negotiations on new international legal instruments were occurring at more or less the same time, and several of those were concluded prior to or at the Rio conference. The United Nations Framework Convention on Climate Change and the Convention on Biological Diversity were signed at Rio, as was Agenda 21—an approximately 850-page text that sets forth strategies for the many complex issues involved in integrating environmental protection and economic development. Yet we know very little about national implementation and compliance with the treaties and other international legal instruments that have been negotiated, despite their importance and growing number. . . .

The project was funded and was under way in 1992. This article presents preliminary observations derived from a project that is very much in midstream. Nevertheless, the quantitative data and written material that are now available through the project and the discussions in the project

From *Global Governance: A Review of Multilateralism and International Organizations,* volume 1, number 2, May-August 1995. Copyright © 1995 Lynne Rienner Publishers, Inc. Reprinted with permission of the publisher.

workshops provide a basis for some tentative generalizations and conclusions.

Why Study Implementation of and Compliance with International Environmental Accords?

International environmental accords—treaties and other international legally binding instruments—have the potential to transform the ways in which humanity uses the planet, the quality of lives all over the world, relations among states, the global economic system, the development paths of advanced and industrializing countries alike, and the differences between North and South. Some speculate that these accords could create international authorities with unprecedented scope and power, predicated on the economic leverage of only a few countries. These accords might impose stringent sanctions on violators or use rewards to induce countries to conform. Conforming could, moreover, reshape a country's energy production, transportation, industrial processes, agriculture, animal husbandry, settlement patterns and migration, and population-growth patterns.

Countries have already negotiated many international treaties and other agreements to protect the environment and to conserve natural resources. While some of these accords existed before the 1972 Stockholm conference, most have been negotiated since then. The rate at which important accords have been proposed and concluded is increasing. The substantive and procedural duties contained in the accords have become more stringent and comprehensive, and the range of issues subject to such accords has expanded. Calls for international treaties and other international legal instruments to protect the global environment will continue and likely accelerate. Indeed, several efforts are in progress. But even if no more accords were negotiated, it would be essential to make those that are in force work effectively.

International accords are only as effective as the respective parties make them. Effectiveness is the result not only of how governments implement accords (the formal legislation or regulations that countries adopt to comply with the accord) but also of how they comply with them (the observance of those regulations and the commitments contained in the international accord). Weak legislation can produce weak compliance, but unenforced strong legislation can have the same effect. One cannot simply read domestic legislation to determine whether countries are complying. While some claim that most states comply with most international treaties most of the time, there are reasons to believe that national implementation of and compliance with international accords are not only imperfect, but often inadequate, and that such implementation as takes place varies significantly among countries. It is not known to what extent environmen-

tal accords have or have not evoked compliance or whether the same factors that presumably motivate compliance with arms control, trade, or
human rights agreements will motivate compliance with environmental
accords.

There is a literature regarding compliance with international accords
concerning arms control, trade, and human rights, and some of the findings in this literature may be applicable to environmental accords. In addition, a general literature exists on enforcement of international treaties and
on enforcement of national environmental laws and regulations.[2] There is
also a broad literature on the impact of international institutions.[3] Studies
of the management of common resources offer additional valuable insights.[4]

Yet there are very few studies of the implementation of and compliance with international environmental accords. The limited studies that do
exist include a notable one by the U.S. General Accounting Office that
looks broadly at compliance of governments with eight international environmental accords and concludes that compliance has been low;[5] a survey
of international environmental treaties and instruments prepared by the
secretary-general of UNCED, which includes a brief description of accord
implementation;[6] a monograph by Peter Sand on global environmental
governance that focuses on the institutional design of international accords
to encourage compliance;[7] and an article by Jesse H. Ausubel and David
G. Victor[8] and a study by David Feldman on the characteristics of international environmental accords that facilitate implementation.[9] None of
these studies focuses on factors at the national level that affect compliance, which is the focus of our study.

There has never been a systematic study of factors affecting compliance at the national level of the international environmental accords into
which countries have *already* entered. Our study takes a first—but we
hope large—step toward drawing from the experience of existing international environmental law those lessons that might instruct us how better to
proceed in the future.

Without better knowledge about the implementation of and compliance with international accords, it is impossible to assess their effectiveness in protecting the global environment or to evaluate the merits of proposed accords. Formally binding international treaties or agreements are
only one of the available instruments for dealing with global environmental issues. One cannot appropriately weigh the advantages of negotiating a
treaty to obtain global environmental goals as opposed to relying on market forces or education without knowing more about what states tend to do
to give effect to the provisions of treaties. Nor is it possible to make sensible suggestions about measures that might be taken to improve the implementation of and compliance with existing and proposed accords. If we
understood these processes better, we should be able to design better

international accords that would enhance the chances of national compliance.

The Stylized View of Compliance and Reality

A traditional, stylized view of international law might maintain that (1) countries accept treaties only when their governments have concluded that they are in their interest; (2) because of that, countries generally comply with treaties; and (3) when countries do not comply with treaties, sanctions are employed both to punish offenders and to serve as deterrents designed to encourage first-order compliance. Reality with respect to many types of treaties, particularly environmental accords, is quite different. While countries might join only treaties that they regard as in their self-interest, there are a variety of reasons countries find them in their interest, and those reasons affect their willingness and ability to comply with them. Governments may choose to accept a treaty because of a desire to jump on an international bandwagon or because of pressures from other governments with leverage over them. Or there may be domestic interests that force the issue. In some cases, countries may enter treaties without intending to modify their behavior significantly so as to comply fully. Even if they intend to comply, some countries may find it difficult or impossible, because they lack the local capacity to do so. Scattered evidence suggests that implementation of and compliance with international environmental accords are often haphazard and ragged. Parties rarely resort to adjudication of violations or employ significant sanctions against noncomplying parties. While blandishments may be used to encourage compliance, these are rarely of major proportions.

Nevertheless, as the experience with human rights treaties so vividly illustrates, over time many countries have gradually begun to do more to implement treaties and improve compliance. The force of environmental accords probably comes not from the possibility of sanctions but from the felt need to coordinate activities affecting the environment and to ensure stable and predictive patterns of behavior that will sustain the commonly held environment.

This less elegant reality of imperfect, varied, and changing implementation and compliance is the starting point for this study. The purpose of the analysis is to discover factors that lead to improved implementation and compliance with treaties that cover environmental issues. We assume that cost-benefit calculations are murky, military sanctions are out of the question, and economic sanctions are exceptional and may violate international trading arrangements. Because of those assumptions, the applicability of the literature with respect to arms control and trade is limited. That with respect to human rights is more relevant. Public goods theory may be more appropriate than game theory for the type of treaties that concerns us. We assume that the propensity of various countries to comply with different treaties will vary and change over time. Our task is to understand the factors that shape that variation and propel the change.

Assessing Implementation, Compliance, and Effectiveness

An essential first step is to have clear definitions of implementation and compliance. *Implementation* refers to measures that states take to make international accords effective in their domestic law. Some accords are self-executing; that is, they do not require national legislation to become effective. But many international accords require national legislation or regulations to become effective. Countries adopt different approaches, ranging from accounting procedures, to incentives to induce compliance, to taxation, to sanctions for noncompliance. This study seeks to identify systematically the various methods that are employed for implementing international accords and to analyze which are used with what effectiveness. In examining steps that have been taken to implement treaties, several questions arise. How comprehensive is the legislation that has been adopted? How much time elapsed before implementing legislation and regulations were adopted? Has the stringency of the legislation changed over time? What factors have affected this change? In many countries, complicated issues of federalism are raised by the implementation of international accords. In those cases, provincial and local-level legislation is also essential.

Compliance goes beyond implementation. *Compliance* refers to whether countries in fact adhere to the provisions of the accord and to the implementing measures that they have instituted. The answer cannot be taken as given, even if laws and regulations are in place. Measuring compliance is more difficult than measuring implementation. It involves assessing the extent to which governments follow through on the steps they have taken to implement international accords. Some measurable factors, such as the staffing and budget of bureaucracies charged with ensuring compliance, the quantity and quality of data that are kept, and the extent to which incentives and sanctions are actually used and imposed, give indications of efforts toward compliance. In the end, however, assessing the extent of compliance is a matter of judgment.

Compliance has several dimensions. Treaties contain specific obligations, some of which are procedural, such as the requirement to report, and others of which are substantive, such as the obligation to cease or control an activity. In addition, preambles or initial articles in treaties place those specific obligations in a broad normative framework, which we refer to as the spirit of the treaty.

Compliance is probably never perfect; substantial compliance is what is sought by those who advocate treaties and agreements. We seek to assess the extent to which substantial compliance is achieved with the procedural and substantive obligations contained in treaties and also with the spirit, or broad norm, involved in the treaty, and to compare the extent of success within and among political units and over time.

Compliance is related but not identical to effectiveness. Countries may be in compliance with a treaty, but the treaty may nevertheless be ineffective in attaining its objectives. And even treaties that are effective in attaining their stated objectives may not be effective in addressing the problems they were intended to address. To illustrate the latter point, compliance with a treaty may result in the cessation of an activity that contributed to pollution, but it might lead to an overall increase of pollution by encouraging other activities as substitutes whose consequences are even worse; or a treaty prohibiting international trade in elephant tusks could effectively stop the trade but have little impact on the decimation of the elephant population.

Table 10.1 shows the several dimensions of implementation, compliance, and effectiveness. Our project is particularly concerned with assessing implementation and compliance. Effectiveness is very important, but until implementation and compliance are better understood, the contribution of treaties to solving international environmental problems cannot be known. Learning about implementation and compliance is an essential first step to learning about effectiveness.

Factors that Affect Implementation and Compliance

Many factors may affect a country's implementation of and compliance with international accords. We are interested in how several interrelated factors affect the extent to which and the way in which countries have met their commitments. These factors include the character of the activity, the character of the accord, country characteristics, policy history, leadership, information, the role of nongovernmental organizations (NGOs), actions of other states, and the role of international governmental organizations (IGOs).

Character of the activity. Environmental accords are about human activities—activities that extract resources, produce pollutants or other emissions, change ecosystems, or reduce biodiversity. Some substances or activities have little economic importance, whereas controlling others has

Table 10.1   International Environmental Accords: Implementation, Compliance, and Effectiveness

I. Implementation

II. Compliance

    A. Compliance with the specific obligations of the treaty
        1. Procedural obligations
        2. Substantive obligations

    B. Compliance with the spirit of the treaty

III. Effectiveness

    A. In achieving the stated objectives of the treaty

    B. In addressing the problems that led to the treaty

consequences for entire economies. Some also have little intrinsic economic value, but the process of compliance can disrupt economic activities in lots of other areas. Some are easy to monitor, while others can be detected only through very intrusive measures. The costs and benefits of regulating substances and activities and their distribution among various social classes and geographical regions can also be important.

The accord itself. The characteristics of the treaty or agreement itself are an important factor. Some issues relate to the process by which the accord was negotiated. By whom and how was the process initiated? What form did the negotiations take? Were issues settled consensually or by majority vote? What was the extent and depth of agreement? The substantive characteristics of the accord also raise important issues. What is the nature of the obligations contained in the accord? Are the duties general or precise? Are they binding or hortatory? What compliance mechanisms are contained in the accords? How does the agreement treat countries that do not join? The Montreal Protocol on Substances That Deplete the Ozone Layer and the Convention on International Trade in Endangered Species obligate parties not to trade controlled substances with countries that are not parties to the agreement. How effective is this provision in inducing compliance? What benefits accrue to signatory countries? What special dilemmas does the accord produce, such as the problem of how an item once placed on the World Heritage Convention's list of protected things ever gets taken off that list?

Country characteristics. The social, cultural, political, and economic characteristics of the countries clearly influence implementation and compliance. We assess the relative importance in shaping a country's actions of its broad political culture, the level of its economic development, and the trajectory and pace of its economic growth. Are there cultural traditions that influence how a country complies? What difference does it make whether the country has a market or a planned economy, or if it is mixed? Does it make a difference in which sector the substance or activity is included? What are the effects of the characteristics of the political system? How strong and effective is the bureaucracy, and what difference does that make? What is the strength of nongovernmental groups, including those engaged in lobbying and domestic and international agenda setting? What is the nature of the legal system? What procedures are required to adopt the regulations or other strategies necessary to implement the agreement?

Policy history. A country's policy history regarding the substance or activity being regulated is another basic factor. What was the country doing about the substance or activity before adhering to the international accord? Had the country already recognized the existence of an environmental problem? What role did the country play in the negotiation of the accord?

Leaders. People make a difference. Some leaders are more committed to and effective in promoting compliance with international environmental accords than others. Some countries have drawn leadership on an issue from the scientific community, while others have not had such communities from which to draw. What are the consequences of changes in and differences among leaders?

Information. It is broadly assumed that the more information there is about an environmental issue and the clearer the understanding of the issue, the more effective implementation and compliance will be. That assumption impels much of the work of international organizations. We want to assess how the availability of information about and the extent of understanding of the environmental issues covered in the treaties affect national implementation and compliance with them.

NGOs. What role do local, national, and international nongovernmental organizations have in determining the compliance of states with international accords? What role, in particular, do international nongovernmental organizations (INGOs) such as Greenpeace or the International Institute for Environment and Development play? What is the role of multinational corporations?

Actions of other states. The actions of other states in implementing and complying with the accord can also affect a state's compliance with an agreement. To what extent have other countries' noncompliance or compliance with the accords affected the willingness of countries to abide by these accords? How does the answer to that question vary with the subject and obligations of the international accord? To what extent can a state be a freeloader under the accord?

IGOs. Finally, international governmental organizations have important roles in promoting the implementation of and compliance with international accords. We investigate how countries relate to the IGOs that have responsibilities for these accords. What importance, if any, was attached to involvement by international organizations such as the United Nations?

These factors can be grouped into four broad headings: (1) characteristics of the activity that the accord deals with; (2) characteristics of the accord; (3) characteristics of the country, or political unit, that is a party to the accord; and (4) factors in the international environment. Figure 10.1 presents a graphic representation of the interaction of those factors with a state's implementation of and compliance with an accord and the effectiveness of the accord.

In examining these factors, we want to test certain hypotheses that are nested within the questions posed in the preceding paragraphs. Some of these hypotheses have been deduced from rational choice assumptions, others have been derived from the existing literature, and still others have been derived from preliminary analyses of empirical data that we have gathered. Some relationships seem obvious. Some have been identified in the assessments by the U.S. General Accounting Office and the secretary-general of UNCED.[10]

Given the realist and rational choice assumptions that undergird game theory, one would expect that the smaller the costs and the greater the benefits associated with the accord, however difficult they may be to calculate, the greater the probability of implementation and compliance. The likelihood of significant sanctions would be included in the prospective cost element of this hypothesis. Since implementation and compliance require monetary and bureaucratic resources, it would seem logical that the larger a country's gross national product and the higher its per capita GNP, the greater the probability of implementation and compliance. Because costly measures can be accommodated with minimal or no redistribution in a period of rapid economic growth, the higher the rate of a country's economic growth, the greater the probability of implementation and compliance. Since domestic group and mass public pressure comprises important mechanisms for promoting implementation and compliance with treaty obligations, several scholars and policymakers have assumed that the more a country adheres to democratic norms concerning political and civil rights and political participation, the greater the probability of implementation and compliance. Many have also assumed that decentralization would promote more-effective compliance.

We expected those hypotheses to be confirmed. We expected them to

**Figure 10.1 International Environmental Accords: Model of Factors
That Affect Implementation, Compliance, and Effectiveness**

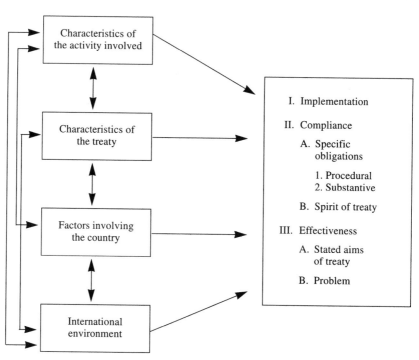

bound other findings. We expected that the variables involved in those hypotheses would explain the largest share of the variance among countries and treaties, but we also were very conscious that it would not be surprising or particularly helpful to those interested in improving compliance for us to discover that rich countries were more likely to comply with treaties than poor countries, or that countries were more likely to comply with those treaties that impose few burdens. Countries cannot be made rich overnight, nor can the burdens that compliance might entail always be eliminated.

Since administrative and bureaucratic capacity is obviously essential for implementing accords, we explore the extent to which such capacity has been and could be increased in ways independent from broader economic, political, and social development. Clearly, the greater the capacity of the political unit to implement the accord, the more likely it is that it will comply. Administrative and bureaucratic capacity depends on economic resources, but it also involves education, technical training and skills, and attitudes.

The relationships that hold greatest fascination for us are those involving international and domestic processes. Game theory and public goods theory provide the foundation for many of the suggestions of these scholars. Factors that one or more of them have stressed are: (1) international momentum toward compliance, which increases the benefits of compliance and the costs and consequences of noncompliance for any signatory state; (2) the amount, quality, and availability of information about the issues involved so that they can be understood; (3) the involvement and/or engagement of domestic officials and bureaucracies so that their personal interests and reputations become issues at stake; and (4) the creation and engagement of communities of interested parties, especially scientists and specialists in the topic, or what Haas has termed "epistemic communities."[11] The first factor involves international processes; the second, international and domestic processes; and the third and fourth, predominantly domestic processes. We are primarily interested in the consequences for implementation and compliance of processes that occur within the lower two boxes on the left-hand side of the diagram in Figure 10.1, those involving the characteristics of the country or political unit that is a party to the accord and those involving the international environment.

Hypotheses concerning those factors are straightforward. With respect to international momentum, the most direct hypothesis is: The greater the number of countries that have ratified an accord and the greater the extent of their implementation and compliance, the greater the probability of implementation and compliance by any individual signatory. Countries have a deep and abiding interest in creating and maintaining a relatively stable and predictable international environment. The more stable and predictable an environment, the higher the costs of disrupting it and, thus, the greater the probability of implementation and compliance. International momentum also has broader aspects, such as the extent to which international public opinion is committed to the issue. International nongovernmental organizations capture and articulate important sections of international public opinion; hence, the stronger and more active the INGOs are in the issue area of the treaty, the greater the probability of implementation and compliance.

With respect to information, the hypothesis is: The greater the flow of scientific and technical information about targeted activities in a form that is understood by governments and public pressure groups, the higher the likelihood of implementation and compliance. Particularly with environmental accords, these actors must rely on scientific and technical information flows to identify and assess risks, address targeted activities, and identify available technical options to enhance compliance.

Hypotheses concerning domestic processes are equally uncomplicated. Two are very important. Because repeated encounters and associations with counterparts as well as concern for reputations have a powerful impact on behavior, the more involved a country's domestic officials and bureaucracies are in the preparation, implementation, and oversight of an accord, the greater the probability of implementation and compliance. Since epistemic communities are deeply committed to the goals of particular accords because of their knowledge and professional interests, the greater the size, strength, and activism of epistemic communities, the greater the probability of implementation and compliance.

Our research efforts focus on these process factors because previous research indicates that they are important. The evidence for them, however, is largely anecdotal. We examine them empirically on a multicountry basis. Since the factors are subject to directed and purposeful modification, policies could be adopted that target them in order to increase implementation and compliance with international environmental accords.

We are also interested in other process factors, such as leadership and the extent of transparency surrounding the activity covered by the accord. Obviously, the more committed a country's leader is to the goals of an accord, the greater the probability of implementation and compliance. Leaders are chosen for many reasons. To some extent, in terms of the focus of this research, a country's choice of leaders is a stochastic process. We study how leaders, whatever their initial inclinations, become more engaged in ensuring compliance with the accord.

Transparency may promote compliance because it makes noncompliance more apparent and makes it easier for international and domestic actors to take actions to encourage and enforce accountability. Transparency is closely linked with the character of the issue covered by the treaty and democratic norms. Cultural factors may affect the acceptability of transparency internally and hence its effectiveness in inducing compliance. We test the hypothesis that transparency promotes implementation and compliance and seek to identify the conditions that bound the hypothesis. We also analyze the extent to which transparency can be promoted.

Stating the hypotheses that have guided our research in such a bald manner may make the project appear overly mechanistic. The project could not have been conducted in a mechanical and simplistic way. Context and institutions are terribly important. The hypotheses are important because they provide a framework that guides and directs the project, useful both as a way of structuring our analyses and guiding comparisons and as a way to link our study with others at a basic, practical level as well as at a theoretical one.

In varying degrees, the factors involved in the hypotheses that are of most concern to us are subject to deliberate manipulation by those who prepare accords and who are responsible for overseeing their implementation and compliance with them. The research seeks to develop a basis for reasoned speculation about how manipulation of these factors might improve implementation and compliance. For example, a broad issue to be

investigated is whether the more a country has been involved in the negotiation of a treaty, the more likely it will be to implement and comply with
the treaty. Or it is possible that a key step in obtaining compliance with environmental treaties from the countries of the South is to improve their indigenous scientific capability so that they can produce independent assessments of environmental problems and evaluate their options for dealing
with them. Or a key step might be to control the behavior of multinational
corporations, which would then exert influence on behalf of environmental
goals in the countries where they operate. Moreover, as has become evident with respect to human rights treaties, compliance with international
accords can change and improve over time, even if compliance was not actually intended by all signing governments at the time of agreement. The
research seeks to understand how improvement might be induced and promoted.

The Research Design: The Countries and the Treaties

To investigate these hypotheses and issues, we have chosen to focus on
eight countries and the European Union (EU) and international treaties
covering five broad areas of environmental concern. We have chosen the
nine political units and the five areas in the hope that the study will yield
knowledge that will have worldwide utility and pertain to most kinds of
environmental accords that may be concluded in the future.

Political Units of Great Importance
and Widely Differing Character

The eight countries selected are Brazil, Cameroon, China, Hungary, India,
Japan, Russia, and the United States. We also include one group of countries, the European Union. These countries have been chosen because they
are very important to the effective implementation of broad international
environmental accords. They include those that have contributed most to
the anthropogenic effects that bring about global change (Japan, Russia,
the United States, and the EU and its members) and others that have the
potential of making major contributions to anthropogenic effects (Brazil,
India, and China).

Cameroon and Hungary were included to illustrate the problems and
processes of implementation and compliance in smaller countries—countries that although their total contribution to global environmental problems may be individually small, when considered as a group constitute by
far the largest number of states in the global political system. This vantage
point is necessary to draw inferences about collective action. The United
States and other large countries can benefit directly by their actions regard-

less of others. But most countries, such as Hungary and Cameroon, cannot, even though collectively countries their size could be more important than the United States. So why do countries that will see the costs so much more clearly than the benefits, due to their relatively small size, become parties or comply?

The EU has been chosen because it increasingly behaves as a state actor through directives and regulations that are applicable in all member states. It represents a new form of governmental organization, one that conceivably could be duplicated elsewhere, such as among the states that constituted the former Soviet Union. It merits study for that reason as well as for the reason that the EU will be a major political and economic actor in forthcoming negotiations. Although the EU is a party to only two of the treaties, most of its twelve member states are parties to all of them.

In the 1990s, those countries included in this study accounted for about three-fifths of the world's population, their GNP constituted about four-fifths of the world product, and they contributed more than two-thirds of the global greenhouse emissions. Table 10.2 presents data that show the importance for environmental issues of the nine political units. They spanned the globe and encompassed a range of forms of political organiza-

Table 10.2   Study of Adherence to International Environmental Accords: The Political Units and Their Characteristics

Country	Population (millions)	GNP per capita (U.S. dollars 1990)	GNP per capita growth rate, 1965–90	CO_2 emissions per capita (tons of carbon)	CFC net use (thousands of metric tons)	Change in forest and woodland
Brazil	150	2,680	3.3	0.38	9	−0.4
Cameroon	12	960	3.0	0.14	0	−0.4
China	1,134	370	5.8	0.59	18	0.0
EU[a]	343	17,058	2.5	2.20	228	1.1[b]
Hungary	11	2,780	—	1.65	1	0.6
India	850	350	1.9	0.21	0	−0.2
Japan	124	25,430	4.1	2.31	58	0.0
Russia	148.7	3,220[c]	—	3.60	—	—
USA	250	21,790	1.7	5.37	197	−0.1
Average	—	8,293	2.8	1.8	63.88	0.08
World average	—	4,964	1.6	1.09	5.4	−0.13
Total	3,022.7	—	—	—	511	—
World total	5,222	—	—	—	659	—

Source: World Bank, *The Environment Data Book: A Guide to Statistics on the Environment and Development* (Washington, D.C.: World Bank, 1993), pp. 10–13.
[a]Not including Luxembourg
[b]Not including Belgium
[c]1991

tion and culture. Furthermore, they included both developed and developing countries, some with mixed-market economies and others that were restructuring centrally planned economies. Finally, some of these countries could be particularly affected by global change.

Five International Environmental Treaties

The five international treaties were chosen to maximize the knowledge that could be gained about ways of managing global environmental change. We deliberately avoided the preconception that the only kind of international environmental agreement that can be entered into is one that regulates emissions; there is considerable variety among these treaties in terms of what they concern and how they deal with it. We have selected only treaties for which there is a significant number of signatories and for which there is already some experience with implementation and compliance. A study of proposed accords that have not yet been implemented would tell us little about what makes for crafting a successful agreement. The five treaties we have chosen include three that deal with the management of natural resources and two that are aimed at controlling pollution. They are:

1. United Nations Educational, Scientific and Cultural Organization (UNESCO) *Convention for the Protection of the World Cultural and Natural Heritage,* 16 November 1972, 27 U.S.T. 37, T.I.A.S. No. 8226 (referred to as the World Heritage Convention). Secretariat, United Nations Educational, Scientific and Cultural Organization, Paris.
2. *Washington Convention on International Trade in Endangered Species of Wild Fauna and Flora,* 3 March 1973, 27 U.S.T. 1087, T.I.A.S. No. 8249 (referred to as CITES). Secretariat, United Nations Environment Programme, Geneva, Switzerland.
3. *International Tropical Timber Agreement,* 18 November 1983, U.N. Doc. TD/Timber/11/Rev. 1 (1984) (referred to as the International Tropical Timber Agreement). Secretariat, International Tropical Timber Organization, Yokohama, Japan.
4. *International Maritime Convention on the Prevention of Marine Pollution by Dumping of Wastes and Other Matter,* 29 December 1972, 26 U.S.T. 2403, T.I.A.S. No. 8165 (referred to as the London Convention and formerly referred to as the London Ocean Dumping Convention). Secretariat, International Maritime Organization, London.
5. *Montreal Protocol on Substances That Deplete the Ozone Layer,* 6 September 1987, 26 I.L.M. 1550 (referred to as the Montreal Protocol), together with the *Vienna Convention for the Protection of the Ozone Layer,* 22 March 1985, 26 I.L.M. 1529 (referred to as the

Vienna Convention). Secretariat, United Nations Environment Programme, Nairobi, Kenya; Secretariat, Montreal Protocol Fund, Montreal, Quebec, Canada. The Vienna Convention is the framework treaty under which the Montreal Protocol was negotiated. We look at this treaty only insofar as it relates to the Montreal Protocol.

The *World Heritage Convention,* 1972, puts international constraints on the use of designated sites within a country. It is a useful model for studying the increasingly common international legal instruments designed to affect a country's behavior toward its own natural and cultural resources. Under the convention, parties nominate sites within their countries for inclusion on the World Heritage List. A meeting of the parties determines whether to include the nominated sites on the list. Once the sites are included, parties are obligated to protect their integrity. If they are in need of financial or technical assistance in doing so, they may receive assistance from the World Heritage Fund, financed by contributions from the parties. A secretariat, which in May 1992 consolidated the separate offices for natural and cultural heritages, administers the convention. Parties vest authority in the elected World Heritage Committee of twenty-one member states, which meets annually and until recently has been primarily devoted to considering proposals to list sites on the World Heritage List. The convention relies on voluntary compliance by the parties. There are no sanctions other than publicity about acts of noncompliance.

The *Convention on International Trade in Endangered Species* (CITES), 1973, is designed to control international trade in endangered species of plants and animals. It is a useful model for studying the technique of protecting the environment by controlling trade in an endangered natural resource or environmentally hazardous product. Under the CITES convention, species are classified into three categories and listed in appendixes: internationally endangered species in which trade is prohibited, species that may become endangered unless trade is controlled, and species not in those two classes but endangered in a particular country that wants the help of others to enforce its control of exports. Under the convention, exports and imports of live specimens listed in the appendixes and of parts and derivatives are to take place only with a permit.

A conference of parties to the treaty meets every two years to review the implementation of the convention and, as appropriate, to revise the categorization of endangered species. A secretariat services the conferences of the parties to the treaty and assists countries in meeting their obligations. It also assists in monitoring trade and helps parties comply with the convention. Inquiries may be conducted into allegations that a species is being adversely affected or that the provisions of the treaty are not being effectively implemented. The conference can review the results of such inquiries and make appropriate recommendations. Publicity is the principal sanction against failures to implement or comply with the treaty, although countries have threatened to invoke trade sanctions.

The *International Tropical Timber Agreement, 1983,* was negotiated to facilitate trade in timber from tropical forests. It includes the major producing and consuming countries and is primarily a commodity agreement. Among its several objectives, however, is "the development of national policies aimed at sustainable utilization and conservation of tropical forests and their genetic resources, and at maintaining the ecological balance in the regions concerned." This goal is to be accomplished by encouraging expansion and diversification of tropical timber trade, improved forest management and wood utilization, and reforestation. To this end, the convention provides for the creation of the International Tropical Timber Organization (ITTO), which functions through the International Tropical Timber Council. The ITTO is charged with monitoring market conditions, conducting studies, and providing technical assistance. The convention is designed to attain its objectives with respect to forest management through development of knowledge, exchange and dissemination of information, and technical assistance.

The ITTO issued on 21 May 1990 the "ITTO Guidelines for the Sustainable Management of Natural Tropical Forests," which are voluntary guidelines for the parties. In the environmental context, national implementation of the convention raises important problems of how to effect substantial changes in the practices of an industry that is central to the economy of countries with tropical forests. It also provides insights into the effectiveness of using information and voluntary measures to induce changes in behavior.

The International Tropical Timber Agreement was drafted to be in force only through March 1994. It has been extended by a resolution of the parties until the new successor agreement goes into effect.

The *London Convention, 1972,* is intended to protect the marine environment from the dumping of certain kinds of pollutants. States are obligated to regulate (or prohibit) dumping of materials that are listed in two annexes and to enforce these measures against vessels or aircraft registered in their territory, flying their flag, or otherwise under their jurisdiction. There is a regular meeting of the parties to review implementation of the agreement and to develop measures with regard to liability, and there are several advisory groups of scientific experts that meet regularly on particular issues. The convention is interesting because it requires states to control the behavior of actors operating in a globally shared resource (the oceans) and to develop measures of accountability.

The *Montreal Protocol on Substances That Deplete the Ozone Layer,* 1987, imposes the most arduous obligations on parties of any of these conventions. It was negotiated within the broad terms of the Vienna Convention, 1985—a framework convention that commits parties generally to take actions to protect both human health and the environment from the adverse effects of activities that modify the stratospheric ozone layer. The Vienna Convention provides for monitoring, the dissemination of information, and research.

The Montreal Protocol requires states that are parties to reduce their consumption of chlorofluorocarbons and to freeze consumption levels of halons. The convention provides target dates, allowing less stringent dates for the developing countries. It provides for regular meetings of the parties and for scientific assessments to be prepared in anticipation of these meetings. At the November 1992 meeting of the parties in Copenhagen, countries agreed to phase out chlorofluorocarbons completely by the year 1996, and halons (except for certain essential uses) by the year 1995, and to add new chemicals to the control list—going well beyond the initial terms of the protocol.

Countries are to report on measures they have taken to implement the protocol. The protocol obligates the parties to establish measures for determining noncompliance with its provisions and for treatment of parties that are found to be in noncompliance. It controls trade in the indicated substances with countries that are not parties to the protocol.

The protocol also recognizes the special needs of the developing countries in implementing the agreement. At the June 1990 meeting in London, the parties agreed to create a new mechanism to provide financial and technical cooperation, including the transfer of technologies, to assist these countries in complying with the control measures of the protocol; that mechanism was established as the Montreal Protocol.

The Montreal Protocol is particularly interesting because of the binding regime it has established for controlling production and consumption of ozone-depleting substances, and for the provision it has made to facilitate compliance by developing countries.

These treaties have been selected for a number of reasons. They involve several key environmental issues connected with global change. They contain a range of types of obligations, and various techniques regarding implementation and compliance. They address both pollution and natural resource problems. They involve issues that occur primarily within states' borders, those that cross borders, and those that are inherently global in nature. These treaties have been in effect a sufficient amount of time, so there is an adequate data base with which to analyze implementation and compliance. Finally, each of the selected states is a party to at least three of these accords, and a majority are parties to all of them. Table 10.3 shows which countries and groups of countries have acceded to which treaties.

Table 10.3   Adherence of the Political Units to International Environmental Treaties as of 1 January 1994 (p = party to treaty)

Political Units	World Heritage	CITES	Tropical Timber	London Convention	Vienna Convention	Montreal Protocol
Brazil	p	p	p	p	p	p
Cameroon	p	p	p		p	p
China	p	p	p	p	p	p
European Union			p		p	p
Hungary	p	p		p	p	p
India	p	p	p		p	p
Japan	p	p	p	p	p	p
Russia	p	p	p	p	p	p
USA	p	p	p	p	p	p

Implementation and Compliance: Some Preliminary Observations

A secular trend toward improved implementation and compliance was visible by 1994. Not all nine political units were doing a better job of implementing and complying with all of the five treaties—indeed, several were not even parties to all of them—but the overall trend was positive. More and more actions have been taken to implement the treaties, and both procedural and substantive compliance have improved. The political units in general are increasingly acting in terms that accord with the spirit of the treaties.

Beyond this secular trend, the political units have also agreed to strengthened and improved treaties. This fact is evident both in the London and Copenhagen supplements to the Montreal Protocol and in the renegotiated International Tropical Timber Agreement.

Those broad points having been made, there are some important qualifications. The performance of some countries with respect to CITES has sharply declined since the mid-1980s. With respect to developing countries, the substantive obligations of the Montreal Protocol are not yet severe. Thus, it would be premature to be extremely optimistic about their performance. Many signs thus far have been positive, but they provide only a weak basis for projecting a positive trend.

Among the five treaties, implementation and compliance seem to be stronger with respect to the Montreal Protocol, the London Convention, and the World Heritage Convention than they are with respect to CITES and the Tropical Timber Agreement. Among the last two, CITES imposes the most stringent obligations of the five accords, and it is the one that has encountered the most serious difficulties in the late 1980s and early 1990s. The Tropical Timber Agreement, with its nonbinding, sustainable forest guidelines, has had the least environmental impact.

No political unit does a perfect job of implementing and complying with the treaties, but the EU, Japan, the United States, and to a lesser extent Russia have done more than the other units in our study. During the past decade, Cameroon has been having the greatest difficulty of the nine political units in implementing and complying with the treaties.

As noted above, even strong implementation and compliance with treaties do not ensure their effectiveness in terms either of meeting the objectives of the treaties or of dealing with the problems that led to the treaties in the first place. In the case of the five treaties that are included in our study, the record is mixed. The Montreal Protocol and the London Convention seem, respectively, to have contributed to a decline in the production and consumption of ozone-depleting substances and in the intentional dumping of wastes in the high seas. The World Heritage Convention appears to have contributed to the preservation of cultural and natural resources. The Tropical Timber Agreement has not yet resulted in the "sustainable utilization" of forest resources, and—unfortunately, despite CITES—there appears to have been, especially since the mid-1980s, an increase in the illicit trade in endangered species. Moreover, while some endangered species have become less critically endangered, others have become more so; but, arguably, the situation could have been even worse absent the treaty.

Revisiting the Model

With these rough assessments as benchmarks, what explains what has happened? The model presented in Table 10.2 grouped the variables we thought might be important into four broad categories: (1) characteristics of the activity involved, (2) characteristics of the treaty, (3) factors involving the country, and (4) the international environment. The model shows that all the factors interact to produce a combined effect on implementation, compliance, and effectiveness. In our discussion, however, for clarity and manageability, the factors must be treated individually. Thus, each of the statements in the following paragraphs requires the qualification "other things being constant."

With reference to the characteristics of the activity involved, our study confirms the conventional wisdom that the smaller the number of actors involved in the activity, the easier it is to regulate it. Because by early 1995 only a limited number of facilities have produced ozone-depleting substances, it has been relatively easy to control the production of those substances as the Montreal Protocol requires. The situation may become more difficult as more production facilities come on-line. The striking contrast between the limited number of facilities that have produced ozone-depleting substances and the millions of individuals who could engage in illicit trade in endangered species contributes to CITES being a much more difficult treaty to enforce than the Montreal Protocol.

Activities conducted by large multinational corporations are also easier to deal with than those conducted by smaller firms that are less visible internationally. Again, the production of ozone-depleting substances provides the example. The large multinational firms are much more subject to the pressure of public opinion and diverse consumers throughout the world than are the smaller, lesser-known firms that engage in much of the timber trade. Obviously, since the characteristics of activities that contribute to environmental degradation are more or less fixed, treaties must address activities whether or not their characteristics facilitate implementation and compliance. To the extent that treaties can decompose problems and define points of attack, these generalizations could be used to shape treaties.

Factors Involving the Treaties

The characteristics of treaties obviously do make a difference. The London Convention, CITES, and the Montreal Protocol impose relatively precise obligations. It is consequently relatively easy to judge whether or not states and other political units are fulfilling these obligations. The World Heritage Convention and the Tropical Timber Agreement are much vaguer; thus, assessing implementation and compliance becomes much more difficult.

Requiring the filing of regular reports is a standard feature that four of the treaties under consideration here, and most others, use to monitor implementation and compliance. Clearly, this is one of the few instruments that is available. Yet it is an instrument that is not well understood. The record of compliance with reporting requirements is spotty at best. Governments, particularly of smaller political units, are extremely overburdened; filing reports is yet one more burden. The locus of the responsibility for preparing the report may be uncertain—is it with foreign offices or with substantive ministries? What is clear is that international secretariats can use the reporting exercise to help them clarify for government officials what the obligations of treaties are and what techniques have been and might be used to fulfill them. Thus, reporting is probably best seen as an educational process rather than a rigorous process of monitoring, and as a tool that enables secretariats, other states that are parties to the treaty, and national and international nongovernmental organizations to intervene to encourage compliance.

It is also clear that even though they have no formal standing under the treaties we have considered, NGOs and multinational corporations can play an important role in providing information about activities that are addressed in international environmental treaties. The TRAFFIC reports on illicit trade in endangered species provide information that governments might find difficult to gather or publish. Greenpeace is an important source of information about ocean dumping. The knowledge that monitoring goes on outside of formal governmental and treaty channels is probably an important restraining factor on governmental actions. The multinational firms that produce ozone-depleting substances sometimes may have had better information than governments about their production. Also, since there are proprietary aspects to this information, these firms have access that governments might not be able to achieve easily. Clearly, the private sector must be engaged if monitoring is to prove effective.

Not surprisingly, for parties to implement and comply with treaties, they must feel that the obligations imposed are equitable. India and China would not become parties to the Montreal Protocol until the agreement about compensatory financing had been reached at the London meeting in 1990. Part of the difficulty with the Tropical Timber Agreement seems to be a sense that burdens are disproportionately imposed on the producer countries; the consumer countries' activities with respect to their forests are unregulated. The new agreement attempts to address this issue by having a separate formal statement regarding temperate forests accompany it.

Factors Involving the Country

The performance of the eight countries and the EU in implementing and complying with the five treaties examined in this study varies substantially across countries and time. The record, however, must be viewed in context. One very important factor shaping how well a country does is what it has traditionally done in the past with respect to the issue in question, including what legislation and regulation it already had in place at the time it became a party to the treaty. For instance, since Japan has had a long tradition of protecting its cultural heritage, becoming a party to the World Heritage Convention did not require vast changes in the way it treated its historical treasures. Its standards may previously have been even above those required by the treaty.

Beyond this, perhaps the most important factor contributing to the variance is administrative capacity. Countries that have stronger administrative capacities can do a better job. Administrative capacity is the result of several factors. Having educated and trained personnel is important. But such individuals usually must have financial support to be effective. For example, while the Indian administrative service is well staffed and well trained, its financial resources are extremely limited, and thus its effectiveness is restricted. Administrative capacity depends on having authority. Administrators whose mandate is narrower than their assigned responsibilities or who are subject to capricious interference cannot do as well as their training and skills would make possible.

Economic factors are important but rather indirectly. The political units in this study have widely varying GNPs per capita that have grown or declined at substantially different rates. Of course, the larger a country's GNP, the more likely it could have a strong administrative capacity; but changes in GNP or the rate of growth of GNP have had little discernible effect on implementation and compliance. Economic collapse and chaos, however, can have a profound effect. In Cameroon and Russia, compliance with CITES seems to have declined since the mid-1980s, and this phenomenon seems to be directly attributable to economic collapse and chaos. Limited government resources and rapid rates of inflation have had an impact on the incentive structure of the individuals who must enforce the provisions of CITES: the customs inspectors. In some instances they have not been paid. In others, they have seen the value of their salaries decline precipitously. Conversely, the value of illicit trade in endangered species has increased. Under the circumstances, the apparent increase in illicit trade in endangered species is perhaps understandable.

Political systems have an effect on implementation and compliance, but, again, the effect is mixed and complex. Large countries have a much more complex task of complying with the obligations of treaties than do smaller ones. There are several levels of political authority in Brazil, China, the EU, Russia, and the United States. In cases where activities that the treaty deals with are widely dispersed—as in CITES, the Tropical Timber Agreement, and the World Heritage Convention—these levels of political authority must be coordinated, which is not always an easy task. Sometimes the authority of the central government, which accepts international obligations, does not reach deeply into local areas. Moreover, these large countries contain within their borders widely different ecological regions, which require variation in the way administration is conducted.

As part of its reform, Russia has attempted to decentralize authority. In the process of decentralization, the authority of Moscow over localities has been weakened. This shift appears to have resulted in a decline in Russia's compliance with CITES. Whether this is the temporary result of an administrative restructuring or a longer-term change is yet to be determined.

Political stalemate and chaos can bring about a noticeable decline in implementation and compliance. These factors seem to have affected Brazil, Cameroon, and Russia.

There are many features of democratic governments that contribute to improved implementation and compliance. Democratic governments are normally more transparent than authoritarian governments, so interested citizens can more easily monitor what their governments are doing to implement and comply with treaties. In democratic governments, it is possible for citizens to bring pressure to bear for improved implementation and compliance. Also, NGOs generally have more freedom to operate in countries with democratic governments. At the same time, however, democratic governments are normally more responsive to public opinion than authoritarian governments. Public opinion is not always supportive of environmental concerns: indeed, the economy is usually the public's greatest concern. Democratic governments allow conflicts about environmental issues to flare. It is probably the case that because of the balance of factors mentioned in this paragraph, democratic governments are more likely to do a better job of implementing and complying with international environmental accords than nondemocratic governments; but this generalization does not always hold, and democratization does not necessarily lead automatically or quickly to improved compliance.

The importance of NGOs has already been mentioned. They play a crucial role in implementation and compliance. They mobilize public opinion and set political agendas. They make information about problems available, sometimes information that governments do not have or would prefer to keep confidential. Often the information they make available is essential to monitoring. They bring pressure on governments directly and indirectly. Because many local and national nongovernmental organizations have connections with NGOs in other countries and INGOs, they are a means of ensuring a uniformity of concern throughout the world. There are also significant transfers of funds among NGOs, so NGOs in poorer countries may have surprisingly extensive resources at their disposal. NGOs have become an instrument for universalizing concern.

Individuals make a crucial difference in the implementation and compliance with treaties. It matters who is the head of state. Brazilian president Fernando Collor took a special interest in the environment, played a major role in having Rio de Janeiro selected as the site for UNCED, and advanced environmental causes within his country. Brazil's compliance with the five treaties improved during his presidency. Russia's prime minister insisted on revealing the Soviet Union's past violations of the London Convention and sought to bring the Russian navy's activities into compliance with the terms of the treaty. Individuals in less exalted positions can also play important roles. Russell Train, as chairman of the U.S. Council on Environmental Quality and administrator of the Environmental Protection Agency, initiated actions within the United States and extended them abroad. He played a crucial role in starting the international momentum in the 1970s. Other individuals through their knowledge, skills, and persistence have played important roles in NGOs. The designation of some heritage sites should clearly be attributed to individuals. Individuals are important also as members of epistemic communities.

The International Environment

The international environment is undoubtedly the most important factor explaining the secular trend toward improved implementation and compliance. Since the Stockholm Conference in 1972, international momentum toward concern for the environment has increased, and it increased sharply starting in the mid-1980s with the publication of the report of the World Commission on Environment and Development, *Our Common Future,* in 1987, and the preparations for the 1992 UNCED meeting in Rio de Janeiro.

The Rio conference was a massive event. It was the largest gathering of leaders of countries in history. It brought together an unprecedented number of NGOs. Significantly, thanks to a decision taken in Working Group III of the Preparatory Commission for UNCED, improving implementation and compliance with international environmental accords was specifically addressed at the conference.

Increased salience for environmental issues was one aspect of the international momentum that developed. The increased salience roused public opinion and mobilized both national and international nongovernmental organizations, and public opinion and NGOs put increased pressure on governments to deal with environmental issues, which enhanced implementation and compliance.

Another aspect of international momentum was that more and more treaties were signed and more and more countries became parties to these treaties. This increase had an effect on implementation and compliance. Governments did not want their countries to be seen as laggards. Moreover, there are practical economic consequences. Once it became apparent that the major countries would stop producing and consuming chlorofluorocarbons, other countries did not want to deal with outmoded technologies. Finally, in the case of a treaty like CITES, it is easier for a government to attempt to enforce its obligations if all of the neighboring countries are also parties.

Figure 10.2 attempts to portray this more nuanced picture of how factors within countries and the international environment affect implementation and compliance. A country's physical conditions, its history, and its culture establish basic parameters that affect implementation and compliance. The economy, political institutions, and public opinion have an effect, but it is generally indirect. These factors operate through proximate variables. In our view, the most important proximate variables are administrative capacity, leadership, NGOs, knowledge and information, and epistemic communities. All these factors, of course, are shaped by the country's preexisting traditions, legislation, and regulations in the area involved. Finally, the international environment, especially in the form of international momentum, is also a proximate variable. And it has been exceedingly important.

What prescriptions do these findings suggest? They underscore the importance of the underlying strength and health of national political-economic systems for efforts to protect the global environment. The strength and health of national political-economic systems are the most important factors; thus, long-term strategies must squarely focus on these issues, as indeed Agenda 21 does. In the shorter run, engaging national leaders in the

Figure 10.2   Factors That Contribute to Lessening or Improving National Compliance with International Environmental Accords

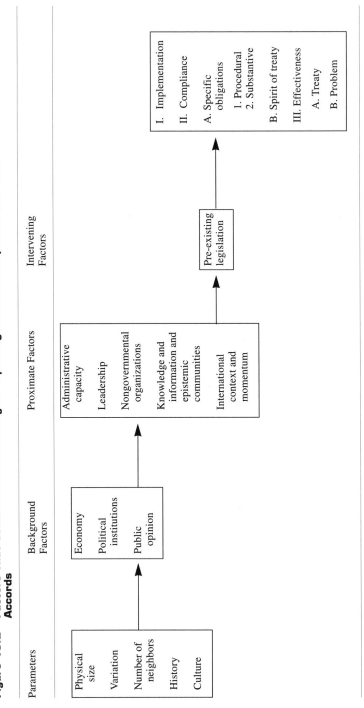

effort to protect and improve the global environment will make a difference. Strengthening national bureaucracies charged with responsibilities for environmental management, supporting international and national nongovernmental organizations that focus on environmental issues, and building epistemic communities all will help. Maintaining and increasing the international momentum for the protection and improvement of the environment is crucial for both its own effects and the stimulus it provides for all the other factors that are important.

Notes

1. Edith Brown Weiss, Daniel B. Magraw, and Paul C. Szasz, *International Environmental Law: Basic Instruments and References* (New York: Transnational Publishers, 1992).

2. Materials on the enforcement of domestic environmental law that are relevant include Keith Hawkins, *Environment and Enforcement* (Oxford: Clarendon Press; New York: Oxford University Press, 1984); and Clifford Russell, Winston Harrington, and William Vaughan, *Enforcing Pollution Control Laws* (Washington, D.C.: Resources for the Future, 1986).

3. See especially David A. Kay and Harold K. Jacobson, eds., *Environmental Protection: The International Dimension* (Totawa, N.J.: Allenheld, Osmun, 1983); Robert O. Keohane, *After Hegemony: Cooperation and Discord in the World Political Economy* (Princeton: Princeton University Press, 1984); Oran R. Young, *Resource Regimes: Natural Resources and Social Institutions* (Berkeley: University of California Press, 1982).

4. See Elinor Ostrom, *Governing the Commons: The Evolution of Institutions for Collective Action* (Cambridge: Cambridge University Press, 1990); and the special issue of *Evaluation Review* edited by Steven Rayner devoted to managing the commons, *Evaluation Review: A Journal of Applied Social Research* 15, no. 1 (February 1991).

5. U.S. Government Accounting Office, *International Environment: International Agreements Are Not Well Monitored*, GAO/RCED 92–43 (January 1992).

6. "Survey of Existing International Agreements and Instruments and Its Follow Up," report by the secretary-general of the United Nations Conference on Environment and Development, A/Conf. 151/PC/103 and Addendum 1 (1992). See also the follow-up, expanded version of the study, Peter H. Sand, ed., *The Effectiveness of International Environmental Agreements: A Survey of Existing Instruments* (Cambridge, England: Grotius, 1992).

7. Peter H. Sand, *Lessons Learned in Global Environmental Governance* (Washington: World Resources Institute, 1990).

8. Jesse H. Ausubel and David G. Victor, "Verification of International Environmental Agreements," *Annual Review of Energy and the Environment* 17 (1992): 1–43.

9. David Lewis Feldman, "Institutions for Managing Global Climate Change," *Global Environmental Change* 2 (1992): 43–58. See also Peter M. Morrisette, Joel Darmstadter, Andrew J. Plantinga, and Michael A. Toman, "Prospects for a Global Greenhouse Gas Accord," *Global Environmental Change* 1 (1991): 209–223. Although the article looks at the process of reaching the agreement, the process has implications for implementation.

10. U.S. Government Accounting Office, *International Environment;* and "Survey of Existing International Agreements."

11. Peter M. Haas, *Saving the Mediterranean: The Politics of International Environmental Cooperation* (New York: Columbia University Press, 1990).

11

Jurisdiction: Changing Patterns of Authority over Activities and Resources

D. W. Bowett

Jurisdiction is a manifestation of state sovereignty. It has been defined as 'the capacity of a state under international law to prescribe or to enforce a rule of law.'[1] There is, of course, a necessary distinction to be drawn between prescriptive jurisdiction and enforcement jurisdiction. The former embraces those acts by a state, usually in legislative form, whereby the state asserts the right to characterize conduct as delictual. Examples would be the enactment of criminal, civil, commercial codes, or regulations governing tax or currency transactions. The latter embraces acts designed to enforce the prescriptive jurisdiction, either by way of administrative action such as arrest or seizure or by way of judicial action through the courts or even administrative agencies of a state. The relationship between the two kinds of jurisdiction is reasonably clear. There can be no enforcement jurisdiction unless there is prescriptive jurisdiction; yet there may be a prescriptive jurisdiction without the possibility of an enforcement jurisdiction, as, for example, where the accused is outside the territory of the prescribing state and not amenable to extradition. Thus, jurisdiction hinges, fundamentally, on the power to prescribe and it is on this aspect of jurisdiction that this essay will concentrate.

A further distinction, common to most legal systems is that between civil and criminal jurisdiction. Assuming that international law contains rules governing the exercise of jurisdiction by states (a matter to be discussed below), the question then arises whether such rules vary according to whether the jurisdiction is civil or criminal. It is on this question that the views of writers differ.

D.W. Bowett, "Jurisdiction: Changing Patterns of Authority Over Activities and Resources," in R. St. J. Macdonald and Douglas Johnston (eds.), *Structure and Process of International Law,* The Hague: Martinus Nijhoff Publishers. Reprinted with kind permission from Kluwer Law International and the author.

It is, of course, true that whereas in matters of crime the courts of a state will always apply the law of that state, in civil matters the 'proper' law to be applied under the rules of the conflict of laws may well be the law of a foreign state. Nevertheless, this difference can scarcely be a sound basis for governing the civil and criminal jurisdictions by different rules of international law, for to concentrate on that one difference is to overlook other important factors.

The first is that, even in litigation between private parties in which the court applies the rules of the conflict of laws, the selection of the proper law is determined by the *lex fori,* the procedure is governed by the *lex fori,* and the rules of public policy of the forum will override. Thus the civil law of the forum, though not necessarily the exclusive law, still influences the outcome of the case.

More important is the consideration that the labels 'criminal' or 'civil' may not accurately reflect any real distinction in the degree to which the prescribing state is exercising its prerogative powers to control conduct. Thus, to take the well-known example of the United States anti-trust legislation, proceedings under sections 1 and 2 of the Sherman Act are manifestly criminal, resulting in fines and imprisonment. In contrast, the proceedings under section 4 are equitable, and those under section 7 of the Sherman Act or section 4 of the Clayton Act for triple damages are civil actions. Yet they all stem from a uniform, regulatory policy by the United States, with effects regarded as coercive by defendants and disobedience to court orders being treated as contempt punishable by criminal sanctions. Thus, the formalistic labelling of certain proceedings as criminal, and others as civil, simply conceals the similarity in nature and purpose of the different legislative provisions. This similarity in purpose between the civil and criminal actions has been frankly recognized by United States authorities. As was stated on behalf of the US Government in testimony before the US Congress Subcommittee on International Economic Policy and Trade on 3 August 1978: 'The basic purposes underlying the private remedies in the Clayton Act are deterrence and compensation. We believe that in the context of the damage remedy these objectives work together to promote a competitive economy. Private damage actions under the Clayton Act supplement the Federal Government's limited enforcement capacity.'[2]

It is suggested, therefore, that what matters is not whether the jurisdiction is civil or criminal, but rather whether the jurisdiction is a manifestation of state policy, designed to confer on the state control over activities or resources to the extent necessary to pursue that policy. The remaining question is whether international law has the function of regulating state jurisdiction and, if so, what rules or principles of international law govern this regulation.

Applicability of Rules of International
Law to Regulate Claims to Jurisdiction

The application of international law to regulate claims to criminal jurisdiction is generally conceded. Indeed, in the case of the *S.S. Lotus* the Permanent Court of International Justice had no hesitation in assuming this general proposition, and the case proceeded on the basis that Turkey's enforcement jurisdiction depended on its prescriptive jurisdiction, and that in turn depended upon such jurisdiction being consistent with international law.[3]

The argument over the application of international law centres around the civil jurisdiction. Mann has argued that there is no essential difference between the competence of a state in criminal matters and the competence in civil matters, that it is the function of international law to prescribe the limits within which a state's rules of private international law may operate (though not the content of those rules), and that the essential criterion should be whether, on the relevant facts, the matter belongs within a jurisdiction because it has a genuine link or close connection with that jurisdiction. Indeed, he regards the issue as inseparable from that of recognition of foreign judgments, and suggests that a foreign judgment may be recognized and enforced precisely because it is a judgment based on a jurisdiction conceded to the courts of the state by the rules of public international law.[4]

For other writers the relevance of public international law is either minimal, or nil, or different than in the case of criminal jurisdiction.[5] This last view is developed by Akehurst, and he demonstrates that civil jurisdiction is frequently assumed on the basis of temporary presence of the defendant, presence of assets (*forum patrimonii*), nationality, domicile or residence, showing little real connection with the forum, but without protest from other states. This may well be true. There may well be evidence that states have not, in practice, insisted upon jurisdiction being backed by evidence of a real connection with the state asserting jurisdiction, however desirable that may be as a rational rule. However, such practice does not, of itself, prove that the rules of public international law have no relevance to civil jurisdiction. While one may concede that the relevance of public international law may be different in criminal and civil matters, that is not to say that it does not exist in civil matters. The argument made here, which is believed to be consistent with Mann's approach, is that where the civil jurisdiction of the state is an instrument of state policy, used as a means of exercising control over activities or resources in the interests of the state, then in principle such jurisdiction ought to be subject to the same governing rules of international law. This would not affect areas of civil jurisdiction concerned solely with the enforcement of private rights. These areas would remain very much within the discretion of the state, asserting jurisdiction largely free of the control of rules of public international law and without protest from foreign states.

The Identification of the Applicable Rules

The general tendency in the literature on jurisdiction is to identify the rules governing jurisdiction in the form of the principles on which jurisdiction is commonly based. These merit some discussion because, as will be seen later, the question which has to be raised is whether these principles do serve satisfactorily as the basis of jurisdiction, or as the basis upon which to determine the propriety of jurisdiction as between different states.

(a) *The Territorial Principle.* This principle may be regarded as the most fundamental of all principles governing jurisdiction. Indeed, the proposition that a state has the right to regulate conduct within its territory would be regarded as axiomatic.

The dynamism and adaptability of the principle in recent years has been quite remarkable. It was recognized, long ago, that the convenient way to handle the jurisdiction over mobile things like ships or aircraft was to link them to a territory, the territory in which they were registered, and this same approach has served more recently for space-vehicles.[6] However, more remarkable has been the way in which the newer problems arising from activities considered to be generally injurious to the community of states have been handled very largely by reference to the territorial principle, and to a lesser extent by the principle of nationality (or personality). Thus, genocide,[7] apartheid,[8] pirate-broadcasting,[9] and the various aspects of terrorism such as hijacking,[10] crimes against internationally-protected persons,[11] and the taking of hostages,[12] and the broad range of terrorist acts covered by the 1977 Terrorist Convention[13] have been dealt with, not by reference to any 'universalist' principle by analogy with piracy, but by relying on the established principles of jurisdiction, principally the territorial principle.

The European Convention on the Suppression of Terrorism is a particularly good example. Articles 6 and 7 provide for an essentially territorial jurisdiction. The utilization of this basic principle in the United Kingdom's implementing legislation, the Suppression of Terrorism Act of 1978, demonstrates how adaptable, with the use of fictions, this basic principle can be. Under section 4 of the Act, acts done in any other convention country are, for purposes of jurisdiction, treated as if done in the United Kingdom: that is the first territorial 'fiction.' There is yet a more sophisticated fiction in section 4(3) in that a national of a convention country (but not a national of the UK) who commits an act in a non-convention country which would be treated as an offence in a convention country may also be deemed to have committed an offence in the United Kingdom: so we have double-transfer of the location of the act, by fiction. It produces a very far-reaching jurisdiction which is in reality extra-territorial but which is treated as territorial by agreement.

It is equally clear that states have relied essentially on the territorial principle to support the jurisdiction necessary to protect their interests in resources actually located outside their territory but conceded by international law to be within the control of the state. The continental shelf doctrine, for example, developed as an assertion of jurisdictional rights, not an assertion of new territorial rights. The 1958 Geneva Convention on the Continental Shelf conceded to the coastal state exclusive sovereign rights for the purpose of exploring and exploiting the shelf resources: Article 77(1) of the Draft Convention on the Law of the Sea (Informal Text) uses exactly the same formula. The manner in which states actually exercised the necessary jurisdiction to assert those exclusive rights was not prescribed by the international texts, but was left to the states, in their discretion. What has commonly been done, as exemplified by the UK Continental Shelf Act of 1964, is to legislate for activities within the shelf limits and, so far as the enforcement jurisdiction is concerned, treat acts or omissions within the shelf area as if they had been committed on the coastal state's own territory. Again, the device is a fiction, but it depends upon the virtual assimilation of shelf and territory for jurisdictional purposes.

With regard to the new concept of the economic zone, the jurisdictional pattern which is emerging is that states will extend throughout the 200 mile zone the legislation previously applied to regulate fisheries or pollution within the territorial sea. This follows the same assimilation of the economic zone and territory, or territorial waters, for the limited jurisdictional purposes which are consistent with the coastal state's rights within the zone. It may be expected that control over activities on artificial islands will follow equally closely the pattern of assimilation adopted for continental shelf installations: they will be treated like territory. The broad assimilation of all these maritime zones with territory adopted by Sri Lanka in 1976 for example, simply extends all relevant territorially-based legislation to the new zone, thus avoiding any serious risk of a jurisdictional gap. The formula used is the following: '... all written laws in force in Sri Lanka shall be read and construed as though the applicability of such laws, wherever relevant, extends to the limits of the contiguous zone, the exclusive economic zone, the continental shelf, or the pollution prevention zone, as the case may be.'[14]

The application of the territorial principle, whether with or without the fictions just described, has always faced the difficulty that proscribed conduct may consist of not merely one but rather a series of acts. In the situation in which some acts occur inside, and some outside the territory, the state will then have to decide whether a crime has been committed within its territory. The general tendency, which accords with common sense, is to ascertain whether one of the constituent elements of the crime has been committed within its territory. This test is reflected in article 693 of the

French Code d'instruction criminelle: 'Est reputée commise sur le territoire de la République, toute infraction dont l'acte caractérisant un de ses éléments constitutifs a été accompli en France.'

There is a quite different situation where a state assumes jurisdiction because the conduct of a party produces 'effects' within its territory. For here there is no suggestion that a part of the conduct constituting the offence occurred within the territory, as in the situation described above: it is conceded, as it were, that all the conduct occurred abroad. The justification for the jurisdiction lies in the view that, where the effects are produced within the territory, the party whose conduct abroad produced those effects is legitimately subjected to the jurisdiction. It is on this basis that the jurisdiction assumed by the United States to give effect to its anti-trust legislation is justified. The US Supreme Court in the celebrated Alcoa case was quite clear that it was dealing with 'conduct outside its borders that has consequences within its borders ...'[15] Subsequent decisions have restated and endorsed the 'effects' doctrine and the validity of jurisdiction on such a basis has in recent years been strengthened by its adoption by Germany and the EEC. Whether the exercise of jurisdiction on this basis can be kept within limits which would safeguard the interests of other states is a difficult question to which we must devote considerably more attention below.

(b) *The Nationality (or Personality) Principle.* There is general agreement with the basic proposition that a state may prescribe for the conduct of its own nationals abroad. Even on its face, however, the proposition requires qualification, for there must be limits on the power of the state of nationality to require conduct on the part of one of its nationals within the territory of another state. One limit which is generally recognized is that the state cannot require conduct illegal under the *lex loci delicti commissi.* However, the idea that a national is subject to the law of his own state *in general* encounters an objection which is much more broadly-based than the specific limit that illegal conduct cannot be required of him. For there is inherent in the notion of a state's domestic jurisdiction, and its counterpart—the principle of nonintervention—the idea that certain matters are only properly regulated by the territorial state. To take an extreme example, for the state of nationality to require its nationals riding motor-scooters to wear crash-helmets, even when driving abroad, strikes one as a manifest absurdity. The objection would not be that the conduct would be illegal abroad, for it is unlikely that it would be, but rather that traffic regulation is patently a territorial power, and there can be no warrant for state A attempting to regulate even the conduct of its own nationals with regard to road traffic in the territory of state B.

The difficulty lies in defining this broader limit. The US Restatement suggests a state may not 'direct a national to engage in activities without regard to harmful consequences to another state.' Yet the substance of the objection is not that there are 'harmful consequences' but rather that the state of nationality is attempting to regulate matters which properly lie within the domestic jurisdiction of another state. Mann seeks to resolve the difficulty by reference to concepts of the 'proper law,' or a 'genuine link,' in the sense that the question to be posed is whether, on the facts, the matter belongs to one jurisdiction or another. In his words, 'The problem, properly defined, involves the search for the state or states whose contact with the facts is such as to make the allocation of legislative competence just and reasonable.'[16]

In this sense, the link of nationality may become no more than prima facie evidence that the person's conduct is properly the concern of the state of nationality. This approach would fit with the tendency to assume jurisdiction over persons who, though not nationals, nevertheless have a residence in a state. In fact many states do levy taxes on the basis of residence, or apply currency regulations to residents,[17] or even military service obligations.[18] Such jurisdiction may appear to be based on the territorial principle, but in reality it is not, for the obligations imposed often bear on the person while abroad. In reality the resident is assimilated to the national because, for the purposes of the particular legislation in question, the resident's links with the state are as close as those of a national.

The situation in which a corporation is deemed to be within the jurisdiction because of the presence there of an affiliate is quite different. For here the defendant corporation is neither a national, nor a resident in the true sense: the corporate separation is disregarded so as to treat the residence of the affiliate as if it were the residence of the defendant. The United Kingdom has opposed the validity of this basis of jurisdiction in its Aide-Mémoire to the EEC Commission in 1969, saying "the separate legal personalities of a parent company and its subsidiary should be respected. Such concepts as 'enterprise entity' and 'reciprocating partnership' when applied for the purpose of asserting personal jurisdiction over a foreign parent company by reason of the presence within the jurisdiction of a subsidiary (and a foreign subsidiary by reason of the presence of its parent company) are contrary to sound legal principle in that they disregard the distinction of personality between parent and subsidiary."[19]

The position is highly controversial. US courts have, for purposes of antitrust legislation, assumed jurisdiction over foreign corporations by reason of the presence of a subsidiary (albeit separate corporate person) within the USA.[20] The essential inquiry, however, is to see whether the foreign corporation is doing business within the United States, via the agency of its subsidiary, so the answer may well turn on the degree of control exercised by the foreign parent. There would seem to be little objection to the state assuming jurisdiction over the conduct of business within its territory. What is not so clear is why this cannot be done by exercising jurisdiction over the local subsidiary or affiliate, without involving the foreign parent company.

Somewhat related problems arise in relation to the assumed power to compel a US corporation to produce documents belonging to a foreign parent or subsidiary, and located abroad;[21] or, indeed to compel a foreign corporation to produce documents located abroad.[22]

However, it can be seen that in relation to corporations, although the jurisdiction of the state of nationality, or incorporation, is clear, there are bound to be problems when this is extended to foreign corporations, ignoring the separation of legal personality, because of evidence of control. The problems obviously diminish when the purpose of the jurisdiction is to regulate the conduct of business by a foreign corporation *within* the state, for there the state can rely upon the territorial principle.

The justification for jurisdiction based upon the passive nationality principle is by no means so clear as in the case of active nationality, for in what circumstances does an injury, civil or criminal, to a national of a state constitute a sufficient concern to the state that it is justified in asserting jurisdiction over it?

The outright rejection of the principle of passive nationality by the US Restatement stands in marked contrast to its rather broad reception elsewhere in civil matters,[23] and its extension in recent years in criminal matters.[24] Thus, the present discordant practice on this aspect of jurisdiction reflects the absence of any clear consensus about the purpose to be served by jurisdiction. In the sphere of civil law it offers to nationals the convenience of suit before their own domestic courts, but may otherwise be highly inconvenient to the foreigner, and even sterile if the foreigner has no assets within the jurisdiction. In the sphere of criminal law it is a claim to jurisdiction which appears weak in comparison to the claim of the territorial state and, indeed, its main justification may be seen in situations, such as crimes aboard aircraft, where the need is seen as being to confer a multiplicity of jurisdictions because of the risk that otherwise no state will exercise jurisdiction.

(c) *The Protective Principle.* There is no doubt of the validity of this principle. What is in issue is its scope. At the core of the principle lies the idea that a state is entitled to protect its security by means of the exercise of its jurisdiction and, understandably, the principle therefore has its primary application in the domain of the criminal law, for conduct threatening the state's security will usually be so serious as to qualify as a criminal act. Commonly, therefore, the principle justifies jurisdiction in respect of political offences such as espionage, sedition, counterfeiting of currency, perjury in relation to official documents such as visas, or attacks against embassies and consulates abroad. There can be little doubt, in this day and age, that a state's security is economic as well as political, so that conduct posing a real threat to a state's economy could be subjected to the state's jurisdiction: indeed, the long-established offence of counterfeiting of currency bears out the legitimacy of extending the principle to conduct with economic consequences.

The doubts relating to the scope of the principle are really two. The first is that states may claim such jurisdiction in relating to conduct which is not generally regarded as criminal at all. It is for this reason that the US Restatement, in defining the principle, adds the proviso 'provided the conduct is generally recognized as a crime under the law of states that have reasonably developed legal systems.[25] The second is that the offences may be so vaguely and broadly defined as to confer a jurisdiction which may not only far exceed that commonly claimed by states but also, because of their vagueness, establish offences which an accused person may not realize he is committing. A prime example is article 161(2) of the Turkish Penal Code which renders liable to imprisonment 'whoever, in time of peace, spreads or relates unfounded or intentional rumours or news so as to cause the excitement and unrest of the public, or engages in activities harmful to national interests '[26] The provision is not confined to nationals, nor to acts committed within Turkey. It is patently impossible for any individual to decide in advance what conduct might be deemed by the Turkish authorities to be harmful to the 'national interests.'

(d) *The Principle of Universality.* By virtue of this principle *all* states would have jurisdiction to try and punish for certain crimes. There are, however, two categories of crimes which should be distinguished. The first is the category which includes crimes under international law, by which is meant those acts or omissions which may be deemed criminal not by reference to some municipal penal code, but simply by reference to international law. The clearest, and non-controversial, illustration of such a crime is piracy: for centuries there has been a true, universal jurisdiction over piracy. This sufficiently indicates the rationale of the jurisdiction. It lies in the view that there exists an accepted, international public policy which regards pirates as *hostes humani generis* and justifies any state in asserting jurisdiction over them.

Beyond piracy, however, the matter is less clear. War crimes are certainly crimes against international law, but it is by no means clear that they are subject to universal jurisdiction. The jurisdiction has been traditionally that of a belligerent power, and the exercise of jurisdiction by Israel in the *Eichmann case* stands out as highly unusual, and probably unfounded. The objection to allowing states generally—neutrals as opposed to belligerents—to assume jurisdiction is really three-fold. First, whereas all nations (or at least all maritime nations) have a real and even commercial interest in having the sea-lanes kept free of pirates, there is no comparable interest in a neutral power to see war criminals punished. Second, the warships of all nations have the right to apprehend pirates on the high seas, so the state asserting jurisdiction will commonly be the state which, because the arrest was effected by its own warship, has the requisite proof to sustain an indictment for piracy. In contrast, the requisite proof for war crimes will be likely to lie either with a belligerent power or the state on whose territory the crime was committed. Third, there will be a strong 'political' element in many war crimes trials, and there must be a risk of this influencing the actions of the state assuming jurisdiction. For example, if the *Eichmann* precedent is valid, why should not Sweden, or Poland, or Yugoslavia indict some former American serviceman for alleged war-crimes in Vietnam? The general antipathy in those countries to the whole American involvement in Vietnam may well serve to prompt the prosecuting authorities to take action and to prejudice any subsequent trial.

The view that the 1949 Geneva Conventions provide for universal jurisdiction, though sometimes asserted, is probably incorrect. For the obligation imposed on all contracting parties to enact municipal legislation so as to make grave breaches of the conventions punishable is *not* the assertion of a universal jurisdiction but merely the provision of the legislative basis for jurisdiction in the event that the contracting party is involved in hostilities as a belligerent.

No universal jurisdiction is provided for in the Genocide Convention and, although some writers take a different view, the better construction of the new conventions dealing with terrorism and apartheid is that they, too, do not sanction a universal jurisdiction. The 1973 Apartheid Convention, for example, provides in article IV that the parties shall prosecute and punish 'in accordance with their jurisdiction.'[27] This therefore relies on the existing heads of jurisdiction and does not make a new category of universal jurisdiction.

Hijacking is another new international crime and in many ways analogous to piracy. Certainly it may be said to injure the interests of states generally in a material, tangible way. Yet, though there is some support for the view that this is a true case of universal jurisdiction, the jurisdictional provisions in article 4 of the 1970 ICAO Hijacking Convention are far from clear.[28] Joyner takes the view that: 'The Hague Convention neither explicitly recognizes aerial hijackings as an offense against customary international law, nor does it specify that states should have universal jurisdiction over offenders.'[29] It would, indeed, be surprising if hijacking were truly a case of universal jurisdiction, for many states have declined to treat it as a crime, or to adhere to the ICAO Convention; it thus lacks the endorsement of universal consent which one would expect to find in a crime for which international public policy concedes universal jurisdiction.

A second, and quite separate category of offences includes those crimes under municipal law (not international law) for which all municipal legal systems make provision. With this category the underlying rationale for universal jurisdiction is that, being crimes which all nations recognize, there is a universal interest in punishing such crimes and maintaining a community-interest in the maintenance of law and order. The idea is by no means new, and harks back to a thesis supported by Grotius[30] and other early writers. Despite its superficial attractions, the thesis neither finds general support in state practice, nor does it commend itself as a very practical proposition. For it overlooks the very real difficulties of criminal trial outside the territory of the state where the crime is committed: difficulties of of language. The idea is much more an argument for extradition than for universal jurisdiction.

Thus, whatever its initial appeal, there are good reasons for not expanding the jurisdictions of states based on the principle of universality.

Purpose and Utility of Rules on Jurisdiction

However trite it may seem, the question of the purpose and utility of the rules or principles on jurisdiction summarized above, needs to be answered. The answer cannot be that these rules serve to indicate *the* state which ought to exercise jurisdiction. For, generally speaking, situations of concurrent jurisdiction are normal enough, so the propriety of a given state exercising jurisdiction is rarely raised in an absolute sense. It is more commonly raised in a relative sense, in the form of a question whether jurisdiction ought to be exercised by state A rather than state B—without disputing that both states can invoke one or other of the principles of jurisdiction to support their claim. Nor can it be supposed that the question is resolved by the simple fact of which state has custody over the accused or can serve a writ on some person within the jurisdiction, so that the better claim is automatically the claim of the state which is in a position to prosecute or sue. For this ignores the fact that, in criminal matters, some states try in absentia. More important, it ignores the fact that jurisdiction over corporations, or in civil matters, will not turn on the simple question of where the accused is physically to be found for purposes of service. For artificial persons exist in many different jurisdictions, and, for purposes of civil jurisdiction over the individual, even the location of his assets may found jurisdiction.

Thus, one is forced to face the question of how to decide whether state A or B has the better claim to jurisdiction. It may, of course, be objected that, given the prevalence of concurrent jurisdiction, there is no need to decide: let both states assert jurisdiction. The objection to this solution is not self-evident. Certainly the objection cannot be that concurrent jurisdiction causes inconvenience to private parties. For the occurrence of concurrent jurisdiction is very common, and in many cases perfectly justifiable. No one would regard the concurrent jurisdiction of flag state and coastal state over a vessel exercising innocent passage as unjustifiable. Yet perhaps the key to this lies in the fact that the jurisdiction of the coastal state is defined and limited to what is necessary to protect its own interest. Nor do large trading companies or multinational corporations regard it as extraordinary or unjustifiable that their activities may be subjected to the jurisdiction of several states, provided these are states in which they actually trade or operate. The real objection, it is submitted, lies in the quite different consideration that the jurisdiction assumed by state A may involve unwarranted interference in matters which have little or nothing to do with state A and are more properly the concern of state B and therefore more properly left to its jurisdiction.

If this is so, it brings us back to a concern about state interests rather than private interests, and the question remains: by what criteria does one assess the propriety of the jurisdiction of state A as against that of state B?

One approach might be to see whether the jurisdiction in question is established on one or other of the recognized principles. That is to say, is it territorial, personal, protective or universal by the standards to be found in state practice? This approach is unlikely to be profitable for two reasons. First, these principles are variously applied by states so there is no uniform standard of application to which reference can be made. Indeed, it is likely that some precedent in state practice could always be found for quite extreme claims to jurisdiction. However, the main reason why this approach is unlikely to be profitable is that it will not answer the crucial question of propriety. Let us assume, for purposes of argument, that state A's claim to jurisdiction can be supported by reference to principle and precedent. This does not necessarily mean that such claim to jurisdiction ought properly to be asserted as against state B, for the test tells us nothing about the degree to which the interests of either state are affected. State A, for example, may well be able to show that, using the 'effects' doctrine, it has territorial jurisdiction. Yet what we need to know is whether these effects are substantial enough that, bearing in mind the interests of state B, this jurisdiction by state A ought to be exercised.

It is suggested, therefore, that rather than rely on the established principles or rules of jurisdiction, one has to go back to the far more basic principles of law which govern relations between states and, of these, there are three that appear relevant.

(a) *Equality of States.* The doctrine of sovereign equality obviously has implications for jurisdiction. The recent formulation of the 'principle of equal rights' in the 1970 Declaration on Principles of International Law concerning Friendly Relations and Cooperation among States suggests something of the kind of limitations on jurisdiction which might result from this doctrine. It refers to the right of states 'freely to determine, without external interference ... their political status and to pursue their economic, social and cultural development ...' This implies, however vaguely, that for state A to assert a jurisdiction which interferes with the political, social or economic development of state B is to exceed the limits of propriety and permissibility. It may also imply a condition of reciprocity in the sense that it would offend against the principle of equality if state A were to assume a jurisdiction it was not prepared to concede to state B.

(b) *The Principle of Non-intervention.* In the terms of the 1970 Declaration: 'No state ... has the right to intervene, directly or indirectly, for any reason whatever, in the internal or external affairs of any other state ...

Every state has an inalienable right to choose its political, economic, social and cultural systems without interference in any form by another state.' This, as with the principle of equality, suggests similar limits to jurisdiction, for the principle of nonintervention is breached by an assertion of jurisdiction which interferes with another state's political, economic, social or cultural system.

(c) *The Principle of Territorial Integrity*. Again, in the terms of the 1970 Declaration, 'Every state has the duty to refrain in its international relations from the threat or use of force against the territorial integrity or political independence of any state ...' This principle has more limited relevance, since problems of jurisdiction rarely involve the use or threat of force. Yet the principle is relevant to the prohibition against one state exercising its enforcement jurisdiction, as by making an arrest or seizing property to enforce a judgment, within the territory of another state without its consent.

However, many types of enforcement jurisdiction will not involve the use or threat of force. The service of process or of a subpoena, the carrying out of investigations, the making of orders for discovery of documents, though they may well take the form of a judicial action, may be of questionable validity not because they involve any threat of force, but rather because they are contrary to the broader principle of nonintervention. This, essentially, was the view taken by the House of Lords *In re Westinghouse Electricity Corporation Uranium Contract Litigation*.[31] It would be perfectly normal for an English Court to give effect to letters rogatory issued by a foreign court: the Evidence (Proceedings in Other Jurisdictions) Act 1975, which gave effect to the 1970 Hague Convention on the taking of evidence in civil or commercial matters, so provided. Yet the evidence showed that it was the intention of the US authorities to convert the evidence so acquired to use as the basis for a criminal prosecution, that is to say, to extend the US Grand Jury investigation extra-territorially into the United Kingdom to ascertain the conduct of Rio Tinto Zinc within England. This was, in effect, to make the English courts privy to the enforcement of American criminal law.

The Attorney-General argued that this was an infringement of the proper jurisdiction and sovereignty of the United Kingdom. The House of Lords accepted this argument, and Lord Wilberforce neatly summarized the conflict of interest in these terms: 'It is axiomatic that in anti-trust matters the policy of one state may be to defend what it is the policy of another state to attack.'[32] The principle of non-intervention, therefore, would prohibit what is in effect the exercise of a prerogative, sovereign power by one state in the territory of another. If the jurisdiction is illegal on that basis, then it matters not that the jurisdiction is exercised by a court, or even by seeking to utilize standard techniques of enforcing judgments of one state's courts via the courts of the state in which the unlawful intervention takes place. Mann puts the point forcibly in the following terms: '... a state has no right to enforce in a foreign court any claim which in substance involves the direct or indirect enforcement of a prerogative right of the enforcing state, or which is made by virtue of the sovereign power ... The crux of the matter lies in the fact that the enforcing state requires compliance with its sovereign demands in foreign countries where its writ does not run and where it cannot be made to run by clothing it into the form of judgments of courts, whether they be its own or those of a foreign country.'[33]

It seems, therefore, that of the three applicable principles the most crucial and fundamental principle is that of non-intervention. The application of this principle is by no means a simple matter, producing clear-cut answers. The very breadth and vagueness of the principle means that its application to a specific problem will require a good deal of judgment and subjective interpretation. Moreover, as suggested above, in many cases the question will not be posed in terms of whether a state's claim to jurisdiction is illegal per se, but of whether it is a 'proper' jurisdiction given the conflicting interests, and claims to jurisdiction, of two or more states. In short, the problem may be the more delicate one of balancing interests rather than of applying the broad principle of non-intervention to the specific facts and producing a clear-cut answer.

The Balancing of Interests as a Technique to Determine the Propriety of Jurisdiction

The area of anti-trust legislation offers a prime example of highly-controversial jurisdiction in which a balancing of interests becomes necessary. For, evidently, what is involved is a conflict of interests, or economic policy between states. This is clearly demonstrated in the *Radio Patents Pool cases*.[34] The US sought, by proceedings within the USA, to hold illegal as in restraint of trade the conduct of Canadian firms being subsidiaries of US firms, in forming a 'pool' of their Canadian patents and agreeing not to licence any manufacture under these patents unless the manufacture occurred in Canada and the licensee agreed not to import from the USA. The US economic policy was clear: laissez-faire, open competition free of restraint. Moreover, it was difficult to deny that the US had subject-matter jurisdiction. Yet, equally, the Canadian economic policy was clear: to promote and protect a domestic radio manufacturing industry. Hence the Canadian protest at what was essentially an attempt to deny to Canada the right to determine the economic policies to govern manufacturing in Canada or, conversely, to make US policies prevail in Canada.

This conflict of economic policy occurs not only in cases before the courts, but also in the action taken by US regulatory authorities such as the Securities and Exchange Commission, the Commodity Futures Trading Commission, the Civil Aeronautics Board and the Federal Maritime

Commission. For example, this last body has sought to challenge the 'conference' agreements reached between shipowners, mostly foreign, designed to rationalize shipping services and avoid uneconomic competition. Yet the jurisdictional conflict is by no means confined to the economic sphere. It has also arisen over matters of foreign policy, as when the US asserted extra-territorial reach for its Foreign Assets Control Regulations to enforce trade embargoes against China, or under the Export Control Act of 1949 to enforce embargoes against the Communist bloc generally.

Thus, without calling into question the right of the USA adopt its own economic or political policies, there is a very large question over the extent to which the USA may impose its economic or political views on foreign parties, or subject activities abroad to regulation in order to promote those policies. The highly subjective nature of the policy decisions involved is well illustrated by the contrast between the US boycott of China, Cuba, and the Soviet bloc and the hostile US reaction to the Arab boycott of Israel. The resentment demonstrated by foreign states was understandably directed to the State Department. Given the separation of powers, the Executive could not directly control the reaction of the courts, but the US courts were by no means unaware of this resentment.

There is no doubt that US courts have become increasingly sensitive to the hostility which is felt abroad when, by using the 'effects' doctrine, the US courts assume an extraterritorial reach for their jurisdiction. In the *Alcoa*[35] judgment in 1945, an effect on US commerce, plus the intention to produce that effect, sufficed to found jurisdiction over foreign companies. In later cases, such as the *General Electric case*[36] or the *Swiss Watchmakers case,*[37] the courts have spoken in terms of 'substantial,' or 'substantial and material' effects. Once one presupposes a substantial interest on the part of the US, the assumption of jurisdiction becomes more tolerable. In the making of orders, American courts have been careful to avoid requiring a foreign party to do anything illegal under the law of a foreign state.[38]

Yet to demand proof of a *substantial* effect, or even to avoid requiring conduct illegal under a system of foreign law is scarcely to weigh competing interests. For even though the effect may be substantial in the US, it may be far more substantial abroad, and no state concerned about an intrusion into its own proper sphere of jurisdiction will be satisfied merely by the plea that nothing *illegal* is being required.

There is, however, some evidence that the US courts, and indeed governmental agencies, are prepared to take a much more comprehensive view of the interests to be weighed. In the celebrated *Timberlane case* in 1976 the US Court of Appeals recognized that, over and above the requirement of substantial effect, there had to be a more comprehensive balancing of interests, including that of comity, thus recognizing the international implications of the assertion of jurisdiction over foreign corporations or acts committed abroad. As Haight has written, "*Timberlane* states that, without more, the 'effects' doctrine of Alcoa is incomplete, because it neither considers the interests of other nations, nor expressly takes into account the full nature of the relationship between the actors and the United States.'[39] In the following years, a serious attempt was made to develop the idea of a 'balancing of interests.' In April 1979 the US Court of Appeals in *Mannington Mills v. Congoleum Corp.*[40] dealt with a suit by a private plaintiff against an American corporation, not a foreign company, for activities overseas. The court identified some ten factors relevant to the requisite balancing of interests, namely: (1) Degree of conflict with foreign law or policy; (2) Nationality of the parties; (3) Relative importance of the alleged violation of conduct here compared to that abroad; (4) Availability of a remedy abroad and the pendency of litigation there; (5) Existence of intent to harm or affect American commerce and its foreseeability; (6) Possible effect upon foreign relations if the court exercises jurisdiction and grants relief; (7) If relief is granted, whether a party will be placed in the position of being forced to perform an act illegal in either country or be under conflicting requirements by both countries; (8) Whether the court can make its order effective; (9) Whether an order for relief would be acceptable in this country if made by the foreign nation under similar circumstances; (10) Whether a treaty with the affected nations has addressed the issue.

By letter of 27 September 1979 the State Department lent its weight to the demand for judicial restraint in the assertion of extra-territorial jurisdiction, in a reply to the Senate Committee on the Judiciary.

> Even where there is a basis in international law for exercising jurisdiction, principles of comity often suggest that forbearance is appropriate. Under these principles, states are obliged to consider and weigh the legitimate interests of other states when taking action and could affect those interests, and should leave the regulation of conduct to the state with the primary interest. Thus, our foreign partners expect that in general they have the right to regulate the climate for investment within their territories and to establish energy and competition policies for their own economies and firms. They expect that the United States will not intrude upon these spheres more than is necessary. We can avoid many unnecessary foreign relations frictions by observing these sound principles, which our enforcement agencies and courts recognize and apply. As one federal court recently stated, 'it is evident that at some point the interests of the United States are too weak and the foreign harmony incentive for restraint too strong to justify an extra-territorial assertion of jurisdiction.' Sometimes, however, US interests and foreign interests in the regulation of certain conduct are both significant. In these circumstances. international law establishes standards for reconciling conflicts of jurisdiction. These standards are not mechanistic or inflexible, but require a good deal of judgment in their application.

The question is whether this approach will prove adequate to prevent the conflict of interests over jurisdictional competence, whether between the USA and other states, or indeed between other states. On present evidence it appears that this approach will not suffice, and there are a number of reasons to support this pessimistic view.

First, there is an inherent difficulty in the balancing of interests being undertaken by the courts of one party, for to ask the US courts to strike an impartial balance between the interests of the US and those of a foreign state is to expect too much of the US courts. The same would be true for other national courts.

Second, it has already proved impossible to get a uniform approach to the balancing of interests, even within the United States.[41]

Third, there are difficulties in getting the foreign state's view of its interests presented adequately to the court. Prior to 1978 the US practice was for the foreign government to communicate its views by Note, and for the State Department then to transmit the Note to the appropriate court. Since 1978, however, at the request of the Supreme Court, the practice has been to encourage the foreign government to file an *amicus* brief, and, indeed, the State Department has urged such governments to submit their views through counsel.[42] This procedure is extremely burdensome for foreign governments, for they have to file briefs, and preferably appear through counsel, each and every time their interests are involved. It is certainly more burdensome than a system whereby general guidelines are negotiated at the political level, and the US authorities institute proceedings only within those guidelines. Such a system of course presupposes that the institution of proceedings is controlled by the US authorities, which is not the case at present since private parties may institute antitrust proceedings.

Fourth, there is the clearest possible evidence that foreign governments are not satisfied with the more considerate approach by US courts, involving the balancing of interests. This evidence is to be found in the legislation being adopted by foreign states to 'block' the extra-territorial reach of the American antitrust and similar legislation. This will be briefly summarized in the following section.

Fifth, to leave the matter to the courts is in any event a questionable solution. For the interests to be weighed are not simply legal interests, but highly-complex political, economic and even social interests which may well be better evaluated elsewhere than in a court of law. In any event, to leave the conflict to resolution by a court is, in a sense, to leave it too late. Evidently, if means could be devised to resolve the conflict elsewhere, without putting the parties to the burden of engaging in litigation, that would be a preferable solution.

Blocking Legislation and Similar Tactics

Perhaps inevitably, states offended by the untoward, and in their view improper, reach of the US jurisdiction have sought a means of self-protection, or perhaps retaliation, by the use of their own prescriptive jurisdiction.

The United Kingdom had reacted to the US Federal Maritime Board's extra-territorial jurisdiction over the shipping conferences and their agreements by passing the 1964 Shipping Contracts and Commercial Documents Act, designed principally to protect British shipowners from US demands for the production of documents and other information. The litigation over the Westinghouse Uranium Contract in 1978, and the lack of success of the British attempt to resolve the conflict through political channels, coupled with evidence of an American determination to take even more stringent measures against the shipping conferences, finally prompted the United Kingdom to enact comprehensive blocking legislation in the Protection of Trading Interests Act 1980. This Act is concerned with measures taken or proposed by a foreign state for regulating or controlling international trade in so far as they apply *outside the territorial jurisdiction* of that state. It empowers the Secretary of State to prohibit the production of documents or information to the courts or authorities of a foreign state (s.2), upon penalty of a fine; it restricts the powers of English Courts to make orders under the Evidence (Proceedings in other Jurisdictions) Act 1975, or to enforce overseas judgments under the Foreign Judgments (Reciprocal Enforcement) Act 1933; and it allows a UK national or resident to sue in an English court for recovery of multiple damages paid under the judgment of a foreign court (s.6); and finally, it allows for the enforcement in England of an overseas judgment which allows recovery of multiple damages (s.7).

Other states are following the lead of the United Kingdom. In Australia there are already two Acts prohibiting the production of certain evidence,[43] and further legislation exists to restrict the enforcement of antitrust laws. In New Zealand there is the Evidence Amendment Act of 1980. And in Canada there is a Bill before Parliament similar to the United Kingdom Act of 1980.[44] On 16 July 1980 France passed legislation restricting the communication of records or information to foreign parties.[45]

There seems little doubt that we are witnessing a growing antagonism towards what are regarded as excesses of jurisdiction, particularly in the area of commercial and economic activities. It is, moreover, an antagonism between states which have in other ways tended to move towards closer co-operation in jurisdictional and judicial arrangements. It is a development which must be regretted and, if possible, checked. The question is how this might be done.

The Resolution of Jurisdictional Conflicts

Theoretically, one avenue of approach might be to try to secure agreement on the principles of jurisdiction, and their limits. It is, however, doubtful whether this approach would be fruitful. As indicated earlier, the states accused of excesses are in fact states which apply rather traditional principles.

The United States, for example, is relying essentially on the territorial principle and, to a lesser extent, the nationality principle. It may be suggested that it is not so much the principles which are disputed but their limits, or perhaps more the manner of their application. Thus, in relation to the nationality principle—itself uncontroversial—the problems really arise with corporations; for the US looks to the nationality of the persons who own the stock in the corporation, whereas the UK looks to the nationality of the corporation. Thus, it is the manner of its application rather than the principle itself which is disputed.

Yet even if the effort were directed to seeking agreement on the limits to the principles, or the manner of their application, it is likely that in many cases, particularly where corporations with activities in both states are involved, the conclusion that both states have some legitimate basis for jurisdiction would seem to be almost inevitable. So the question really becomes one of deciding whether, assuming a valid basis for jurisdiction to exist, it would be reasonable or proper for one state to exercise its jurisdiction in a particular way. There may well be quite different answers according to whether one is concerned with the imposition of criminal penalties, or discovery of documents, service of documents, the taking of evidence, or enforcing private rights. Moreover, if the balancing of interests between states is to be thorough and perceptive, it becomes impossible to arrive at such a balance by the application of a set of principles or rules. The principles or rules on which jurisdiction is commonly based—territoriality, personality, protective, universal—cannot, in themselves, provide the necessary balance of interests. Nor, indeed, can the principles of nonintervention or equality. What these principles of law can provide is the legal context within which the many factors have to be assessed. The range of factors already used is, as we have seen, both extensive and different from the principles and rules; and even the category of factors already used should not be regarded as an exclusive or closed category.

Thus, the 'balancing' has to be achieved by the exercise of either judicial or negotiating skills: it cannot be achieved by legislation, whether on the national or international plane, that is, via municipal legislation or a treaty.

As to the choice between using judicial or negotiating skills to achieve the right balance, the experience so far would suggest that the negotiating skills are to be preferred. The process of negotiation should be much more flexible than the use of a judicial process, and eminently more suitable to the area of economic or commercial conflicts of interests. This has been recognized by the US courts. In some cases the 'weighing' of interests advocated in the *Timberlane case* has simply not been attempted[46] and in the US District Court Judge Marshall has stated frankly that 'the judiciary has no expertise or perhaps even authority to evaluate the economic and social policies of foreign governments.'[47]

Some progress would appear to have been made in the direction of negotiation or consultation. For example, Canada and the USA, established an Anti-Trust and Consultation Procedure under the 1959 'understanding.'[48] Australia, too, has agreed in principle in August 1980 to joint consultations with the USA. The OECD, through its Restrictive Business Practices Committee, has also advocated prior consultation as the most appropriate procedure,[49] and has itself begun an intensive study of the jurisdictional problems inherent in the control of restrictive business practices.

In principle, the technique of consultation could be adapted to suit varying degrees of commitment. There could be bilateral consultation without more although this would seem somewhat pointless unless, in the result, the Party threatening to exercise jurisdiction could withdraw the threat as a result of being satisfied during the consultation that, in the light of the interests of the other Party, its exercise of jurisdiction would be improper. There could also be the form of multilateral consultation which one finds in GATT,[50] whereby the 'complainant' and the 'defendant' states support their positions before a Panel of States and ultimately benefit from the collective view of the contracting Parties as a whole. Obviously this would need an organization like GATT or OECD to be effective, but it does have the advantage of subjecting the positions of the two parties directly involved to the scrutiny, and perhaps the more objective evaluation, of a group of interested (though not directly involved) states. Even more advanced, one could envisage consultation between the Parties in the form of a conciliation exercise, with the Parties receiving the advice of the conciliation panel although not strictly bound by it.

Whatever the form of consultation adopted, it will be a somewhat sterile exercise unless, in the result, the parties could modify their intentions with regard to jurisdiction. The difficulty is that, on present evidence, there seems little indication that the United States can modify its intentions.

Assuming that the United States does agree that it ought not to foist its own views about the right way to manage a domestic economy on other states (in itself a questionable assumption) what can be done to introduce a change? The ideal solution would be revision of all the legislation which has produced the extra-territorial reach which has occasioned so much protest: but it may be doubted whether this is a practical course. An alternative would be for the US Department of Justice, or the other regulatory authorities, to modify their policies: so, in effect, they would not institute proceedings against foreign parties unless, as the result of the process of consultation, it was thought proper to do so.

The real problem would lie, however, in the fact that, although the anti-trust legislation is designed to promote governmental policy, its enforcement does not lie solely with the governmental agencies. So long as private suits are possible, and particularly the suits for treble damages that have caused such antagonism, the problem would not be solved merely by a change in the US governmental policies on enforcement. Thus the onus lies on the United States to initiate the necessary changes, internally, and no improvement of techniques of consultation or elaboration of guidelines will do much to resolve these conflicts until the United States is prepared to lay the basis, internally, for an accommodation with foreign states. There is little evidence of a willingness to do this, so conflicts of jurisdiction are likely to remain with us for a long time to come.

Notes

1. American Law Institute, Re-Statement of the Law, Second (1965): Foreign Relations Law of the United States, ch. 1, s. 6, 20.
2. Department of Justice press release, 3 August 1978: repr. in 73 AJIL (1979), 130–131. The Clayton Act of 1914, together with the Federal Trade Commission Act 1914, Suppl. the Sherman Act.
3. PCIJ, Ser. A, no. 10(1927).
4. Mann, "The doctrine of jurisdiction in International Law," RC (1964) I, 44–46 and 73–76.
5. Akehurst, "Jurisdiction in International Law," 46 BYBIL (1972–1973) 170–177.
6. Treaty on Principles governing the Activities of States in the Exploration and Use of Outer Space, art. 8: 61 AJIL (1967), 644.
7. UN Convention on the Prevention and Punishment of the Crime of Genocide, adopted by the GA, 9 December 1948: 78 UNTS 27.
8. UN International Convention on the Suppression and Punishment of the Crime of Apartheid, adopted by the GA, 30 November 1973: 13 ILM (1974), 50. Art. 5 asserts no new basis for GA, jurisdiction but refers simply to trial by a 'competent tribunal of any state party.'
9. The 1965 Agreement on the Prevention of Broadcasts transmitted from Stations outside National Territories, sponsored by the Council of Europe, relies on the territorial and personality principles, providing for punishment of persons within the territory who give aid to, or finance, the actual broadcasters: 4 ILM (1965), 115.
10. Convention for the Suppression of Unlawful Seizure of Aircraft, 16 December 1970: 10 ILM (1971), 133; Convention for the Suppression of Unlawful Acts against Civil Aviation, 23 September 1971: 10 ILM (1971), 1151.
11. UN Convention on the Prevention and Punishment of Crimes against Internationally-Protected Persons, including Diplomatic Agents, adopted by the GA, 14 December 1973: 13 ILM (1974), 41. Art. 3 bases jurisdiction on the principles of territoriality and personality, active and passive.
12. International Convention against the taking of Hostages, adopted by the UN GA, 17 December 1979 (UN Doc. A/34/819 (1979), 5). Art. 5 of this Convention provides for jurisdiction which is either territorial or based on nationality, active and passive.
13. Convention of 27 January 1977: *European Treaty Series,* no. 90.
14. Churchill, Nordquist, Lay, *New Directions in the Law of the Sea,* V, 322.
15. *US* v. *Aluminum Company of America and Others,* 44 F. Suppl. 97; 148 F. 2d. 416.
16. Mann, *Supra* note 4, p. 44.

17. E.g., the UK Exchange Control Act 1947.

18. The US Military Selective Service Act 1971, s. 3 confined military service to resident aliens on an immigrant visa. The earlier Universal Military Training and Service Act 1951 had applied to all resident foreigners, but France protested and in 1943 passed legislation retaliating against Americans: see Rousseau, *Droit international public* (1977), III, 137–141.

19. Cited Brownlie, *Principles of International law* (1979), 310–313.

20. *US* v. *US Alkali Export Assn.* 1946–1947 *Trade Cases,* s. 57, 381 (SDNY 1946); *US* v. *ICI* 100 F. Suppl. 506 (SDNY 1951).

21. An issue in the 1953 *Oil Cartel* Grand Jury Investigation: see Fugate, op. cit., 116.

22. As in the *International Paper case* 72 F. Suppl. 1013 (SDNY 1947).

23. E.g., in France, where art. 14 of the Civil Code confers jurisdiction on French courts over contractual obligations with a French national, even though the contract is made abroad with a non-resident foreigner. For criticism of this provision see Mann, loc. cit., 77; De Winter, 'Excessive Jurisdiction in Private International Law' 17 ICLQ (1968), 706–707.

24. As in the Tokyo Convention on Offences and Certain Other Acts committed on Board Aircraft, 1963: 58 AJIL (1964), 566. Art. 4 confers jurisdiction on a state where the offence has been committed by *or against* a national or permanent resident of that state.

25. US Restatement, s. 33 (1).

26. *Turkish Criminal Code, The American Series of Foreign Penal Codes* (1965).

27. 13 ILM (1974), 50.

28. Art. 4(1) sets out three heads of jurisdiction, i.e., where the offence is committed on an aircraft registered in the state, where the aircraft lands in the state with the offender on board, and where the aircraft is leased to a lessee doing business in or residing in the state. However, para. 2 provides: 'Each Contracting State shall likewise take such measures as may be necessary to establish its jurisdiction over the offence in the case where the alleged offender is present in its territory and does not extradite him ...' If this establishes a universal jurisdiction, what is the point of setting out the narrower heads of jurisdiction in the first paragraph?

29. Joyner, *Aerial Hijacking as an International Crime* (1974), 180.

30. *De Jure Belli ac Pacis,* vol. 2, ch. 21, paras. 3–6.

31. [1978] 2 WLR 81; [1978] 1 All. E.R. 434: and see the *Westinghouse Uranium Contracts Litigation* before the US Court of Appeals, Tenth Circuit, in which the US Court quashed an order for discovery against a Delaware Corporation with its corporate office in Canada. (17 ILM (1978), 77).

32. At p. 448.

33. Loc. cit., 142, 147.

34. *US* v. *General Electric Co.* 170 F. Suppl. 596 (SDNY 1962).

35. 44 F. Suppl. 97; 148.

36. (1949), 82 F. Suppl. 753; (1953), 115 F. Suppl. 835.

37. (1963), *Trade Cases,* s. 77, 414, 457.

38. *US* v. *ICI Ltd.* 105 F. Suppl. 215 (SDNY 1952); *Mannington Mills Inv. v. Congoleum Corp.* 595 F. 2d. 1289; *US* v. *Standard Oil Co. (N.J.)* 1969 *Trade Cases* ss. 72, 742.

39. Proceedings, ASIL (1977), 223.

40. 595 F. 2d. 1287 (3rd Cir. 1979).

41. See the case of *Westinghouse Uranium Contracts Litigation* 17 ILM (1978), 77.

42. See Letter of Mr. Owen, Legal Adviser to the State Department to the Associate Attorney-General, dated 17 March 1980: 74 AJIL (1980), 665.

43. Foreign Proceedings (Prohibition of Certain Evidence) Act 1976: no. 121 of 1976; Foreign Proceedings (Prohibition of Certain Evidence) Amendment Act 1979: no. 13 of 1979.

44. Bill C-41 (1980). Section 8 of this bill also has the very novel 'claw-back' remedy, allowing the Canadian citizen to recover multiple damages awarded in a foreign jurisdiction. Canada had much earlier Statutes protecting business records: i.e., the Business Records Protection Act 1947 (Ontario) and the Business Concerns Records Act 1947 (Québec).

45. Law no. 80-438 (19890), J.O. 1799. See 75 AJIL (1981), 382–386.

46. See *General Atomic Co.* v. *United Nuclear Corporation,* decision of Supreme Court of New Mexico, 29 August 1980; *Dominicus Americana Bohio* v. *Gulf and Western* (1979) 473 F. Suppl. 680.

47. Cited by the Australian Attorney-General, Mr. Peter Durack QC before the Australian Parliament in 1981 during the Second Reading of the Foreign Anti-Trust Judgments (Restriction of Enforcement) Amendment Bill 1981.

48. H.C. Deb. (Canada), 1969, I, 574–575; Henry, 'The US Anti-Trust Laws: a Canadian viewpoint,' 8 *Canadian YBIL* (1970), 249–283, at p. 270.

49. See Recommendation of the OECD Council of 5 October 1967, 8 ILM (1969), 1309.

50. See Dam, *The GATT* (1970), ch. 10; Jackson, 'GATT as an Instrument for the Settlement of Trade Disputes,' *Proceedings, ASIL* (1967), 144.

PART 2.5

International Law as
Operating System:
International
Legal Structures

12

International Dispute Settlement and the Role of International Adjudication

Richard B. Bilder

Some Characteristics of International Adjudication

International adjudication involves the reference of a dispute or group of disputes, by agreement of the parties, to either an *ad hoc* arbitral tribunal or a permanent judicial court for binding decision, normally on the basis of international law. In the case of reference to an arbitral tribunal, the parties by special agreement must usually establish not only the issue to be arbitrated but also the machinery and procedure of the tribunal itself, including the method of selection of the arbitrator or arbitrators. In the case of reference to judicial settlement by a permanent judicial body, such as the International Court of Justice, the machinery and procedure of the tribunal, including the method of selection of the judges of the court, are already established by existing international instruments—such as the Statute and the Rules of the International Court—and the tribunal is already in being.

It is well-established that, absent special agreement, a state is under no international legal obligation to submit a dispute with another state to impartial arbitral or judicial settlement. However, if a state does consent to arbitration or judicial settlement of a dispute with another state, it is bound by that decision and the appropriate tribunal may exercise jurisdiction according to the terms of such consent. A state's consent to adjudication may apply either to a particular existing dispute with another state or to all or particular categories of dispute that may arise in the future; that is, a nation's consent to adjudication may be, and often is, given by agreement in advance.[1] Since a tribunal's jurisdiction to decide a particular dispute is

Reproduced with permission, Richard B. Bilder, "International Dispute Settlement and the Role of Adjudication," in *The International Court of Justice at the Crossroads* 155 (Lori Damrosch, ed., 1987), © The American Society of International Law.

entirely dependent upon the consent of the parties, it will usually, before considering the merits, have to determine that such consent in fact exists.

It is important to remember that adjudication is only one of many possible ways of dealing with international disputes. The usual and accepted methods of peaceful settlement are those listed in Article 33 of the U.N. Charter—negotiation, inquiry, mediation, conciliation, arbitration, judicial settlement, resort to regional agencies or arrangements and resort to U.N. or other international organization dispute-settlement procedures. In essence, this list of methods reflects a spectrum of techniques ranging from so-called "diplomatic means," which give control of the outcome primarily to the parties themselves, to so-called "legal means," such as arbitration or judicial settlement, which give control of the outcome primarily to a third party or parties.

Negotiation is clearly the predominant, usual, and preferred method of resolving disputes and is normally an essential part of any dispute-settlement process, even if other techniques are also involved. Thus, adjudication is often preceded, accompanied by, or arranged through some kind of negotiating process. Moreover, international arbitral or judicial decisions often embody compromises reflecting strong elements of negotiation or mediation among the arbitrators or judges, at least some of whom may see their role as safeguarding the interests or representing the point of view of one or another party. More generally, the various techniques are not mutually exclusive, and a particular process of dispute settlement will often combine different methods. As Professor Schachter points out: "Flexibility and adaptability to the particular circumstances are the essential characteristics of these various procedures. There is little to be gained by seeking to give them precise legal limits or procedural rules as a general matter."[2]

In deciding whether to use adjudication as a way of resolving a particular international dispute, the states involved will have to weigh its advantages and disadvantages against those of alternative available methods.

Is Adjudication Necessary for an Effective Legal Order?

The vision of an international legal order in which all international disputes are subject to binding adjudication has strongly influenced thinking about international law. Not surprisingly, national legal systems have furnished the model for how people think about a legally regulated international society. In national jurisprudential thinking, adjudication has traditionally been accorded a preeminent status among dispute-settlement techniques; indeed, it has generally been assumed that the hallmark and *sine qua non* of an effective domestic legal system is the compulsory settlement of disputes by permanent courts. Consequently, this is the goal many have set for the international legal system as well. Subjecting nations to the rule of law has often been equated with subjecting their behavior to the judgment of impartial international tribunals. For Americans in particular, an historical experience in which courts have played an important role in forging and maintaining an effective federal system has suggested that international courts might play a similar role in helping to establish an effective international system.

By this standard, achievement of an effective legal order remains elusive. As indicated, it is a fundamental principle of international law that no state need submit its disputes to impartial adjudication unless it wishes; unless all states involved in a particular dispute have given their consent, an international arbitrator or court has no jurisdiction to decide the dispute. But states have generally been reluctant to give such consent. While nations often pay lip service to the ideal of judicial settlement, they have in practice referred relatively few significant disputes to impartial tribunals. Much thought has been devoted to ways by which nations may be encouraged to make more use of international courts.[3] But thus far none of these has seemed to work very well.

While there are good arguments for encouraging more use of international adjudication, a brief comment on the role of courts in national legal systems and the supposed analogy between the domestic and international legal orders may be helpful.

First, while adjudication plays a significant role in national legal orders, there is growing evidence that this role is probably different than commonly assumed. Recent studies, at least in the United States, suggest that the great mass of disputes are settled in other ways than by formal court decision. Most disputes never reach the courts. This is particularly the case with disputes between parties who have, and expect to continue, long-term relationships with each other; clearly, such relations might be disrupted by resort to the courts. Moreover, most disputes that do reach the courts are settled before the court reaches a final decision. And even where a judicial judgment has been obtained, the matter may ultimately be settled in ways other than the judgment indicates. Indeed, there is growing evidence to suggest that lawsuits function primarily as a spur to private settlement, and that judges function significantly as mediators in encouraging such settlements as well as in their more formal roles as deciders of disputes. Consequently, legal scholars, and some law schools, have been giving increasing attention to examining the role of nonadjudicatory techniques in the functioning of the legal order, and to devising new and innovative alternative-dispute-resolution techniques to meet social needs.

Certainly, the fact that most disputes are settled otherwise than by court decision is also true of the international legal order; indeed, given the reluctance of states to submit their disputes to adjudication, most international disputes must necessarily be settled by non-judicial means if they are to be settled at all. What is missing in the international system, however, is the potential spur to good-faith negotiation and negotiated settlement provided by courts with compulsory jurisdiction.

Paradoxically, the prevalence of non-judicial settlement in the domestic legal system may result in part from the availability of judicial settlement; each party knows that the cost of its failure to settle may be the other party's recourse to the courts, with all the uncertainty that entails. Moreover, the possibility of recourse to a court may restrain the parties from taking too extreme or unreasonable adversarial positions in their negotiations; each will know that excessively strained legal arguments, or those made in less than good faith, may be exposed in an eventual judicial opinion, or may even prejudice or embarrass its case. Indeed, the prospect of eventual judicial decision necessarily affects the way the parties think about the law; inevitably, they will bargain and assess the value of various settlement proposals in terms of how they think a court will decide.

But in the international legal system the prospect or threat of eventual judicial settlement is usually missing, and the pressures for good-faith negotiated settlement may consequently be less significant. Absent any likelihood that a third party will authoritatively review a party's arguments, there will be little check on its unilaterally advancing any interpretation or legal position it wishes, so long as its argument has even the flimsiest "legalistic-sounding" support. Moreover, thinking about settlement in terms of the merits of the respective claims is more awkward—for without a prospect of eventual adjudication, it may make little sense to try to predict what a court will do. Finally, it is worth noting that, even if a dispute reaches international adjudication, the approach of the international tribunal is likely to be somewhat different from that of a domestic tribunal. For, unlike domestic courts, international tribunals have only occasionally seen their role as including encouraging or mediating negotiated settlements between the parties. Perhaps more activism by international courts in this respect would be useful.

Second, it is in any case open to question whether national legal systems, involving the ordering of a wide variety of relations between millions or hundreds of millions of individuals coexisting in a close-knit national society, are in fact appropriate models for an international legal system, designed to meet very different problems of order and cooperation among some 170 nation states. The special characteristics of the international political order—and in particular the inevitability of continuing interactions and relations among its members—may suggest the appropriateness of legal institutions, techniques and responses very different from those found within national legal orders. We are beginning to realize that there is no *one* way in which a legal system must work; instead, there are a number of ways of organizing a legal order, more than one of which may do the job effectively.

Third, the character of international tribunals and concept of international adjudication are not quite the same as their domestic counterparts. For one thing, the general absence of formal mechanisms for enforcement of international arbitral or judicial judgments is very different from the situation in national legal systems; there is no international "sheriff." Even if, as is the case, most such judgments are in fact complied with, questions of compliance and effectiveness will inevitably tend to color the way states, the public and probably arbitrators and judges themselves view international adjudication.

Moreover, an international tribunal typically includes not only "neutral" arbitrators or judges but also arbitrators or judges who it is assumed will reflect the views or even represent the partisan interests of the various parties. A tripartite arbitral tribunal, for example, will usually be made up of one arbitrator appointed by each of the parties and a third "neutral" arbitrator selected by agreement of the two "national" arbitrators. And, under the Statute of the International Court, judges are elected by the U.N. Security Council and General Assembly bearing in mind "that in the body as a whole the representation of the main forms of civilization and of the principal legal systems of the world should be assured." While judges of the nationality of a party retain their right to sit on a case, if the Court in any case does not include a judge of the nationality of any of the parties, that party may choose an *ad hoc* judge to sit as a judge in the case. Finally, judges of the International Court do not have life tenure but are elected for only a nine-year term; while they may be reelected, ultimately they must go home!

This suggests that what we mean by impartiality in international adjudication, and perhaps how we expect an international tribunal to deal with a case, differ somewhat from our expectations of national courts. In international adjudication, impartiality is more a function of the composition and balance of the tribunal as a whole than of the neutrality of every single arbitrator or judge. Moreover, given the fact that judges who are assumed to reflect the parties' interests are deliberately included on an international tribunal, it is not surprising that the decision of such a tribunal will often embody strong elements of negotiated compromise. Professor Schachter comments:

> The fact that judges often reflect particular state interests is, of course, at variance with the ideal of objectivity of the judicial function. Yet it is not unreasonable to regard the reflection of national or group interests as appropriate and advantageous for an international court in a divided and heterogenous world.[4]

Finally, as we have seen, international adjudication is only one among many possible international dispute settlement techniques; in practice, most international disputes—including legal disputes—are resolved by nonadjudicatory rather than adjudicatory techniques. Thus, however desirable a greater willingness of states to use adjudication may be, effective international legal order can be, and in fact has been, maintained even in its absence. Certainly, any paucity of effective international adjudication is neither reason for despair nor an excuse for avoiding national obligations to respect and encourage the rule of law and to settle disputes by peaceful means.

Some Advantages and Disadvantages of Adjudication

From the standpoint of the interests of individual nations and the international legal order, adjudication offers both potential advantages and disadvantages as compared with other dispute-settlement techniques.

It may be useful to spell these out for several reasons. First, it may indicate the kinds of things officials are likely to consider in deciding whether to submit a dispute to adjudication. Second, it may more particularly suggest some of the reasons why nations have been reluctant to use adjudication as an international dispute-settlement technique, and possible ways of overcoming this reluctance. Third, it may suggest those particular kinds of disputes which are likely to be either more or less appropriate for resolution through adjudication. Finally, it may be helpful in better understanding and assessing present and potential U.S. policy decisions concerning the acceptance of the compulsory jurisdiction of the International Court of Justice.

Any list of *pros* and *cons* can at most be only suggestive. It will be evident that some of the categories suggested here are overlapping, and a number are "two-sided"—that is, what is an advantage to one nation may be a disadvantage to another, or what one nation may see as a virtue of adjudication in one situation, it may view as a defect in another. Moreover, the list is only theoretical, and it will depend on the situation whether any of the potential advantages or disadvantages of adjudication actually accrue in practice. Indeed, experience suggests that fears concerning the possible risks of adjudication, in particular, are largely unfounded.

Possible Advantages of Adjudication

(1) *Adjudication is dispositive.* At least ideally, an arbitral or judicial ruling decides and puts an end to the dispute. It is often more important to the parties that a dispute be settled than that it be settled in a particular manner or in the best possible way. This is, of course, also true of a negotiated settlement. But where negotiations are for some reason unsuccessful (for example, because internal political pressures make it impossible for one party to compromise, or negotiations are at an impasse and an agreed settlement

proves unattainable), adjudication provides an alternative way in which the parties can put the matter behind them—*res judicata*—and move on to other things.

(2) *Adjudication is impartial.* The basic idea of third-party adjudication is that a neutral and uninvolved third party is at least more likely to decide the dispute in a fair and just way, free of distorting influences produced by the biases, interest or disparate power of the parties themselves. Even if, as has been suggested, some international arbitrators or judges may have predispositions, the balance of power on an international tribunal will usually be held by neutral judges, and thus the decision of the tribunal as a whole is likely to be impartial. The concept of impartial dispute settlement reflects basic human attitudes concerning procedural fairness, which are embodied in natural law principles and the general principles of law recognized in the legal systems of almost all nations. Consequently, decisions reached by impartial processes assert a strong claim to acceptability and legitimacy, both by the parties themselves and the broader international community.

(3) *Adjudication is principled.* An impartial arbitrator or judge will presumably decide the dispute on the basis of neutral legal or equitable rules or principles—"the rule of law"—rather than the parties' respective power or the judge's bias or arbitrary whim. The normal practice of requiring the third-party decider to articulate the reasons for the decision buttresses this expectation. This, again, reinforces the likelihood of acceptability of the decision.

(4) *Adjudication is authoritative.* To the extent the parties have consented to third-party adjudication of a dispute, the tribunal is respected, and its procedures are fair, the decision is likely to be viewed by the international community as authoritative. An authoritative decision will have the effect of legitimating the prevailing party's claim and buttressing expectations of and pressures for compliance with the judgment. Even absent compliance, the judgment, by legitimating the winning party's claim, may strengthen its bargaining posture vis-à-vis the losing party in further negotiations or justify its taking of retorsional, retaliatory or other self-help measures to protect its interests or enforce its now authoritatively-proclaimed rights. In the U.S.-Iran *Hostages* case, for example, the U.S. considered it useful to seek and obtain an authoritative declaration of the illegitimacy of Iran's actions despite doubts whether Iran was likely to comply with such a judgment, and the judgment may have been helpful in bringing about a final resolution of the matter.[5] Similarly, Nicaragua considered it useful to seek and obtain an authoritative declaration of the illegitimacy of U.S. support of the *contras* and other actions against Nicaragua, despite doubts as to whether the U.S. will comply with the judgment.[6]

(5) *Adjudication is impersonal.* Since the decision is by a third party, neither of the governments of the parties themselves can be held directly responsible for the outcome. There are probably a number of disputes

where governments are relatively indifferent as to the outcome and would normally be willing to negotiate a compromise settlement, but where, for internal political or other reasons, they are unable to concede or even compromise the issue in negotiations. Third-party settlement is a politically useful way by which foreign offices can dispose of such problems without taking direct responsibility for concessions.[7] In effect, they can "pass the buck" for not "winning" the dispute to the third-party tribunal—"Don't blame us, blame the judge." The tribunal, for its part, can invoke principles of impartiality and commitment to decision by neutral principles of law as a shield against personal criticism.

(6) *Adjudication is serious.* Because adjudication is generally understood to be a complex, expensive and rather intimidating business, involving significant risks for any party invoking it, a nation's proposal to submit a dispute to adjudication shows both the other party and the international community that it takes the matter very seriously and is prepared to go to considerable lengths to pursue its claim. It is certainly a good way of getting people to pay attention to the claim! Moreover, it shows that that party really believes in the legitimacy of its claim, since it is prepared to submit it to impartial judgment. Conversely, a refusal by the other party to accept an offer to submit the dispute to adjudication will raise doubts among the other party's own citizens and in the international community more broadly about the legitimacy of that other party's position: "If it really thinks it's right, then why isn't it willing to let an impartial court decide the matter?" Thus, simply threatening or bringing an action in an international court may in itself buttress a party's credibility and bargaining strength in further negotiations, force the other party to give the claim more serious attention, and increase pressure on the other party by other nations or the international community to settle the dispute.

(7) *Adjudication is orderly.* The well-established structure of the adjudicative process provides a framework for the orderly presentation and development of the opposing arguments concerning the dispute. Where complex and difficult factual and technical questions are involved—as may be the case, for example, in land or maritime boundary disputes—the adjudicative process may facilitate a more orderly and thorough examination of the issues than might otherwise be the case. Adjudication also typically requires at least some contact and cooperation between the parties. At the least, this may lead to a more thorough examination of the issues by each party and a fairer disposition of the controversy. Conceivably, it may lead to a better understanding by the parties themselves of the respective merits of each other's positions concerning the issues in dispute, and to their own negotiation of a settlement.

(8) *Adjudication may reduce tensions and buy time.* Agreement to submit a dispute to adjudication demonstrates the parties' commitment to a peaceful and fair settlement and can, in some cases, "depoliticize" the dis-

pute. (However, as indicated below, it can also sometimes have the opposite effect.) Moreover, awkward or dangerous disputes may sometimes be contained through delay, and resort to judicial settlement may be a politically acceptable way of buying time.[8] That is, by taking the dispute to adjudication, the parties can give the appearance of remaining firm in their respective positions and "doing something," while still privately hoping that, during the lengthy period of preparation and hearings, new possibilities of negotiation may be opened up by events (for example, a change of government in the other party) or the passage of time.

(9) *Adjudication can be precedential and help develop international law.* An authoritative arbitral or judicial decision not only settles the dispute before the tribunal but may provide at least some guidance to both the parties and other states as to how they and others should conduct themselves in the future—that is, as to the relevant rules and expectations of the international society concerning particular kinds of international behavior.[9] Judicial decisions can have this law-clarifying and developing effect as a practical matter despite the fact that, as a technical legal matter, they are considered not to have precedential effect. The precedential effect of any particular ruling will vary, of course, depending on the particular issues before the tribunal, the nature and prestige of the tribunal, who the parties are, and the quality of the tribunal's reasoning.

(10) *Adjudication is system-reinforcing.* As indicated, impartial adjudication is widely seen as symbolizing the international rule of law, and a nation's willingness to submit a dispute to judicial settlement is generally taken as the test of its respect for and commitment to international law. To the extent many or most states demonstrate such a commitment, the expectation that others will also do so and will respect and comply with law is reinforced, and the international legal system as a whole is strengthened. Conversely, if many or most states refuse to submit disputes to impartial settlement by law, or show contempt for international adjudicative processes or institutions, respect for international law and its effectiveness in regulating international relations and promoting order will be weakened. Moreover, the prospect that a dispute may be subject to adjudication is likely to increase the relevance and contribution of law in promoting a negotiated peaceful settlement. As has been suggested, the possibility of recourse to, and eventual decision by, an impartial tribunal may serve to discourage the parties from taking legally-unreasonable adversarial positions in negotiations, provide a useful reference point for them to assess the potential value of each other's settlement proposals, and encourage their negotiation of a settlement since each party will realize that, should it fail to settle, it must face the risk of an adverse decision by the judicial tribunal. In a broader sense, adjudication helps give meaning and reality to international law by providing it with authoritative interpretation and practical consequences.

Possible Disadvantages of Adjudication

(1) *Adjudication involves the chance of losing.* The most important drawback of adjudication is that it involves the possibility of an adverse decision. Submission to third-party settlement means that parties give up control over outcomes, which foreign office officials are understandably hesitant to relinquish. Many nations are simply unwilling to take the chance that they may lose, particularly when the dispute involves what they consider important or "vital" national interests. If there is any alternative, states will prefer to avoid this risk. Moreover, if one party to a dispute is in a stronger bargaining position than the other, there may, other things equal, be little reason for it voluntarily to give up this advantage by agreeing to adjudication. (Conversely, if a state is in a weaker bargaining position than its adversary, it may consider it has little to lose and can only gain by resort to adjudication.) Or, if what one party seeks is essentially legitimation or public support of its position (which may in practice be the principal advantage it can hope to gain from a favorable arbitral or judicial decision), it may be easier, politically preferable, and less risky to seek such an endorsement from a political body, such as the U.N. General Assembly, than from an arbitral or judicial tribunal. Of course, the risks of adjudication may depend in part on other factors, such as its unpredictability or the possibility of bias of the tribunal, to which we now turn.

(2) *Adjudication is unpredictable.* The outcome of adjudication may be difficult to predict either because there are no relevant rules of international law or because, as is often the case, existing rules are ambiguous or uncertain. Indeed, were it otherwise, there would be little point in the nation likely to lose agreeing voluntarily to submit the dispute to adjudication; in a sense, uncertainty is what makes the game worth the candle. Moreover, even apart from the problem of deliberate bias by the tribunal, letting a third party decide a matter always involves an element of chance. No matter how careful the parties are in selecting an arbitrator or judge, no matter what the judge's reputation, any judge may simply fail to understand the issue, have unconscious biases, try to avoid responsibility or criticism by "giving something to each side" or compromising, or simply reach a wrong decision through incompetence or wrong or inadequate reasoning. Adjudication may be a good way of getting a decision and disposing of a problem. But it is no guarantee the decision will be the "right" or most just one.

(3) *Adjudication may not be impartial.* The premise of adjudication is that the arbitrator or judge will be impartial. However, as previously suggested, the process of selection of international judges may be influenced by political factors, and international tribunals typically include judges of the nationality of the parties. Thus, it is not unlikely that at least some judges may have predispositions favoring one party's position or not be impartial.

States have indicated that they are very concerned whether particular tribunals will in fact be impartial. For example, commentators from socialist and Third World countries have frequently suggested that the International Court is too "western-oriented." In contrast, the United States and Canada recently insisted, as a condition of submission of the *Gulf of Maine* case to the International Court, that the case be heard by a panel of "western" judges.[10] Perhaps most dramatically, the recent U.S. withdrawal from the *Nicaragua* case, and then from acceptance of the compulsory jurisdiction of the Court, appears to have been based at least in part on the charge that many or most of the present members of the Court are predisposed against U.S. interests, or at least against the interests of rich and powerful states.

If, as may be the case, international tribunals are increasingly being asked to deal with issues in which the applicable law consists more of broad principles and standards than of specific rules, any such predispositions on the part of judges could arguably have more significant consequences. While judicial predispositions may have relatively little scope to manifest themselves in disputes like the *Hostages* case where the relevant rules (in that case, of diplomatic immunity and protection) are precise and clear, the situation may be different where a tribunal is called upon to apply much broader and less precise principles such as "equitable apportionment," "appropriate compensation," or the scope of prohibitions on the use of force, in which there is much room for judicial flexibility.

The technique of international arbitration, in which the parties have more control over selection of the members of the tribunal, and, in particular, must usually agree on selection of the "neutral" arbitrator, is, of course, less likely to raise this problem.

(4) *Adjudicative settlement is imposed.* In contrast with a settlement reached by the parties themselves through negotiated agreements, a judicial tribunal imposes its own settlement on the parties. Even where a state has initially consented to adjudication, traditional notions of sovereignty and national pride and honor may make it resist the idea that an international arbitrator or court can appropriately rule on that state's behavior or tell it how it should behave or what it must do. Non-judicial dispute settlement techniques, of course, again avoid this problem, since each party must agree to any final settlement.

(5) *Adjudicative settlement may be illusory or superficial.* A tribunal must necessarily focus narrowly on the immediate "legal" issue before it, which may, in fact, have little to do with the actual underlying causes of the dispute at hand or the true source of contention between the parties. In cases where the "legal" issue is only the symptom or symbol of a far more complex problem, the tribunal's judgment may not really settle, and may even exacerbate, the dispute. This problem may be particularly acute in situations where one party is an unwilling litigant before the tribunal, refuses to appear or withdraws, or otherwise indicates its unwillingness to consider

a decision as dispositive. The claim that such wider (and allegedly non-justiciable) "political" issues were at stake was raised both by Iran in the U.S.-Iran *Hostages* case and by the U.S. in the recent *Nicaragua* case.

(6) *Adjudication is adversarial and potentially escalatory.* Despite efforts by the international community to encourage judicial settlement, being "taken to court" may in practice be regarded as a hostile and unfriendly act—something which persons or nations who are or want to be friends or continue doing business generally do not do. As previously suggested, where one party to a dispute does not wish impartial adjudication, efforts by the other party to force judicial settlement may increase bad feeling, discourage further negotiation, and inhibit alternative attempts to reach solutions. Moreover, once a lawsuit is brought, the case, rather than the dispute behind it, may become the focus of the parties' grievances. "Winning the case" and maintaining national honor may become more important than finding a sensible solution to the problem through a negotiated compromise.

(7) *Adjudication may freeze the dispute and the parties' options.* Once a dispute is brought to court, the dispute will become at least to some extent outside the control of the parties. As indicated, the case may acquire its own dynamic, and "winning" the case becomes the goal. For example, lawyers rather than diplomats are likely to assume a leading role in further decisions. The tribunal may hand down interim restraining orders, further constraining one or both of the parties' actions. In some cases, the tribunal may permit the matter to drag on unduly, locking the parties into long-term contention and further exacerbating tensions. In other cases, the tribunal may have little choice but to move swiftly and remorselessly towards decision, even if it is in the parties' mutual interest that the dispute sit a while, and perhaps with time and changing circumstances and perceptions fade away. Moreover, the fact that adjudication is usually public and often newsworthy may in itself serve to freeze the parties' positions, give the dispute a public prominence and significance neither desires, and obstruct possibilities for a compromise settlement.

(8) *Adjudication is inflexible.* In theory, adjudication is a zero-sum game—one party wins, the other party loses. But many problems intrinsically may be not amenable to such all-or-nothing solutions, or, in any event, may be better resolved by compromise than by a "win-lose" decision. If a dispute has persisted over time, it will usually mean that there is at least some merit in the positions of both parties (or at least a sincere belief by each in the merit of its position). Where two states are necessarily involved in continuous interactions and long-term relations, a decision which legally disposes of a particular dispute but leaves one party feeling it has been treated unfairly may ultimately do more harm than good. In this case, feelings of resentment and attempts to compensate in other areas for what is perceived as an unjust decision may hamper future working relationships between the parties or even alienate the losing party from the

legal or political system. Where such a result is likely, techniques which permit the reaching of mutually acceptable and politically-viable compromise settlements may be more useful and appropriate.

As noted, international arbitrators and courts in practice often do seem to reach what are in effect compromise solutions. But there is no consensus that this is what they *ought* to be doing. Indeed, decisions which too blatantly reflect a compromise may lose credibility and acceptability.

(9) *Adjudication is conservative.* Since adjudication is, at least in theory, only law-applying, it looks for principles of decision to what the law "is" rather than what the law "ought to be." It is interesting to note that nations have rarely agreed to permit international tribunals to decide disputes simply on the basis of equitable considerations (*ex aequo et bono*) rather than law, although it would be open to them to do so.

Thus, where what one party is really demanding—perhaps with good reason—is a change in the law, judicial tribunals have difficulty providing an adequate or acceptable resolution of the dispute.[11] Indeed, should a tribunal attempt to develop the law creatively to meet new attitudes or problems, it may face the charge that it is too "activist" and exceeding its appropriate function. Unless tribunals are willing to exercise a creative law-developing role, and states are willing to recognize and accept the appropriateness of their doing so, international adjudication may have little to offer nations seeking change and demanding what they regard as a fairer and more just international legal order and society.

(10) *Adjudication may be inconvenient and costly.* Arbitral or judicial proceedings may be complex, time-consuming, and expensive and may divert the energies of high-level officials from other important duties. For poorer nations, the legal costs of hiring sophisticated counsel (usually from western countries) may be significant. Delays may be substantial; it is not uncommon for the decision of a case to take a number of years.[12]

(11) *Adjudication may be too precedential.* The precedential nature of adjudication can pose risks as well as advantages. A party may be relatively indifferent to the outcome of a particular minor dispute, but not indifferent to the potentially precedential effect of a decision on other similar or analogous disputes, either with the same or other parties, which may be of much more significance. In such case, the risk that the tribunal may reach a finding or pronounce some principle prejudicial to a nation's broader interests or other more important disputes may be greater than its interest in settlement of a particular dispute warrants.

(12) *Adjudication may be ineffective.* Absent more effective international procedures for the enforcement of international arbitral or judicial decisions, a nation may be uncertain whether, even if it secures a favorable judgment, the judgment will be carried out. This will, of course, be particularly the case where one party is an unwilling litigant before the tribunal and has indicated that it will not respect the judgment. Moreover, international tribunals have typically been less flexible and creative in shaping

appropriate remedies than have national courts. In practice, however, most arbitral or judicial judgments—at least those in cases where the parties have clearly consented to jurisdiction—have been complied with. And, as previously suggested, a party may in some cases be as interested in the tribunal's declaration of the legitimacy of its claim as in actual enforcement or compliance with the judgment.

(13) *Adjudication may be used for propaganda or harassment purposes.* A nation may be concerned that other unfriendly nations may abuse any available judicial processes by bringing frivolous suits in order to embarrass or harass it. In justification of its recent withdrawal from the *Nicaragua* case, the U.S. stated that: "Nicaragua's suit against the United States . . . is a blatant misuse of the Court for political and propaganda purposes."[13] Fears of possible abuse clearly lay behind the U.S. Senate's recent decision to advise and consent to U.S. ratification of the Genocide Convention only with a reservation that the U.S. would not be bound by the "compromissory clause" in the Convention which would permit any party to refer disputes as to the application or interpretation of the Convention to the International Court for decision; the Senate indicated its concern that, absent such a reservation, states unfriendly to the U.S. might use this provision to institute in the Court suits accusing the U.S. of "genocide," simply in order to embarrass or harass it.

However, it is not easy clearly to distinguish a "proper" from an "improper" use of the Court. Certainly, nations seem often to have a largely "political" or "propaganda" purpose in mind in resorting to the Court, in the sense that they usually hope, by legitimating their claim, to bring the force of adverse international community opinion to bear on the other party's actions. As indicated, the United States, with some success, used the Court in just this way against Iran in the *Hostages* case, and Nicaragua undoubtedly had such a purpose in mind in bringing its *Nicaragua* case against the United States. Again, the U.S. has itself on several occasions used the Court simply to bring publicity to its grievance against another nation, as when it filed a series of suits in the 1950s against Soviet bloc countries protesting the shooting down of U.S. aircraft near or over their territory. The U.S. was well aware that, given the obvious absence of Soviet consent to the Court's jurisdiction, the Court would be compelled to dismiss the actions, as it promptly did.[14]

Some Advantages and Disadvantages of Adjudication by a Court as Contrasted with *Ad Hoc* Arbitration

As indicated, international practice distinguishes between adjudication by ad hoc arbitrators and by established and permanent courts, such as the International Court of Justice.

Possible Advantages of a Court

Some advantages of a permanent court are:

(1) *A court is convenient and readily available.* In contrast to the situation with respect to arbitration, there is no need for the parties resorting to a permanent international court to establish a special tribunal to deal with the dispute or to negotiate the tribunal's composition, rules or procedure. This can be particularly useful where a state is seeking judicial help on an urgent basis—for example, interim measures of protection—to prevent a *fait accompli* by the other party to the dispute. Moreover, many of the costs of the institution can be widely shared within the international community. More broadly, the ready availability of an international court, and the prospect that another party can invoke its jurisdiction, may in itself serve to discourage illegal behavior, forestall conduct which might give rise to disputes, or lead to the negotiated settlement of any disputes which do arise.

(2) *A court is likely to be more independent and professional.* An arbitral tribunal is typically composed of individuals who serve as arbitrators only part-time and occasionally, and who work together only for the single case or a short period of time. In contrast, judges on a court have guaranteed tenure, work together on a series of cases over a number of years, and have a public and professional commitment to the judicial role. Consequently, judges are less dependent than are arbitrators on the need to please a particular constituency in order to be selected for their job, more insulated from outside pressures, and more likely to be impartial. Indeed, a court, as a continuing institution, is likely to develop its own internal norms and group pressures, imposing and reinforcing special standards of impartiality and professional commitment on its member judges, who as long-term participants in this special "club" are likely to take their judicial role particularly seriously. Finally, continuing judges are more likely, with long experience over time, to develop the special understanding, skills, judgment, and wisdom which competent professional adjudication requires.

(3) *A court has more opportunity to develop the law in a consistent way.* Despite the formal absence of any doctrine of precedent in the international legal system, a court is more likely to be sensitive to its law-creating role and to develop a consistent jurisprudence. This has certainly been the case with the International Court, which through both its decisions and advisory opinions has contributed significantly to the clarification and development of international law,[15] and with other courts such as the European Court of Human Rights, which has contributed importantly to the growth of international human rights law.

(4) *A court is a salient symbol of the availability of adjudication as a means of peaceful settlement.* The very existence of an international court may serve to remind disputing nations of the possibility of resorting to the court as a way of resolving their differences. The prestige, availability, and

ease of access of a court may make it politically more difficult for one party to resist another's proposals to submit a dispute to adjudication as a way of peaceful settlement.

(5) *A court symbolizes the ideal of the rule of law in the international system.* As previously noted, the concept of the rule of law has been widely equated with the availability of impartial adjudication; a permanent court expresses this ideal in a concrete institution. This has been the case with the International Court, which for many people throughout the world, has come to represent humanity's aspirations for an ordered, peaceful and just international society, functioning under the rule of law. Whatever may in fact be the actual role of the Court, there is little doubt that it functions as the most obvious public symbol of the reality of international law.

Possible Disadvantages of a Court

Some disadvantages of a permanent court are:

(1) *A court's composition is fixed and out of the control of particular parties.* If one party believes that the members of a court are biased or considers them as lacking needed expertise or unacceptable for other reasons, it will be unwilling to resort to that court. While some flexibility with respect to the selection of judges for a particular dispute may be possible, as with the International Court's special chamber procedures, it is questionable how far such procedures may be stretched without undermining the court's reputation, cohesion and dignity. Where the issues involved are highly technical and complex, as in commercial disputes or disputes involving technical fields such as aviation, the law of the sea, commodity agreements or telecommunications, the parties may prefer to use arbitral or specialized tribunals which include judges with special expertise. The 1982 U.N. Law of the Sea Convention, for example, provides for several types of such specialized tribunals.

(2) *A court's procedures may be relatively inflexible.* Unlike arbitration, where the parties may by agreement shape the tribunal and its procedure exactly as they wish to meet their particular dispute-settlement needs, a court's flexibility in this respect is likely to be limited.

(3) *A court may be more available, prestigious, public and precedential than one or both parties desire.* Because a court is likely to be more prestigious, visible and newsworthy than an *ad hoc* arbitral tribunal, a party's risks from going to the court and facing a possibly adverse judgment or ruling of law are increased. Certainly, it will be more difficult for a losing state to attack or refuse to comply with a court's judgment, or to argue that any rule it enunciates is not entitled to weight. For a party brought before the court unwillingly, on the basis of a general advance consent, this may pose particularly acute problems.[16] If the tribunal has express or inherent implied authority to issue restraining orders or interim measures of

protection, potentially interfering with or embarrassing a nation's pursuit of its foreign policy objectives, these risks are increased.

The Role of International Adjudication

This discussion suggests that the acceptability and usefulness of adjudication will vary with the circumstances of each particular dispute. But, in addition, it may suggest some broader conclusions:

First, international adjudication is likely to continue to play only a limited role in the settlement of international disputes for some time to come. As indicated, international adjudication requires consent by *both* countries. There will undoubtedly continue to be some situations where both parties consider the benefits of adjudication to outweigh its risks and are willing to consent to judicial settlement, most frequently either by special agreement or through compromissory clauses in specific treaties. But given alternatives, the parties to a dispute will usually prefer to use non-adjudicative methods of settlement which entail fewer risks and over which they can exercise some control.

Second, it follows that the prospects for widespread acceptance of the general compulsory jurisdiction of the International Court under the Optional Clause of Article 36(2) of the Court's Statute—at least, unless coupled with broad reservations—do not at the moment seem bright. Many nations are clearly concerned that such a broad commitment would produce few practical gains in terms of immediate national interest, and might pose significant, if not yet clearly perceived, risks in an uncertain future. The recent U.S. experience in the *Nicaragua* case can only serve to heighten awareness of such risks. Given the availability of alternative methods of dispute settlement, many nations may see little reason to take a chance.

In theory, one might expect a particular reluctance to accept compulsory jurisdiction by powerful nations, or at least nations which see themselves as likely to be in a superior bargaining position in the kinds of disputes that they think might arise. Conversely, one might expect a greater willingness to accept compulsory jurisdiction by (1) less powerful nations, which may see impartial adjudication more as a protection than a risk; (2) nations which see themselves as unlikely to be involved in disputes affecting significant national interests; (3) traditionally idealistic nations which regard the support and development of a stronger international order as an overarching national interest; and perhaps (4) some nations which tend to accept such obligations primarily to look "law-respecting," either without serious consideration or without real commitment. In practice, however, it has not always worked out this way; some more powerful nations, such as the United Kingdom, have seen a commitment to compulsory jurisdiction as in their national interest, and many smaller or less powerful countries, particularly from the Third World, have been unwilling to accept the compulsory jurisdiction of the Court.

Third, the reluctance of states to consent to adjudication does not mean either that international law is ineffective or that the international legal system does not work. It is clear that international law continues to play an essential role in avoiding and resolving international disputes, and that most international disputes are in fact settled, albeit by other means than adjudication.

Fourth, while adjudication may not be the best way of resolving *every* dispute, there are clearly a number of situations in which adjudication, or at least the availability of adjudication, can perform a very useful dispute settlement function. In practice, most disputes do *not* involve issues of significant or "vital" national concerns. In these cases, while each party may prefer to "win" the dispute, the stakes involved are limited and either can afford to lose. Adjudication is one good way in which the parties can achieve their most important objective in these situations—getting rid of the dispute. Indeed, to the extent that states can be assured that a commitment to adjudication will be restricted to less vital issues, they will be more willing to agree, even in advance, to adjudication. Thus, nations have frequently been willing to agree to compromissory clauses providing in advance for compulsory jurisdiction over disputes arising out of treaties concerned with specialized matters of clearly defined scope and limited import, such as commercial treaties.

Moreover, we have seen that international tribunals, simply by being available, may help avoid, or induce the settlement of, disputes. Even if states choose only infrequently to invoke the International Court's jurisdiction under the Optional Clause or compromissory clauses in relevant agreements, that does not mean such commitments are useless. On the contrary, since each party to a dispute covered by such provisions knows that the other can resort to the Court, a party that wishes to avoid adjudication will have more incentive to reach a negotiated settlement. That is, where the parties have conferred potential jurisdiction on an international tribunal, their decisions and bargaining, like those of parties to domestic disputes, will be more likely to occur "in the shadow of the law." J.G. Merrills comments:

> . . . the value of arrangements for dispute settlement is not to be judged solely by the cases. For a provision for compulsory arbitration by its very existence can discourage unreasonable behavior and so may be useful even if it is never invoked.[17]

Because adjudication can be a particularly useful tool in our tool box of dispute-settlement techniques, it is important that it be kept ready at hand, easily available, and employed to the fullest whenever its use is warranted. Even if adjudication is not a panacea for problems of world order, it makes sense to do all that we can to strengthen and encourage the greater use of judicial institutions, and to improve their ability to respond in flexible ways to nations' dispute-settlement needs.

Fifth, more consideration could usefully be given to expanding the advisory jurisdiction of international tribunals. Governments have been reluctant to accept binding judicial settlement since they see legally binding judgments as posing special potential risks—even though such fears may be unrealistic and unlikely to come to pass. Advisory or non-binding adjudication, on the other hand, can offer many advantages of impartial third-party decision while reducing some of its most significant risks. In most cases, an advisory decision may in fact provide a mutually acceptable basis for resolution of the dispute; however, each party will have the assurance that, should its worst fears be realized and the decision prove unacceptable, it can legally refuse to comply with it, incurring only limited public relations costs. While binding adjudication may in principle be preferable, non-binding adjudication may in some situations be the most that one or both parties will agree to—and, in that event, better than nothing. The thus far successful experience of the newly formed Inter-American Court of Human Rights with advisory jurisdiction is suggestive in this respect.

Finally, it bears repeating that, for many people, international adjudication symbolizes the rule of law in international affairs. Whatever the truth may be as to how the international legal system actually works, public judgments as to the relevance and effectiveness of international law are at least in part based on whether the public sees international courts, and particularly the International Court of Justice, as playing a significant role in international dispute settlement. If many states—particularly important ones—are willing to submit their disputes to impartial settlement and show respect for the International Court, this will be taken by the public as meaning that international law is in itself relevant and worthy of respect, and the public will believe in and support international law. If, on the other hand, important states show indifference or contempt for international adjudication and the Court, the public is likely to conclude that international law is meaningless—a joke—and withdraw its belief and support.

If this is true, it has policy implications for any nation concerned with international law. Such a nation, in making decisions regarding adjudication and the International Court, must take the symbolic impact as well as the more immediate benefits and costs of its actions into account. For example, such a nation might wish to consider referring some disputes to the Court in order to support its prestige, even if adjudication involves some risks and other techniques might be preferable. Certainly, a state which values international law would want to think long and hard before deliberately taking action likely to diminish respect for international adjudication or the Court.

Conclusion

What is the relevance of this discussion to U.S. policy and, in particular, an assessment of the Administration's recent decision to withdraw U.S. acceptance of the compulsory jurisdiction of the International Court under Article 36(2) of the Statute of the Court?

First, it suggests that the question of acceptance of the compulsory jurisdiction of an international tribunal such as the International Court is a legitimate issue, on which opinions may differ. I believe that the benefits to the U.S. national interest of acceptance of the compulsory jurisdiction of the Court far outweigh the risks. But it is certainly open to the U.S. government or any other government to strike a different balance concerning the respective advantages and disadvantages of such acceptance and conclude otherwise.

Second, it may suggest some of the reasons why the U.S. and other nations have been reluctant to accept the compulsory jurisdiction of the Court, and thus the types of measures or safeguards which might serve to overcome such concerns. Many nations have seen risks in accepting the Court's compulsory jurisdiction. Nevertheless, a number of them, including until very recently the U.S., have found it possible to accept the Court's compulsory jurisdiction with appropriate reservations protecting them from those particular risks they found unacceptable. A more careful analysis and deeper understanding of the risks of most concern to the present Administration may suggest forms of reservation which could adequately protect U.S. interests and make a resumed U.S. acceptance possible.[18]

Third, it may place the practical consequences of U.S. acceptance or non-acceptance of the Court's compulsory jurisdiction in some perspective. While adjudication and the Court can play an important role in international dispute settlement, the effectiveness of the international legal system will not stand or fall on what any particular U.S. administration decides to do or not to do in this respect. U.S. withdrawal from the Court's compulsory jurisdiction may arguably, as I believe, have been a bad decision—unwise and unnecessary substantively, based upon unpersuasive reasons, and, in the way it was done, needlessly damaging to our national reputation, the Court, and the international legal system. But it does not mean that international law will become irrelevant, that international disputes will cease to be resolved, or that the Court will disappear. Despite the U.S. withdrawal, the shared national interests in predictability and order which lead most nations to support an international legal system will persist; nations will continue as in the past to settle their disputes primarily by non-judicial techniques (but on occasion through resort to adjudication or the Court); and the Court will continue to serve a useful and respected function and do useful work. In any case, U.S. withdrawal from the Court's general compulsory jurisdiction under the Optional Clause has not, at least as yet, included a similar withdrawal from existing U.S. commitments to the compulsory jurisdiction of the Court under the compromissory clauses of the many specific bilateral and multilateral treaties to which the U.S. is a party.

Finally, this discussion may suggest some of the reasons why I and many others[19] believe that support of the International Court of Justice and a resumed acceptance of its compulsory jurisdiction are in the U.S. national interest.

From the foundation of the Republic, the principle of respect for law has been a firm tenet of U.S. foreign policy. In particular, our nation over many years has led the way in promoting the impartial arbitration of international disputes. The American people, and every previous national administration, have generally believed that our country's and our children's future would be brighter in a world governed by law than one where disputes were resolved by power and coercion. Moreover, we have generally been aware that, in view of the importance of the U.S. in international affairs, there is little likelihood that an effective international legal order can be achieved without firm U.S. commitment and participation. Perhaps a few nations can hope to "free-ride" on an international legal system supported by most others—invoking the benefits of international law when it is to their advantage but ignoring the law when respect for law seems at the moment inconvenient or disadvantageous. But this course is not open to our country. For, if we choose not to play by the rules of the game, there may not be any game left worth playing.

One of the principal ways in which the U.S. has demonstrated its commitment to international law has been through support for the International Court. This policy has recognized not only the Court's potential practical usefulness in advancing immediate U.S. foreign policy interests, as in our use of the Court in the *Hostages* crisis, but also the Court's broader contribution in settling international disputes, in developing international law, and as a symbol of the ideal of international order. U.S. acceptance of the Court's compulsory jurisdiction in 1946, even if limited, reflected an appreciation of the importance of such a U.S. commitment, particularly in encouraging other nations to do likewise. This position was sustained for 40 years, under seven different presidents, up to the present.

As the *Nicaragua* case shows, U.S. acceptance of the compulsory jurisdiction of the International Court cannot be risk-free; few national (or private) decisions are. But despite the *Nicaragua* case, the risks of such acceptance, particularly if limited by appropriate and reasonable reservations and conditions, seem small compared with the long-run benefits the U.S. stands to gain. Certainly, one of the most significant of these benefits is that, by resuming support of the Court, we will be helping to preserve, and hopefully strengthen, the role and usefulness of the Court and international legal order for our nation's future—a future in which the Administration's concern with Nicaragua may turn out to be but a passing and only dimly-recalled memory.

Our national interest urgently requires a reconsideration of this question by both the Administration and Congress, with a view to renewed U.S. acceptance of the Court's compulsory jurisdiction.

Notes

1. There are some 250 agreements, bilateral and multilateral, containing compromissory clauses or other provisions conferring on the International Court of Justice jurisdiction over disputes as to the interpretation or application of the agreements. See 1983–84 *Y.B.I.C.J.* 51–56, 92–108. Of these, the U.S. is a party to about 75.

2. Oscar Schachter, "International Law in Theory and Practice," 178 *Rec. des Cours* 10 at 205.

3. See L. Gross (ed.), *The Future of the International Court of Justice* (2 vols., 1976) and Allot, "The International Court of Justice," in Waldock (ed.) *International Disputes: The Legal Aspects* (1972).

4. Schachter, *supra*, p. 70.

5. United States Diplomatic and Consular Staff in Tehran, 1980, *I.C.J.* 3. But the State Department Legal Adviser at the time of the hostage crisis has said: "Although I regard the Court's pronouncements as having served a useful purpose in terms of mobilizing world opinion and persuading our allies to join with us in the imposition of at least some modest economic sanctions against Iran, it must also be recognized that both the judgment and the economic sanctions added to the complexity of unraveling the dispute between the two governments." R. Owen, "The Final Negotiation and Release in Algiers," in W.Christopher, ed., *American Hostages in Iran: The Conduct of a Crisis* 301 (1985).

6. *See Nicaragua* case (Jurisdiction), Judgment of November 26, 1984, and *Nicaragua* case (Merits), Judgment of June 27, 1986.

7. This is probably the case regarding many arbitrations and judicial decisions dealing with relatively minor territorial disputes, such as the *Island of Palmas* arbitration (U.S. v. Neth), *Hague Ct. Rep.* 2d (Scott) (Perm Ct. Arb. 1928), 2 *R. Intl. Arb. Awards* 829, *see generally* Jessup, "The Palmas Island Arbitration," 22 *A.J.I.L.* 735 (1928); and the *Clipperton Island* arbitration, 2 *R. Int'l Arb. Awards* 1105 (French); 26 *A.J.I.L.* 1390 (1932) (Eng. transl.), *see generally* Dickinson, "The Clipperton Island Case," 27 *A.J.I.L.* 130 (1933).

8. The acceptance of arbitration by Chile and Argentina in the *Beagle Channel* arbitration seems to have been motivated, at least in part, by a desire to descalate tensions and seek compromise. Portions of the award and relevant documents pertaining to the arbitration appear in 1 J. Wetter, *The International Arbitral Process: Public and Private* 276–404 (1975). For the further evolution of this dispute and its eventual settlement, *see* 17 *I.L.M.* 634, 738–53, 1198–1205.

9. The legal principles affirmed by the Court in the *Nicaragua* case, for example—including its condemnation of the aggressive use of force, coercive intervention, and violations of the humanitarian rules of armed conflict—clearly are considered by the Court as applicable not only to the U.S. but to every nation in the world.

10. For text of Special Agreement, *see* 20 *I.L.M.* 1378 (1981) and for Order of Jan. 20, 1982, *see* 1982 *I.C.J.* 5(11–13). For final decision in the case *see* 1984. *I.C.J.* 246. For discussion, *see* Brauer, "International Conflict Resolution: The ICJ Chambers and the Gulf of Maine Dispute," 23 *Va. J. Intl. L.* 463 (1983).

11. *See e.g.*, Prime Minister Trudeau's explanation in 1970 of Canada's decision, upon enacting its Arctic Waters Pollution Prevention Act, to withdraw pollution control issues from its consent to I.C.J. compulsory jurisdiction, discussed in Bilder, "The Canadian Arctic Waters Pollution Prevention Act: New Stresses on the Law of the Sea," 69 *Mich. L. Rev.* 1 (1970) at 25–26 ("What is involved . . . is the very grave risk that the World Court would find itself obliged to find that coastal states cannot take steps to prevent pollution. Such a legalistic decision would set back unreasonably the development of law in this critical area. . . . We will not go to court until such time as the law catches up with technology.").

12. For example the *Barcelona Traction* case (Belgium v. Spain), 1970 *I.C.J.* 3, took eight years to reach decision, and the *South West Africa* case (Ethiopia and Liberia v. South Africa), 1966, *I.C.J.* 6, took six years. In neither case did the Court render a judgment on the merits.

13. U.S. Department of State, "U.S. withdrawal from the Proceeding Initiated by Nicaragua in the International COurt of Justice," Jan. 18, 1985, 85 *Dept. St. Bull.* No. 2090 (March 1985).

14. *See Treatment in Hungary of Aircraft and Crew of the U.S.*, 1954, *I.C.J.* 103; *Aerial Incident of 10 March 1953*, 1956 *I.C.J.* 6; *Aerial Incident of 7 October 1952*, 1956 *I.C.J.* 9; *Aerial Incident of 4 September 1954*, 1958 *I.C.J.* 158; *Aerial Incident of 7 November 1954*, 1959, *I.C.J* 276.

15. On the contributions of the Court to international law, *see, e.g.*, H. Lauterpacht, *the Development of International Law by the International Court* (1958).

16. The U.S. faced just such problems as a result of the Court's Judgment of 27 June 1986 in the *Nicaragua* case, in which the Court found U.S. support of the *contras* and certain other actions against Nicaragua in violation of international law. As indicated, as of the time this is written, it is too early to predict whether the decision will in fact embarrass the Administration's policy of providing support for the *contras,* or affect public or congressional attitudes with regard to that policy.

17. J. G. Merrills, *International Dispute Settlement* (1984), 88.

18. Suggestions have been made for various types of reservations to meet the Administration's concerns. They include reservations excluding from the jurisdiction of the Court matters involving national security or the use of force or referred to other dispute-resolution procedures or under consideration by the U.N. Security Council; excluding jurisdiction when the applicant party's declaration of acceptance of the Court's compulsory jurisdiction was made for the purpose of filing the individual suit; and providing for the possibility of denunciation of the U.S. acceptance with immediate effect. Suggestions have also been made for modification or elimination of certain U.S. reservations in its 1946 declaration of acceptance, particularly the multilateral treaty (Vandenberg) reservation and the "self-judging" domestic jurisdiction (Connally) reservation. *See, e.g.*, D'Amato, "Modifying U.S. Acceptance of the Compulsory Jurisdiction of the World Court," 79 *A.J.I.L.* 385 (1985); D'Amato, "The U.S. Should Accept, by a New Declaration, the General Compulsory Jurisdiction of the World Court," 80 *A.J.I.L.* 331 (1986); Gardner, "U.S. Termination of the Compulsory Jurisdiction of the International Court of Justice," 24 *Col. J. Transnat'l L.* 421 (1986); and Morrison, "Reconsidering United States Acceptance of the Compulsory Jurisdiction of the International Court of Justice," 148 *World Affairs* 63 (1985).

19. *See, e.g.*, letter to the *N.Y. Times,* Feb. 1, 1986, from Professor Anthony

D'Amato and Keith Highet, speaking for some 40 distinguished colleagues in international law, expressing "deep professional concern regarding the Government's decision" and expressing the view that "The U.S. should re-establish its long-standing commitment to international law and the peaceful settlement of international disputes by carefully considering the adoption of a new or amended instrument of general adherence to the World Court's compulsory jurisdiction."

13

WTO Dispute Procedures, Standard of Review, and Deference to National Governments

Steven P. Croley and John H. Jackson

Introduction

I ncreasing international economic interdependence is obviously becoming a growing challenge to governments, which are frustrated by their limited capacities to regulate or control cross-border economic activities. Many subjects trigger this frustration, including interest rates, various fraudulent or criminal activities, product standards, consumer protection, environmental issues and prudential concerns for financial services. Although it has been said that "all politics is local," it has also been said, with considerable justification, that "all economics is international."

The Uruguay Round's result (including the Agreement Establishing the World Trade Organization (WTO)) is one important effort to face up to some of the problems associated with interdependent international economic activity. Central and vital to the WTO institutional structure is the dispute settlement procedure derived from decades of experiment and practice in the GATT, but now (for the first time) elaborately set forth in the new treaty text of the Dispute Settlement Understanding, as part of the WTO charter. Over the last fifteen years, many countries have come to recognize the crucial role that dispute settlement plays for any treaty system. It is particularly crucial for a treaty system designed to address today's myriad of complex economic questions of international relations and to facilitate the cooperation among nations that is essential to the peaceful and welfare enhancing aspect of those relations. Dispute settlement procedures assist in making rules effective, adding an essential measure of predictability and effectiveness to the operation of a rule-oriented system in the otherwise relatively weak realm of international norms. Thus, the GATT contracting parties resolved at the 1986 launching meeting of the Uruguay Round (at Punta del Este) to deal with some of the defects and problems of existing dispute settlement rules. The result of that resolve was the new DSU.

Yet dispute settlement by an international body such as GATT or WTO panels treads on the delicate and confusing issue of national "sovereignty." Even if one recognizes that some concepts of "sovereignty" are out of date or unrealistic in today's interdependent world, the word still raises important questions about the relationship of international rules and institutions to national governments, and about the appropriate roles of each in such matters as regulating economic behavior that crosses national borders. The GATT dispute settlement procedures have increasingly confronted these questions, including the degree to which, in a GATT (and now WTO) dispute settlement procedure, an international body should "second-guess" a decision of a national government agency concerning economic regulations that are allegedly inconsistent with an international rule.

To pose a concrete example: Suppose that a government applies certain domestic product standards, perhaps for reasons of domestic environmental policy, in a manner that causes some citizens (or foreign exporters) to argue that the government action is inconsistent with certain WTO norms (such as rules in the WTO Technical Barriers to Trade Agreement). Suppose also, however, that a national government agency (or court) determines that the national action is *not* inconsistent with WTO rules, and another nation decides to challenge that determination in a WTO proceeding. It would seem clear that the international agreement does not permit a national government's determination *always* to prevail (otherwise the international rules could be easily evaded or rendered ineffective). But should the international body approach the issues involved (including factual determinations) *de novo,* without any deference to the national government? Certainly, it has been argued in GATT proceedings (especially those relating to antidumping measures) that panels should respect national government determinations, up to some point. That "point" is the crucial issue that has sometimes been labeled the "standard of review."

This issue is not unique to GATT or the WTO, of course; nor even to "economic affairs," as literature in the human rights arena indicates.[1] Even so, during the past several years the standard-of-review question has become something of a touchstone regarding the relationship of "sovereignty" concepts to the GATT/WTO rule system. Indeed, in the waning months of the Uruguay Round, the standard-of-review issue assumed such importance to some negotiators that it reached a place on the short list of problems called "deal breakers"—problems that could have caused the entire negotiations to fail. This was particularly odd, given that the issue was one that only a few persons understood, and that was virtually unnoticed by almost all the public or private policy makers concerned with the negotiation. Clearly, certain economic interests were deeply concerned, most notably those in the United States who favored greater restraints on the capacity of the international body to overrule U.S. government determinations on antidumping duties, and who were perceptive and economically endowed enough to carry their views deeply into the negotiating process. And those views cannot be easily dismissed. In many ways they go to a central problem for the future of the trading system—how to reconcile competing views about the allocation of power between national governments and international institutions on matters of vital concern to many governments, as well as the domestic constituencies of some of those governments. They also raise important "constitutional" questions about international institutions and the potential need for "checks and balances" against misuse or misallocation of power in and for those institutions.

For immediate purposes, however, we want to focus on the more particular question of proper standard of review for a WTO panel when it undertakes to examine a national government's actions or rulings that engage the issue of consistency with the various WTO Agreements and are subject to the WTO's DSU procedures. We will not here explore another interesting standard-of-review question—pertaining to the review by the new WTO Appellate Body established under the DSU of a report by a first-level panel acting under the DSU. In this appeal procedure, the Appellate Body's review is limited to "issues of law covered in the panel report and legal interpretations developed by the panel." The difficult question will be how to distinguish questions of law from other questions (fact?). But it seems clear that the standard of review of the first-level panel as it examines national government actions and determinations is a question of law, and so could very well come before the Appellate Body at some point, probably quite early in the evolution of the WTO.

Naturally, the standard-of-review issue is one that many legal systems face. Indeed, some negotiators drew on certain national-level legal doctrines for analogies to use in the GATT/WTO context. For example, the matter has been the subject of considerable litigation, and Supreme Court attention in the United States, and the European Union Court of Justice in Luxembourg has faced similar issues in its jurisprudence. In fact, one of the questions that interests us most is whether it is appropriate to draw an analogy from national-level jurisprudence—specifically, from U.S. jurisprudence—for help in determining the scope or standard of review of an international body over national-level activity.

We proceed here, then, as follows. In part II, we explore briefly the GATT context of the question, remembering that Article XVI:1 of the WTO Agreement mandates that GATT jurisprudence will "guide" the jurisprudence and practice of the WTO. In part III, we look at the new WTO Agreements relevant to the standard-of-review question, and consider their potential meaning against the backdrop of some of the history of the Uruguay Round negotiation. In part IV, we turn to the jurisprudence of U.S.

administrative law, which has struggled for many decades with a somewhat similar standard-of-review question, associated in recent years with the U.S. *Chevron* doctrine, explained in part IV. In part V, we explore some of the basic policies underlying the *Chevron* doctrine and argue that those policies do not find easy application in the context of an international proceeding. Finally, in part VI we briefly draw some tentative conclusions and suggest some avenues that may be useful for considering the approach of the WTO panels.

Background: Illustrative GATT Panel Jurisprudence

Clearly, the desire of some negotiators to deal explicitly with this subject in the Uruguay Round was influenced by their reaction (or that of their constituencies) to some GATT panel cases, especially antidumping cases, in which observers felt the panels had overreached their authority and been too intrusive in disagreeing with national government authorities. Thus, it is worth noting some of the GATT panel reports that addressed this question or topics related to it.

In fact, a very early GATT working party discussed this subject in 1951 in a case involving a complaint by Czechoslovakia against a U.S. escape clause action that had raised tariff barriers on the importation of "hatter's fur." The working party concluded in favor of the United States, reasoning as follows:

> 48. These members were satisfied that the United States authorities had investigated the matter thoroughly on the basis of the data available to them at the time of their enquiry and had reached in good faith the conclusion that the proposed action fell within the terms of Article XIX as in their view it should be interpreted. Moreover, those differences of view on interpretation which emerged in the Working Party are not such as to affect the view of these members on the particular case under review. If they, in their appraisal of the facts, naturally gave what they consider to be appropriate weight to international factors and the effect of the action under Article XIX on the interests of exporting countries while the United States authorities would normally tend to give more weight to domestic factors, it must be recognized that any view on such a matter must be to a certain extent a matter of economic judgment and that it is natural that governments should on occasion be greatly influenced by social factors, such as local employment problems. It would not be proper to regard the consequent withdrawal of a tariff concession as *ipso facto* contrary to Article XIX unless the weight attached by the government concerned to such factors was clearly unreasonably great.[2]

By contrast, in a case brought by Finland against New Zealand's application of antidumping duties on imports of transformers, the panel ruled in 1985 that New Zealand authorities had not sufficiently established the validity of a "material injury" determination, a ruling that rejected New

Zealand's contention that neither other contracting parties nor a GATT panel could challenge or scrutinize that determination. The panel said that to refuse such scrutiny "would lead to an unacceptable situation under the aspect of law and order in international trade relations as governed by the GATT."[3] The panel in this connection further noted that a similar point had been raised, and rejected, in the 1955 report of the panel on complaints relating to Swedish antidumping duties. The 1985 panel shared the view expressed by the 1955 panel that "it was clear from the wording of Article VI that no anti-dumping duties should be levied until certain facts had been established." The 1985 panel further pointed out, again quoting the 1955 panel: "As this represented an obligation on the part of the contracting party imposing such duties, it would be reasonable to expect that that contracting party should establish the existence of these facts when its action is challenged."[4]

To examine another example, in a case against Korea's antidumping duties on polyacetal resins, the United States challenged the Korean Government's determination of injury. Korea argued that "it was not the task of the Panel to second guess the KTC [Korean government body] . . . [T]he Panel's job was not to conduct a de novo investigation nor to attach its own weights to the different factors."[5] Nevertheless, relying on language in the relevant GATT antidumping agreement, the panel decided that the KTC's injury determination before the panel did not meet the requirements of the treaty language. Other cases have raised similar issues and, indeed, the criticism of the panel's approach in some cases is clearly what engendered the U.S. effort to obtain some limitations on the "standard of review" in the Uruguay Round negotiations.

Some later cases, however, seemed to take a more restrained view of a panel's authority. In the 1994 case of U.S. restrictions on imports of tuna, for instance, the panel noted:

> The reasonableness inherent in the interpretation of necessary was not a test of what was reasonable for a government to do, but of what a reasonable government would or could do. In this way, the panel did not substitute its judgement for that of the government. The test of reasonableness was very close to the good faith criterion in international law. Such a standard, in different forms, was also applied in the administrative law of many contracting parties, including the EEC and its member states, and the United States. It was a standard of review of government actions which did not lead to a wholesale second guessing of such actions.[6]

Similarly, in the prominent cases of twin complaints by Norway against the U.S. antidumping and countervailing duties on imports of Atlantic salmon, the panel in both cases ruled mostly in favor of the United States, finding that the U.S. action was not inconsistent with its GATT obligations, and seemed quite cautiously restrained in its approach (too restrained, some argue). The Government of Norway wrote a letter criticizing the panel's approach, to which the panel replied, saying, inter alia, that "the panel found it inappropriate to make its own judgement as to the relative weight to be accorded to the facts before the USITC."[7]

Thus it can be seen that the standard-of-review question is recurring and delicate, and one that to some extent goes to the core of an international procedure that (in a rule-based system) must assess a national government's actions against treaty or other international norms. Indeed, a more detailed review of these and other cases would show that quite a few concepts invoked by panels over the years relate to the broader question of the appropriate relationship of international dispute settlement proceedings to national government actions. With such broader questions in mind, we turn to the more particular question of the appropriate standard of review for GATT/WTO panels, focusing especially on antidumping.

The Law and Negotiating Context of the WTO

Relevant Texts

The Uruguay Round texts contain several different explicit or implied references to the standard-of-review question. The most prominent of these is found in the Anti-Dumping Agreement in Article 17.6. This provision, which applies *only* to antidumping measures, reads as follows:

> In examining the matter referred to in paragraph 5:
> (i) in its assessment of the facts of the matter, the panel shall determine whether the authorities' establishment of the facts was proper and whether their evaluation of those facts was unbiased and objective. If the establishment of the facts was proper and the evaluation was unbiased and objective, even though the panel might have reached a different conclusion, the evaluation shall not be overturned;
> (ii) the panel shall interpret the relevant provisions of the Agreement in accordance with customary rules of interpretation of public international law. Where the panel finds that a relevant provision of the Agreement admits of more than one permissible interpretation, the panel shall find the authorities' measure to be in conformity with the Agreement if it rests upon one of those permissible interpretations.

Article 17.6 is not the only provision bearing on the standard of review. Also relevant are two Ministerial Decisions taken at the final Ministerial Conference of the Uruguay Round at Marrakesh, Morocco, in April 1994, and made part of the text of the Uruguay Round Final Act. These state, respectively:

DECISION ON REVIEW OF ARTICLE 17.6 OF THE AGREEMENT ON IMPLEMENTA-
TION OF ARTICLE VI OF THE GENERAL AGREEMENT ON TARIFFS AND TRADE
1994

Ministers decide as follows:

The standard of review in paragraph 6 of Article 17 of the Agreement on Implementation of Article VI of GATT 1994 shall be reviewed after a period of three years with a view to considering the question of whether it is capable of general application.

DECLARATION ON DISPUTE SETTLEMENT PURSUANT TO THE AGREEMENT ON IM-
PLEMENTATION OF ARTICLE VI OF THE GENERAL AGREEMENT ON TARIFFS AND
TRADE 1994 OR PART V OF THE AGREEMENT ON SUBSIDIES AND COUNTERVAIL-
ING MEASURES

Ministers recognize, with respect to dispute settlement pursuant to the Agreement on Implementation of Article VI of GATT 1994 or Part V of the Agreement on Subsidies and Countervailing Measures, the need for the consistent resolution of disputes arising from anti-dumping and countervailing duty measures.

As both of these passages suggest, the antidumping provisions were not uncontroversial, for the Ministerial Decisions seem both to limit the application of those provisions, and to raise questions about how they fit into the overall jurisprudence of the WTO. To understand the source of that controversy, one must read these texts, Article 17.6 in particular, in the light of their negotiating context and history. That history, as we understand it, was briefly as follows.

Negotiating Context

Some government representatives thought it would be wise to have language constraining the standard of review by a GATT or WTO panel, and believed that U.S. administrative law jurisprudence provided a useful model for this constraint. As explained in more detail below, the U.S. jurisprudence seemed to suggest an approach whereby the courts (absent definitive statutory language to the contrary) would show deference to administrative actions by the executive branch of government, if those actions were based on a "reasonable interpretation" of the statute. Thus, negotiators suggested that the international rules of procedure should restrain WTO panels from ruling against a nation if its approach or interpretation was "reasonable."

This suggestion provoked opposition from at least two quarters. First, it drew opposition from many nations that felt such a rule would overly constrain panels while giving too much leeway to national governments to act in a manner inconsistent with the purposes of the WTO Agreements. In addition, many believed that a "reasonable" standard would allow different nations to develop different approaches to the international rules of the WTO Agreements, thus reducing consistency and reciprocity, and potentially allowing many different national administrative versions of the same treaty language.

Second, the "reasonable" standard worried certain other interests who wanted to ensure the effectiveness of many rules of the WTO, particularly those in the intellectual property area. These interests also believed that the "reasonableness criteria" would constrain panels too much, and make it difficult to successfully challenge objectionable practices that were inconsistent with various WTO rules.

In the tense moments of the final days of the negotiations, several compromises were reached. First, the text of Article 17.6 was reworded to use the word "permissible" rather than "reasonable" as justification for a national approach, *but* (a very big "but") this provision was preceded by the language of the first sentence in 17.6(ii), which we discuss below. No less important, the negotiators compromised so that the limiting language on standard of review would apply only to the antidumping text (which attracted the proposals in the first place), and not necessarily to other dispute settlement cases before the WTO panels. The Ministerial Decisions quoted above reflect the divisions of opinion on these issues by calling for consideration in three years of whether Article 17.6 "is capable of general application," and "recognizing" the "need for consistent resolution of disputes" with regard to "anti-dumping and countervailing duty measures." As to the general approach for panels (outside the antidumping area), while there are no provisions in the DSU explicitly concerning the "standard of review" as such, some language may be construed as relevant. The most interesting, perhaps, is found in DSU Article 3.2: "Recommendations and rulings of the DSB [Dispute Settlement Body] cannot add to or diminish the rights and obligations provided in the covered agreements." This language could be interpreted as a constraint on the standard of review, but possibly not to the extent of Article 17.6 of the Anti-Dumping Agreement.

The Fruits of Compromise

Now to focus on the structure of Article 17.6 of the Anti-Dumping Agreement itself. The key language is in paragraph 6(ii), quoted above. This was the compromise language of the Uruguay Round negotiators. What does it mean? A better understanding of its meaning must await future panel decisions. (Thus, early cases may be enormously important in this regard.) But, at least on the face of it, subsection (ii) seems to establish a two-step process for panel review of interpretive questions. First, the panel must consider whether the provision of the agreement in question admits of more than one interpretation. If not, the panel must vindicate the provision's only permissible interpretation. If, on the other hand, the panel determines that the provision indeed admits of more than one interpretation, the panel shall proceed to the second step of the analysis and consider whether the national interpretation is within the set of "permissible" interpretations. If so, the panel must defer to the interpretation given the provision by the national government.

Note that, in the first step of the analysis, subsection (ii) instructs the reviewing panel to consider the interpretive question, mindful of "the customary rules of interpretation of public international law." According to negotiators, this admonition is a direct albeit implicit, invocation of the Vienna Convention on the Law of Treaties. Interestingly, however, it is not clear in light of that Convention whether or how a panel could ever reach the conclusion that provisions of an agreement admit of more than one interpretation. This is true because the Vienna Convention provides a set of rules for the interpretation of treaties—defined as any "international agreement[s] concluded between States in written form and governed by international law" and thus clearly including the GATT/WTO—aimed at resolving ambiguities in the text. Articles 31 and 32 of the Vienna Convention are particularly relevant here. Article 31, "General rule of interpretation," sets forth a set of rules guiding the interpretation of the text of a treaty. Article 32, "Supplementary means of interpretation," provides additional guidelines for any case in which application of the rules in Article 31 still leaves the meaning of a provision "ambiguous or obscure," or when it renders a provision "manifestly absurd or unreasonable." Article 32 suggests, in other words, that the application of Article 31 should in many cases resolve ambiguities, and that where the application of Article 31 does not do so, Article 32's own rule—"[r]ecourse . . . to supplementary means of interpretation, including the preparatory work of the treaty and the circumstances of its conclusion"—will resolve any lingering ambiguities.

Thus, it is not clear what sort of ambiguity in an agreement's provision is sufficient to lead a reviewing panel to the second step of the analysis contemplated in Article 17.6(ii). Once a panel has invoked Articles 31 and 32 of the Vienna Convention, it presumably will have already settled on a nonambiguous, nonabsurd interpretation. Article 17.6 thus raises several questions about the relationship between it and Articles 31 and 32: Is any ambiguity whatsoever sufficient to move a panel to consider the range of permissible interpretations? Or does a provision admit of more than one interpretation for the purposes of Article 17.6(ii) after application of Article 31, but before application of Article 32? Or does a provision admit of more than one interpretation for the purpose of Article 17.6(ii) only after application of both Articles 31 and 32? In short, just which sort of ambiguity is sufficient to trigger a panel's deference? Without answering these questions, Article 17.6(ii) does, at least on the surface, suppose that a panel could somehow reach the conclusion that a provision admits of more than one permissible interpretation, for the second sentence of paragraph 6(ii) would otherwise never come into play. Indeed, some of the negotiators seem to feel that this is precisely the case; there never can be resort to the second sentence. Others, however, mostly proponents of the original "reasonable" language who desire more constraint on panels, argue to the contrary.

The U.S. Jurisprudence: A Valid Source of Analogy?

As already suggested, an apparently similar standard-of-review issue, raising analogous questions, figures prominently in U.S. administrative law (the same is probably true for other countries as well). In U.S. law, that issue concerns the level of deference that federal courts reviewing decisions made by federal administrative agencies will exercise toward those decisions. Until fairly recently, and broadly speaking, reviewing courts exercised considerable deference with respect to agencies' "factual" determinations, and accorded less deference to agencies' "legal" decisions. This two-tiered approach reflected a familiar division of function between the separate branches of government, according to which agencies were to handle the more or less "technical" aspects of statutory implementation, while courts were to ensure that agencies exercised their authority within the boundaries of the law. This bifurcated approach also followed the U.S. Administrative Procedure Act's direction for courts to "decide all relevant questions of law," which itself reflected traditional understandings of the proper roles of courts and agencies. Traditionally, judicial deference to agencies' legal determinations required special justification, whereas deference to factual determinations did not. That general rule was altered, however, in 1984, when the U.S. Supreme Court handed down its decision in *Chevron U.S.A., Inc. v. Natural Resources Defense Council, Inc.*, in which the Court articulated a new standard of review for agencies' interpretations of law—the *Chevron* doctrine.

The Chevron *Doctrine*

Courts applying the *Chevron* doctrine face two sequential questions, often referred to as "step one" and "step two" of *Chevron*. First: Has Congress "directly spoken to the precise question at issue,"[8] or is the statute interpreted by the agency "silent or ambiguous"?[9] To answer this question, the reviewing court applies the "traditional tools of statutory construction."[10] If, upon applying those traditional tools, the reviewing court concludes that Congress has indeed spoken to the precise issue in question, then "that is the end of the matter";[11] the court will hold the agency faithful to Congress's will, as unambiguously expressed in the statute.

If the court concludes instead that the statute is "silent or ambiguous" with respect to the interpretive question at issue, then the reviewing court proceeds to a second question—step two: Is the agency's interpretation of the statute a "reasonable" or "permissible" one? If the court determines that the agency's interpretation is not reasonable, then the court will supply one. If, however. the court determines that the agency's interpretation is reasonable, the court will defer to the agency's interpretation, even if—and this is the bite of the *Chevron* doctrine—the agency's interpretation is not one the court itself would have adopted had it considered the question on its own.

At least at first glance, then, the *Chevron* doctrine is straightforward: It instructs courts to defer to agencies' interpretations of law if and only if the statute in question is ambiguous and the agency's interpretation is reasonable. A close reading of *Chevron,* however, reveals that the doctrine itself is ambiguous, not least of all with respect to exactly how much interpretive ambiguity is necessary to proceed to step two. Will any statutory ambiguity suffice, or must the provision in question be utterly ambiguous, even after the reviewing court's application of the traditional tools of statutory construction, before the court will move on to address the reasonableness question? The best answer may be somewhere in between. What is clear is that *Chevron* provides sufficient leeway for lower courts to find ambiguities, or not, as they will. Accordingly, while lower courts cite and apply *Chevron* and its progeny routinely, their decisions vary widely with respect to what constitutes sufficient ambiguity to trigger step two of the doctrine.

According to many U.S. administrative law scholars, the *Chevron* doctrine constituted a significant shift of power from courts to agencies.[12] As explained shortly below, the shift is commonly justified by reference to some of the most important principles underlying U.S. administrative government—expertise, accountability and administrative efficiency. But, first, the important surface similarities between the *Chevron* doctrine in U.S. administrative law, on the one hand, and the standard of review set forth in Article 17.6 of the Anti-Dumping Agreement, on the other, deserve careful attention.

Chevron *and Article 17.6(ii)*

For one thing, *Chevron* requires a federal court to defer to an agency's interpretation of an ambiguous statutory provision so long as that interpretation is "reasonable" or "permissible," even if the reviewing court would have interpreted the statute differently had it considered the question in the first instance. Similarly, Article 17.6 requires a GATT/WTO panel to defer to a party's interpretation of an ambiguous Agreement provision so long as that interpretation is "permissible," even if (by direct implication) the reviewing panel would have adopted an alternative interpretation had it considered the question originally. Second, the *Chevron* doctrine instructs courts to employ the "traditional tools of statutory construction" when determining whether the statutory provision in question is "ambiguous" in the first place. Article 17.6, for its part, instructs panels to apply the "customary rules of interpretation of public international law" when determining whether the Agreement provision in question "admits of more than one permissible interpretation." Third, as noted, the *Chevron* doctrine is somewhat unclear about the level of ambiguity that is required to trigger step two of the *Chevron* analysis and, accordingly, lower courts vary widely on their approach to this issue. Article 17.6, similarly, is unclear about how panels will ever get to "step two" of the 17.6 standard, given the section's implicit invocation of the interpretive rules set forth in the Vienna Convention on the Law of Treaties.

Finally, and most fundamentally, both *Chevron* and the standard-of-review issue in Article 17.6 bear important implications about the distribution of legal and political authority. In the U.S. administrative regime, *Chevron* spelled an important shift of interpretive power from federal courts to agencies (and, thus, to the President). According to the conventional wisdom, whereas courts previously had most of the authority to resolve ambiguities in legislation, now agencies have significant authority to determine what Congress meant. Unless agencies exercise that authority unreasonably, courts must go along.

While this wisdom is sound so far as it goes, *Chevron*'s allocation of power is probably more complicated and more subtle than the conventional view suggests. Because reviewing courts have significant leeway to find, or not to find, a step-one ambiguity, courts retain significant power to vindicate or invalidate agencies' interpretive decisions. This is true because where courts' *Chevron* analyses end at step one, agencies often lose, and where the analyses proceed to step two, agencies usually win. Thus, courts retain an important check on agency authority, even though as a formal matter agencies and not courts have the authority to pass on the interpretive question initially. *Chevron* ties courts' hands only insofar as step one requires a court to defer to an interpretation it would have invalidated otherwise. *Chevron* shifts power *to* courts, however, insofar as step one allows a court to defer to what it considers a preferred interpretation of a statute that, under the pre-*Chevron* regime, the court would not have been able to support. In sum, *Chevron* comes with offsetting effects on federal judicial power: Reviewing federal courts "lose" in the sense that they must defer to unwelcome agency interpretations that, before *Chevron,* they could have invalidated; but they "gain" in the sense that they are permitted to vindicate welcome interpretations that, before *Chevron,* they would have been required to invalidate. What is more, courts hold the key to *Chevron*'s step two—given that the reviewing court itself decides at step one whether there is an ambiguity of sufficient proportions to proceed to step two.

While *Chevron*'s (re)allocation of interpretive authority between agencies and courts is complex, Congress's power almost certainly was curtailed as a result. This is so because, after *Chevron,* there are more interpretations of statutory provisions that courts can potentially uphold; again, some interpretations that courts would have been required to invalidate before *Chevron* will now be upheld. As a result, Congress must now speak with greater specificity, or run the risk that an agency will interpret a statute, with judicial blessing, in a manner that pre-*Chevron* courts would have said Congress did not intend.

Chevron-*Type Deference and Interpretive Authority in the GATT/WTO Context*

In the GATT/WTO context, the standard-of-review question implicates a similar allocation of interpretive power—among countries that first interpret a disputed provision of the Anti-Dumping Agreement, GATT/WTO panels hearing disputes, and members party to the Anti-Dumping Agreement. Here, too, the issue is complex and subtle. On the one hand, if panels were to interpret Article 17.6 as requiring considerable deference to a member's interpretation of a provision, disputing members would enjoy greater authority vis-à-vis GATT/WTO panels. On the other hand, if panels were to interpret Article 17.6 as requiring considerable deference where a provision admits of more than one interpretation, *and* as providing them with considerable leeway to determine whether a provision does admit of more than one interpretation, then panels themselves would enjoy significant power both to invalidate interpretations (under step one of 17.6) they deemed undesirable and to vindicate interpretations (under step two of 17.6) they deemed desirable. What is more, the power of WTO members, analogously to the power of Congress, would be compromised under a *Chevron*-like application of Article 17.6. Some of the members' intentions—specifically, those that were ambiguously, but nevertheless ascertainably, expressed in the Agreement—would not necessarily be vindicated under a *Chevron*-like interpretive framework. Indeed, beneficiaries of antidumping duty orders probably sought a *Chevron*-like standard of review for precisely this reason—so that panels would be less powerful. As suggested above, such interests no doubt thought that a *Chevron*-type standard, by making it more difficult for panels to invalidate a party's interpretation as contrary to the intent of the GATT/WTO membership, would effectively allocate power to GATT/WTO disputants and away from the members collectively. But to reiterate, since panels will decide what is ambiguous, the result of the standard could conversely shift more power *to panels.*

None of this is to suggest, however, that Article 17.6(ii) should be interpreted like the *Chevron* doctrine, whatever hopes may or may not have motivated certain negotiators. At least two important differences distinguish the standard of review embodied in 17.6 from *Chevron* deference.

First, Article 17.6(ii) uses the word "permissible," which may not be identical in meaning to "reasonable" or "permissible" as construed in U.S. law. In U.S. law, the essential test for step two of the *Chevron* analysis is whether the agency's interpretation is "rational and consistent with the statute," a test that agencies can quite easily pass. Second, the "customary rules of interpretation of public international law" referred to in Article 17.6 certainly are by no means identical to the "traditional tools of statutory construction" in U.S. domestic law, the latter being more quickly consulted and more open-ended than the former (especially, as indicated above, with regard to legislative history). As already explained, Articles 31 and 32 of the Vienna Convention aim at resolving any facial ambiguities in treaty text. In U.S. law, in contrast, it is well understood that application of the traditional tools of statutory construction can exacerbate as much as eliminate statutory ambiguities.

These important differences notwithstanding, at least some GATT/WTO disputants and negotiators have recognized both the analogy between *Chevron* and the standard of review for international panels, and the specific doctrinal and theoretical similarities between *Chevron*'s and Article 17.6's approaches to those analogous issues. In fact, the *Chevron* doctrine seems likely to shape the perspective of U.S. disputants in particular, for whom it is such a familiar and influential doctrine in their home regime. Thus the question arises, and will arise in future panel cases, about how far the *Chevron* analogy can be sustained in the context of GATT/WTO panel review. Should future GATT/WTO panels exercise *Chevron*-like deference? Or should they instead interpret the word "permissible" rather narrowly and/or apply the Vienna Convention's rules governing treaty interpretation in such a manner as to be very reluctant ever to conclude that an agreement provision "admits of more than one interpretation"? Part V is a first attempt to consider this crucial question.

Policy Consideration:
The Limits of the *Chevron* Analogy

Some Common Justifications for Chevron *Deference*

One traditional justification for greater judicial deference to agencies on legal questions in the U.S. administrative regime is that of agency expertise—the "expertise argument." This justification comports with traditional understandings about the respective roles of the different branches of government and agencies' place in modern government. Agencies, on this view, are the technical experts that put into operation the policy judgments made by legislators. Indeed, technical expertise is the raison d'être of agencies; by focusing on a particular regulatory field. or sector of the economy, agencies can do what Congress lacks the time and other institutional resources to do. *Chevron* itself, which presented the question whether the statutory term "stationary source" referred to an entire pollution emitting plant or, rather, to every single smokestack within such a plant, supplies an apt example of when an agency's special technical expertise can aid statutory interpretation. According to the expertise argument, agencies are deemed to understand even the legal ramifications of the problems agencies are created to work on. Admittedly, the dichotomy between legal and factual questions may at times be difficult to maintain, but that observation argues as much in favor of as it does against *Chevron* deference.

Agency expertise, however, is not the only common justification for *Chevron*-type deference. Sometimes the doctrine is justified also on democratic grounds. According to the argument from democracy, it is agencies, not courts, that are answerable to both the executive and the legislative representatives of the citizenry. Because judges are not elected, while presidents and legislators are, and because agencies but not judges are accountable to the President and to Congress, judicial deference to agency decisions enhances the political legitimacy of the administrative regime.

Finally, *Chevron* may be justified also in the name of administrative efficiency or coordination. Before *Chevron,* different federal courts in different jurisdictions could interpret the same statutory provision differently. Multiple interpretations by different federal courts would mean that the statute "said" different things in those different jurisdictions. Such confusion could be eliminated by appellate review, but agencies faced uncertainty pending review, and the possibility of different interpretations across different appellate circuits remained. Because multiple agencies do not typically interpret the same statutory language, however, *Chevron* deference allows the agency charged with administering a statute to interpret that statute. One agency, rather than many federal courts, now resolves ambiguities in the statute that the agency in question is charged to administer. Such interpretive streamlining not only reduces uncertainty but also promotes regulatory coordination. Once an agency has settled on a reasonable interpretation, it can act on the basis of that interpretation nationally.

These three arguments are not offered here to supply an unassailable normative defense of the *Chevron* doctrine; whether *Chevron* was a welcome development in U.S. administrative law is a debatable question beyond the scope of the present analysis. While these common justifications resonate with some of the most fundamental principles, underlying administrative government, they do not necessarily exhaust the argument that might be offered on behalf of *Chevron*. Each of the above justifications is subject to serious objection when applied to international review, however.

Chevron-*Type Deference and GATT/WTO Panels*

Whatever the doctrine's ultimate merits or demerits, *Chevron*'s central concept of "reasonableness" has at the very least a surface appeal. In fact, across many substantive areas of U.S. law, legal rules impose in one form or another requirements that are satisfied by reasonableness; where parties have acted in a reasonable way or have adopted reasonable positions, legal institutions and legal rules do not interfere. In the GATT/WTO context, the permissibility standard of Article 17.6 has a similar commonsense ring. The WTO Anti-Dumping Agreement will invariably raise many complicated interpretive questions involving a variety of underlying factual and legal issues. So long as a member's interpretation of the Agreement is permissible—within the realm of the plausible, in some general sense—deference on the part of reviewing panels may be sensible. After all, members may reasonably disagree about the meaning of the Agreement's provisions, and unless GATT/WTO panels have some privileged access to the meaning of the Agreement, there may be no reason to substitute a panel's interpretation for that of one authority. In addition, a deferential posture on the part of antidumping panels may help guard against panel activism more generally. Whatever the merits of *Chevron* in U.S. administrative law, then, do not the doctrine's general justifications also argue for a *Chevron*-like standard of review in the context of the Anti-Dumping Agreement?

Return first to the expertise argument, which justifies a deferential standard of review on the grounds that agencies are experts within their respective statutory domains. In the GATT/WTO context, there is probably no analogous rationale, certainly not one as strong. That GATT/WTO members have superior information to GATT/WTO panels about the meaning or ultimate aim of the Agreement's provisions seems implausible. Nor is any particular GATT/WTO member an "expert" relative to any other. GATT/WTO members undoubtedly have their own incentives to become experts about the meaning of the Agreement, but none can plausibly claim expertise over any other.

Granted, disputing parties who have made decisions facing a GATT/WTO panel challenge almost surely have vastly more *factual* information than reviewing panels do. Because panels themselves lack many fact gathering resources, they are ill-positioned to second-guess a party's factual determinations. Article 17.6(i), appropriately, reflects this reality by establishing a rather deferential standard of review of factual conclusions. That standard provides that panels shall ask only whether an authority's factual determinations were "proper" and whether an authority's evaluation of those facts was "unbiased and objective." If these conditions hold, a panel is to defer to the authority's view of the facts, "even though the panel might have reached a different conclusion." But parties' technical superiority over factual matters does not justify a deferential standard of review for authorities' interpretation of the Agreement's provisions. National authorities probably do not bring to a dispute any specialized understanding that renders them specially qualified to ascertain the legal meaning of *international agreements,* in the same way that the EPA's specialized understanding of environmental regulatory issues arguably renders that agency specially qualified to ascertain the meaning of "stationary source."

This leads to a second and related distinction between the posture of agencies and GATT/WTO members. In stark contrast to administrative agencies, GATT/WTO members are not specifically charged with carrying out the GATT/WTO. To be sure, members are obligated to fulfill their responsibilities under the WTO Agreement. In that limited sense, GATT/WTO members are charged with administering the GATT/WTO. But no country or combination of countries was ever delegated the responsibility of implementing the WTO Agreement in the way that administrative agencies are charged with implementing their statutes. Countries party to an antidumping dispute are not delegates whose technical expertise specially qualifies them to make authoritative interpretive decisions. They are, rather, interested parties whose own (national) interests may not always sustain a necessary fidelity to the terms of international agreements. Thus, while there may well be reasons for panels to defer to an authority's permissible interpretation of the WTO Agreement, expertise of parties to a panel dispute is probably not among them.

The same is true for the argument from democracy. Indeed, this argument cuts in the opposite direction from *Chevron,* once transplanted to the GATT/WTO context. Unlike agencies, national authorities that are parties to an antidumping dispute are not accountable to the GATT/WTO membership at large. GATT/WTO panels, not disputing parties, are the membership's delegates. Panels are delegated the authority to try to vindicate the political decisions—the compromises, the trade-offs—made by members as a whole. Therefore, while GATT/WTO panels resemble courts, and while they are asked to adjudicate claims between competing national parties, their interpretation of any WTO Agreement will *not* displace the interpretations of any body that is accountable to the membership—will not, in other words, displace interpretations by others who can plausibly be said to be representatives of the GATT/WTO membership. The argument in *Chevron* that judges should defer to the interpretive decisions made by those accountable to the citizenry's representatives simply has no analogue in the GATT/WTO antidumping context.

The observation that national authorities, unlike agencies, are not accountable to the membership at large speaks to the very purpose of the dispute settlement process, indeed the GATT/WTO Agreement itself—an agreement that, at bottom, seeks to overcome the significant coordination or collective-action problems that its membership otherwise faces. Absent the Agreement (or one like it), individual members have an incentive to erect trade barriers that may "benefit" them individually, to the greater detriment of other members. Furthermore, absent some dispute settlement process for keeping members faithful to the Agreement, members have similar incentives to apply the Agreement in ways "advantageous" to them. Further still, absent a standard of review for legal questions that prohibits self-serving interpretations of the Agreement that are *arguably* but not *persuasively* faithful to the text, members have an incentive to erode the Agreement through interpretation. In this light, respecting the policy preferences and judgments of the GATT/WTO constituency argues against, not in favor of, a *Chevron*-like standard of review.

Indeed, the fundamental problem with attempting to transplant a *Chevron*-like national standard of review to the GATT/WTO context is that such an approach overlooks the basic fact that in an international proceeding the underlying legal problem is rather different: Whereas in a national procedure the court is reviewing a national administrative action or determination under the national law, such as a statute, the international body has the task of ascertaining the meaning and application of an international norm. The question before the international body generally is whether the interpretation of an agreement underlying a national government's action is actually consistent or inconsistent with that agreement. This is not necessarily the same question as that faced by the national courts, at least in some legal systems. Of course, the international rule may be the applicable national rule if the treaty has direct "statutelike" application (if, for example, the treaty is self-executing), and the international rule may also have a role in influencing national interpretations of national law. But in many cases, at least in the United States, the courts are reviewing *national* law, which is determinative of the outcome of the national case, even if that determination proves to be inconsistent with *international* obligations. The international body, on the other hand, is charged with interpreting and applying the international norms engaged by the case. Accordingly, in almost all cases the parties to the dispute at the international process (nation-state governments) are different from the parties in the national case, which may be private firms, or subordinate parts of the government.

The efficiency argument fares no better in justifying a deferential standard of review. Whereas in the U.S. administrative law setting there is typically little danger of multiple interpretations of the statutory language by several different agencies, in the GATT/WTO setting multiple interpretations of agreement provisions is precisely one of the problems that panel review is designed to ameliorate. For in the GATT/WTO context it is highly likely that multiple countries will confront interpretive questions about one and the same GATT/WTO provision. The danger of multiple interpretations of the same provision as a threat to reciprocity thus seems considerable; as already observed, the Agreement itself is a response to a serious international coordination problem. At the same time, there seems to be little threat that the new GATT/WTO panels will render multiple and incompatible interpretations of the same agreement provision. Even though GATT/WTO panels are composed (at least at the initial stage) on an ad hoc basis, and even though, strictly speaking, GATT/WTO cases do not constitute binding precedent on subsequent GATT/WTO panels, the jurisdiction of these panels (in contrast to that of U.S. federal courts) is not confined to specific geographical regions. Moreover, while the principle of *stare decisis* does not govern GATT/WTO dispute settlement, panels very often make authoritative references to previous panels' decisions relating to the same or similar issues, and multiple panels' consistent treatment of a given issue over time can assume the force of a "practice" that guides panel interpretation of the Agreement. Here again, then, the GATT/WTO context presents an inverse situation as compared to U.S. administrative law: Whereas in the U.S. domestic context *Chevron* deference shifts interpretive power away from multiple courts and to one agency, similar deference in the antidumping context would shift interpretive power away from one institution and to multiple and varied parties to the GATT/WTO, each with a different culture and legal institution.

Of course, to argue that expertise, accountability and efficiency do not counsel in favor of a *Chevron*-like application of Article 17.6(ii) is not to argue that a *Chevron*-like approach is ultimately unjustifiable. Rather, the argument here is that some of the most common and most powerful justifications of the *Chevron* doctrine carry very little weight once transplanted to the context of GATT/WTO dispute settlement. To the extent that the *Chevron* doctrine influenced the drafting of Article 17.6, consideration of the appropriateness of that approach is in order. If Article 17.6 is to be applied in a *Chevron*-like way, its justification must come from outside the *Chevron* paradigm. We conclude with one possible justification.

Conclusion: Sovereignty and Standard of Review in International Law

While the analysis here has focused on scope of review in the GATT/WTO antidumping context specifically, the basic question considered reaches beyond the process of GATT/WTO dispute resolution itself. The standard-of-review question is faced at least implicitly whenever sovereign members of a treaty yield interpretive and dispute settlement powers to international panels and tribunals. Moreover, as national economies become increasingly interdependent, and as the need for international cooperation and coordination accordingly becomes greater, the standard-of-review question will become more and more important. The difficulty is clear: On the one hand, effective international cooperation depends in part upon the willingness of sovereign states to constrain themselves by relinquishing to international tribunals at least minimum power to interpret treaties and articulate international obligations. Recognizing the necessity of such power does not lessen the importance at the national level of decision-making expertise, democratic accountability or institutional efficiency. On the other hand, nations and their citizens—and particularly those particular interests within nation-states that are reasonably successful at influencing their national political actors—will want to maintain control of the government decisions.

Such parties may at times invoke the principle of national "sovereignty" to justify a deferential standard of review in the international context. At the same time, national authorities may also resist relinquishing interpretive power to GATT/WTO panels on the grounds that doing so compromises their sovereignty. Admittedly, the word "sovereignty" has been much abused and misused; nevertheless, if the term refers to policies and concepts that focus on an appropriate allocation of power between international and national governments, and if one is willing to recognize that nation-states *ought* still to retain powers for effective governing of national (or local) democratic constituencies in a variety of contexts and cultures—perhaps using theories of "subsidiarity"—then a case can be made for at least *some* international deference to national decisions, even decisions regarding interpretations of international agreements. After all, if the decisions and policy choices of national political and administrative bodies (such as the Commerce Department and the ITC in the United States) are too severely constrained by panel interpretation of the Agreement, those bodies and their constituencies will understandably resist. Important sovereignty values, in short, will inevitably come into conflict with the values underlying the newest embodiment of the GATT/WTO dispute settlement process. And there is no *a priori* reason why coordination values must in *every* case across every context, trump sovereignty values. Some trade-off is necessary.

Yet merely identifying important sovereignty values does not by itself provide a persuasive argument justifying deferential panel review. Standing alone, the argument that deferential review is necessary to protect authorities' national sovereignty fails to acknowledge that some balance between authorities' interest in protecting their sovereignty, on the one side, and the broader interest in realizing the gains of international coordination, on the other, must be struck. The argument proves too much, in other words, as it unwittingly challenges the very rationale of the GATT/WTO itself.

We thus approach the end of our analysis by identifying a major problem without recommending any easy solution. The problem is how to formulate and articulate the necessary mediating principle or principles between the international policy values for which a dispute settlement is desired, on the one hand, and the remaining important policy values of preserving national "sovereign" authority both as a check and balance against centralized power, and as a means to facilitate good government decisions close to the constituencies affected, on the other hand. Our appeal is to the dual propositions that the national-level approach to the standard-of-review issue, specifically a *Chevron*-like approach, does not provide appropriate analogies for the international approach, but that there is nevertheless an important policy value in recognizing the need for some deference to national government decisions. A reasonable, nuanced approach by the WTO panels is important for the credibility of the WTO dispute settlement system, and such an approach will lessen the dangers of inappropriate unilateral reactions by governments and citizen constituencies of nation-state members of the WTO. It should be obvious that this approach is needed for virtually all types of cases and not just those in antidumping or other specified categories.

Of course, we do not here prescribe any particular standard of review for panels considering national governments' interpretations of treaty obligations. Time and experience with particular cases will likely clarify the appropriate standard, or standards (since these may vary with different subject matters). Indeed, perhaps all that is required is that panels (including appellate panels) perceive and show sensitivity toward the issues involved when an international body reviews the legal appropriateness of national government authorities' actions. In this connection, panels should keep the relevant purposes, strengths and limitations of their institution in mind.

For example, panels should be cautious about adopting "activist" postures in the GATT/WTO context. For one thing, the international system and its dispute settlement procedures, in stark contrast to most national systems, depend heavily on voluntary compliance by participating members. Inappropriate panel "activism" could well alienate members, thus threatening the stability of the GATT/WTO dispute settlement procedure itself. Relatedly, panels should recognize that voluntary compliance with panel reports is grounded in the perception that panel decisions are fair, unbiased and rationally articulated.

Quite apart from these concerns, panels would be well advised to be aware also of the potential shortcomings of the international procedures, shortcomings that sometimes relate to a shortage of resources, especially (but not only) resources for fact-finding, as well as to the need for a very broad multilateral consensus. Moreover, panels should also recognize that national governments often have legitimate reasons for the decisions they take. At times, for example, such governments can justifiably argue that an appropriate allocation of power should tilt in favor of the national governments that are closest to the constituencies most affected by a given decision. More generally, panels should keep in mind that a broad-based, multilateral international institution must contend with a wide variety of legal, political and cultural values, which counsel in favor of caution toward interpreting treaty obligations in a way that may be appropriate to one society but not to other participants.

Notwithstanding these (and other) reasons for "judicial restraint," panels must at the same time understand the central role that the GATT/WTO adjudicatory system plays in enhancing the implementation, effectiveness and credibility of the elaborate sets of rules the WTO was created to maintain. Successful cooperation among national authorities to a large extent rests with the institutions given the responsibility to help carry out the WTO's dispute settlement procedures. Thus, when a particular national authority's activity or decision would undermine the effectiveness of WTO rules, or would establish a practice that could trigger damaging activities by other member countries, panels will undoubtedly show it less deference.

Notes

1. R. St. J. Macdonald, *Margins of Appreciation,* in European System for the Protection of Human Rights, ch. 6 (R. St. J. Macdonald, Franz Matscher & Herbert Petzold eds., 1993); *see also* Thomas A. O'Donnell, *The Margin of Appreciation Doctrine: Standards in the Jurisprudence of the European Court of Human Rights,* 4 Hum. Rts. Q. 474 (1982).

2. GATT Dispute Settlement Panel, "Hatter's Fur Case", Report on the Withdrawal by the United States of a Tariff Concession Under Article XIX of the GATT, 1951, paras. 8–14, GATT Sales No. GATT/1951–3 (1951), *portions reproduced in* John H. Jackson & William J. Davey, Legal Problems of International Economic Relations: Cases, Materials and Text 556 (2d ed. 1986).

3. GATT Dispute Settlement Panel, New Zealand—Imports of Electrical Transformers from Finland, GATT, Basic Instruments and Selected Documents [BISD], 32d Supp. 55, 67, para. 4:4 (1985) [hereinafter New Zealand Transformers].

4. New Zealand Transformers, *supra* note 3, at 68, para. 4:4.

5. GATT Dispute Settlement Panel, Korea—Anti-Dumping Duties on Imports of Polyacetal Resins from the United States, GATT Doc. ADP/92, para, 57 (1993) [hereinafter Korea Resins].

6. GATT Dispute Settlement Panel, United States—Restrictions on Imports of Tuna, GATT Doc. DS29/R, para. 3.73 (1994) [hereinafter Tuna II].

7. GATT Dispute Settlement Panel, United States—Imposition of Anti-Dumping Duties on Imports of Fresh and Chilled Atlantic Salmon from Norway, GATT Doc. ADP/8, at 232 (1992); GATT Dispute Settlement Panel, United States—Imposition of Countervailing Duties on Imports of Fresh and Chilled Atlantic Salmon from Norway, GATT Doc. SCM/153, paras. 209–12 (1992). Many GATT panel cases discuss this question of "deference." *See, e.g.,* United States—Section 337 of the Tariff Act of 1930, BISD, 36th Supp. 345 (1990); Korea Resins, *supra* note 22, paras. 208–13; United States—Taxes on Automobiles, GATT Doc. DS31/R, paras. 5.11–5.15 (1994); United States—Imposition of Countervailing Duties on Imports of Fresh and Chilled Atlantic Salmon from Norway, GATT Doc. ADP/8, paras. 43–67 (1992).

8. *Chevron,* 467 U.S. at 842.

9. *Id.* at 843.

10. *Id.* n.9; *see also* KMart Corp. v. Cartier, Inc., 486 U.S. 218, 300 (1988) (Brennan, J., concurring); NLRB v. United Food & Commercial Workers Union, Local 23, 484 U.S. 112, 123 (1987); INS v. Cardoza-Fonseca, 480 U.S. 421, 446 (1987).

11. *Chevron,* 467 U.S. at 842.

12. *See, e.g.,* §3.3. Kenneth Culp Davis and Richard J. Pierce Jr., Administrative Law Treaties (3d. 3d. 1994).

14

Obstacles to the Creation
of a Permanent War Crimes Tribunal

Christopher L. Blakesley

F rom time to time, a need arises to prosecute individuals who commit
war crimes. A permanent war crimes tribunal may be appropriate to satisfy this need, but only if it meets certain protective criteria. While survey-
ing the problems inherent in past war crimes tribunals, this article addresses
procedural and structural foundations upon which a permanent international criminal tribunal could be established.

General Problems for the
Establishment of a Permanent Tribunal

Individual liability for war crimes is difficult to enforce and is un-
likely to be accepted uniformly by states.

Individual criminal responsibility is the cornerstone of any international
war crimes tribunal. Nuremberg Principle I provides that "[a]ny person
who commits an act which constitutes a crime under international law is
responsible therefor and liable to punishment."[1] Acts by heads of state or
other government officials, even if committed in an official capacity, may
not constitute an immunity defense to or mitigate criminality. These officials, therefore, could also be held responsible for offenses committed pursuant to their orders. Additionally, liability for criminal negligence may be
imposed on a person in a position of authority who knew, or had reason to
know, that his or her subordinates were about to commit a war crime, and
who failed to take whatever action was necessary and reasonable to prevent, to deter, or to repress its commission. The same liability must hold for
failure to prosecute those who commit such offenses. Will nations unilaterally agree to such liability? If not, are they liable pursuant to customary

Reproduced with permission from *Fletcher Forum of World Affairs*, 18, 1 (1994).

international law or general principles? Who or what institution will be able to impose this liability on them?

A permanent tribunal challenges the sovereignty of the individual member-states of the United Nations.

Crimes under international law and those under domestic law are not mutually exclusive. The jurisdiction of any international criminal tribunal would be co-extensive in some areas with domestic courts. Under certain circumstances, for example, murder may be a crime under both domestic and international law. While a permanent international tribunal would be unlikely to pursue ordinary killings falling within domestic jurisdiction, the extent to which it theoretically could do so—and therefore the amount of discretion left to it to determine its own jurisdiction—would depend on whether and to what extent the court's subject matter jurisdiction was specifically limited. For example, the statute creating the Ad Hoc Tribunal for Crimes Against Humanitarian Law in the Former Yugoslavia (hereafter, the "Ad Hoc Tribunal") purports to limit that tribunal's jurisdiction. Nevertheless, the statute appears to have expanded the scope of humanitarian law, which traditionally followed the Hague and Geneva rules, by adding some crimes not included in the Hague and Geneva Conventions. By expanding the definition of humanitarian law, the scope of the tribunal's subject matter jurisdiction has also expanded.

The combination of an expanding scope of humanitarian law and a permanent court with more general jurisdiction than an ad hoc tribunal suggests inevitable conflict between the proposed international tribunal and domestic criminal courts. Article 9 of the Ad Hoc Tribunal statute provides for concurrent jurisdiction of the international tribunal and domestic courts, but gives the international tribunal primacy. Article 10 particularizes that primacy. While this arrangement may well be appropriate in the particular circumstances in the former Yugoslavia, the primacy of a permanent tribunal may be unacceptable to some U.N. member states.

Both the Nuremberg Trials and the Ad Hoc Tribunal address war crimes. But for the fact that in both instances, agents of the sovereign itself were engaged in widespread violations of international humanitarian law, the creation of a criminal tribunal with international jurisdiction would not have been deemed appropriate, even on a short-term basis. This accommodation may not be extended to a permanent war crimes tribunal, where subject matter jurisdiction may tend to expand. A permanent tribunal, once established, would quite predictably operate in a different fashion. Freed from the strict limits of ad hoc jurisdiction, it could interpret its own jurisdiction as it deemed necessary. In the United States and European Community, such primacy has meant that the "higher court" seeks to assert its superiority in fact over lower courts of the affected states. As the higher court extends its jurisdiction, the sovereignty of the affected states has historically been eroded. How would the jurisdictional relationship between domestic courts and a permanent tribunal affect state sovereignty?

The structure of a permanent tribunal based on the continental model would conflict with American Constitutional protection of liberty.

While more familiar concerns about the guarantees of individual liberty are addressed below, the conflict between the continental model and the U.S. Constitution's principle of separation of powers must also be addressed. This bedrock principle was understood by both supporters and opponents of the Constitution to be the essential guarantee of liberty. According to the principle, drawn from the eighteenth century French philosopher Montesquieu, there can be no liberty unless the legislative, executive, and judicial powers are separate from each other.

In the Ad Hoc Tribunal, which follows the continental model, the court has a judicial organ and a prosecutorial organ. While it is specified, as discussed below, that these two organs be independent of each other, American Constitutional experience casts doubt on the efficacy of such "parchment barriers." Traditional American Constitutionalism distrusts the good intentions of fellow citizens in positions of power, insisting instead upon institutional barriers to contain their ambitions. That distrust would be greater in a permanent international war crimes tribunal because of the mixture of legal and cultural backgrounds. The absence of structural protections based on separation of powers may be acceptable in an ad hoc tribunal whose competence is narrowly circumscribed by statute, but their absence is unlikely to be universally acceptable for a permanent tribunal.

Complicating Factors

The problems facing a permanent war crimes tribunal are many and varied. The Nuremberg and Tokyo trials were prosecuted by the victorious Allies against Nazi and Imperial Japanese conduct. The offenses were not applied to the Soviets, who also committed pre-arranged "acts of aggression" in their invasions of Poland and the Baltic States, and whose treatment of ethnic or national minorities could well have been considered to fit any definition of "crimes against humanity." Nor were they applied to the bombing of Dresden, Tokyo, Hiroshima, or Nagasaki, or to other Allied conduct including treatment of prisoners and submarine warfare. The offenses were drafted to apply only to the defeated enemies.

No doubt, one can now draft offenses in a neutral fashion, avoiding the restrictive language of Nuremberg which made those trials appear hypocritical. If done, however, the law must apply to leaders of every nation. Professor Alfred Rubin notes: "[u]nless the law can be seen to apply to

Israel's leaders as well as to leaders of various Arab factions, to George Bush (who ordered the invasion of Panama) as well as Saddam Hussein (who ordered the invasion of Kuwait), it will seem hypocritical again."[2]

Will a permanent tribunal have the resources and capability to try the mass of war crimes that occur around the world? If not, how will a permanent tribunal be impartial in deciding which offenses to prosecute and which to ignore? If the "law" is not to be applied to all persons against whom there exists equivalent evidence, the tribunal's verdicts may be perceived as political manipulation rather than justice.

Will the tribunal prosecutor have the capacity to bring charges against citizens of his or her own nation or its "allies"? If the prosecutor is a person chosen by the General Assembly, will the Western powers be satisfied? If chosen by the Security Council, will the Third World be satisfied? Is there any acceptable way to limit the discretion of the prosecutor? If a tribunal were created by convention, could the nations of the world agree on a prosecutor and judges?

Similarly, will the permanent tribunal be supported, even, or especially, if it is evenhanded when it decides which offenses to prosecute? Can a permanent tribunal be created that can prosecute all significant war crimes and not offend the nations which must support it? This problem relates to sovereignty and whether nations, through their governments, will abide sending their high governmental or military officials to the tribunal for prosecution. If they do not, the tribunal will appear impotent. What can the international community do to nations who refuse to cooperate? What about any U.N. forces who committed war crimes? Would the tribunal prosecute them? Perhaps most seriously, there is no assurance that such a tribunal would *deter* war crimes. Indeed, could the tribunal avoid sending the message that, once a country engages in war, it must do anything to eliminate the evidence of war crimes? This would not be the message the tribunal wishes to send.

If one focuses on the current legal order and the practicalities of international law, one may wonder whether the creation of a permanent war crimes tribunal is feasible or even whether it is inherently inconsistent with that law and that order. Would such a tribunal achieve its goals or actually be inimical to them? Would it risk establishing a legal system wherein war criminals are neither effectively prosecuted nor the victims and witnesses protected? Would the human rights and civil liberties of the accused individuals be protected?

Historical and Conceptual Background

Efforts to establish an international criminal tribunal are not new, although they have intensified recently. One wonders whether this history of so many attempts and so few successes suggests that the time is ripe for a permanent tribunal, or that a complete change in the international system is required before one will succeed. Professor Cherif Bassiouni reports that "the first prosecution for initiating an unjust war is reported to have been in Naples, in 1268, when Conradin von Hohenstaufen was executed for that offense."[3] The "modern" idea of establishing an international criminal court could be said to have been launched in 1899 with the Hague Convention for the Pacific Settlement of International Disputes.

The 1919 Versailles Treaty was another early step toward establishing a war crimes court. The face of the treaty provided for the prosecution of Kaiser Wilhelm II for a supreme offense against the "international morality and the sanctity of treaties" and for war crimes charged against German officers and soldiers. Also in 1919, the Allies established a special commission to investigate the responsibility *"for acts of war"* and crimes against *"the laws of humanity."* The Report of the Commission contained the following conclusion: "All persons . . . who have been guilty of offences against the laws and customs of war or the laws of humanity, are liable to criminal prosecution."[4] This provision was developed in response to the killing of an estimated one million Armenians by Turkish authorities and the Turkish people, supported or abetted by the state's public policy. There can be no doubt that those who committed such atrocities knew they were committing a crime. Moreover, a review of some state practices and of the views of scholars demonstrates that there was an understanding that crimes against humanity existed. The opposition of the United States however, *prevented* the Commission's report from including this type of conduct among the offenses that an international criminal court would prosecute. Subsequently, the Treaty of Sèvres, which was the 1920 Treaty of Peace between the Allies and the Ottoman Empire, provided for the surrender by Turkey of such persons as might be accused of crimes against "the laws of humanity," but unfortunately, in 1923, the Treaty of Lausanne, gave them amnesty.

Between the two world wars, a wave of terror swept Europe, mostly in connection with nationalist claims in the Balkans. In 1936, Adolf Hitler emphasized the international community's inability to prosecute or sanction crimes against humanity when he said, "And who now remembers the Armenians?" Indeed, it is particularly revealing that he would preface his policy of exterminating Jews, Gypsies, and Slavs by revealing that the absence of interest by the world community in effectively prosecuting such conduct, and in creating appropriate international structures to enforce this proscription, gave him the comfort of knowing that he might succeed in genocide, as others had in the past. In 1937, the League of Nations adopted a Convention Against Terrorism; an annexed Protocol provided for the establishment of a special international criminal court to prosecute such crimes. India was the only country to ratify the Convention, which never entered into force.

After World War II, it became obvious that crimes against peace, war crimes, and what became known, with the London Charter of 8 August 1945, as "crimes against humanity" had been committed. The London Charter established the International Military Tribunal (IMT) at Nuremberg, which was designed to prosecute major war criminals in the European Theater. In 1946, a similar international military tribunal was established in Tokyo to prosecute major Japanese war criminals in the Far Eastern theater.

Since World War II, there have been many examples of conduct that would fit the Nuremberg principles and which could have been tried in a war crimes tribunal. During the Vietnam War, atrocities were committed by both sides. The depredations of the Khmer Rouge in Cambodia are infamous. The Iraqi Air Force appears to have bombed villages in Kurdistan with both mustard gas and nerve gas. The former Soviet Union is alleged to have booby-trapped dolls belonging to Afghan Mujahideen children. The macabre list could go on and on.

In 1989, the General Assembly urged consideration of the establishment of an international criminal court. This recommendation was predicated on growing international concern for drug trafficking, and an initiative taken in 1987 by the Soviet Union, which proposed the development of such a tribunal in order to investigate acts of international terrorism. The International Law Commission (ILC) was requested to prepare a report and, in 1990, proposed the creation of an international criminal court. The Sixth Committee of the General Assembly subsequently addressed the issue in 1991, and proposed that the issue be studied further.

On 8 April 1993 the International Court of Justice (ICJ), in response to the suit filed by Bosnia and Herzegovina, called upon Serbia and Montenegro to "immediately . . . take all measures within their power to prevent commission of the crime of genocide . . . whether directed against the Muslim population of Bosnia and Herzegovina or against any other national, ethnical, racial, or religious group." This was an interim decision, wherein the Court noted that facts were still in dispute. It was also unable to render a decision in relation to disputed rights falling outside the ambit of the Genocide Convention.

The creation of the Ad Hoc Tribunal for crimes against humanitarian law was the culmination of several earlier Security Council resolutions adopted in reaction to reported depredations in the former Yugoslavia. In early 1992, Resolution 771 called for preliminary investigations. Resolution 780 of 6 October 1992 created a "War Crimes Commission," which analyzed the information garnered by the earlier investigations, conducted its own investigations, and reported its findings to the Secretary-General. Subsequently, the Secretary-General recommended that the

Security Council create the Ad Hoc Tribunal. On 11 February 1993, the Security Council adopted this recommendation and called for the creation of the Ad Hoc Tribunal in its Resolution 808.

Security Council Resolution 808, paragraph 1, provides: "an international tribunal shall be established for the prosecution of persons responsible for serious violations of international humanitarian law committed in the territory of the former Yugoslavia since 1991." Thus, the temporal and territorial jurisdiction of the Tribunal are limited to conduct since 1 January 1991 in the territory of the former Socialist Federal Republic of Yugoslavia, including its land surface, airspace, and territorial waters.

The Legal Basis and Authority to Establish a Permanent Tribunal

The usual and most appropriate method for establishing an international criminal tribunal would be a convention, whereby nations would establish the court and approve its statute. All member states would likely be under a binding obligation to take whatever action is required to enforce the statute under the U.N. Charter, Chapter VII.

Article 41 of the U.N. Charter provides: "The Security Council may decide what measures not involving the use of armed force are to be employed to give effect to its decisions, and it may call upon the members of the United Nations to apply such measures." Article 42 adds: "Should the Security Council consider that measures provided for in Article 41 would be inadequate or have proved to be inadequate, it may take such action by air, sea, or land forces as may be necessary to maintain or restore international peace and security. Such action may include demonstrations, blockade, and other operations by air, sea, or land forces of Members of the United Nations." The argument is that if the use of force is allowed as a "measure" under Article 42, *a fortiori,* the creation of an ad hoc international criminal court should also be allowed. In "the particular case of the former Yugoslavia, the Secretary-General believes that the establishment of the International Tribunal by means of a Chapter VII decision would be legally justified, both in terms of the object and purpose of the decision [as indicated in the purpose statement in his report] and of past Security Council practice."[6]

The Ad Hoc Tribunal for the former Yugoslavia provides a contemporary example of the application of international law for war crimes prosecution. The Secretary-General's Report relating to the atrocities there noted that the creation of the Tribunal for the prosecution of the alleged breaches of international humanitarian law will apply existing law, including the Geneva Convention of 12 August 1949, and that the Security Council would not be creating law or purporting to legislate. Is this assertion accurate? Where, besides in the Geneva and Hague Conventions, would these crimes be found? Would they be found with sufficient clarity to satisfy due process concerns? Would the Secretary-General's assertions hold for a permanent war crimes tribunal?

Specific Tribunal Characteristics

Propriety

A tribunal will only be acceptable if it proceeds in a manner that is beyond reproach. Basic notions of fairness and human rights in relation to investigation, prosecution, and trial are paramount. Any tribunal unscrupulous in protecting the accused from abuses and deprivation of civil liberties would be a dangerous institution. Justice Jackson summed up the importance of this point in his opening statement during the Nuremberg Trial.

> Before I discuss the particulars of evidence, some general considerations which may affect the credit of this trial in the eyes of the world should be candidly faced. There is a dramatic disparity between the circumstances of the accusers and the accused that might discredit our work if we should falter, in even minor matters, in being fair and temperate.
>
> Unfortunately, the nature of these crimes is such that both prosecution and judgment must be by victor nations over vanquished foes [*a problem not faced by the Ad Hoc Tribunal for the former Yugoslavia*].
>
> . . . We must never forget that the record on which we judge these defendants is the record on which history will judge us tomorrow. To pass these defendants a poisoned chalice is to put it to our lips as well. We must summon such detachment and intellectual integrity to our task that this Trial will commend itself to posterity as fulfilling humanity's aspirations to do justice.[7]

International Human Rights Law provides the minimum standards for protection of an accused person. Increasingly, U.S. requests for extradition and hand-overs under Status of Forces agreements have been overridden by international and foreign courts, which have ruled that international human rights provisions take precedence. In two of the cases, concerns over capital punishment in the United States have resulted in litigation in which courts outside the United States have held that turning persons over to states with the death penalty would in certain circumstances violate provisions of international human rights conventions. International human rights conventions contain analogues to many of the protections guaranteed by the U.S. Constitution, including the right to fair trial, to "equality of arms" and access to court, to the presumption of innocence, to the right to confrontation, and to the right to counsel of choice. Though some of the international human rights protections meet, and even exceed, U.S. Constitutional standards, some do not. Article 20(1) of the Statute for the Ad Hoc Tribunal provides that the "[t]rial chambers shall ensure that a trial is fair and expeditious and that proceedings are rendered in accordance with the rules of procedure and evidence, with full respect for the rights of the accused and due regard for the protection of victims and witnesses." The accused's Geneva Law and human right to consult a lawyer and to have adequate time to prepare a defense must be ensured. To be acceptable, this protection must be applicable to the entire trial process.

Subject Matter and Territorial Jurisdiction

Article 4 of the Statute for the Ad Hoc Tribunal for the former Yugoslavia provides for jurisdiction over the crime of genocide, and Article 5 covers "crimes against humanity," which includes *other inhumane acts.*" The Statute takes some license on "crimes against humanity," adding some crimes that are not included in the Geneva Convention (IV). Perhaps at one time, the phrase "other inhumane acts" was imprecise, and would have posed a potential problem vis-à-vis the principle of *nullum crimen sine lege.*[8] It is necessary that whatever conduct is covered be clearly and explicitly "proscribed by relevant international law."[9] With some 22 categories of international crimes, representing 314 international instruments enacted between 1815 and 1988, none of which properly defines in criminal law terms the offenses proscribed nor the elements thereof, it is necessary that the offenses be codified or otherwise clearly defined. If not, their vagueness will violate notions of due process.

Articles 2 through 5 of the Statute, in order to be more specific, provide for jurisdiction over grave breaches of the Geneva Conventions of 1949, violations of the laws or customs of war, genocide, and crimes against humanity. The Secretary-General noted that only crimes which have clearly and beyond any doubt become part of customary law may be prosecuted. These laws include the law applicable in armed conflict as embodied in the Geneva Conventions of 12 August 1949 for the protection of War Victims; the Hague Convention (IV) of 18 October 1907, Respecting the Laws and Customs of War on Land, and the Regulations annexed thereto; the Convention on the Prevention and Punishment of the Crime of Genocide of 9 December 1948; and the Charter of the International Military Tribunal of 8 August 1945.

It should be noted that no reference is made in the Statute to Protocols I and II to the Geneva Conventions. This omission raises the additional question, which will commonly be at issue, of whether the conflict on the territory of the former Yugoslavia is international or internal. If it is internal or not "armed conflict," and Protocols I and II are not incorporated, or not otherwise part of customary international law, then only Common Article 3 of the Geneva Conventions applies. Common Article 3 mentions nothing of rape or other offenses that are specified in Articles 2 through 5 of the Statute of the Ad Hoc Tribunal.

A related problem is whether conduct must have been "committed in armed conflict." Both the Nuremberg and Tokyo Tribunals required that "crimes against humanity" be committed "in execution of, or in connection with" another crime in the relevant Charter of the Tribunal. This is a serious problem, which caused the Nuremberg Tribunal *not* to prosecute for those offenses committed in Germany against German nationals or residents prior to 1939. The definition of "armed conflict" is nuanced and difficult. I would argue, however, that certain offenses, even not committed during armed conflict, are established as international crimes against humanity in customary international law, but this distinction would pose serious problems for a "War Crimes Tribunal."

International conventions that purport to create international "crimes" have been a problem in an arena where "crimes" are usually poorly defined. Crimes against humanity were explicitly recognized in the Nuremberg Charter and Judgment, and in Control Council Law Number 10. These rules have become part of customary international law and, indeed, articulate "general principles of law recognized by civilized nations." Note that "rape" was *not listed* in the Nuremberg Charter, but *is listed* in Law No. 10, which (attempting to delimit rape as a crime only when specified) further deleted "in execution of or in connection with any crime within the jurisdiction of the Tribunal." Furthermore, the phrase "[a]trocities and offenses included *but not limited* to [murder, etc.]" was substituted to expand the range of crimes qualifying as "crimes against humanity." The Secretary-General argues that these offenses include crimes aimed at any civilian population, and are prohibited regardless of whether they are committed "in an international or internal armed conflict."[11] Other inhumane acts of a "very serious" nature, proscribed by relevant international law, refer to willful killing, torture, and rape, committed as part of a widespread or systematic attack against any civilian population for political, racial or religious grounds. Does "very serious" as found in paragraph 48 of the Statute really differ from "serious"? Does Article 5's phrase "in ... armed conflict" mean *during* armed conflict? Has the Ad Hoc Tribunal really avoided the dilemma faced by the Nuremberg and Tokyo Tribunals?

In the conflict in the territory of the former Yugoslavia, such inhumane acts as "strategic" rape have been lumped together with so-called "ethnic cleansing." Widespread and systematic rape and other forms of sexual assault, including forced prostitution, should probably be given separate recognition. The Ad Hoc Tribunal will have the authority to prosecute persons responsible for the following crimes when committed in an armed conflict and directed against any civilian population: murder; extermination; enslavement; deportation; imprisonment; torture; rape; persecutions on political, racial and religious grounds; and other inhumane acts. It remains to be seen whether that Tribunal will be able to obtain the persons of the accused, acquire sufficient evidence, and successfully prosecute those brought to trial. It remains further to be seen whether a permanent tribunal could do so.

How would a permanent tribunal's jurisdiction be worked out? This is a serious problem. The most efficient approach internationally would be to have exclusive jurisdiction in the tribunal for the named offenses. The least efficient approach would allow the state of the nationality of the defendant or the state on whose territory the offense occurred to have primacy. The Ad Hoc Tribunal for the former Yugoslavia opted for concurrent jurisdiction. While concurrent, the Ad Hoc Tribunal's jurisdiction is also primary, so that at any stage of the procedure, the Tribunal may formally request the national court(s) to defer to the Tribunal's competence. The Tribunal's rules of procedure and evidence govern the specifics of this concurrent relationship. The problem with this approach, of course, is the diminution of state sovereignty. States would tend not to become parties. Would nations run the risk of having their nationals sent to be tried by judges possibly from enemy or rogue nations? On the other hand, a more limited approach would make the court dependent on recalcitrant leaders of states which had been involved in the violations. Either way, a permanent tribunal would face serious problems.

Rights of the Accused

It is axiomatic that any international tribunal must fully respect all of the internationally recognized standards regarding the rights of the accused at all stages of the proceedings. It would seem that this means *at least* the rights contained in Article 14 of the International Covenant on Civil and Political Rights. Would these be sufficient? These rights include:

1. All persons shall be equal before the International Tribunal.
2. In the determination of charges against him, the accused shall be entitled to a fair and public hearing, subject to Article 22 of the Statute.
3. The accused shall be presumed innocent until proven guilty according to the provisions of the present Statute.
4. In the determination of any charge against the accused pursuant to the present Statute the accused shall be entitled to the following minimum guarantees, in full equality:
   (a) to be informed promptly and in detail in a language which he understands of the nature and cause of the charge against him;
   (b) to have adequate time and facilities for the preparation of his defence and to communicate the counsel of his own choosing;
   (c) to be tried without undue delay;

(d) to be tried in his presence, and to defend himself in person or through legal assistance of his own choosing; to be informed, if he does not have legal assistance, of this right; and to have legal assistance assigned to him, in any case where the interest of justice so requires, and without payment by him in any such case if he does not have sufficient means to pay for it;

(e) to examine, or have examined, the witnesses against him and to obtain the attendance and examination of witnesses on his behalf under the same conditions as witnesses against him;

(f) to have the free assistance of an interpreter if he cannot understand or speak the language used in the International Tribunal;

g) not to be compelled to testify against himself or to confess guilt.

Extradition. There must be an extradition treaty (or an analogue) and implementing legislation. The U.S. Supreme Court has held that extradition is not possible without an applicable extradition treaty. Thus, it is necessary that some form of an extradition-type treaty be entered into and that it receive the advice and consent of the Senate. It will be necessary that the treaty call for the "extradition" (or other legal rendition) of a fugitive to the tribunal for trial. Would this be an extradition? Is extradition the appropriate vehicle? Whatever it is called, would a rendition be an extradition, as called for by U.S. jurisprudence, when a fugitive is being sent to an international tribunal rather than another state? These are questions that will likely be answered in the affirmative, but may have to be addressed by the courts in the United States. This problem may be obviated by the promulgation of a law that provides for extradition or rendition to the tribunal. This law could authorize the rendition and cover the incidents and issues relating to that rendition. It could be argued that the U.N Charter, via the above-mentioned provisions and Article 25 thereof, could function like an extradition treaty.[12] Could such a law even require certain protections for the accused? It could be considered, at least, as a treaty-based mechanism for the rendition of individuals. One must ask whether this approach will be upheld under the Supreme Court jurisprudence, if a fugitive were to be requested from the United States.

The Supreme Court has insisted on an extradition treaty because the relevant statute so requires. A statute alone, therefore, may be sufficient for extradition (assuming that a *prima facie* case is established for surrender). A statute is necessary because of the principle that individuals cannot be apprehended without general legislative authorization. It is certainly necessary in the United States that there be enabling or implementing legislation for this to work. Apparently, the Council of Europe is working on model implementing legislation for Europe.

In order to bring an individual accused of war crimes to trial in countries of the common law tradition, sufficient evidence to establish "probable cause" must exist. Probable cause relates to the decision to arrest or to hold a person over for trial or to extradite him to serve an already extant conviction and sentence. Europeans often disagree with the use of the probable cause standard for extradition, and may oppose it for a war crimes tribunal.

The principle of non-bis-in-idem. This principle, whereby no person shall be tried twice for the same offense, must be incorporated into the statute of any war crimes tribunal. Thus, given the primacy of the Tribunal's jurisdiction, subsequent trial before a domestic court should be forbidden. Even this principle poses problems. What should happen if: (a) the characterization of the act by the national court did not correspond to its characterization under the tribunal statute, or (b) considerations of impartiality, independence or effective means of adjudication were not guaranteed in the proceedings before the national courts? Should the Tribunal decide to assume jurisdiction over a person who has already been convicted by a national court? If so, would this violate *non-bis-in-idem*? Would the Tribunal's taking into consideration the extent to which any penalty imposed by the national court has already been served resolve the problem?

Article 10(2)(b) of the Ad Hoc Tribunal for the former Yugoslavia indicates that retrial may take place if the "national court proceedings were not impartial." This language probably refers to a situation of the kind suggested by the clause's next phrase, which speaks of the accused being "shielded from international criminal responsibility." Would a new prosecution violate *non-bis-in-idem*? There may be situations where the International Tribunal would be more protective of the human rights of the accused than would be a given domestic court, which may not be "impartial" or "well-disposed." Take, for example, the worries of Justice Jackson, the chief U.S. prosecutor during the Nuremberg Trials noted earlier, and more recently the trials of two Bosnian Serbs sentenced to death for war crimes in Bosnia-Herzegovina. The defendants were convicted after confessing, although their confessions were not corroborated, were withdrawn, and the defendants claimed that they had been given under torture and repeated beatings. Scars and markings found on their bodies were consistent with the claims of torture. Even if these individuals actually committed the crimes, can the international community afford the alleged method of arriving at the "truth"?

The substantive defenses to war crimes must be maintained. *The superior orders defense* acknowledges that soldiers must obey their superiors. Obviously, if superior officers have the power to inflict punishment, pain or death on a soldier who refuses to obey, duress may be involved, although duress is actually a separate defense. In addition, the American Bar Association (ABA) Task Force on the Ad Hoc Tribunal for the former Yugoslavia recommended that superior orders should be a legitimate defense if "a defendant acting under military authority in armed conflict did not know the orders to be unlawful and a person of ordinary sense and understanding would not have known the orders to be unlawful." It is hard to conceive, however, of a situation in which the grave breaches covered by the statute of a war crimes tribunal would not be understood to be illegal.

Duress is traditionally a separate defense from superior orders. It would likely be considered only a mitigating factor when combined with the superior orders defense, where superior orders are conjoined with circumstances of coercion or lack of moral choice. Other standard criminal law defenses, such as minimum age or mental incapacity, for example, would be determined by the Tribunal itself. Certainly, criminal liability would obtain for complicity in such crimes.

In the case of the former Yugoslavia, the ABA Task Force has recommended that mitigation due to duress should be the *only* type of mitigation allowed under superior orders. This recommendation is sound, but as duress is a distinct defense, it should be separated from the superior orders defense. The mistake-of-law type of superior orders defense should be eliminated and duress retained. It is true that the aspect of the superior orders defense that gives rise to the lack of "moral choice" is a duress-like defense. This relationship was recognized at the Nuremberg Trial, although literally excluded in the London Charter. A second aspect or type of superior orders defense is that based on "ignorance of the illegality." The U.S. Military Field Manual formulates its mistake-based superior orders defense on that basis.[13] Should both types of defense be allowed if a war crimes tribunal were created, or should only duress be allowed, as the ABA suggests?

The right of confrontation.   *Ex-parte* affidavits or video-taped depositions should not be admissible in trial, because their use is inconsistent with the right of the accused to "examine, or have examined, the witnesses against him."[13] This right is protected under Article 21(4)(e) of the Statute of the Ad Hoc Tribunal, although unfortunately that article does not include the right to confrontation, which is broader than the specific right to cross-examine. The Ad Hoc Tribunal's article, taken verbatim from Article 14(3)(e) of the International Covenant on Civil and Political Rights, would likely be used in a permanent war crimes tribunal. Is this right the same as that of a defendant to confront the witnesses against him? Does it include the concomitant right to cross-examine those witnesses? The ABA Task Force concludes that the right is concomitant to cross-examination. This relationship is *not self-evident,* however, especially given the broad "civil law" practice of allowing the judge to do the questioning (not always so vigorously as the Anglo-American trial attorney). Moreover, during the

Nuremberg Trials, where cross-examination was actually allowed, it was generally ineffective because of defense counsels' lack of experience.

However, there is *serious tension* between the preliminary and essential responsibility of a tribunal to ensure a fair trial that comports with due process and the *obligation to protect victims and witnesses*. To provide protections for the accused, as discussed above, without adequate safeguards for victims of war crimes, rape, and torture risks not only severe psychological harm to those victims, but even jeopardizes their very lives and those of their family members. The perpetrators of such crimes often have militia or other forces available to intimidate or harm the witnesses and victims. In the case of the former Yugoslavia, the ABA Task Force suggested that any derogation from the principle *against the use of ex-parte* affidavits should be limited to permitting their use as corroborative evidence in cases involving sexual assault against women, and that an *ex-parte* affidavit might be used at the investigatory stage, but not at trial.

Professor M. Cherif Bassiouni has strong reservations about the use of the U.S. model of confrontation and cross-examination without adequate safeguards for rape and torture victims. First, these procedural safeguards may be easily abused and cause distortion of the "truth-seeking" process. Second, the U.S. model disregards the legitimate rights and interests of the victim-witness. Third, the model assumes that other mechanisms in society will protect the victim-witness, which is unlikely in an international tribunal. Finally, the model lends itself to the further victimization of witnesses, including assassination and other forms of reprisals and harassment. Hence, while it is clear that human rights norms require some sort of "confrontation-type" examination (or the right to "have examined"), there is disagreement over what that means and should mean in the international tribunal context. Whatever approach one takes presents serious problems.

In a meeting held under the auspices of the International Scientific and Professional Advisory Council (ISPAC) in Spain on 3 May 1993, several recommendations were made with a view to protecting victims and witnesses while still providing for the accused's right to confrontation. Suggested protections included adding the following passage to Article 21 (*Rights of the Accused*) paragraph 4(e) of the Statute for the Ad Hoc Tribunal: "With regard to child witnesses this examination will be restricted to questions through the Tribunal only. In other cases where the International Tribunal considers it appropriate for the protection of the witness, it may similarly restrict the questioning." Article 18 (*Investigntion and Preparation of Indictment*) paragraph 3 was to be amended to include: "The views and concerns of victims shall be presented and considered at appropriate stages of the proceedings where their personal interests are affected, without prejudice to the accused and consistent with the other rules of the International Tribunal." Further, it was recommended that the

Tribunal "[take] into account the victims' needs for privacy and their special sensitivities. For example, screens or facilities for giving evidence from a separate room and separate waiting areas for defence and prosecution witnesses can be provided for protection. In this context, child victims should be offered special protection and interview procedures." These recommendations are to be taken into consideration in drafting the *Rules of Procedure and Evidence* and the general administrative structure of the Ad Hoc Tribunal, based on the notion that the United Nations ought to be prepared to incorporate the essence of its *Declaration on Victims* into this effort. These improvements should also be applicable to any permanent tribunal. The artistry and wisdom with which this is done will weigh heavily on the success or failure of the tribunals.

Even if done well, would these safeguards be sufficient for the victims, the witnesses, and the accused? Providing some of the traditional Anglo-American safeguards for the accused without establishing serious protective measures for victims will simply ensure that no victims will come forth, or if they do, that the risk of harm will be significant. Not including them will render the tribunal suspect. The international community would run the risk of facing another fiasco such as that at the Leipzig Trials. The result may be no serious or important convictions, but plenty of trauma for the victims and witnesses.

Standard of proof for conviction. The reasonable doubt standard has been the controlling standard for conviction in common law nations for over 200 years. The perception and understanding of this standard in the United States is that the evidence be sufficient to establish that there is no reasonable hypothesis or explanation of the evidence other than that of the defendant's guilt. It is a difficult burden to meet, as it should be when a person's life or liberty is at stake. The equivalent standard was recently applied by the Israeli Supreme Court in the *Demjanjuk* case. "Civilian" countries, on the other hand, generally are opposed to it, although on the continent, even the great German Lutheran jurist, Baron Samuel Pufendorf (1632-1694) linked the concept of *"conscience"* (similar to the French notion of *"intîme conviction"*) to notions of moral certainty and of proof beyond a reasonable doubt. "Modern" "civilian" states do not follow this model, and would oppose its adoption for a war crimes tribunal. Not this model, and would oppose its adopting the reasonable doubt standard will cause problems for countries of the common law tradition.

Appellate and Review Proceedings

A war crimes tribunal will not be viable or appropriate unless it provides meaningful appellate review. The Secretary-General's Report on the former

Yugoslavia and the associated Statute recognize the fundamental nature of the right to appeal, as incorporated in the International Covenant on Civil and Political Rights. Thus the Ad Hoc Tribunal will have an appellate process whereby a person convicted (or the prosecution) will be able to appeal errors on questions of law that would invalidate the decision, and on errors of fact which would occasion a miscarriage of justice. The Appellate Chamber may reverse, affirm, or revise the decisions of the Trial Chambers by way of decision rendered publicly and accompanied by a reasoned opinion, to which other opinions, either concurring or dissenting, may be appended. The decision of the Appellate Chamber is final.

The fact that there is but one level of review is problematical. Also, would allowing the prosecution more than an interlocutory appeal of errors of law which would trigger a new trial for the same offense, violate the principle against double jeopardy? It would seem so. To comport with the protection against double jeopardy, the tribunal should allow this prerogative.

Organization and Composition of the Permanent Tribunal

An international war crimes tribunal would likely be organized along the lines of a continental court, as was the Ad Hoc Tribunal. It would be composed of a judicial or adjudicative organ, a prosecutorial organ, and a secretariat. The prosecutorial organ would investigate allegations, prepare indictments, and prosecute persons allegedly responsible for committing the relevant violations. The tribunal would have Trial Chambers, where the Judicial Organ would hear cases, and an Appellate Chamber for appeals. The Chambers could be composed of a number of (say, eleven) independent judges, no two of whom would be nationals of the same nation. Three judges should serve in each of the two Trial Chambers and five would serve in the Appellate Chamber. Professor Ed Wise has noted that it would have been much easier and less expensive to follow the old Anglo-American tradition of a single judge riding circuit. Unfortunately, this approach is not generally accepted around the world. The Secretariat would be the administrative arm of the tribunal to service the other two branches.

A judge should oversee and rule on the sufficiency of indictments, to decide whether an accused will be bound over for trial. That judge should not sit on a trial panel. This is appropriate for purposes of protecting the integrity of the system, but it poses problems in relation to availability of judges at the trial stage. When judges have decided on the indictment, they should be disqualified to hear the trial. Given the large number of indictments and, hence, the likely large number of trials, this will certainly cause logistical and time-delay problems with trials. In fact, since they sit in panels, when one member of a panel is disqualified from hearing the trial, the whole panel is so disqualified. In this sense, it might have been better to have totally separate panels: one available only for preliminary matters and another for trials.

The ABA has recommended that Ad Hoc Tribunal judges be removed for cause upon a super majority vote of the Security Council, and that no member of the Security Council have a veto over any removal decision. The Task Force also wisely recommended that two or more alternate trial judges and one alternate Appellate judge be appointed, to avoid inflexibility. Will either the majority of the General Assembly or the "major powers" be amenable to such a rule for a permanent tribunal?

Continental Justice Systems and Protection of the Accused

While continental criminal justice systems have built-in protections for individuals accused of crime, even in the best of circumstances they are not as expansive as the constitutional protections in the United States. The defendant will be deprived of fundamental fairness (in the U.S. sense of substantive due process), equal protection, effective assistance of counsel, the right of confrontation, and other rights. Without the application of these protections, the U.S. Constitution and courts require the convictions to be overturned. Accordingly, there may be serious difficulty participating in the creation of a system that does not comport to U.S. Constitutional mandates, then sending U.S. nationals to be prosecuted therein. Thus, a serious tension exists between the criminal justice models competing for adoption in a war crimes tribunal.

The French system for protection of the accused is similar to other systems in Europe. The French criminal investigation in the usual non-absentia prosecution is undertaken, theoretically, by either a *juge d'instruction* (investigating judge) or a *procureur* (prosecutor, who is trained in exactly the same way and has the same authority and responsibility as a sitting judge). Indeed, the *procureur* is called *un magistrat debout* or standing judge. The system is designed with the goal of providing a prosecutor who is sensitive to his or her obligation to protect civil liberties as well as to protect the state against criminals. The protections are built into the person and office of this judicial official. In reality, the *police judiciaire* (who are actually the regular police, functioning as "judicial," or investigative, police) conduct the actual investigation in most cases, under the supervision of the *procureur.* Much of the evidence is obtained without counsel being available to the defendant, until he or she formally becomes a "suspect." The protection of counsel is thus provided much later than in the U.S. system, because the judicial official provides the protection.

In some very serious and sensitive prosecutions, the investigation is conducted by the *juge d'instruction* who, at least in theory, is not a prosecutor at all. Thus, the protection of the accused is built into the investigative stage, through the person and expertise of the *juge d'instruction* or *procureur.* This protection is based on trust. *A serious problem with this approach,* from the U.S. Constitutional perspective, is that the American system assumes that any investigator (even a judicially trained one) will eventually develop a theory of the case and will be influenced by that theory. While this influence is understandable and normal, the U.S. system recognizes it and protects against the dangers it poses by allowing vigorous defense counsel to represent the defendant from the early stages of the investigation. Continental systems are based on the good faith efforts of governmental officials and the police; the U.S. system is not dependent on trust, but calls for zealous, independent defense. Adoption of either system will cause problems for the other.

Another problem with the European model is the use of the *dossier.* The dossier is the entire package of documentary evidence obtained during the investigation. Though it includes reports and records of all investigations, examinations, and statements of expert and other witnesses, much of it is in the form of simple police reports, written by the investigating officer. It is all admissible in a continental trial (although most of it would not be admissible in a U.S. trial). Indeed, the dossier is not only available to the chief judge, but is heavily utilized and relied upon by that judge in running the trial and rendering the ultimate decision. The trial, therefore, is generally very brief. Although the judge allows the defendant to make a statement and to pose questions to witnesses upon whose testimony the documents are often based, in many instances, by the time the actual trial begins, the conviction is virtually assured. Thus, the essence of a continental trial (including the protections of the accused and the ultimate conclusion, the *"objective truth"* of whether the accused committed the offense), takes place at the pre-trial stage.

The jury system in Europe is also unlike that in the United States. The French jury, for example, is generally made up of nine individuals. There is also a three-judge panel, including the chief judge, who deliberates and votes with the jury. It is possible that the lay members of the jury, not being lawyers and deferring to the social and legal authority of judges, may be influenced by the three-judge panel and by its control over deliberations. The chief judge, being armed with the entire dossier, certainly has the power and authority to influence the jury's deliberations and their ultimate *intîme conviction.*

A judgment of conviction in Europe is not required to be based on the *"reasonable doubt"* standard. A continental judge or jury, rather than determining that the evidence must rule out all other reasonable hypotheses except guilt, must simply arrive at an "intimate conviction" (*une intîme conviction*) that the individual committed the crime alleged. This means simply that the trier of fact must *know* in his or her heart that the defendant committed the offense. The judge's *intîme conviction* of guilt or innocence is based on that judge's thorough knowledge of all the evidence in the dossier. There are virtually no restrictions on the type of evidence allowed into the dossier and eventually into trial. The impact of the dossier being available to the judge, whether or not each witness is presented at trial for testimony, is tremendous.

Trial in absentia.   Some continental Europeans have argued for the use of the trial *in absentia.* The Nuremberg Charter specifically provided for such trials. This provision would certainly accommodate the difficulty such a tribunal would face in being able to obtain custody of persons accused of war crimes. Trials *in absentia,* however, would be anathema to common law systems. Some of the arguments against trials *in absentia,* presented below, apply to continental criminal justice systems in general.

In a trial *in absentia,* the defendant, in addition to his absence, has neither a right to a jury nor a right to counsel *at any time.* The French *Cour d'Assises* (the French Court in which serious crimes—analogues to U.S. felonies—are tried), for example, simply verifies that the formalities were met, then renders its decision. No witness is heard and only written documents of the dossier are consulted. In addition, the dossier remains available for any subsequent trial.

Even the human rights protections mandated by international law as applied through the French and other continental legal systems for regular trials (albeit probably inadequate for U.S. Constitutional purposes) are *not available* for trials *in absentia.* Most nations abrogate prior convictions *in absentia* and allow a new trial once custody of the defendant is obtained. The abrogation of the prior conviction *in absentia* and the retrial of the defendant, however, *do not* address the deficiencies of trial *in absentia* nor erase the human rights violations associated with the procedure.

Protections of the accused in his "new trial."   European law generally requires that a conviction *in absentia* be purged or abrogated when the "convicted" individual is returned for a *"new trial."* But the impact of the prior conviction *in absentia* is *enormous.* The "retrial" in the continental systems of a person already convicted *in absentia* is devoid of any constitutional protections compatible with U.S. standards. Thus, no assurance that the individual sent to the tribunal would be accorded due process *compatible with U.S. standards* could be made.

The problems are in the nature of the continental system, the nature of a continental trial, and the record of prior conviction as it is used in that trial. Although the formal conviction is abrogated, the dossier is retained and is available for use in the new trial. This may mean, if a given witness is not available to be presented in open court, that the impact of the evidence exists, without opportunity to cross-examine or even to confront all witnesses against the defendant. Moreover, the judge absolutely controls and presents the case, ultimately participating with and affecting the jury. The judge presents the evidence, calls the witnesses, and questions them in a manner consistent with his or her vision or theory of the case. Thus the judge, though "objective," will not necessarily provide the same rigorous challenge to the witnesses that a zealous advocate does for his or her client in the United States. This reality, coupled with the influence of the dossier, make it clear that the protections afforded a defendant under U.S. Constitutional standards are simply not available in the trial in continental systems, especially when the trial follows a prior conviction *in absentia*. It is likely that a war crimes tribunal would follow the European model. This choice would prove difficult for the United States and other common law nations to accept.

Sending an individual to the tribunal for trial will be analogous to extradition. Furthermore, the United States, if it participates, will have contributed to the creation of a tribunal that will be constitutionally deficient. Can the Treaty Clause of the Constitution (Article 7, §2) justify U.S. participation in a tribunal that does not meet due process standards? A trial must proceed in a manner that is beyond reproach from the point of view of fairness and the protection of human rights. If U.S. courts are not scrupulous in protecting accused individuals from abuses and deprivation of civil liberties, Americans will ultimately be unwitting participants in such violations, condemning the viability and integrity of the U.S. extradition process, tainting American cooperation in criminal matters, and eroding U.S. Constitutional principles.

Justice Jackson's statement regarding fairness in investigation and prosecution, quoted above, applies to a war crimes tribunal today. Americans compromise themselves when they deliver someone up for prosecution in a system that does not comport with U.S. standards of justice. Trial after a conviction *in absentia* is certainly one of those situations, but so may be a trial in the first instance. First, for conviction, the standard of proof "beyond a reasonable doubt," discussed above, must be required. Yet, it is not the standard on the continent and its omission is especially harsh for a trial involving a conviction *in absentia*. Second, in either situation, no counsel would be present at many critical stages of the procedure. Similarly, *ex-parte* affidavits, police reports, and other evidence nonadmissible in a U.S. trial, taint an original trial or retrial even further. The use of this evidence is inconsistent with both the U.S. Constitution and the right of "confrontation" in Article 14(3)(e) of the International Covenant on Civil and Political Rights, which the United States has just recently ratified.

Can a permanent war crimes tribunal proceed in a manner that the United States can accept and that brings credit to the international legal system? It must be, and must be perceived to be, effective in obtaining and prosecuting perpetrators of crimes in a manner that guarantees the international human rights protections afforded accused individuals. Dangers abound: difficulty in obtaining evidence in a manner that comports with protections guaranteed accused persons; difficulty in obtaining custody of accused individuals; difficulty in protecting victims of the atrocities while obtaining meaningful and usable evidence against accused persons. Many other crucial problems face a war crimes tribunal. Their proper resolution is indispensable.

Conclusion

This paper has attempted to present a balanced analysis of the problems facing the creation of a permanent war crimes tribunal. The problems are daunting, especially from the perspective of a U.S. civil libertarian. Inherent problems of such a tribunal's encroachment on sovereignty prevent some scholars from accepting the possibility of its existence at all. The inherent tension between effectively obtaining custody of, gathering evidence against, and prosecuting those accused of war crimes creates another imposing set of problems and barriers. Is it possible to avoid having the tribunal become a political tool? If so, is it possible to ensure that the tribunal will be able to obtain custody of fugitives to prosecute in sufficient numbers to make it meaningful? If not, it will be perceived as being a hollow shell. If it is able to obtain sufficient numbers of accused individuals, will it be able to prosecute and convict them while protecting their rights and those of the victims and witnesses? Will the exercise be substantive and important for the protection of human rights and the prevention and prosecution of war crimes and other crimes against humanity, or will it be a symbolic gesture? If it is a symbolic gesture, will it promote or detract from those laudable goals?

Notes

1. The Charter and Judgment of Nuremberg recognize five principles: I.) as indicated in the text; II.) "The fact that domestic law does not punish an act which is an international crime does not free the perpetrator of such crimes from responsibility under international law"; III.) "The fact that a person who committed an international crime acted as Head of State or public official does not free him from responsibility under international law or mitigate punishment"; IV.) "The fact that a person acted pursuant to order of his government or of a superior does not free him from responsibility under international law. It may, however, be considered in mitigation of punishment, if justice so requires"; V.) "Any person charged with a crime under international law has the right to a fair trial on the facts and law." "Nazi Conspiracy and Aggression Opinion and Judgment, Nuremberg, 30 September 1945," reprinted in 41 *A.J.I.L.* 186–218 (1946); see also J. Spiropoulos, "Special Rapporteur,

Formulation of Nuremberg Principles," 2 *1950 Yrbk. Int'l L. Comm.* 181, 191–193.

2. "International Crime and Punishment," 33 *The National Interest* 73 (1993).

3. M. Cherif Bassiouni, "International Law and the Holocaust," 9 *Cal. W. Int'l L. & Pol.:* 335, 337, n 12 (1993).

4. "Report of the Commission on the Responsibilities of the Authors of the War and on Enforcement of Penalties for Violations of the Laws and Customs of War, Conference of Paris 1919," Carnegie Endowment for International Peace, Division of International Law, Pamphlet No. 32 (1919), reprinted in 14 *A.J.I.L.:* 94 (Supp. 1920).

5. "Case Concerning Application of the Convention on the Prevention and Punishment of the Crime of Genocide (*Bosnia and Herzegovina v Yugoslavia [Serbia and Montenegro]*), request for the indication of provisional measures, (1993) *I.C.J. Reports* 3, 31 *I.L.M.* 890 (1993) (wherein Bosnia and Herzegovina filed suit against Serbia and Montenegro" for violating the Genocide Convention" and other illegal conduct in violation of customary international law).

6. Secretary-General's Report, at paras. 24, 27 (noting for example, Security Council Resolution 687 [1991] and subsequent resolutions relating to the conflict between Iraq and Kuwait).

7. Justice Robert H. Jackson, Chief Counsel for the Prosecution in the Nuremberg Trials, *Opening Statement,* delivered 20 November 1945, quoted in Telford Taylor, *The Nuremberg Trials,* 167–69.

8. No crime without law. A similar maxim is *mulla poena sina lege*—no punishment without law.

9. See, e.g., Ex Parte Quirin, 317 U.S. 1, 27–31 (1942); quoted in "I.M.T. at Nuremberg, Opinion & Judgment," reprinted at 44 *A.J.I.L.* 172, 220 (1947).

10. Secretary-General's Report, at paras. 34, 35.

11. Secretary-General's Report, para. 47.

12. Article 25 states, "The Members of the United Nations agree to accept and to carry out the decisions of the Security Council in accordance with the present Charter."

13. The mistake-based defense excuses or mitigates liability when a reasonable person would not have known the conduct was illegal; duress excuses or mitigates liability when coercion eviscerates moral choice.

14. Article 14(3)(e), International Covenant on Civil and Political Rights.

15. The *Leipzig Trials* (1921–22) were the first major international attempt to punish war criminals. See "German War Trials: Report of the Proceedings Before the Supreme Court in Leipzig," 16 *A.J.I.L.* 628 (1922) (note that they were tried before German tribunals). They essentially failed. The Allies succumbed to political considerations, which were allowed to thwart efforts of the prosecution. The German defendants were cheered as they left the tribunal, while the Allies were derided and mocked.

16. The term "civilian" is used here to denote those nations which derive their legal systems from the "civil code" tradition, which began with the French *Code Napoléon.*

17. Samuel Pufendorf, *Of the Law of Nature and nations* (C.H. Oldfather & W.A. Oldfather, trans. 1688); Pufendorf, along with other international law publicists including Grotius, Suarez, and de Vattel, contemplated the transnationality of justice.

PART 3.1

International Law as
Normative System:
To Regulate
the Use of Force

15

Self-Defense
and the Rule of Law

Oscar Schachter

S elf-defense on the international level is generally regarded, at least by international lawyers, as a legal right defined and legitimated by international law. Governments, by and large, appear to agree. When they have used force, they have nearly always claimed self-defense as their legal justification. Governments disputing that claim have usually asserted that the legal conditions of self-defense were not met in the particular case. However, despite the apparent agreement that self-defense is governed by law, the meaning and validity of that proposition remain open to question. There are some who challenge the basic idea that the security of a state—its self-preservation—can and should be subjected to international law. Others question whether under present conditions the ideal of a rule of law can be applied on the international level to national security decisions. My aim in this essay is to explore some aspects of the problem raised by these challenges to the applicability of international law to claims of self-defense. It is not my intention, I should add, to consider specific interpretations of self-defense.

An Inherent and Autonomous Right?

The idea of self-defense as an inherent and autonomous right has roots in two distinct schools of thought. One is traditional naturalist doctrine, expressed, for example, in Grotius's words that "[t]he right of self-defence . . . has its origin directly, and chiefly, in the fact that nature commits to each his own protection . . . ."[1] Preservation of the self was regarded as a natural right of the state, as of individuals, that could not be abrogated or limited by positive law. The United Nations Charter has been said to reflect this in characterizing self-defense as an "inherent right." The French expression, equally authentic, is *droit naturel;* in Spanish, it is *derecho inmanente;* and in Russian, *neotemlemoe pravo* (indefeasible right).

While acknowledging that the concept "inherent right" has natural law origins, many authorities on international law reject the idea that the right of self-defense exists independently of positive law and cannot be altered by it.[2] The International Court of Justice in its 1986 Judgment in the *Nicaragua* case, noting that Article 51 of the UN Charter recognizes a "natural" or "inherent" right of self-defense, said that "it is hard to see how this can be other than of a customary nature, even if its present content has been confirmed and influenced by the Charter."[3] However, the fact that the Court and international legal scholars consider that self-defense is governed by positive law has not obliterated an opposing conception of self-defense as an autonomous, nonderogable right that "exists" independently of legal rules. That conception, I believe, continues to influence popular and official attitudes concerning national security.

A second intellectual root of the proposition that self-defense cannot be governed by law is the belief in the subordination of law to power. This point of view was expressed forcefully by Dean Acheson, an eminent lawyer and former Secretary of State, in remarks to the American Society of International Law. He admonished international lawyers for debating the legal propriety of the U.S. "quarantine" in the Cuban missile crisis of 1962. The action taken by the United States was, in his view, "essential to the continuation of [its] pre-eminent power."[4] Law, he declared, "simply does not deal with such questions of ultimate power. . . . The survival of states is not a matter of law."[5] While these words may be interpreted in various ways, their main purport clearly was to emphasize that self-defense could not be governed by law when a grave threat to the power of a state or to its way of life was perceived by that state.

As might be expected, Acheson's emphatic denial of the relevance of law to the use of force did not commend itself to international lawyers generally, however divergent their legal opinions. But Acheson's position can hardly be considered as aberrant. It is in keeping both with the widely held view that the preservation of the state has precedence over positive law and with the "practical" understanding that it must be left to each state to decide what is necessary for its own self-defense. The latter position was given formal expression in the well-known statements made by the United States and France in connection with their adherence in 1928 to the Kellogg-Briand Treaty for the Renunciation of War. They each declared then that a state claiming self-defense "alone is competent to decide whether circumstances require recourse to war in self-defense."[6] The other signatories apparently accepted the same interpretation.

International lawyers concerned with the integrity of the legal commitment to renounce war in the 1928 Treaty were quick to see the danger of according exclusive competence to the state claiming self-defense. Hersch Lauterpacht, writing not long after the conclusion of the Kellogg-Briand Pact, declared that a claim that self-defense was not subject to objective evaluation could not be accepted in law. He wrote: "Such a claim is self-contradictory inasmuch as it purports to be based on legal right and at the same time, it dissociates itself from regulation and evaluation of the law."[7]

This statement of Lauterpacht was quoted with approval by Judge Stephen M. Schwebel in his dissenting opinion to the 1986 ICJ Judgment in the *Nicaragua* case. Schwebel placed much weight on Lauterpacht's analysis to support his conclusion that claims of self-defense were, in principle, justiciable. That analysis, as presented in Lauterpacht's classic work, *The Function of Law in the International Community,* likened self-defense in international law to the corresponding right in municipal law. In both cases, Lauterpacht said, the right was "absolute" in the sense that no law could disregard it.[8] Moreover, a state, like an individual, would have to decide in the first instance whether the immediate use of force in defense was necessary. However, the right is "relative" inasmuch as it is presumably regulated by law. "It is regulated to the extent that it is the business of the courts to determine whether, how far, and for how long, there was a necessity to have recourse to it."[9] Lauterpacht was aware, of course, that on the international level, states resisted submitting disputes regarding use of force to judicial process. That state of affairs, he argued, was in contradiction to the emerging law regulating use of force.[10] States could not have it both ways: if they did not accept the principle of justiciability, the legal dimension of self-defense would disappear and with it the regulation of force by law.

Lauterpacht's position received judicial support in the Judgment of the International Military Tribunal in Nuremberg in 1946. The Tribunal was confronted with the argument on behalf of the German Nazi leaders that Germany had acted in self-defense and that every state must be the judge of whether in a given case it has the right of self-defense. (Ironically, this argument accorded with the U.S. position taken in connection with the Kellogg-Briand Pact.) The Nuremberg Tribunal rejected that contention, observing that "whether action taken under the claim of self-defense was in fact aggressive or defensive must ultimately be subject to investigation or adjudication if international law is ever to be enforced."[11]

This forthright statement of the Nuremberg Tribunal was doubtless in keeping with the United States views in 1946. However, in the 1980s, the *Nicaragua* case produced doubts as to the justiciability of claims of self-defense. The U.S. position, as it developed, was not entirely clear or free from ambivalence. In 1984 U.S. counsel had argued to the Court that the United States alone was in a position to determine the necessity of the "defense" measures it had taken against Nicaragua in the particular circumstances of that case, an argument noted and approved by Judge Schwebel.

Nevertheless, the United States did not argue that self-defense was necessarily beyond legal evaluation and, as the Court observed, it did not claim that international law was not relevant or controlling in the case. The U.S. arguments against admissibility were addressed to other grounds, including the argument that the Security Council had exclusive competence to pass on the legality of the use of force.

After the Court ruled against the United States on the jurisdictional issues, the official U.S. stand appeared to move toward the same position as that expressed in 1928—namely, that questions of the necessity of defense were ultimately reserved to the defending state alone. This shift is suggested by statements made in congressional hearings on the withdrawal by the United States of its acceptance of compulsory jurisdiction. In explaining why the United States would not and should not submit to the International Court's jurisdiction in regard to its use of force in self-defense, the Legal Adviser of the Department of State declared that the exercise of self-defense could not be subject to the decision of the Court inasmuch as the national security of the United States was involved.[12] Such matters are the ultimate responsibility assigned by our Constitution to the President and the Congress."[13]

That statement can be read as rejecting any "external" authority to judge the legitimacy of American defense measures, a position that would contradict the idea of self-defense as a right defined by law. It is arguable that the U.S. position did not entirely exclude third-party determinations because it recognized the competence of the UN Security Council (an "external" body) to pass upon claims of self-defense. But since the United States has a veto in the Council, it remains ultimately the judge of its own cause, at least as far as the formal decisions are concerned. On the other hand, the fact that the United States recognizes the authority of the Council to discuss the legitimacy of self-defense measures is, in some measure, a weakening of its claim that it alone can be the final judge of the necessity of its defense measures. The Council, of course, is a political body charged with maintaining peace and security; it is not required to decide legal issues.

Underlying this apparent ambivalence in the U.S. position is the evident fact that the United States is not prepared to concede in respect of other states that they, too, can exclusively determine the necessity and legitimacy of their self-defense actions. To do so would mean that objections to such actions as the Soviet use of force in Czechoslovakia and Afghanistan would have to be based on purely political grounds. This line of argument would be much less effective in mobilizing world opinion than the argument that the basic norms of the Charter have been violated by the unlawful use of force. To say that each state is free to decide for itself when and to what extent it may use arms would remove the principal ground for international censure, and, in effect, bring to the vanishing point the legal limits on unilateral recourse to force. This is surely not the considered position of the United States, notwithstanding the rebuffs it has received in the International Court and UN organs.

The Influence of Community Judgment

That states generally do not welcome international scrutiny of their defensive measures is hardly surprising. This attitude is especially marked when armed force is actually used, even though seen by the user as legitimate self-defense. The drafters of the UN Charter sought to meet this problem by requiring, in Article 51, that each member immediately report to the Security Council measures taken by it in the exercise of the right of self-defense. This requirement, though explicit and unambiguous, has rarely been observed by states using force. However, the failures to report have not precluded the Council from considering, and in some cases passing judgment on, such claims when the matter was raised by states that questioned the legality of the use of force. The Council has rejected claims of self-defense in several cases (notably against states whose policies were generally disapproved).[14] No resolution has been adopted explicitly upholding a claim of self-defense, though in a few cases a resolution or the Council's failure to act has been construed by commentators as tacit approval or toleration of the use of force in question.[15] The Council, more often than not, has been precluded by the veto from reaching formal decisions on the validity of such claims. Most of those cases were then considered by the General Assembly, which, unfettered by the veto, generally condemned the alleged self-defense action as a Charter violation.[16] In no such case, however, has the target state accepted the UN decision as binding upon it.

One could say that this shows that each state remains the ultimate judge of its own cause in matters of self-defense; but it also shows that states using force do not escape community judgments even though they seek to avoid them. In actuality, appraisals of the legality of state conduct, especially in regard to the use of armed force, are made in a variety of non-judicial contexts. Since 1945, each time a state has used armed force outside its borders, its lawfulness has been subject to third-party judgment. Such judgments have been made by other governments, expressed individually or in collective political bodies. They have also been made by the community of international lawyers, by organs of opinion, by political parties and by other nongovernmental organizations. There is, in this sense, no escape from the judgments of the interested communities. They vary, to be sure, in their quality, their objectivity and their impact on the conduct of the state in question. The processes as well as the results are uneven. Yet it is clear that, in the end, no state is actually the *sole* judge of its own cause when it claims to have used force in self-defense.

Certainly, these various judgments are not binding or enforceable in the way judicial judgments are supposed to be. Moreover, their objectivity may be questioned because they often appear to be influenced more by political attitudes than by legal standards. But these deficiencies are not the whole story. Votes in international bodies show that the reactions to use of force are not always dictated by political affinities in disregard of facts and law. States that are friendly to, or even closely allied with, an accused state have not hesitated to cast their vote against that state when the issues were clear. Even the most powerful states have not been immune to censure by states that normally would follow their lead. The overwhelming majorities that have censured the USSR for its invasion of Afghanistan and condemned the United States for its actions in Grenada and Nicaragua are notable examples.[17] Clearly, international violence is not a matter of indifference to the world; nor is it considered to be solely a political problem. States accused of illegality take pains to show their conduct to be legitimate self-defense. They are mindful of the political costs of adverse opinion even though they may persist in the questionable use of force. It is significant that accused states do not deny they are bound by international rules; they rest their justification on factual assessments or interpretations that would bring them within the law. The International Court of Justice took note of this tendency in its 1986 Judgment in the *Nicaragua* case, declaring that it confirmed the general acceptance of the rules on force as binding law.

Of course, such "acceptance" does not fully answer the perennial question of whether the legal principles significantly influence states in their planning or use of force. Political analysts often regard the legal justifications as after-the-fact rationalizations that have little, if any, effect on the actual decisions. They maintain that, at bottom, such decisions are based on considerations of power and interest, which nearly always prevail over contrary legal restraints. This broad generalization, which is probably widely accepted, raises more questions than it answers. In particular, it leaves open the critical issue of whether the limitations on the use of force are considered generally to serve the national interests and the security of states. To counterpoise "interest" and "law" as conflicting factors in this context is misleading. Even on the premise of an essentially anarchical, Hobbesian conception of international society, the coexistence of independent states and their mutually beneficial intercourse are seen to require some restraints on the unilateral recourse to force. Hence, the position of states that self-defense as defined by international law is the only ground for the unilateral use of force is not in itself inconsistent with the realist thesis of national self-interest. It is realistic in recognizing that international violence has not been eliminated by the legal prohibitions in the United Nations Charter or by its collective security provisions and that, consequently, a right of self-defense must be legitimized. It also recognizes, through the right of collective self-defense, that the targets of aggression may require armed assistance by other states.

Recognizing these rights as exceptions to the general prohibition on force necessarily presupposes that the exercise of the right is limited by law. If this were not the case and each state remained free to decide for itself when and to what extent it may use force, the legal restraint on force would virtually disappear. It surely cannot be said that this result is perceived to be in the national interest of states generally or, for that matter, in the interest of the most powerful states. Neither the United States nor the Soviet Union can realistically consider it in the national interest to recognize the unlimited right of each to use force. They cannot therefore accept a self-judging conception of the right of self-defense without, in effect, licensing the other state to resort to force whenever it chooses to do so.

To say that self-defense must be regulated by law does not assume that general rules are sufficient in themselves to ensure the security of all states. The UN Charter and other relevant agreements make it quite clear that the maintenance of peace and security requires more than agreement on principles of law. Decisions must be taken in specific cases. States must react in words and deeds to claims of self-defense when force is used. Such responses are not automatic or foreordained; they involve acts of will and, therefore, assessments of interest and power. Governments rarely, if ever, make such decisions "solely" or "purely" on legal grounds; they are not expected to behave like a court. But whatever factors determine such decisions, once made they become part of the law-shaping process, influencing expectations as to the acceptability of future actions influencing use of force. Most governments recognize this. Whether or not they are themselves involved in the particular conflict, they are aware of the implications for other conflicts and often of their own interest in avoiding the spread of hostilities. Legality matters to them, not only as rhetoric to win support, but also as a factor to be taken into account as part of the effort to contain violence and reduce the risks of escalation.

Defensist Principles and the *Lex Specialis*

A critical question affecting both law and policy on self-defense concerns the degree of uncertainty or indeterminacy that inheres in the proclaimed legal limits. Some indeterminacy results from the key standards of necessity and proportionality, concepts that leave ample room for diverse opinions in particular cases. Other sources of uncertainty can be traced to differing interpretations of the events that would permit a forcible defensive action.

Varying views have been advanced by governments and scholars relating to the kinds of illegal force that would trigger the right of an armed defensive response. While strong positions have been taken by nearly all states against "preventive" or "preemptive" war, some uncertainty remains as to threats of force that credibly appear as likely to result in imminent attack. Other issues, highlighted by the *Nicaragua* case, concern the illegal use of force through subversion, supply of arms, and logistic support of armed forces as sufficient ground for defensive response It is not entirely clear to what extent self-defense responding to an armed attack embraces the use of force as a deterrent to future attacks. Nor is there agreement on the circumstances that would permit a state to intervene (or "counterintervene") in an internal conflict under the principle of collective self-defense. Even more unsettling is the uncertainty about the first use of nuclear weapons, the targeting of civilian centers and the proportionality of retaliatory action.

These controversial issues indicate that the rules of self-defense fall far short of a code of conduct that would provide precise "hard law" for many cases likely to arise. Even though governments have a stake in securing clarity as to what is permitted and forbidden, there are obvious limits to achieving that objective. General formulas accepted as law are subject to continuing interpretation and, therefore, to fresh arguments as to what the law should be. Concrete situations create new perceptions and "accomplished facts." At times, the line between violations and emerging law may be difficult to draw, made more difficult by the absence of judicial authority and the great disparities in power in the international community. Lawmaking authority does not reside in majorities in international assemblies, even though large majorities cannot usually be ignored. Powerful states—that is, those with the ability to control the outcome of contested decisions—may determine patterns of conduct for other states, as well as for themselves. But their ability to do so is limited by the checks and balances inherent in the distribution of power and, in particular, by the nuclear setoff. Clearly, the two superpowers are not all-powerful hegemons able to exercise complete control over the use of force by weaker states, not even by all those close to their borders. The rough parity of power between them undoubtedly contributes to restraint. It does not eliminate, however, the struggles within states that erupt beyond their borders or the localized hostilities between neighboring states that threaten to spread. The application of legal rules in these cases and the formulation of new rules derived from practice "accepted as law" are not decided by the great powers alone. . . .

Notwithstanding its relative indeterminacy, self-defense as a legal norm can have an ascertainable relationship to the policies and actions of governments. The "defensist" principle—namely, that self-defense is the only legitimate reason to use force against another state—has been expressed as the strategic policy of most states. Evidence for this is not only found in governmental statements to international bodies, where they may be expected. Recent studies by political scientists and students of military strategy confirm the practical implications of defensist doctrine.[18] When states proclaim the principle of self-defense as governing the use of force, they have a stake in its credibility to other states and to their own citizens. For such states to be credible, their training and contingent planning must reflect a defensist strategy. Their good faith can be tested by their willingness to consider ways to reduce threats and resolve conflicts without using force. Hence, a defensist posture is not merely one of restraint but a source of policy that goes beyond the essentially negative rules of the law. It has obvious implications for such protective activities as monitoring and inspection. It calls for limitations on weaponry and balance among adversaries. The danger that systems which purport to be defensive may be perceived as offensive and therefore "destabilizing" becomes a matter of central concern. The most obvious consequence of defensist doctrine is that states no longer consider that they may invade other states for objectives that were considered in prior periods as legitimate and appropriate. Thus, the naked use of force for economic gain, or to avenge past injustices, or civilize "inferior" people, or vindicate honor, or achieve "manifest destiny," is no longer asserted as national policy. Seen in the perspective of history, this is a profound change in the relations of states.

I do not mean to suggest that power—or more precisely, relative power differentials among states—no longer matters. Acceptance of the legal norm of self-defense as the sole legitimate use of force has not eliminated military strength as a major factor in the relations of states. States will react, as they have in the past, to perceived power imbalances that are seen as threatening their present position and vital interests. Disparities in power may involve implied or sometimes express threats of force to influence behavior of other states. Armaments and military alliances are considered necessary and legitimate responses to such threats. Neither the Charter nor customary law imposes limits on the size or composition of armed forces or on military pacts for defense. States are legally free to deploy their forces as they choose within their territories or in the territories of consenting states. They are also entitled to deploy armed force in areas beyond national jurisdiction (notably, the high seas), except insofar as they have entered into treaties to limit such activity. The military establishments and the protective measures of states are governed, by and large, by national defense policies and the "politics of security," rather than by the international law governing use of force and self-defense.

Even so, international law is not entirely excluded. It becomes relevant to national security policy in different ways, all rooted in the idea that force should not be used or threatened except in self-defense. States that accept this defensist principle, as nearly all claim to do (though future exceptions cannot be ruled out), are faced with heavy costs—political as well as economic—when they seek security by unilateral action. Such costs may be reduced by mutual arrangements with possible adversaries. But the choice may involve the so-called security dilemma, namely, the likelihood that unilateral measures intended to increase a nation's security decrease the security of others, whereas joint measures, although less costly, involve a measure of insecurity because of the fear of violations by the other parties. The risks contribute to the complexities of international negotiations concerning mutual security. Whatever the dynamics of such negotiations and the obstacles encountered in particular cases, we now find many arrangements, bilateral and multilateral, that involve reciprocal restraints on national military activity. They extend to kinds of weapons, deployment of forces, military exercises, testing and in some cases size of forces.[19]

When these arrangements are embodied in treaties, they are readily seen as part of international law, as instances of a *lex specialis* governing specific activities for the states that are parties. Of course, states may also agree on restraints in instruments that are not treaties, such as political declarations or gentlemen's agreements or by tacit understandings expressed in reciprocal practices. Although these are not regarded as legal commitments, they are observed and relied upon as long as the states concerned have a common interest in maintaining the arrangement. Violations may be treated in these cases substantially the same as they are treated in respect of treaties. They may be grounds for protest or for terminating the arrangement or for countermeasures. The difference between nontreaty regimes and treaties may be important for domestic constitutional processes, but the distinction may not make any significant difference in the observance of the rules and restraints. In some cases, nontreaty practice becomes "special" custom recognized as legally obligatory customary law for the states concerned. Even apart from this, the distinction between the formal treaty obligations and the "rules of the game" based on tacit understandings and practice may not have very much practical significance.

The point I wish to underline is that national security policies premised on defense have produced a variety of international arrangements that enable states, particularly potential adversaries, to impose limits on their military establishments and activities in the well-founded expectation that others will do the same. The costs of self-defense are thereby reduced, though states still have to seek means of dealing with the risks of violation. Provision may be made for verification, consultative procedures, countermeasures and dispute settlement. Such measures strengthen the understanding that the restraints are not simply arrangements of convenience to be broken at will. It is surely not inappropriate for governments as well as international lawyers to treat these regulatory arrangements as part of the body of international law, as rules of conduct, and not merely as transient power bargaining.

The more controversial questions of self-defense have been raised by actions and claims that would expand a state's right to use force beyond the archetypical case of an armed attack on the territory or instrumentality of that state. Such expanded conceptions of self-defense are exemplified by the following uses of force by states claiming self-defense:

(1) the use of force to rescue political hostages believed to face imminent danger of death or injury;[20]

(2) the use of force against officials or installations in a foreign state believed to support terrorist acts directed against nationals of the state claiming the right of defense;[21]

(3) the use of force against troops, planes, vessels or installations believed to threaten imminent attack by a state with declared hostile intent;[22]

(4) the use of retaliatory force against a government or military force so as to deter renewed attacks on the state taking such action;[23]

(5) the use of force against a government that has provided arms or technical support to insurgents in a third state,[24]

(6) the use of force against a government that has allowed its territory to be used by military forces of a third state considered to be a threat to the state claiming self-defense;[25]

(7) the use of force in the name of collective defense (or counterintervention) against a government imposed by foreign forces and faced with large-scale military resistance by many of its people.[26]

As indicated by the footnote references, these seven categories summarize situations that have occurred in recent years. The list is not complete; other extended self-defense claims have been asserted by governments to justify their use of force or to threaten such use in some situations.[27] Nearly all the cases have been discussed in UN bodies and, although opinions have been divided, it is clear that most governments have been reluctant to legitimize expanded self-defense actions that go beyond the paradigmatic case. Thus, no UN resolution has approved the use of force in any of the cases that I have listed. In the few cases where resolutions were adopted that passed judgment on the legality of the action, they denied the validity of the self-defense claim. In many cases, resolutions were not adopted, but the majority of states that addressed the issue of lawfulness criticized the actions as contrary to the Charter. Few ventured to defend the legality of the self-defense claim. Of course, political sympathies influenced the votes of many of the states, but, as I observed earlier, in several notable cases, allied or friendly states joined in condemnation of the actions. In at least some of these cases, and perhaps all of them, the opposition to the self-defense claims appeared to be based in part on a difference of view as to the facts. In many cases, assertions of the state claiming self-defense were simply not believed; in some cases, factual claims of *both* sides to the dispute were treated with the utmost skepticism.

The uncertainty surrounding the factual claims and the not insignificant political motivations are reasons that condemnation by governments in the UN bodies cannot always be accepted as persuasive on the issue of lawfulness. On the other hand, such condemnations cannot be ignored; they warrant consideration as relevant appraisals. Moreover, from a broader perspective, the general reluctance to approve uses of force under expanded conceptions of self-defense is itself significant. Such reluctance is evidence of a widespread perception that widening the scope of self-defense will erode the basic rule against unilateral recourse to force. The absence of binding judicial or other third-party determinations relating to use of force adds to the apprehension that a more permissive rule of self-defense will open the way to further disregard of the limits on force. It is true that some international lawyers believe that legitimate self-defense should be construed more liberally. They argue that the absence of effective collective remedies against illegal force makes it necessary, indeed inevitable, that states take defensive action on the basis of their own perceptions of national interest and capabilities. In addition to the imperatives of national security, they cite the responsibility of powerful states to maintain international order. They stress that the words of the Charter should be interpreted "in context" so as to yield "reasonable" meanings required by the "purpose and object" of the text.[28] Unilateral acts that stretch the meaning of self-defense are treated as "state practice," although there is no general *opinio juris* to support their acceptance as law. Hence, conduct that violates text and earlier interpretations can be viewed as new or emerging law based on the efficacy of accomplished facts in shaping the law. Some of these arguments, if accepted, would extend the concept of self-defense so broadly as to allow almost any unilateral use of force taken in the name of law and order. There is no evidence that governments by and large would favor this result. On the contrary, the records of the United Nations, as already mentioned, show strong resistance to widening self-defense to permit force except where there has been an armed attack or threat of imminent attack. It does not seem likely that this resistance will disappear in the foreseeable future.

This does not mean, of course, that the law of self-defense will remain static. The kaleidoscopic events of our era will continue to create new pressures for resort to force. The role of international law cannot be limited to repeating the old maxims. What its role should be calls for further consideration. In the next section, I offer some thoughts and suggestions.

Enhancing Security Through Law and Institutions

To begin with, a clear distinction should be maintained between law as an expression of common policy and purpose and the use of law for rationalization of state action. If law is to operate as a limit on national power, it will lead to judgments of legitimacy that diverge from a particular state's perception of national interest at a given time. True, such divergence may be reduced by redefining or widening the conception of national interest to include the long-term interest in stability and order. But changing the conceptions of national interest is easier said than done. In a concrete case, national leaders and their citizenry may hold to their particular view of state interest, even though clearly incompatible with the law and the "enlightened" views of others. To conclude that law must yield to such judgments of national interest negates the idea of law as a restraint on state conduct. This is not to say that international law can replace the continuing task of defining national interests and the defense needs of a state. That there may be a conflict between such national goals and the restraints of international law must be acknowledged. Recognizing such tension is an important step toward reconciliation of the competing interests.

One path toward reducing the tension between defense needs and legal rules of restraint lies in the specific agreements referred to earlier as the *lex specialis*. Such agreements may be explicit or they may be tacit. They may even be legally nonbinding (as are gentlemen's agreements) and still relied upon for mutual compliance. By moving from the abstract level to the concrete, states can achieve rules of behavior that are perceived to support the common interests in security and reduced defense costs. Such agreements, it is true, may be frangible, but while they last, they add to the sense of security. De Gaulle once remarked that "treaties are like roses and young girls; they last while they last." That they do not last forever is no reason to minimize them. Indeed, like some fashions, they would be intolerable if they did not change.

Specific agreements concerning defense rarely go beyond reciprocal negative restraints when the parties are adversary. In contrast, agreements among states that share a common defense interest tend to involve more positive cooperation. But adversary states that are apprehensive about the threat of others may also benefit from arrangements that entail cooperation, such as exchanges of information and other confidence-building procedures. Some of the recent arms limitation agreements between the superpowers are steps in that direction.[29] Other agreements between former adversaries provide for cultural relations, free movement of persons, normal trade.[30] Agreements of that kind can create a sense of diffuse reciprocity and generalized commitment that strengthens compliance. In the current parlance of political science, they may become "security regimes."

The adoption of such treaties and regimes for particular areas or activities would not exclude a continuing reference to the general principles of self-defense set forth in the Charter and authoritative customary law. If such principles are to be treated as law rather than after-the-fact rationalization, they must be applied to concrete cases in a disciplined and consistent way. This process entails an analysis that takes rules seriously and does not "deconstruct" them, making all meanings permissible. Legal reasoning helps to limit purely subjective interpretation. Textual exegesis, original intent, relevant context, evolving purposes, and practice "accepted as law" are elements in such reasoning. So are applicable doctrine and basic postulates of law. These elements cannot be reduced to a single governing factor. Every legal analysis, moreover, must take account of the complexity of the particular situations and their relationship to the dominant ends of the law in question. Yet the factual uniqueness of each case cannot obliterate the limits set by the general rules. If law is to be relevant, a state's right of self-defense in a particular situation must have as its necessary corollary recognition of the right of all other states in comparable cases.

This proposition not only is implicit in the idea of juridical equality; it also underlines the need for criteria that are generally recognized and accepted as authoritative. Ad hoc judgments that are purportedly based entirely on the facts and an undefined standard of "reasonableness" tend to be largely determined by crypto-criteria that reflect particular preferences and values. Such judgments are not likely to help clarify the line between permissible and impermissible conduct carried out in the name of self-defense. Furthermore, they will be perceived as lacking justification based on norms that the community of states—not just part of it—has accepted.

It is true that standards for determining the legitimacy of defense will necessarily be somewhat abstract. They will not be fully determinate for they will have to be interpreted and applied to individual cases. Facts, analysis and deliberation will be required to reach appropriate conclusions that take into account both standards and circumstances. A process of reasoning involving the interaction of principle and situation (i.e., casuistry in its favorable sense) is required. Moreover, that process and the continuing reflections of governments and international lawyers extend beyond the elaboration of established doctrine. They involve, as they should, the development (or construction) of more specific standards appropriate for changing circumstances. To some extent, such standards emerge through the responses of states faced with new situations. This type of ongoing law-generating process calls for continuing appraisal by international lawyers, as well as by governments.

Of equal importance to the elaboration of standards are the processes for application of the standards to particular cases. International lawyers earlier in this century emphasized the preeminent value of judicial determination and many urged the extension of the compulsory jurisdiction of the

International Court. The more hopeful among them envisaged the Court as an arbiter of major disputes, not excluding acts of aggression. The Nuremberg Judgment reinforced that image. In the 1950s, American lawyers, generally conservative, called for the "rule of law" through compulsory jurisdiction of the International Court.[31] Leaders such as Eisenhower and Nixon favored greater use of the Court. But as most governments failed to respond, the Court was increasingly seen to be marginal, limited to technical legal disputes. With the Tehran *Hostages* case and, more dramatically, the *Nicaragua* case, the Court was seized of disputes involving force. Its decisions in the *Nicaragua* case produced misgivings (as well as support) and they also gave rise to a rather more profound debate than had previously occurred on the role of adjudication and on compulsory jurisdiction.[32] (Not at all profound and, one would hope, quickly forgotten were the diatribes against the Court.) Notwithstanding the criticism of the *Nicaragua* decision by U.S. officials and some lawyers, the role of the Court remains on the international agenda.

The recent, rather sweeping assertion by some U.S. lawyers that no case involving force is appropriate for the Court might not be persuasive if agreement can be reached on some categories of such claims. It will be recalled that in the 1950s the United States itself sought to bring to the Court claims among from the shooting down of its planes in Eastern Europe.[33] The *Hostages* case against Iran would not have been admissible if the United States earlier had excluded cases involving force from its treaty commitment.[34] Having these cases in mind, it hardly seems perilous for a state to agree to adjudication of cases involving acts of force such as shooting incidents or isolated attacks, under reciprocally binding acceptances of compulsory jurisdiction. Officials distrustful of international tribunals, especially in matters affecting security, sometimes argue that the Court should not be "burdened" with consequential disputes likely to be seen as political. On the other hand, we should not overlook the value of a judicial decision holding a state accountable in a matter of some consequence. The *Hostages* case against Iran is a pertinent example. The assumption, sometimes made, that the Court needs to be "protected" against important controversies is surely open to question. It is unlikely that a tribunal limited to minor technical disputes would fulfill the need and expectations for an authoritative judicial organ. The International Court would not be greatly respected if it became the international equivalent of a small-claims court. I see no good reason for international lawyers now to argue for the principle *de maximis non curat praetor.*

Nevertheless, we must be wary of assuming that recourse to a court will resolve all disputes reducible to legal issues. In a technical (or Pickwickian) sense, this may be true. Every dispute can be construed as a question of whether conduct objected to is permissible or not under international law; hence, logically all disputes are susceptible to judicial determination. But this reasoning obviously misses the reality of disputes that, in substance, are not about differences in the meaning of the law. A court will not truly resolve such disputes even if given jurisdiction. We must reconcile ourselves to the fact that, at best, judicial regulation of armed conflicts will remain peripheral, most likely limited to cases arising out of specific incidents of limited scope and duration.

Clearly, we must look beyond the Court in order to reinforce the accountability of states for improper resort to force. The heart of that effort lies in fact-finding, review and appraisal by international agencies in a variety of contexts. With regard to self-defense, accountability requires respect for the obligation under Article 51 to report armed action claimed to be defensive. To give effect to that obligation, governments must report the facts openly and truthfully. This would impose limits on secrecy, though in some cases military necessity might be an acceptable ground for limited reporting. Accountability can also be given effect in many situations by monitoring and verification arrangements, particularly by international agencies. The renewed interest in treaties that provide for verification and monitoring is promising. There is surely ample room for more extensive use of observers, truce supervisors and peacekeeping forces to assist in determining the facts in disputes about the use of force and self-defense. Institutional procedures, such as those of the UN Security Council, the regional organizations and the international secretariats, require strengthening to ensure that factual reporting and monitoring are effective. The deliberative processes of international organs require adaptation for the appraisal of facts and the claims of the disputing parties. Obviously, these various steps are not the exclusive province of the international lawyers, though the skills of lawyers in regard to procedures of fact-finding and dispute settlement would be helpful.

It is tempting to lawyers to call for the rule of law in international affairs. The temptation is not resisted in this essay, though much of it is concerned with the obstacles to realizing the ideal. The relationship of national security and international law is inevitably complicated and fluid. I have not tried to simplify it, but I have accepted a basic premise—namely, that the right of self-defense, "inherent" though it may be, cannot be autonomous. To consider it as above or outside the law renders it more probable that force will be used unilaterally and abusively. No state or people can face that prospect with equanimity in the present world. The answer, in part, is that self-defense must be regarded as limited and not only legitimated by law. To give this conception reality requires more than juridical doctrine. It demands, as I have suggested, a structure of accountability built upon obligations, procedures and institutions. The political will that is necessary depends on understanding both the danger of unbridled force and the necessity of legal and institutional control. Recent events, as I have noted, offer some promise of that development. It is through such concrete measures that international law may in time strengthen the national security of all states.

Notes

1. H. Grotius, De Jure Belli Ac Pacis, bk. II, ch. I, pt. III, at 172 (Carnegie Endowment trans. 1925) (1646).

2. *See* H. Kelsen, The Law of the United Nations 791–92 (1950); D. Bowett, Self-Defence in International Law 187 91958); Ago, Addendum to Eighth Report on State Responsibility to the International Law Commission, [1980] 2 Y.B. Int'l L. Comm'n, pt. 1 at 13, 66–67, UN Doc. A/CN.4/SER.A/1980/Add.1; Y. Dinstein, War, Aggression and Self-Defence 169–72 (1988).

3. Military and Paramilitary Activities in and against Nicaragua (Nicar. v. U.S.), Merits, 1986 ICJ Rep. 14, 94, para. 176 (Judgment of June 27).

4. Acheson, Remarks, 57 ASIL Proc. 13, 14 (1963).

5. Id.

6. U.S. note of June 23, 1928, *quoted in* H. Miller, The Peace Pact of Paris 213, 214 (1928).

7. H. Lauterpacht, The Function of Law in the International Community 179–80 (1933).

8. H. Lauterpacht, *supra* note 8, at 180.

9. *Id.*

10. *Id.* at 181.

11. Judgment of the International Military Tribunal at Nuremberg, 1946, 1 Trial of German Major War Criminals Before the International Military Tribunal 208 (1947).

12. Sofaer, Statement, in *U.S. Decision to Withdraw from the International Court of Justice: Hearing Before the Subcomm. on Human Rights and International Organization of the House Comm. on Foreign Affairs,* 99th Cong., 1st Sess. 27–28 (1985).

13. *Id.* at 30.

14. For example, self-defense claims made by Israel for attacks against Palestinian organizations based in Jordan and Lebanon were rejected by the Security Council in the following resolutions: SC Res. 228 (Nov. 25, 1966); SC Res. 265 (Apr. 1, 1969); SC Res. 270 (Aug. 26, 1969); SC Res. 279n (May 12, 1970); SC Res. 313 (Feb. 28, 1972); SC Res. 332 (Apr. 21, 1973); SC Res. 347 (Apr. 24, 1974). *See also* SC Res. 488 (June 18, 1831) (condemning Israeli air attack which destroyed the Osiraq nuclear reactor in Iraq in 1981). The general Assembly rejected the Soviet Union's self-defense claim to justify the intervention in Afghanistan in 1980. GA Res. ES-6/2 (Jan. 14, 1980). In addition, South Africa has been condemned for its attacks against neighboring states. SC Res. 393 (July 30, 1976); SC Res. 387 (Mar. 31, 1976).

15. For example, the Security Council resolution that noted the invasion of the Falkland Islands by Argentina in 1982 demanded the immediate withdrawal of all Argentine forces from the Falkland Islands. No reference was made to the withdrawal of British forces. A clear implication was that the British had legitimately exercised the right of self-defense. The resolution was adopted by 10 votes to 1 (Panama), with 4 abstentions. SC Res. 502 (Apr. 3, 1982). The Israeli rescue action in Entebbe, Uganda was criticized in the Security Council (and also defended). When a draft resolution censuring Israel was not put to a vote, the Council's nonaction was seen as an indication that the rescue mission was not a violation of Article

2(4). *See* Schachter, *International Law in the Hostage Crisis: Implications for Future Cases,* in American Hostages in Iran 325, 331 (1985).

16. The General Assembly may indicate its disapproval of a doubtful self-defense claim in a more indirect manner, as by refusing to accept the credentials of a regime imposed by illegal resort to force, for example, Kampuchea. *See* GA Res. 34/22 (Nov. 14, 1979); and 37/6 (Oct. 28, 1982).Conversely, the United Nations has refrained from condemning the use of force under a questionable claim of self-defense when the end result of the action was not considered reprehensible. For example, the Tanzanian invasion of Uganda in 1979 and its continued occupation were not censured by the General Assembly or by the Organization of African Unity. *See* N. Ronzitti, Rescuing Nationals Abroad Through Military Coercion and Intervention on Grounds of Humanity 102–06 (1985).

17. GA Res. 37/73 (Nov. 29, 1982) (condemnation of the Soviet Union for its invasion of Afghanistan); GA Res. 38/7 (Nov. 2, 1983) (condemnation of the United States for its invasion of Grenada); SC Res. 562 (May 10, 1985) and GA Res. 40/188 (Dec. 17, 1985) (condemnation of the United States for its trade embargo against Nicaragua); GA Res. 41/31 (Nov 3, 1986) (calling for U.S. compliance with the ICJ's Judgment in *Nicaragua* case).

18. M. Ceadel, Thinking About War and Peace 72–88 (1987); The Conventional Defense of Europe (A. Pierre ed. 1986); Stockholm International Peace Research Institution, Policies for Common Security (1985).

19. Existing treaties include those establishing nuclear-free zones, prohibiting proliferation, and limiting size and number of weapons. *See, e.g.,* Treaty on the Non-Proliferation of Nuclear Weapons, July 1, 1968, 21 UST 483, TIAS No. 6839, 729 UNTS 161; Treaty on the Limitation of Anti-Ballistic Missile Systems, May 26, 1972, U.S.-USR, 23 UST 3435, TIAS No. 7503; Treaty on the Elimination of Their Intermediate-Range and Shorter-Range Missiles (the INF Treaty),Dec. 8, 1987, U.S.-USR, S. Treaty Doc. No. 11, 100th Cong., 2d Sess. (1988), *reprinted in* 27 ILM 84 (1988); Treaty for the Prohibition of Nuclear Weapons in Latin America, Feb. 14, 1967, 22 UST 762, TIS No. 7137, 634 UNTA 281 (the United States is not a party).

20. Rescue actions were undertaken by Israel in Entebee, Uganda in 1976 and by the United States in Iran in 1980. An earlier rescue mission was carried out in Stanleyville in the then Congo by Belgium. For discussion of legal issues, see Schachter, *supra* note 19, at 1629–32.

21. E.g., the U.S. bombing of Libya. *See* Dep't St. Bull., No. 2111, June 1986; GA Res. 41/38 (Nov. 20, 1986); Statement of U.S. representative to UN Security Council, *excerpted in* Contemporary Practice of the United States, 80 AJIL 632, 633–36 (1986).

22. E.g., the Israeli action against Egypt in 1967. *See* Dinstein, *the Legal Issues of Para-War and Peace in the Middle East,* 44 St. John's L. Rev. 466, 469–70 (1970).

23. E.g., the Israeli military invasion of Lebanon in 1982. *See* SC Res. 509 (June 6, 1982); and GA Res. ES-7/9 (Sept. 14, 1982). *See also* Feinstein, *The Legality of the Use of Armed Force by Israel in Lebanon,* 20 Isr. L.Rev. 362 (1985); Mallison, *Aggression or Self-Defense in Lebanon?,* 77, ASIL Proc. 174 (1983).

24. E.g., the U.S. support of the resistance (contras) in Nicaragua. *See Nicaragua* case, 1986 ICJ Rep. 14; *see also* Moore, *The Secret War in Central America and the Future of World Order,* 80 AJIL 43 (1986); Rowles, *"Secret Wars," Self-Defense and the Charter, id.* at 568.

25. E.g., the U.S. blockade of Cuba in 1962. *See* McDougal, *supra* note 19; Wright, *The Cuban Quarantine,* 57 AJIL 546 (1963).

26. An example is the military aid to the resistance in Afghanistan given by Pakistan and the United States. *See* J. Collins, The Soviet Invasion (1986). On the legal claim of the USSR, see Dowsald-Beck, *The Legal Validity of Military Intervention by Invitation of the Government,* 56 Brit. Y.B. Int'l. L. 189 (1985).

27. For example, self-defense has been cited as justification for military action to recover "lost" territories that were allegedly taken by illegal force. India's seizure of Goa and Argentina's attempt to occupy the Malvinas-Falkland Islands are in point.

28. *See* M. S. McDougal & F. Feliciano, Law and Minimum World Public Order 207–61 (1961); Moore, "the Legal Tradition and the Management of National Security," in *Toward World Order and Human Dignity* (W. H. Reisman & B. Weston eds. 1976).

29. See note 20 *Supra.*

30. E.g., Treaty of Peace, Mar. 26, 1979, Egypt-Israel, Art. III, 18 ILM 362, 364 (1979). The Helsinki Final Act of 1975, *supra* note 20, provided for a broad range of cooperative relations—economic, cultural, exchange of information, etc.—among former adversaries.

31. *See* Rhyne, *The Athens Conference on World Peace Through Law,* 58 AJIL 138 (1964); Franck & Lehrman, *Messianism and Chauvinism in America's Commitment to Peace Through Law,* in The International Court of Justice at a Crossroads 3, 6, 15–17 (L. Damrosch ed. 1987) [hereinafter Damrosch].

32. *See* Damrosch, *supra* note 21, especially articles by Bilder, Weiss, Damrosch, Gordon and Highet. *See also Appraisals of the ICJ's Decision: Nicaragua v. United States (Merits),* 81 AJIL 77 (1987); Scott & Carr, *The ICJ and Compulsory Jurisdiction, id.* at 57.

33. *See* Schachter, *Disputes Involving the Use of Force,* in Damrosch, *supra* note 21, at 223.

34. United States Diplomatic and Consular Staff in Tehran (U.S. v. Iran), 1980 ICJ Rep. 3 (Judgment of May 24).

16

International Law and the Recourse to Force: A Shift in Paradigms

Anthony Clark Arend and Robert J. Beck

The point is that international law is not higher law or better law; it is *existing* law. It is not a law that eschews force; such a view is alien to the very idea of law. Often as not it is the law of the victor; but it is law withal and does evolve.[1]

Daniel Patrick Moynihan

Introduction

When the framers of the United Nations Charter met in San Francisco, they hoped to establish a new world order—one in which the recourse to force would be severely restricted. To this end, they formulated the United Nations Charter paradigm for the *jus ad bellum*. Three components set the parameters of this paradigm: 1) a legal obligation; 2) institutions to enforce the obligation; and 3) a value hierarchy that formed the philosophical basis of this obligation.

The first of these components, the legal obligation, was embodied in Article 2(4) of the Charter. States were to refrain from any threat or use of force against the political or territorial status quo or in any other way against the principles of the United Nations. The only exceptions to this general prohibition were 1) force used in self-defense as defined in Article 51, and 2) force authorized by the Security Council in accordance with the provisions of Chapter VII.

The second component, the international institutions, were established under Chapter VII of the Charter. Under these provisions, the Security Council is empowered to investigate international conflicts and determine

Anthony Clark Arend and Robert J. Beck, *International Law and the Use of Force,* London: Routledge, 1993, pp. 177–202. Reprinted with permission of Routledge and the authors.

if there is a threat to the peace, a breach of the peace, or an act of aggression. If the Council so determines, it is further authorized to take collective action against the recalcitrant state.

The third element of the Charter paradigm is the underlying value hierarchy. When the Charter was drafted, even though the framers proclaimed many goals for the new international organization, its preeminent goal was the maintenance of international peace and security. This goal of peace was to take priority over other goals of justice. Justice was to be sought, but not at the expense of peace. Given the experience of the first two world wars, the framers believed that more damage was done to the international system by taking up arms to fight for justice than by living with a particular injustice.

The preceding analysis reveals, however, that since the Second World War, a number of significant developments have challenged the validity of this Charter paradigm. These include such problems as the failure of international institutions and the emergence of new values concerning the recourse to force. Although most international legal scholars would contend that these post-war developments represent serious threats to the Charter paradigm, few would claim that they are indicative of a paradigmatic shift. We reject this contention. Our conclusion is that in the world since 1945, a new legal paradigm has indeed emerged: a 'post-Charter self-help' paradigm. This paradigm, we argue, is at present the best framework for understanding the contemporary law relating to the recourse to force. But even as this second paradigm may currently describe existing law, recent events in the Middle East, Eastern Europe, Central America, Africa, and elsewhere suggest that a third paradigm may be emerging, a 'prodemocratic' paradigm.

This chapter will attempt to provide an analytical framework for understanding these conclusions. In order to do so, the first section will outline the contours of the post-Charter self-help paradigm. The second section will explore the possible emergence of a new, pro-democratic paradigm. Finally, the third section will examine the future direction of the *jus ad bellum* and make recommendations for its development.

The Post-Charter Self-Help Paradigm

Not long after the Charter was adopted, changes in the international system began to challenge the efficacy of this framework for the recourse to force, leading ultimately to the emergence of a new paradigm. In order to understand the nature of this paradigm, let us examine three elements: 1) the failure of Charter institutions; 2) the emergence of a new value hierarchy; and, 3) the changed legal obligation.

The Failure of Charter Institutions

Since 1945 several major problems have developed with the system for the collective use of force established by the Charter. These include the veto, the inability to establish formal mechanisms for collective action, and the general rejection of limited collective security. Even though world leaders and scholars made efforts to respond to these problems, these efforts showed little promise. Using the General Assembly as a substitute for the Security Council only really worked in the case of Korea. And in that case, the Security Council has already authorized the initial action. In subsequent uses of force, the Assembly has not been able to respond effectively to challenge an act of aggression. Similarly, the use of regional arrangements has not proved very successful. Such arrangements have responded only selectively to uses of force by states and have frequently been perceived as little more than a fig leaf for great power actions. Finally, peacekeeping, which developed in the wake of the failure of limited collective security, cannot be considered as a substitute. Peacekeeping explicitly recognizes that collective action to fight aggression is unlikely. It comes into play only after the hostilities have ceased and the parties consent to international supervision. Peacekeeping is thus not a legitimate alternative to the Chapter VII approach to collective enforcement.

In short, in the post-Charter period, international institutions have failed to deter or combat aggression. The international community has faltered in its efforts to address this profound problem.

A New Value Hierarchy

As observed previously, the Charter paradigm for the recourse to force was predicated upon the assumption that 'peace' was more important than justice. In the post-1945 world, however, states have repudiated this hierarchy of values. In many diverse sectors of the international system, claims have been made that force against the existing political and territorial order may, at times, be justified. These claims seem to have manifested themselves in three different ways: 1) claims to use force to promote self-determination; 2) claims to resort to 'just' reprisals; and, 3) claims to use force to correct past 'injustices.'

These claims suggest that the members of the international system have rejected the philosophical underpinnings of the Charter paradigm. Rather than believing that more injury to world order occurs when force is used to pursue just goals, states have come to believe that, at certain times, it is better to break the peace in the name of justice, than to live with the injustice. At times, justice must take precedence over peace.

A Changed Legal Obligation

The Death of Article 2(4)

The failure of Charter institutions to enforce norms relating to the recourse to force and the changing value hierarchy have obliged many scholars to re-think the status of the contemporary *jus ad bellum*. In short, scholars have been compelled to ask whether Article 2(4) is still good international law. We have argued that a putative norm is a rule of international law only if it is authoritative and controlling. As a consequence, for Article 2(4)'s pro-scription to be regarded as genuine law, its authority and control must be clearly demonstrated.

A review of scholarship and practice suggests three fundamental approaches to this question. The first has been labelled the 'legalist' approach; the second the 'core interpretist' approach; and the third the 'rejectionist' approach.[2] This section will examine each of these three approaches in turn and conclude that the 'rejectionist' approach reflects most accurately the reality of the international system.

The Legalist Approach.   A significant number of international publi-cists might be considered 'legalists.'[3] These legal scholars, while recogniz-ing that problems exist, adhere to the basic belief that the principle enunci-ated in Article 2(4) is still good law. To make this argument, they stress several points. First, they argue that the norm remains authoritative since no state has explicitly suggested that Article 2(4) is not good law. As Pro-fessor Louis Henkin has explained '[n]o government, no responsible offi-cial of government, has been prepared to pronounce it dead.'[4] Thus, be-cause states have not explicitly repudiated Article 2(4), its authority continues.

Second, legalists argue that despite the problems of Article 2(4), the norm remains controlling of state behavior. Here, they contend that despite violations of the norm, it has *for the most part* exerted a restraining influence on state behavior. In the words of Professor Henkin, 'the norm against the unilateral national use of force has survived. Indeed, despite common misimpressions to the contrary, the norm has been largely observed'.[5] One aspect of this legalist argument seems to be that while it is easy to count the times that a particular norm is violated, it is quite difficult to identify the times when a norm exerted a controlling influence, when states refrained from forcible action because of Article 2(4)'s proscription. Another aspect of this argument is that since most states are not, in fact, using force in violation of the Charter, the norm is generally controlling of behavior.

Finally, the legalists argue that Article 2(4) must be understood as a *treaty* obligation for those states that have ratified the United Nations Charter and not just as an obligation under customary international law.

Hence, the procedure for a normative change is much more specific and defined. Professor Edward Gordon has argued that

> [t]he rule embodied in Article 2(4) is not just a freestanding rule of customary law; it is also a formal treaty obligation. States may withdraw their consent to be bound by treaty obligations, but may not simply walk away from them.[6]

Explains Gordon, '[t]he existence of an operational code [read 'state practice'] different from the formal commitment may be cause for withdrawing state consent, but it does not supplant the process for withdrawing consent called for by the treaty or by treaty law generally.'[7] Although recognizing that treaties may be 'replaced' if they are 'not followed,' Gordon contends that 'an observer's inference that they are lagging behind actual practice is too subjective and fragile a criterion to replace the formal evidence of withdrawal of state consent as an indicator of the continuing force of treaty obligations.'[8] In other words, states must formally terminate a treaty for it to cease to binding; mere non-compliance is insufficient.

While there is a certain logic in these arguments advanced by the legalists, there are also problems. First, although it may be true that no state has explicitly declared that Article 2(4) is not good law, this fact alone does not mean that the norm is necessarily authoritative. For obvious political reasons, states have not overtly argued that the Charter norms are invalid. States have on numerous occasions claimed the right to use force in circumstances that are, nevertheless, clearly antithetical to the principle enshrined in Article 2(4). Given these claims, it seems incorrect to contend that states still hold 2(4) in very high esteem. Admittedly, the provision may still command some perceptions of legitimacy, but they seem to be far below those required for a healthy rule of law.

Second, the arguments advanced by the legalists for the controlling nature of Article 2(4) also seem to be inconsistent with realities of the international system. Certainly not every state violates Article 2(4), and certainly it is difficult to judge when a particular state's behavior was influenced by the existence of 2(4). Nevertheless, the norm has been violated frequently and with impunity in some of the most important cases of state interaction. Even though legal scholars may disagree as to the precise list of such violations of Article 2(4), there is broad agreement that numerous violations have taken place. . . .

Even Professor Henkin, in arguing that Article 2(4) is still valid, was forced to deal with a number of these instances. He explains:

> the norm against unilateral force has been largely observed. With the exception of Korea (in some respects an 'internal war'), the brief, recurrent Arab–Israel hostilities in 1956, 1967, and 1973, the flurry between India and Pakistan over Kashmir in September 1965, the invasion of Czechoslovakia by Soviet troops in 1968, [and in the footnote he says: 'One might

add, unhappily, Ethiopia–Somalia and Vietnam–Cambodia–China in 1978–79'], nations have not engaged in 'war,' in full and sustained hostilities or state-to-state aggression even in circumstances in which in the past the use of force might have been expected.'[9]

These 'exceptions,' and others that have taken place since the time Henkin's book was written, are profound exceptions, not simply minor incidents. These uses of force would seem rather clearly to indicate that when a state judges other foreign policy goals to be at stake, it will generally *not* allow itself to be circumscribed by the prohibition of Article 2(4).

Finally, the legalists' use of the treaty-nature of Article 2(4) is problematic. Even though Article 2(4) is a treaty provision, the same test for determining the validity of customary international law can also be employed. If a treaty provision is greatly lacking in authority and control, it seems quite logical to argue that the provision is no longer authentic 'international law.' In the decentralized system that exists today, international law is constituted through state practice. In 1945, fifty-one states chose to enunciate a particular rule relating to the use of force by ratifying the United Nations Charter. Since then, these states and over one hundred additional ones have, through their actions, chosen to change this rule. Even though there have been no formal acts that have attempted to change the written words of Article 2(4), the behavior of these states has been sufficient to effect a change.

The 'Core Interpretist' Approach.   Another approach to understanding the status of Article 2(4) has been called the 'core interpretist' approach. The 'core interpretists' argue that although the narrow, legalistic interpretation of Article 2(4) no longer represents existing law, a 'core' meaning of the Article that is still authoritative and controlling can nevertheless be identified.[10] Naturally, these scholars differ as to what represents this 'core' meaning. Some suggest that the 'core' is very large. They contend that the basic prohibition contained in Article 2(4) is still valid, except as modified by authoritative interpretations confirmed in state practice. Thus, every unilateral use of force is prohibited unless it can be demonstrated that the accepted interpretation of the Charter allows for an exception. These 'core interpretists' argue that permissible exceptions would include such uses of force as anticipatory self-defense, intervention to protect nationals, and humanitarian intervention.

Other 'core interpretist' scholars take a slightly different approach. They contend that the 'core' of Article 2(4) is much smaller. For example, Professor Alberto Coll suggests that

> insofar as there is a remnant of a legal, as opposed to a moral obligation left in article 2(4), it is a good faith commitment to abstain from *clear aggression* that involves a disproportionate use of force and violates other principles of the Charter.[11]

According to Coll,

> [c]lear aggression and the content of article 2(4) and article 51 would, in turn, be defined by reference to established traditions of normative reasoning, such as prudence and just war doctrine, in an open interpretative process similar, in fact, to that already underlying state decisionmaking on the use of force in many situations.[12]

He explains that '[u]nder this interpretative process, *clear aggression* would encompass different typologies of coercive acts which various traditions of ethical reasoning, throughout different periods of history, have condemned in the strongest terms as unlawful and morally reprehensible.'[13] Thus using Coll's approach, 'clear aggression' could include the use of force to gain territory, to achieve political domination, and to perpetrate genocide. The activities of Nazi Germany and Imperial Japan that inaugurated the Second World War would be the most obvious examples of such 'clear aggression.'

But whatever the precise nature of the 'core' that the various scholars identify, the important aspect of this approach is that it continues to affirm Article 2(4) as the existing *jus ad bellum*. All the writers of this school would contend that *some* version of Article 2(4) represents the law, and would reject arguments that 2(4) is now dead. One reason for this desire to hold on to even a shred of Article 2(4) is a belief that rejecting the norm entirely might be premature because states do refrain from certain uses of force. Consequently, such rejection could actually contribute to the dissolution of whatever restraining influence 2(4) still exerts. Another reason seems to be the symbolic nature of 2(4). For many 'core interpretists,' Article 2(4) represents a goal, an aspiration of the post-Second World War era. To claim that it is no longer law, would be to claim that prohibiting the unilateral resort to force was no longer a noble goal worth pursuing.

But despite these laudable aspirations, there is one major problem. Holding on to Article 2(4) may actually be doing more harm than good to the international legal system. Given the severely weakened authority of 2(4) and its manifest lack of control, to use Article 2(4) in any way to describe the law relating to the recourse to force may simply be perpetrating a legal fiction that interferes with an accurate assessment of state practice. It may indeed be true that some 'core' of the Article 2(4) prohibition may remain, such as a prohibition on the use of force for territorial aggrandizement. But the problem is that Article 2(4) was designed to be much more than simply a prohibition on the use of force for that narrow purpose. One of the radical aspects of 2(4) was that it went beyond the Kellogg-Briand Pact, which prohibited recourse to 'war,' by prohibiting *all* uses of *force* that were against the territorial integrity or political independence of a state or otherwise inconsistent with the purposes of the United Nations. Moreover, it even prohibited *threats* of force. In other words, the Article

2(4) prohibition was much broader than simply the 'core.' If only this small sub-set of Article 2(4) still remains, it does not seem appropriate to describe the law by reference to the full set.

The 'Rejectionist' Approach.   The third possible approach to the status of Article 2(4) has been called the 'rejectionist' approach. To take this approach would be to argue that Article 2(4) does not in any meaningful way constitute existing law. The contention would be that because authoritative state practice is so far removed from any reasonable interpretation of the meaning of Article 2(4), it is no longer reasonable to consider the provision 'good law.'

The classical elaboration of the rejectionist approach can be found in Professor Franck's 1970 article on the death of Article 2(4).[14] At the time, Professor Franck argued that '[t]he prohibition against the use of force in relations between states has been eroded beyond recognition.[15] This erosion, according to Franck, was due to three main factors: 'the rise of wars of "national liberation",' 'the rising threat of wars of total destruction,' and 'the increasing authoritarianism of regional systems dominated by a super-Power.[16] But, he explained, '[t]hese three factors may . . . be traced back to a single circumstance: the lack of congruence between the international legal norm of Article 2(4) and the perceived national interests of states, especially the super-Powers.[17] In short, as states have come to value goals other than those expressed in Article 2(4), the authority and control of the norm have essentially disappeared. As Professor Franck put it in 1970: 'The practice of these states has so severely shattered the mutual confidence which would have been the *sine qua non of* an operative rule of law embodying the precepts of Article 2(4) that, as with Ozymandias, only the words remain.'[18]

Twenty years later, in his *The Power of Legitimacy Among Nations,* Franck reaffirmed his 'rejectionist' understanding of Article 2(4). Acknowledging the egregious lack of control of putative rules dealing with the use of force, he commented:

> the extensive body of international 'law,' oft restated in solemn texts, which forbids direct or indirect intervention by one state in the domestic affairs of another, precludes the aggressive use of force by one state against another, and requires adherence to human rights standards simply, if sadly, is not predictive of the ways of the world.[19]

Later, Franck compared Article 2(4) and the one-time US Government mandated 55-mile per hour national speed limit. Observing that while both rules possess 'textual clarity,' they, nevertheless, 'do not describe or predict with accuracy the actual behavior of the real world.'[20] He explained that their determinacy is undermined by a popular perception that they can't mean what they so plainly say. The irrationality of the rules—their incoherence: a failure to be instrumental in relation to the purposes for which they were devised—causes us to believe, and act on the belief, that they have become indeterminate. The rules, therefore, have lost some of their compliance pull.[21]

Apart from Professor Franck, no other major international legal scholar has *explicitly* taken this approach. Yet despite this lack of support, the 'rejectionist' approach seems to offer the most accurate description of the contemporary *jus ad bellum*. The legalist approach seems too removed from the realities of the international system and the core interpretist approach seems to do little more than perpetuate a legal fiction. Based on what states have been saying and what they have been doing, there simply does not seem to be a *legal* prohibition on the use of force against the political independence and territorial integrity of states as provided in even a modified version of Article 2(4). The rule creating process, authoritative state practice, has rejected that norm.

The Post-Charter Obligation

If Article 2(4) is in fact dead, a larger question remains: what norms have developed in the post-Charter era to replace it? In other words, what rules of behavior have states constituted that *are* regarded as authoritative and are, in practice, controlling? Based on state behavior, several conclusions can be drawn about legal principles that seem to have emerged to fill the gap caused by the death of Article 2(4). The following section will set out these conclusions. We will employ here a 'positivist' approach to international law. That is, we assume that unless a restrictive norm of law can be established prohibiting a particular use of force, states are permitted to engage in that use of force. In short, for any use of force to be prohibited, an authoritative and controlling *proscription* must exist.

Our proposal does not purport to offer the only acceptable formulation of the law; rather, it seeks merely to present one possible description of the post-Charter *jus ad bellum*. In order to do so, we will first discuss those circumstances under which recourse to force seems to be lawful. Then, we will examine those circumstances under which recourse to force appears to be unlawful.

Lawful uses of force

1. Self-defense (including anticipatory self-defense and reprisals). The first circumstance in which the unilateral use of force would seem to be lawful in a post-Article 2(4) legal system would be self-defense. This is not particularly controversial. Individual and collective self-defense has always been explicitly permitted under Article 51 of the Charter. The major change would be the addition of anticipatory self-defense and reprisals.

Before the Charter was adopted, states had the right under customary international law to use force in self-defense even before an armed attack occurred if it could be demonstrated that such an attack were imminent and that no other recourse was available. With the demise of Article 2(4), it is reasonable to assume that this preexisting right would be rehabilitated. There seems to be no consensus on a rule prohibiting force undertaken for that purpose.

In addition to anticipatory self-defense, it would also seem that reprisals would be permissible. States have also been suing a broadened definition of self-defense to justify reprisals. There seems to be a belief on the part of states conducting such actions that they are proper to punish and deter certain prior illegal acts of the target state, even though such initial acts do not rise to the level of an armed attack. While not all states have endorsed the use of force for these purposes, there appears to be no clear agreement on an authoritative norm prohibiting reprisals.

2. Promotion of self-determination.   In light of the growing preference for 'just' uses of force, the use of force to promote self-determination would also seem to be lawful. But since different states have defined self-determination in different ways, it would be impossible to restrict this right to the promotion of a particular 'type' of self-determination. It would, in other words, be difficult to claim that using force to promote 'pro-democratic' self-determination would be permissible, but using force to promote 'pro-socialist' self-determination would be impermissible. Consequently, there would seem to be a right for states to use force to promote self-determination *however* they define it. This would mean that such action as the Soviet 'liberation' of Czechoslovakia and the American 'liberation' of Panama would be lawful. It would also mean that it would be permissible to provide assistance to either side in a civil conflict, with the determination being made by the intervening party as to which side was acting in the true interests of self-determination.

This use of force to promote self-determination is obviously much more controversial than self-defense. It actually constitutes a clear use of force against the political independence and territorial integrity of a state. Nevertheless, as demonstrated earlier, states have come to regard a just pursuit of self-determination as a proper use of force, at least when it is their definition of self-determination. Once again, there seems to be no restrictive rule prohibiting such use of force.

3. Correction of past injustices.   Finally, it would seem to be lawful to employ force to correct injustices that had been inflicted on a particular state at a particular time in the past. This means that if one state had previously seized the territory of another state, had endangered the nationals of that state, or had violated some other major norm of international law, the aggrieved state could use force to rectify the situation. This new rule would legalize such actions as the Argentine invasion of the Falklands and, if they had been done today, the British, French, and Israeli invasion of Egypt in 1956, and the Arab invasion in 1973.

This use of force to correct past injustices also clearly involves action against the political and territorial status quo. States seem to feel, however, that the status quo is often unjust, and that in the absence of other effective means to correct the situation, they have the right to take the matter into their own hands.

Unlawful Uses of Force: Territorial Annexation

If states have come to acknowledge that force may properly be used to promote self-determination and to correct past injustices, very little would seem to be prohibited. In fact, in a world without Article 2(4), the only thing that does seem to be proscribed is the use of force for pure territorial aggrandizement. States still appear to believe that it is illegitimate to use force solely for the purpose of gaining territory.

Perhaps the most dramatic example of this belief can be seen in the response of the international community to the August 1990 Iraqi invasion of Kuwait. When Iraq invaded and annexed Kuwait, it justified its actions on the basis of Arab unity. Claiming that colonial borders had been unjustly drawn, the Iraqi Revolutionary Command Council proclaimed that it had 'decided to return the part and branch, Kuwait, to the whole and origin, Iraq, in a comprehensive, eternal and inseparable merger unity.' Yet despite this apparent claim of correcting a past injustice, the international community squarely condemned the invasion and annexation. On August 2, the United Nations Security Council adopted Resolution 660 condemning the invasion by a vote of 14–0, with Yemen not voting. Four days later the Council acting under Chapter VII of the Charter, imposed economic sanctions on Iraq by a vote of 13–0, with Cuba and Yemen abstaining. Shortly thereafter, following Iraq's claim of annexation, the Council unanimously adopted Resolution 662. This Resolution reiterated the Council's demand 'that Iraq withdraw immediately and unconditionally all its forces' from Kuwait, and decided 'that annexation of Kuwait by Iraq under any form and whatever pretext has no legal validity, and is considered null and void' and demanded 'that Iraq rescind its actions purporting to annex Kuwait.' On November 30, after much negotiation, the Council adopted Resolution 678 authorizing states to use force in Iraq did not comply with the demanded withdrawal.

The Security Council's actions in this case are quite telling. Even though Iraq's actions were veiled in claims of 'justice,' the Council did not hesitate in condemning the invasion and purported annexation. The justification undoubtedly was too much of a transparent 'pretext' for a simple effort at territorial aggrandizement, reminiscent of justifications used at the beginning of the Second World War. The reaction would indicate a strong perception on the part of the overwhelming majority of states that uses of force for pure territorial aggrandizement are impermissible. Moreover, the fact that such uses of force have been quite rare in the post-War era, indicate that this norm does have a high degree of control.

But what all this suggests is that the legal structure that has emerged from the ashes of Article 2(4) may simply be a modified regime of 'self-help.' Under such a regime, states can lawfully use force to promote self-determination as they define it and to correct what they perceive to be injustices. For these purposes they possess a *competence de guerre,* akin to that possessed by states before the adoption of the League of Nations Covenant. Under this paradigm, however, one use of force *is* prohibited— force for territorial annexation. Of course even here, state could claim that they were acing for other 'just' reasons when their actual goal was pure territorial acquisition.

An Assessment of the Post-Charter Obligation

If the international legal system has moved toward a modified regime of self-help in the post-Charter period, is this evolution good? Does this type of legal arrangement further the general goals of international law? Assuming that one of the main purposes of international law is to promote stability and regularity in the relations among states, the answer would quite clearly be *no.* Self-determination and justice are extremely subjective terms. They can mean virtually anything a particular state chooses them to mean, and they can be used to justify virtually any use of force. In the world of 'just' causes, one person's liberator is another person's oppressor, and one person's freedom fighter is another person's terrorist.

The problem, however, is that while self-determination can mean almost anything, Article 2(4) has already been stripped of any real meaning. In light of state practice, to contend that it is still good law is to make *it mean* virtually anything. Recognizing that Article 2(4) is dead may not be very satisfying, but it may be accurate. The normative framework suggested above certainly does not represent the most desirable legal regime, but it may reflect the *existing* legal regime.

The Post-Cold War Era: A New Paradigm?

Critics of the preceding analysis of the post-Charter self-help paradigm might contend that the discussion has assumed the existence of a particular type of international system. The paradigm, it could be argued, seems to assume the continuance of the Cold War and its attendant evils—lack of superpower cooperation, widespread superpower intervention, and the like. Now that the tumultuous year of 1989 has brought an end to the Cold War, the paradigm no longer depicts reality. With the collapse of the Soviet Union, increased cooperation among the permanent members of the Security Council, the rising capital of the United Nations, and the great movements toward democracy, a *laissez-faire* approach to the use of force no longer seems accepted. Instead, it could be argued, a new 'pro-democratic' paradigm is coming to describe the law relating to the recourse to force.

This section will examine the arguments supporting the existence of this would-be paradigm. It will do so by exploring the possible emergence of a new value hierarchy and a 'new' legal obligation. . . .

The Emergence of a New Value Hierarchy?

In the Post-Charter Self-Help paradigm, justice is valued above peace. States are claiming the right to use force to promote certain 'just' goals. The major difficulty with this formulation is that different groups of states have: offered differing and often contradictory definitions of what a 'just' goal is. With the ending of the Cold War, however, it could be contended that an international consensus is emerging around certain acceptable 'just' goals. Specifically, it could be argued that in light of recent developments, there is a consensus that it is proper to use force to promote democratic self-determination in the western sense of the term.

This argument could be made in two steps. First, with the decline of the ideological confrontation between the East and the West, there is growing international agreement on what constitutes an 'illegitimate' regime. Such a regime would be one that engages in gross violations of human rights as enumerated in the Covenant on Civil and Political Rights or one which has come to power in total disregard of constitutional processes. Hence, the pre-1989 regimes in Panama, East Germany, Bulgaria, Czechoslovakia, and Romania, to name a few, could be regarded as illegitimate. In support of the notion that agreement on the illegitimacy of certain regimes transcends the East-West divide, proponents of this contention would cite Gorbachev's attitude regarding the Eastern European regimes. They would argue that in his calls for change in Eastern Europe and his tacit acceptance of such change, he reflected a new thinking on the part of the Soviet Union's leadership that those regimes were, in fact, illegitimate. Second, because there could be near universal agreement that a particular government is illegitimate, it could be contended that there is an emerging belief that it is becoming permissible to use force against such regimes to promote the self-determination of the peoples.

Although this argument is only in the initial stages of development, one American scholar, Thomas Franck, has attempted to suggest its contours. Professor Franck argued that states 'are gradually coming to agree on a *right* to democratic governance, or freedom from totalitarianism.'[22] He explained that

> [w]hatever decent instincts came to cluster around the magnet of 'self-determination,' creating a widely-accepted exception to article 2(4), must now carry forward, in the post-colonial era, to imbue a new inter-nationally-recognized human right to political freedom.[23]

And, according to Franck,'[k]in to such a right would be another: a right of the democratic members of the international community to aid, directly or indirectly, those fighting for their democratic entitlement.'[24] These 'democratic entitlements,' explained Franck, 'are already spelled out in international instruments, in particular the Covenant on Civil and Political Rights, which may now be regarded as customary international law.'[25] But Franck believes that

> [w]hen the most basic of these rights have been found to have been violated—and *only* then—an enunciated international consensus might now be ready to form around the proposition that the use of some levels of force by states could be justified to secure democratic entitlements for peoples unable to secure them for themselves.'[26]

In short, justice would still be valued over peace, but the definition of justice would not be as subjective as in the self-help paradigm.

The Emergence of a 'New' Legal Obligation?

Based on these institutional and attitudinal changes, it could be argued that a 'new' legal obligation regarding the recourse to force is in the process of emerging. Following Franck, it could be contended that the international community is coming to accept one just cause for the recourse to force aside from self-defense—intervention to remove an 'illegitimate' regime. With the decline of competing ideologies, there is developing a consensus around what constitutes such an illegitimate regime and a growing acceptance of the permissibility to use force, if necessary, to remove such a regime. If this is indeed becoming the case, then the paradigm depicting the *jus ad bellum* may be shifting away from the post-Charter self-help paradigm to a new pro-democratic paradigm. Under such a paradigm, force would be permissible in two circumstances: to engage in individual and collective self-defense and to promote 'pro-democratic' self-determination.

While such a paradigmatic shift may occur at some point in the future, at present, it seems exceptionally premature to assert its imminent arrival. This is true for a number of reasons. First, despite the dramatic developments in Eastern Europe and the former Soviet Union, there still seems to be no real international consensus as to what constitutes an 'illegitimate' regime. While it is true that an apparent agreement developed regarding the illegitimacy of certain Eastern European governments, there seems to be no such consensus with respect to the rest of the world. If fidelity to the International Covenant on Civil and Political Rights is used as a determinant of legitimacy, a substantial number of countries fall short. Even following the remarkable developments of 1989, the human rights organization Freedom House lists fifty-nine states as 'not free.'[27] These states comprise over two billion people and come from nearly every area of the world. Clearly, if over one-third of the states in the international system maintain regimes in which significant political rights and civil liberties, as defined in the West, are denied, it is impossible to argue that there is some consensus on democratic legitimacy.

Second, even assuming there were some emerging agreement on legitimacy, there is clearly no consensus developing on the efficacy of the use of force to remove such a regime. A case in point would be the invasion of Panama by the United States. Even though one argument raised by the United States centered around the illegitimacy of the Noriega regime, there was near universal condemnation for the American action. While certain states believed that the government of Manuel Noriega was indeed illegitimate, there seemed to be a general rejection of US contentions that this illegitimacy gave rise to a unilateral right to invade the country. If this was the case with respect to Panama, it is difficult to envision many other cases in which there could be agreement on the permissibility of force to remove an anti-democratic regime.

In short, despite the dramatic changes that have taken place in international politics over the last several years, there does not yet seem to be the international consensus necessary to support the existence of a pro-democratic paradigm. States have not yet come to accept a *jus ad bellum* that permits intervention for only one particular type of self-determination aimed at removing illegitimate, anti-democratic regimes.

The Future of the *Jus Ad Bellum*

Three Possible Scenarios

In light of the preceding analysis, it is contended that there has been a definite paradigm shift in the post-Charter period. The Charter prohibition on the recourse to force as established in Article 2(4) is simply no longer authoritative and controlling. States have chosen to reject this strict proscription in favor of a more permissive norm that prohibits force only in cases of action aimed at territorial aggrandizement and allows forcible efforts to promote self-determination as it is variously defined, to carry out a just reprisal, and to correct a past injustice. Despite the changes that have taken place in the international system, states have not yet reached a consensus on a more restrictive norm limiting permissible intervention to cases involving 'pro-democratic' self-determination. In other words, the post-Charter self-help paradigm, for good or ill, still describes the existing law relating to the initiation of force.

Given this conclusion, where is the law going? Is the international system evolving toward a pro-democratic paradigm or not? While it is impossible to answer this question with any certainty, three scenarios seem plausible.

First, it is conceivable that there will be no significant change in the post-charter self-help paradigm. States may continue to claim the right to use force to correct injustices and promote self-determination as they determine.

While there may be increased great power cooperation, this does not necessarily indicate that all states will refrain from acting to promote self-determination. It should be noted, for example, that even while the Soviet Union was allowing the East European states to go their own way, the United States was acting forcefully in Panama. Moreover, the changed nature of Europe may have little to do with the actions of states in other parts of the world. Islamic states, African states, and others may continue to be motivated by diverse definitions of self-determination and justice and may, when appropriate, use force to realize these claims.

A second possible scenario involves the ultimate acceptance of the pro-democratic paradigm. Even though the international system has not yet come to accept a definition of a legitimate regime, it is possible that the international community is evolving toward such definition. Before 1945, human rights was not even a legitimate topic of conversation in international discourse; now, even though definitions of human rights vary greatly, the notion that individuals have certain rights in the international system is generally accepted. It is possible that over time more refinements will be made in this area of the law and the provisions of instruments such as the Covenant on Civil and Political Rights will begin to be reflected in practice. This may then give rise to an accepted notion of legitimacy and a concomitant right to intervene to promote such legitimacy.

Finally, there is even a possibility that Article 2(4) could be rehabilitated. The recent actions by the United Nations in the Gulf may indicate a willingness to return to a more restrictive approach to force. Even though the Iraqi invasion is an easy case because it involved obvious aggression for territorial aggrandizement, it is possible that the effect of the UN response will be a reinvigoration of the norm. With the world apparently rallying around the Charter in this case, the effect may be to encourage states to be more supportive of Charter norms in the future. Having committed themselves as a matter of principle in this case, states may be more inclined to defend the honor of Article 2(4) in the future. If this were to occur, it could lead to a new consensus on the unilateral use of force. Article 2(4) could actually become reflective of authoritative state practice.

A Recommended Jus Ad Bellum

Whether these or other plausible scenarios will come about is likely to remain unclear for some time. What is clear, however, is that the current post-Charter self-help regime leaves much to be desired. A system that provides very little in normative restraints on the recourse to force, that allows states to use force to promote self-determination and justice as they may choose to define them, is destructive of world order. For policy makers, a course of action that would promote the return to something more closely resembling Article 2(4) would seem to make sense.

Given the recent developments in the United Nations system, the greater potential for great power cooperation, and the commitment of the international community in the Iraqi conflict, the possibility of reestablishing the Charter framework for the recourse to force seems greater than at any other time since 1945. In consequence, we would recommend the following framework for the law relating to the recourse to force. This proposal, we believe, would move the international system closer to a more stable and predictable normative structure. First, we will set out our suggestions for lawful uses of force. Next, we will examine what we believe should be regarded as unlawful uses of force. Finally, we discuss four advantages of our proposal: its clarity of language; its treatment of the changed nature of international conflict; its recognition of the need for limited self-help; and its capacity to enhance international order.

Lawful Uses of Force

Self-defense

As under the Charter paradigm, self-defense would be a permissible ground for states to take recourse to force. Our proposal sets out three explicit circumstances under which a state may lawfully use force to defend itself: armed attack; imminent attack; and indirect aggression.

1. Armed attack. First, states would be allowed to use force in response to an overt armed attack. This would simply reaffirm the language of Article 51. When one state engaged in a clear, obvious armed attack against another, the victim state would have the right to respond with force. The only restriction on this right of the aggrieved state would be the traditional requirements of necessity and proportionality.

2. Imminent attack.   Second, states would be allowed to use force to respond to an 'imminent' armed attack. It seems only logical to assert that states need not be required to wait until the bombs drop or the troops cross their borders before they can take defensive action. Given the technology of modern weaponry, the right of *effective* self-defense could become meaningless if a state were required to weather a first hit before it could respond. In accepting anticipatory self-defense as a permissible ground for the use of force, we posit that the burden of proof should fall upon the state exercising this right. The state must demonstrate that an armed attack is truly 'imminent' and that its preemptive action is necessary.

3. Indirect aggression.   The International Court of Justice held in the *Nicaragua* case that indirect aggression could rise to the level of an 'armed attack,' engendering a right of self-defense under Article 51. One of the main difficulties with the Court's decision was that it set the threshold of armed attack unduly high.

We accept the notion that indirect aggression can, in some cases, be tantamount to an armed attack. We would, however, propose a lower threshold than that suggested by the International Court of Justice. In our view, indirect aggression (subject to certain qualifications) can be regarded as an armed attack in three instances: covert actions, interventions in civil/mixed conflicts, and certain terrorist actions.

Covert action. While every covert action not undertaken in self-defense is delictual, not every one constitutes an 'armed attack.' It is impossible to determine with absolute precision when a covert action rises to the level of an armed attack. We nevertheless believe that a reasonable assessment of a covert action's character can be made on the basis of three interrelated factors: the nature of the activities; the severity of the effect of the activities; and the temporal duration of the activities.

Nature of activities. We believe that a host of covert activities could rise to the level of an armed attack. These would include such state actions as assassination, destruction of buildings, attacks against military and civilian targets, sabotage, and other acts of violence. The critical common denominator in all these would be their fundamentally *violent* nature. Covert actions such as bribery of public officials and financial support for political movements would be excluded from this category. Although these non-violent actions would be illegal violations of the sovereignty of the target state, we do not consider them to be equivalent to an armed attack. In short, the necessary precondition for an armed attack is *violence.*

Severity of effect. The effect of the violent covert activities in question should be comparable in severity to the effect of an overt armed attack. This level of severity would obviously vary with the nature of the action. Sabotaging a single small building that contained a limited amount of military equipment would not rise to the level of an armed attack. Assassinating a state's president, destroying a major military compound with explosives, or poisoning a water filtration plant would.

Temporal duration. A third factor to be weighed is the temporal duration of covert activities. A one-time covert act producing an effect of great severity might by itself be sufficient to constitute an armed attack. Activities producing effects of lesser severity, however, might only constitute an armed attack if they were part of an ongoing pattern of behavior. If the head of state were assassinated, that one act per se could be equated to an armed attack. The isolated destruction of a single small building might not be sufficient to be considered an armed attack; nevertheless, the destruction of a number of such structures over a period of time could be sufficient.

Support of rebels. At what point does outside state support of a rebel movement rise to the level of an armed attack? This question proved to be one of the most contentious ones debated during the Central American conflict of the 1980s. In order to answer this inherently difficult question, three inter-related factors must be weighed: the nature of outside support; the severity of the effects of outside support; and the attributability of the effects to the intervening state.

Nature of support. As noted above, the International Court of Justice in Nicaragua set the 'armed attack' threshold at a very high level. Specifically, it held that only the introduction of 'armed bands' or 'mercenaries' into a target state would rise to the level of armed attack. We disagree. We contend that a whole *range of actions* could cross the armed attack threshold: a state's provision to rebels of significant financial support; a state's provision of weapons and ocher equipment, intelligence, command and control support, and training; and, of course, a state's introduction of armed bands and mercenaries.

Severity of effect. In determining whether a state's actions constitute an armed attack, the *intention* of the intervening state is not dispositive. Nor, moreover, is the *amount of aid* provided by the intervening state to the rebels. The key element in determining whether a state's support of rebels engenders the right of self-defense is the *effect on the target state* of the outside support. The degree of outside support for rebels must be sufficient to produce 'substantial effects' within the target state. Any 'effects' akin to those caused by a conventional attack by regular armed forces should be regarded as 'substantial' ones. As with covert actions, a temporal factor should affect the determination of what constitutes substantiality. 'Substantial effects' could be the result of a single prominent action or of a series of lesser actions undertaken over a period of time.

Attributability of effects to the intervening state. Unlike effects produced by covert action, effects produced by a state's support of rebels are not directly caused by the intervening state. The intervening state merely provides various forms of assistance to the rebels; the rebels, in turn, undertake actions producing effects within their state. Accordingly, for an 'armed attack' to be attributable to the intervening state, the effects within the target state must be demonstrated to be *directly linked* to the intervenor's assistance. For example, if it were proven that an intervening state provided munitions and logistical support to rebel forces, and that those forces employed that assistance in raids against government targets tantamount to an overt armed attack, then the intervening state should be considered to have effectively committed an 'armed attack.' Under such circumstances, the victim state could use force in self-defense against the intervening state.

Terrorist action As with covert action, every terrorist act is delictual, though not every terrorist act constitutes an 'armed attack.' It is impossible to determine precisely when a terrorist act rises to the level of an armed attack. We nevertheless believe that a host of terrorist acts can do so. Depending on the attendant circumstances, these might include such actions as assassination, destruction of buildings, attacks against military and civilian targets, and sabotage.

A terrorist act is distinguished by at least three specific qualities:

    a. actual or threatened *violence;*
    b. a *'political'* objective; and
    c. an *intended audience.*

Random acts of violence performed without deliberate political objectives should not be considered 'terrorism,' even if they do inspire 'terror.' Neither should non-violent acts, done for political purposes and directed at a specific target group. Nor, properly speaking, should politically-motivated acts of violence, when undertaken without any particular audience in mind. Accordingly, an 'act of terrorism' should be considered *'the threat or use of violence with the intent of causing fear in a target group, in order to achieve political objectives.'*

In order to justify a forcible state response, the effect of the terrorist act or acts in question must be comparable to the effect of an overt armed attack. This 'armed attack threshold' varies with three interrelated factors: the *locus* of the terrorist act; the *temporal duration* of the terrorist act; and the *severity of injury* the act inflicts upon the state.

Locus. The locus of a terrorist act may be either within a responding state's territory or outside it. Though scholars have generally not isolated this factor, we believe that it is a critical variable for determining the 'armed attack threshold.' Because it violates a state's 'territorial integrity,' a terrorist act occurring within a state's borders constitutes an inherently greater injury to that state's sovereignty than does an identical act abroad.

Temporal duration. A second factor to be weighed is the temporal duration of terrorist acts. A terrorist act can be a single, isolated occurrence or part of an on-going pattern of behavior. The latter variety of act, irrespective of its locus or severity, is more likely to rise to the level of an 'armed attack' because it causes a continuing injury to the state.

Severity of injury to the state. The 'severity' of injury to the state caused by a terrorist act can range across a broad spectrum of acts, although where precisely an act should be placed on this spectrum is debatable. At one end of the spectrum are acts causing injuries of minor severity to the state. We believe that these acts would include ones such as the temporary detention of a private citizen, the destruction of a private citizen's property, or the destruction of a limited amount of government property. Even the killing of a single national could be considered an act inflicting an injury of minor severity upon *the state.* To contend this is not to diminish the tragic results of such an act; rather, it is to underscore that the severity of the act should ultimately be evaluated in terms of its effect upon the state *per se.*

At the other end of the spectrum are acts causing injury of major severity to the state. We believe that these acts would consist of ones which strike at the core of a state's sovereignty. These would include the assassination of a government official, the destruction of a major government installation, or the killing of a large group of nationals *qua* nationals. While we believe that the killing of one national, or perhaps a small number of them, should not be regarded as inflicting severe injury to the state, we nonetheless contend that the killing of a large group of nationals should be so regarded. When a large number of nationals are attacked solely on the basis of their nationality, such an attack on what can reasonably be considered an embodiment of the state's sovereignty would seem to cause the state an injury of major severity.

In assessing whether the 'armed attack threshold' has been reached, the locus of the act, its temporal duration, and the severity of injury it inflicts upon the state must be considered simultaneously. As each of these three factors varies, so, too, will the assessment of whether an 'armed attack' has occurred. For example, an attack of a given severity occurring abroad might not be tantamount to an 'armed attack,' while one of equal severity occurring within a state's territory might be. Because an act within a state's borders self-evidently violates that state's 'territorial integrity,' it is reasonable to posit a lower standard for 'severity' for terrorist acts occurring there than for acts occurring outside a state's territory. Similarly, a single act producing an injury of great severity to the state might by itself be sufficient to constitute an armed attack, whereas activities producing injuries of lesser severity might only constitute an armed attack only if they were part of an ongoing pattern of behavior. In addition to the question of which terrorist acts engender a right of forcible response is the question of what entities constitute permissible *targets for a self-defense response.* There are two such possible targets: the terrorist actor itself; or a state related in some way to the terrorist actor..

We submit that a self-defense response should be permitted against a terrorist actor under three circumstances. First, force may be employed by a victim state if the terrorist actor is located in that state's jurisdiction or in an area beyond the jurisdiction of any state: for example, the high seas or the airspace over the high seas. Second, a state may take forcible action against a terrorist actor located in another state's jurisdiction if that 'host state' is unable or unwilling to take steps to suppress that actor. Lacking evidence of 'host state' support or sponsorship of the terrorist actor, a victim state may not use force against host state targets *per se*. Rather, its action must be limited to the terrorist actor alone. Third, a victim state may employ force against a terrorist actor located in a state which is supporting or sponsoring the activities of the terrorist actor.

Depending on the circumstances, a self-defense response should also be permitted against a state involved with a terrorist actor. Here, we propose an 'attributability' requirement similar to that which we advanced for state support of rebels. A state may support or sponsor terrorist actors. In either of these cases, the effects produced by a state's action are not *directly* caused by the state. Instead, the state merely provides various forms of assistance to the terrorist actors; the terrorists, in turn, undertake actions producing effects on the victim state. Accordingly, for an 'armed attack' to be attributable to the sponsoring or supporting state, the effects on the victim state must be demonstrated to be *directly linked* to the state's assistance. For example, if it were proven that a state provided munitions and logistical support to terrorist actors, and that those terrorists employed that assistance in an action reaching the 'armed attack threshold,' then the sponsoring or supporting state should be considered itself to have effectively committed an 'armed attack.' Under such circumstances, the victim state could use force in self-defense against the terrorist-linked state.

Intervention to protect nationals

Provided that four criteria are satisfied, a state should be permitted to intervene to protect its nationals. First, the nationals of the intervening state must be in imminent danger of loss of life or limb. Second, the target state must be unwilling or unable to protect the nationals of the intervening state. Third, the purpose of the intervention must be limited to the removal of the threatened nationals. The intervention must not be used as a pretext for any other activities in the territory of the target state. Fourth, the force used in the intervention must be proportionate to the mission of removing the nationals. No force may be used beyond that which is required to accomplish that limited task.

Force authorized by the Security Council

Finally, as in the Charter paradigm, force authorized by the Security Council would be permissible.

Unlawful Uses of Force

Aside from the uses of force detailed above, all other uses of force by a state would be prohibited. This would include the use of force to gain territory, to correct past injustices, and to promote self-determination. As noted above, there is virtually universal agreement that the use of force for territorial aggrandizement is currently illegal. To permit such a use of force would be to destroy all vestiges of international order. In addition, even though the post-Charter self-help paradigm seems to allow the use of force to correct injustices and to promote self-determination, we believe that the terms 'injustice' and 'self-determination' are excessively subjective. Were states allowed to use force to promote their own brands of justice and self-determination, nearly any use of force could be legitimized.

Advantages of Our Proposed Jus Ad Bellum

Our proposed *jus ad bellum* may not constitute the 'ideal' regime. Nevertheless, it represents a significant improvement over both the Charter paradigm and the existing post-Charter self-help paradigm. The advantages of our proposal can be evaluated in the light of four criteria: its clarity of language; the degree to which it addresses the nature of international conflict; the degree to which it recognizes the need for limited self-help; and its capacity to enhance international order.

First, our suggested *jus ad bellum* eliminates some of the interpretation problems of the Charter framework. In particular, the proposal attempts to deal with the meaning of Article 51 and the nature of an 'armed attack.' It allows for an explicit recognition of several categories of action that may give rise to the right of self-defense including imminent attack and indirect aggression. Our approach includes a number of subjective elements; nevertheless, we believe that it contains fewer than other approaches.

Second, our proposal addresses the changed nature of international conflict. It responds to both civil and mixed conflicts and to the problem of state-sponsored terrorism. As noted throughout our work, these types of conflict have been prominent features of the post-Second World War system. Any legal framework must specifically address these varieties of conflict if it is to be effective.

Third, our framework recognizes the need for self-help for the protection of nationals. It acknowledges that states are frequently unable to receive the cooperation of the target state when their nationals are in danger and that sometimes they may be required to engage in unilateral action to extricate their citizens. Our proposal would legitimize such action, subject to the criteria set out above.

Fourth, our proposal recognizes the critical importance of a restrictive *jus ad bellum* for international order. As we have consistently emphasized, the post-Charter self-help paradigm is destructive. It is far too subjective and allows states excessive justifications for the resort to force. If international law is to promote international stability, the normative framework for the recourse to force must be as limited and objective as possible. In our proposal, we consider all uses of force to correct past injustices and to promote self-determination to be impermissible. Although any given use of force for these purposes could indeed be just, it seems impossible to devise any realistic criteria that would be both reasonably objective and acceptable to all states. Accordingly, we support a strict prohibition on the unilateral recourse to force for these purposes.

If a particular incident were to arise in which states claimed that force should be used either to correct an injustice or to promote self-determination, we believe that the Security Council would be the most appropriate body to consider the issue. If the Council determined then that the matter were so grave that it constituted a threat to the peace, the Council could authorize forcible measures. Such a multilateral approach would, in our view, be far more preferable to the unilateralism of the post-Charter self-help paradigm. It would not eliminate the subjective aspects of defining justice or self-determination. However, before any forcible action could be undertaken, it would require Security Council endorsement.

Notes

1. D. Moynihan, *On the Law of Nations.* 19 (1990).

2. Arend, 'International Law and the Recourse to Force: A Shift in Paradigms,' *Stan J. Int'l L.* 27: 1 (1990).

3. Although it is nearly impossible to categorize scholars as *absolutely* falling into a particular school, some individuals seem to be more clearly 'legalists.' Such scholars would include: Michael Akehurst, Ian Brownlie, and Louis Henkin. See, M. Akehurst, *A Modern Introduction to International Law:* 256–261 (6th ed. 1987); I. Brownlie, *International Law and the Use of Force by States* (1963); L. Henkin, *How Nations Behave:* 135–164 (2nd ed. 1979).

4. Henkin, 'The Reports of the Death of Article 2(4) Are Greatly Exaggerated,' *Am. J. Int'l L.* 65: 544, 547 (1971).

5. L. Henkin, *How Nations Behave:* 146 (2nd ed. 1979).

6. Gordon, 'Article 2(4) in Historical Context,' *Yale J. Int'l L.* 10: 271, 275 (1985).

7. Ibid.

8. Ibid.

9. L. Henkin, op. cit.: 146.

10. This seems to be the approach taken by the majority of international legal scholars. Such scholars would include Derek Bowett, Myres McDougal, John Norton Moore, W. Michael Reisman. See, D. Bowett, *Self-Defence in International Law* (1958); M. McDougal and F. Feliciano, *Law and Minimum World Public Order* (1961); Moore, 'The Secret War in Central America and the Future of World Order,' *Am. J. Int'l L.* 80: 43, 80–92 (1986); Reisman, 'Coercion and Self-Determination: construing Charter Article 2(4),' *Am. J. Int'l L.* 78: 642 (1984).

11. Coll, 'The Limits of Global Consciousness and Legal Absolutism: Protecting International Law from Some of its Best Friends,' 27 *Harv. J. Int'l L.* 27: 509, 613 (1986).

12. Ibid.: 620.

13. Ibid.

14. Franck, 'Who Killed Article 2(4)? Or: Changing Norms Governing the Use of Force by States,' *Am. J. Int'l L.* 64.

15. Ibid.: 835.

16. Ibid.

17. Ibid.

18. Ibid.: 809.

19. T. Franck, *The Power of Legitimacy Among Nations:* 32 (1990) (footnotes omitted).

20. Ibid.: 78.

21. Ibid.

22. Franck, 'Secret Warfare: Policy Options for a Modern Legal and Institutional Context,' Paper presented to the Conference on Policy Alternatives to Deal with Secret Warfare: International Law, US Institute of Peace, March 16–17, 1990: at 17.

23. Ibid.: 17–18.

24. Ibid.: 18.

25. Ibid.

26. Ibid. Professor Franck has further developed these ideas. See, Franck, 'The Emerging Right to Democratic Governance,' *Am. J. Int'l L.* 86: 46 (1992).

27. 'Survey Update,' insert in *Freedom at Issue* 112 (1990).

28. Professor John Norton More has consistently emphasized the point that for the right of self-defense to be meaningful, it must be a 'real' right. States must be able to provide for 'effective' self-defense. See Moore, 'The Use of Force in International Relations: Norms Concerning the Initiation of Coercion,' in J. Moore, F. Tipson and R. Turner, *National Security Law:* 85, 87–89 (1991).

PART 3.2

International Law as
Normative System:
For the Protection
of Individual Rights

17

The UN's Human Rights Record: From San Francisco to Vienna and Beyond

Philip Alston

How Far Has the United Nations Come Since 1945?

U nder the shadow of the tragedy in Bosnia and of the inability of states, acting alone or collectively, to end the continuing gross violations, it is tempting to conclude, in despair, that the United Nations human rights program has entirely failed. But while not denying the all-too-evident shortcomings of international mechanisms in relation to events occurring only a couple of hundred miles away from Vienna, it is nevertheless essential to maintain some sense of perspective in assessing the overall picture. For that purpose, we need to acknowledge both the good news and the bad news. We need to ask not only how far we still must go to establish an effective response to human rights violations, but also how far we have come since the signing of the United Nations Charter in San Francisco in 1945, which committed states to promote respect for human rights.

Clearly, historical surveys cannot be a major preoccupation when massive, blatant, and often all too vividly, documented violations continue in many parts of the world. By the same token, however, it is necessary to appreciate what has been achieved in order to know where to go and how we might get there.

When the Universal Declaration of Human Rights was adopted in 1948 as a "common standard of achievement for all peoples and all nations," virtually all governments said the standards were not to be legally binding upon them. At that time, no specific human rights violations, apart from slavery, genocide, and gross abuses of the rights of aliens, were effectively proscribed. Virtually all states shielded themselves happily behind Article 2(7) of the UN Charter in arguing that human rights was strictly an internal

Reprinted from *Human Rights Quarterly* 16 (1994) 375–390 © 1994 by The Johns Hopkins University Press.

affair for the state concerned. While a UN Commission on Human Rights was set up, governments entirely dominated its work. Independent experts were accorded no role whatsoever and NGOs were restricted, in formal terms, to stiff, cameo appearances. The Commission's mandate was largely confined, in practice, to the drafting of new treaties and other legal instruments. Governments wasted no time in declaring in 1947, that the Commission had "no power" whatsoever to respond in any way to violations of human rights.' They did, however, agree to establish a procedure that would channel the thousands of complaints the United Nations received annually. This bureaucratic maze was subsequently dubbed by John Humphrey (who struggled valiantly as the head of the UN's human rights Secretariat) as "the world's most elaborate waste-paper basket."[1]

In 1948 many governments had specifically rejected proposals to adopt binding treaty obligations and, by 1953, the United States had informed the world that it would have nothing to do with any human rights treaty the UN might adopt. The US indicated that such efforts as were then underway should be sidelined and its efforts helped to ensure that they were—for over a decade. When the drafting of the two International Human Rights Covenants was finally completed, in 1966, it took another decade before a mere thirty-five states ratified them and brought them into operation. Thus, the UN's initial foray into the human rights area was far from promising.

Today, however, [more] than fifty years after the adoption of the UN Charter, very significant progress has been made. The standards contained in the Universal Declaration are, in practice, applicable to every state, whatever its formal attitude to their legal status. The view that human rights violations are essentially domestic matters, while still put forward in an almost ritual manner from time to time, receives very little credence from the international community. A vast array of international standards, the most important of which are the six "core" human rights treaties,[2] supplements the Universal Declaration. In addition to the six expert treaty bodies created by the United Nations to supervise the compliance of states parties with their obligations under those treaties, regional human rights conventions and implementing machinery have been set up in Europe, the Americas, and Africa. The United Nations has also created a complex array of other, additional monitoring mechanisms.

In the mid-1960s the Commission on Human Rights began responding to human rights violations, albeit in a very limited number of situations. Since 1979, when the magnitude of unanswered atrocities forced it to go beyond the "unholy trinity" of South Africa, Israel, and Chile, the Commission has gradually and persistently expanded both the number and diversity of countries subjected to public monitoring as well as the range and intrusiveness of the procedures it has been prepared to apply. NGOs and the victims of human rights violations now participate in ever-increasing numbers in the work of one or more of the bodies set up by the Commission or its Sub-Commission. Indeed, governments attest to the increased potential effectiveness of the UN by the lengths to which they go in order to achieve membership of the Commission and to influence its deliberations, as well as by the occasional harshness of their denunciations of its actions.

Most recently, the United Nations has become heavily involved in the administration of human rights programs of unprecedented scope and importance in countries such as El Salvador, Cambodia, and Haiti. What began as electoral assistance has developed into a major activity. In addition, the UN has provided technical assistance in the human rights field to a significant number of countries.

In brief, the international human rights system has developed to an extent that was inconceivable by the vast majority of observers in 1945. Even at the time of the first World Conference on Human Rights, held in Teheran in 1968, not a single treaty monitoring body was in existence. Moreover, no procedures existed for investigating violations, other than for Southern Africa and the Occupied Territories in the Middle East. States were simply not held accountable, except when outrageous violations coincided with the short-term political interest of at least two of the three geopolitical blocs. Indeed, during the past twenty-five years the United Nations system has made immense progress. Of course, it is by no means sufficient and we must acknowledge the enormous inadequacies as well.

How Far Does the United Nations Still Have to Go?

As Amnesty International stated to the World Conference, we must also "face up to the failures" of the United Nations in protecting human rights. Because these failures have been well documented elsewhere,[3] it must suffice to merely take note of some of them in the present article. They include:

• Many serious situations have been neglected by UN bodies, either completely or for many years. Moreover, a handful of powerful countries continues to enjoy a degree of *de facto* immunity from sustained scrutiny, except perhaps in relation to the most truly egregious violations of human rights.

• The mandates given to different "investigative" and "humanitarian" procedures remain subject to a complex array of restraints of both a substantive and procedural nature.

• The techniques available to theme and country rapporteurs to mobilize the shame which might end specific violations remain singularly underdeveloped.

• The follow-up measures accompanying these procedures are too often ineffectual and many of the governments targeted have succeeded in ignoring them, or made only token gestures in response.

• The UN system, broadly defined, continues to isolate human rights concerns within a narrow sphere of activities, despite some recent break-throughs.

• In relation to certain issues, very little progress has been made; they include most notably economic, social and cultural rights, minority rights, and women's rights.

• The financial and human resources available to carry out the various UN mandates are lamentably inadequate.

But despite the many shortcomings of United Nations human rights endeavors, there are grounds for optimism. International public opinion and the work of international and domestic NGOs can greatly influence the positions taken by governments and can create conditions in which international organizations can become more effective. In addition, developments in communications make it increasingly difficult for governments to stem the flow of information from local groups to international "umbrella" human rights groups and inter-governmental monitoring bodies. These developments relate less to the impact of CNN-type media coverage of horror situations than to the effect of the development of wireless technologies that eliminate the dependence upon governmentally-controlled lines of communication. Because of their low cost, relative ease of use, and the difficulty of impeding their use, wireless technologies potentially offer small groups in remote and previously inaccessible areas a degree of direct access to the international community that had previously been available only to large well-resourced urban groups with established international links.

Seven Dilemmas That Have Inhibited Reform Efforts

Human rights debates within the United Nations for many years centered on questions which, although highly controversial from a political perspective, were not particularly complex in conceptual or practical terms. For example, the condemnation and even the definition of practices such as torture, disappearances, and arbitrary executions were relatively straightforward matters, provided only that a political majority could be obtained. In some cases, particularly those relating to racial discrimination in general, and apartheid in particular, this did not prove unduly difficult. By contrast, issues such as minority rights, religious tolerance, democracy and rights of participation, economic and social rights, and women's rights were much more complex and were generally avoided, except for the purposes of ritual incantation when that proved necessary or expedient. In institutional terms, the procedures that existed for responding to violations were so basic, even primitive, that reforms did not need to be very sophisticated to constitute

significant progress. And finally, the attitudes of the three principal geopolitical groups—the West, the East (Communist countries), and the Third
World—were generally depressingly predictable.

Today the challenges, and their possible solutions, are much more con-
voluted. Many of the issues that have belatedly reached the active international agenda are much less susceptible to clearcut solutions. This is in part
because the problems are systemically entrenched and thus represent a fundamental challenge to ruling elites, and also in part because their ramifications are far-reaching and by no means confined to a single country.
Existing institutional arrangements are highly complicated and conceal an
array of overlapping and replicative arrangements and inefficiencies,
achieved after prolonged negotiations among states and subsequently sanctioned by tradition. The geopolitical blocs, for all their valiant attempts to
regroup, have become far less coherent—and thus much less predictable—
in terms of their preparedness to embrace serious reforms of the human
rights regime.

Partly because we are accustomed to a relatively straight-forward and
predictable system within which the possibilities for change were very limited, and partly because of a simple paucity of imagination and lack of
openness to innovation, the human rights community now appears largely
paralyzed in the face of the major challenges that now confront it. This
inability to move beyond the old certainties is best illustrated by reformulating some of the major challenges in terms of the dilemmas which many
in the human rights community consider them to present. Seen in these
terms, the challenges can be made to look more like dangerous nettles
which will only sting those who are foolish enough to grasp them, thereby
setting back the cause of human rights. One alternative, which then
becomes more attractive, is simply to avoid addressing the difficult
issues—to cling to the status quo for fear that any attempt at reform or any
reopening of the decisions already taken would only threaten achievements
which have been so hard won.

Such fears are by no means always without foundation. For example, it
would be foolhardy at best to contemplate redrafting or updating the
International Bill of Human Rights. In relation to various other matters,
however, the fears have been overstated and it is important that they do not
stifle the thinking and political, legal, and diplomatic creativity that is necessary to fashion a more effective and incisive international human rights
regime.

Seven dilemmas are particularly pertinent in this regard:

(i) While it is desirable to acknowledge the relevance of different cultural, philosophical, social, and religious factors in relation to the
application and interpretation of human rights norms, many are reluctant to do so for fear that this would undermine the fundamental principle of universality. As a result, the quest for a glib formula which will

dispose of the issue in a manner that is deemed acceptable to the principal geopolitical actors assumes overriding importance. Thus the outcome achieved at Vienna[4] is considered to be highly satisfactory, despite the extent to which it glosses over the debate that is desperately needed if the human rights movement is to move to a more sophisticated plane.

(ii) While economic, social, and cultural rights must be recognized as human rights, many Western human rights proponents have been reluctant to do so for fear that the status of civil and political rights would inevitably suffer in what they perceive to be a zero-sum game. In effect, what one side gains, the other must lose; for it is assumed that there cannot be mutual gains.

(iii) While international human rights standard-setting efforts have sometimes been duplicative, imprecise, or incomplete, there is a reluctance to acknowledge this problem, as a prelude to tackling it, for fear that the status of international standards in general would be undermined.

(iv) While the need for anticipatory or preventive approaches, such as the provision of advisory services to governments, is widely recognized, many activists are reluctant to explore the means by which such approaches can be rendered effective for fear of undermining the UN's indispensable monitoring role.

(v) While the dire need to rationalize some of the procedural and institutional arrangements in the human rights field is acknowledged, there is considered to be too great a risk that an attempt to do so will be hijacked by those who wish to reduce, rather than enhance, the effectiveness of the bodies or procedures concerned. As a result, a patchwork quilt of considerable complexity serves to confuse or deter many potential "consumers" of these procedures and to diminish the pressures to develop procedures that will be truly effective.

(vi) While it is conceded that human rights considerations should be factored into the full range of UN activities, concerns that this will dissipate protection efforts, or that existing institutional sensitivities will be offended, are used to justify a failure to explore innovative new approaches.

(vii) While it is clear that the role of both national and international NGOs should be significantly enhanced within the UN system, efforts to do so are either not pursued at all or are radically diluted on the grounds that more assertive approaches would provide opponents with an opportunity to reduce even further the role currently accorded to NGOs.

It cannot be denied that within each of these dilemmas there is significant cause for concern. Any attempt at reform can be hijacked and, in the human rights area in particular, that risk is always present. But it is surely counterproductive to treat each and every one of these issues as a Pandora's box which must forever remain closed for fear that, if ever opened, it will wreak havoc upon those who dared to do so. Such an approach only delays the constructive consideration of complex but crucial issues. These issues ultimately must be addressed if progress is to be made towards a truly effective international regime capable of transcending many of the shortcomings of existing arrangements.

The remainder of this article elaborates on the importance of several of these issues in the context of what a recent Amnesty International statement has termed the "divergences of opinion [over] crucial matters" that confront the World Conference.[5] They are: universality, indivisibility, and North-South solidarity.

Universality

In the Bangkok Declaration, adopted at the World Conference Regional Preparatory Meeting in April 1993, the Asian states "recognize that while human rights are universal in nature, they must be considered in the context of a dynamic and evolving process of international norm-setting, bearing in mind the significance of national and regional particularities and various historical, cultural and religious backgrounds."[6] Many observers have characterized this as constituting, in effect, a back-door repudiation of the principle that the standards contained in the International Bill of Rights apply equally to all nations and cultures. In fact, both positions have some substance, despite their apparent irreconcilability.

The challenges are fivefold. In the first place, the international community must insist, as both the Bangkok Declaration and the Jakarta Summit Meeting of the Non-Aligned Movement[7] have recognized, that the standards contained in the International Bill of Rights are universally applicable to all nations. The World Conference largely met this challenge by adopting the Vienna Declaration. To give substance to this commitment, governments should have agreed to mount a concerted worldwide campaign to achieve universal ratification by the year 2000 of the six core United Nations human rights treaties. In the end, the Vienna Declaration and Programme of Action stop well short of this step, even though universal participation in these treaty regimes would be the best possible context in which to pursue a systematic discussion of the relevant issues.

The second challenge is to recognize the need to take account of cultural diversity. Once we move beyond the core, physical integrity rights, the nature of the society, its traditions and culture, and other such factors become highly pertinent to any efforts to promote and protect respect for the rights concerned. We must recognize that the reflexive, often dogmatic, admonitory, and homogeneous approach that is appropriate to such core violations will simply be less productive, and achieve far less enduring results than a more sensitive, open, and flexible approach which situates the goals sought within the society in question. The precise requirements of what is often termed the right to democracy is a case in point. Human rights efforts will be enriched, not compromised, by an approach that is, in appropriate respects, more probing, more self-conscious, and more eclectic than that which many countries have achieved to date.

The third challenge is related to the second. It is essential to recognize that there are conflicts among rights and that the resolution of such conflicts requires greater openness about the difficulties involved and a more concerted attempt to accommodate the different values involved. The human rights movement must move beyond the metaphor of rights as trumps that simply override all competing considerations, and acknowledge that the actual equation is rather more complicated. Religious rights and women's rights are a case in point, although there are many others as well. This is by no means to suggest, however, that the non-human rights dimensions of a problem should be put on a par with those that clearly are covered by universal norms.

The fourth challenge is to compel governments to go far beyond the evasive generalities that continue to characterize most claims that certain rights are not applicable in some societies. This tendency is epitomized by, but by no means limited to, many of the reservations that have been lodged to the Convention on the Rights of the Child and the Convention on the Elimination of All Forms of Discrimination against Women. It is one thing to specify a carefully-defined area in relation to which a state wishes to reserve its position; it is entirely another to formulate open-ended reservations which can then be interpreted to exempt the government concerned from any obligation that it finds distasteful. The extent to which the latter approach has proliferated in recent years, and the difficulty which the relevant international bodies have had in getting an effective grip on the problem, have served to make it into a challenge of major proportions.

The fifth challenge is, for NGOs and others in particular, to begin to scrutinize claims of relativism in terms of their foundations within the cultural, philosophical, or religious traditions of societies. Many claims made have no foundation whatsoever in such traditions. Instead they reflect no more than the age-old tendency of governments to justify the cynical and self-interested proposition that their own citizens neither want nor need the protection of human rights.

Some human rights activists will consider the introduction of greater complexity and the abandonment of absoluteness where it is not justified as a step backwards. It is, in fact, the opposite. It reflects the growing importance, maturity, and sophistication of the international debate and signifies that international human rights principles are at last starting to infiltrate themselves into the more deeply-rooted social, cultural, and legal norms of diverse societies. Until that process begins to succeed, the human rights revolution will remain little more than an aspiration, however noble.

Indivisibility

Another principle of truly fundamental importance which is said to be under siege at present is that of indivisibility. This principle holds that two sets of rights—economic, social, and cultural rights, and civil and political rights—are of equal importance. For a variety of compelling reasons, the United Nations recognized from the outset—in the Universal Declaration in particular—that neither set of rights could be accorded priority over the other. But that has not deterred various governments, NGOs, and others from arguing, when it suits them, that one set of rights is, in practice, a prerequisite to enjoyment of the other. All such arguments must be rejected. They are without either legal or empirical foundation and threaten to destroy the only basis upon which an international consensus on human rights will ever be possible.

When governments make these arguments, they are, in essence, attempting to justify the denial of basic human rights. When commentators make these arguments, such as *The Economist's* attack on economic rights as mere goals and its admonition to the West to ignore them in the rights debate,[8] they should draw a reasoned and powerful response from the human rights community. When they are made by NGOs they are particularly damaging and demand a strong response.

It is thus regrettable that attacks by human rights NGOs on the very notion of economic, social, and cultural rights have all too often been met with a resounding silence on the part of other NGOs. To take an example, the then Executive Director of the largest and most influential of the US-based groups—Human Rights Watch—wrote in early 1993, before his retirement from that position:

> The view that economic and social questions should also be thought of in terms of rights was not solely confined to the Soviet bloc. It is reflected in several provisions of the Universal Declaration of Human Rights and in an International Covenant on Economic, Social and Cultural Rights . . . . Moreover, human rights activists in a number of Third World countries, especially in Asia, have long held the view that both kinds of concerns are rights. Their argument has not proved persuasive in the West, however, and none of the leading international nongovernmental groups concerned

with human rights has become an advocate of economic and social rights.[9]

This statement, which at that time reflected the approach that had been adopted by Human Rights Watch for over a decade, is wrong on every count. Far from being a Soviet creation, the formulations on economic rights contained in the Universal Declaration have their clear, immediate origins in concepts proposed by President Roosevelt and in specific formulations put forward by a Committee of the American Law Institute in 1944. Such rights are by no means confined to one covenant but are contained in every one of the major UN treaties other than the Civil and Political Rights Covenant, as well as in separate regional treaties in Europe and the Americas. Suggesting that economic rights are some sort of Asian delicacy demonstrates either stunning ignorance or blind prejudice. Every Western country, except the United States, is a party to the relevant treaty. It is greatly to the credit of Human Rights Watch that it has, in the course of 1993, signalled not only its commitment to ratification by the United States of the International Covenant on Economic, Social and Cultural Rights, but also its preparedness to address those rights when they arise within the context of their existing mandate.

While the vast majority of the major international NGOs have clearly endorsed the validity of economic, social, and cultural rights, very few of them have done anything constructive about these rights. It is time to remedy this deficiency. Not every NGO should concern itself with these rights, but none should pretend to be basing its work on international standards if it rejects those rights *per se*. Moreover the NGO community must, if it is to retain its immense credibility, encourage the emergence of more groups that are committed to the promotion of economic, social, and cultural rights. Until that happens, the allegation of selectivity will be valid when applied to the NGO community as a whole, even though it cannot justifiably be levelled against any individual NGO.

The first priority is to take those governments that insist on the fundamental importance of economic and social rights at their word. Those governments that have not ratified the relevant Covenant must immediately be prevailed upon to do so. It must be said, without equivocation or reticence, that advocacy of these rights coupled with a failure to accept any legal obligations to respect them does not demonstrate a genuine commitment.

Once formal international obligations have been accepted, the second priority is to ensure that governments establish appropriate domestic arrangements to monitor the enjoyment of these rights and to provide at least some means by which they can be formally vindicated (whether by individuals or groups) at the national level. The great majority of governments have not yet taken either of these steps and NGOs have permitted many of them the luxury of ratifying the Covenant and doing very little by way of follow-up. A campaign should be launched to hold governments accountable in this regard.

The third priority is to begin drafting an Optional Protocol to the Covenant which would permit the submission of complaints alleging serious violations of economic, social, and cultural rights. This exercise will: (a) fill the existing vacuum, as a result of which international procedures effectively exclude these rights from their purview; (b) bring the debate over these rights to bear upon real-life situations and to move beyond the determinedly abstract character of past debates; and (c) provide the specificity of focus which is required to enable the development of meaningful jurisprudence in this area. In this respect, the statement contained in the Vienna Programme of Action encouraging "the Commission on Human Rights, in cooperation with the Committee on Economic, Social and Cultural Rights, to continue the examination of optional protocols" to the Covenant is an important step in the right direction.[10]

Solidarity

The North-South dimension of the human rights debate is of fundamental importance but it continues to be pursued largely by means of exercises in shadow boxing. The rhetoric of both sides has often been quite similar—as has been their failure to focus on specifics. Thus, for example, the North identifies "solidarity" as the key element in the Declaration on the Right to Development—"solidarity between industrialized countries and their developing partners, solidarity in every country with the most disadvantaged."[11] On the other hand, the South calls the right to development "universal and inalienable" and argues that the main obstacles to its realization "lie at the international macroeconomic level."[12] Neither side has been prepared to go beyond such generalities and render the debate meaningful in human rights terms.

NGOs have all too often indulged this evasiveness, preferring to contribute to a North-South slinging match rather than devising benchmarks against which the positions of both sides can be evaluated. One such benchmark, UNDP's "20/20 proposal," would restructure the budgets of developing nations to ensure a 20 percent allocation for priority social sector programs, and industrialized countries would ensure that 20 percent of their overseas development assistance is devoted to human priority concerns (economic and social rights). Despite the stunning modesty of the latter goal, it is still far from being met. Similarly, little has been done to identify clear criteria against which to measure authentic human rights sensitivity on the part of the international financial institutions. Instead, we usually hear competing, and equally unhelpful, calls to increase aid radically or to terminate it abruptly, all in the name of human rights.

Integration

It is paradoxical that, as a result of the UN's growing responsiveness to previously long-ignored calls for human rights concerns to be integrated into other activities (such as development cooperation, peacekeeping, and other forms of dispute settlement), it is now necessary to emphasize that such integration must have its limits. Authentic human rights fact-finding and monitoring cannot be an integrated part of advisory services or technical cooperation. The differences between the two types of activity are fundamental and the distinction must be retained. Similarly, while peace-keeping, the exercise of "good offices" functions, and conciliation efforts are important and should reflect integrated human rights components, they cannot be substitutes for human rights monitoring, nor is it appropriate in most instances to combine responsibility for the different functions in the same entity. Rather, in many situations, human rights monitors are needed to scrutinize the human rights promoting activities of technical advisers, peace-keepers, and others, rather than being replaced by them. Similarly, the UN system should address the need to vest a central coordinating role in relation to all human rights matters in a single entity, whether it be the Centre for Human Rights, a High Commissioner for Human Rights, or some other effective alternative.

The Role of Nongovernmental Organizations

When the Universal Declaration was being drafted, a heated debate took place between East and West over whether human rights derived from the inherent dignity of humankind or were merely entitlements granted by governments. Philosophical considerations aside, neither position accurately reflects reality; human rights are in fact extracted from governments by popular movements and what are now known as NGOs. Indeed, no well-informed observer would doubt that NGOs have been instrumental in contributing to many of the breakthroughs that have been achieved in the international human rights regime. Thus, some governments have every reason to want to minimize the role and privileges accorded to NGOs. Recent threats in this regard are not new.

The remainder of this article considers, in a critical but constructive manner, some of the challenges that lie ahead for NGOs. One such challenge is for international NGOs to encourage and assist the evolution of domestic NGOs. Any such help must be non-paternalistic and be provided on terms set by the grassroots groups. Far too little attention has been paid in the past to what might be done to build up indigenous capacity. Too many Western NGOs act as though they believe that respect for human rights in the world will be won or lost in a handful of Western capitals. In the same vein, it is necessary not to over-state the importance for domestic groups to be actively engaged vis-à-vis international forums. The work in such forums is undoubtedly important but it does not require the direct involvement of every small domestic group, many of whose scarce resources would better be spent at home.

NGOs active at the international level need to become both better coordinated and more systematically critical. Both challenges are difficult in practice. NGOs must become better coordinated in forums such as the Commission on Human Rights and its Sub-Commission. If not, NGOs, because of their sheer numbers and diversity, will be relegated to a mere sideshow role which can safely be ignored by the governmental representatives and the press to whom their efforts should be directed. Clearly, NGOs must be more effective in pooling resources, reducing unhelpful repetition, enabling better targeting, and encouraging greater specialization. In the absence of such strategies, governments looking for excuses to hobble NGOs will not find the task as difficult as it should be.

One is struck in looking at the NGO movement by its homogeneity of tactics and approaches. While in some respects this is desirable, in others it is not. Where are the equivalents of Greenpeace or ACT UP at one end of the spectrum, and the World Resources Institute and other environmental think tanks at the other? Perhaps the relatively limited range of the spectrum helps to explain why NGOs are not always as critical as they should be. There is, for example, a tendency to consider the work of international organizations on the terms that they set themselves rather than on the basis of more objective, or NGO-determined, criteria. This is illustrated by the response to UNESCO's work in the field of human rights education. In recent years UNESCO has failed dismally in this domain. It has convened conference after conference and adopted one platitudinous, banal declaration or program of action after another. In concrete terms, UNESCO has achieved little more than the diversion of NGO energy and resources into futile activities. In the meantime the dire need for a sustained and serious international human rights education campaign remains unaddressed. Yet NGOs have, for the most part, played along with this nonsense instead of developing a detailed, constructive, public critique of UNESCO's shortcomings which could serve as the basis for reinvigoration of its work.

Another illustration is the Commission on Human Rights' 1503 procedure for examining, on a confidential basis, situations of gross violations. While views differ as to whether it has outlived its undoubted historical usefulness, there can be little doubt that it has been rendered needlessly ineffectual by some of the procedural approaches that it has followed. Yet NGOs have not sought to mount a campaign to achieve any of the much-needed reforms. They have, almost without exception, gone along with its many flaws.

But, in conclusion, the need to enhance the role and effectiveness of

NGOs vis-à-vis the UN program is by no means a one way street in which all of the responsibility lies with the NGOs themselves. The United Nations must address in a constructive and systematic fashion the need to accord NGOs the status and rights that they deserve as full partners in a common endeavor. It makes no sense, for example, that local and national NGOs are, virtually by definition, excluded from consultative status with the Economic and Social Council, especially at a time when they are coming to be seen as vital partners in a genuine dialogue with governments.

Notes

1. John Humphrey, "The United Nations Commission on Human Rights and its Parent Body," in *René Cassin: Amicorum Discipulorumque Liber,* ed. Karel Vasak (Paris: Pedone, 1969), 1:110.

2. These include the International Covenant on Economic, Social and Cultural Rights; the International Covenant on Civil and Political Rights; the International Convention on the Elimination of All Forms of Racial Discrimination; the Convention on the Elimination of All Forms of Discrimination against Women; the Convention on the Rights of the Child; and the Convention against Torture and Other Cruel, Inhuman or Degrading Treatment or Punishment.

3. Amnesty International, "Facing Up to the Failures: Proposals for Improving the Protection of Human Rights by the United Nations" (London, Dec. 1992, AI Index: IOR 41/16.92); Ian Martin, "The Promotion of Human Rights and Prevention of Human Rights Violations," Council of Europe Doc. CE/CMDH (93) 6 (1993).

4. Paragraph 1 of the Vienna Declaration (UN Doc. A/Conf.157/22 of 6 July 1993) states that:

The World Conference on Human Rights reaffirms the solemn commitment of all States to fulfill their obligations to promote universal respect for, and observance of, all human rights and fundamental freedoms for all in accordance with the Charter of the United Nations, other instruments relating to human rights, and international law. The universal nature of these rights and freedoms is beyond question.

5. "Issues at the UN World Conference on Human Rights," Doc. IOR 41/WU 02/93 (29 March 1993).

6. A/CONF.157/PC/59. ¶ 8.

7. "The Jakarta Message: A Call for Collective Action and the Democratization of International Relations," NAC 10/Doc.12/Rev.1 (6 Sept. 1992), ¶ 18 ("We reaffirm that basic human rights and fundamental freedoms are of universal validity.").

8. "The Blue and the Red," *The Economist,* 8 May 1993, 21–22.

9. "Aryeh Neier, "Human Rights," in *The Oxford Companion to Politics of the World,* ed. John Krieger (New York: Oxford University Press, 1993), 403.

10. The Vienna Declaration and Programme of Action" reproduced in "Report of the World Conference on Human Rights: Report of the Secretary-General," UN Doc. A/CONF.157/24 Part I (13 Oct. 1993), Part II, ¶ 74.

11. World Conference on Human Rights: Position Paper by the European Community and its Member States, April 1993, ¶ 10.

12. Bangkok Declaration, ¶ ¶ 17–18.

18

Sovereignty Is No Longer Sacrosanct: Codifying Humanitarian Intervention

Jarat Chopra and Thomas G. Weiss

O ne word explains why the international community has difficulty countering [human rights] violations: "sovereignty." The distinguishing feature of a new order established by the Treaty of Westphalia, it obscured humanitarian intentions of earlier founders of international law;[1] However, developing guidelines for the forcible delivery of assistance, beyond historical and recent experience, can break the human rights-sovereignty deadlock in a system where states remain the principal actors.

In the bloody aftermath of the Persian Gulf War, the United Nations Security Council passed Resolution 688 on April 5, 1991, which insisted "that Iraq allow immediate access by international humanitarian organizations to all those in need of assistance in all parts of Iraq to make available all necessary facilities for their operations." This effectively authorized two major relief operations, "Safe Haven" and "Provide Comfort." In spite of host government hostility and widespread reluctance in the region and in UN circles, some 13,000 U.S. troops and 10,000 soldiers from twelve other nations delivered 25 million pounds of food, water, medical supplies, clothing, and shelter to protected areas carved out of northern Iraq.

Several observers labeled these efforts "humanitarian intervention," resuscitating a conceptual debate on the subject.[2] The intervention in Kurdistan reflected growing public outrage with African countries—particularly in the Horn-where both governments and rebels had deprived civilians of international succor as part of their war arsenals. But intergovernmental discussion was divided during the 1991 General Assembly. Representatives of developing countries were particularly sensitive about reform of the UN humanitarian assistance machinery as a possible "Trojan horse" for big-power intervention after the Cold War.

Originally published by the Carnegie Council on Ethics and International Affairs in *Ethics and International Affairs* 6 (1992): 95–117.

Traditionally, sovereignty has been interpreted to exclude interference in local affairs, thereby preventing international responses to atrocities such as genocide by the Khmer Rouge or gassing of Kurds by the Iraqi government. Hence, the creation of havens in Kurdistan was a watershed and precedent. But deep suspicion of the event highlighted practical inadequacies of humanitarian intervention. The Iraq case was unique and another bad example on which to base general principles; and more significantly, it illustrated that there is no mechanism in place to distinguish national interests. In his last annual report on the work of the organization," former UN Secretary-General Pérez de Cuéllar called for reinterpretation of the Charter principles of sovereignty and noninterference in domestic affairs to allow for intervention on humanitarian grounds, as well as identification of the objective conditions under which it should be carried out.

In the past, debate about humanitarian intervention had been primarily among legal scholars, who affirmed the validity of the concept but disagreed on whether or not to codify the objective conditions under which it should be carried out.[3] The principal shortcoming was vulnerability to abuse: powerful states with ulterior motives would be able to intervene in weaker states on the pretext of protecting human rights. The legal debate continues, with Oscar Schachter, for example, stopping short of referring to Resolution 688 as an authorization for humanitarian intervention: "it is unlikely that most governments would approve a broad right of the United Nations to introduce troops for humanitarian purposes against the wishes of the government."[4] At the same time, he argues that the UN could override reluctant host governments by invoking enforcement procedures under Chapter VII of the UN Charter.

Current debate has moved beyond lawyers to include diplomats, politicians, and political scientists. Most of these practitioners and analysts, however, have little understanding of the essential legal quality and background of humanitarian intervention. It is the working hypothesis of this article that greater familiarity with international legal arguments would not only clarify debate but assist in developing a mechanism to guarantee, by force if necessary, the access of innocent civilians to international assistance. "Humanitarian" and "intervention" are contradictions when viewed through the prism of sovereignty, but it is our contention that the two can be reconciled by examining closely the sources of underlying authority for both sovereignty and human rights.

While battles are not won by relying on lessons from previous wars, new international principles necessarily build on experience. The current, largely political, debate about humanitarian intervention represents a step backward from the conceptual progress made during an extensive legal debate two decades ago. The present focus is on "intervention" *per se* and, therefore, sovereignty, while previously domestic jurisdiction as an issue was considered secondary to preventing the abuse of humanitarian justifications. The preoccupation with intervention, and whether it is permissible on humanitarian grounds, is a red herring; it ignores the practical concern for adequate measures to prevent states from using human rights to camouflage ulterior motives.

Legal debates in the 1960s and 1970s over the codification and objective criteria of humanitarian intervention paralleled earlier arguments about the definitions of "war" in the 1928 Kellogg-Briand Pact and "aggression" under the 1945 UN Charter. Since no definition could be sufficiently comprehensive, it was argued in both cases that potential aggressors would be able to navigate between provisions and circumvent the letter of any prohibition. Instead, without defined parameters states found that they did not have to navigate at all to contravene the spirit of the prohibition. For example, in 1931 Japan invaded Manchuria and declared that since a formal state of war did not exist its actions were not inconsistent with the 1928 Pact. Similarly, Italy invaded Abyssinia in 1936 without any formal declaration.

Whether the Kellogg-Briand Pact prohibited only formally declared war, or measures involving force short of war as well, Article 2(4) of the UN Charter rectified this discrepancy by forbidding "the threat or use of force." It still permitted and described exceptions in the form of self-defense (Article 51) and collective action (Chapter VII). But unacceptable aggressive uses of force were not defined for fear that states would abuse such a definition and also because the Charter's more general prohibition was thought to redress the restrictiveness of the term "war."

Since the Second World War, the nature of conflict has increasingly moved away from interstate territorial disputes to more complex internal insurgencies. Foreign economic and political coercion replaced massed armies, and intervention was often based on requests from governments with questionable legitimacy. In the absence of specific Charter directions, states were able to avoid the international characterization of their actions as "aggression." Superpowers intervened in their spheres of influence—the United States in the Americas and Vietnam, and the Soviet Union in Eastern Europe and Afghanistan; as did lesser powers in theirs—Cuba in the Caribbean and Africa, and India on the sub-continent. They resorted to justifying such actions as assistance to legitimate governments.

Efforts to clarify the threat or use of force prohibited under Article 2(4) included the 1974 passage of General Assembly Resolution 3314 on the "Definition of Aggression." It proved not to be comprehensive and excluded disputed categories of force in the interest of agreement. States have not been able to manipulate the letter of the provisions included, however, and instead have relied on elastic interpretations of entirely separate, lawful justifications for using force, such as self-defense or invitation by host governments. States have had to flout openly these provisions, and this has made unilateral uses of force easier to condemn since the first determination of "aggression" by the Security Council in 1976, when South Africa invaded

Angola. Definitions restrict by raising barriers and thereby reducing incidents. While determined efforts cannot be deterred by rules, coordinated responses to the clearly labeled "aggression" of Iraq's invasion of Kuwait is a dramatic illustration of what condemnation can entail in the post-Cold War era.[5]

The legal debate concerning humanitarian intervention has remarkable similarities, particularly whether objective criteria of the concept should or could be codified. Comprehensiveness and fear of abuse were as prevalent as in the earlier debates about war and aggression. There are essentially four lines of reasoning against codification:[6]

(1) Experimentation with the concept throughout history has failed, since justifications for intervention have not had humanitarian results. For example, the Crimean War was provoked by Russia asserting in 1853–54 the right to protect Christians persecuted by the Sultan of the Ottoman Empire. Far from supporting Russia, Great Britain and France intervened to protect Turkish sovereignty and independence. In 1931, one of Japan's justifications for invading Manchuria was on humanitarian grounds. Hitler invaded Czechoslovakia in 1938 claiming to protect ethnic Germans who, he maintained, had been denied the right of self-determination and were suffering mistreatment under the Czechs. More recently, the Indian Army intervened in the Jaffna peninsula to provide aid to the besieged Tamil minority, but airdrops and the presence of some 55,000 troops failed to produce anything other than continued civil war and are more readily explained by Indian domestic politics than humanitarian sentiments.

(2) Codification would lead to further abuse as states could base their actions on interpretations of legal provisions, rather than mere rhetorical proclamations. As such, law would be used by the strong against the weak. It would serve power politics and no longer be law to protect the weak from the strong.

(3) Whatever the objective conditions identified, it would still be impossible to distinguish between action sincerely based on humanitarian grounds and ulterior motives of self-interest. Intentions cannot be identified without access to the policy-making mind of the state, which is hardly accessible in multilateral diplomacy.

(4) The value of codification is minimal because legal systems allow for mitigating circumstances. In fact, humanitarian intervention by a disinterested state would not be inconsistent with existing international norms, which seek to restrict only harmful conduct. It is further argued that the prohibition on the use of force and intervention under Charter Article 2(4) is fragile enough and

so often breached that codification of another exception would only erode it further.

At the same time, there are four arguments, largely mirror images of the above, in favor of codification:[7]

(1) The concept of humanitarian intervention has not been sufficiently tested in history precisely because there has been an absence of objective criteria identified. Besides, there have been a number of successes beginning as early as 480 B.C., when Prince Gelon of Syracuse demanded that the Carthaginians halt child sacrifices to Saturn.

(2) Clearly defined parameters would inhibit states from easily characterizing their abusive actions as humanitarian-driven. Through codification, a high degree of proof could be demanded from states claiming this right of intervention. As such, powerful states would be restricted and the weak protected from insincere motives.

(3) Moreover, if an intervention fulfilled the objective criteria of codification, it would not matter if state action had been motivated by a concurrent self-interested policy.

(4) As with any law, codification would restrict abuse, not merely affirm acceptable conduct. By further clarifying unlawful conduct, codification would strengthen the general prohibition on the use of force. If the terms "territorial integrity" and "political independence" that figure so prominently in Charter Article 2(4) were not interpreted to include the protection of human rights, then they would be inconsistent with the spirit of the Charter, which provides for both. In fact, without such codification there persists a glaring contradiction in the Charter, rather than protection of both domestic jurisdiction and human rights.

This legal debate was largely static during the 1980s, until political developments reshaped the arguments and placed the issue once again prominently on the global agenda. Theoretical questions about the acceptability of humanitarian intervention remained secondary to the practical problem of how it should be conducted.

While the right of humanitarian intervention was not on the agenda, human rights were central international concerns. In the four decades since the signing of the UN Charter and adoption of the Universal Declaration of Human Rights, boundaries of state sovereignty became more and more porous, as any number of technical, economic, and environmental challenges demonstrated. Moreover, areas that formerly were considered entirely domestic, such as minority and individual rights, became subject to external scrutiny. This led to a growing body of international conventions, rules, and norms aimed at regulating the humanitarian behavior of states. Following the creation of several prominent nongovernmental organizations, like Amnesty International, Jimmy Carter placed human rights at the center of his presidential platform. While controversy was not lacking, human rights became viewed as less Western and more universal. But until recently the capacity of the international community to respond when such norms are violated has been meager.

However, 40 years of international norms-creation led to the possibility of and need for norms-implementation. In December 1988 the General Assembly adopted Resolution 43-131, which formally recognized the rights of civilians to international aid and the role of nongovernmental organizations in natural disasters and similar emergencies. Two years later, General Assembly Resolution 45-100 reaffirmed these rights and provided specific access corridors of "tranquility" for humanitarian aid workers. With the passage of Security Council Resolution 688 a few months later, the issue of humanitarian intervention was thrust squarely onto the political agenda of states when the acute problems of some 1.5 million Kurds were interpreted as a threat to international peace and security.

In the process, however, the finely tuned legal debate has been forgotten in the defensive reaction of many developing countries to "another form of intervention." The old shibboleths of noninterference in the domestic affairs of governments and the inviolability of sovereignty have been cited instinctively, with increasing frequency and inadequate reflection.

Can the protection of human rights justify setting aside inherent organizing principles of the international system? Bold proponents of the cause, including former UN Secretary-General Pérez de Cuéllar, call for limited acceptance of the idea. However, we have taken a step backward because the issue of codification has became secondary to whether or not the basic right of humanitarian intervention exists. The political debate has lost sight of plausible answers to the following practical questions: What has sovereignty been and what is it now? What is its relation to human rights? What are the objective criteria of humanitarian intervention? It is to these questions that we now turn.

Sovereignty is pivotal in determining whether or not to intervene on humanitarian grounds. Intervention implies violation or intrusion upon authority; and while authority, like sovereignty, is an abstraction, its concrete form consists of territorial boundaries. Controversy over crossing borders occurs not only because they represent the extent of local political control, but because the right to this control is a sacred underpinning of international order as currently understood. Hence, significant legal instruments have been concluded that prohibit action which is considered threatening to the overall system.

However, sovereignty is a legal fiction that continues to evolve.

Perceiving it as immutable and beyond question requires resort to selective memory, a tendency in international fora. The family, the tribe, and the city all did quite well without it. Yet the widespread view persists that it is the best mechanism for organizing human society at the global level. The inability of sovereignty to reflect adequately the effective self-development of international society has relegated it to increasing conceptual and practical irrelevance in such fields as trade, famine, and environment. For the protection of human rights too, there has been a perceptible movement away from the anachronism of exclusive domestic jurisdiction.

Nation-states have been the principal building blocks of the international system, and their measure of legitimacy as states has been the attribution of sovereignty. As the only abstraction, sovereignty is special in the list of criteria of statehood. The 1933 Montevideo Convention on the Rights and Duties of States lists three others: a permanent population, defined territory, and a government. While a state, as any collective construct, is something more than the sum of its parts, sovereignty transforms it into an absolute. Hinsley points out that sovereignty is not a fact, like energy or power; it is a quality of a fact. Sovereignty is a characteristic of power that relegates its holder to a place above the law. A sovereign is immune from law and only subject to self-imposed restrictions.[8]

While the Treaty of Westphalia is the usual point of departure for historians, the origins of sovereignty were properly in the Roman Empire. The Hellenistic monarchies were restricted by the Greek notion of law as something more valid than the community or its rulers. As such, the king "personified law" since his will amounted to the rules of order. This was different from the divinity of the ruler in the Near East and ancient India, where the king may have governed by the grace of gods but was, like his subjects, subordinate to the external laws of the universe, or dharma. In the Roman Empire, however, it was argued that the source of law must be above the law, and hence the emperor was so regarded. This essential element of sovereignty emerged at the end of the first century.

The rebirth of sovereignty in the nation-state is customarily dated from the end of the Thirty Years War in 1648. Despite attempts during the Middle Ages, such as by the Carolingians and the Holy Roman Empire, to unify and centralize authority, large concentrations of secular power never attained the distinct feature of sovereignty. Its metaphorical implications of immutability, inviolability, perfection, and transcendence were monopolized by the church, on which the emperor relied for legitimacy. Eventually, following three decades of war between Catholics and Protestants, the Peace of Westphalia separated the powers of church and state. In so doing, it transferred to nation-states the special godlike features of church authority. Nation-states inherited the pedigree of sovereignty and an unassailable position above the law that has since been frozen in the structure of international relations.

Whether the power structure of nation-states ever accurately reflected textbook characteristics, sovereignty is no longer sovereign, the world has outgrown it. The exclusivity and inviolability of state sovereignty are increasingly mocked by global interdependence. Electronic communications and media have fostered conscious and unconscious identification among all of humanity. Convenient and accessible transportation has facilitated mass movements of people and, consequently, the increasing de-linkage (psychologically and physically) of populations from territory. The atomic age extinguished boundaries between destruction and the destroyer. Satellites that penetrate "space above any territory of the globe, regardless of 'sovereign' rights over air spaces and duties of 'non-intervention,'" serve to emphasize the new openness and penetrability of everything to everybody."9 "The common heritage of mankind," enshrined in the 1979 Convention on the Moon and Other Celestial Bodies and the 1982 Convention on the Law of the Sea, "marks the passage from the traditional postulate of sovereignty to that of cooperation."10 Interconnectedness has entered the consciousness of public opinion and has been expressed through popular concern for the environment, human rights, and health— including the AIDS epidemic. That the most powerful economies in the world, the G-7, must act in concert on major policies reflects increasing awareness of global financial integration.

At the same time, the fiction of sovereignty has remained greatly intact. The exclusivity of sovereignty has meant that nation-states have been the only members of the international community and the sole "reference points" of international law. In the eyes of the law, individuals do not exist independently of states. There has been no adequate mechanism for redressing state abuse in a system meant ultimately for human welfare.

The direct application of international law to individuals, however, has begun to evolve and circumvent the once impermeable membrane of sovereignty. This is the principal consequence of attributing rights, as well as duties, to human beings. Also, there is direct participation by individuals in the international system: bodies like the International Court of Justice (ICJ) or the International Law Commission (ILC) are composed of specialists who, "whilst appointed by governments, sit in their individual capacities as experts."11 The UN Secretary-General has an influential independent capacity under Article 99 of the Charter.

Other non-state actors also have become influential participants in international processes. Throughout the past four decades, the personalities of international organizations have been affirmed and their capacity to enter into relations with other subjects of international law has grown. Business companies have enjoyed limited status as persons under international law. The mandate system of the League of Nations, the UN trusteeship system, and the concept of self-determination are expressions of the personality of non-states, or pre-states. National liberation movements—the Palestine

Liberation Organization (PLO) and the South West Africa People's Organization (SWAPO) prior to Namibian independence—were given observer status in the General Assembly. The proliferation of nongovernmental organizations in the last few decades has resulted in a privatization of diplomacy and the realization that local citizens cannot be excluded from the international system. In October 1990 the UN General Assembly admitted the International Committee of the Red Cross (ICRC) as its first NGO with observer status, while many others hold consultative status with the Economic and Social Council. Moreover, Namibia in 1989 and Nicaragua in 1990 held the most extensively civilian-monitored elections in history.

Revolutions in technology and information, as well as the appearance of important actors without the attributes of sovereignty, have diminished the relevance of sovereignty for states. As such, the criteria of statehood have shifted to include more complex subjective standards, and not only the objective characteristics of territory, population, government, and sovereignty. Is there a willingness and ability to observe international law? Is the regime in power racist or unlawfully constituted? That a state's legitimacy can determine its sovereignty gives this term a completely new meaning.

The supremacy of sovereignty over law is untenable. Sovereignty as a transcendent source of law is supposed to operate hierarchically between ruler and ruled; it is not supposed to function horizontally, or relatively with other sovereigns. Sovereign equality supposedly prevented developing or legitimating *primus inter pares*. The flaw in the theory of sovereignty is that it was a unitary concept operating in a community: mutual respect implied not being sovereign at all. As such, it is universally recognized that in conflicts between laws of a national sovereign and international law, the latter prevails.

The principle of unanimous voting in the League of Nations became decision making by majority in the UN. This means that sovereign states can be bound against their will by the votes of other states. The veto power of the permanent members of the Security Council vitiates the sovereignty of all other members because by definition one cannot be more sovereign than another. Paradoxically, decolonization eroded the concept because newly emerging small states were forced to rely on community laws for security. In any case, the natural law tradition within international legal thought always perceived the ultimate source of law as *supra*national, for only the law is sovereign: "the public interest (state necessity, reason of state, or whatever) cannot be invoked against the law, except to the extent that the law itself so allows."[12]

What then has sovereignty become (or perhaps, what has it always been)? There are two interpretations, one through international law and the other political. Under international law, there are not degrees of sovereignty; it either exists or it does not. The narrow standard of traditional sovereignty forms a threshold: once nations achieve a kind of critical mass, they are catapulted to a transcendent status through recognition by other members of the states club.

Legal sovereignty cannot be partially redefined or refined. Even when international lawyers account for factual challenges they retain the classic formula.[13] If the standard of definition is not met, sovereignty does not exist. When NGOs, corporations, and revolutionary movements interact directly with states, both non-states and states are considered to operate as legal equals. Employing the logic of the law, either both or neither are sovereign.

Fear of attributing recognition [had] been a primary reason for Israel's refusal to meet with the Palestine Liberation Organization, or the general hesitation of government officials and senior staff members of international secretariats to meet with insurgents or to consider national liberation movements entitled to protection under the humanitarian laws of war. When non-states gain personality, statehood is no longer an exclusive status; and sovereignty verges on operational irrelevance. Moreover, if collective enforcement under Chapter VII of the UN Charter is acceptable intervention, then states are not absolutely inviolable, nor therefore sovereign. Even if sovereignty is said still to operate in pockets at the highest levels of government, current challenges to the concept lead to the conclusion that it is gradually becoming a dead letter of international law.

Political scientists and theorists of international relations have formulated a corruption of sovereignty, which they perceive in terms of degrees. By redrawing strict parameters to include challenges, sovereignty is not seen as incompatible with individual rights, non-state actors, or permeable boundaries. It is possible to be more or less sovereign. Sovereignty becomes an elastic term that refers to a category of social and political organization that is linked geographically to delimited territory. As such, it has no special meaning other than a contextual one. In contrast to international law's objective, largely standardized threshold, political scientists view limits as determined subjectively. Hence, humanitarian interventions, non-state actors, international organizations, and human rights could all be included as exceptions to the anomaly of partially absolute sovereignty.

During the 1991 General Assembly debate on emergency assistance in wars, redefinitions of sovereignty were apparent. The ICRC argued: "In terms of the existing right to assistance, humanitarian assistance cannot be regarded as interference. Far from infringing upon the sovereignty of states, humanitarian assistance in armed conflicts, as provided for by international law, is, rather, an expression of that sovereignty." At the same session, the Soviet Union noted that reservations about "humanitarian intervention" can be addressed by reformulating the issue as "humanitarian solidarity."

Proponents of humanitarian intervention can, and usually do, rely on one of two arguments, both of which lead to the same conclusion. To maintain the traditional concept of sovereignty is to accept its obsolescence and recognize that the emperor has no clothes. If sovereignty is dead, humanitarian intervention does not violate a sacred principle. On the other hand, if humanitarian intervention is permitted as part of an expanded definition of sovereignty and solidarity, then it does not conflict with the remainder of sacrosanct sovereignty.

Eliminating sovereignty from the lexicon of international relations in the foreseeable future is unlikely, however, for state-centered power structures will not agree easily to part with the basis for their status quo. Moreover, sleights of hand and redefinitions that include humanitarian intervention would perpetuate the fiction of sovereignty and continue to slow the acceptance of such rapidly developing concepts as cross-boundary environmental protection. One way to circumvent sovereignty altogether is to explore why human rights constitute a legitimate justification for intervention and how codification could prevent abuse in this area.

Future acceptance of "humanitarian intervention" is linked to a conceptual and practical capacity to reconcile its two conflicting halves. Running through the United Nations Charter are two contradictions: (i) sovereignty and human rights and (ii) peace and justice.

Explicit Charter provisions illustrate the first contradiction. Article 2, paragraph one, bases the organization on the principle of sovereign equality of all member states; paragraph four prohibits the threat or use of force against any state; and paragraph seven protects from UN intervention "matters which are essentially within the domestic jurisdiction of any state." At the same time, preceding these provisions are the first words of the Charter preamble: "We the Peoples of the United Nations determined . . . to reaffirm faith in fundamental human rights, in the dignity and worth of the human person, in the equal rights of men and women. . . ." Article 1(3) then states that "the Purposes of the United Nations are . . . to achieve international cooperation in solving international problems of an economic, social, cultural, or humanitarian character, and in promoting and encouraging respect for human rights and for fundamental freedoms for all without distinction as to race, sex, language, or religion." Under Articles 55 and 56, members are committed "to take joint and separate action in cooperation with the Organization" for the promotion of "equal rights and self-determination of peoples," including "universal respect for, and observance of, human rights." In Article 68, the Economic and Social Council "shall set up commissions . . . for the protection of human rights." Article 76(c) states that a basic objective of the trusteeship system is "to encourage respect for human rights and for fundamental freedoms for all. . . ."

The second contradiction is apparent in the following questions: Are human rights exclusively within the domestic jurisdiction of states or are they an international concern with community jurisdiction? What is the separation of powers? Should the prohibition on the threat or use of force against states be applicable to violence against human beings? Or, for that matter, is the threat or use of force against states permissible for the protection of human rights? Which authority is superior, state jurisdiction over individuals within its boundaries, or international jurisdiction over inalienable human rights?

Underlying these questions is the perennial conflict between peace and justice, stability and change. The avoidance of war, or at least the control and centralization of violence, is central to the Charter. Order, ideally maintained through Chapter VII enforcement mechanisms, was considered the best means to peace. Order, however, amounted to the maintenance of the status quo, which enabled "those who already 'have' to secure their privileges and . . . encourage[d] the 'have nots' to accept their lot."[14] Seeking justice often implied disorder, instability, and therefore the scourge of war. Order and the hope for peace normally outweighed the concern for justice. Sovereignty and human rights were reconciled through a similar hierarchical interpretation of Charter provisions.

The concept of humanitarian intervention could not develop if respect for sovereignty (and the prohibition on intervention) always superceded humanitarianism. As sovereignty and the prohibition against outside intervention protecting it have been eroded, human rights have grown in clarity, strength, and breadth. The evidence of 40 years suggests that this trend will continue, but it has not reached the point yet where human rights systematically outweigh sovereignty. Occasionally, however, they do, and the intervention on behalf of the Kurds in Iraq was a watershed. While the reversal in priorities was only temporary, the event was a dramatic harbinger that reflects the pace of humanitarian developments.

Four decades have been spent defining human rights, and they are now clearer as a justification for action than ever before. Human rights norms are reaching a point where they can be implemented and enforced. In the last decade, the United Nations "has developed an impressive array of new enforcement machinery—machinery that is not widely known but has fundamentally changed what the United Nations can and does accomplish to aid individual victims of human rights violations."[15] This machinery includes:

•Establishing a variety of specialized theme mechanisms (a Working Group and several independent rapporteurs) to take effective action (often on an emergency basis) wherever there are problems regarding several critical human rights problems that affect individuals: disappearances, summary executions, torture, and religious intolerence.

•Appointing numerous Special Rapporteurs (or Representatives) to examine conditions in individual countries. Afghanistan, Chile, El Salvador, Iran, and Romania are among the current ones.

•Establishing and expanding the activities of new supervisory committees that monitor compliance with human rights treaties, several of which have new optional complaint mechanisms through which individuals can seek redress.

•Substantially expanding the advisory services program that provides technical assistance in human rights.

•Developing a major initiative to expand UN public information on human rights in a new world campaign designed to advance awareness of rights and awareness of the UN machinery through which individuals can claim their rights.

Moreover, in August 1991 the United Nations Observer Mission in El Salvador (ONUSAL) became the first military-civilian operation with the task of monitoring human rights abuses. The General Assembly convened a world conference on human rights in 1993. The importance of human rights is highlighted in recent proposals for restructuring the secretariat, including one of four new deputy secretaries-general responsible solely for humanitarian and human rights issues.

Reversing the conventional priority of sovereignty over human rights, however, would not automatically reconcile internal contradictions in the term "humanitarian intervention." In practice, the concept of intervention would still imply violating sovereign authority without having identified a higher authority on which the supremacy of human rights rest. Questioning the source of authority for human rights invites responses from many angles of a traditional split in jurisprudence: positivism considers international law to be derived fundamentally from the will of states, while natural law maintains that there is a higher authority than sovereignty. For positivists, human rights exist only because states permit them to exist; and as sovereignty is the source of rights, it will always be the higher authority. This is contrary to the spirit of the movement toward increased respect for human rights, since as a formulation it is self-defeating. Natural law is the best means by which state abuse of human rights can be challenged; but one of the reasons that human rights have not yet gained primacy is that their source of authority is more difficult to identify than the concrete mechanisms of state. Identifying the source of natural law is an ancient problem, but one that merits increased attention today. From this can be deduced the legitimacy and authority for the concept of human rights, as well as for their protection.

While both sovereignty and the source of natural law are absolutes, they differ in their formulations. The former is quantified in secular terms manifested as the state; the latter is a qualitative determination of basic goods. Thomas Aquinas's "treatise on law" in the *Summa Theologica* consolidated much of the earlier thought on this subject since Plato's *Republic* and Aristotle's *Nicomachean Ethics.* His definition of natural law is encapsulated in a condensed phrase, *participatio legis aeternae in rationali creatura:* the participation of the eternal law in rational creatures. It is an operation between our capacity to understand and existing universal laws. This principle is comparable to the Tao, or way, of Lao Tzu; Cofucian rites or "style of life"; Hindu and Buddhist dharma, or right action; Islamic Sunna, or model behavior of the Prophet; Japanese giri, or rules of behavior. Aquinas's "account of the source of natural law thus focuses first on the experienced dynamisms of our nature, and then on the intelligible principles which outline the aspects of human flourishing, the basic values grasped by human understanding."[16]

The authority for natural law is what ought to be. It is very much the purpose of law to restrict possible destructive action. Allott states that "Law constrains or it is a travesty to call it law. . . . Law transcends the power of the powerful and transforms the situation of the weak or it is a travesty to call it law."[17] While what human rights ought to be has largely been enumerated, clarification of how it ought to be enforced has only begun.

Whether values are universal or culturally or even individually specific is a question that emerged from the earliest human social relations. It is linked to the basic duality that divides all philosophy, religion, and ideology: diversity and unity, the individual and the collective. Despite these persisting dilemmas, there is not disagreement about whether in principle humanitarian intervention is acceptable. The crux of the issue is fear of abuse and how the danger can be mitigated to make the pill of intervention easier to swallow.

Swallowing is particularly difficult for Third World states. Their representatives draw obvious parallels to the unpalatable power of imperialists who intervened on the basis of "principles" such as "civilization," "white man's burden," and "manifest destiny." The fact that in the present international system those with the resources to intervene are former colonial powers or large and traditionally obtrusive neighbors does not facilitate discussion. Nonetheless, there are two starting points for dialogue—codification and decision making. The codification of objective criteria of the circumstances in which humanitarian intervention should be carried out and the type of operation it should be is the first premise. The second is that decisions about humanitarian intervention must be made exclusively on a genuinely collective basis.

Some authors have attempted to identify lists of objective criteria. Lillich enumerates five conditions that would validate humanitarian intervention: immediacy of violation of human rights; extent of violation of human rights; invitation to use forcible self-help; degree of coercive measures employed (i.e., proportionality); and relative disinterestedness of acting state. Moore adds five qualifications: an immediate and extensive threat to fundamental human rights, particularly a threat of widespread loss of human life; a proportional use of force which does not threaten greater destruction of values than the human rights at stake; a minimal effect on authority structures; a prompt disengagement, consistent with the purpose of the action; and immediate full reporting to the Security Council and appropriate regional organizations.[18]

In the context of relief for man-made disasters, Minear has set down nine operational principles governing humanitarian, assistance: recognition of the importance of safeguarding human life, including redefining its relationship with sovereignty; motives for assistance missions must be transparent to affirm legitimacy; response to assistance needs must be consistent in each case, and therefore automatic and not selective; assistance must be provided comprehensively to all categories of persons in need, and not according to artificial distinctions such as between "refugees" and "displaced persons"; success of assistance operations depends on local popular participation, or mutuality; civilian management is preferable for civilian humanitarian initiatives; increasing fidelity to international law; disaster prevention measures and methods of peaceful conflict resolution should be fostered to avoid the need for intervention after the fact; and there must be accountability by the assistance donor, as well as by host governments to their own populations.[19]

An essential problem with codification that has re-emerged in the current debate, however, is the desirable degree of specificity: the enumeration of appropriate circumstances might exclude unforeseen situations requiring assistance which do not fall strictly within any agreed categories. As mentioned earlier, definitions cannot be exhaustive, nor can they be extensive without becoming too restrictive. At the same time, flexibility requires general provisions, which are then open to abuse. The best way to overcome this dilemma and reduce the danger of abuse is to restrict humanitarian intervention exclusively to the category of collective action as understood in Chapter VII of the UN Charter. Prohibiting it as a form of self-help would circumvent the unreliability of unilateral interventions.

To circumscribe illegitimate justifications, the United Nations should have sole responsibility for determining the existence of humanitarian crises, in the manner that it has monopoly to "determine the existence of any threat to the peace, breach of the peace, or act of aggression" under Article 39. Furthermore, direction or conduct of humanitarian operations should be only a United Nations activity, ideally through Chapter VII of the Charter. In the absence of Article 43-47 agreements for a standing UN force and adequate military capacity, much greater thought needs to be given to clarifying the meanings of "collective action" and "subsidiary organ."

"Collective" must mean the subordination of command and control of sovereign armed forces to a centralized instrument, authorized to act by the larger community in the event of a crisis. Action through international organization, or multilateralism, is distinct from multinational action, which amounts to individual states independently cooperating in a particular venture, effectively as a form of self-help. Particularly, collective action is conducted according to standard operating procedures devised and agreed to prior to a crisis, and which are consistently applied whatever the configuration of subjective interests of community members. The importance of "collective" is not necessarily in the operation, which may be executed by one or two or many states, but in the decision to act as well as the continued direction of the operation. Given the U.S.-led coalition's prosecution of the Gulf War and the lack of reporting once the decision to authorize "all necessary means" was taken, the nature of centralized command and control has assumed a greater importance.

Under Article 7(2) of the UN Charter, the principal organs of the organization, including the Security Council, can appoint an agent or establish "such subsidiary organs as may be found necessary." The Charter nowhere defines "subsidiary organ," but Kelsen argues that it can include a collegiate body, a single individual or member state, or a group of members.[20] This raises the question of whether the Security Council can delegate the execution of enforcement measures—as a category of tasks distinct from others—to a "subsidiary organ." While the Charter is unclear, it would seem that the answer is affirmative if three conditions are met: First, it should be clear that the state or group of states is acting on behalf of the world organization and that the link between the two is direct. Second, given that the command of the operation is not functionally part of the UN administration, the instructions from the organization to its agent must be clear, specific, and incontestable. Finally, the agent must be directly responsible to the authority of the organization. Avoiding the kind of inadequate contact between the United Nations and allied forces in Kurdistan after resolution 688 has made imperative a formalization of sub-contracts for humanitarian relief to subsidiary organs.

While the United Nations should develop its professional capacity to conduct such operations on its own to avoid any dispute as to the collectivity or legitimacy of actions called for by the Security Council, it might well begin by strengthening its humanitarian assistance mechanisms for interventions not involving uses of force. Coordination of assistance efforts is a significant step toward collective action and regulation of motives. Recent examples include the Special Emergency Programme for the Horn of Africa (SEPHA) and the Special Coordinator for Emergency Relief Operations in Liberia (UNSCOL).

Among the decisions of the 1991 General Assembly was the appointment of a single humanitarian aid coordinator with the authority, at least in principle, to respond to governments and opposition groups that deny assistance to suffering civilians. Resolution 46–182 also creates new and useful institutional mechanisms, including a special new $50 million fund, a standing interagency committee in Geneva, unified appeals, and a new roster of expertise.

Observers have criticized the United Nations for inefficiency and duplication, because individual agencies are more concerned with their particular objectives and fund-raising needs than with delivery. The harmonization of efforts among intergovernmental and nongovernmental organizations is an imperative, and the new coordinator and institutional machinery, when backed by the Secretary-General and the five permanent members of the Security Council, should be able to better coordinate activities. . . .

The struggle toward a law of humanitarian intervention is a twofold task: to mollify contradictions between human rights and intervention and to codify norms so that humanitarianism cannot be used to justify unacceptable and self-interested interventions. Overcoming the abuse of humanitarianism as a justification for ulterior motives is the common ground in the debate and a useful starting point for discussion. Drawing upon both the analysis of humanitarian intervention and re-examination of legal meanings of terms in a political context provides the means to build bridges and act. Legal definition and political agreement together provide the means to unify "justice" and "peace" through humanitarian action. [Javier Perez de Cuéllar] in his final report on the work of the organization, arrived at a similar conclusion: "We need not impale ourselves on the horns of a dilemma between respect for sovereignty and the protection of human rights. The last thing the United Nations needs is a new ideological controversy. What is involved is not the right of intervention but the collective obligation of states to bring relief and redress in human rights emergencies."[21]

The Bush administration devoted much rhetorical attention to developing a strong underpinning of international law for the so-called new world order. It also devoted a significant amount of energy and military might to multilateral diplomacy and the implementation of international decisions. There is now a rare opportunity to harness this rhetoric and place long-standing humanitarian concerns at the center of international decision making. The erosion of sovereignty and the emergence of a human rights regime converge, when it is finally possible to enforce growing recognition of individuals' rights of access to humanitarian aid, irrespective of their governments' permission.

Missing still, however, is what Third World representatives refer to as a lack of moral authority for humanitarian intervention. Recent thinkers have looked beyond sacrosanct sovereignty and the state toward social organization based on culture or society, defined in their widest senses. As these subvert sovereignty, we must better understand the human desire for absolutes, inherent in both individuals and communities. For us to transcend the dictates of sovereignty, we must articulate an ethical vision and so reshape human relations with authority.

While human needs do not as yet override sovereignty in all instances, the latest resolution of the General Assembly nonetheless takes a significant step along the path of establishing more rights for the afflicted. This process is a continuation of the efforts by the ICRC to protect prisoners, the wounded, and innocent civilians from states during wartime. In the past few decades, humanitarian NGOs have taken matters into their own hands and resorted to cross-border operations, and intergovernmental organs have sought inroads in defining the rights of innocent civilians in war zones. But binding international legal instruments have not kept pace.

With the humanitarian intervention in Iraq and the recent debate at the United Nations, the international community appears perched on the brink of a new era. The international community is moving toward codification of principles and identification of the appropriate conditions under which humanitarian imperatives will override domestic jurisdiction.

Notes

1. Theodor Meron, "Common Rights of Mankind in Gentili, Grotius and Suárez," *American Journal of International Law* 85 (1991), pp. 110–16.

2. See Mario Bettati, "The right to Interfere," *The Washington Post*, April 14, 1991; Thomas G. Weiss and Kurt M. Campbell, "Military Humanitarianism," *Survival* 33 (Sept./Oct. 1991), pp. 451-64; Brian Urquhart, "Sovereignty vs. Suffering," *The New York Times,* April 17, 1991.

3. See for instance, Richard B. Lillich, ed., *Humanitarian Intervention and the United Nations* (Charlottesville: University Press of Virginia, 1973); Richard B. Lillich, "Forcible Self-Help by States to Protect Human Rights," *Iowa Law Review* 53 (1967), p. 325; J.P.L. Fonteyne, "The Customary International Law Doctrine of Humanitarian Intervention," *California Western International Law Journal* 4 (1974), p. 203; Chilstrom, "Humanitarian Intervention Under Contemporary International Law," *Yale Studies in World Public Order* 1 (1974), p. 93.

4. Oscar Schachter, "United Nations Law in the Gulf Conflict," *American Journal of International Law* 85 (1991), p. 469.

5. For a general discussion, see Thomas G. Weiss and Meryl A. Kessler, *Third World Security in the Post–Cold War Era* (Boulder: Lynne Rienner, 1991). For specific case studies, see Thomas G. Weiss and James G. Blight, eds., *The Suffering Grass: Superpowers and Regional Conflict in Southern Africa and the Caribbean* (Boulder: Lynne Rienner, 1992).

6. See Thomas M. Franck and Nigel S. Rodley, "After Bangladesh: The Law of Humanitarian Intervention by Military Force," *American Journal of International Law* 67 (1973), p. 275; Ian Brownlie, *International Law and the Use of Force by States* (Oxford: Clarendon Press, 1963), pp. 338–42; Ian Brownlie, "Thoughts on Kind-Hearted Gunmen," in Lillich, *Humanitarian Intervention,* pp. 139–48; Tom J. Farer, "Humanitarian Intervention: The View From Charlottesville," in *ibid.,* pp. 149–64.

7. See for instance, Lillich, "Forcible Self-Help," pp. 325–51; John Norton Moore, "The Control of Foreign Intervention in Internal Conflict," *Virginia Journal of International Law* 9 (1969), pp. 261–64; Myres McDougal and Michael Reisman, "Response by Professors McDougal and Reisman," *International Lawyer* 3 (1969), p. 444; H. Lauterpacht, *International Law and Human Rights* (London: Stevens, 1950), pp. 120–21; L. Oppenheim, *International Law: A Treatise,* ed. H. Lauterpacht, 8th ed. (London: Longmans, 1955), pp. 667–72.

8. F. H. Hinsley, *Sovereignty,* 2nd ed. (Cambridge: Cambridge University Press, 1986). chap. I. This historical discussion is from chap. II. See also, Allott, *Eunomia,* para. 16.15 *et seq.*

9. John H. Herz, quoted in R. P. Anand, "Sovereign Equality of States in International Law," *Receuil des Cours,* 1986–II, pp. 31–32.

10. Antonio Cassese, *International Law in a Divided World* (Oxford: Clarendon Press, 1986), p. 391. On the concept of "the common heritage of mankind" generally, see chap. 14.

11. D.W. Bowett, *The Law of International Institutions* (London: Stevens & Sons, 1975), p. 354. Also, see chap. 12.

12. Philip Allot, *Eunomia: New Order for a New World* (Oxford: Oxford University Press, 1990), para. 11.28.

13. W. Michael Reisman's concept of "popular sovereignty" is no less sovereignty traditionally conceived than state sovereignty. "Sovereignty and Human Rights in Contemporary International law," *American Journal of International Law* 84 (1990), pp. 866–76.

14. Ali A. Mazrui, *Cultural Forces in World Politics* (London: James Currey, 1990), p. 22. Mazrui also distinguishes between peace and justice on religious grounds: by adopting peace over justice, the UN Charter allied itself with the Christian God of love, whose Son was regarded as a Prince of Peace, while the God of Islam and Judaism has been a God of justice.

15. John Tessitore and Susan Woolfson, eds., *Issues Before the 45th General Assembly of the United Nations* (Lexington: UNA–U.S.A./Lexington Books, 1991), p. 119–20.

16. John Finnis, *Natural Law and Natural Rights* (Oxford: Clarendon Press, 1980), p. 403.

17. Allott, *Eunomia,* p. xvii.

18. For a definition of a threshold below which humanitarian intervention might be triggered, see Theodor Meron and Allan Rosas, "A Declaration of Minimum Humanitarian Standards," *American Journal of International Law* 85 (1991), pp. 375–81; Lillich, "Forcible Self-Help," pp. 347–51; Moore, "Control of Foreign Intervention," p. 264.

19. Larry Minear, "A Strengthened Humanitarian System for the Post-Cold War era," testimony before the Select Committee on Hunger of the U.S. House of Representatives at a hearing entitled "The Decade of Disasters" The United Nations' Response," in Larry Minear, Thomas G. Weiss, and Kurt M. Campbell, *Humanitarianism and War: Learning the Lessons from Recent Armed Conflicts,* Occasional Paper #8 (Providence, RI: Thomas J. Watson Jr. Institute for International Studies, 1991), pp. 36–42.

20. Hans Kelsen, *The Law of the United nations: A Critical Analysis of Its Fundamental Problems* (London: Stevens & Sons Ltd., 1950), p. 138. See also discussion of issues that follows, as well as p. 149. *et seq.* on states and individuals as UN "organs."

21. UN Doc. A/46/1, p. 10.

PART 3.3

International Law as
Normative System:
For the Protection
of the Environment

19

The International
Protection of the Environment

Alexandre Kiss

Introduction

E nvironmental protection as such is a relatively recent issue in international law. Although international conventions have been concluded
with the intention to protect determined species—birds,[1] fur seals,[2]
whales,[3] and so on since the beginning of this century, and even though
more general actions have been undertaken to ensure the conservation of
nature in determined areas[4] or to prevent the pollution of specified rivers,[5]
lakes[6] or marine zones[7] since the 1930's, the concept of an endangered
biosphere which should be protected is relatively new. The end of the
1960's can be considered as the beginning of a new consciousness of the
fragility of the thin layer on, above, and under the surface of our planet
where all life is concentrated. This understanding leads to an extension of
the tasks which international law should fulfill. Legal means are necessary
to solve the problem of environmental protection and above a certain
dimension such problems are necessarily international ones. All the components of the natural environment are interrelated: from this point of view
neither air, nor oceans, rivers or wildlife can be divided into segments
according to existing borders, so that the pollution and other sorts of environmental harm are propagated regardless of state sovereignty and its limits. But there are also numerous interactions among the different components of the natural environment: an important part of ocean pollution
comes from the land, carried by rivers or by the air; ocean pollution can
have an impact on climates and on the production of oxygen; wildlife is

Alexandre Kiss, "The International Protection of the Environment" in R. St. J.
Macdonald and Douglas Johnston (eds.), *Structure and Process of International
Law*. The Hague: Martinus Nijhoff, 1983, pp. 1069–1094. © Martinus Nijhoff Publishers. Reprinted with kind permission from Kluwer Law International and the author.

391

endangered by the pollution of the soil, of waters, and so on. Thus the influence of a given nuisance can affect indirectly many other components of the global environment. The conclusion may be drawn that the protection of the earth's environment must be not only international but also global.[8]

Economic considerations also demand international cooperation in the efforts to safeguard the environment. The cost of anti-pollution measures taken in one country can lead to distortions in the conditions of international trade, so that there is a need for the harmonization of national legislation in this field.

It may be considered that environmental law exists as such since the second half of the 1960's and that, in particular, international environmental law appeared about 1968 with the first proclamation of general principles concerning water conservation[9] and air pollution control[10] and with the decision of the UN General Assembly to organize a world-wide conference on the protection of human environment. The result of this decision was the Stockholm Conference convened in June 1972, which can be regarded as a milestone in the short but rather rich history of international environmental law.

As a matter of fact, this history is rich in developments of various kinds. With the Stockholm Conference an impulse has been given to the development of world-wide legal rules and principles: efforts have been made to draft conventions with a universal scope, for ocean pollution control,[11] for the protection of wildlife[12] and on several other topics.[13] Unfortunately, the efforts failed on several points, so that one may wonder if the new trend which characterizes the last years, and which tends to the development of international environmental law in regional frames is not the most realistic one. Anyway, there seems to be a general understanding that this law should be further developed simultaneously at a universal, at regional and at national levels. The tools for such development should be not only international treaties, whether general or regional, but also principles, guidelines and other non-binding texts which could be transformed at a later stage of the evolution into binding ones, at the level where this is the most appropriate.[14]

Another transformation of the young international environmental law can be more forecasted by the present, mostly new, problems and trends, than observed on the basis of generalized facts. Like national environmental legislation, international environmental law started with a sectorial approach according to the main components of the environment: the principal legal instruments concerned fresh water pollution control, the protection of the sea against pollution, that of wildlife, and so on. Certain international instruments reflected a more global approach, since they had to combat effects which could affect any area, like radiations,[15] but they were rather exceptional. Now we understand better the interrelations between the components of the environment: soil, watercourses, seas, atmosphere, wildlife, so that the necessity of a more global approach is more and more recognized. On the other hand, we now know better that radioactive substances[16] and chemicals[17] can produce harmful impacts on any of the environmental components—or on several of them at the same time, so that a more global approach is more and more frequently necessary. This globalization of environmental law cannot be separated from another evolution, which is even more characteristic and which is still more important for a theoretical study on international environmental law: the growing integration of the protection of the planet's environment in the more general concept of protecting and managing the natural resources of mankind.

At the same time as the consciousness that the biosphere can be degraded or even destroyed, the understanding appeared that the earth's resources are limited. Several years later the oil crisis was a powerful indicator in this regard and the conception of a world where the balance between a growing population and the limited natural resources threatens to be broken, can less and less be avoided. The various components of natural environment, such as fresh water, clean air, the ocean's living resources, the ozone layer, wild fauna and flora, and so on are parts of the natural resources which should be protected, that is, managed and equitably shared. The consequences of such an understanding on international environmental law and, in particular, on the theory of that law system, cannot be underestimated.

A theoretical approach of such a new and rapidly transforming system as international environmental law is necessarily a difficult one. Since theories should be based on realities, as a matter of fact this approach cannot be a simple, but a complex one, taking into account the different basic concepts which exercised an influence on the formation of this new part of international public law. It should not be forgotten that the respective effects of such concepts may vary during the development: the influence of some of them may become stronger or weaker according to the evolution of facts, international situations, but also of scientific and economic factors, and, last but not least, of our conceptions of the present world.

It seems that the international legal rules which may be considered as constituting the international law of the environment originate from three roots: traditional international law, the concept of shared resources, and the new, emerging conception of common interest of mankind.

Traditional International Law

Traditional international law is still based on the concept of state sovereignty. In this regard the main environmental problem is the deterioration of a state's environment by activities taking place outside the limits of its jurisdiction. This problem is generally known under the term 'transfrontier pollution.'

The Notion of 'Transfrontier Pollution'

However, the concept of transfrontier pollution is not as clear as it might appear at the first glance. The term 'transfrontier' could be considered as implying only limited areas along state borders, that is, the transfrontier pollution could be interpreted as a phenomenon linked with relationships between neighbouring countries. In this case, it would concern only two or three states and probably a zone not broader than 20-30 kilometres on each side of frontiers which separate two countries. As a matter of fact, in the treaty practice, the term 'transfrontier' has been given a very broad interpretation, so as to include any form of pollution which has adverse effects in another country. Such a conception is reflected, in particular, in the International Convention on Long-Range Transboundary Air Pollution, signed on 13 November 1979, in Geneva, by thirty-five states, including all European countries but also Canada and the United States. Long-range transboundary air pollution has been defined in this instrument as meaning: 'air pollution whose physical origin is situated wholly or within the area under the national jurisdiction of one State and which has adverse effects in the area under the jurisdiction of another State at such a distance that it is not generally possible to distinguish the contribution of individual emission sources or groups of sources.'[18]

The term 'pollution' might also be interpreted in different ways. When strictly understood, it does not imply certain other forms of the deterioration of the natural environment which, for instance, disturb biotopes or destroy the conditions of wildlife. On the other hand, 'pollution' could be interpreted as including only situations where an effective damage has already been done and thus excluding damage which might result in the future from a continuing harmful influence—for example, low-rate air pollution or water pollution, the effects of which will be manifest only after a certain period of time—and, which is even more important, excluding risk caused by particularly hazardous activities.

A definition given by a recommendation of the Organization for Economic Cooperation and Development adopted on 14 November 1974 which formulates several principles concerning transfrontier pollution seems to meet this problem since it proposes a broad definition of pollution. According to this text, pollution means 'the introduction by man, directly or indirectly, of substances or energy into the environment resulting in deleterious effects of such a nature as to endanger human health, harm living resources and ecosystems, and impair or interface with amenities and other legitimate uses of the environment.'[19]

Such a broad interpretation seems to be generally accepted by now. The definition of pollution given by the Draft Convention on the Law of the Sea which can be considered as a synthesis of the former definitions, uses the terms: 'the introduction by man, directly or indirectly, of substances or energy into the marine environment, which results or is likely to result in such deleterious effects as to harm to living resources and marine life, hazards to human health, hindrance to marine activities . . . impairment of quality for use of sea water and reduction of amenities.'[20] Thus, long-term effects as well as environmental risk seem to be covered by the term 'pollution' which should be given the same interpretation when it is used in the conception 'transfrontier pollution.' Such an interpretation may be considered as producing important effects on the nature of international responsibility for environmental prejudice.

Applicable Rules

The problem of transfrontier pollution can be met theoretically in three different ways, which will be considered here as three hypothesis. The first of them is that international law does not include any rule forbidding such an interference in the environment of foreign states, the second one consists in assuming that there is no specific rule concerning transfrontier pollution, but a general principle prohibits to cause damage on foreign territory, while the third possibility is that there are specific rules concerning transfrontier pollution.

(1) The admission that there is no rule at all which would prevent a state to cause a damage—and in particular an environmental prejudice—to other states amounts to the recognition of absolute sovereignty of each state over its territory, like the conception reflected by the Harmon doctrine.[21] Still, even if such a theory could be upheld, the opposing interests lead to the need to recognize that a solution must be found to solve the conflict between sovereign rights. Such a solution could result from the theory of the abuse of right, according to which no one should use his right in an arbitrary manner or in such a way that the consequences which may result from it for other states' rights are out of proportion with the benefit of the holder of the right. This would mean concretely that the pollution of an international watercourse by one river state which causes damage to the lower state should not be accepted if such a pollution can easily be avoided or if the benefit which results from this method of waste disposal for the upper state is without common measure with the damage caused to the other one.

The theory of abuse of right has been mentioned several times in connection with transfrontier pollution. One should not forget in this regard the very nature of the theory itself. Whether it is applied as a positive international law norm, or even when it only remains as a background element of legal thinking, the principle that a state should not make abuse of its rights is an evolutive concept. Continuing application of the theory—whether explicit or not—to a determined problem may lead to the emergence of a new specific rule which prohibits the acts amounting to an abuse, such as harmful pollution of the atmosphere or of international watercourses. Such specific rules can be integrated into the general customary law of nations, but they can also be included in treaty provisions between the concerned states. At the end of the evolution one should thus naturally find solutions which are considered here as being the second and the third hypothesis, that is, the existence of a general rule of international law and that of specific rules.

(2) Transfrontier pollution can also be prohibited by international legal rules which protect in general the territory of a state against all damaging intervention from outside. The basic rule has been formulated by the International Court of Justice in the *Corfu Channel* case, stating as a principle of international law of general applicability 'every state's obligation not to allow knowingly its territory to be used contrary to the rights of others.'

It is thus admitted that there is an obligation resulting from the general rules of international law to respect other states' rights, which overrides the territorial sovereignty of the state when a damaging action is taking place. The same principle results from the *Trail Smelter* arbitration, but there it has been formulated in such a way that it can also be understood as amounting to a specific rule prohibiting transfrontier air pollution.[22] Anyway, there seems to be little doubt about the absolute obligation of states to respect the territory of their fellow states, although when acts by private persons are concerned, the implementation of this obligation may raise problems which we will treat under the heading of international responsibility for transfrontier pollution.

(3) Although such a general obligation exists, during the last decade the number of specific rules related to transfrontier pollution has increased with a speed unusual in international law. The general obligation not to cause damage to the environment outside the limits of territorial jurisdiction has been formulated in Principle 21 of the 1972 Stockholm Declaration on the Human Environment as follows: 'states have, in accordance with the Charter of the United Nations and the principles of international law, the sovereign right to exploit their own resources pursuant to their own environmental policies, and the responsibility to ensure that activities within their jurisdiction or control do not cause damage to the environment of other states or of areas beyond the limits of national jurisdiction.'

The Stockholm Declaration is not binding, but this principle has been included in various subsequent international instruments, such as the Charter of Economic Rights and Duties of States and the Program of Action in the Field of the Environment adopted in 1973 and in 1977 by the Council of the European Communities. Article 194(2) of the draft Convention on the Law of the Sea reflects the same principle, but the most representative text in this regard is the preamble of the Convention on Long-Range Transboundary Air Pollution, adopted in Geneva on 13 November 1979. According to it, Principle 21 of the Stockholm Declaration 'expresses the common conviction that states have . . . the responsibility to ensure that activities within their jurisdiction or control do not cause damage to the environment of other states or of areas beyond the limits of national jurisdiction.'

This last formulation, speaking of a 'common conviction' of states, makes one think of one of the constituting elements of international customary law. Indeed, it is necessary that states have the conviction that a norm applied in international practice is a part of positive international law. Although the preamble of the Geneva Convention, which announces this 'common conviction' is not a mandatory text in itself, like preambles in general, this formula can nevertheless be considered as a valuable testimony of the consciousness that the obligation outlined in the Stockholm Declaration exists. The repetition of the same principle in various international texts, even if none of them is legally binding, can be considered as equivalent of a constant practice, the more so since two arbitral awards, given in the *Trail Smelter* case and in the *Lake Lanoux* case[23] had posed formerly the same rule and since no international practice opposed to this principle has been proved so far. Thus, it may be concluded that Principle 21 of the Stockholm Declaration formulates a customary international law rule, which can be considered as being the general foundation for the prohibition of transfrontier pollution.

Further, rules concerning transfrontier pollution in general have also been developed in regional frameworks. The most advanced of them have been drafted by the Nordic Council, an organization of Scandinavian states, and are inserted in the Nordic Environmental Protection Convention, signed in Stockholm on 19 February 1974. This Convention can be considered as a model, since it includes not only the general principles to be applied in case of transfrontier pollution, but since it also establishes special procedures to prevent it or to remedy it. However, the geographic scope of this convention is limited to four countries.

A broader territorial asset can be found in OECD which adopted general principles on transfrontier pollution including the principles of previous information and consultation, of equal right of hearing for the populations concerned, and of non-discrimination in the application of national legislation to polluting activities which may produce harmful effects on the environment of other states.[24] These rules are formally not binding, but they may be considered as the formulation of emerging norms of international environmental law.

International Responsibility

International responsibility for transfrontier pollution has often been studied by scholars. According to traditional international law principles, its theoretical fundament is that a transfrontier pollution results from an illegal act. Thus, international liability should be applied in all the three hypothesis which have been formerly examined: prohibition of the acts which cause such a pollution by the principle forbidding abuse of right, by a general rule protecting the states' territory or by a specific rule forbidding transfrontier pollution.

Even if one admits that a state which would cause by the fault of its proper organs considerable damage to the environment of another state is liable in international law, there remain cases where the application of the rules of international responsibility in this field raises three questions: (1) can international responsibility be invoked when no actual damage has been caused but where only a risk of damage exists?; (2) is a state liable for transfrontier pollution caused by private persons resident on its territory? and; (3) what is the legal nature of international liability for transfrontier pollution?

The answers to these questions can be outlined as follows: (1) International liability for risk means in this field that even without any actual damage to the environment of a foreign country, a state would be liable for activities which could possibly cause such a damage. It does not seem that on the whole general international law recognizes the principle of international liability for risk. Authors who are the most favourable to international liability for risk consider it necessary to qualify the activity which produces a specially high level of risk 'hazardous activities' or even 'ultra-hazardous activities.'[25]

If international law admits that international liability can result from such activities, two further questions should be answered: how to assess the risk and how to evaluate the compensation which might be asked for by the threatened state. As far as the first question is concerned, the notion of environmental risk should first be considered. Both definitions of pollution which have been quoted in the present study include the risk of pollution as being a possible element of the pollution. The OECD principles use the concept of the introduction by man, of substances or energy into the environment resulting in deleterious effects of such a nature as to endanger human health, harm living resources and ecosystems and impair or interfere with amenities and other legitimate uses of the environment. It is clear that if this definition requires concretely some deleterious effects, it does not necessarily imply that damage has already occurred: the nature of such effects may amount in itself to pollution. Moreover, the concept of risk is stressed by the use of the word 'endanger.' The definition given by the Draft Convention on the Law of the Sea goes still further in this way since it takes into account not only acts actually resulting in deleterious effects, but also those which are 'likely to result' in such effects. Moreover, this text speaks of 'hazards to human health' which implies the concept of risk even more than the terms 'endanger human health.'

In these circumstances, the main question is how far such a risk can be assessed for the purpose of establishing international liability. The general uncertainty of environmental damage assessment in cases of pollution in general and transfrontier pollution in particular is rather well known, although all the consequences which result from it do not seem to be often taken into account by the doctrine. The situation is even more complex when only the risk of such a damage is at hand, since then the mere release of pollutants into international watercourses or into the atmosphere could be enough to found international liability if it is of a nature to endanger human health or to harm the environment, without taking into account the fact that in concrete cases the pollutant might not have reached the frontier. The mere existence of a nuclear plant in the proximity of the border could also be considered as allowing a claim for compensation. When applying the Law of the Sea Conference's draft definition the risk could mean that an outburst from an off-shore oil rig in the territorial waters of a country could found in itself the liability of the state, even if the waters of a neighbouring state do not suffer in reality any pollution damage resulting from it. One may wonder whether it is realistic to think that states would accept liability on such premises.

The second question is how, in such circumstances, in the absence of any material damage, compensation should be calculated. The only basis for it could be to take into account the cost of the preventive measures which the state, feeling threatened, has already taken: that is, the construction of anti-nuclear shelters or other devices near a nuclear power plant on the border, the preparation and transport of personnel and of anti-pollution material in coastal zones which could be affected by an oil spill on the sea coming from the waters of another country, and so on. Here again, so far there are no indications that states are ready to accept to pay for such expenses to other states.

Still, the inclusion of the risk of environmental damage into the definition of pollution is frequent in international legal texts. One is tempted to deduce that such texts do not necessarily mean that the principle of liability for environmental risk is recognized as a part of positive international law. Most of those instruments concern international cooperation in order to control transfrontier pollution and aim not at the compensation, but at the prevention of harmful effects of transfrontier pollution by establishing adequate international or national procedures. (For example, respectively information, consultation, mutual assistance between governments and authorization of polluting activities, of dumping, and so on inside states.) None of such instruments link transfrontier pollution with international liability and some explicitly refuse any such linkage.[26] It might thus be concluded that a claim for compensation for a mere environmental risk has little chance to be accepted by the potential polluter.

(2) As far as the state responsibility for acts of private persons is concerned, it is a well-established principle of international law that such responsibility is a function of that state's control over the activities concerned. Thus, if transfrontier pollution caused by activities which are directly developed by state organs or by legal entities depending on the state (that is, where public authority can directly decide) generally found international responsibility, the problem is more complex when private polluters are at stake. Of course, such persons must also respect the international obligations of the territorial state. However, the implementation of international obligations by the state itself, with the aim of imposing them on all residents, deserves closer examination.

As a rule, states must ensure the respect of their international obligations on their territory by taking the most appropriate and the most effective measures. They generally adopt specific legislation to this effect. In the field of pollution control quite often such submits activities harmful to the environment to prior authorization.[27] The granting under certain conditions or the refusal of the authorization to allow the state to fulfil its international obligations in the case of a possible transfrontier pollution. However, the concrete problem may then arise how far pollution produced outside national jurisdiction should be taken into account when delivering such an authorization. If no authorization procedure exists, the state will be obliged to prevent transfrontier pollution by other ways and it has been submitted that if it fails in this obligation, its liability is by definition a strict one.[28]

These circumstances lead to the question how far in reality a state can cope with its international obligations only by using the power with which it is normally invested inside its frontiers, that is, how far the legislative instruments available to a state allow it to control transfrontier pollution originating from its territory. As a matter of fact, a distinction should be made in this regard between different situations according to the legal technique to be used to prevent pollution, it being understood that the choice of such a technique results from the characteristics of the pollution to be controlled.

Legal rules relating to pollution control can be based on the act which causes pollution. It will then establish emission standards for discharges of polluting substances into the atmosphere or into water, or it will adopt quality standards for determined substances like chemicals. In such situations, whatever the consequences of the pollution may be and wherever such consequences may be produced, inside or outside the jurisdiction of the territorial state, such rules are to be applied to any polluting activity on the state's territory. One can even imagine that the prevention of transfrontier effects is an incidental one, the principal aim being to control pollution inside the state frontiers.

The situation looks different when the polluter's country adopts a legislation based on the consequences of polluting activities, for instance when it introduces quality standards for a given segment of the environment, like air, watercourses, lakes, and so on. This means the adoption of rules prescribing that the pollution of a given segment should not be higher than a determined level. One may wonder in such situations how far the consequences of the pollution produced outside the state territory can be taken into account, and, to begin with, how they can be assessed. Here two international law problems, which are as a matter of fact complementary, arise: the extra-territorial effects of national legislation related to pollution control, and the sovereignty of foreign states. The first would limit any effect of national legislation to the territory of the state, the second prohibits any act of national authorities on the territory of any foreign state-even the assessment of damages produced there. The well-known case of the noise caused by the Salzbourg airport in German territory illustrates the difficulties which can result from such principles in transfrontier pollution cases.[29]

As a conclusion, it may be stated that the implementation of the obligation which every state has, not to allow that facts or activities taking place under its jurisdiction cause transfrontier pollution, may raise very concrete legal problems. No wonder that in such circumstances states endeavour to draft specific rules in order to meet legal questions raised by such pollution. Such an attitude was also recommended to the parties to the *Trail Smelter* arbitration by the award and it has been stressed that this recommendation is perhaps the most important contribution of that award to the development of international environmental law.[30] Anyway, this method has been adopted by Austria and the Federal Republic of Germany to settle the dispute resulting from the nuisances which the proximity of the Salzbourg airport has produced in German territory.

(3) As for the nature of international liability for transfrontier pollution, it may be stated that authors often propose strict liability.[31] Precedents taken in other fields, such as responsibility for damage caused by objects launched into the outer space or for nuclear activities, are invoked in favour of such a solution, which is in theory far the best of all, without any doubt.

However, it should not be forgotten that the only field where strict liability has been really adopted in inter-states relations is that of the damage caused by space objects. All the other examples generally referred to concern relations between private persons and tend to ensure that the victim of nuclear accidents[32] or of marine pollution by oil[33] will obtain a minimum of compensation by means of redress supplied by municipal law systems. As a matter of fact, states seem to be rather reluctant not only to accept international law rules establishing strict liability for transfrontier pollution, but even to accept any international law rule by which they could be held responsible for environmental damage. Hence a general trend to shift the problem of compensation for transfrontier pollution to another level, the inter-individual one, where civil law-solutions—strict liability combined with the designation of the responsible and a financial guarantee system—allow the victims of a transfrontier pollution to be compensated for the prejudice really suffered, at least below determined limits.

These difficulties in the implementation of the general rules resulting from the 'transfrontier pollution approach' make it doubtful whether in concrete cases redress for damage caused by such pollution can be ensured with a probability which allows dissuasive, that is, preventive effects. Although general rules and in particular international responsibility may turn out useful in certain cases, the general conclusion is rather that without a specific, detailed international legislation, the international protection of the environment cannot be ensured. Such specific rules should be, of course, founded on the general principles of international law and on the general norms prohibiting transfrontier pollution, but they must tend above all to the establishment of a better cooperation between neighbouring states. Such a cooperation should include mutual information, consultation, the use of the best procedures to ensure that concerned private persons will accede to adequate legal remedies, the equitable application of existing environmental legislation to facts detrimental to the environment of the neighbouring country, and so on.[34] However, these elements lead in reality to another approach, which is based not on state sovereignty, but on the concept of 'shared natural resources.'

It may be added that even understood in a positive way and developed into a coherent system, principles and rules resulting from the 'transfrontier pollution approach' could never solve all the environmental problems: they could never ensure, for instance, the protection of the high seas, of Antarctica, and of the outer space from pollution, nor that of the living resources in general, wherever they may be. Such objectives need different, more general approaches.

The Concept of Shared Resources

The concept of shared natural resources has been mainly developed in Latin America.[35] Its fundament is the common concern which a limited number of states—two or more but not too many—have in a given resource, so that they should share the benefit which might result of its use in an equitable manner. As a matter of fact, such benefit could be diminished or even annihilated for one or more of the concerned countries if another, or several others, use the resource taking into account only its or their exclusive interests. The classical example is an international watercourse where the upper river states pollute the water in such a way that lower river states cannot use it normally.

The concept of shared resources meets resistence on behalf of certain states which do not want to admit that others have a part in their natural resources, like oil or minerals, while, in the meantime, there is a clear evolution in international environmental law toward the acceptance of principles based on this concept. The reason for this opposition is probably that no clear distinction has been made between shared *environmental* resources and other natural resources: a general consensus could probably be reached much easier for the former, including mainly atmosphere, rivers, lakes, underground water, certain marine areas, wild fauna and flora and landscapes.

Limited in its scope to environmental resources, the concept of shared resources appears quite often in positive international law, in particular in treaties concerning watercourses[36] and in some cases river basins[37] prohibiting the pollution of such waters. Various forms of cooperation between concerned states may also be considered as expressions of the shared environmental resource concept. It may be referred to international legal rules providing for standard setting,[38] for the establishment of special commissions, or the use of existing bodies in order to control the pollution of rivers and lakes[39] or, in the field of the protection of wild fauna and flora, to conservation measures taken in determined areas which are the habitat of shared biological resources[40] Quite a number of regional treaties aiming at the protection of determined marine areas are also to be mentioned; they concern the protection of the Baltic,[41] of the Mediterranean Sea,[42] the Persian Gulf,[43] and the West African coasts[44] from pollution.

Thus, a first point can be made: in quite a number of situations the concept of shared environmental resources has inspired states which, as a result, established or intensified cooperation for the conservation of determined environmental resources. In certain cases, such cooperation covers not only the preservation of a certain quality of the environment or of some segments of the environment, but it has also quantitative aspects by fixing the part of the shared resource which each concerned state can appropriate.[45]

A further step in the evolution was the attempt to formulate, on the basis of existing experience in bi- or multilateral frameworks, general principles which should govern not only particular situations but which should be applied at a world-wide level every time that two or more states share a natural environmental resource. This task has been undertaken by a group of experts instituted by the UN Environmental Program. After lengthy discussions, on 8 February 1978 a text including 15 principles has been adopted with a title which shows the difficulties of the undertaking: 'Draft Principles of Conduct in the Field of the Environment for the Guidance of

States in the Conservation and Harmonious Utilization of Natural Resources Shared by Two or More States.'

This text is fundamentally based on the Stockholm Declaration on the Human Environment of 1972 and may be considered as a development of that declaration. It stresses several of the Stockholm principles, such as the need of cooperation, when necessary by the conclusion of bilateral or multilateral agreements, with a view to controlling, preventing, reducing or eliminating adverse environmental effects which may result from the utilization of shared resources, as well as the sovereign right to exploit the resources and the responsibility to ensure that activities within the state's jurisdiction or control do not cause damage to the environment of other states or of areas beyond the limits of national jurisdiction. The main obligation for each state is to avoid to the maximum extent possible and to reduce to the minimum extent possible the adverse environmental effects beyond its jurisdiction of the utilization of a shared natural resource. Here again, not only the damage to the environment, but also the threatening of the conservation of a shared renewable resource and the endangering of the health of the population of another state have to be taken into account.

A number of specific obligations should result from these principles for states sharing a natural resource. They should make environmental assessments before engaging in any activity with respect to a shared natural resource which may create a risk of significantly affecting the environment of another state or states sharing that resource. Concerned states should exchange information and engage in consultations on a regular basis on the environmental aspects of the shared resource. Plans to initiate which can be relevant in this regard should be notified to the concerned state or states, consultations should be held, joint scientific studies and assessments should be organized, and in emergency situations the concerned states should inform each other and cooperate. Further, the Draft Principles proclaim the necessity for states, when considering, under their domestic environmental policy, the permissibility of domestic activities to take into account the potential adverse environmental effects arising out of the utilization of shared natural resources, without discrimination as to whether the effects would occur within their jurisdiction or outside it. It is also stated that states should endeavour to provide persons in other states who have been or may be adversely affected by environmental damage resulting from the utilization of shared natural resources with equivalent access to and treatment in the same administrative and judicial proceedings, and make available to them the same remedies as are available to persons within their own jurisdictions who have been or may be similarly affected.

Unfortunately, this text has two major weaknesses. First, the states participating in its drafting were unable to agree on a definition of the concept of 'shared natural resources,' although the following wording was proposed: 'The term "shared natural resource" means an element of the natural environment used by man which constitutes a biogeophysical unity and is located in the territory of two or more states.' In the second place, although UNEP's Governing Council has approved the Draft principles, the UN General Assembly reserved its approval so far. Nevertheless, the Draft Principles on Shared Natural Resources may be considered as a good formulation of emerging principles of international environmental law, the more so as they are based on elements of positive international law existing in bilateral or multilateral frameworks.

It may be pointed out that these elements often concern transfrontier pollution situations. Thus, the question may be asked, what is the difference between international rules resulting from the two different approaches? The answer seems to be that the concept of transfrontier pollution is, in its original formulation, a negative one, prohibiting the violation of foreign sovereignty. That of the 'shared natural resources' implies more than just peaceful coexistence with respect to the right of others: it means that the concern of other states has to be taken into account and that states sharing a natural resource have a common responsibility for the conservation of that resource, independently of immediate interests. It is normal in these circumstances that in most cases the application of the 'shared resource concept' results in active international cooperation between concerned states, including the adoption of specific rules for the use of the shared resource.

As a matter of fact, in certain aspects the 'transfrontier pollution concept' appears to be overtaken not so much by this second approach in itself, but by the necessity of cooperation which results from the very nature of the international action tending to protect the biosphere. This necessity has been felt from the beginning. One of the earliest and most fundamental texts in this field, the Principles Concerning Transfrontier Pollution adopted as a recommendation by the Council of OECD on 14 November 1974 explains in its preamble that the principles are 'designated to facilitate the development of harmonized environmental policies with a view to solving transfrontier pollution problems.' It is also characteristic that the first of the principles proclaimed is international solidarity the implementation of which is a concerted policy. Other principles adopted in this recommendation are essentially the same, although more detailed, as the Draft Principles on Shared Resources, and can be considered as the forerunners of the latter.

It may thus be concluded that cooperation between concerned states is an inevitable consequence of the 'shared resources' concept. Such cooperation involves in most cases the adoption of specific treaty rules and the institution of international organs in order to determine the attitude which states have to adopt when using the natural resource shared with others.

Of course, the question of international responsibility can arise also in this field. The infringement of mutually agreed binding international rules, whether resulting from treaties or from the practice of international organs constitutes a violation of international law. Thus it generates international responsibility which has to be established in the light of the relevant treaty provisions, like the violation of any other international obligation. However, the enforcement of treaty rules by international responsibility seems to be much easier than that of the general principles applicable to transfrontier pollution analysed earlier, since the answer to most of the major problems is already given by the text of the treaty itself, which states exactly the obligations of the contracting parties.

Although the 'shared resources concept' constitutes a further step in the development of international environmental law, when compared to the 'transfrontier pollution,' one should not forget that its scope is limited. In fact, it concerns only determined environmental resources, such as a watercourse, a lake, sometimes a river basin or a regional sea. Other, larger problems are also to be solved and therefore a broader concept is needed, which still presents, however, some analogies with the 'shared resources approach.'

The Concept of Common Concern of Mankind

A number of treaty rules as well as of non-mandatory principles aiming at the protection of the environment cannot be considered as resulting from either of the concepts formerly envisaged. They do not protect the sovereignty of states and are related only incidently to transfrontier pollution, like, for example, the 1972 London Convention prohibiting the pollution of the sea by dumping of wastes and other matter. On the other hand, although their aim is equally the protection of common interests, their scope is much broader than environmental resources shared by two or several states, like watercourses, or a given marine area; the scale of the protected interests is much larger here, since the whole of mankind is concerned. It may thus be considered that a different concept is at stake which aims at the protection of the common concern of mankind. This concept underlies the 1972 Stockholm Declaration on Human Environment. Its best expression is probably Principle 2 according to which, 'The natural resources of the earth including the air, land, flora and fauna and especially representative samples of natural ecosystems must be safeguarded for the benefit of present and future generations through careful planning or management, as appropriate.'

A number of international texts contain more detailed rules. Even a superficial examination shows that these can be divided from a legal point of view into two categories: international rules which aim at the protection of the environment outside the territorial jurisdiction of any state, and those which tend to protect the environment inside the states' territorial jurisdiction.

(a) The first category of such rules concerns what is often called the 'commons' and what is more and more considered as forming the essential part of the 'common heritage of mankind': high seas and the atmosphere above it,[46] outer space,[47] Antarctica,[48] to which new elements are likely to be added, like climate and the stratospheric ozone layer.[49] The protection of the environment of such areas is mostly to be ensured by international treaties with a universal scope, but regional conventions may also be relevant in this regard like, for example, conventions concerning land-based pollution of the sea, the effects of which are important for the pollution control of the ocean as a whole. Indeed, so far the only international treaties concerning this aspect are regional ones.[50]

(b) A relatively new trend in international law consists in adopting conservation measures for certain elements of the environment which are located inside the limits of state jurisdiction. Such measures result mostly of treaties with a world-wide scope which aim at the conservation of wild life by controlling the international trade in endangered species of wild fauna and flora,[51] by protecting migratory species,[52] or by providing for the conservation of areas which are particularly important as ecosystems or as the habitat of wild species[53] However, regional treaties can have the same object insofar they concern only species living in limited areas.[54] The common characteristic of such treaties is to oblige the contracting states to ensure under their jurisdiction the conservation of determined elements of the environment which are considered as essential not only for themselves, but also for the rest of the world. One may quote here a paragraph of the preamble of the UNESCO Convention for the Protection of the World Cultural and Natural Heritage, of 16 November 1972, which reminds us that 'parts of the cultural or natural heritage are of outstanding interest and therefore need to be preserved as part of the world heritage of mankind as a whole.'

Whether such international rules are to be applied in areas which are not under state jurisdiction, or inside the territorial jurisdiction of states, they are different from the majority of international treaties. Their main characteristic is that they are in a way unilateral as far as the obligations they impose on the contracting parties are concerned: by adopting such treaties, such states accept only obligations. They have to act, to prohibit, to cooperate with others, without any direct counterpart. This is different from what has been considered as being the essential part of the written law of nations, the contractual obligations accepted by states on a basis of reciprocity. Here no immediate advantage results for a single contracting state: their objective when concluding such a treaty is not to acquire new competences or some direct benefit for themselves or for their nations; their motivation is the common concern for the conservation of the natural resources of the earth.

Of course, there is a state interest, but it is a rather remote one which results from the understanding that there is a solidarity of the whole of mankind which has to face certain dangers together. Thus the benefit for contracting states is that their nationals will live in the present and in the future in a less deteriorated biosphere, as a result of a restriction of the freedom to act accepted by all the other states as well as by themselves. The expression and the implementation of such a common concern is more in conformity with traditional international law as far as areas are concerned where no territorial state jurisdiction can be exercised. For such areas, the only means to adopt international rules is the conclusion of treaties by the whole international community representing the common concern of mankind—or which, anyway, should be supposed to do so. The extension of conservation rules to the area under state jurisdiction is, on the contrary, a phenomenon which shows that a new element appeared in the law of nations.

This new motivation and the international rules which express it are particularly characteristic of the effort to conserve the environment, which at a certain level is a task for the whole of mankind. However, the common concern of mankind has appeared before the 'environmental era' with the conclusion of other international conventions—and with the adoption of other international rules of a different nature—having the same characteristics, that is, not providing for any direct counterpart for the states to which they impose obligations. Such international instruments can be found in what can be called the 'humanitarian field' which appeared as early as the seventeenth century with the protection of human beings against religious discrimination, followed later on by the combat against slavery and against prostitution, then by the elaboration of rules tending to the 'humanization' of war. After World War I, labour legislation appeared and at the end such obligations were generalized with the adoption of world-wide rules as well as regional ones concerning the protection of fundamental human rights and freedoms. Here also no immediate benefit results for the contracting states in counterpart of the burden which is imposed to them: the only motivation which can explain the acceptance of such rules is the conscience of what can be called the common concern of mankind.

These considerations might lead to a much-discussed distinction between 'traités-contrats' and 'traités-lois' and even, presumably, they can be identified with this category of conventions. Some authors deny that such a distinction presents any relevance for international law. An in-depth discussion of the theoretical interest of the question is outside the scope of the present study. However, it seems to be possible to submit that all the international rules tending to the protection of the environment are not merely motivated by the need to protect the environment of states in the respect of their sovereign rights or even by the understanding that shared resources should be used in an equitable manner. The recognition that there is a different source of inspiration, the common concern of mankind, for a part of the norms which compose international environmental law, and even for a growing part of it, tends to the globalization of some of the aspects of this matter. At the present stage of evolution, one of the tasks seems to be to develop world-wide rules on the basis of existing experience gained in regional frameworks, it being understood that at the following stage new regional rules should be based on universal ones which have been established in this manner. Such a globalization is in conformity with the very nature of the environment which cannot be cut into portions, whether small or great, even if geographical differences have to be taken into consideration. Such an evolution also corresponds to the pattern which has been followed in the 'humanitarian field' where the globalization of norms has been recognized as a necessity, even when the implementation sometimes is easier in regional frameworks.

One could also ask the question whether the 'common concern of mankind' approach does not imply that specific legal implementation techniques are used. This seems to be the case, in particular, of the 'reporting system,' which means that the contracting states address to an international organ designated to this effect periodical reports on the way in which they have implemented the obligations resulting for them from a treaty, and that such reports are discussed in that organ.[55] Even if the latter adopts conclusions concerning such reports, no other sanction than a purely moral one is at hand: a condemnation shows that the state did not respect its treaty obligations and usually no other consequence results from the procedure. Such a moral sanction can be justified only when a higher interest is at stake and when the mere establishment of the facts implies that a state did not fulfill a duty which is considered as a fundamental one by the international community.

These considerations imply that the actual role of traditional rules concerning international responsibility is rather restricted in the enforcement of international norms protecting the environment when such norms result from the concept of 'common concern of mankind.' Liability exists, of course, at least in principle, and can be used for any breach of clearly defined treaty obligations, but one should not forget that often treaties concerning the conservation of the environment provide more for cooperation, for the establishment and implementation of programs of action, for the exchange of information and so on, than for rules which are enforceable in the traditional sense of the word. This also explains why specific legal techniques are often used for their implementation.

Conclusion

It has been stressed that the consciousness of environmental problems is quite recent. The understanding that our planet is in danger has raised problems which have to be solved at different levels, the international one probably being the most important. Such problems constitute a real challenge to international law. It is normal that the first reaction of doctrine was to try to find out how existing, well-assessed approaches could be used in this new field. The application and the development of fundamental rules, like state sovereignty, lead to the 'transfrontier pollution concept.' A more recent source of inspiration, the existence of local and regional solidarities, which is in reality an extra-legal fact, was an incitement to understand that shared natural resources should be used on an equitable footing, at least as far as environmental aspects of such use are concerned. This permitted the emergence of new international principles, such as the obligation of states sharing a natural resource to inform each other of relevant facts, situations and projects, to consult each other, to cooperate in the control of facts which could deteriorate the environment, and to treat the residents of other concerned states on an equal footing with respect to foreseeable or established environmental risk or damage. However, the world-wide level could not be avoided for solving environmental problems, the more so as consciousness of the global character of some of the main environmental problems is growing. Hence the role of a concept, that of the common concern of mankind, which already had been used in some other fields, and which seems to correspond to the character of an increasing part of the problems, became relevant. This evolution does not mean that one or another of the three approaches is likely to disappear or should disappear. Rather, it seems to mean that their respective importance has to be clearly understood when international protection of the environment is at stake and that further evolution may lead to changes in this equilibrium.

Notes

1. As early as in 1902 a Treaty for the Protection of Birds Useful to Agriculture has been signed in Paris, on 19 March. (Internationales Umweltrecht, Multilaterale Verträge, W.E. Burhenne & E. Schmidt-Verlag (eds.), Berlin, no. 902:22/1).

2. USA-UK, Washington, 7 February 1911 (De Martens-Triepel, 3rd Ser. vol. v, 717); Great Britain, Japan, Russia, USA, 7 July 1911, (Op. cit., 720). Internationales Umweltrecht, see note 1, no. 957:11, etc.

3. Convention for the Regulation of Whaling, Geneva, 24 September 1931 (Int. Umweltrecht, see note 1, no. 931:71).

4. See, e.g., the Convention Relative to the Preservation of Fauna and Flora in their Natural State, London, 8 November 1933, applied principally in Africa and India (op. cit., no. 933:83), and the Convention on Nature Protection and Wild Life Preservation in the Western Hemisphere, Washington, 12 October 1940 (op. cit., no. 940:76).

5. USA-Canada, Washington, 11 January 1909, *AJIL* (1910), suppl., 239; Belgium-UK (Concerning Tanganyka and Ruanda-Urundi), London, 22 November

1934 (De Martens-Triepel, 3rd Ser. vol. XXXVI, 83); Poland-USR, Moscow, 8 July 1949, UNTS, vol. 37, 25, etc.

6. Agreement on the Protection of Lake Constance against Pollution, Steckborn, 27 October 1960 (Int. Umweltrecht, no. 960:80); Convention Concerning the Protection of Lake Leman Against Pollution, Paris, 16 November 1962, (Revue générale de droit international public, 1963, 630), etc.

7. International Convention for the Prevention of the Pollution of the Sea by Oil, London, 12 May 1954 (Int. Umweltrecht, no. 954:36).

8. A. Kiss, 'Survey of Current Developments in International Environmental Law,' IUCN (Morges, 1976), 12.

9. Water Charter, proclaimed by the Council of Europe on 6 May 1968.

10. Declaration of Principles on Air Pollution Control, adopted by the Committee of Ministers of the Council of Europe on 8 March 1968.

11. Convention on the Prevention of Marine Pollution by Dumping of Wastes and Other Matter, adopted in London on 29 December 1972; International Convention for the Prevention of Pollution from Ships, London, 15 January 1974. (UNEP, Selected Multilateral Treaties in the Field of the Environment, A. Kiss (ed.), Nairobi, (1981), respectively 283 & 311).

12. Convention on International Trade in Endangered Species of Wild Fauna and Flora, Washington, 3 March 1973, Selected Multilateral Treaties, 289; Convention on the Conservation of Migratory Species of Wild Animals, Bonn, 23 June 1979 (op. cit., 479).

13. UNEP, Draft Principles of Conduct in the Field of the Environment for the Guidance of States in the Conservation and Harmonious Utilization of Natural Shared by Two or More States, approved by the UNEP Governing Council on 19 May 1978 by decision 6/14 (UNEP/IG.12/2) and Aspects Concerning the Environment Related to Offshore Drilling and Mining within the Limits of National Jurisdiction, adopted by the UNEP Working Group of Experts on Environmental Law in February 1981 (UNEP/GC.9/5/Add.5, an. III, published in Environmental Policy and Law (1981), 50).

14. This is one of the major conclusions of the Ad Hoc Meeting of Senior Government Officials Expert in Environmental Law, held in Montevideo from 28 October to 6 November 1981.

15. Treaty Banning Nuclear Weapon Tests in the Atmosphere, in Outer Space and Under Water, Moscow, 5 August 1963 (Selected Multilateral Treaties, 185).

16. See the Regulations of the International Atomic Energy Agency, inter alia on the transport of radioactive materials, IAEA, Bulletin, vol. 21, no. 6 (December 1979), 2 ff.

17. See Eckard Rehbinder, 'Control of Environmental Chemicals,' in; IUCN, Trends in Environmental Policy and Law (Gland, 1980), 212–213.

18. Art. 2(b), Selected Multilateral Treaties, 493.

19. OECD and the Environment (Paris, 1979), 108.

20. Art. 1(4), A/CONF.62/WP.10/Rev.3.

21. See on this 'doctrine' J. Ballenegger, La pollution en droit international (Droz, Genève, 1975), 56–57; Julio A. Barberis, Los recursos naturales compartidos entre Estados y el derecho internacional (Madrid, 1979), 16–18.

22. See a summary of this case in A. Kiss, 'Survey,' 43–46 (note 8).

23. Arbitration between France and Spain, Award of 19 November 1956, UN Reports on Arbitral Awards, vol. XII, 285, at p. 303.

24. Recommendation adopted on 14 November 1974, C(74)224.

25. W. Jenks, 'Liability for Ultra-Hazardous Activities in International Law,' Recueil des cours de l'Académie de droit international, vol. 117 (1966 :); A

Randelzhofer & B. Simma, 'Das Kernkraftwerk an der Grenze,' in" *Festschrift für* Friedrich Berber, Müchen (1973), 389–432.

26. See, e.g., the Convention on Long-Range Trans-boundary Air Pollution, Geneva, 13 November 1979, to which a footnote has been added in a rather unaccustomed way, in order to make it clear that 'this Convention does not contain a rule on State liability as to damage.'

27. A comparative study on national legislation in the member states of the European Economic Community shows that such rules are quite frequent (ENV/223/74,rev. 2). Cf. Handl, 558. One should also be reminded that UNEP's experts on environmental law have recommended a licencing system for offshore mining and drilling (UNEP/GC.9/5/Add.5, an. III).

28. G. Handl, "State Liability for Accidental Transational Environmental Damage by Private Persons," *AJIL* (1980) 564–565.

29. In this case the Austrian authorities refused access to non-residents in Austria to preliminary public procedures concerning the extension of the Salzbourg airport near the German frontier. The complaint of residents in Freilassing, the neighbouring city on the German side of the border, both Germans and Austrians, has been rejected by the Administrative Tribunal on 30 May 1969 which held that Austrian legislation could not be applied in these circumstances outside Austrian jurisdiction. The problem had been settled during the judicial procedure by a bilateral treaty signed on 19 December 1967, which, however, entered into force only on 17 May 1974. Compensation is provided for in favour of the victims of the nuisance caused in German territory by the airport. See I. Seidl-Hohenveldern, 'A propos des nuisances jues aux aéroports limitrophes, le cas de Salzbourg et le traité austro-allemand du 19 décembre 1967,' Annuaire français de droit international (1973), 890–894.

30. L.F.E. Goldie, 'A General View of International Environmental Law,' The Hague Academy of International Law, Colloquium (1973), 71.

31. Goldie, 73–73; Handl, 564; Dupuy, 158 ff and International Liability for Transfrontier Pollution, IUCN, Trends in Environmental Policy and law (Gland, 1980), 377.

32. Convention on Third Party Liability in the Field of Nuclear Energy, Paris, 29 July 1960; Convention on Civil Liability for Nuclear Damage, Vienna, 21 May 1963.

33. International Convention on Civil Liability for Oil Pollution Damage, Brussels, 29 November 1969.

34. See the Principles Concerning Transfrontier Pollution, adopted by OECD as a Recommendation on 14 November 1974/C(74)224/ which embodies all these principles.

35. See principally: Julio A. Barberis, *Los recursos naturales compartidos entre estados y el derecho international* (Madrid, 1979).

36. Such obligations result quite often from treaties related to boundary waters. See an enumeration of 15 such treaties in A. Kiss, 'Survey,' 73–74 (see note 8), and of about 10 other treaties concerning specific watercourses (ibid., 74).

37. See, e.g., the Agreement Concerning the Niger River Commission and the Navigation and Transport on the River Niger, Niamey, 25 November 1964, (Selected Multilateral Treaties, 186). Cf. J.A. Barberis, 23–26.

38. See, e.g., art. 17 of the Agreement between Poland and the German Democratic Republic Concerning Navigation in Frontier Waters and the Use and Maintenance of Frontier Waters, Berlin, 6 February 1952, art. 17, UNTS, vol. 304, 168; art. 27 and ans. I and II of the Treaty between Belgium and the Netherlands Concerning the Improvement of the Terneuzen and Ghent Canal, Brussels, 20 June

1960, UNTS, vol. 432, 19; arts. 2–4 and ans. I & II of the Agreement between Canada and the USA on Great River Lakes Water Quality, Ottawa, 15 April 1972, International Legal Materials (1972), 694; Convention for the Protection of the Rhine against Chemical Pollution, Bonn, 3 December 1976, Selected Multilateral Treaties.

39. A Kiss, 'Survey,' 75–76 enumerates 21 treaties including provisions which establish special commissions or give competence to existing bodies in such matters (see note 8).

40. See, e.g., art. 4 of the Statute Relating to the Development of the Chad Basin, 22 May 1964, signed in Fort Lamy (Journal official de la République Fédérale du Cameroun, 15 September 1964); the Convention on Fishing and Conservation of the Living Resources in the Baltic Sea and the Belts, Gdansk, 13 September 1973 (Selected Multilateral Treaties, 308), etc. Treaties concerning the régime of frontiers concluded by the USSR with its neighbours often contain provisions concerning wildlife. Examples are given in A. Kiss, 'Survey,' 90 (see note 8).

41. Convention on the Protection of the Baltic Sea Area, Helsinki, 22 March 1974 (Selected Multilateral Treaties).

42. Convention and Protocols for the Protection of the Marine Environment against Pollution in the Mediterranean, Barcelona, 16 February 1976 and Athens, 17 may 1980 (resp. Selected Multilateral Treaties, 422 and Internationales Umweltrecht no. 980:37 see note 1).

43. Kuwait Regional Convention for Cooperation on the Protection of the Marine Environment from Pollution, 23 April 1978 (Selected Multilateral Treaties, 160).

44. Convention for Cooperation in the Protection and Development of the Marine and Coastal Environment of the West and Central African Region, Abidjan, 23 March 1981 (UNEP/IG.22/7).

45. See, e.g., the agreement between Canada and Norway on Sealing the Conservation of the Seal Stock in the North-West Atlantic, Ottawa, 15 July 1971, FAD, Fisheries Circular, no. 326, FIRD/C 326, 62, or par. 1 of the Annex to the Convention for the Conservation of Antarctic Seals, London, 11 February 1972, International Legal Materials (1972), 251.

46. See the London Convention on the Prevention of Marine Pollution by Dumping of Wastes and Other Matter, 29 December 1972 (Selected Multilateral Treaties, 283) as well as the International Convention for Prevention of Pollution from Ships, London, 2 November 1973 (Selected Multilateral Treaties, 311), and arts. 192–237 of the Draft Convention on the Law of the Sea (A/CONF. 62/WP.10/Rev. 3 and Corr. 1-3).

47. Art. 9 of the Treaty on Principles Governing the Activities of States in the Exploration and Use of Outer Space, London, Moscow and Washington, 27 January 1967, (UNTS, vol. 610, 205); art. 7 of the Agreement Governing the Activities of States on the Moon and Other Celestial Bodies, 18 December 1979, (International Legal Materials, 1979, 1434).

48. Art. 9 of the Antarctic Treaty, Washington, 1 December 1959, UNTS, vol. 402, 71.

49. An Ad Hoc Meeting of Senior Government Officials Expert in Environmental Law, held in Montevideo from 28 October to 6 November 1981 has designated the protection of the ozone layer as one of the major subject areas to be considered for the elaboration of international rules. A Draft Convention is to be submitted in January 1982 to an intergovernmental meeting.

50. Art. 6 of the Convention on the Protection of the Marine Environment of the Baltic Sea Area, Helsinki, 22 March 1974 and an. II to the Convention (Selected

Multilateral Treaties, 380, 384); Convention for the Prevention of Marine Pollution from Land-Based Sources, Paris, 4 June 1974 (op. cit., 404); art. 8 of the Convention for the Protection of the Mediterranean Sea against Pollution, Barcelona, 8 February 1976, (e.g., 423) and Protocol for the Protection of the Mediterranean Sea Against Pollution from Land-Based Sources, Athens, 17 May 1980 (Internationales Umweltrecht, 980:37 see note 1); art. 6 of the Kuwait Regional Convention for Cooperation on the Protection of the Marine Environment from Pollution, 23 April 1978 (Selected Multilateral Treaties, 461); art. 7 of the Convention for Cooperation in the Protection and Development of the Marine and Coastal Environment of the West and Central African Region, Abidjan, 23 March 1981 (UNEP/IG./22/7, 25-26). However art. 207 of the Draft Convention on the Law of the Sea (note 14) provides for the protection of the marine environment against land-based pollution.

51. Convention on International Trade in Endangered Species of Wild Fauna and Flora, Washington, 3 March 1973 (Selected Multilateral Treaties, 289).

52. Convention on the Conservation of Migratory Species of Wild Animals, Bonn, 23 June 1979 (op. cit., 289).

53. Convention on Wetlands of International Importance, especially as Waterfowl Habitats, Ramsar, 2 February 1971, (op cit., 246) and UNESCO Convention Concerning the Protection of World Cultural and Natural Heritage, Paris 23 November 1971 (op. cit., 274).

54. See, e.g., the African Convention on the Conservation of Nature and Natural Resources, Algiers, 15 September 1968, (op. cit., 107) and the Convention on the Conservation of European Wildlife and Natural Habitats, Bern, 19 September 1979 (op. cit., 492).

55. A. Kiss, 'Mechanisms of Supervision of International Environmental Rules, in: *Essays on the Development of the International Legal Order* (Sijthoff & Noordhoff, 1980), 109. See also, in particular, art. 12(2) of the 1973 Washington Convention on International Trade in Endangered Species (note 76) and art. 11 of the 1973 London Convention for the Prevention of Pollution from Ships (note 46).

20

Responsibility for Biological Diversity Conservation Under International Law

Catherine Tinker

Introduction

The international law on biological diversity has developed along with scientific understanding and now embodies an ecosystem approach to the conservation of the variety of life. The ecosystem concept and a basic sense of state responsibility not to harm the environment was formulated in 1972 in the Stockholm Declaration and later, in the World Charter for Nature. Since Principle 21 of the Stockholm Declaration, the concept has crystallized in customary international law, but it did not appear in binding treaty law until the United Nations Convention on Biological Diversity (the Convention or Treaty) entered into force in 1993. Earlier wildlife protection treaties contained some aspects of the approach that was later adopted in the Biodiversity Convention. For example, the Ramsar Convention adopted a habitat and sustainable use approach to the conservation of wetlands; the World Heritage Convention has been a factor in some national development plans that were altered to avoid damage to listed sites,

The nature of state responsibility under Principle 21, which is not to harm the territory of other states or the territory beyond national jurisdiction, is still evolving. One way of implementing the goals contained in Article 3 of the Biodiversity Convention is to apply the precautionary principle, which requires restraint of any human activity that may adversely affect biodiversity. The precautionary principle in international environmental law is one response to the popular recognition that preventive action in the face of scientific uncertainty about future harm is necessary. The precautionary principle lowers the burden of proof required for blocking proposed or existing activities that may have serious long-term harmful consequences. There is no agreement on the content of the precautionary

Reprinted with permission of *Vanderbilt Journal of Transnational Law.*

principle nor is there consensus on whether a principle, rather than an approach, has actually emerged. "Nevertheless, countries have begun to develop precise and useful formulations of the principle in specific contexts."[1]

There is tremendous scientific uncertainty about the loss of biodiversity caused by various human activities, both lawful and unlawful. The numbers and types of life forms that exist as genes, species, sub-species, microorganisms, and bacteria in various ecosystems and habitats are a vast unknown. In the face of this, the precautionary principle requires an even greater degree of restraint in human activity to conserve and sustainably use biodiversity. Perhaps, for now, the precautionary principle should mandate a policy of "no action." Such an interpretation would be consistent with those who have called for a clarification of the notion of responsibility and prevention in environmental concerns. As one author has asserted, "[i]t is no longer sufficient to talk of state responsibility for environmental damage. The context must change to reflect state responsibility for the preservation of global environmental well-being."[2]

Traditional international lawmaking or standard-setting is an inherently slow process. This is particularly true in international environmental law where there is very little consensus surrounding existing norms. Soft law, customary law, and treaties are needed to set standards and define legally-binding duties and obligations based on the precautionary approach. Existing environmental treaties need to be enforced and additional states urged to ratify them. To ensure the highest degree of compliance, the principle of precautionary action to avoid environmental harm must be recognized in international law as a means of fulfilling states' obligations to conserve, sustainably use, and equitably share biodiversity.

The United Nations Convention on Biological Diversity codifies a line of soft law and international custom to create hard law in the treaty. The obligations accepted by states party to the Convention are threefold: conservation of biodiversity; sustainable use of biological diversity; and equitable sharing of biodiversity benefits. States party to the Convention are mandated to establish national legislation and plans. In order to fully comply with the treaty, these internal laws and development plans must take into account the responsibility accepted under the Principle 21 language and the jurisdictional scope article, Article 4. Arguably, to fully comply with the letter and spirit of the Convention, states must apply the precautionary principle in their decision-making processes and whenever they take action under national legislation and development plans.

Full application of the principle of precautionary action may require states to forego the short-term financial opportunities available from resource depletion and loss of biodiversity in order to secure long-term human benefits for the planet and future generations. For those developing countries in which poverty, disease, and starvation make it almost impossible to forego short-term but destructive gains, the Convention offers means of financing biodiversity conservation projects and the transfer of appropriate technology. In the meantime, the Convention requires states to monitor, study, and catalogue the rich storehouse of genetic variety contained in their rainforests, coral reefs, wetlands, deserts, and coastal zones. When greater scientific certainty about the effect of human activity on ecosystems and habitats is achieved, planners, lawyers, and diplomats may be better able to balance conservation and sustainable use of biological diversity. In the meantime, the lack of full scientific certainty should not be used as a reason for postponing measures to avoid or minimize a threat of significant reduction or loss of biological diversity.

International attention should be drawn to formulating global responsibility for biodiversity conservation and sustainable use. The Convention on Biological Diversity echoes Principle 22 of the Stockholm Declaration with a weak reference to the need to study state liability. It may be fruitful for such a study to follow the guidance of two other Stockholm Declaration principles. Principle 4 states that "[humanity] has a special responsibility to safeguard and wisely manage the heritage of wildlife and its habitat, which are now gravely imperiled by a combination of adverse factors. Nature conservation, including wildlife, must therefore receive importance in planning for economic development." Principle 5 states that "[t]he non-renewable resources of the earth must be employed in such a way as to guard against the danger of their future exhaustion and to ensure that benefits from such employment are shared by all [humanity]." The arguments for global conservation of biological diversity are weighted in favor of intangibles: aesthetics or preservation of open space or potential value for generations not yet born, based on equity or fairness.

This article analyzes the legal issues that attend fulfillment of the ambitious objectives of the Convention on Biological Diversity. This article also notes areas of ambiguity in the Convention, which remain to be clarified, and emphasizes responsibility for loss of biodiversity and prevention of that loss. Part II explores the failure of the traditional international law of state responsibility and liability to adequately protect the environment. Part II also reviews the U.N. International Law Commission's work on draft articles that incorporate a preventive or precautionary approach, specifically the draft articles on state responsibility and liability for environmental harm from lawful activities. This article suggests that a more appropriate legal approach is the application of the precautionary principle, which seeks to prevent harm rather than determine liability and damages after harm has occurred.

Part III argues that as greater scientific knowledge is achieved, the precautionary principle should be applied to all proposed human actions that may cause a loss of biodiversity, alter ecosystem and habitats, or affect genetic material. The article concludes that the principle of precautionary action may be seen as the means of enforcing the Biodiversity Convention and used as a procedural test to decide whether a proposed use of biodiversity is sustainable. Ultimately, the real test of the Convention on Biological Diversity will be the extent to which its provisions safeguard the planet's rich biological diversity, and the extent to which humans can undertake development projects without irrevocably destroying their global genetic heritage.

State Responsibility and Liability

Under traditional concepts of international law, the doctrine of state responsibility developed to address the relationship between a given state and citizens of other countries. The concept of state responsibility presupposes a clear legal duty or international plane or an obligation arising under treaty or the customary law. The state-alien example implicates the international principle of nondiscrimination against aliens and treaty obligations involving the treatment of diplomatic persons or the right of innocent passage. In the early 1970s, the concept of state responsibility was broadened to include any internationally wrongful acts.

The problem for international law is to interpret the concept of state responsibility in the environmental context. The U.S. understanding of international law is codified in the *Restatement (Third) of the Foreign Relations Law of the United States*, which states that a nation is obligated to take necessary measures to ensure that activities within the jurisdiction or control of that state conform to "generally accepted" international rules or standards. Even in the absence of an injury, a state is responsible to all other states for any violation of this obligation and for any resultant significant injury to "the environment of another state or to its property, or to persons or property within that state's territory or under its jurisdiction or control." The application of the broad language of Section 601, however, is limited by the state's obligation to take only "such measures as may be necessary, to the extent practicable under the circumstances. . . ."

"Generally accepted" international obligations and rules of conduct related to international environmental law now require, inter alia, the conservation and sustainable use of biological diversity and nonrenewable natural resources. At the same time, pressures for resource development and short-term economic gain encourage a broad range of public and private activities that adversely affect the environment, either now or in the future. In the area of generally accepted international obligations, state responsibility is triggered by the *de minimis* duty to observe the principle of *sic utere tuo ut alienum non laedas*[3] Thus, states have a general duty to prevent uses of their territory that cause significant harm to other states. A state causing transboundary pollution is obligated to take reasonable measures to protect neighboring states from harm and to compensate them for damage. In addition, there may be obligations *erga omnes;*[4] the *Restatement* contemplated these obligations as they apply to areas beyond national jurisdiction and they are described by the International Court of Justice in the *Barcelona Traction* case.

The International Law Commission's Approach: State Responsibility for Internationally Wrongful Acts

The United Nations International Law Commission (I.L.C.) differentiates internationally wrongful acts from activities not contrary to international law. The first give rise to state responsibility. The second give rise to liability for injurious consequences. It is well established in international law that breach of a rule of international law entails state responsibility for an internationally wrongful act. The I.L.C.'s 1980 Draft on State Responsibility specified: "There is an internationally wrongful act of a State when conduct consisting of an action or omission is attributable to the State under international law; and that conduct constitutes a breach of an international obligation of the State."

The I.L.C. approach to state responsibility is to differentiate between "primary rules" and "secondary rules" of conduct that specify the action or refusal to act, which triggers state responsibility. Primary rules are obligations; secondary rules determine the legal consequences of failure to abide by primary rules. Secondary rules "specifically [deal] with the issues of responsibility and liability, although these issues cannot always actually be separated from the operation of the primary rules."[5] Allott has taken issue with the possibly meaningless distinction between primary and secondary rules and with the amount of time that has been invested over the past four decades in belaboring the point. Allott charges that the resultant delay in the formulation of the I.L.C. draft on state responsibility, "is doing serious long-term damage to international law and international society."[6] Even more seriously, Allott charges that the I.L.C.'s process and states' substantive approach to state responsibility virtually assure that states will not be held accountable for their actions.[7]

Under traditional public international law, three threshold questions are used to determine state responsibility: Was there a duty under international law? Was the duty breached? Can responsibility be attributed to a state for the violation of international law? Acts by nonstate entities, such as a citizen or official for whose acts a state is not responsible, do not give rise to state responsibility. Through the doctrine of attribution, however, a state can be responsible for the acts of its own citizens against another state.

The I.L.C. maintains that state responsibility attaches only to internationally wrongful acts. Although the violation of a clearly-defined treaty obligation or an unequivocally recognized norm of customary law clearly constitutes an internationally wrongful act, the I.L.C. has neither listed nor defined other potentially wrongful acts. Under the I.L.C. rubric, state responsibility is triggered when a state commits an international delict, regardless of whether any injury results. Once a state accepts binding duties, any failure to observe them necessarily amounts to a breach of international obligations. The breach may provoke a variety of responses, ranging from state protests to formal diplomatic expressions of displeasure and censure throughout the world community.

A state may raise a defense to its breach of an international obligation; in I.L.C. parlance, these defenses are known as 'conditions precluding wrongfulness." The defenses include necessity, prior consent, self-defense, and *force majeure*. They may be raised in many situations, including a failure to observe the precautionary principle that causes transboundary pollution or degradation of biological diversity. Because the international obligation at issue is one that requires the state to balance competing interests, almost every state can be expected to raise a defense such as necessity. Here the difficulty of defining and applying the precautionary principle becomes apparent. If the precautionary principle is merely a guideline to actions that may accomplish other goals, then it cannot be a primary rule or an obligation for purposes of state responsibility analysis. The application of the precautionary principle may be seen as a consequence of attempting to fulfill a primary obligation.

Although state responsibility does not arise unless there is a breach of an international obligation, the breaching action or inaction must be attributable to the state. Difficulties of attribution are inherent in the concept of objective responsibility, because a state is always liable for the acts of its officials and organs, even when they act *ultra vires*.[8] Brownlie notes that Grotius viewed the *culpa* as the proper basis of state responsibility.[9] Brownlie, however, moved beyond the confines of fault to a more realistic test when he wrote that one 'need not qualify responsibility of a state for an internationally wrongful act by the negligence (*culpa*) or intention (*dolus*) of the actor."[10] In the I.L.C.'s consideration of objective state responsibility, negligence or fault is not generally important for determining state responsibility or establishing an internationally wrongful act. After several years of inattention to the topic of state responsibility, in 1993 the I.L.C. formally adopted articles on cessation, reparation, restitution in-kind, compensation, satisfaction and assurances, and guarantees of nonrepetition, and included exceptionally detailed commentaries to the articles.

Consideration of whether to include a draft article on "international crimes" was postponed until the I.L.C.'s 1994 session. International crimes include internationally wrongful acts that are considered "essential for the protection of the fundamental interests of the international community" as a whole.[11] In its list of proposed international crimes, draft Article 19(3)(d) includes the serious breach of an international obligation of essential importance for the safeguarding and preservation of the human environment. Thus, according to the proposal, massive pollution of the atmosphere or of the seas would constitute an international crime. The I.L.C. remains divided on this controversial subject. Some members consider the same serious acts to be wrongful acts or to be violations of *erga omnes* obligations. From this perspective, there is no need to use the label "crimes." In contrast, other I.L.C. members consider the same acts to be crimes and believe that "crimes" is an appropriate label.

The International Law Commission's Approach: Liability of States for Injurious Consequences of Acts Not Contrary to International Law

If an exporting state—or a company within its jurisdiction or control—failed to obtain prior informed consent from the importing state and shipped hazardous biotechnology products, such an activity could be considered an internationally wrongful act, and thus trigger state responsibility regardless of whether any harm occurred. On the other hand, the shipment could be considered an activity not contrary to international law, which could only trigger liability for the exporting state if there were injurious consequences. The need to fit the facts of a given situation into these particular categories—whether the distinction is meaningful or not—arises from the decision of the I.L.C. to split the issue into two separate topics: state responsibility for internationally-wrongful acts, consisting of both primary and secondary obligations; and international liability for injurious consequences of activities not contrary to international law.

On a theoretical level, it is not clear that the conceptual basis on which it—liability for injurious consequences of activities not contrary to international law—is distinguished from state responsibility is either sound or necessary. On a more practical level, it is questionable whether it represents a useful basis for codification and development of existing law and practice relating to environmental harm, the field in which the Commission has mainly located the topic. From either perspective, it is liable to seem at best a questionable exercise in reconceptualising an existing body of law or, at worst, a dangerously retrograde step that may seriously weaken international efforts to secure agreement on effective principles of international environmental law.

The I.L.C. draft on liability for the injurious consequences of activities not contrary to international law states that civil liability will attach when four factors are present. There must be: (1) human activity; (2) the activity must be within the territory or control of a state; (3) the activity must be capable of giving rise to harm; and (4) there must be actual harm to persons or things within the territory or control of another state. Unlike the doctrine of state responsibility, which can attach even in the absence of harm, the concept of liability requires actual harm. Most commentators agree that the harm must be "substantial" or "serious," because state liability should not attach to minor incidents. There are several unanswered questions surrounding the draft. These questions include the draft's intended meaning of "control" and whether the draft applies when a state fails to act to remove a natural danger.

The I.L.C.'s current approach to liability is to "focus on prevention of harm from activities that constitute a particular risk." The I.L.C. begins by clarifying that the scope of the article includes lawful activities that "create a risk of causing significant transboundary harm through their physical consequences." The I.L.C. defines risk to include both "a low probability of causing disastrous harm and a high probability of causing other significant harm." The I.L.C. then goes on to address prior authorization, risk assessment, and measures to minimize risks.

States are most likely to be deterred from causing environmental harm if some standard of liability is imposed. Whether the system is grounded in strict liability or negligence is of considerably less importance. If international law adopts a liability system, states will be liable for environment damage caused by both public and private actors, regardless of whether the harm occurs within another state or beyond the boundaries of national jurisdiction. The liability approach best protects the rights of innocent victims of environmental harm because it shifts the burden of proof and makes it possible to collect prompt, adequate, and effective compensation once injury is established. Of course, the most effective way to protect the rights of the innocent is to prevent the harm or destruction from occurring in the first place.

One of the most difficult issues facing the I.L.C. is whether to impose a strict liability system or a fault-based system. For a number of obvious political and financial reasons, states are reluctant to adopt strict liability and therefore lack the will to negotiate an environmental liability protocol.[12] On the other hand, "the very absence of responsibility or liability provisions may be essential to the success of many environmental protection agreements."[13]

The meaning of strict liability and absolute liability in the context of activities affecting the environment is particularly relevant to hazardous or ultrahazardous activities and has created substantial problems for the I.L.C. The most visible ultrahazardous activity is nuclear and there is precedent for finding liability in cases where nuclear operations have caused environmental damage. The treaties pertaining to nuclear accidents have adopted a variety of approaches. Other treaties have addressed the harms caused by such specialized problems as objects that fall to earth from outer space.

The I.L.C. has had considerable difficulty addressing ultrahazardous activities. The I.L.C. created a working group and later adopted the group's recommendations. In essence, the I.L.C. is attempting to create consensus within itself on the basic issues of prevention and remediation.[14] If general consensus does develop, the I.L.C. will be able to move on to consideration of the specific mechanisms that should be used to address ultrahazardous risks.[15]

The Precautionary Principle and the International law of Biological Diversity

Traditional models of international law and state responsibility focus upon ensuring compensation for transboundary damages and do not adequately address the challenges arising in international environmental law. The classic model poses a bilateral conflict between one state as actor and another state as victim, with significant physical harm occurring across national boundaries attributable to the first state. Emerging conflicts over the fundamental assumptions and value choices inherent in the "sustainable development" and "sustainable use" of nonrenewable natural resources located within a given state do not fit the bilateral paradigm. Presently, unless some transboundary damage is implicated, no state may raise a legal objection to the domestic environmental policies of any other state. Within the confines of their own borders, international law permits each state to deplete or injure its natural resources, to destroy its gene pool, species, and habitats, and to otherwise harm its environment. Thus, the traditional model of international environmental law creates a jurisdictional problem.

A second problem is that the long-standing "duty and damages for breach" model is inherently reactive and simply cannot prevent the loss of biological diversity, the despoliation of Antarctica, or the destruction of the ozone layer. Although the reactive model once may have been an appropriate response to transfrontier air or water pollution, today a growing number of environmental problems do not fit the mold of narrowly-defined transfrontier pollution and duties imposed on single states. International relations in the field of environmental protection have developed mostly in multilateral frames.

A new, more preventive model is needed to protect transnational ecosystems and the global commons. Under the new model, proponents of development will bear the burden of proving, before they proceed, that the planned use is sustainable and that no harm will result from proposed development. Only compliance with standards based on the precautionary principle and international cooperation will provide the necessary protection for the planet. Ultimately, achieving conservation and sustainable use of biodiversity and nonrenewable natural resources will require changes in human production and consumption. Certain groups or individuals in society will have to sacrifice short-term gains for long-term benefits and to consider meeting the basic needs of future generations as well as those of the present. International law and state responsibility doctrines must necessarily expand to reflect this new imperative for precautionary approaches to human activity and their regulation.

The Precautionary Principle

The precautionary principle has been defined in two ways. It has been defined as an international application of the German law principle of precautionary action (*vorsorgeprinzip*). It has also been defined as the variety of regulatory approaches adopted by governments to implement the *vorsorgeprinzip* principle; efforts to control emissions at their source by using best available technology are one example of this definition in practice. The precautionary principle can be used as a theory and justification for environmental strict liability; this perspective is rooted in the tort law goal of providing compensation to victims of harm. The precautionary principle also may be understood more broadly as a duty to take precautionary action and to avoid risk. In practice, the precautionary principle informs a substantive duty of care that requires environmental impact assessments or other regulatory investigations prior to permitting given actions.

The phrase "the precautionary principle" has appeared in a number of international instruments. Its meaning varies from "its weakest formulations ... to its strongest [in which] it can be seen as a reversal of the normal burden of proof, as in the Oslo Convention Prior Justification Procedure."[16] Several recent United Nations documents, including the 1992 Rio Declaration, have articulated the precautionary principle: "In order to protect the environment, the precautionary approach shall be widely applied by States according to their capabilities. Where there are threats of serious or irreversible damage, lack of full scientific certainty shall not be used as a reason for postponing cost-effective measures to prevent environmental degradation." In another formulation, the preamble to the U.N. Convention on Biological Diversity also refers to the precautionary principle, but omits phrases such as "according to their capabilities" and "cost-effective" measures, which qualify the language of the Rio Declaration. The Biodiversity Convention declares its intentions by, "[n]oting also that where there is a threat of significant reduction or loss of biological diversity, lack of full scientific certainty should not be used as a reason for postponing measures to avoid or minimize such a threat." In the Biodiversity Treaty, the language of obligation has been softened by using "should" to replace the mandatory "shall" used in the Rio Declaration. Other references to the precautionary principle appear in recent multilateral treaties, conference declarations, and regional agreements, especially in agreements related to oil pollution of the North Sea. It has been noted that the precautionary principle turns away from the "assimilative capacity" approach to environmental pollution, and recognizes the limitation to scientific knowledge on ecosystems.

Each of these formulations of the precautionary principle gives rise to different applications of the international law of state responsibility and liability. At its strongest, the precautionary principle may be interpreted to prohibit virtually all uses of natural resources and all human activities in certain ecosystems. Such a moratorium could continue indefinitely, until sufficient scientific knowledge developed about the effects of proposed activities or uses. At its weakest, the precautionary principle may be merely hortatory language that is intended to guide states as they adopt national legislation and plans. This permissive approach to resource use and human activity creates a balancing of interests that makes it possible for developmental and quality of life considerations to outweigh the need to conserve biodiversity and take other preventive action. Although the international community may strive to achieve an expansive application of the precautionary principle in the future, the permissive interpretation dominates the status quo.

The precautionary principle has appeared as soft law in numerous conference declarations and other statements of what governments think international law should be. In the absence of strong evidence of state practice and *opinio juris,*[17] such as an explicit statement from a high-level government minister that precautionary measures were adopted because they are mandated under international law, it is difficult to conclude that the precautionary principle is currently customary international law. Examples of national legislation that refer to the precautionary principle or that are implicitly based on such a principle are insufficient to demonstrate a binding international legal obligation.

Apart from any sense of legal obligation under international law, there are many subjective variables that may affect a state's choice of precautionary action. Precautionary actions may save money in several situations: when there is a great likelihood that damages will occur; when damages, while unlikely, will be of great magnitude should they occur; and when a large number of people are likely to be injured if the harm is not prevented. The type or degree of damage contemplated and the ease of adopting precautionary measures may also induce precautionary action, particularly if there is public demand or political support for precautionary action. A state may act voluntarily based on a moral or ethical imperative. It may also voluntarily adopt a precautionary course for economic reasons. Sometimes it is more cost-efficient to prevent damage than to wait for damage to occur and pay the resulting costs.

It is never easy to say precisely when a rule crystallizes into customary international law. There is no convenient bright line test or formula to apply; the number of years that have elapsed since the original articulation of the principle and the number of times the principle has been quoted in soft law documents are not dispositive. To find the *opinio juris,* it is always necessary to locate the reasons for state practice. Similarly, if states adopt the language of international instruments that are neither binding nor intended to be binding upon the parties, then the mere fact that states have adopted that language is insufficient to prove that a customary rule of international law exists.

If a state happens to follow such a nonbinding principle, it may not necessarily believe that it was under a legal compulsion to do so and may not accept that it could be liable for breach under international law for failing to follow the law. To structure the definition of customary international law otherwise would be to erase the difference between nonbinding and binding international law, and to eliminate the incentive for states to join the soft law declarations from which international environmental law frequently evolves. For purposes of this article, it is not necessary to definitively state whether the precautionary principle is or is not customary law. Rather, the question is whether the precautionary principle affects the international law of state responsibility and liability when the principle is or becomes law, either through treaty obligations or through the future development of customary international law.

The relationship between state responsibility and the precautionary principle has yet to be fully defined. The first element of state responsibility is the existence of a clear legal duty or obligation that gives rise to the concept of an "internationally wrongful act." The second element is a breach of the legal duty. The next step is evaluation of possible defenses to the breach. Finally, compensation for victims of the breach must be determined.

The first element is the crux of the relationship between the precautionary principle and state responsibility. If the precautionary principle has not yet risen to the level of a legal duty or obligation, then it is difficult or even impossible to move on to the problems of breach, defenses, and compensation. Certainly, it may also be impossible to deter harmful behavior.[18] Because the concept of environmental harm is relatively new m international law, there are few clearly-defined internationally wrongful acts that could trigger state responsibility. As principles of international environmental law become recognized as binding law through customary law and treaty law, more obligations will exist. Breach of those obligations may then lead to state responsibility. At present, a state's failure to follow the precautionary principle is not an internationally wrongful act that can trigger state responsibility. Even when a state is obligated by treaty to observe the precautionary principle, an internationally wrongful act has not necessarily occurred. It is necessary to examine the precise language of the treaty obligation. If the treaty says "should" instead of "shall," the offending state is not bound. Similarly, state obligations are often conditioned by phrases such as "to the extent practicable" and "according to their capabilities." Treaties frequently require adoption of only those preventive measures that are "cost-effective." Another problem in the relationship between the precautionary principle and the law of state responsibility is that some treaties referring to the precautionary principle are quite new and have not entered into force. In such situations, it is impossible to gauge the extent of compliance to be expected from states parties, or to imagine extending the obligation to states not party to the treaty. If the treaty is regional, it is difficult to draw out a clear rule of international law with "global applicability." Furthermore, the problem remains: how to determine what action must be taken to fulfill the obligation.

One starting point is to consider the relationship between the ' precautionary principle and Principle 21 of the Stockholm Declaration. It may be possible to achieve compliance with Principle 21 through observation of the precautionary principle. Principle 21 of the Stockholm Declaration is an example of an international environmental text containing the principle of state responsibility. It states that all nations have a responsibility to ensure that activities under their jurisdiction or control do not cause damage to the environment of other states or to areas beyond national jurisdiction. Principle 21 should be read in conjunction with Principle 22, which calls for the development of international law "regarding liability and compensation for the victims of pollution and other environmental damage. . .."

The Stockholm Declaration can also be read as a policy shift. Some developed nations addressed newly-recognized global environmental problems and, at the same time, some developing nations asserted sovereignty over their own natural resources. The broadening of the responsibility concept can be seen both in the second clause of Principle 21 and in the World Charter for Nature, in which states accepted the responsibility principle in relation both to other states and to nature itself. Perhaps the notion of state responsibility to nature will be further extended in the future to include a state's responsibility to international civil society. The foregoing discussion demonstrates that the principle of precautionary action may be considered a secondary obligation or a consequence of the states' primary responsibility not to harm the territory of another state or the territory beyond national jurisdiction. It remains to be seen whether Principle 21 applies to harms that occur within a state's own territory.

Efforts to link Principle 21 to states' responsibility not to breach international obligations are supported by the recommendations of the World Commission on Environment and Development. The Brundtland Report noted that "recognition by states of their responsibility to ensure an adequate environment for present as well as future generations is an important step toward sustainable development." The Brundtland Report defined international environmental obligations the breach of which triggers the duty to pay compensation by saying that states have a responsibility toward their own citizens and to other states. While the Brundtland Report provides a road map for the future development of general principles of international environmental law, it is not a source of binding legal duties or obligations for states.

The Brundtland Commission convened a group of legal experts that drafted one obligation on state responsibility and a second obligation on "liability for transboundary environmental interferences resulting from lawful activities"; the International Law Commission divided consideration of the two subjects in a similar manner. The main object of the liability article clearly is payment of compensation for transboundary environmental harm. Indeed, the article seems to assume that the cost of preventing harm or reducing the risk is so great that prevention is realistically impossible. In Article 11, the state responsibility article of the Brundtland Commission's legal experts group report, the mandate is much broader than in Article 21. Under Article 11, the state must cease the internationally wrongful act and restore the *status quo ante* as far as possible. Where appropriate, the state must give satisfaction and pay compensation for harm caused by its breach of international obligations.

In order to identify the possible impact of the precautionary principle upon the international law of state responsibility, it is necessary to examine the nature of the obligations that the precautionary principle as international law would create. Given the uncertainty over the scope and meaning of the precautionary principle and the extent to which it obligates a state to act, violation of the precautionary principle presently does not constitute a breach of international law. This section suggests that the precautionary principle may develop into its own treaty and customary norm. If this occurs, the precautionary principle will be analytically similar to the duty to warn and the duty to mitigate; through these duties a link will be forged between state responsibility and the obligation not to harm the territory of another state or the territory beyond national jurisdiction.

The Precautionary Principle and Biological Diversity

International biodiversity law and policy objectives are strongly affected by ideas concerning the value of biodiversity and the root causes of biodiversity loss. These same value judgments affect related national and regional policies and laws. Valuing biodiversity is difficult because little is understood about genes, species, and ecosystems. First, biodiversity has direct economic value from products derived from biodiversity, such as medicines or new breeds of animals or plants. Second, biodiversity has indirect value, such as ecotourism.

Third, biodiversity possesses options value, because it offers uses not yet known but of value to future generations. Fourth, biodiversity possesses existence value, which is drawn from the mere continuance of life forms in and of themselves, without regard for their economic utility. In addition to these economic, aesthetic, and ethical values, biodiversity has ecological and scientific value, because it is a storehouse of genes and micro-organisms that may permit organisms and ecosystems to recover from various afflictions. The World Charter for Nature recognized humanity's powerful impact upon the environment, the benefits of biodiversity, and the causes of biodiversity destruction.

Given the potential transboundary impact of the loss of biodiversity and the attendant mitigation costs, loss of biodiversity is clearly a matter of international concern. Furthermore, human activity is undeniably responsible for the accelerating loss of global biodiversity. Human activity is rapidly altering both terrestrial and aquatic ecosystems at an unprecedented and alarming rate. Human impact far exceeds the impact of catastrophic natural events, such as periodic fires, floods, and pestilence, that have occurred since prehistoric times. Although the planet possesses a remarkable ability to recuperate from natural disasters and even some human-made disasters, many authorities agree that the planet has reached the limits of its endurance.

Conditions of poverty are the impetus for the governments of developing countries to seek an improved quality of life for their citizens. This legitimate and worthy goal must be counterbalanced by the need to prevent further loss of biodiversity or, at the least, to make informed choices reflecting both long-term and short-term costs and benefits. Importantly, the Rio Declaration repeated the World Charter for Nature's concern for unsustainable consumption and production patterns.

The Convention on Biological Diversity requires party states to draw up national plans and legislation to achieve the Convention's objectives. If a state produces a plan claiming to address the conservation and sustainable use of biological diversity, that state has fulfilled its Convention obligations. At present, no mechanism exists to assess the substantive adequacy and consistency of national plans with the goals of the Convention. Without this important oversight mechanism, it is nearly impossible to charge a state party with breach of its Convention obligations. Similarly, until clear international standards of sustainability are developed, it is impossible to gauge the effects of a state's plan or a proposed activity on the long-term conservation and sustainable use of biological diversity.

The Convention also failed to explain its relationship to other treaties, such as the Convention on International Trade in Endangered Species and the Ramsar Convention. Under the specific language of the treaty, the general "last in time rule"[19] of treaty interpretation and preemption does not apply. Determining the effect of an action taken under multiple international instruments is difficult. The Law of the Sea Treaty clearly trumps the Biodiversity Convention according to the Convention itself. But under earlier conservation and wildlife treaties, it is much less certain whether a decision from the Conference of the Parties (COP) overrides a decision by the treaty body of a different instrument. The interrelationship and overlapping jurisdiction of various U.N. bodies also creates problems. For example, the location of the forests issue is being debated in numerous fora including the COP to the Convention on Biological Diversity; the U.N. Commission on Sustainable Development (CSD); the Global Environment Facility (GEF); the U.N. Food and Agriculture Organization (FAO); and other treaty bodies. Although this may be a salutory multi-fora approach to a complicated problem, it may also permit special interests to "forum-shop" for a receptive audience.

New treaties and soft law declarations of the past two decades and states' increasingly serious reports on their environmental protection activities have created an international environmental law that is strong and growing. The goals of conservation, sustainable use, and equitable benefit-sharing have at last elicited common efforts at the local, national, and international levels that are mutually reinforcing, as will be seen in the next subsection's examination of the international law on biodiversity.

"Soft Law," Customary International Law, and Treaty Law Related to Responsibility for Biodiversity

Commentators frequently refer to international conference statements that represent international consensus or aspiration as "soft law,"[20] a legal form that is not actually binding on states. Soft law is the newest and most common form of law-making in the international system; it frequently appears in new areas of international law-making in which obligations are not dependent upon custom. International soft law states global goals and public expectations. Once the expectations are stated, they may lead to increased public pressure, and ultimately states may recognize the soft law goals as enforceable international prohibitions. Examples of soft law include declarations and resolutions by conferences on the ministerial level or head of state level, multi-disciplinary meetings of scholars or professionals, and U.N. General Assembly resolutions. Even if soft law declarations are not initially binding, they indicate the direction in which the international community is interested in moving and how far states are willing to go.

The U.N. World Charter for Nature, adopted by the General Assembly in 1982, is a good illustration of a "soft law" that formulated a rule and caused some countries to follow the rule as a matter of policy. The General Assembly "expressed its conviction that the benefits which could be obtained from nature depended on the maintenance of natural processes and on the diversity of life forms and that those benefits were jeopardized by the excessive exploitation and the destruction of natural habitats." The General Assembly also "solemnly invited Member States, in the exercise of their permanent sovereignty over their natural resources, to conduct their activities in recognition of the supreme importance of protecting natural systems, maintaining the balance and quality of nature and conserving natural resources, in the interests of present and future generations."

The World Charter for Nature was adopted against this background as a statement of aspirations. The Charter contained a number of far-reaching significant statements regarding the relationship of human beings to other forms of life and the consequences of human activity for natural resources. Some of these statements were dropped or altered significantly in the UNCED documents and in the Biodiversity Treaty ten years later. The general principles in the World Charter for Nature included respect for nature, preservation of global genetic resources, global conservation, and sustainable use.

Customary international law is another recognized method of international lawmaking. The central problem in customary international law is determining whether and when a rule has reached the point of universality and legality. Although the traditional two-pronged test of customary international law searches for evidence of state practice and evidence of *opinio juris,* the test does not necessarily provide a simple answer. Principle 21 of the Stockholm Conference on the Human Environment provides a useful case study of the long road leading to becoming customary international law. Principle 21 provides that "[s]tates have . . . the sovereign right to exploit their own resources pursuant to their own environmental policies, and the responsibility to ensure that activities within their jurisdiction or control do not cause damage to the environment of other states or of areas beyond the limits of national jurisdiction." This statement is the result of a long progression that began with the appearance of the general idea of the principle in the *Trail Smelter* arbitration, a decision with no precedential value in any judicial forum. *Trial Smelter's* principle was repeated in a decision of the International Court of Justice in the *Corfu Channel* case, and later included as part of the declaration of the 1972 Stockholm Conference. The principle was repeated more strongly in the "soft law" World Charter for Nature resolution. Each of these steps was evidence that at some point, Principle 21 had become customary law. Finally, the principle became hard law when it was included in the U.N. Convention on Biological Diversity.

The language that became Principle 21, and later Article 3 of the Convention on Biological Diversity, changed slightly through its various incarnations. The *Trail Smelter* arbitration decision said that no state has the right "to use or permit the use of its territory in such a manner as to cause injury by fumes in or to the territory of another or the properties or persons therein, when the case is of serious consequences and the injury is established by clear and convincing evidence." The *Corfu Channel* case expanded the general principle to recognize every state's obligation not to knowingly allow its territory to be used for acts contrary to the rights of other states. The Stockholm Declaration was much more specific and prohibited states from activities that, "cause damage to the environment of other States or of areas beyond the limits of national jurisdiction." The U.N. General Assembly revised the principle's language somewhat. The "soft law" World Charter for Nature appeared and announced that "[s]tates and, to the extent they are able, other public authorities, international organizations, individuals, groups and corporations shall . . . [e]nsure that activities within their jurisdictions or control do not cause damage to the natural systems located within other States or in the areas beyond the limits of national jurisdiction. . . ."

Although the World Charter for Nature changed the term "environment" to "natural systems," it still limited the prohibition against harm to areas "within other States or in the areas beyond the limits of national jurisdiction." This jurisdictional scope limitation persisted in later formulations, including the Biodiversity Treaty. The addition of a phrase referring to both nations' developmental and environmental policies emphasizes the concern for sustainable development that was articulated first, and most effectively, in the Brundtland Report. This concern for sustainability characterized the UNCED documents, including the Rio Declaration, Agenda 21, and the U.N. Convention on Biological Diversity.

In its next incarnation, Principle 21 appeared in the Rio Declaration, and said:

> States have, in accordance with the Charter of the United Nations and the principles of international law, the sovereign right to exploit their own resources pursuant to their own environmental and developmental policies, and the responsibility to ensure that activities within their jurisdiction or control do not cause damage to the environment of other States or of areas beyond the limits of national jurisdiction.

The recognized test for whether Stockholm Principle 21 has become customary law is the traditional inquiry of evidence of both state practice and *opinio juris*. Evidence of state practice can be found in the presence of statements made by governments since 1972 that support Principle 21; in the inclusion of the principle in other treaties or formal declarations; and in the decisions of arbitral panels and judicial bodies that cite or rely on the principle. *Opinio juris* is evidenced by the writing of jurists who claim to have found an acceptance of Principle 21 in major legal systems around the world, as well as by a number of bilateral and regional agreements that have referred specifically to the Stockholm Declaration in their texts. Each of these documents establishes that states are following Principle 21 in practice and believe themselves to be obligated.

Statements and declarations by the U.N. General Assembly and other multilateral conferences that include the text of Principle 21 can also be cited as proof that the principle has indeed crystallized into customary law. Principle 21's language has been copied countless times in other declarations and resolutions. Moreover, when Principle 21 was codified in the Biodiversity Treaty, it earned international acceptance. Once codified in a treaty, Principle 21 is separately binding on all parties to the treaty, regardless of whether it is customary law.

Since Principle 21 was codified in the Biodiversity Treaty, it becomes necessary to define the meaning of Principle 21 in that context. The existence of states' rights implies that states have a corresponding moral, ethical, and increasingly legal responsibility. The principle of sovereignty guarantees the right of a state to act. Principle 21 balances that right with a state's duty to protect the environment within its jurisdiction or control and to prevent transboundary harm. This responsibility necessarily limits a state's right to use its natural resources with unfettered discretion. Similarly, international law restricts a state's right to use force at will through the requirements of necessity and proportionality. States' absolute sovereignty is already restricted by the global imperative to survive in the face of grave threats to the planet's soil, water, and air. Absolute freedom of consumption without regard for environment costs and nonsustainable means of production are also becoming the target of restrictions under international law and policy.

States may find themselves increasingly under prohibitions regarding the protection or sharing of scarce natural resources, under both permissive and prohibitive systems of laws. As described above, in a permissive system, everything that is not prohibited is permitted and states' sovereignty is absolute. In a prohibitive system, everything not explicitly permitted is assumed prohibited unless clear pension can be found from some supranational source. Principle 21 as binding customary law appears to be a permissive system, tempering states' absolute rights with only the responsibility not to harm the territory of another or territory beyond national jurisdiction. Both the precautionary principle and Principle 21 of the Stockholm Declaration as contained verbatim in the Biodiversity Convention embody the concept of responsibility and need to consider sustainability.

The shift toward prevention and responsibility, and away from the notion of liability and compensation after harm occurs, is a crucial step in accepting the fundamental concept of international biological diversity. Once the basic premises of responsibility and sharing are accepted, resources can be redirected to find the means to achieve these ends. Some possible solutions include transfer of environmentally-sound technology, access to genetic resources, and distribution of some of the royalties from successful genetically-derived products to the source countries and local communities. Greater international cooperation will benefit those who participate; countries may choose not to share, but they will be denied access to valuable resources.

Protection of biological diversity requires more than species preservation. Scientists have discovered the importance of ecosystems; they act both as corridors between habitats that support endangered species and as rich depositories of unidentified organisms. It is inadequate to measure the value of an "ecosystem by reference to its utility for human beings, because it is impossible to value uses that have not yet been imagined. Utility valuation also fails to account for the intrinsic value of ecosystems and life forms. The degree of environmental harm and the true cost of biodiversity loss are important in decision-making and risk analysis; they also have implications for any future liability and compensation regime. Given the present inability to accurately value biodiversity, it is best to adopt a preventive approach rather than to risk unknown harm. The precautionary principle does not require absolute scientific certainty as a prerequisite to preservation of an area or species that may be irreparably harmed before it is fully understood.

The new United Nations Convention on Biological Diversity attempts to balance interests on a global level and represents a general commitment to the conservation and sustainable use of biodiversity. In an effort to clarify the interests being balanced, the Convention carefully defines biological diversity, biological resources, and biotechnology. Although the Convention codifies Principle 21, it does not resolve the problem of liability for the loss of biodiversity.

The parties to the Biodiversity Convention accepted a binding obligation to conserve biodiversity and received an affirmation of their sovereign right to use forests, wetlands, and other ecosystems for development, tempered by the requirement of sustainable use. This obligation was a new departure for developing countries. In return for guaranteed access to the genetic resources located in genetically rich developing countries, developed countries accepted an obligation to share the benefits of biotechnology. The final compromise, then, endorsed both the conservation of biodiversity and its sustainable use. To some, this trade-off has ominous overtones. The Third World Network, an Indian nongovernmental organization, fears that the North is attempting to preserve its access to the South's genetic resources. Thus, the South would supply the "raw material for the [North's] next industrial revolution," in the North's privately-held biotechnology industry.

International law does not yet possess state responsibility or means of calculating appropriate damages for the accidental or willful destruction of biodiversity. Nevertheless, since the Convention on Biological Diversity entered into force in December 1993, it is plausible that the international law of precautionary action may rise to the level of a duty, which can trigger state responsibility when breached. The breach may occur when states fail to regulate activities within their jurisdiction or control or cause damage in areas beyond national jurisdiction. In order to achieve the conservation and sustainable use of biological diversity, it may be necessary to use the international legal system to regulate or restrict development patterns in accordance with the precautionary principle.

When a state breaches its duty to uphold the precautionary principle, Article 3 of the Convention on Biological Diversity offers a basis for assessing the state's responsibility. Although the duty applies only to extraterritorial harm, the Convention's article on jurisdictional scope may give rise to responsibility for a state's activities, regardless of where the effect occurs. The Convention's jurisdiction varies somewhat. The Convention's jurisdiction over components of biodiversity is consistent with Principle 21 and extends only to harms caused in the territory of other states or in the territory beyond national jurisdiction. The Convention's jurisdiction over processes and activities is considerably broader and leaves room for further interpretation of responsibility beyond the transborder context. Such an extension of jurisdictional scope is inherently necessary to the conservation of biological diversity.

New principles of international environmental law have developed quickly in recent years in response to global imperatives for sustainable development; nowhere is that trend more noticeable than in the formation of international law on biodiversity. The United Nations Convention on Biological Diversity, which entered into force as binding international law on December 29, 1993, has been ratified by 127 nations. The first Conference of the Parties took place in late 1994, formally adopting many of the interim institutional and financial mechanisms for the operation of the treaty established when the treaty was opened for signature during the United Nations Conference on Environment and Development in June, 1992. A declaration adopted at the close of the first COP noted that states party to the Convention on Biological Diversity regard it "as much more than just a set of rights and obligations: it is a global partnership with new approaches to multilateral cooperation for conservation and development. . . ."

The U.N. Convention on Biological Diversity represents a new style of treaty negotiation, in that the Convention's subject matter is very broad and the Convention was negotiated with unusual speed and openness. Other features also contribute to the treaty's uniqueness. First, the treaty pioneers an ecosystem approach to conservation that moves beyond the species-specific or habitat-specific approaches of earlier conservation treaties, including those on migratory birds, wetlands, and trade in endangered species. Second, both the preamble and the body of the treaty emphasize the participation of women, local communities, and nongovernmental organizations (NGOs) in biodiversity protection. This language is a significant departure from most other multilateral instruments, which address only the role of the states party to the treaty. The Convention's identification of nonstate actors is a recognition that successful implementation of the treaty will require cooperation from many sectors.

Third, the initial formulation of the treaty was marked by the initiative and contributions of NGOs; indeed, the first draft of the treaty was prepared by an NGO. Fourth, the Biodiversity Treaty is unique, because the text of Stockholm Principle 21 appears verbatim as Article 3; marking the first time this language has appeared in binding international law, rather than in "customary law" or "soft law." The idea of national sovereignty over resources is balanced or tempered to some degree by the requirement that each state accept its responsibility not to harm the territory of any other state or the territory beyond its own national jurisdiction. Finally, the treaty represents a trade-off of mutually beneficial goods, a trade-off that is possible because both developing and developed states have something of value that the other group wants.

Although it is too early to tell how effectively the treaty will be implemented, there is cause for some optimism. The Convention calls for the study of the creation of a Clearinghouse Mechanism for Technical and Scientific Cooperation, which would share knowledge on biological diversity and promote cooperation. In addition, the Convention establishes the Subsidiary Body on Scientific, Technical, and Technological Advice (SBSTTA). On-going discussions at the two meetings of the Intergovernmental Committee on the Convention on Biological Diversity and at the first COP centered on the institutional and organizational entities needed to implement the Convention, as well as on related concerns such as financial mechanisms, intellectual property rights, and biosafety. Most of the NGOs in attendance at the meetings on the Convention in 1993 and 1994 called for efforts to address the relationships between poverty, unsustainable production and consumption, unequal trade relations, and biodiversity; the discussions did not, however, directly address these underlying causes of biodiversity loss.

By the end of the first COP, many of the organizational issues required to set up a new treaty were resolved. The United Nations Environment Programme (UNEP) was designated the appropriate institutional body to function as the Secretariat, and the rules of procedure were established. Finally, the work of the next three years was divided into topics and compiled as the Medium Term Programme of Work of the Conference of the Parties 1995-1997. Despite progress at the first COP, many aspects of the Biodiversity Treaty remain open to interpretation. These gray areas include: state responsibility for prevention of loss of biodiversity; the meaning of "sustainable use" of biological diversity; the extent of a party's obligations to enforce the treaty's objectives through domestic laws; the relationship of the Convention to other wildlife and habitat treaties; and the relationship of the COP and Secretariat to other U.N. bodies whose mandates include aspects of biodiversity.

Conclusion

New international environmental law principles, including sustainable development and recognition of serious human threats to the global environment, have created new applications for the doctrines of state responsibility and liability, although states' environmental obligations under international law remain ill-defined. It is difficult to reconcile most activities threatening loss of biological diversity with the I.L.C.'s language on state responsibility for "primary" and "secondary" obligations and "internationally wrongful acts." Furthermore, the concept of "injurious consequences arising from acts not contrary to international law" appears to be of limited use when only ultrahazardous activities are examined. The concept's use is limited, because biodiversity loss most frequently occurs through the accumulation of ordinary human activities that affect an ecosystem.

Principle 21's concept of state responsibility links sovereign power and privilege with general obligations not to harm the territory of another state or the area beyond national jurisdiction. The legal principles relevant to air, space, aircraft, and maritime boundary disputes are considerably less relevant to problems involving micro-organisms and migratory species. Similarly, territorially-based concepts are not very useful in assessing states' responsibility when they fail to regulate multinational commercial entities that destroy or unsustainably exploit biodiversity resources. One option is to define such commercial activities as internationally wrongful or otherwise prohibited under international law. Unfortunately, this step is unlikely to occur. Another option is to recognize the precautionary principle as a means to comply with state responsibility not to harm the environment. Failure to adopt national plans or procedures incorporating a precautionary approach may then trigger international responsibility or liability.

In other words, a state's duty to take precautionary action may be seen as one of a cluster of procedural norms similar to the duties to warn other states, to mitigate damages. and to assist in case of emergency. For example, the Rio Declaration reaffirms a state's obligation to provide early notification in an emergency and when activities may have a significant transboundary impact. The Rio Declaration also affirms a state's obligation to assist in the event of such emergencies. Moreover, some states are required by treaty to provide both early notification of risk to other states and assistance to other states in the event of a nuclear accident. The goal of these procedural norms is to make information widely available to local communities and to the international community so that states can make informed choices and undertake appropriate responses. A state wishing to comply with the principle of precautionary action may do so by incorporating environmental impact assessment procedures in national planning and legislation.

At the 1992 United Nations Conference on Environment and Development (UNCED), participating states affirmed the importance of environmental impact assessment (EIA) procedures as an integral part of the development process. Currently, more than fifty nations require EIA as a matter of domestic law; and sixteen states of the United States have adopted laws that are more substantive than the National Environmental Protection Act (NEPA). In addition, international organizations, such as the World Bank, have adopted EIA procedures as part of their decision-making process. The popularity of EIAs is due in large measure to their proven effectiveness in anticipating and mitigating the adverse environmental impacts of development projects, and their usefulness in providing environmental information to decision-makers. Moreover, EIA procedures often give potentially affected local communities an opportunity to participate in the decision-making process.

The widespread acceptance of environmental impact assessments is demonstrated by the passage of the Espoo Convention on Environmental Impact Assessment in a Transboundary Context, which was opened for signature in 1991. As of mid-1995, twenty-eight states have signed the convention; a majority of Western and Eastern European states, the United States, and Canada are among the signatories. The Convention requires parties to "take all appropriate and effective measures to prevent, reduce, and control significant adverse transboundary environmental impact from proposed activities." To comply with the Convention, states must notify potentially affected states of environmental dangers, and must consult with affected states to reduce or eliminate adverse environmental effects. The use of EIAs, then, may be one way to implement the precautionary principle in national and international law and policy. It is an approach with particular relevance to the conservation and sustainable use of biological diversity.

Another conceptual way to approach the goal of biodiversity conservation under international law, as explored *supra* in Part II, is through state responsibility and liability. The current limitation of obligations not to harm territory within the jurisdiction of another state or beyond the national jurisdiction does not fully protect global biodiverse resources, for states may still destroy such resources within their territorial boundaries under existing international law. What is needed in the future, then, is to extend responsibility to all states to conserve and sustainably use such resources as a global storehouse of genetic information or medicine chest, separate and apart from claims of sovereign rights, unless subject to the balances and tradeoffs negotiated in the Convention on Biological Diversity.

Applying the principle of state responsibility in areas beyond national

jurisdiction, such as Antarctica and the high seas, creates an opportunity to apply the doctrine of state responsibility in a context free from the claims of sovereign rights. The U.N. Convention on the Law of the Sea (LOS) offers a plan that is tailored for the maximum preservation of humanity's common heritage. Similarly, Antarctica offers the chance to preserve a unique ecosystem of "enormous scientific, ecological, spiritual, and aesthetic importance."[21] The Madrid Protocol to the Antarctic Treaty "implicitly adopts the precautionary principle of environmental planning."[22] In the concept of pollution on the high seas, "[d]octrine and practice . . . now evidence the existence of a parallel obligation to prevent harm to the shared resource of the high seas environment. . . . The 1982 LOS Convention [codifies a duty] as the obligation to act with 'due regard' for other states."[23]

The concept of "internationally wrongful act" creates problems for the application of traditional notions of state problems responsibility for environmental damage. Because clear norms of international environmental law have not yet been fully and universally recognized, the application of the doctrine of state responsibility is not particularly useful at this time. Thus, "[i]t may be concluded that, with respect to transfrontier pollution, the principle of state responsibility is undergoing a process of development and consolidation, but it is not yet to be considered to have hardened into a rule of international law."[24] As discussed by the I.L.C., much serious environmental harm can result from activities that are not "wrongful" in themselves, but whose cumulative effect is disastrous. The international system still awaits the development of an international law on liability and compensation for victims and a broader concept of state environmental responsibility. Obviously, the best strategy for a state that is mindful of its responsibility is to avoid a breach of international obligations entirely or to adopt preventive measures. It is the duty of the international community to develop a full understanding of those obligations.

The creation of international environmental law has led to the recognition of certain legal obligations, such as states' responsibility not to harm the territory of another state and the territory beyond national jurisdiction. This responsibility should be expanded to address threats to global resources and biodiversity even when the threats occur within the territory of individual states. The new international environmental legal system should encourage states to observe their obligations to conserve and sustainably use the environment. In cases where it is difficult to know whether an activity is sustainable the best course for legislators and policy makers is to apply the precautionary approach and prevent environment harm. States that take their environmental responsibilities seriously, comply with their treaty obligations, and strengthen their national regulatory systems need not fear the establishment of international standards and an extended notion of state environmental responsibility. The international community soon must formulate a clear understanding of state environmental responsibility that is proactive and designed to minimize risk. The duty to take precautionary action is becoming customary international law. As such, it offers one way for states to undertake sustainable development, to uphold Stockholm Principle 21, to conserve and sustainably use biological diversity, to protect areas beyond national jurisdiction, and to meet other global obligations. In the process, states' and citizens' self-interest in adopting precautionary measures will become apparent as the Biodiversity Convention is implemented and other sources of international law develop.

Notes

1. Edith Brown Weiss, *International Environmental Law: Contemporary Issues and the Emergence of a New World Order,* 81 Geo. L.J. 675, 690 (1993).

2. Susan H. Bragdon, *National Sovereignty and Global Environmental Responsibility: Can the Tension Be Reconciled for the Conservation of Biological Diversity?,* 33 Harv. Int'l L.J. 381, 391 (1992).

3. This phrase is roughly translated as a form of the golden rule or good neighborliness—an injunction to use one's property in a manner that does not injure another's property. It is related to the civil law concept of "abuse of rights." One classic example of the principle is the idea that neighbors may not build "spite fences" to separate themselves from one another.

National laws also contain "the doctrine that makes an otherwise proper exercise of one's property rights wrongful unless the use [sic] compensates the person who is injured by the use." Louis Henkin et al., International Law: Cases and Materials 1380 (3d ed. 1993). *See also* James Barros & Douglas M. Johnston, The International Law of Pollution 74–76 (1974).

4. *Erga omnes* obligations are obligations owed to the international community as a whole, rather than just to another state.

5. Francisco O. Vicuña, *State Responsibility, Liability, and Remedial Measures Under International Law: New Criteria for Environmental Protection,* in Environmental Change and International Law 124, 128 (Edith Brown Weiss ed., 1992).

6. Philip Allott, *State Responsibility and the Unmaking of International Law,* 29 Harv. Int'l L.J. 1, 1 (1988).

7. *Id.* at 16.

8. [T]he public law analogy of the *ultra vires* act is more realistic than a seeking for subjective *culpa* in specific natural persons who may, or may not, 'represent' the legal person (the state) in terms of wrongdoing. . . . the state also bears an international responsibility for all acts committed by its officials or its organs which are delictual according to international law, regardless of whether the official organ has acted within the limits of his competency or has exceeded those limits." Ian Brownlie, Principles of Public International Law 437–40 (4th ed. 1990) (citing Estate of Jean-Baptiste Caire v. United Mexican States, 5 R.I.A.A. 516, 529–31 (1929)).

[T]here is no need to show fault in the sense of malicious intent or negligence on the part of the state officials responsible for the action of inaction. . . . [O]pinions of eminent authorities such as Lauterpacht, Verdross and Eagleton . . . have favoured the Grotian view that State responsibility rests on "the conception of States as moral entities accountable for their acts and omissions in proportion to the *mens rea* of their agents, the real addressees of international duties. . . ."

Oscar Schachter, International Law in Theory and Practice 203 (1991) (quoting Hersh Lauterpacht, Private Law Sources and Analogies 173 (1970)).

9. Brownlie, *supra* note 8, at 437.

10. *Id.* at 437–39. Negligence and fault are, however, pertinent when determining reparations. *Id.*

11. *Report of the International Law Commission on the Work of its Twenty-Eighth Session,* U.N. GAOR, 28th Sess., Supp. No. 10, U.N. Doc. A/28/10 (1976), *reprinted in* 2 Y.B. Int'l L. Comm'n 95, U.N. Doc. A/CN.4/SER.A/1976/Add.1 (pt. 2) (1976).

12. In fear of possible liability for environmental harm from their own activities, no state is leading the charge to impose international liability. For example, following the Chernobyl accident, one might have expected states such as Sweden to bring a case against the U.S.S.R. at the International Court of Justice for damage suffered within their state. In reality, no such case was brought. This suggests Sweden is concerned that it too could be subject to third party claims, such as those resulting from acid rain pollution damage.

13. Jutta Brunnée, *The Responsibility of States for Environmental Harm in a Multinational Context—Problems and Trends,* 34 Les Cahiers de Droit [C. de D.] 827, 845 n.96 (citing A. Rest, *New Tendencies in Environmental Liability/Responsibility Law,* 21 envtl. Pol'y & L. 135 (1991) (supporting the adoption of instruments of legal responsibility and liability)).

14. In other words, the Commission will focus first on preventive measures in respect of activities creating a substantial risk of harm, and then on remedial measures after harm has occurred. The goal is to create, in this manner, agreement in the Commission on basic elements of its work on the topic.

15. It remains to be seen whether this procedure will enable the Commission to free itself of the difficulties it has faced. If so, the Commission may be able to focus on various approaches, including insurance schemes of the type contained in the International Convention on Civil Liability for Oil Pollution Damage and the 1971 International Convention on the Establishment of an International Fund for Compensation for Oil Pollution Damage. These instruments reflect a market-oriented socialization of the risk with regard to one class of undeniably useful, indeed essential, activities known to be ultrahazardous in terms of their potential damage.

16. David Freestone, *The Precautionary Principle,* in International law and Climate change 21, 30 (Robin Churchill & David Freestone eds., 1991).

17. The *opinio juris communis,* or expression of a legal obligation, relates to a nation's perception of its duties. Proof of obligation can be found in decisions of national courts, and in statements by leaders and jurists as to the legal effect of a declaration, etc.

18. Deterrence theory posits that a change in behavior will occur when the threatened consequences of an act become too painful or expensive, and when it is clear that such consequences will occur. Deterrence works only if the consequences are sufficiently unpleasant.

19. The "last in time rule" provides that in the case of a direct conflict between a treaty and a federal statute, the last in time will prevail.

20. Alexandre C. Kiss, Survey of Current Developments in International envi-

ronmental Law 23 (1976) (citing Rene J. Dupuy, *Droit déclaratoire dt Droit Programmatoire: de la Coutume Sauvage à la Soft Law, in* l'élaboration Du Droit International Public 132 (1975)). See also Christine M. Chinkin, *The Challenge of Soft Law: Development and Change in International Law,* 38 Int'l & Comp. L.Q. 850 (1989); Panel, *A Hard Look at Soft Law,* 82 Proc. Am. Soc'y Int'l L. 317 (1988).

21. David J. Bederman, *The Antarctic and Southern Ocean Coalition's Convention on Antarctic Conservation,* 4 Geo. Int'l Envtl. L. Re. 47, 47 (1991).

22. Bederman, *supra* note 21, at 49.

23. *See* Brian D. Smith, State Responsibility and the Marine Environment: the rules of Decision (1988), at 89.

24. Jutta Brunnée, Acid Rain and Ozone Layer Depletion: International Law and Regulation (1986). at 113 (citing Lothar Gündling, *Verantwortlichkeit der Staaten für grezüberschreitende Umweltbeeintäctigungen,* 45 Zeitschrift Fur Auslandisches Offentliches Recht und Volkerrecht [Zaörv] 265, 273 (1985)).

PART 3.4

International Law as
Normative System:
Managing the Commons

21

Looking Back to See Ahead: UNCLOS III and Lessons for Global Commons Law

Christopher C. Joyner and Elizabeth A. Martell

I n December 1973 the Preparatory Conference for the Third United Nations Conference on the Law of the Sea (UNCLOS III) convened in New York. Representatives from 150 states were in attendance as the Conference was charged by the United Nations General Assembly with preparing a comprehensive international agreement on the law of the sea, by consensus if possible.

On December 10, 1982, after nearly 9 years, the product of 11 substantive UNCLOS III sessions—a treaty of some 200 single-spaced pages, consisting of 17 parts with 320 articles and 9 annexes—was opened for signature in Montego Bay, Jamaica.[1] UNCLOS III negotiations formally came to a close with a new instrument for governing the world's oceans proffered for legal adoption by the international community. Yet while 117 states became signatories to the new 1982 Convention on that December day, many other governments continued to harbor real frustration and dissatisfaction with the final legal product. Included among those disgruntled governments were several of the most important international maritime actors, including the United States, the United Kingdom, Italy, and the Federal Republic of Germany.

The UNCLOS III experience has been aptly described as "the largest, most technically complex, continuous negotiation attempted in modern times."[2] The Conference was negotiated on the basis of consensus, as a package deal, with the understanding by participants that such an approach required that no reservations to the final treaty be permitted. Appreciating this, several aspects of the 1982 United Nations Convention on the Law of the Sea (1982 Convention) have already entered into customary international law. It also is true that the treaty itself entered into force in late 1994 with the requisite 60 ratifications deposited. Nevertheless, the Convention did not embody a wholly successful outcome. In retrospect, the 1982 Convention fell victim to a North-South, developed-developing world ideological schism that detracted from the participating governments' ability to make it universally accepted conventional law. Certain political and economic residues of that schism remain to complicate the implementation of contemporary ocean law.

This article examines precedents for making future international global commons law that can be derived from the experience of the UNCLOS III negotiations and their progeny, the 1982 Convention. To this end, the following section undertakes a brief historical review of UNCLOS III. In so doing, those provisions in the Convention deemed offensive to the developed world are analyzed. The next section, "Lessons for Future Commons Law Negotiations," appraises the status of the law of the sea today, in light of the promulgation of the 1994 Implementation Agreement.[3] In particular, an assessment is made to determine if consensus exists among governments on whether the seas are properly deemed *res nullius* or *res communis*. Further, a comparison is made of the intent of the UNCLOS III participants regarding the customary international legal effects of the Convention's provisions with the current understanding and application of those provisions, especially the concept of the exclusive economic zone (EEZ).

Lessons that have applicability for the creation of future commons law creation can clearly be drawn from the UNCLOS III negotiations. In the section, "Rethinking Approaches to Commons Law Negotiations," a number of important lessons are presented, as are several options that might be contemplated by states in negotiating future commons law. Clearly, the consensus method used to formulate the 1982 Convention is not the only means available to states, and it remains arguable whether the global conference is the most appropriate means to negotiate a treaty of such a sweeping, universal character.[4] In the conclusion, the query is posed as to whether a binding global commons regime can be negotiated by all states, accepted and ratified by all states, and then actually be made to fulfill its stipulated, multifaceted purpose. Admittedly, the conclusion may be hardheaded and even less than optimistic. Still, the UNCLOS III experience suggests cause for caution in this regard.

It is important at the outset to appreciate what is meant by the notion of a global commons area. A *global commons* is an area beyond the limits of national jurisdiction to which all peoples have free and open access. Such commons are generally meant to include the oceans, outer space, and Antarctica. In environmental policy, the "tragedy of the commons" is a much-repeated metaphor of what can happen when a common resource is overexploited by too many people.[5] The long-term result of a short-run strategy of overuse is exhaustion of the common area's resources, to the detriment of everyone. While the traditional accounting of the tragedy of the commons tells of herdsmen grazing their sheep on a village green, today the exploitation frequently is performed by large corporations and governments, with a critical component of the (over)exploitation of the global commons being technological. Until technology reaches a level where resources of the global commons areas can be profitably and easily exploited, such exploitation will remain limited. Harvesting marine living resources in this century exemplifies the point. Since the 1940s, technological developments have made it possible for ocean fisheries to be overharvested. Today, only a half-century later, the world's fisheries have been severely depleted. Whereas the living resources of the ocean were once viewed by Hugo Grotius as inexhaustible, in 1995 they are so threatened that a "usually quiet player on the world stage" may feel compelled to take unilateral and legally suspect action to protect stocks off its coasts, as the recent tension between Canada and Spain so dramatically illustrates.[6]

A vital element of the global commons problem is environmental. As long as the oceans are regarded as a commons, users have scant incentive to accept responsibility for their pollution or other degradation, or at most, will accept only a modicum of the costs imposed on the entire global community. The traditional view of Grotius held that the resources of the seas were inexhaustible. The oceans would remain forever free of being polluted in wholesale fashion since human activities could affect the seas to a limited degree.[7] This view held that the seas were so vast and so fluent, with such extraordinary remedial capabilities, that they could be used safely as a toilet for the world's wastes. Today, this view seems hopelessly naive. Again, the issue of marine pollution is inextricably linked with technological advances. Between 1964 and 1974, for example, the world commercial deadweight shipping tonnage doubled from 150 million tons to more than 308 million tons.[8] With increased maritime traffic came increased marine pollution.

The accepted legal definition of a commons area rests on the notion of *res communis,* that is, something belonging to all. During the UNCLOS III negotiations, the developing states endeavored to have the seas beyond the limits of national jurisdiction legally declared—in the 1967 phrase of Malta's representative to the United Nations, Arvid Pardo—the "common heritage of mankind."[9] This understanding of the concept of common heritage rests on *res communis* and refers to "an undivided asset to be shared by all nations irrespective of their technological capabilities and to be managed by the United Nations," rather than by any particular state.[10] Pardo's original conception of the high seas and deep seabed as the common heritage of mankind was intended to operationalize *res communis* for all of the world's people. The oceans and their bounty were to be shared by all, and everyone was to share in the benefits derived from use of the oceans.[11]

With regard to ocean resources, the legal notion of *res communis* is set against the concept of *res nullius,* which holds that things belonging to no one are available for appropriation by anyone capable of recovering them.

The distinction here is important, simply because if the ocean belongs to all people and all people have the right to use the oceans, how could any particular person or state legally justify a special right of exploiting and consuming ocean resources for their own personal gain? If the oceans belong to all, how could only a few lawfully exploit and profit from marine resources? The conflict became drawn between contrary conceptions of ocean property rights and the technological ability to exploit resources of the seas.

The *res nullius* interpretation traditionally has been applied to high seas resources and it was this conception that the developed states applied to the seabed during the UNCLOS III negotiations. With regard to the deep seabed, the practical difficulties of obtaining effective occupation (particularly the requirement of establishing permanent settlement) make it highly unlikely that any one state could stake a sovereign claim to any portion of the ocean floor. Consequently, the debate over whether the ocean floor is legally *res nullius* versus *res communis* may have been overstated. Whichever precept applies in principle, developed states obviously retain a great advantage over the developing world in exploitation capacity, unless and until their technological and capital advantage is somehow offset. The distinction between *res communis* and *res nullius* as applied to the deep seabed proved to be irreconcilable at UNCLOS III. While developed states espoused laissez-faire, free-trade principles, Third World states denounced the fact that in the modern era, "open access meant equal access to the valuable resources of the commons in name only."[12] The philosophical lines had been drawn for a protracted ideological confrontation.

UNCLOS III Revisited

By the mid-1960s, when several governments began seriously discussing the possibility of a new conference to standardize sea law, the need for an updated convention had become clear. Although the first and second Geneva Conference meetings had taken place less than a decade earlier, they had proved ineffective in establishing a lasting, much less universal, regime for the oceans. The most pressing maritime issue seen by the two superpowers at the time was the threat to over 100 strategic straits posed by the proliferation of unilateral state claims to territorial seas and economic zones beyond the then accepted 3-mile territorial sea limit. The United States and the former Soviet Union both wanted to maintain the largest possible extent of high seas area as the first substantive session of UNCLOS III began in Caracas in June 1974.

For their part, the states of the developing world welcomed the opportunity to participate in negotiating a new law of the sea. Many of them had achieved independent status subsequent to UNCLOS I and II, and thus had been unable to exercise their sovereignty in fashioning ocean law during those earlier conferences.[13] Additionally, developing countries were driven by the ideological imperative during the mid-1970s of establishing a new international economic order (NIEO) that would address the perceived inequities inherent in the current global distribution of resources. As one authoritative commentator has observed, "Consistent with their criticism of the laissez-faire ideology of traditional international law, Third World countries challenged its corollary, the principle of the freedom of the seas, as developed by the more powerful and now technologically superior maritime states."[14] Even before the UNCLOS III negotiations began, the ideological clash had begun to take shape. This schism had been foreshadowed in 1970 by the split 62 in favor, 28 in opposition, with 28 abstentions vote in the UN General Assembly on Resolution 2574D, the so-called "Moratorium Resolution."[15] This resolution, which had aimed to forestall the national freedom of seabed mining pending establishment of an international regime, was opposed by major maritime powers and others as "the declaration of a mere 'paper majority.'"[16]

The agenda of UNCLOS III was impressive in legal scope and issue-area breadth. The scope of the items negotiated at the Conference is unprecedented in international negotiations, as it encompassed a variety of disparate themes—political, legal, economical, technological, informational, and military, among others. The agenda also revealed a split between the developed states, led by the United States and the former Soviet Union as global maritime powers, and the developing world. Initially the United States would have preferred only a limited review of ocean law issues, since its main interests involved expanded coastal state jurisdiction. By 1970, however, the United States had realized that the newly independent developing countries refused to consider the question of "creeping jurisdiction" in isolation from ocean resource issues. Consequently, the United States acceded to a comprehensive conference.[17] The capacity to set the agenda for international negotiations may well be an instrument of state power that developed nations can wield to ensure that their environmental concerns are addressed, as some observers have suggested.[18] In the case of UNCLOS III, however, that ability seems to have been wanting by the two superpowers, to their eventual regret.

A gentleman's agreement at the outset among participants decided that the negotiations at UNCLOS III should proceed on a consensus basis.[19] It was understood by the participants that all governments involved might well be obliged to sacrifice one goal in favor of gaining others. Indeed as Robert Friedheim has noted, "Both the United States and the Soviet Union recognized that under the basic consensus rule the treaty would have to be a package, and they would therefore have to offer trade-offs on issues of lesser salience to get favorable outcomes of issues of higher salience."[20] Thus the Convention was negotiated as a "package deal," with the stipulation in

Article 309 that no reservations to the final draft would be permitted. While the issue linkages contained in the Convention served to enlarge the potential scope of the new regime for the seas,[21] the terms of the package were ambiguous. Many governments came to view the original package deal as being a trade-off of navigational rights for expanded coastal state jurisdiction. Others perceived the trade-off in more general terms, especially as navigational guarantees in exchange for access to resources.[22] These differing perceptions led to a breakdown in communications and eventually to diplomatic deadlock as the negotiations drew to a close in 1982.

It should be noted that in the corpus of international environmental law, UNCLOS III provides a somewhat unusual case owing to the actual degree of scientific certainty about its environmental provisions. Other negotiations designed to protect some aspect of the environment often have been compelled to operate under a cloud of uncertainty and without consensus in the scientific community about either the causes of or the optimal solutions to a recognized problem. In some cases, the very existence of a real environmental threat has been questioned.[23] Negotiations at UNCLOS III took place in a very different atmosphere, largely because the period between the late 1960s and the late 1970s was an era marked by several prominent disasters for the ocean environment, including the wrecks of the tankers *Torrey Canyon* in 1967 and *Amoco Cadiz* in 1978.[24] International attention became riveted on the fate of the oceans from man-made pollution. Yet while protection of the marine environment and the preservation of the ocean's living resources certainly are components of the 1982 Convention, and extensive ones at that,[25] the Convention does not endeavor to establish specific provisions aimed at protection. Rather, it relies on statements of general principles.[26] It directs states to enact national laws to protect the marine environment and its inhabitants from land- and sea-based sources of pollution,[27] as well as to establish and work within regional and global institutions, including the International Maritime Organization, to preserve the ocean environment.[28]

There was, of course, a considerable body of international environmental law dealing with conservation and pollution control already on the books. Yet the 1982 Convention itself is remarkably short on specifics, given the clarity about the issues involved. This lack of specifics likely reflects the suspicions and doubts in the North-South debate over the proper assignment of state responsibility for shouldering the costs of conservation: Should there be equal assignment of responsibility, or proportional assignment based on level of development?[29] While a deliberately ambiguous approach may be preferred by governments negotiating a treaty so as to ensure its acceptability by all participants, a convention that merely "invites states to be good citizens, but does not define what good citizenship means, beyond not polluting,"[30] leaves much to be desired in terms of policy implementation and its actual international enforcement.

Scientific uncertainty can undermine the chances for successfully negotiating an international environmental protection regime. Still, even absent the difficulty of having to deal with scientific uncertainty, the treaty product of UNCLOS III was compromised for other reasons. The final draft of the Convention was rejected largely on ideological grounds by the Reagan administration early in 1982, leaving other Conference delegates stunned and frustrated. After nearly a decade of negotiations, the desire to conclude the Conference was strong. Representatives of the Group of 77, while persistently adamant on seabed issues, had made compromises in the recent sessions and were not willing to make further concessions to the United States.[31] The Conference concluded without agreement to its composite negotiated product by the most visible and important global maritime actor, the United States.

Although the United States had entered into the UNCLOS III negotiations with the preeminent goals of securing navigational freedom and straits passage for its military and commercial ships—goals which were realized in the language of the 1982 Convention—the entire package was jettisoned by the United States because of Part XI, which concerned deep seabed mining. Mining resources of the deep seabed initially had not been a major objective for the United States in the negotiations, and in fact both the U.S. Navy and the Department of Defense had entered the negotiations with a willingness to compromise on other aspects of sea law in order to obtain navigational security. Indeed, these departments had "preferred linkage because it appeared to permit trading other issues for assurances of free access for military forces."[32] By 1982, however, ideological forces had coalesced in the new administration to sink the agreement. In a real sense, a more fervent, committed kind of conservative political ideology had risen to power with the Reagan administration. It affected every issue of domestic and foreign policy, and the law of the sea proved no exception.[33]

The North-South debate first hinted at in the 1969 General Assembly vote on the Moratorium Resolution had now grown into an ideological impasse. Under the leadership of the Group of 77, land-based producers of the minerals found in the polymetallic nodules of the sea—most of them from developing countries—joined with other Third World states against prospective deep seabed mining states, particularly the United States. On April 30, 1982, the first, only, and final vote on the Convention was taken, with 130 states in favor, 4 opposed, and 17 abstaining.[34] As one analyst tersely put it, "The end of UNCLOS could hardly be called its finest hour."[35] The treaty for the law of the sea had been consummated, at a cost of turning off participation by most Western states.

The ideological confrontation thus had been joined. There were on the one hand the Western industrialized states, led by the United States, who advocated private, free-enterprise capitalism. For them, the deep seabed retained its traditional legal status of being *terra nullius*. On the other hand, there were the developing countries in the Group of 77, who wanted an international authority to manage and regulate deep seabed mining. For this group the seabed was the common heritage of mankind, the resources of which should be exploited, with derived revenues being distributed to poor, needy governments.

The unanimous 1970 Declaration of Principles (G.A. Resolution 2749) and the eventual law of the sea instrument confirmed that the seabed beyond the limits of national jurisdiction is not a *res nullius*. The Declaration of Principles also affirmed that it has become an unchallengeable principle of international ocean law that this area cannot be appropriated unilaterally. This fiat is explicitly set out and secured by Article 137 of the 1982 Convention.[36] The question, of course, turns on allocation of the resources of the seabed. Today the sea, "including the surface of the water, the water column, the seabed, and all minerals and organisms found therein, is regarded as a juridical unity, subject to a single constitutive regime governing its use, a view supported by traditional jurisprudence as well as by the language of the 1958 and 1982 conventions."[37] The clear conclusion suggests that if the oceans are viewed as *res communis*—something held in common by all—then it follows that legal restrictions on the exploitation of exhaustible resources are mandated. The key question then is whether these restrictions apply to third parties outside the juridical obligations of the 1982 Convention.

Before the 1994 Implementation Agreement was produced, a debate arose over whether the 1982 Convention constituted an "objective regime" that would have applicability to third parties. One argument went that since the United States had participated in the UNCLOS III negotiations with the acknowledged recognition that the end product would be a package deal, that government was bound by the principle of estoppel. The United States and its allies "implicitly represented to other States that they would accept Part XI along with the other new rules in the Convention, or they would forego these rules entirely."[38] Since other governments had made concessions in their interests based on this assumption, the United States and its allies should be estopped from rejecting Part XI while accepting the other sections of the treaty. Nonetheless, referring to Article 35 of the Vienna Convention, which affirms that treaties require consent to be binding, some observers have suggested that until a treaty is ratified by the "specially affected states," it cannot be said to "constitute a binding customary regime."[39] With particular regard to ocean law,

> [w]hile UNCLOS, in many respects, represents a codification of prior customary international law, and in some cases, a progressive development now probably on its way to establishing new customary norms [including the concept of the exclusive economic zone], this cannot be said of UNCLOS' seabed regime.[40]

Thus strong support surfaced for the U.S. contention that while many aspects of the 1982 Convention might be exercised as customary international law, such was not the case with respect to the deep seabed mining regime. The law of the sea in the Convention was clearly customary and universally applicable. The law of the seabed was new, untested, and nascent in state practice.

On the other hand, the *res communis* principle might be viewed as a peremptory norm, as defined under Article 53 of the Vienna Convention.[41] This situation would suggest that the Convention did indeed establish an objective regime for the seabed that would be binding on the United States, even without its consent. As James Morell opined, "The nonappropriation element of the *res communis* principle—mandatory in nature regardless of whether an ocean use is exhaustible or not, although some exclusive rights of use may be allocated under an international regulatory regime in the former case—is thus a true peremptory norm."[42] The implication here is that, because manganese nodules are an exhaustible resource found in an area designated *res communis,* they should be properly governed under a multilateral regulatory regime. Consequently the proposed establishment of an alternative competitive mining regime would contravene the status of *res communis,* and thus violate the peremptory norm.[43]

In any event, shortly after the Convention was opened for signature in December 1982, several of its aspects already were deemed reflective of customary international law, including the innovative concept of the EEZ contained in Part V of the Convention.[44] The *travaux preparatoire* for the 1982 Convention suggest that this interpretation runs contrary to what the negotiators had intended.[45] Indeed when the U.S. intention not to sign the Convention became known, the president of UNCLOS III, Tommy Koh, insisted that the Convention was an integral package and that "it is not possible for a State to pick what it likes and to disregard what it does not like."[46] Even so, as one legal scholar has noted, "[T]here is actual evidence supporting the view that the 'package deal' argument will not carry great weight before an international tribunal."[47] By way of example, in both the *Tunisia/Libya* and *Malta/Libya* cases,[48] the International Court of Justice accepted that the EEZ exists as customary law quite apart from the EEZ regime that was created in Part V of the 1982 Convention. This probably was attributable in large part to the broad acceptance of 200-nautical-mile fishery and conservation zones implemented by many coastal states during the 1970s, before the EEZ had become accepted as a legal construct.

Lessons for Future Commons Law Negotiations

A number of lessons that may supply insight into the most effective ways and means to negotiate global commons regimes can be realized from the

UNCLOS III experience. These lessons also suggest where problems may be confronted and how opportunities may be seized in the course of future commons negotiations.

1. *To be successful, agreements cannot exclude specially affected states.* Article 34 of the Vienna Convention on the Law of Treaties asserts that "a treaty does not create either obligations or rights for a third State without its consent."[49] Accordingly, to achieve their intended purposes, commons law agreements cannot exclude specially affected states (i.e., those governments that have particular national stakes in the treaty's purpose and effects). That the 1994 Implementation Agreement to the 1982 Convention was felt necessary substantiates this realization. This addendum was negotiated to permit United States participation basically on its own terms, by eliminating or negating the offensive provisions of Part XI.[50] Only decisions that take into consideration the interests of those states particularly affected by the treaty are likely to generate sound and acceptable norms of behavior. As one authoritative commentator put it, "Decisions that emerge largely from the rhetorical imperatives of multilateral bodies or national ideologies are likely to produce fustian and divergent practices."[51] This is no doubt true. The latter sort of decision appears more likely to emerge when a large multilateral conference convenes and "creates a temptation to regard the assembled participants as representatives of all mankind dispatched to enunciate global community policy on its behalf. . . . The result is a rhetorical pressure to cast issues in terms of community values."[52] Such self-imposed global responsibility expands the realm of states that conceivably could be "specially affected"—at least in a philosophical sense—by a commons agreement.

Whether a state is specially affected by an international agreement largely becomes a matter of self-definition. The most important considerations in the law of the sea, from the early vantage point of the United States, were those that dealt with navigational freedom and straits passage. As the UNCLOS III negotiations continued, however, the U.S. delegation reformulated its hierarchy of national interests until the issue of deep seabed mining took on greater salience. While the seabed mining companies themselves clearly had an interest in negotiating a favorable convention, most outside observers disagreed with the Reagan administration's perception of the balance of U.S. interests.[53] Of course, such observers were not making U.S. foreign policy decisions. While many scholars may question and disagree with the U.S. government's own notions of its interest hierarchy, self-perception by the decision-makers of a special interest remains the most important factor.[54]

This lesson, if carefully applied to future commons law negotiations, may result in fewer binding treaties being presented for signature. It may also foster an increase in the number of nonbinding statements of principle or similar documents that permit a specially affected state to put on a show of support for the effort while not committing itself to be bound by the terms of the agreement. For example, at the United Nations Conference on Environment and Development (UNCED) in Rio de Janeiro in 1992, the negotiations did not produce a treaty on deforestation but rather a statement of principles on forestry issues.[55] This reflected the reluctance of the major affected states, particularly Indonesia, Malaysia, and Brazil, to accept a binding treaty with any restrictive substance. Yet UNCLOS III also illustrated the potential liability that comes with the exclusion of such states, particularly when specially affected states are also the ones that would bear substantial costs of the regime. In April 1982, those governments that abstained or voted against the draft law of the sea convention contributed some 60% of the total United Nations budget,[56] an economic consideration that cannot be ignored.

2. *Issue linkage may improve the chances of success if used judiciously, but it can backfire.* The 1982 Convention was, of course, negotiated as a "package deal." Evidence emerges from the UNCLOS experience that issue linkage can work as a sound negotiating strategy to expand the zone of agreement for participants.[57] Elliott Richardson, the U.S. representative to UNCLOS III during the Carter administration, agrees and put it neatly: "Where a country is asked to do more or give up more than its self-interest would warrant, it must be offered positive incentives to sacrifice for the larger good."[58] That suggestion seems quite reasonable, especially if the country is also a state specially affected by the agreement.

The difficulties involved in negotiating the 1982 ocean law instrument suggest, however, that it may not be an ideal paradigm to use for all other environmental negotiations. With regard to establishing a climate change convention, for example, the UNCLOS III negotiations model appeared to suggest that the political, economic, and diplomatic costs of covering all aspects of climate change in one agreement far exceeded the benefits of the comprehensiveness obtained.[59] It was the very comprehensiveness of the 1982 Convention that ultimately eroded its support. This realization has prompted the conclusion that the elimination of issues may serve as a means to preserve and strengthen negotiating blocs.[60] This, of course, is the principal intent and design of the 1994 Implementation Agreement: to remove the objectionable seabed mining portions of the Convention so that the rest of the instrument could be considered and implemented on its own considerable merits.

Another suggestion on the question of issue linkage and delinkage might be to increase the incentive structure for parties. Instead of subtracting issues that could undermine a comprehensive convention, the provision of greater economic incentives by one side could thereby encourage the other side to accept the treaty or at least make constructive compromises. Such incentives might include linking loans to environmental protection, or establishing environmental assistance programs, or pursuing debt-for-nature swaps.[61] Such linkages could be established on a bilateral or multilateral basis and integrated into the formal provisions of the agreement.

When the United States walked away from the 1982 Convention, the Third World was in no mood to renegotiate the sensitive terms of the treaty. It appeared as though the United States had attempted to use a shake-down tactic rather than a linkage tactic. Whereas the latter is a quid pro quo approach and should produce a mutual advantage, the former is "one-sided extortion by means of threats,"[62] with the express intent of producing a winner at the expense of the other side. Since the United States recognized that its status as a specially affected state would undermine the establishment of an effective, universal regime for the seas if it did not participate, the Reagan administration sought to use that leverage to gain concessions from the developing states majority. It is possible that the incoming U.S. negotiators in the Reagan administration were not aware that other governments were weary of negotiating and thus they miscalculated the degree to which further concessions might be wrung. It also is possible that the Reagan administration concluded that might makes right and the United States did not need a law of the sea treaty containing an internationally socialistic seabed mining regime. Though plainly a cynical view, that is the impression left by the administration's ultimate legal attitude and policy position.

The basic lesson is that a bird in the hand is probably worth two in the bush. Pressing issue linkage too hard and too far can lead to mutual loss. As one commentator on negotiations has observed,

> There is a risk that constantly pushing to find additional value through linkages can create a climate that Roger Fisher describes as a "stingy bargaining environment"—in which each side always holds out for more, even after satisfying their fundamental interests. This stance can become self-defeating if the parties turn down "good" agreements that they actually have in hand in favor of theoretically superior outcomes.[63]

The lesson is that, at a certain point, governments must recognize that they have gained all that can be won from issue linkage. This realization, of course, is a subjective calculation. Accordingly, since governments frequently fail to act as fully rational actors and misperceptions by policymakers can happen, miscalculations are bound to occur. The fact that so many commentators feel that the United States should have accepted the 1982 Convention supports the conclusion that the Reagan administration miscalculated the extent to which other states were willing to exchange further concessions for U.S. participation.

   3. *The consensus approach to negotiation tends to expand the time and effort required to reach a successful agreement.* The consensus approach to negotiations recognizes the sovereign equality of states and, in theory, that

collective choice can be a useful means to achieve a positive sum outcome without the alienation and divisiveness that come with casting votes to formally declare positions. An agreement based on consensus also may acquire special status as being reflective of customary law. While the UNCLOS III negotiations proceeded on a consensus basis for nearly 9 years, in April 1982 the United States forced a vote on the acceptability of the Convention text. This act reflected the fundamental understanding by the U.S. government that an international agreement reached by consensus carries relatively greater weight in creating customary international law than an agreement that proceeds according to a majority-rule procedure.[64] When a formal opportunity is presented for "objectors" to officially assert their view, the case is made for those governments to elude being legally bound to an international agreement without their consent.

At the same time, consensus decision making attributes disproportional influence to critics and can be very costly in time and effort.[65] The consensus approach allows all participants to share a voice in the final product of the negotiations. This means that in formulating a global ocean regime, the disparate interests of nearly 160 states had to be taken into consideration. Clearly these 160 states did not share a common agenda, a fact attributable to conflicting ideological, political, and economic interests. The dilemma for all international negotiations is that in most cases, as it was at UNCLOS III, some issues are of particular importance to all states, which reduces the possibility for compromise and increases the complexity of the process. As one authority on ocean law and policy observed, "On any issue of importance, no state [is] willing to be excluded from a negotiation or to allow its interests to be represented by others."[66] Governments cannot be condemned for exercising caution when confronted with a possible loss of their sovereignty. Still the result of such a sentiment is an increase in the effort, patience, and time required to reach an agreeable consensus outcome.

4. *Protracted, drawn-out negotiations risk being overtaken by technological and political changes.* When negotiations are conducted over a prolonged period of time, they may be outstripped by technological and political changes in the international milieux. There are at least two elements to this impact of change. First, the problem of "foreseeability" of technological developments suggests that to remain relevant, international negotiations must be both timely and appropriate for the issue at hand. Because the pace of technological developments is so rapid today, it is understandable why the Group of 77 countries were acutely concerned that the potential bonanza of mineral riches on the seabed would be harvested before those developing governments were able to participate and share in that exploitation. Even so, the intensity of objections to the provisions in Part XI ultimately helped to undermine U.S. support for the entire Convention. James Sebenius pointed out that, "In the earlier days of the LOS negotiations the official view generally held that, in the absence of a treaty, navigational

rights would erode and conflict would generally increase."[67] As negotiations continued, however, the United States elected a succession of new leaders until one took office who believed that there was a viable alternative to the Convention. That alternative did not include U.S. participation in the Convention, either as a party or even as a signatory.

On the other hand, technological or other circumstances that arise during the course of a negotiation or before it comes into force might make concluding an agreement easier. In the case of deep seabed mining, the United States has only limited economic and security interests, since both the demand for and prices of the nodular minerals have declined over the past decade. Thus at present the market does not appear likely to make deep seabed mining commercially viable before 2030, and in all probability, even much later than that." In theory this change in the international setting should have made the Convention more economically palatable to the United States by the early 1990s, even without the 1994 Implementation Agreement. The implementation instrument, however, supplied the legal guarantees necessary to protect U.S. interests in a future regime for mining the deep seabed, whenever that might occur.

5. *The ideological divide between the North and the South must be given due weight.* Since the 1982 Convention entered into force in late 1994, the concept of the common heritage of mankind has become fixed as a part of conventional international law. The association of the common heritage of mankind with the NIEO during the 1970s made it repulsive to many industrialized states, but its inclusion in the 1982 Convention was necessary to secure Third World cooperation. Similar compromises probably will be required in future international commons law negotiations and therefore must be anticipated. The fact remains, as Lawrence Susskind points out, that more than 2 decades after its formulation, the NIEO aspiration has not been fully abandoned by developing countries. Susskind logically believes that continued pressure on the North by the South to achieve the NIEO agenda could give the less developed world sufficient leverage to temper demands of the industrialized world.

> If the South makes meeting its earlier economic goals a quid pro quo for its willingness to participate in collective efforts to respond to environmental threats, all progress on the environmental front will come to a halt. If, however, the South's objectives can be linked strategically (perhaps *opportunistically* is a better word) with Northern efforts to achieve environmental protection and sustainable development, then the impetus for sustained global cooperation may finally be provided.[69]

This possibility suggests that the governments of the South can play their ideological trump card, but should do so only with due caution. While the industrialized governments of the North must recognize the needs and

goals of their neighbors to the South, the Third World also has an obligation to be willing to compromise. Sustainable development must be a two-
way street, if it is to work for the betterment of national economies and the
protection and preservation of global commons areas.

6. *Since national interest and global equity open conflict, governments
most consider the long-term consequences of their immediate actions.* This
lesson is similar to the previous one, but it places the onus squarely on the
developed world, which is the chief beneficiary of global inequity today.
The text of the 1982 Convention is notable for its efforts to incorporate the
notion of global equity into its provisions. For example, the treaty recognizes the needs of geographically disadvantaged and landlocked states. The
Convention text in Part XI attempted to redress the balance of interests
between the technologically advanced states and the less-developed world
in the sea-bed mining regime, although it went too far in the view of the
United States and other miners. The upshot, of course, was the Implementation Agreement 12 years later. Even so, its assertion that the deep seabed
and its resources are the common heritage of mankind underscores the precept that "first-come, first-served" is not an acceptable principle of economic justice. Obtaining global equity implies genuine acknowledgment
that a principal source of First World wealth was colonial or imperial
exploitation, and that all peoples have the right to enjoy a certain, minimal
standard of living, regardless of whether they live in Northern Europe or
sub-Saharan Africa. A just international arrangement "nullifies the contingencies and biases of historical fate," in the words of philosopher John
Rawls.[70] Instead of calling for the equitable distribution of resources yet to
be exploited, as the 1982 Convention does, conceptions of global equity
frequently mandate redistribution of resources today.[71] This is a debate that
goes beyond the scope of this study, however, though it no doubt will
impact heavily on future commons law negotiations.

In the future it is conceivable that sets of treaties may have to be considered simultaneously, or individual treaties might have to be placed in the
context of a larger North-South global bargain. To a certain extent, this was
the road taken to the Rio Summit in 1992. Negotiating such a bargain
would require taking considerations of global equity into account. Hence
the evolution of "sustainable development" as a critical component of a
new global environment order. The key point in the fifth lesson above was
that North and South must recognize each other's ideological agendas and
be truly willing to compromise on certain points. The key point in the sixth
lesson is that at times producing global equity may demand more concessions from the developed states than from the Third World. Yet because
governments often view their national interests in utilitarian, zero-sum
terms, it may be difficult for leaders to rally the political will necessary to
transcend immediate goals and recognize a long-term interest in creating a

global community based on principles of justice.[72] That is to be expected in an international system composed of sovereign states motivated by self-serving national interests.

An example from the Convention illustrates this point. Since the EEZ concept is customary international law today, it is fair to conclude that the United States benefited greatly in economic terms from the UNCLOS III process, without paying any economic or ideological costs that the Reagan administration associated with Part XI and the international regulation of deep seabed mining. In this case it is easy to recognize that certain economic benefits were obtained by an apparently inequitable policy. On the other hand, there were long-term costs incurred by the United States in terms of international political tension and ill will. These costs had come in relationships with the Third World, which had sought to use the UNCLOS III negotiations to redress global inequities, as well as with a number of Western allies, who might have gone along with the treaty absent U.S. pressure. Obviously, the long-term costs are less tangible and more difficult to empirically measure than are the economic gains reaped by the United States. They are costs nonetheless. When making international policy, leaders should define their national interests to take into account the costs incurred when global equity is undermined.

Rethinking Approaches to Commons Law Negotiations

Approaches to negotiating global environmental law for the commons fall into two categories. The first involves a comprehensive strategy that links several issue areas under one negotiating umbrella.[73] This view toward international environmental law is bolstered by the emerging understanding that ecosystems must be preserved as systems for environmental action to be optimally effective. Such a holistic approach also may help overcome the North-South problems discussed above. The incremental approach to crafting environmental regimes puts pieces of the ecological puzzle together, though not in either a uniform or unitary fashion. Problems are dealt with on an ad hoc basis. A comprehensive strategy would aim for an overarching relationship between North and South—one that could link together issues of process and substance through a comprehensive international negotiation. The second strategy instead takes a more piecemeal approach to negotiations. The philosophy behind this approach is that issue linkage may increase the benefits for all participants in a negotiation, but it also may undermine the possibility for consensus. The UNCLOS III negotiations illustrate the potential for difficulty and obstruction that may result from linking too many issues.

As one of some 200 sovereign actors, an individual state, even a large and influential one, often has little control over setting the agenda for international negotiations. This is illustrated well by the UNCLOS III process, where the unified South through the Group of 77 was able to include agenda items that the North would have preferred to leave out. Further, the forum for negotiations is also usually removed from the control of individual governments. In the early, prenegotiation stage of UNCLOS III, for example,

> many governments initiated studies on a large number of the ocean-use problems, many of which required more than unilateral acts for solution. In dealing with particular problems—fisheries, the continental shelf, pollution—shipping and naval rights analysts often recommended technically sound solutions which they hoped could be achieved unilaterally, bilaterally, or regionally. They recommended going to a universal conference only if unilateral, bilateral, or regional efforts had failed, or were likely to fail, and they preferred returning to a universal forum only if the issues could be grouped into "separate packets."[74]

All this notwithstanding, the developing countries seized the time and opportunity to convene a near-universal conference. The intimation here suggests that the selection of agenda items for consideration and the type of negotiating found to be used can be of critical importance in producing a successful outcome for parties.

As already mentioned, the opinions of specially affected states should be given due regard in the negotiations. One can compare the eagerness of states to gain control over the zones off their coasts with the relatively small number of states that perceived a direct interest in Part XI of the Convention. Where the negotiations focused on food, energy, and military issues, the assembled states were able to reach a near consensus. The fact that consensus broke down over polymetallic nodules implies that multilateral negotiations have greater chances for success when the immediate national stakes are both high and broadly distributed.[75] Recognizing the ideological basis of this breakdown in consensus, resort to issue-linkage could raise the stakes so high for all parties that abandoning negotiations will be seen as producing a net loss for both North and South. The likelihood is that future environmental treaties may well have to be tied to explicit pledges about aid flows, trade, and debt in ways unlike the past. Perhaps given the recent global acceptance of free market principles exemplified in the 1994 Implementation Agreement, ideological aversion to such linkages will wane in the developed world as states in the South learn to frame their demands in liberal, rather than socialist, terms.

At least five approaches are available for pursuing commons law negotiations and each has its own strengths and deficiencies. Each approach, or combinations of them, can provide strategies for negotiating international agreements affecting the oceans, outer space, or the Antarctic. Much obviously depends on the nature of the commons agreement, the particular governments involved, and the international circumstances affecting the negotiations.

1. *Construct a framework convention, with provisions for additional protocols.* One strategy involves negotiating a framework convention with the understanding that one or more additional related protocols eventually will be attached to it. In many instances, a piecemeal approach may make agreement more likely than would a comprehensive approach to the same agenda, such as the UNCLOS III strategy on the law of the sea. By breaking the general subject down into manageable pieces, the convention-cum-protocols strategy can sidestep the negative results of issue-linkages experienced in the course of the law of the sea negotiations. The more ambitious the goals are, the more issues upon which participating governments must reach agreement. A strategy designed to augment a framework agreement allows for more gradual, deliberate piece-by-piece commons law to evolve. In this manner, governments have more time to appreciate the legal and political merits in adding new measures later to the new regime.

The initial framework convention may be lacking in specifics. Still, it can become the first step in involving a government in the negotiating process on an important issue. Subsequently, a negotiating history among states may make future negotiations on the issue area more likely. In many cases the framework convention requires governments to demonstrate serious intent to participate in subsequent protocol arrangements in order to become a party to the general agreement. Even so, separate parts may be negotiated without any specific requirement to become party to all of them.[76]

The open-ended nature of this approach permits negotiators more flexibility in taking future developments into account. Such a strategy might have helped overcome the difficulties encountered with the seabed mining provisions of the 1982 Convention. While the Convention as a whole deals with contemporary marine activities, the seabed regime focuses with great specificity on future contingent activities. In such a case, a more suitable approach might have been to establish a framework regime. Later when serious interest in resource development surfaces, an international regulatory system could then be set up to manage any anticipated development. One example of an agreement that did use the framework convention-plus-protocols approach was the 1976 United Nations Environment Programme's (UNEP's) Regional Seas Convention, which has been followed in subsequent UNEP regional seas conventions.[77] Similarly the 1985 Vienna Convention for the Protection of the Ozone Layer set out a general framework for monitoring, exchanging information, and facilitating scientific research.[78] It was succeeded by the 1987 Montreal Protocol, a more detailed document that established a sophisticated regime for controlling chemical depletion of the ozone layer.[79]

2. *Encourage and improve international coordination of national plans.* International coordination of national conservation plans allows governments to retain a certain functional sovereignty over global commons environmental protection. Unlike the above-mentioned strategy of negotiating a framework convention plus protocols, under this coordination approach future protocols are not anticipated when the framework agreement is established. Instead states merely agree to establish their national plans within a structure of international oversight, perhaps complemented with an international monitoring component. This approach could be especially useful when governments agree on the need to deal with an environmental problem, but cannot reach agreement even on a vague framework convention calling for future protocols, or on who should bear how much of which burdens. Examples of such an approach being utilized include the 1992 Framework Convention on Climate Change[80] and the 1992 Convention on Biological Diversity.[81]

One element in the debate over the preservation of global commons areas and their resources turns on the issue of whether governments are more likely to adopt forward-looking, conscientious policies in zones that are formally recognized as falling under their exclusive jurisdiction, as opposed to the policies they adopt toward the commons areas. The establishment of the system of EEZs put under national jurisdiction and control the environmental management of a substantial portion of what in large part formerly had been high seas areas, as well as 90% of the world's fisheries. Depletion of fish stocks has continued apace, however, even though international agreements outside the 1982 Convention have been negotiated to curb unsustainable harvesting of stocks. Continued overfishing suggests that state governments have difficulty controlling the actions of their own nationals. It also indicates that such a loose arrangement that allows governments to set their own quotas (within "reasonable" limits or similar such language) may be too weak. While it is necessary to be cognizant of state sovereignty, if states are unwilling to take on the responsibility for implementing needed conservation measures, the commons environment ultimately will suffer. This realization suggests that incentives, perhaps through issue-linkages, might be sought to make reluctant states more amenable to agreeing to and upholding a more binding convention.

3. *Pursue regional arrangements.* Regional arrangements have been established to deal with many environmental issue areas, including fishing on the high seas,[82] outer space law,[83] and conservation in the Antarctic.[84] A regional approach could help to avoid cultural and ideological conflicts that have emerged in the past when governments at different levels of economic development have met for discussions in an international forum. Regionalism might improve the chances for achieving a successful outcome to the negotiations. On the other hand, because levels of economic

development of states within a geographical region tend to be similar, a regional approach to negotiating multilateral agreements also could solidify the schism of the world into haves and have-nots.

Resort to a regional arrangement might be more viable in situations where a global convention is perceived as being too unwieldy or too time-consuming to negotiate. In such a situation, "[r]ather than wait for universal consensus, groups of countries with analogous interests and capabilities may wish to pursue agreements among themselves,"[85] perhaps but not necessarily under the aegis of a framework treaty. Active involvement of the United States in the ocean law negotiations began in a regional setting, under the umbrella of the Organization of American States (OAS) in the 1940s. The United States was badly outnumbered in the OAS forum, however, and so shifted negotiations to the United Nations framework.[86] This strategy eventuated into the 1958 and 1960 Geneva Conferences on the Law of the Sea, then to the UNCLOS III experience, and ultimately the negotiations that led to promulgation of the 1994 Implementation Agreement.

4. *Pursue a strictly unilateral approach.* In certain circumstances, states might be better off if they opt to pursue an independent course of action rather than adhere to a wider convention or international regime. A government considering unilateral action may be in a situation where there is no international agreement to which it can become a party.[87] If there is in fact no global regime in a certain issue area, a unilateral approach might be the only option for a government that feels the need to take some constructive action and is unable to garner support for an international treaty on that issue. Paradoxically, a state can be punished for pursuing a unilateral approach to environmental protection if its action is seen to interfere with trade practices under the General Agreement on Tariffs and Trade (GATT).[88] Moreover even if the provisions of GATT are not at issue, a government pursuing an independent policy of environmental protection may find itself at a distinct economic disadvantage relative to less "green" states. A government also may be concerned that a subsequent international agreement will require further action without giving the proactive state credit for its previous environmental accomplishments.[89] Clearly, there are both costs and benefits for a government considering unilateral action when no international agreement exists for dealing with the environmental problem in question.

A government confronts different considerations when an international regime is already in place. A precedent now exists demonstrating the advantages of unilateral action in the UNCLOS III negotiations. The United States was able to reap the current benefits of its EEZ and continental shelf resources while avoiding the costs of acceding to Part XI of the Convention. In retrospect, this strategy appears successful since the 1994 Implementation Agreement substantially revised the offensive portions of the 1982 text to be more compatible with a free market economic philosophy. As one authority has tersely posited, "[R]ejection of the Convention by the United States reflects a belief that unilateralism is a viable policy alternative when backed by military force, the *res communis* principle and budget deficits notwithstanding."[90] The United States was fortunate and seems to have emerged relatively unharmed from its solo ocean law course throughout the past decade. It is not unreasonable to conclude, however, that pursuing a unilateral approach in place of participating in a complex international regime such as the Convention might well carry high costs, as many observers had predicted the United States would discover soon after its refusal to sign the agreement in 1982.[91]

While it might be possible for a government to establish bilateral and multilateral arrangements that obtain benefits or rights analogous to those contained in a broader agreement, without paying the legal costs of being obligated to that general agreement, certain political advantages and economic benefits may be lost in exchange for those rights. Moreover, the government acting unilaterally may encounter contrary states who are disinclined to grant such rights or who insist on asserting their own interpretation of that international law.[92] A government considering such a unilateral approach would have to conduct its own cost-benefit analysis to determine if the costs involved in participating in the regime truly outweigh the costs it would incur by taking a solo national approach. The fact remains that for any government, be it a maritime power or a geographically disadvantaged state, the fundamental problems of ocean law essentially are global, not national or regional. Sooner or later, law of the sea questions will have to be resolved on a global basis if maritime commerce and use of ocean resources are to proceed in a peaceful, stable international climate.

5. *Pursue a parliamentary diplomacy approach.* The last realization leads back to the negotiating strategy pursued at UNCLOS III, namely what Friedheim termed "parliamentary diplomacy."[93] Of course, there are certain problems of international relations that cannot be effectively resolved absent securing universal or near-universal consent among states. Although many environmental problems can be addressed on a regional or even a unilateral basis, the world's commons areas present a special case and often require a more comprehensive and global strategy.

A parliamentary diplomacy approach works by consensus based on the sovereign equality of all states. It also assumes that outcomes can be bargained, which will increase the benefits for all participants; that is, outcomes of parliamentary diplomacy are not zero-sum. To increase their bargaining power, states with common interests often join together and create the opportunity for shaping "complementary (overlapping) and contradictory interests (cross-cutting cleavages)."[94] Given the complexity associated with large-scale, multilateral conferences that adopt a universal approach, parliamentary diplomacy frequently involves the use of a package deal—a trade-off strategy that simplifies the process of achieving consensus on key issues without adopting a majority-rule procedure,[95] as seen in UNCLOS

III. Consensus permits obtaining agreement without having to vote on an issue, an act that inevitably casts a formal split between parties in a negotiation.

The high issue-density of establishing a comprehensive maritime regime revealed to governments that a universal approach was necessary to avoid uneven participation in the ocean regime as evinced after the first two UNCLOS meetings. The failure to reach universal agreement on the final text of the 1982 Convention strongly suggested that a convention on global climate change would be better pursued by using another approach. The parliamentary diplomacy approach appears most successful when governments are formulating new law, since an extensive body of existing law frequently can complicate the process of codifying norms in one document.

Conclusion

In the absence of a universally accepted regime for the oceans, governments are forced to conclude limited bilateral and multilateral agreements or to act unilaterally to achieve their national interests. For example, in lieu of the protections offered by the Convention, the United States adopted the Freedom of Navigation Program in 1979 to globally protect navigational rights. The program

> combines diplomatic action and the operational assertion of navigational rights. [It] emphasizes the use of naval exercises to discourage state claims inconsistent with customary international law, as reflected in the Convention, and to demonstrate the U.S. resolve to protect navigational freedoms proclaimed in that agreement.[96]

Given what is currently known about the costs and benefits accrued from seabed mining, pursuing such a unilateral strategy now seems to involve substantial military, financial, and political costs in return for minimal economic benefits. Further in an era of diminishing naval strength, "the United States is confronted with increasingly diverse claims to sovereignty over ocean areas by coastal and island states, claims that are inconsistent with the terms of the 1982 Convention."[97] These claims are asserted by a diverse collection of states and pertain to a wide assortment of maritime issues, affecting all regimes of the oceans.

It remains arguable whether the current proliferation of unilateral claims is comparable to the cacophony of claims asserted during the period between the World War II and the 1960s. In this regard the 1982 Convention has stabilized ocean law, even without universal ratification. It also is probably true that had the Convention been more widely accepted in 1982, the costs confronting the United States today in protecting its freedom of navigation would be much lower. The United States chose to reject the Convention out of a belief that the most important provisions already were customary law. This assumption is being challenged today.

As a maritime superpower, the United States, and all states for that matter, benefit most when ocean law is stable and regular. Widespread ratification of the 1982 Convention undoubtedly will increase order and predictability by facilitating international adaptability to new circumstances, fostering accommodation of interests among states, narrowing the scope of maritime disputes to more manageable proportions, and providing the ways and means to resolve these disputes. If not binding on all states, the influence of the 1982 Convention will be gravely weakened and the U.S. interest in order and stability will be undermined. The Convention is a framework agreement for ocean law. If governments are unwilling to participate even within that general framework, the prospects for cooperation on narrow issue-areas would seem to be diminished.

The basic question that must be addressed is whether a global commons regime can be negotiated, accepted by all or most states, and then actually be made to fulfill its agenda. There are tools that can be used to facilitate negotiation of such an agreement, such as the resort to linking and subtracting issues. The fact that commons areas are best governed by a regime in which all states participate is obvious. It is equally true that environmental issues are best dealt with systemically, by recognizing the complexity and interdependence of the web of life in a particular ecosystem. The dilemma turns on reconciling the need for universal participation by states with conflicting interests. It also comes down to satisfactorily resolving the vast array of issues that must be considered in concluding such a regime.

While each case obviously is different, a spate of environmental treaties has been promulgated in recent years that reveals a clear trend. Transboundary air pollution, acid rain, biological diversity, transboundary movement and disposal of hazardous wastes, global warming, protection of wetlands, conservation of species, ozone depletion, and many other environmental issues have been addressed through special international agreements. A progressive attitude has evolved stemming from a steep learning curve in the international community, which seems to suggest great promise for future negotiations on global commons issues. If governments can incorporate the lessons of UNCLOS III into their negotiating strategies, and then prudently employ those strategies to keep international law genuinely applicable to managing the commons areas, that optimism may prove to be warranted.

Notes

1. *The Law of the Sea: United Nations Convention on the Law of the Sea with Index and Final Act of the Third United Nations Conference on the Law of the*

Sea (New York: United Nations, 1983), [hereinafter cited as 1982 Convention]

2. Robert L. Friedheim, *Negotiating the New Ocean Regime* (Columbia, SC: University of South Carolina Press, 1993), 5.

3. G.A. Res. 48/263 (July 28, 1994), Agreement relating to the Implementation of Part XI of the United Nations Convention on the Law of the Sea of 10 December 1982.

4. The meaning of "appropriate" in this context simply refers to the likelihood of a successful outcome (i.e., the promulgation of a widely ratified international legal instrument).

5. See Garrett Hardin, "The Tragedy of the Commons," *Science* 162 (Dec. 13. 1968), 1243-1248.

6. Anne Swardson, "Canada, EU Reach Agreement Aimed at Ending Fishing War," *Washington Post,* April 16, 1995, A21.

7. Friedheim, *Negotiating the New Ocean Regime,* 14.

8. United Nations Department of Public Information, *A Quiet Revolution: United Nations Convention on the Law of the Sea* (New York: United Nations, 1984). 34.

9. See U.N. GAOR 22d Sess., U.N. Doc. A/6695 (17 August 1967). Pardo suggested that the General Assembly should internationalize the seabed beyond a narrow territorial sea by either reinterpreting or amending the 1958 Continental Shelf Convention, and that this international seabed should be placed under international management.

10. Robert L. Bledsoe and Boleslaw A. Boczek, *The International Law Dictionary* (Santa Barbara: ABC-Clio, 1987), 189.

11. See Arvid Pardo, "Who Will Control the Seabed?," *Foreign Affairs* 47 (1968), 123-137.

12. Friedheim, *Negotiating the New Ocean Regime,* 17.

13. See, e.g., United Nations. *A Quiet Revolution,* 4, 6.

14. Boleslaw Boczek, "Ideology and the New Law of the Sea," *Boston College International and Comparative Law Review* 7 (1984), 10.

15. U.N.G.A. Res. 2j74 (XXV), text reprinted in 9 I.L.M. 419-423 (1970).

16. Dennis W. Arrow, "Seabeds, Sovereignty, and Objective Regimes," *Fordham International Law Journal* 7 (1984). 169. 179.

17. Markus Schmidt, *Common Heritage or Common Burden?* (Oxford: Clarendon Press, 1989). 43.

18. See Andrew Hurrell and Benedict Kingsbury, "Introduction," in Andrew Hurrell and Benedict Kingsbury, eds., *The International Politics of the Environment* (Oxford: Clarendon Press, 1992), 37.

19. "Declaration Incorporating the 'Gentleman's Agreement' made by the President and Endorsed by the Conference at its 19th Meeting on 27 June 1974," in Rules of Procedure, U.N. Doc. A/Conf. 62/36 (July 2. 1974), Appendix.

20. Friedheim, *Negotiating the New Ocean Regime,* 33.

21. See Lawrence Susskind, *Environmental Diplomacy: Negotiating More Effective International Agreements* (New York: Oxford University Press. 1993), 87.

22. Schmidt, *Common Heritage or Common Burden?,* 29.

23. For example, Wilfred Beckerman argued that "according to the latest scientific consensus, such as it is, the damage done by the predicted climate change will be nothing like as great as is widely believed and certainly not the inevitable global catastrophe scenario hawked around. . . . There is plenty of time to think and to weigh up the costs and benefits of alternative courses of action." "Global Warming and International Action: An Economic Perspective," in Hurrell and

Kingsbury, *International Politics of the Environment,* 288. Compare another article from the same volume: "If it is important to prevent climate change, it is important to begin now." The article offered several approaches to negotiating an agreement and suggests essential elements to the eventual treaty. Elliot L. Richardson, "Climate Change: Problems of Law-Making," in ibid., 170.

24. United Nations, *A Quiet Revolution,* 3.

25. See 1982 LOS Convention, arts. 192-237.

26. 1982 Convention, art. 194(1), for example, illustrates the point.   While asserting that states "shall" take action, the passage is quite general in describing what states "shall" actually do, leaving the specific obligations of states wide open to interpretation.

27. For example, 1982 Convention, arts. 207-212.

28. For example, 1982 Convention, arts. 197, 200, 202. 207-212.

29. Friedheim, *Negotiating the New Ocean Regime,* 181.

30. Ibid., 183.

31. Ibid., 39.

32. Joseph S. Nye, Jr.. "Political Lessons of the New Law of the Sea Regime," in Bernard H. Oxman, et al., eds., *Law of the Sea: U.S. Policy Dilemma* (San Francisco: Institute for Contemporary Studies, 1983), 115.

33. Schmidt, *Common Heritage or Common Burden?,* 259.

34. The four votes in opposition were cast by Israel, Turkey, the United States, and Venezuela. The abstentions came from Western European states and the Soviet Eastern European bloc.

35. Schmidt, *Common Heritage or Common Burden?,* 254.

36. 1982 Convention, art. 137.

37. James B. Morell, *The Law of the Sea: An Historical Analysis of the 1981 Treaty and Its Rejection by the United Stares* (Jefferson, N.C.: McFarland & Co.. Inc., 1992). 175.

38. Stephen Vasciannie, "Part XI of the Law of the Sea Convention and Third States: Some General Observations," *Cambridge Law Journal* 48 (March 1989), 1, 97.

39. Arrow, "Seabeds, Sovereignty, and Objective Regimes," 215.

40. Ibid., 226.

41. Vienna Convention on the Law of Treaties, May 23, 1969, U.N. Doc. A/CONF.39/27, reprinted in 8 I.L.M. (1969). See Morell, *The Law of the Sea Convention,* 183.

42. Morell, The Law of the Sea Convention, 185.

43. Ibid., 189.

44. As Bernard Oxman, a former vice-chairman of the U.S. Delegation to the Conference, stated in 1983, "Except perhaps for the provisions on deep seabed mining and the settlement of disputes, the stipulations of the convention are already regarded by some government and private experts as generally authoritative statements of existing customary international law applicable to all states." Bernard Oxman, "Summary of the Law of the Sea Convention," in Oxman, et al., *Law of the Sea,* 148.

45. See Vasciannie, "Part XI of the LOS Convention," 94 (at note 43) for examples.

46. Quoted in James K. Sebenius, *Negotiating The Law of the Sea* (Cambridge: Harvard University Press. 1984), 93.

47. Vasciannie, "Part XI of the LOS Convention," 95. See also Schmidt, *Common Heritage or Common Burden?,* 12.

48. *Case Concerning the Continental Shelf (Tunisia/Libyan Arab Jamahiriya)*

1982, reprinted in 21 I.L.M. 225 (1982) and *Case Concerning The Continental Shelf (Libyan Arab Jamahiriya v. Malta),* 1985, reprinted in 24 I.L.M. 1189 (1985).

49. Vienna Convention. art. 34.

50. See Christopher C. Joyner. "The United States and the New Law of the Sea," *Ocean Development and International Law,* 27 (1996), pp. 41-58.

51. Bernard Oxman, "The Two Conferences," in Oxman, et al., *Law of the Sea,* 140.

52. Ibid., 134.

53. Ken Booth, Law, Force and Diplomacy at Sea (London: George Allen & Unwin, 1985). 29.

54. See "Statement by Expert Panel: Deep Seabed Mining and the 1982 Convention on the Law of the Sea," *American Journal of International Law* 82 (1988), 367, which concluded that, *"[T]he United States has limited economic and security interests in deep seabed mining.* But the United States shares the compelling interests in all states in achieving universal agreement on a comprehensive law of the sea, which requires agreement also on a regime for the deep seabed." (authors' emphasis). Compare with Sebenius, *Negotiating the Law of the Sea,* 82, who observed that, "[A]fter noting that 'those extensive parts dealing with navigation and overnight and most other parts of the convention are consistent with United States interests,' President Reagan said that he rejected the treaty because of his 'deep conviction that the United States cannot support a deep seabed mining regime with such major problems.'"

55. Statement of Principles for a Global Consensus on the Management, Conservation, and Sustainable Development of All Types of Forests adopted at the United Nations Conference on Environment and Development Rio de Janeiro, June 13, 1992.

56. Obviously. this is explained by the fact that the largest United Nations contributors—the United States, Western Europe, and Japan—fell into this category. Note, however, that both Japan and France signed the Convention within a short period of time, so they cannot properly be said to have been excluded.

57. Susskind, *Environmental Diplomacy,* 87.

58. Richardson, "Climate Change," 176.

59. Susskind, *Environmental Diplomacy,* 89.

60. Ibid.

61. Richardson, "Climate Change," 176.

62. Susskind, *Environmental Diplomacy,* 98.

63. Ibid., 93.

64. Morell, *The Law of the Sea,* 83.

65. Friedheim, *Negotiating the New Ocean Regime,* 33.

66. Ann Hollick, *U.S. Foreign Policy and the Law of the Sea* (Princeton, NJ: Princeton University Press, 1981). 378.

67. Sebenius, *Negotiating the Law of the Sea,* 83.

68. See Jonathan I. Charney, "The United States and the Revision of the 1982 Convention on the Law of the Sea," *Ocean Development and International Law* 23 (1992), 286.

69. Susskind, *Environmental Diplomacy,* 94 (emphasis in original).

70. John Rawls, *A Theory of Justice* (Cambridge, MA: Harvard University Press, 1971), 378.

71. See, e.g., Charles Beitz, *Political Theory and International Relations* (Princeton, NJ: Princeton University Press, 1979).

72. Obviously, scholars and practitioners who view international politics through a classical realist or a neorealist lens would dispute the basic point that nor-

mative considerations should play a role in formulating so-called national interest. They would not agree that a "just" (i.e., incorporating notions of equity such as we have mentioned) global arrangement ipso facto, must be in any given state's long-term best interests. For discussion of these considerations, see Christopher C. Joyner, "International Law and Foreign Policy: Rethinking the Academic Relevance of Normative Reality," paper prepared for the Conference on International Law and Australian Foreign Policy, University of New South Wales Australian Defense Force Academy, Canberra, July 10, 1995.

73. Gareth Porter and Janet W. Brown, *Global Environmental Politics* (Boulder, CO: Westview Press, 1991), 145-152.

74. Friedheim, *Negotiating the New Ocean Regime,* 29.

75. Oxman, "Summary of the LOS Convention," 139.

76. Edith Brown Weiss, "International Environmental Law: Contemporary Issues and the Emergence of a New World Order," *Georgetown Law Journal* 81 (1993), 675, 688.

77. See Barcelona Convention for the Protection of the Mediterranean Sea Against Pollution, February 16, 1976, in 15 I.L.M. 290; Barcelona Protocol Concerning Cooperation in Combatting Pollution of the Mediterranean Sea by Oil and Other Harmful Substances in Cases of Emergency, February 16, 1976, in 15 I.L.M. 306; Barcelona Protocol for the Prevention of Pollution of the Mediterranean Sea by Dumping from Ships and Aircraft, February 16. 1976, in 15 I.L.M. 300.

78. Convention for the Protection of the Ozone Layer. March 22, 1985, in 26 I.L.M. 1529 (entered into force September 22, 1988).

79. Montreal Protocol on Substances that Deplete the Ozone Layer. September 16, 1987, 26 I.L.M. 1550 (entered into force January 1, 1989).

80. Framework Convention on Climate Change, opened for signature June 4, 1992, 31 I.L.M. 849 (1992).

81. Convention on Biological Diversity, opened for signature June 5, 1992, 31 I.L.M. 818 (1992).

82. For example, the 1982 Convention for the Conservation of Salmon in the North Atlantic, done at Reykjavik March 2, 1982, entered into force October 1, 1983, T.I.A.S. No. 10789. The 1966 International Convention for the Conservation of Atlantic Tunas established regional commissions to coordinate state activities. See International Convention for the Conservation of Atlantic Tunas, done May 14, 1966, 20 U.S.T. 2887, T.I.A.S. No. 6767, 673 U.N.T.S. 63.

83. For example, the Convention of 1976 for the Establishment of a European Space Agency, adopted by several states in Western Europe, and the Agreement of 1976 on Cooperating in the Exploration and Use of Outer Space for Peaceful Purposes, adopted by nine communist states.

84. See Christopher C. Joyner, "Fragile Ecosystems: Preclusive Restoration in the Antarctic," *Natural Resources Journal* 34 (Fall 1994), 879-904.

85. Richardson, "Climate Change," 178.

86. Hollick, *U.S. Foreign Policy and the Law of the Sea,* 377.

87. See, e.g., Peter M. Haas, "Protecting the Baltic and North Seas," in Peter M. Haas, Robert O. Keohane, and Marc A. Levy, eds., *Institutions for the Earth: Sources of Effective International Environmental Protection* (Cambridge, MA: Massachusetts Institute of Technology Press, 1994), 134-141 (discussion of leader and laggard states).

88. 61 Stat. Part 5, A12, 5j U.N.T.S. 187, T.I.A.S. No. 1700. For instance, in 1991 a GATT panel found against the United States for its imposition of trade restrictions (under the U.S. Marine Mammal Protection Act of 1972 [86 Stat. 1027 (1972), as amended by 104 Stat. 4467 (1990) and codified at 16 U.S.C. 1361 ff]

against Mexico for that country's continued use of purse-seine nets to catch tuna. and in the process taking incidental catches of dolphins. See "General Agreement on Tariffs and Trade: Dispute Settlement Panel Report on United States Restrictions on Imports of Tuna," 30 I.L.M. 1594 (1991).

89. Lawrence Susskind and Connie Ozawa. "Negotiating More Effective International Environmental Agreements," in Hurrell and Kingsbury, *International Politics of the Environment,* 162.

90. Morell, *The Law of the Sea,* 206. It is not clear that this belief in "right through might" was as uniform as Morell suggests. See, e.g., Schmidt *Common Heritage or Common Burden?,* 266, who notes the Department of Defense's recognition that a unilateral policy based on force (i.e., that "might makes right") may carry diplomatic and political costs.

91. For example, Sebenius in his *Negotiating the Law of the Sea,* 93-94, opines that "It is . . conceivable that certain states would seize on U.S. repudiation of the convention as an excuse to impose selectively special costs, taxes, requirements, or regulations on vessels flying the U.S. flag. . . . Beyond outright discrimination, however, lies the prospect that without its support for the whole treaty, the very consensus [on navigational freedoms] the United States is relying on will erode."

92. Kathryn Surace-Smith, "Note: United States Activity Outside of the Law of the Sea Convention," *Columbia Law Review* 84 (1984), 1032, 1058.

93. Friedheim, *Negotiating the New Ocean Regime,* 5.

94. Ibid., 47.

95. Ibid., 73–74.

96. George Galdorisi, "The United Nations Convention on the Law of the Sea: A National Security Perspective," *American Journal of International Law* 89 (1995), 208, 210.

97. Ibid., 211.

22

Tensions in the Development of the Law of Outer Space

Katherine Gorove and Elena Kamenetskaya

The laws pertaining to activities in outer space developed rapidly during the more than two decades following the first satellite launching and led to the emergence of a new field of international law—international space law. Although the development of new laws governing outer space activities has tapered off in the 1980s and early 1990s, the conduct of space activities has still resulted in the accumulation of a vast amount of space law.

Several trends in the pursuit of these activities have greatly affected the law and brought about long-standing debates over what to regulate and how to regulate. Clearly, the most important of these trends is the increase in commercial opportunities arising from outer space activities, which has created a burgeoning desire in private entities to engage in space-related activities and resulted in a larger number of space ventures. Yet because of the expense of pursuing activities in outer space which may or may not have commercial results, states have had to pool their financial and technical resources to ensure that their expenditures on space activities do not vastly outweigh the benefits of space activities, at least as perceived by the public. Because of the need to justify the expense of space activities, more countries are expressing an interest in carrying out activities, such as participating in manned space flights, to pique the interest of the public and keep their support.

The possibility of commercial uses for outer space activities has led to an increase in national space laws as states have had to legislate domestically either to carry out international treaty obligations or to oversee private parties' activities in outer space. This trend has also evoked demands from countries without space capabilities for measures of "equity," which have been particularly evident in the debate over the meaning of the concept of "common heritage of mankind," the demands for allocation of positions in the geostationary orbit and the use of radio frequencies, the protection of the space environment for future spacefarers, and the insistence on formalizing guidelines for international cooperation. In addition, debate over whether air and outer space should be delimited has intensified, with some states wanting assurances of sovereignty over their air space. These trends and tensions, among others, will demand substantive international dialogue and cooperation.

Although some states may favor postponing such cooperation, the advent of manned space flights and the increase in orbital debris, along with other problems arising from space activities, necessitate cooperation. What follows is a discussion of each of these areas of legal tension, a discussion of the need for international cooperation, and, finally, a discussion of possible long-term cooperative mechanisms which could facilitate dialogue between states. A particular effort will be made to show the areas in which U.S. and Russian views have changed through the years and how their positions have shifted vis-à-vis developing countries.

Legal Regulation on International and National Levels

International law rapidly developed to meet the challenge of the space age.[1] The fact that all states could be or were affected by space activities and that the spacefaring powers occasionally needed the tacit consent of third-party states to conduct their activities (for example, acquiescence of neighboring states whose air space was traversed on missions to and from outer space) meant that legal regulation was and is essential. Consequently, international space law now includes a plethora of different multilateral and bilateral agreements.[2] From the outset of space exploration, legal regulation of space activities was of an interstate character, because for years only states, not private entities, participated in space exploration. The reason for this was two-fold: first was the high cost of space exploration, resulting in the need to combine national efforts on the state level; and second was a close interdependence of space exploration with the interests of defense, economics, and politics.

This initial "state" orientation of space activities is clearly reflected in the principal international treaty pertaining to the exploration and use of outer space, the Treaty on Principles Governing the Activities of States in the Exploration and Use of Outer Space, Including the Moon and Other Celestial Bodies (Outer Space Treaty). Its Article VI places international responsibility for national activity in space on states, regardless of the nature of the entity that carries out the activity.

Some authors contend that this article limits the realm of subjects of space activity to the states themselves.[3] In fact, Soviet doctrine had generally espoused that doctrine. Clearly, however, the more pragmatic view in line with the wording of the provision, as well as with state practice, is that Article VI merely requires the state to ensure that activities of private entities comply with international law. The current Russian position has shifted dramatically on this issue in recent years, particularly in light of its ability to offer commercial launch services.

Unfortunately, however, only in the last ten years have scholars begun to study the interrelationship between states' internal regulation of private participation in space activities and the corresponding international regulation or guidelines for such activities.

During the 1980s, states' interest in national regulation became acute. During that time, the increased opportunities for commercial space ventures resulted in the participation by a large number of private firms and other nongovernmental entities. These factors and others necessitated national regulation of the participation of "private persons" in space exploration, with respect to their rights and obligations and their relationship to the state. In order to assure compliance with Article VI, states provided guidelines and issued licenses to private corporations to engage in various space activities.

Nevertheless, far less national legislation exists than interstate regulation, although domestic space legislation has steadily increased as international space law has developed. Several countries, most notably the United States, France, the United Kingdom, and Sweden, have adopted national laws and regulations governing space activities. In a number of other states—for example, Brazil—norms guiding space activities are included in legislation on telecommunications or in other specialized legislation. Other states have adopted provisions on the competence and structure of their national space agency or council (the majority of state members of the European Space Agency, some states in central and eastern Europe, and others).

The United States has quite a panoply of legislation pertaining to space activities—more so than other countries. The first landmark U.S. Space legislation was the National Aeronautics and Space Act (NASAct) of 1958. Other laws of major importance are the Communications Satellite Act of 1962, the Land Remote-Sensing Commercialization Act of 1984, and the Commercial Space Launch Act with amendments. In fact, some states within the United States have also developed legislation, effective only within that state, to encourage certain types of space activities.

In addition to the congressionally enacted laws, numerous departments and agencies within the U.S. federal government have been authorized to issue regulations pertaining to space activities. The President can also issue presidential executive orders, pronouncements, policy statements, directives, and determinations. Not only are there laws and regulations relating to space activities, but a large number of administrative proceedings coming before federal agencies have resulted in decisions with respect to policies, standards, licensing, and procedures having an impact on space activities. A small body of cases within federal or state courts has slowly developed; some were brought by appeal from an agency ruling, particularly the Federal Communications Commission; others originated directly in state or federal courts on other issues of space law, such as liability for damage from explosions or loss of satellites.

Regrettably, the huge space program of the Soviet Union had no specific non-classified legislation applying to space activities. Instead, it had a multitude of rules and regulations adopted by various ministries and agencies which were inaccessible to the public. For years, lawyers in the Soviet Union advocated the passage of a unified body or code of space law. Only in 1991 was such a draft formulated, sent to one of the committees of the Supreme Soviet for further study, and published in the main legal journal of the country.

With the break-up of the Soviet Union, the appearance of a number of sovereign states, and the establishment of the Commonwealth of Independent States, the situation is changing. Now different international treaties must provide the framework for Commonwealth states interested in pursuing those joint space activities which seem economically, scientifically, technically, and politically reasonable. On December 30, 1991, nine of the eleven members of the CIS concluded the first of these treaties (the "Minsk Agreement"). In July 1992, the Ukraine also joined the Minsk Agreement. This is the first legally binding document pertaining to space exploration for most of the former Soviet republics. The Agreement emphasizes the significance of space science and technology for the participants' development and the need of combining efforts to ensure effective space research and exploration serving the interests of science, the national economies, and defense. Basically the Agreement aims to regulate joint efforts of parties in the exploration and use of outer space, with an interstate space council to oversee joint activities. With respect to interstate programs with military and dual purpose (military and civilian) space facilities, the joint strategic armed forces would be in charge. The Minsk Agreement also regulates the utilization of space facilities, provides for financing, and solves a number of other questions of common interest to those CIS states choosing to participate.

In addition to operating within the framework of the Minsk Agreement, it is logically foreseeable that the former republics of the Soviet Union, particularly Russia, would develop their own domestic space legislation. In Russia, for example, it was recently recognized at the highest political level that having national regulation of space activities was a necessity; and the first draft of a Russian space act is thus being formulated. The current version of the draft determines the goals and guiding principles for the conduct of space activities, the structure and competence of supervisory organs,[4] the financing of space activities, the legal status of space objects and astronauts, and the allocation of liability and responsibility for the exploration and use of outer space. As with the NASACT, the Russian draft space act could form the basis of further and more specific domestic space legislation.

What remains to be seen, however, is the effect of the increase in domestic space legislation around the world. This increase could in turn lead to codification of norms or practices in international treaties for other nations to follow when developing their internal standards. In the alternative, diversity among nations in their treatment of space-related activities could prevail. There may be advantages and disadvantages to harmonization of municipal laws. For example, carriers are often favored unduly when nations negotiate uniform conditions of carriage. With competition in the provision of launchers, customers may benefit from individual negotiation of the allocation of risk, rather than an allocation set by treaty. On the other hand, harmonization of municipal laws protecting intellectual property developed in outer space could be crucial to encouraging international research efforts, as well as efforts to combat problems of space debris and questions of liability. Nevertheless, such international standardization might be difficult, since states in the forefront of technical developments may fear inhibiting future developments.

In the initial period following efforts by the Soviet Union and the United States toward developing principles of space law—embodied in the Outer Space Treaty, the Rescue and Return Agreement, the Liability Convention, and the Registration Convention within a relatively short period of time—the United States showed some reluctance to codifying further and more specific principles of space law. Instead, the U.S. preferred to wait until the need for codification was demonstrated. In contrast, the Soviet Union supported further specificity in the law of outer space, particularly with respect to delimitation between air and outer space. Yet, although the Soviet Union and the U.S. disagreed with one another over the necessity and substance of further law, neither wanting to hinder space exploration, both disagreed with the position of developing countries who were in favor of codifying numerous areas of space law in a manner beneficial to developing nations. Consequently, the two countries were prompted to side together in the context of developed versus developing country debates, in which the latter countries persistently called for the establishment of an international regulatory framework to govern space utilization. With Russia's increasing interest in commercial possibilities in the space area, the two countries' positions should become more closely intertwined.

The Drive for Equity

The primary reason for the insistence by developing countries on an international regulatory framework has been their desire to share in any benefits that may accrue from space activities. Their claims in the space law field were a manifestation of their general demand for a New International Economic Order (NIEO). More specifically, the developing countries wanted some type of "equity," as reflected in their drive for (1) acceptance of the "common heritage of mankind" concept or at least a sharing in the benefits received from space activities; (2) access to the geostationary orbit; (3) intergenerational equity, or environmental protection for outer space so as to prevent cluttering of outer space with debris; and (4) formalizing or institutionalizing international cooperation. The discussion of the first three positions follows; the fourth issue will be addressed in the last section of this chapter.

Common Heritage of Mankind

The Outer Space Treaty contains several provisions relevant to mankind. First and foremost, Article I, paragraph 1, provides that the exploration and use of outer space, including the moon and other celestial bodies, "shall be carried out for the benefit and the interests of all countries, irrespective of their degree of economic or scientific development and shall be the *province of all mankind*" (emphasis added). This duty is followed by Article I, paragraph 2, which provides that outer space and celestial bodies "shall be free for exploration and use by all states without discrimination of any kind, on a basis of equality" and that "there shall be free access to all areas of celestial bodies." The Article also provides for the "freedom of scientific investigation." At the same time, Article II prohibits "national appropriation" of outer space, including the moon and other celestial bodies, "by claim of sovereignty, by means of use or occupation or by any other means."

The Moon Agreement, which is in force for only a small number of nations and none of the space powers, goes beyond the Outer Space Treaty in providing a characterization of the legal status of the natural resources of the moon and other celestial bodies. Unlike the Outer Space Treaty which makes no mention of natural resources, the Moon Agreement in Article 11 specifically provides that such resources are the "common heritage of mankind." While the concept of "common heritage of mankind" may be compared to the phrase "province of all mankind" used in the Outer Space Treaty, the common heritage concept is given much more substance by the Agreement. It obligates the parties to establish an international regime to govern the exploitation of natural resources as such exploitation is about to become feasible. As a complementary obligation, the Agreement requires the parties to inform the Secretary-General of the United Nations, as well as the public and the international scientific community, to the greatest extent feasible and practicable of any natural resources they may discover on the moon. In addition, the Agreement repeats the non-appropriation clause of the Outer Space Treaty.

Some states, mostly developing countries, claim that the provisions in the Outer Space Treaty, when coupled with these provisions of the Moon Agreement, have acknowledged that under customary international law the whole of outer space is to be regarded as the common heritage of mankind.[5] Accordingly, the developing countries call for a framework which would: (1) prevent developed countries from unilaterally exploiting common resources in situations where developing countries do not yet have the necessary technology or financing; (2) guarantee the direct participation of lesser developed countries ("LDCs") in international management and exploitation of these resources; and (3) distribute the subsequent benefits primarily to aid developing countries.[6] In sum, they advocate for outer space and other areas outside the territory of any one state a framework similar to that of the law of the sea, with its alleged internationalization of the exploitation of seabed resources and with a regulated system for participation and benefit-sharing by LDCs.

In contrast, developed states, first of all, refuse to acknowledge that the common heritage of mankind concept is customary international law. They also point out that the Moon Agreement has not been adopted by any of the major spacefaring nations[7] and that the treaties to which most nations are parties do not include this phrase. Therefore, they conclude that the framework sought by the LDCs is not required by space law. They also note the observations of numerous scholars that the notion of common heritage of mankind has been reflected in different concrete ways in various fields of law. For example, no temporary moratorium exists on the exploitation of space resources, as has been argued to exist for seabed resources. Unlike in the law of the sea, there is no broadly accepted treaty in the space law field creating an international authority to oversee exploitation of resources. The notion has also been treated in a different manner under the Antarctic system.

Both the United States and the Soviet Union have traditionally supported the view associated with developed states, although in the early stages of the drafting of the Moon Agreement, the United States accepted the "common heritage of mankind" language proposed by the developing countries, while the Soviet Union opposed the language. By the time the United States realized the connotations and implications of the phrase, it was too late in the drafting process to reverse its position. The Soviet Union ultimately agreed to the language, forecasting that the phrase would be problematic. Since the consensus adoption of the Moon Agreement, neither country has agreed to the interpretations of the phrase. Nonetheless, the Soviet Union has frequently seemed more willing to interpret its obligations within an institutionalized framework of cooperation, as reflected, for example, in its proposals for a World Space Organization. Nevertheless, such a proposed World Space Organization would not provide for the mandatory transfer of technology or a mandatory sharing of benefits in a precise fashion-contrary to the claims of the developing countries who regard them as essential concomitants of the definition of the common heritage of mankind. Russia's current policy seems to be consistent with the earlier Soviet position.

Another issue that frequently becomes linked with the debate over the meaning and relevance of the "common heritage of mankind" is the interpretation of the non-appropriation clause of the Outer Space Treaty. That phrase is legally binding on all space powers and possibly on all states, if regarded now as a part of customary international law. Developing countries contend that the Outer Space Treaty's non-appropriation provision prohibits the removal of resources from the moon or other celestial bodies, except for scientific reasons. They cite the Moon Agreement's stipulation that the "natural resources in place" are subject to the non-appropriation principle as merely indicative of customary international law. Moreover, some nations argue that the use of orbital slots in the geostationary orbit also violates the principle because the regulatory regime of the International Telecommunications Union (ITU) permits use of the orbit/spectrum resource for an indefinite period of time.

Developed countries have argued that the language suggests, on the contrary, that an entity can acquire sole ownership over natural resources removed from the moon's surface and that only resources "in place" cannot be subject to appropriation. In addition, they point out that occupying an orbital slot does not suggest permanent appropriation, because a geostationary satellite does not occupy a specific area of outer space for very long, since it is constantly in motion. Consequently, no one nation would be able to exercise exclusive control over an orbital slot.

In recent years, the common heritage of mankind issue has come up indirectly before the U.N. Committee on the Peaceful Uses of Outer Space (UNCOPUOS) under the relatively new agenda item, "consideration of the legal aspects related to the application of the principle that the exploration and utilization of outer space should be carried out for the benefit and the interests of all states, taking into particular account the needs of developing countries."[8]

This new agenda item was the result of a compromise between developed and developing countries. Within the Legal Subcommittee of UNCOPUOS, the Group of 77 (representing developing countries) had originally suggested a proposal for an agenda item dealing with "Access by States to Benefits of the Exploration and Uses of Outer Space." With their proposed agenda item, they envisioned four areas for further study: (1)

relevant provisions of space law related to the access of states to the benefits of space activities; (2) the question of access by states to the benefits of space activities in various areas of applications of space sciences and technology; (3) the concept of resources to be shared under Article I; and (4) the concepts of "benefits" and "interests" and means for the distribution of "benefits."

Developed countries, on the other hand, had other proposed agenda items completely unrelated to a study of Article I. After extensive negotiations, a compromise was reached, whereby in essence the developing countries succeeded in placing an item on the agenda which pertained more specifically to their concerns and interests. Subsequently, extensive discussion ensued as to what work was to be included within the ambit of the proposal, and eventually it was agreed to have a survey undertaken of national legal frameworks, international agreements, and other documents pertaining to the Article I agenda item. With this new agenda item, the developing nations seem to be pressing for a set of legal principles which would institutionalize international cooperation and thereby place upon the more developed nations a positive obligation to act. Although this attempt to formalize cooperation will be discussed in more detail below, the purpose seems to be to create a definition of treaty obligations under Article I which would require a sharing of benefits from space exploration. In other words, since the debate over the legal status of the "common heritage of mankind" language has not progressed in the manner developing nations wished, the countries have revived the debate with the same goals in mind but put the debate in the context of Article I of the Outer Space Treaty.

The developed countries interpret the provision on the new agenda item to preclude changes in the existing economic or legal conditions for traditional freedom of space exploration and access to international resources. Accordingly, these developed states believe that the language encompasses only some "equitable" changes in the distribution of financial and other economic benefits derived from the exploitation of resources of outer space which perhaps would benefit developing countries. They believe that these changes will be determined by those states exploiting the resources in a manner to be negotiated at a future point in time with the non-spacefaring nations. It is clear that neither Russia nor the United States would look kindly upon suggestions involving a systematic sharing of benefits, but would rather look to equitable notions at a future point in time when tangible benefits are being received.

Two other concepts that are occasionally tied with discussions of the "common heritage of mankind" or of Article I of the Outer Space Treaty are those of equitable access and intergenerational equity.[9] Equitable access relates primarily to access to the geostationary orbit: which, in turn, is tied to notions of intergenerational equity in the sense that future access is in part dependent on the issues of space debris.

The Geostationary Orbit

Our solar system contains numerous natural resources which remain untapped—minerals, rare elements, and even the weightless vacuum. Not all of the resources have been identified or located. Although most are inaccessible at this time, one of the most important space resources is relatively easy to gain access to and to use—the geostationary orbit.[10] This resource differs from most others in that it is reusable. The only constraint attached to the geostationary orbit is its size, with the result that the demand for the resource could exceed the supply.[11] Currently, only one-tenth of the theoretical slots for locating satellites in the geostationary orbital arc are occupied. Additionally, some scientists have stated that technology will continue to advance, allowing for more satellites to share the same orbital area. Nevertheless, although orbital saturation is not a significant danger, having access to the locations which provide needed services and coverage is scarce. Rather, technology must also allow for increased use of the radio spectrum, particularly since more countries will likely gain the ability to have their own satellites and the demand for the orbit and spectrum could increase correspondingly.

Thus, the spatial limitation of the geostationary orbit and the radio spectrum means that one day the orbit could become crowded, rendering access difficult, expensive, or next to impossible for use by latecomers. As a result, non-spacefaring nations have pressed for some form of *a priori* planning.

Some of these non-spacefaring nations, the equatorial states, have claimed sovereignty over the segments of the geostationary space located directly above their territories. The substance of this claim is contained in the Bogota Declaration, which provides that this space is regarded as an integral part of the underlying countries' territory and as "a natural resource" over which they exercise full and exclusive sovereignty.[12] Thus, the stationing of satellites within this section of the geostationary orbit would be subject to the prior and express consent of the equatorial states.

Other non-spacefaring nations are concerned that the orbit will become saturated and, instead of claiming sovereignty, contend that the segments of the orbit must be considered "the common heritage of mankind." Presumably, as discussed above, this could mean that an international agency should be created to regulate the use and exploitation of the orbit/spectrum resource in the interests of the world community. It could also mean that orbital slots should not be allocated among all user states now, because they should be kept empty now to allow for easy future access.

In stark contrast, developed countries currently using the resource are resisting the efforts to set aside the orbit/spectrum resource for latecomers, preferring practical necessity over philosophical equality. On the whole, they have in practice taken a first-come, first-served approach to the exploitation of the geostationary orbit. They note that even if a country does not own and operate a satellite in a particular slot, that country currently has the ability to lease a transponder on the satellite to serve its needs. If the developed countries did not take advantage of the available slots, the developing countries would not have this benefit.

The compromise between these sides has resulted in the inclusion of the term "equitable access" in many recent international instruments. This term has developed over the past twenty years as various resolutions have attempted to deal with access to radio frequencies.

In 1973, the term "equitable access" appeared for the first time in an international agreement binding on the parties. The 1973 International Telecommunications Convention in Article 33(2) stipulated that:

> In using frequency bands for space radio services Member shall bear in mind that radio frequencies and the geostationary satellite orbit are limited natural resources, that they must be used efficiently and economically so that countries or groups of countries may have equitable access to both in conformity with the provisions of radio regulations according to their *needs and the technical facilities at their disposal.*[13]

Thus, two crucial preconditions of equitable access were set forth in Article 33 of the 1973 ITU Convention—"need" and "availability of technical facilities." In addition, the International Frequency Registration Board's ("IFRB") responsibilities were expanded to include the geostationary orbit, giving teeth to Article 33. These two provisions from the 1973 Convention provided a new legal basis for access to the "orbit/spectrum resource."

During the 1979 World Administrative Radio Conference (WARC), the requirement of equitable access was reiterated in Resolution 3, which noted the limited nature of the orbit, the increasing demand for the resource, and the need for "equitable access to" and "efficient and economical use" of the resource by all countries "as provided for in Article 33 [of the ITU Convention of 1973] and Resolution 2." Resolution 2 repeated an earlier resolution adopted in 1971 which stated that "the radio frequency spectrum and the geostationary satellite orbit are limited natural resources" which should be used "effectively and economically." In addition, the Resolution provided that "all countries have equal right in the use" of the orbit/spectrum resource and that such use "can start at various dates depending on the requirement and readiness of technical facilities of countries." The Resolution also highlighted that registration of one's orbit/spectrum "should not provide any permanent priority" and that it "should not create an obstacle to the establishment of space systems by other countries." Consequently, the 1979 WARC was tremendously important in terms of defining equitable access in that it suggested for the first time that future needs and abilities were relevant and that the "first-come, first-served" approach would not be determinative in deciding future allocation of the orbit/spectrum resource.

Simultaneously, Resolution 3 requested what eventually became a two session WARC ("WARC-ORB '85" and "WARC-ORB '88"), "to guarantee in practice for all countries equitable access to the geostationary-satellite orbit and the frequency bands allocated to space services. The WARC-ORBs, however, did not commence until 1985.

In the meantime, the 1982 ITU Convention (the Nairobi Convention) modified Article 33's preconditions for equitable access. The 1982 ITU Convention deleted the phrase in Article 33(2) of the 1973 ITU Convention "according to their needs and the technical facilities at their disposal" and substituted the words "taking into account the special needs of the developing countries and the geographical situation of particular countries." This change was preceded by a similarly worded addition to Article 10, paragraph 3(c) of the Convention requiring the IFRB, in furnishing advice to members, to take into account "the needs of Members requiring assistance, the specific needs of developing countries, as well as the special geographical situation of particular countries."

In 1985 and 1988 the Orbital WARCs,[14] as called for by the 1979 Resolutions, were held, attempting to "guarantee in practice for all countries equitable access." The two primary results were an Allotment Plan that gave each country one orbital location within a predetermined arc to use with the frequency bands identified for allotment planning (only the Fixed Satellite Service bands) and improved procedures. The Allotment Plan came into force in March 1990.

Some writers say that the Plan appears to have balanced flexibility with a long-term guarantee of access and made provisions for multilateral planning meetings to be monitored by the ITU's Administrative Council. Others contend that yet another non-agreement has resulted which will cause massive inefficiencies. In the year following WARC-ORB '88, a Plenipotentiary Conference was held in Nice. One of the decisions of the Conference was to adopt a Constitution and Convention to replace the 1982 Nairobi Convention. Nevertheless, the 1989 ITU Constitution, the "Nice Constitution," basically reiterated Article 33 of the Nairobi Convention (1982) with virtually no change, except that the word "rationally" was added as another requirement for using the radio frequencies and geostationary orbit.

In light of the recent Orbital WARCs, the meaning of equitable access has been partially resolved for the foreseeable future. Equitable access does not mean equality of orbital slots, and it does not mean that the spectrum used now has to cease being utilized until some time in the future when a developing country may need it. Nevertheless, for now some guarantee of access to the orbit/spectrum resource for late arrivals has been secured;

they can use at least one orbital position within a predetermined arc and bands for up to 800 MHz of bandwidth. Thus, all participants have equitable access to the orbit/spectrum resource. This access, however, will have to be sought and agreed to at the time when the particular situation and need arises, meaning that "what is considered to be 'equitable' will have to include, in part, considerations of economy and efficiency."[15] In addition, the provisions of Articles I and II of the Outer Space Treaty have been clarified by the Space WARCs in that if the ITU can "effectively make dispositions allowing for the exploitation and use of the orbit/spectrum resource for a limited period, this can only mean that no legal person . . . can effectively assert sovereignty-based exclusive claims or proprietary rights to the indicated resources."[16]

In spite of this seeming resolution, a number of developing countries have advocated the establishment of a special legal regime to regulate access and utilization by all states; some have suggested that the Legal Subcommittee working with the ITU could contribute to the establishment of such a regime, while others have stated that the ITU is the appropriate body. Their goal is to develop a legal regime which would implement a system of preferential rights in cases of competing requirements. It seems doubtful, however, that the developed nations would agree to have this issue discussed in detail before UNCOPUOS, in addition to the ITU. Moreover, developed counties consider the "equitable access" issue settled for now. Clearly, neither Russia nor the United States would want to be limited in their satellite usage, whether governmental or commercial.

In conclusion, it can be said that the first-come, first-served principle was true in the short-term, but not in the long-term, and no longer has legal significance. The Conference's conclusions may mean that equity as defined in the context of the geostationary orbit will be used in other areas of space law, perhaps in the implementation of principles pursuant to the Article I agenda item. Clearly, in the same way that the developing countries opposed the first-come, first-served approach, Russia and the U.S. are likely to oppose such an implementation.

Environmental Protection of Outer Space

Equity has also been a factor in the drive by developing countries and non-space powers to get Russia and the United States to take action toward protecting the environment and, particularly, to deal with the problems of space debris. The idea of intergenerational equity in the environmental context has affected the respective equation to the extent that non-space nations fear that the orbit will be so cluttered that access will become difficult and/or expensive. Moreover, the concept clearly suggests that harm to the Earth's space environment, as well as to its surface and air space environment must be avoided, if not to protect this generation, then to protect future generations. Not only has there been concern about chemical, biological, and radiological pollution, but there has been increased awareness of the problems posed by the accumulation of debris[17] in outer space. Objects ranging from defunct satellites, burnt-out motors, and mission-related objects, to nuts, bolts, and paint flecks are circling the Earth at various altitudes. The debris can cause an enormous amount of damage as demonstrated by the *Challenger*'s window being destroyed by a mere paint chip approximately 0.2 millimeters in diameter. Although most of the debris reentering the atmosphere will vaporize in the upper atmosphere, some debris will not, but will instead strike the Earth's surface.[18] The impact of both nuclear and non-nuclear material could possibly cause severe damage if inhabited areas are hit.

Unfortunately, none of the international space treaties provides much help in combatting the problem of space debris. Although the Outer Space Treaty and the 1972 Convention on the International Liability for Damage Caused by Space Objects (Liability Convention) provide some limited protection for outer space, the moon, and celestial bodies, also referred to as the "space commons," many gaps in coverage exist. This is particularly true if specific damage to a state has not occurred.

As noted above, Article VI of the Outer Space Treaty mandates international responsibility for national activities in outer space, irrespective of whether such activities are carried out by governmental or nongovernmental entities. This provision makes the state responsible for private activities. In addition, Article VII of the Outer Space Treaty makes a state launching an object into outer space liable for injuries caused by that object to another state or to natural or juridical persons, whether on earth, in the air, or in outer space. Article VII has been supplemented by the Liability Convention, which in Article II provides for strict liability for "damage" occasioned by a launching state's space object to the surface of the earth or to aircraft in flight. The same Convention in Article III provides for a negligence standard when the damage is caused "elsewhere than on the surface of the earth to a space object" or to "persons or property on board such a space object." These two provisions for liability apply only if "damage" as defined in the Liability Convention's Article I has occurred. "Damage" means the "loss of life, personal injury or other impairment of health; or loss of or damage to property of states or of persons, natural or juridical, or property of international intergovernmental organizations."

Clearly, these provisions can be helpful when specific damage has occurred to a specific person or property and where the source of the damage can be identified. For debris, however, it would be difficult to locate the source of, for example, the paint chip which caused the damage. General or specific damage to the space environment from chemical, biological, or radiological contamination or large amounts of debris would not fall within the Liability Convention's definition of "damage," since the space commons is not the property of states, persons, or organizations. Damage as defined in the Liability Convention would not appear to cover the over-cluttering of the lower earth orbit, threatening other states' space activities and rendering them more expensive. Consequently, there is a problem in terms of holding states liable for damage caused to the space commons.

Insofar as the states' duties to the space commons are concerned, they appear to be vague. Article IX of the Outer Space Treaty imposes an obligation on the states parties to avoid harmful contamination of the moon and other celestial bodies. Article IX could be interpreted to apply to outer space as well, the obligation being only "to avoid *harmful contamination.*"[19] That phrase is not defined in the Treaty, and it is not clear whether it means debris or some type of biological contamination. In addition, Article IX requires states parties to prevent the introduction into the earth's environment of extraterrestrial matter which may cause adverse changes. This provision would not apply to debris of terrestrial origin. Also, the phrase "adverse changes" is not defined, nor is it stated when states should think it necessary to adopt appropriate measures and what those measures should be.

Not to be overlooked is a general provision in Article IX which stipulates that states parties shall conduct their activities in outer space "with due regard to the corresponding interests of all other States Parties to the Treaty." Also under Article XI, if a state party has reason to believe that an activity planned by another state party would cause "potentially harmful interference" with its activities "in the peaceful exploration and use of outer space," it "may request consultation" with the potentially interfering state. Nonetheless, the other state party's obligation to consult exists only when it has a reasonable belief that its activities "would cause potentially harmful interference" to another state party's activities. Presumably, in such a case, if the state decided not to consult, it would be in breach of its international treaty obligations. Inasmuch as the Treaty does not provide for a strong dispute settlement procedure, the state could maintain that it was not in breach.

Apart from this, the "common interest" provision in Article I and some other general provisions in the Outer Space Treaty require compliance with international law and call for promotion of international cooperation. These provisions could possibly be of some help in holding a state generally responsible for injury caused by its debris to the space commons.

The Moon Agreement, to which, as noted earlier, the major spacefaring nations are currently not parties, would be more helpful. The Agreement would create an important new obligation for states to avoid harmful effects on the environment of the earth irrespective of the type of activity causing harm. In other words, while the Outer Space Treaty requires states to avoid harm to the environment only through contamination, the Moon

Agreement includes other ways as well. Nevertheless, this treaty still fails to define major terms. Also, some authors have noted that Article 1 of the treaty states that it applies to the moon, orbits, and trajectories in or around it and other bodies in the solar system. This would imply that the treaty still leaves parts of outer space unprotected. The Agreement, however, adds more specific procedures and requirements for consultation if a state party believes that another party is not fulfilling the obligations incumbent upon it or that another state party is interfering with its rights.

There can be no question that the lacunae in international space law for the protection of the "space commons" must be addressed, either specifically through a new space treaty or in the general context of protecting the areas outside the jurisdiction and control of states, *i.e.,* the "international commons," through international environmental law.

International environmental law when coupled with the space treaties may provide some help in imposing duties upon states—party and nonparty to the various applicable treaties—with respect to protecting the space commons. Several treaties are relevant in this context. The Convention on the Prohibition of Military or any Other Hostile Uses of Environmental Modification Techniques provides that a state party "undertakes not to engage in military or any other hostile use of environmental modification techniques having widespread, long-lasting or severe effects as the means of destruction, damage or injury to any other State Party." It defines the term "environmental modification techniques" as referring "to any technique for changing—through the deliberate manipulation of natural processes—the dynamics, composition or structure of the Earth, including its biota, lithosphere, hydrosphere and atmosphere, or of outer space." The Treaty Banning Nuclear Weapons Tests in the Atmosphere, in Outer Space and Under Water also relevant in that one of its purposes is to "put an end to the contamination of man's environment by radioactive substances."

Apart from treaties concerning environmental protection, a fair amount of customary international environmental law exists which could provide more help. The Restatement of Foreign Relations Law has summarized the duties owed by a state to areas outside its jurisdiction and control as follows:

> A state is obligated to take such measures as may be necessary, to the extent practicable under the circumstances, to ensure that activities within its jurisdiction or control: a) conform to generally accepted international rules and standards for the prevention, reduction, and control of injury to the environment of areas beyond the limits of national jurisdiction; and b) are conducted so as not to cause significant injury to the environment of areas beyond the limit of national jurisdiction.[20]

The foregoing standard would bolster the duties contained in the Outer Space Treaty. States would have to abide by those "generally accepted international rules and standards," even if they were not contained in treaties to which they were party, effectively extending a spacefaring state's environmental obligations to "areas beyond national jurisdiction." The Restatement standard would carry the obligations under the Liability Convention one step further, prohibiting "significant injury" to "the environment of areas beyond the limit of national jurisdiction," *i.e.*, the space commons.

Although drawing upon international environmental law strengthens the international space law provisions protecting the space commons, it is clear that more attention needs to be devoted to protecting the commons. It is particularly imperative to search for solutions to the problem of debris in the geostationary orbit ("orbital debris"). Countries must reduce the number of objects in orbit either by placing fewer satellites in that orbit or by removing dead satellites from the orbit. Currently, the latter would be extremely expensive. To require that countries take either step requires agreement on a set of practices, principles, or standards.

Consideration of the space debris problem up to now has not received sufficient support internationally to be placed on the agenda of the Legal Subcommittee of UNCOPUOS, with a particular lack of interest on the part of the United States and Soviet Union (and now Russia). This is more than likely because of the expenditures involved in adequate remedial measures. Proposals to place debris on the agenda have been supported by several nations, most notably Sweden and the Netherlands. Recently, the General Assembly, in Resolution 46/45, stated that space debris could be an appropriate subject for discussion by UNCOPUOS in the future. Even if support remains insufficient for studying the question within the Legal Subcommittee, it could be possible to establish an international experts group on space debris within the Scientific and Technical Subcommittee, since that forum has already been considering the debris situation in relation to nuclear power sources.

The French have expressed interest in setting up an international monitoring agency which would monitor debris using an extensive satellite system. The main drawback to such a proposal, however, is the cost involved. Perhaps an alternative would be to organize a framework for cooperation among national organizations and international organizations, where all organizations would monitor and exchange data collected, perhaps delivering such data to an organization assigned the task of compiling it and making it available to all interested states.

Scientists have pointed out that the present problem of possible collisions in space is almost entirely a problem of debris particles unnecessarily created in orbit by explosions of rocket upper stages. Therefore, they argue that rocket upper stage design and operation changes must be found to eliminate further break-up and that any intentional explosions should be limited to low altitudes, where disintegration is more rapid. They also note that in the long run the problem of overcrowding will occur at higher altitudes and then active de-orbiting or retrieval will be necessary.

Consequently, the first step to be taken would be to collect data on the steps currently taken by spacefaring nations to deal with space debris. In the meantime, scientists could gather additional data on the more than 7,000 man-made objects that are trackable and many more times that number of objects that are untrackable to get some ideas as to possible scientific solutions.

In addition, the U.N. could call upon member states to adopt legal and technical measures directed at the minimization of space debris. In the long run, states could draft international agreements to combat the problem of debris or amend existing agreements or develop a Protocol to the 1967 Outer Space Treaty to define terms in a way that debris would be covered by the current treaties. Or, as some authors have suggested, states could use the principles developed by the World Commission on Environment and Development as a model to follow.[21]

The preferred approach in the near term, at least until a broader consensus could be reached, would be to develop Standards and Recommended Practices (SARPS) similar to those included in the Annex to the Chicago Convention for the establishment of the International Civil Aviation Organization. These would have the advantage of being flexible recommendations, yet would serve as guidelines on ways to avoid causing environmental harm. Because such standards are technically not binding, the United States and Russia might be more willing to participate in their formulation. At the same time, they could serve as a basis for the development of customary international law which could eventually lead to treaty codification. The difficult question would be under whose auspices SARPS would be developed: the UNCOPUOS, the ITU, United Nations Environmental Programme (UNEP), or an independent or governmentally appointed group of experts which would bring the SARPS to the UNCOPUOS in a manner in which UNCOPUOS would not have to pass upon them.

Undoubtedly, a further study of the appropriate regulatory framework is essential. Even if standards are developed, there will be a need to establish a framework for providing compensation to parties injured by space debris in cases in which the debris is from an unidentifiable source. Some have suggested the establishment of an international insurance regime or an international fund to compensate victims of damage caused by unidentifiable space debris.[22] Both funds would be based upon the size of a launching state's space activities.

Although developing countries, as well as other non-space powers, are concerned about the issue, they have not been able to make this topic an agenda item in UNCOPUOS, largely because of U.S. opposition. Instead of waiting until the rest of the world or a space disaster forces action, the U.S.

together with other states should decide on action now, which as a minimum could be in the form of recommended practices.

Delimitation of Air and Outer Space

The first satellite flight engendered many political and legal questions for international lawyers and policy makers to face. Although perhaps the number of problems has been exaggerated, it is certain that one of the first challenges encountered as a result of man's entry into outer space was to define the point at which air space ends and outer space begins in order to determine the extent to which a state could assert sovereignty over its air space and thus control an activity.

There is no natural division defining the border between the atmosphere and outer space. For doctors, space begins at a low altitude within dozens of kilometers, where the lymph glands of a human being begin to swell without special protection. Physicists and chemists, in contrast, find elements of the atmosphere at altitudes well above several hundred kilometers. These two regions, the atmosphere and outer space, have completely different legal regimes. Yet, the precise dividing line has escaped precise physical description and defied legal delimitation. Countries have still not been able to agree on whether to establish a legal division between the two regions.

The question of delimitation has been discussed and scrutinized at length in both legal and scientific literature as well as in international forums, including the United Nations. Its interrelationships with military, political, and scientific-technical interests of states complicate any final resolution. Apparently, all major arguments have been expressed, and the positions of all sides are clear, yet no agreements have been reached.

Beginning in 1967, the question of the demarcation of the atmosphere and outer space came under consideration in the UNCOPUOS and its Legal Subcommittee. Because of French and Italian proposals put forward that year, the Legal Subcommittee requested UNCOPUOS's Scientific-Technical Subcommittee to consider scientific and technical criteria related to the delimitation of air and outer space. Examining different aspects of the problem, the Scientific-Technical Subcommittee concluded that it could not yet define scientific and technical criteria which would permit a precise demarcation between the two areas. Although UNCOPUOS emphasized the necessity of further examination of this question, the answer of the Scientific-Technical Subcommittee had a negative impact on discussion of the delimitation question, although the issue was put on the Legal Subcommittee's agenda in 1969. Additionally, other U.N. organs and a few international organizations continued to examine different aspects of this problem. Some of these entities began to focus attention on the technical characteristics of satellite flight, such as the perigee of orbits. They concluded that perigees of satellites below one hundred kilometers above sea level were a rare exception and that subsequent scientific-technical progress would have an insignificant effect on the perigee of future satellites.

After these studies were published, a large number of states and scholars came out in favor of delimiting air and outer space at the minimum altitude of orbiting artificial Earth satellites. This approach definitively reduced the number of possible criteria used to determine the boundary between the air and outer space. The question that remained was whether such spaces should be delimited. If so, at what altitude should this be done—the minimum altitude of the perigee of a satellite's orbit or at some other fixed height? If outer space should be delimited, then should one use a functional approach in order to differentiate space activities? An analysis of the discussion of this question in the Legal Subcommittee indicates differences in the positions of the Soviet Union and the United States, as well as differences between the approach of developing countries and that of the United States.

In addition to literature arguing that delimitation of air and outer space is premature, the literature and practice of states reflect two contradictory approaches to the question: "functional" and "spatial." Functionalists do not propose to establish a boundary between air and space, but rather to solve problems arising from the need to regulate air and space activities. One of the more consistent followers of this approach is the Canadian lawyer Nicolas M. Matte. Matte approaches the air and outer space from a legal point of view as a single sphere in which air/space activity occurs.[23] The place of the activity is irrelevant; rather, the key factor is the nature of the activity. Therefore, if it is a "space activity," it will remain a space activity, even if the respective flight crosses the sovereign air space of a foreign state. As a result, outer space laws apply to it. Matte accepts the concepts of freedom of outer space and/or state jurisdiction and control over its air space as long as they are understood in terms of "functional freedom" and/or "functional sovereignty." Functional sovereignty would allow for states to control their security to the extent that functional freedom could be exercised, allowing for access to outer space. The functional approach, however, would require defining terms such as "space activity" or "space flight." Although no state has submitted a substantial proposal using this approach to the Legal Subcommittee in recent years, Russia in 1992 submitted a document posing a number of questions for discussion if a functional approach were to be formulated.

The advocates of the "spatial" approach contend that a precise delimitation is essential. Proponents note the differences between legal regimes for air and outer space. Developing country proponents stress that states need assurance of sovereignty over their air space to preserve territorial integrity and security. Other proponents appear to advocate a demarcation to ensure that states do not further their claims of sovereignty to include portions of space lying in outer space. Those advocating this approach recognize, however, that the lowest perigee of an orbiting spacecraft lies in outer space.

In Russian literature, the spatial approach to the problem of demarcation between the air and outer space has prevailed. In general, the Soviet Union had supported in principle the establishment of a boundary by treaty at an altitude of 100-110 kilometers above sea level. The Soviet Union also brought to the Legal Subcommittee several proposals drawing upon initiatives of other states and international organizations. One of the more recent compromise proposals provided:

> While not resolving in advance the question of the need to establish a boundary between air space and outer space and without prejudice to the final position concerning the upper limit of State sovereignty, general agreement might be reached to the effect that:
> 1. Any object launched into outer space shall be considered as being in outer space at all stages of its flight after launch at which its altitude above sea level is 110 kilometers or more.
> 2. Space objects of States shall retain the right to fly over the territory of other States at altitudes lower than 110 kilometers above sea level for the purposes of reaching orbit around the Earth or proceeding on a flight trajectory beyond the confines of that orbit, and for the purpose of returning to Earth.[24]

Some states considered this proposal to be the basis for compromise and a useful interim solution. In spite of this, the UNCOPUOS arguments have continued, with some countries wishing to have this item dropped from the Subcommittee's agenda or to reduce the time allocated to it.

Basically, the United States holds neither the spatialist nor functionalist view, but believes instead that discussions of delimitation between air and outer space are premature. The negative reaction of the United States to this question has increased since the expansion of the space shuttle program and the advent of an aerospace plane. The underlying U.S. concern is that technology could be hindered by delimitation and that the absence of agreements has not yet led to international tension. For example, a futuristic aerospace plane might travel at low heights (reaching the fringes of outer space) or a new generation of satellites may circle the earth at altitudes lower than the altitude currently possible. If there were a formalized delimitation, both activities could fall within the ambit of air space and require the underlying countries' permission for passage. Moreover, with an exact demarcation, states might increase their claims to sovereignty over their air space and limit space objects' ability to traverse their air space; in addition, complaints of technical violations of the demarcation line might arise.

Opponents of the U.S. position believe that this question needs to be resolved, particularly in light of space technology which permits reusable spacecraft to land in aircraft mode, and the future advent of aerospace vehicles which would be able to operate in air and outer space. Some of these opponents believe that such a demarcation, whether spatial or functional, would keep states from making claims to the portions of outer space directly above their territory on the grounds of sovereignty over air space and would thus decrease the likelihood of future international tensions. In contrast, other states want to delimit in order to assert strong claims of sovereignty over all of their air space.

Vast differences between the U.S. and Soviet approaches have not always existed. Before 1979, the Soviet Union had also thought that delimitation was premature. Not until after the Bogota Declaration and the 1976 technical report on the lowest perigees of satellites did the Soviet Union shift its position. It appears that one of the major reasons for the shift was that the Soviet Union was concerned that the equatorial nations' claims to the geostationary orbit could possibly affect the conduct of space activities and thus that the best method to counter their demands would be to define the two areas. Although the U.S. had the same concerns, the U.S. continued the former approach of no demarcation point. The U.S. appeared to have a greater concern that once the Legal Subcommittee acknowledged a specific line above which is presumed to be outer space, the equatorial countries would claim that the area below that point is presumed to be air space and correspondingly would assert strong claims to exclusive sovereignty over activities occurring in that area, thus limiting technology and perhaps access to outer space. Perhaps Russia's continued lack of concern stems from the large area of land occupied by the CIS which would allow the countries operating under the Minsk Agreement to launch a space object without necessarily crossing a non-participating state's air space. In contrast, smaller spacefaring nations clearly would have to traverse other states' air space.

In practice, a general international custom has taken shape, which the United States would not dispute. The altitude of the lowest perigee orbit of artificial Earth satellites (currently approximately 100-110 km above sea level) lies at a point in outer space, and states may transit through air space to reach this point. Nevertheless, the fact that custom recognizes the perigee point as a point in outer space does not *ipso facto* mean that below that altitude is air space, with corresponding air space rights. Such a custom, however, has developed not only because states have silently acquiesced to it, but also because it has been expressly recognized. For example, foreign states have not protested a single launch or flight of a space object (which occurs several hundred times a year) as a violation of their sovereign air space. In fact, in the first ten to fifteen years of space flight, states launching satellites and spacecraft (primarily the U.S. and Soviet Union) were congratulated by others. Moreover, legal literature supports this view.[25]

In conclusion, the fact that states have acknowledged as customary international law that the altitude of the lowest perigee orbit of artificial earth satellites lies at a point in outer space "does not mean that states may not have different points of view relating not only to more precise treaty enforcement of this border, but also to the very necessity of such enforcement at present."[26] Currently, the 1992 Russian working paper seems to be the best proposal for focusing current discussion on this long-standing agenda item, because a functional approach would be far more likely to be accepted at some point by those countries which would have traditionally opposed any delimitation.

Legal Problems Arising from Manned Space Flight

Yuri Gagarin once said that the profession of the astronaut would become "the most important space profession." Since 1961 more than two hundred manned flights have been completed and the number of countries representatives of which have made their space flights is increasing steadily. Active participation of humans is essential to the exploration and use of outer space. Humans carry out complicated experiments and research and generate enthusiasm for space activities. In addition, enabling man to live for long periods of time in outer space and observing his adaptability provides valuable research for scientists. The more that outer space is explored and techniques for prolonging human existence in space improve, both in terms of safety of the spacecraft and in terms of medical knowledge, the larger the number of legal problems that demand resolution.

Many norms governing manned space flights are already reflected in international space law, primarily in the Outer Space Treaty and the Rescue and Return Agreement. These norms are mainly aimed at the implementation of Article V of the Outer Space Treaty, which declares that states "shall regard astronauts as envoys of mankind in outer space and shall render to them all possible assistance in the event of accident, distress, or emergency landing." Nevertheless, the existing norms do not solve the multitude of questions and problems pertaining to manned space flight. The fact that the norms devoted to the regulation of manned space flight are reflected in different international agreements makes their implementation very difficult and calls for the conclusion of a new international agreement specifically devoted to manned space flight.

During consideration of a new agenda item for the Legal Subcommittee of UNCOPUOS in the mid-1980s, the Soviet delegation proposed to include questions of regulating the legal status of the personnel of space objects, in particular those personnel involved in international space flights.

The U.K. delegation at the same session of the Subcommittee also suggested formulating a document aimed at insuring the safety of manned space objects and rendering assistance to them where there are objects in distress in outer space. Unfortunately, because of developing countries' desire to see some sort of examination of issues related to their benefiting from space exploration (see discussion above), this topic was not placed on the agenda. Nevertheless, the wording of the new agenda item pertaining to the interpretation of Article I of the Outer Space Treaty is so broad that its framework could include the elaboration of a draft international agreement on manned space flights.

In 1988 scholars engaged in space law from the Institute of State and Law of the Academy of Sciences of the USSR, the Research and Study of Space Law and Policy Center at the University of Mississippi Law Center, and the Institute of Air and Space Law in Cologne, Germany, initiated a common research project aimed at drafting a Convention on Manned Space Flights. This project, lasting for several years and successfully completed in 1990 was the first time researchers had cooperated in the formulation of an unofficial international draft space agreement. During these years seven drafts were formulated until a final agreement was reached which represented a compromise among the different points of view advanced by the participants.[27] The main objective of the project was to initiate and promote international discussion in the hope that they would lead to negotiations among states either in the UNCOPUOS or elsewhere. As a first step the draft convention was published in the journals of the cooperating participants, presented in October 1990 to the Board of Directors of the International Institute of Space Law (IISL), and then submitted by the IISL to the Legal Subcommittee of UNCOPUOS. Since this draft represents the result of years of study on the part of three groups, the discussion in this section will focus on some of the draft's provisions.

The draft convention contains a number of important provisions. First, the draft defines terms such as "manned space object," "manned space flight," "international manned space flight," and "crew."

"Manned space object" means "a space object on which a person or persons effect a space flight." The term "manned space flight" means "a flight of a space object with a person or persons on board from Earth to outer space or in outer space and extends to the embarkation, launch, in orbit, deorbit, reentry, landing and disembarkation phases." It is interesting to note that the definition of "manned space object" does not clarify the point at which an object ceases to be a space object for purposes of the Liability and Registration Conventions. The definition of "manned space flight" also does not answer the question as to whether a part of a space object is still a space object or whether debris is a space object. "International manned space flight" is defined as "a space flight in which persons of at least two or more States or of an international organization participate." Therefore, even if all participants are from the same state, the fact that one participant is representing an international organization renders the flight an international one.

Although consideration had been given to defining the terms "astronaut" and "personnel" in the draft convention, the Agreement instead created a new term: "crew." "Crew" is defined as "persons who effect professional activities during a space flight. Clearly, this term would include astronauts who engage in professional activities. One of the authors of the draft convention has stated that, in retrospect, this definition may prove confusing, because the definition does not make it clear that the professional activities must relate to the mission in order for the individual to be "crew."

Although the drafters had difficulty in defining "astronaut" and "personnel," they felt that it was still necessary to provide for coverage of persons who were passengers on a manned spacecraft. Currently, Article VIII of the Outer Space Treaty provides for jurisdiction and control over "personnel" of a space object. Article V of the Outer Space Treaty deals with assistance for "astronauts" in distress and Articles 1 through 4 of the Rescue and Return Agreement apply only to "personnel." The absence of the definition of the term "passenger" is a severe gap in the law, particularly with the advent of the aerospace plane, which will be able to carry passengers. The draft agreement in Article VI devoted to mutual assistance in space has provided a certain coverage for this gap by recognizing that "any person in outer space" is an "astronaut within the meaning of Article V of the Outer Space Treaty" and is "part of the personnel of a spacecraft within the meaning of Article V of the Outer Space Treaty and the Rescue Agreement." So this coverage was given, according to the understanding of the drafters, for the purpose of mutual assistance in order to safeguard the life and health of persons during space flight, in the event of accident, distress, or emergency landing. Remaining undefined is the definition of passenger: an authorized participant in the space flight or any noncrew person.

The draft convention provides that registration of manned space objects must be carried out in accordance with the provisions of the Registration Convention. Consequently, a manned space object shall be registered by the launching state, and separate flight elements may be registered by different states. Because multiple registration is excluded, states must jointly determine which one shall register the manned space object or a flight element in an international manned space flight.

In addition, the draft convention clarifies some issues of jurisdiction and control. Currently, these problems have to be solved in light of Article VIII of the Outer Space Treaty, which provides that a state on whose registry an object launched into outer space is carried "shall retain jurisdiction and control over such object, and over any personnel thereof while in outer space or on a celestial body." This provision does not cover all the problems of jurisdiction and control. For example, it does not regulate the exercise of jurisdiction over an object and its personnel when on the high seas, in the air space of a foreign state, or in any other place beyond the limits of the jurisdiction of any state. The draft convention specifically covers this gap. According to the draft, a state of registry retains jurisdiction and control over manned space objects or elements and over any persons thereof "while in outer space or on a celestial body, or on the high seas, or in any other area beyond the limits of the jurisdiction of any state." It is interesting that the drafters failed to reach agreement on the question of jurisdiction over space objects and persons present in the air space of a foreign state.[28]

A special article of the draft is devoted to the regulation of the rights and obligations of persons participating in manned space flights. In general, the preparation of the flight, the determination of composition and functions of the crew, and the participation of other persons, as well as their rights and obligations, fall within the competence of the state exercising jurisdiction and control. At the same time, the draft convention defines the main functions, rights, and obligations of the "commander of the manned space object." For example, the commander shall "(1) provide for the safety and well being of all persons on board, and (2) provide for the protection of the space flight elements and any payload carried or serviced by the manned space object." The commander "shall have sole authority throughout the flight to use any reasonable and necessary means to achieve this end." The authority of the commander extends to all persons participating in the space flight irrespective of their nationality, and the directions of the commander are subject to implicit execution by all participants in the flight.

Serious attention is given in the draft convention to ensuring safety and mutual assistance in space. Thus, according to the draft, the activities connected with the exploration and use of outer space and celestial bodies shall be conducted in a way which "ensure, to the highest degree possible, the safety of the persons involved." In addition, "[i]n order to avoid harmful space debris, pollution, contamination and harmful changes to the environment of the Earth, and in particular, to avoid risks therefrom to manned space flight, the State Parties shall study the feasibility of appropriate measures and shall make the respective information available to the Secretary-General of the United Nations for dissemination to all interested states."

In accordance with Article V of the Outer Space Treaty and the Rescue and Return Agreement, crew "shall render all possible assistance, including, if necessary, the provision of shelter on their manned space to persons who are experiencing conditions of distress in outer space or on celestial bodies." To facilitate such assistance states "shall study and exchange information on possible steps to ensure the compatibility of manned space objects and technical means for carrying out rescue operations in outer space."

Other articles of the draft are devoted to problems of responsibility, liability, intellectual property, consultations, and settlement of disputes.

Of course, the suggested draft convention is not the only possible way of solving all main problems of the regulation of manned space flights. Some of its provisions could be changed or altered; the draft could be developed or extended. Nevertheless, this draft should be seen as a suitable foundation for the elaboration of an international agreement on manned space flights. Cooperation is and will be increasingly important for manned space flights. Although perhaps ad hoc agreements can work for a specific joint project where respective rights and obligations are determined by contract, parties to the specific arrangement would be well served if all countries were bound by a set of obligations vis-à-vis their space objects and personnel. In addition, it is clear that definitional gaps need resolution within the context of an international agreement and not only on an ad hoc basis. Thus, parts of the draft convention could serve as a basis for dealing with those issues that cannot be or should not be solved contractually in a specific case.

Mechanisms for Cooperation in Space: Perspectives and Problems

International cooperation in the exploration and use of outer space was essential from the beginning of the space era. Despite the unfavorable international political climate, cooperation achieved significant results, on both a multilateral and a bilateral basis. Cooperation ranged from drawing up rules governing space activities, to research and development, to the commercial exploitation of space applications. Some cooperation was intergovernmental, while other incidences involved private entities; some was of a bilateral nature, other multilateral. Beginning in the 1970s, however, interest in developing a mechanism for cooperation in space grew noticeably. Two methods for such cooperation were advanced. The first was an expansion of the activities of existing organizations and the creation of new organizations with specific mandates, such as INTELSAT or INTER-SPUTNIK. The second was the creation of a universal space organization for developing cooperation in all phases of space exploration. In practice, the former method has been adopted. Although the two methods do not contradict, but rather complement one another, the second method for cooperation has not yet come to fruition.

Nevertheless, since the 1950s, scholars have proposed creating a universal space organization.[29] The early proposals were quite different from more recent proposals, in that at that time scholars thought that the creation of one organization would be sufficient to handle all aspects of space co-operation and exploration. More recent proposals instead suggest a dual approach, proposing the creation of a universal space organization, taking into account the activities of the U.N. and other existing space organizations. Nevertheless, many of these proposals are quite general, and only some address the goals, tasks, structure, and authority of such an organization.

The Soviet Union officially proposed the creation of a World Space Organization (WSO) for the first time in the 1980s. This proposal was submitted to the U.N. Secretary-General initially, and more detailed proposals were later introduced in the UNCOPUOS. Unfortunately, for a long period of time, with the exception of one or two small publications,[30] there was no detailed analysis of these initiatives, no examination of the pluses and minuses of these proposals, and no serious criticism of the additions and changes to them either in literature or in international forums, including the UNCOPUOS or UNCOPUOS's Legal Subcommittee.

Those advocating the establishment of a WSO, as had been proposed by the Soviet Union, believe that the increasing interdependence required of states wishing to benefit from activities in outer space necessitates an organization which could serve as the center of a broad international cooperative effort in space exploration for peaceful purposes, facilitating access to space activity for all countries. They contend that a global space organization would be able to accomplish global tasks that regional organizations are either incapable or unwilling to perform. They suggest that the creation of a WSO, closely interacting with the U.N., would become the center of cooperation in space exploration and would give space exploration a new impetus.

The distinctive characteristic of the proposed WSO would be that the organization could not only coordinate the activities of member states, but could engage directly in the exploration and use of outer space; all states could be members. For this purpose, the WSO draft charter provides that the WSO "can lease, acquire or create necessary elements of a scientific-industrial basis, including spacecrafts, equipment, initial installations, surface resources, compression stations, and laboratories."

Nevertheless, the proposal to create a WSO has received a mixed reaction, with some for it, some against it, and others hesitating. Several of the Western nations are not interested in establishing a WSO, fearing that technological development might be stifled by bureaucratic red tape. The U.S., in particular, seems to fear that the organization would become entwined with political issues and theoretical arguments pertaining to a number of issues, including peaceful versus military uses of space. In addition, several members of the European Space Agency believe that the creation of a WSO would duplicate the function of existing space organizations. Moreover, many of the Western countries fear that they would foot most of the bill for such an organization and thus that it would be too costly.

Interestingly, in addition, some of the developing countries have a rather passive reaction, although it would appear that the WSO's mandate would give all countries, particularly the developing countries, a chance to engage in space activities and would allow for "the distribution of benefits arising from space activity." Moreover, there is a proposal connected with the WSO to create a development fund for financing international projects that will primarily fulfill the goals of giving aid and assistance to developing countries in the area of space exploration. Sixty percent of the fund would be contributed by states most actively involved in space activity; thirty percent of the fund would come from the fees of WSO members who engage in space activities, and the remaining ten percent would come from the fees of the remaining members of the WSO or some other as yet undetermined source approved by the Assembly. Although a similar mechanism does not exist in any other proposed or existing multilateral space organization, many questions related to the creation of a WSO need additional study and must be defined more precisely, including those of financing and of the interaction between the WSO and other space organizations.

Recently, the French Centre National de la Recherche Scientifique (CNRS) organized a working group to complete a study on the advantages or disadvantages of a World Space Organization for cooperation and the subject areas for coverage, as well as a proposal for structure. They noted that because the international scene has changed dramatically with the end of the Cold War, a number of new requirements have developed which call for international cooperation. For example, the growing number of spacecraft requires coordination for launches, orbit, and reentry; the development of programs for planetary exploration pursued jointly by developed countries; and operational activities such as the remote sensing of natural resources, weather forecasting, environmental monitoring, and launch services. Because of the nature of space activities, entailing high costs, sometimes affecting national security or involving competition, and sensitive political and economic considerations, the report concluded that there is no prospect of setting up a World Space Organization with broad powers. The report argued, however, for setting up a limited World Space Organization which would not be operational and which would not be used for commercial ends. It suggested that the tasks of such an organization should be confined to tasks that cannot be undertaken through other forms of international cooperation. Examples are drawing up international rules and monitoring compliance with them; gathering technical information on space activities; and circulating data gathered in the course of such activities, such as data relating to environmental monitoring. The working group suggested that to accomplish these tasks a United Nations Centre for Space, which was planned as part of UMSPACE-82 could be revived. This would mean that the organization would be attached to the United Nations, would be streamlined and flexible, and, for some tasks, would incorporate the existing structures of the U.N. Outer Space Affairs Division, the UNCOPUOS, and its subcommittees.

The working group's detailed report and analysis is bound to stimulate extensive discussions and further studies. Clearly, this proposal could provide an inexpensive and workable solution to fill gaps in organizational frameworks for space activities.

The reluctance of some of the developed nations to take any steps of this nature may remain, however. The reason is that pursuant to the new agenda item pertaining to "consideration of the legal aspects related to the application of the principle that the exploration and utilization of outer space should be carried out for the benefit and the interests of all states, taking into particular account the needs of developing countries," the developing countries have recently begun a drive for an institutionalization of international cooperation.

Some of the principles sought by developing countries in institutionalizing cooperation in the outer space field include a proviso that all states "should have access to the knowledge and applications derived from the exploration and use of outer space on an equitable, non-discriminatory and timely basis," and that this should be done through international cooperation. In addition, a most-favored-nation clause and system of preferences for developing countries was demanded, so that conditions offered to one state in a specific field of cooperation in outer space would have to be established with other countries where similar programs of international cooperation exist; reciprocity could not be asked from developing countries. Also included was a provision to share with developing countries on an "equitable basis the scientific and technological knowledge necessary for the proper development of programmes oriented to the more rational utilization and exploration of outer space."

With developing countries seeking to formalize cooperation in this manner, there will probably be an increase in the reluctance of the United States to agree to the creation of any new international organization unless the mandate is extremely specific. On the other hand, the proposal of the Soviet Union for a WSO, if Russia were to push for it again, would more than likely satisfy to a large extent the developing countries' demands in this area. Nonetheless, as noted earlier, the WSO is extremely unlikely for financial reasons. Consequently, it seems that the manner of cooperation suggested by the CNRS working group's report could be one of the most realistic proposals for the near future and that in any case it requires a more detailed and objective analysis.

Conclusion

In the preceding discussion an attempt has been made to review briefly some of the areas of legal tension, as well as the need for international cooperation in the fields of international space law. Particular attention has been paid to the areas in which U.S. and Russian positions have changed through the years and to the manner in which their positions have shifted with respect to the developing nations.

While the United States and the Soviet Union led the drive toward developing principles of international space law, in more recent years the United States has shown some reluctance to codify further and more specific principles of space law unless the need for such codification is demonstrated. At the same time, the Soviet Union/Russia has supported further specificity in the law of outer space, but not to the extent called for by the developing nations.

In spite of the differences between the Soviet Union and the United States in a number of areas of space law, their opinions had to merge because of the challenges presented by these claims of developing nations. Such a confluence was inevitable as well in light of financial cuts of space activity, both in Russia and the U.S.A. Both wanted to be able to pursue space activities without much hindrance, either for reasons of prestige or commercial use. At the same time, the area of manned space flights can serve as a good example of true cooperation, at an informal level, in the drafting of a convention without prompting from the developing nations.

Currently, Russian and U.S. interests, particularly those relating to commercial uses, are merging. In addition, both countries are facing large budgetary constraints. It would thus seem that cooperation will increase on the topics of interest to them and that their reluctance to heed the calls for equity as perceived by the developing nations will strengthen.

The two primary areas discussed in this chapter which entail extensive international cooperation and further the establishment of practices or standards include (1) manned space flight and (2) the question of protection of the space commons and the treatment of space debris. Although the issues of delimitation and access to the geostationary orbit are important, they do not call for as much attention by the United States or Russia. Of course, the Legal Subcommittee of UNCOPUOS can continue to discuss the question of delimitation, probably in the context of the most recent Russian working paper. At the same time, issues of the geostationary orbit can continue to be dealt with within the ITU when problems with the implementation of the current standards arise. Clearly, cooperation for the protection of the space environment and conclusion of a treaty on manned space flight does not mean that a new world space organization is necessary. Nor does it require that a new limited space organization be established immediately. Rather, it suggests that both topics should be put on the Legal Subcommittee's agenda to be studied by groups of experts who could in turn draft a treaty on manned space flight and establish standards and recommended practices for the protection of the space environment.

Notes

1. The primary treaties were adopted within years of the first rocket launching; the four broadly accepted space treaties were adopted in 1967, 1969, 1973, and 1976. *See infra* note 2.

2. The five major international agreements drafted by the United Nations Committee on the Peaceful Uses of Outer Space (UNCOPUOS) include: Treaty on Principles Governing the Activities of States in the Exploration and Use of Outer Space, Including the Moon and Other Celestial Bodies, Jan. 27, 1967, 18 U.S.T. 2410 [hereinafter Outer Space Treaty]; Agreement on the Rescue of Astronauts, the Return of Astronauts and the Return of Objects Launched Into Outer Space, Apr. 22, 1968, 19 U.S.T. 7570 [hereinafter Rescue and Return Agreement]; Convention on International Liability for Damage Caused by Space Objects, Mar. 29, 1972, 24 U.S.T. 2389 [hereinafter Liability Convention]; Convention on Registration of Objects Launched Into Outer Space, Jan. 14, 1975, 28 U.S.T. 695 [hereinafter Registration Convention]; and Agreement Governing the Activities of States on the Moon and Other Celestial Bodies, Dec. 5, 1979, 18 I.L.M. 1434 (1979) [hereinafter Moon Agreement].

3. On this question, *See* Pravovye Problemy Polyotov Cheloveka v Kosmos (Legal Problems of Manned Space Flight) 176–99 (V.S. Vereshchetin ed. 1986). J. Kolossov, *On the Problem of Private Commercial Activities in Outer Space,* 27 Proc. Colloq. L. Outer Space 66, 66–71 (1985) (International Institute of Space Law [hereinafter IISL] proceedings from Lausanne, Switzerland meeting in 1984) [hereinafter Kolossov, *Private Activities*].

4. According to the Decree of the President of Russia of February 25, 1992, a new organ—the Russian Space Agency—was established for the purpose of effective utilization of space facilities in Russia in the interests of social and economic development of the country, security, and furthering Russian international cooperation. This agency will have a number of tasks, including the implementation of state space policy, the formulation of draft state space programs in cooperation with other concerned state organs, the coordination of commercial space projects, and the development of international cooperation. *See* Rossiyskaya Gazeta, Feb. 27, 1992.

5. A. Cocca, *Common Heritage of Mankind: A Basic Principle of the International Legal System,* 31 Proc. Colloq. L. Outer Space 89 (1989) (IISL proceedings from Bangalore meeting in 1988) offers an overview of the development of the concept.

6. *See* D. Goedhuis, *Problems of Frontiers of Outer Space and Air Space,* in 1982 Recueil Des Cours d'Academie de Droit International [R.C.A.D.I.] 371; G. Danilenko, *The Concept of the "Common Heritage of Mankind" in International Law,* 13 Ann. Air & Space L. 247 (1988).

7. Part of the reason for the non-adoption of this Agreement had been countries' fears of the creation of an international authority with jurisdiction over exploitation.

8. *See* Report of the Legal Sub-Committee of the Work of its Twenty-Seventh Session (14–31 March 1988), U.N. Doc. A/AC.105/411, Apr. 8, 1988 [hereinafter 1988 Report] at 10, ¶ 41.

9. *See* B. Nagy, *Common Heritage of Mankind: The Status of Future Generations,* 31 Proc. Colloq. L. Outer Space 319 (1989) (IISL proceedings from Bangalore meeting in 1988), who argues that future generations constitute part of mankind, and, therefore, they are entitled to benefit from resources deemed to be the common heritage of mankind. In this light, he suggests that half of the non-

renewable natural resources should be allotted to the foreseeable future (defined as the first seven generations) and the other half to all of the other generations. With respect to non-renewable resources, he would have two principles prevail: the conservation of options and the conservation of quality. In order to achieve these aims "mankind which is more than the aggregation of states and the future generations should have their own representation, not mediated through the existing states." *Id.* at 319.

10. A satellite orbiting the earth above the equator which at an altitude of approximately 36,000 km will revolve almost concurrently with the earth, appearing stationary from the earth, uses this orbit.

11. The geostationary orbit (GSO) is actually a band around the earth with three dimensions and a finite volume, approximately 30 km thick and 150 km wide.

12. On December 3, 1976, this declaration was made by eight equatorial countries: Brazil, Colombia, Congo, Ecuador, Indonesia, Kenya, Uganda, and Zaire. *See* ITU Document WARC-BS, 81 E of Jan. 17, 1977. By 1988, a number of these states were claiming "equitable access" to the geostationary orbit instead of proprietary rights.

13. ITU, International Telecommunications Convention, art. XXXIII(2), T.I.A.S. No. 8572 (1973) (emphasis added).

14. World Administrative Radio Conference on the Use of the Geostationary Satellite Orbit and the Planning of Space Services Utilizing It (a 2 part conference) [hereinafter WARC-ORB '85 and WARC-ORB '88].

15. Christol, *The Legal Status of the Geostationary Orbit in the Light of the 1985–1988 Activities of the ITU,* 32 Proc. Colloq. L. Outer Space, 215, 221 (1990) (IISL Proceedings from Malaga, Spain meeting in 1989).

16. *Id.* at 220.

17. It is difficult to define what debris is. Schwetje defines debris as "spent spacecraft, their used rocket stages, separation devices, shrouds, clamps and the products of deliberate or accidental explosions." *See* F.K. Schwetje, *Space Law: Liability and Space Debris, In* Environmental Aspects of Activities in Outer Space 29, 31 (K.H. Bockstiegal ed.) (1990) (compilation of papers presented at an International Colloquium held in Cologne, Germany on May 1, 1988, now published as Volume 9 of Studies in Air and Space Law).

18. Some debris in farther orbits, not the lower earth orbit (LEO), actually remains in place for far longer than the debris in LEO. The atmosphere slows down objects traveling in LEO, resulting in a faster rate of decay which speeds the cleansing of the orbit. The debris in farther orbits then not only causes overcrowding of that orbit, but also increases chances of collisions. *See* Matte, *Environmental Implications and Responsibility in Use of Outer Space,* 12 Ann. Air & Space L. 419, 424 (1989).

19. *See* S. Gorove, Studies in Space Law: Its Challenges and Prospects 162–163 (1977).

20. *See* Restatement (Third) of Foreign Relations Law of the United States, at § 601. Although part of this summarization of the law is derived from the *Trail Smelter Arbitration,* which has been given different and sometimes conflicting interpretations, *see* M. Lachs, Environmental Aspects of Activities in Outer Space 187, a number of international documents and statements of experts groups incorporate this standard.

21. A Cocca, *Protocol on Environmental Consequences of Activities in Outer Space, in* Environmental Aspects of Activities in Outer Space 109, *supra* note 20, at 121–122. *See also* M. Williams, *Customary International Law and General Principles of Law, in id.* at 153, which addresses many of the problems involved in

the application of customary international law to the environmental aspects of space activities.

22. Hurwitz, *An International Compensation Fund for Damage Caused by Space Objects,* 24 Proc. Colloq. L. Outer Space 201. *See also* B. Hurwitz, State Liability For Outer Space Activities (1992); S. Hobe, *Space Debris: A Proposal for its International Regulation,* 24 Proc. Colloq. L. Outer Space 194, 199.

23. N. M. Matte, Aerospace Law.

24. U.N. Doc. A/AC.105/L. 168 ann. III, June 5, 1987; *see also* U.N. Doc. A/AC.105/L.112, June 20, 1979, and U.N. Doc A/AC.105/C.2/L.139, April 4, 1983.

25. *See, e.g.,* B. Cheng, *"Space Objects," "Astronauts," and Related Expressions,* 34 Proc. Colloq. L. Outer Space 17. Cheng states that outer space can be said to begin arguably at an altitude of 96 kilometers above the earth, clearly so at 110 kilometers above, and definitely so at 130 kilometers. *Id.* at 26.

26. G. N. Danilenko, *Granitsa mezhdu vozdushnym i kosmicheskim prostranstvom v sovremennom mezhdunarodnom prave* (The Boundary Between Airspace and Outer Space in Contemporary International Law), 9 Sovetskoye Gosudarstvo I Pravo 73 (1984).

27. *See* reprint in 18 J. Space L. 209 (1990); and 1 Sovetskiy Zhurnal Mezhdunarodngo Prava 75–81 (1991).

28. Obviously, their failure to reach agreement stems from the lack of consensus internationally on whether there should be delimitation of air and outer space. *See* discussion *supra,* section IV.

29. The first ideas on the creation of space organization were expressed in the legal literature of the late 1950s. Problemy Kosmicheskogo Prava (Problems of Space Law) 172 (1961). Later literature includes E.G. Vasilevskaya, Pravovye Problemy Osvoyeniya Luny I Planet 13–14 (Legal Problems of Opening Up the Moon and Planets) (1974); V.S. Vereshchetin, Mezhdunarodnoye Sotrudnichestvo v Kosmose, Pravovye Voprosy (International Cooperation in Space: Legal Questions) 129 (1977); H. DeSaussure, *Evolution Towards an International Space Agency,* 19 Proc. Colloq. L. Outer Space 32–41 (1977) (proceedings from Anaheim, California meeting in 1976); D. Myers, *A New International Agency to Coordinate the Actions of States in Outer Space: Some Preliminary Suggestions,* 19 Proc. Colloq. L. Outer Space 414–416 (1977) (proceedings from the Anaheim, California meeting in 1976); J. Tamm, *Should an International Outer Space Agency Be Established?,* 13 Proc. Colloq. L. Outer Space 53–60.

30. E. Kamenetskaya, *International Space Law: New Institutional Opportunities, in* Perestroika and International Law. Current Anglo-Soviet Approaches to International Law at 172–184 (1990); B. Khabirov, *Through Cooperation in Space Towards Understanding and Peace on the Earth,* 32 Proc. Colloq. L. Outer Space 38 (1989) (proceedings from Bangalore meeting in 1988).

PART 3.5

International Law as
Normative System:
To Regulate
Economic Activity

23

International Economic Law: Reflections on the "Boilerroom" of International Relations

John H. Jackson

Introduction

T he pace of international economic activity and the developing interdependence of national economies is head spinning. Governments increasingly find it difficult to implement worthy policies concerning economic activity because such activity often crosses borders in ways to escape the reach of much of national government control. This can be true for subjects as diverse as insurance, brokerage, product health and safety standards, environmental protection, banking, securities and investment, professional services such as medical or law, and many more. . . .

First, I will make some general observations about international economic law and its characteristics. Second, I will briefly reflect on developments in the Uruguay Round. Third, I will suggest some broader implications of the Uruguay Round and other activities of international economic law, namely the problems posed today for government regulation of international economic behavior. Finally, I will offer a few conclusions.

Some General Observations About International Economic Law

At the outset, it is appropriate to ask what we mean by "international economic law." This phrase can cover a very broad inventory of subjects: embracing the law of economic transactions; government regulation of economic matters; and related legal relations including litigation and international institutions for economic relations. Indeed, it is plausible to suggest that ninety percent of international law work is in reality international economic law in some form or another. Much of this, of course, does not have the glamour or visibility of nation-state relations (use of force, human rights, intervention, etc.), but does indeed involve many questions of international law and particularly treaty law. Increasingly, today's international economic law issues are found on the front pages of the daily newspapers.

One of the problems for a law teacher in this field, is what to include in a course. Clearly my co-authors, other colleagues and I have decided to focus on the core "system" aspects of international economic regulation. what I often call the "constitution." This avoids too much of a "smorgasbord" approach of sampling many varied subjects and also represents a priority choice that downplays the transactional law and focuses more on *regulation* by government institutions. including both national and international institutions.[1] We recognize, however, that there are other worthy views on these choices.

Another problem for the legal scholar is the choice of subjects for research and the approach to that research. Again, I will reveal some of my predilections. These preferences are to shape research so as to be useful for the "active users," the legal professionals (government or private) who must regularly cope with international law concepts and legal rules. This is a "policy research" preference rather than a "theory" preference, although obviously there are many situations in which theory has important relevance to policy. But such theory needs to be "good theory," and generally I feel good theory must be tested, most often by empirical observation. Thus, there is a strong component of empiricism in my preferences.

In trying to describe international economic law, I would like to mention four characteristics about the subject:

1) International Economic Law (IEL) can not be separated or compartmentalized from general or "public" international law. The activities and cases relating to IEL contain much practice which is relevant to general principles of international law, especially concerning treaty law and practice. Conversely general international law has considerable relevance to economic relations and transactions. It is interesting, for example, to compare the number of cases handled by the GATT dispute settlement system (approximately 250)[2] to those handled by the World Court (approaching 100). Numbers don't tell the whole tale, but there certainly are some GATT cases that have had as profound consequences on national governments and world affairs as have ICJ cases. The GATT cases are rich with practice relating to the general question of international dispute resolution, and some of this practice has broader implications than simply for the GATT (and now WTO) system itself.

2) The relationship of international economic law to national or "municipal" law is particularly important. It is an important part of understanding international law generally, but this "link," and the interconnections between IEL and municipal law are particularly significant to the

operation and effectiveness of IEL rules. For example, an important question is the relationship of treaty norms to municipal law, expressed by such phrases as "self executing" or "direct application."

3) As the title phrase—international economic law—suggests, there is necessarily a strong component of multi-disciplinary research and thinking required for those who work on IEL projects. Of course, "economics" is important and useful, especially for understanding the policy motivations of many of the international and national rules on the subject. Obviously, it is just as important to understand some of the criticisms of economic analysis, and to treat with skepticism some of the economic "models." Likewise, there are alternative value structures which should balance some economic notions of "efficiency." Thus, various lifestyle choices, and certain long-range value objectives can at least appear, and perhaps actually be, contradictory to some economic objectives, at least as some of those economic objectives are phrased by certain writers.

In addition to economics, of course, other subjects are highly relevant. Political science (and its intersection with economics found generally in the "public choice" literature) is very important, as are many other disciplines, such as cultural history and anthropology, geography, etc.

4) As previously noted, work on IEL matters often seems to necessitate more empirical study than some other international law subjects. Empirical research, however, does not necessarily mean statistical research, in the sense used in many policy explorations. For some key issues of international law there are too few "cases" on which to base statistical conclusions (such as correlations), so we are constrained to use a more "anecdotal" or case study approach. This type of empiricism, however, is nevertheless very important, and a good check on theory or on sweeping generalizations of any kind.

Since this often requires a study of particular cases, or at least of certain groups of cases, with considerable quantitative elements, it is frequently necessary to master a considerable amount of detail to understand some of the interplay of forces affecting international economic relations and the law concerning those relations. What does all this imply for research? As many of us represented in this volume realize already, our task in selecting priorities for research and successfully carrying out such research is not easy. Empiricism, multi-disciplinary approaches, and the breadth of legal understanding to relate not only general international law principles with IEL, but also both with national constitutional and other law, create quite a burden.

Some of these points remind me of an experience I had recently which I will share with you. About a year or two ago I received a call from a journalist editorial writer of one of the major U.S. national papers. He had been trying to understand something about dumping cases which were prominently in the news, and he had been referred to me by a mutual friend. We talked for more than an hour on the telephone about the essential attributes of the international dumping rules, as well as the way the United States applies those rules in its national law. We worked through some hypothetical cases illustrating the difficulties and the "tilts" in the rules and their administration. As any of you who have had to grapple with this subject know, this comes fairly quickly to the "mego" stage ("my eyes glaze over"). However, my caller gallantly mastered the logic, and finally at the end he said "Boy, this certainly is the boiler room of international relations!"

Uruguay Round Developments:
An Example of Research Needs

At this time shortly after the completion of the GATT Uruguay Round negotiation, it is almost unthinkable to write about the subject of this paper without some reference to that round and to what it means for this subject.

I for one, have been greatly impressed with the achievements made in the Uruguay Round. We are all aware of the difficulties encountered in this Round which caused a prolongation of the negotiation. The 1988 failure of the Mid-Term Review Ministerial Meeting in Montreal, as well as the 1990 "impasse" at the Brussels Ministerial Meeting did not give cause for optimism about the Round. Nevertheless, in December 1991 the then GATT Director-General Arthur Dunkel directed a coordinated effort of secretariat officials and diplomats to achieve a complete draft of the status of the negotiation at that time. This "Dunkel Draft" was flawed in many respects, but it was the first time that nations and their officials could have an overall look at what was being done. Two years later, after a number of national elections, economic difficulties, and other political changes, the resulting agreement achieved in December 1993 is extraordinary, and largely based on the "Dunkel text." This achievement has now entered into force.

I will not here go through an inventory of each of the achievements.[3] We are all familiar with the importance of incorporating into the trading system the subjects of trade in services, as well as intellectual property protection. Likewise, we know the difficulties of bringing GATT discipline to agriculture, and we admire that at least a start has been made in that respect. Other achievements include significant market access with impressive tariff cutting, a start towards remedying problems in the textile trade, a more complete integration of developing countries into the rule oriented system, and new "codes" for subsidies, safeguards, and product standards.

Perhaps the most significant achievement. however, at least from the point of view of this group, is the result of the Uruguay Round concerning institutions. Not only has an impressive new set of dispute settlement procedures been put forward, but a new charter for an international organization-the World Trade Organization (WTO)—has been approved as a sort of "capstone" for the many complicated provisions of the negotiation results.

The previous institutional structure (GATT) was frail and beset by what I have often called "birth defects." We recall that the GATT was never intended to be an organization, but evolved into one because of the failure (shortly after 1948) of nations to ratify and put into effect the then drafted charter for an ITO—International Trade Organization. As the defects and weaknesses of the GATT institutional structure became more apparent, just during a period of time when the problems of international economic relations became more aggravated, it was clear to world leaders that an improvement was needed in the institutional structure, and I believe the WTO Charter represents such improvement.

The new charter is not perfect by any means and certainly is not an ITO. The new charter is more a "mini-charter," which is designed to carry forward the practices and customary procedures that have been developed through trial and error within the GATT system for more than forty years. Indeed, in many ways the new charter better protects the institutional structure and the sovereignty of the members than did the GATT structure with its defects. Many practices which under GATT were merely customary, such as the "consensus" technique of decision making, have now been partially defined and embodied in treaty language, with fall-back procedures that will help protect against misuse of power or institutions. The WTO will facilitate implementation of the Uruguay Round by extending an institutional umbrella to the new subjects, and by reinforcing the "single package idea" of the Uruguay Round. (All the principal treaty agreement clauses will now become required for each WTO member, unlike the results of the Tokyo Round where nations could more or less pick and choose among ten or so "side agreements.")

The new dispute settlement procedures will for the first time establish a unified set of procedures for disputes of all types under the various WTO agreements, and will embody these procedures for the first time in a legal text (as compared to the rather imprecise views about customary practice that tended to prevail before). If the new procedures work, certain specific defects of the system, such as the blocking of panel reports, will be overcome, substituting instead an ingenious appellate procedure almost unique in international law.

I think it is difficult to over emphasize the potential significance of these achievements. The Uruguay Round itself has been the most ambitious of the trade rounds under GATT, and would be a success with half of its achievements. When you add to this a number of other current developments including the deepening and broadening of the European Union, the implementation of the North American Free Trade Agreement (NAFTA), and the developments of the economies "in transition," such as the parts of former Soviet Union and of mainland China, I think it is plausible to argue that we are witnessing a watershed shift and the most profound change in international economic relations. institutions, and structures since the origin of the Bretton Woods System at the end of World War II.

What the WTO will face in the future is still not clear. High on the priority list of many persons' agenda is a thorough consideration of the policies of environmental protection as they relate to international trade. Additionally, considerable work on the relationship of competition policy (antitrust) and trade rules is suggested. Embedded in the Uruguay Round results is a very extensive work agenda, because many of the agreements call for follow-up activity on, for example, services, agriculture. subsidies, and intellectual property. Perhaps further down the road there will be demands on the WTO system to consider the relationship of other important subjects to the world trade rules, including labor standards, human rights, and other "link" issues now forming an important part of the trade questions. Further study on some of the goals and assumptions of trade economics will undoubtedly be undertaken, and a number of issues we might call "cultural clash issues" will be given attention, including internal economic structures of distribution and retail trade, gender equality and other questions of discrimination, and the relationship of political structures and democracy to successful long term trading relationships.

Sovereignty, Subsidiarity and Society or The Problem of Regulating International Economic Behavior

I would like now to turn to some tentative and more fundamental thinking about our subject. To some extent, I am trying to anticipate what may be important directions for scholars and thinkers relating to international economic law in the future.[4]

I start with the observable circumstances of a world that is becoming increasingly intertwined and interdependent. Some call this "globalization." The manifestations are many. As you look at some of the major developments during the last few years, including the completion of NAFTA, the Uruguay Round completion itself (awaiting implementation), the intricate and remarkably detailed bilateral negotiations between the United States and Japan (some in the context of the Structural Impediments Initiative—SII), the directions of the European Union towards greater integration in Europe, and the remarkable developments of the economies in transition, including Russia and the former partners of the Soviet Union, China, and indeed many developing countries, we can see many manifestations of this greater "globalization." If you examine in particular some of the language in NAFTA, such as that in Chapter 11 or Chapter 18, it is truly astonishing how deeply the treaty norms "intrude" into what has previously been termed "sovereign prerogative." The deepening regulation in Europe confirms that trend, and to a somewhat lesser extent, but nevertheless on a much broader scale, some of the Uruguay Round achievements (particularly the potential of the services agreement and the intellectual property agreement) point to a similar direction.

These efforts respond to a major problem of today's international relations, namely: the difficulty of government regulation of international economic behavior. Whether it is a banking scandal such as BCCI, or the difficulty of harmonizing certain consumer or food product standards, or the differential effects of taxes, social security, medical insurance, and labor immobility, there is today hardly any subject that can be said to be effectively controlled by a single national sovereign. This, of course, is frustrating to many national government leaders, since in many circumstances it prevents them from effectively fulfilling their constituents' needs or desires. Sometimes an attempt to "go it alone" can simply generate counter-responses from other countries, such as escalating tariffs, competitive devaluation of currencies, "race to the bottom" in connection with regulatory standards or taxation, and other difficulties. Many economists analyze these problems as the "prisoner's dilemma," which when analyzed under game theory techniques suggests the need for international cooperation.

In these circumstances, governments often find (as they do internally) that various worthy policies are conflicting. The trade liberalization policies are designed to promote enhancement of world welfare and to preserve the peace against rancorous economic quarreling. Often, however. these policies appear to conflict with environmental goals, human rights norms, and labor standards. When these "dilemmas" of policy conflict occur within a nation-state, they must be ironed out through governmental institutions of that nation. When these similar conflicts occur on an international scale, then we must look to international institutions for this task. Unfortunately, the international institutions are notably weaker than most national institutions. Clearly then, there is an important field of policy research and endeavor in exploring the techniques, mechanisms, and institutions for providing the necessary international cooperation.

Some Conclusions

I think you can now see some of the directions my thinking takes us. Legal scholars as well as economists and political scientists must struggle with these problems using different types of governmental activity: unilateral, bilateral, regional, or multilateral. They must try to appraise the longer term effectiveness of these various levels of activity, and they must try to assist policy makers in determining appropriate courses of action. The legal scholar, however, has a particular, and I would say more important role. In a broad sense what we are struggling with is the development of the "constitutional law" of international economic relations. By this I refer to the international economic or trade system as a whole, and the institutional structures which allow it to operate effectively. Thus, we face issues for which the lawyer's role is, at least partly, to help protect the longer range constitutional provisions from certain short-term or ad hoc expediency temptations of governments or other players in that system, and to help shape the direction of that constitutional development.

Very important to this "constitutional" approach, is the question of appropriate allocation of power, and the protection against the misuse of power. The needs for international cooperation lead to the development of international organizations, but such organizations can be misused and their power abused. For example, leadership of an organization can be unresponsive and relatively self-perpetuating (given the diplomatic difficulties of selection of leaders in the context of more than one hundred nations participating). Such leaders, or power structures within organizations can cause a misallocation of the resources of the organization (such as for a marble headquarters, or an inappropriately high percentage of expenditures for low priority activity). There have even been some occasional allegations of fraudulent activity. Furthermore, some countries which are heavy contributors resent being outvoted by large numbers of mini-states which are arguably irresponsible because the projects the latter favor do not require any contribution by them.

This also brings us to the question of sovereignty and subsidiarity. In some peoples' eyes, sovereignty is an outdated idea. Insofar as sovereignty implies the right of governments to do what they will, including torture their own citizens, I believe most people would recognize that the ancient concepts are no longer viable today. In addition, the actual circumstances of the "globalized market" impose realistic constraints on the unilateral exercise of "sovereignty" to solve certain problems. Some would argue that we should virtually do away with the concept of sovereignty. On the other hand, there may be a newer approach to defining sovereignty that could be significant and worthwhile. This would embrace the idea that the concept of national sovereignty is really part of "subsidiarity" (a term often discussed in Europe) meaning that sovereignty in this sense is a claim that the appropriate allocation of power among different levels of government leads to a conclusion that certain types of decisions should be made only at the national level and not in an international organization or cooperative mechanism. The concept of subsidiarity, however. could go further. It could lead to a conclusion that other kinds of decisions must be *elevated* to the international level. In addition, it could lead to the conclusion that sub-national, regional or even cultural units should be endowed with the exclusive power to make certain kinds of decisions.

Connected with these issues are dozens of more detailed legal issues regarding the structure of a charter for an international organization and the procedures for various kinds of decision making. These include whether voting should be by majority or a super-majority, whether there should be "veto rights," whether voting should be weighted, and whether there should be some small "steering group" power centers.

In addition, an increasingly important issue for these constitutional problems of "international governance," is the dispute-settlement procedures and mechanisms associated with them. Particularly with reference to international economic relations, I have argued elsewhere that a "rule-oriented" approach is very significant.[5] Such an approach gives additional predictability and stability such that millions of individual entrepreneurs and investors will have a higher degree of confidence in the decisions which they make. This can lower transaction costs. lower certain risk premiums that might otherwise apply, and thus better allocate investment or market decisions so as to enhance world welfare. These rules and their evolution can also be a major mechanism for mediation between conflicting policy goals of the international economic system.

There are certainly many other institutional and "constitutional" issues that can also be addressed by IEL scholars including some of the detailed questions involving secretariats, privileges and immunities, budget making, the role of officials in organizations, and activity of such officials such as mediation and good offices. The relationship of trade institutions to the monetary organizations and the Bretton Woods System clearly needs more attention. . . .

To close, the reader can probably see that these remarks and reflections confirm some descriptions of me as an exponent of the "pragmatist school" of international law scholarship. I would also add the phrase "normative realist." Like many scholars, I feel the pressure of responsibility for moving the subject forward despite the difficulty and limitation of resources, and despite the sometimes pessimistic viewpoint that mere "realism" can engender.

Notes

1. John H. Jackson, William Davey, and Alan Sykes, Legal Problems of International Economic Relations (3d ed. 1995).

2. *See* Robert Hudec, Enforcing International Trade Law: The Evolution of the Modern GATT Legal System 417–585 (1993) (indexing 207 GATT complaints from July 1948 to November 1989).

3. *See* John H. Jackson, *Managing the Trading System: The World Trade Organization and the Post-Uruguay Round GATT Agenda, in* Managing the World Economy: Fifty Years After Bretton Woods Ch. 3, 131–52 (Peter B. Kene & Institute for International Economic eds., 1994).

4. John H. Jackson, *Alternative Approaches for Implementing Competition Rules in International Economic Relations,* 177–200, Aussenwirtschaft—Swiss Rev. Int'l Econ. Rel. No. 2/94 (St. Gallen Switzerland, 1994).

5. *See* John Jackson, The World Trading System, (1989) at 85–88.

24

The Charter of Economic Rights and Duties of States and the Deprivation of Foreign-Owned Wealth

Burns H. Weston

I n a parable drawn from *The Trial,* Franz Kafka once etched the following chilling profile:

> Before the Law stands a doorkeeper on guard. To this doorkeeper there
> comes a man from the country who begs for admittance to the Law. But
> the doorkeeper says that he cannot admit the man at the moment. The
> man, on reflection, asks if he will be allowed, then, to enter later. "It is
> possible," answers the doorkeeper, "but not at this moment." Since the
> door leading into the Law stands open as usual and the doorkeeper steps
> to one side, the man bends down to peer through the entrance. When the
> doorkeeper sees that, he laughs and says: "If you are so strongly tempted,
> try to get in without my permission. But note that I am powerful. And I
> am only the lowest doorkeeper. From hall to hall keepers stand at every
> door, one more powerful than the other. Even the third of these has an as-
> pect that even I cannot bear to look at." These are difficulties which the
> man from the country had not expected to meet; the Law, he thinks,
> should be accessible to every man at all times. . . .[1]

The message of this parable is fundamental, I believe, to a proper understanding of the Charter of Economic Rights and Duties of States, adopted
by the UN General Assembly by an overwhelming vote of 120 to 6 with 10
abstentions in December 1974 as a centerpiece of what has come to be
called the "New International Economic Order" (NIEO). Signaling the end
of complete Northern hegemony and the emergence of a new interdependence of power and wealth, this NIEO Charter raises fundamental questions about what is fair and just, quintessentially legal and moral questions
that, in Ali Mazrui's well-chosen words, mirror a Third World "caught
between the indignity of charity and the ambition of economic justice."[2]

Reproduced with permission from 75 *AJIL* 437 (1981), © The American Society of
International Law.

It is from this general perspective that one should approach Article 2 of the NIEO Charter and, in particular, its subparagraph 2(c), which purports to affect the Law of State Responsibility as it impinges upon the nationalization, expropriation, or other deprivation of foreign-owned wealth. Article 2 reads in its entirety as follows:

> 1. Every State has and shall freely exercise full permanent sovereignty, including possession, use and disposal, over all its wealth, natural resources and economic activities.
>
> 2. Each State has the right:
>
> (a) To regulate and exercise authority over foreign investment within its national jurisdiction in accordance with its laws and regulations and in conformity with its national objectives and priorities. No State shall be compelled to grant preferential treatment to foreign investment;
> (b) To regulate and supervise the activities of transnational corporations within its national jurisdiction and take measures to ensure that such activities comply with its laws, rules and regulations and conform with its economic and social policies. Transnational corporations shall not intervene in the internal affairs of a host State. Every State should, with full regard for its sovereign rights, co-operate with other States in the exercise of the right set forth in this subparagraph;
> (c) To nationalize, expropriate or transfer ownership of foreign property in which case appropriate compensation should be paid by the State adopting such measures, taking into account its relevant laws and regulations and all circumstances that the State considers pertinent. In any case where the question of compensation gives rise to a controversy, it shall be settled under the domestic law of the nationalizing State and by its-tribunals, unless it is freely and mutually agreed by all States concerned that other peaceful means be sought on the basis of the sovereign equality of States and in accordance with the principle of free choice of means.

A break from the past seems clear. The so-called public purpose (or public utility) doctrine is disregarded. The "doctrine of alien nondiscrimination" is ignored. And the much heralded international law principle of compensation appears to be "domesticated," *i.e.,* rejected as an *international* regulatory norm. Provoking not a little consternation and complaint among capital-exporting constituencies,[3] the provision is a vivid demonstration, even if primarily a symbolic one, of the central NIEO demand for restructured perspectives and patterns of international economic order, as most recently, albeit rather ineffectually, evidenced by the General Assembly's 11th Special Session on international development issues (which anticipated the upcoming "global negotiations" on international cooperation and development).

A preliminary reassessment of the issues fundamentally at stake in this discrete realm therefore seems needed. Accordingly, I shall proceed first and briefly with the failure of Article 2 to incorporate the "public purpose" and alien nondiscrimination doctrines, and then shall consider in some detail two questions that I believe must be asked about the compensation issue which Article 2 does address: (1) whether Article 2(2)(c) *is* or *is not* an authoritative statement of existing international law (*lex lata*); and (2), assuming *arguendo* a negative answer to the first issue, whether Article 2(2) (c) *should* or *should not* be recognized as an authoritative statement of international law (*de lege ferenda*). The key issues thus may be seen to divide between law and policy.

Article 2 and the Public Purpose Doctrine

It is neither surprising nor shocking that Article 2 omits mention of the public purpose doctrine, *i.e.,* the contention that foreign property, rights, and interests cannot be "taken" except for reasons of public necessity or utility. Although early declared by Grotius to be a limitation upon a sovereign's power of eminent domain, and while understandably incorporated into many domestic systems to protect against executive and legislative abuse, the doctrine has found scant support in practice as a "rule" of international law whose violation *independently* engages international responsibility. Research has yet to reveal any international legal dispute that has turned on the public purpose issue alone. In 1962, the General Assembly itself embraced the doctrine in its Resolution 1803 (XVII) on Permanent Sovereignty over Natural Resources. Yet, as even the doctrine's erstwhile proponents now concede, "there is little authority in international law establishing any useful criteria by which a State's own determination of public purpose can be questioned."[4] This conclusion, I believe, is realistic. Moreover, no matter what legal effect one may ascribe to the NIEO Charter, it is amply reinforced not only by Article 2, but also by many of the remaining Charter provisions which similarly favor unfettered economic sovereignty as a basis for ordering international economic affairs. The point is not that foreign-wealth deprivations should not be taken in the public interest, but, as Hans Baade has observed, in "*whose* public interest, as determined by whom."[5]

Article 2 and the Alien Nondiscrimination Doctrine

For all its disabilities, the so-called public purpose doctrine does serve nevertheless to remind us that what or why something is wanted commonly conditions both our perspectives about the permissibility of given initiatives and the correctness of individual and group responses to them. So basic is this question of motives or objectives to all legal systems, indeed, that one might greet without too much alarm the omission in Article 2 of the doctrine of alien nondiscrimination, *i.e.,* the contention that resident aliens are entitled to *at least* the same protection of their persons and property ("vested rights") as local law affords to nationals. Long honored in customary practice, judicial decisions, and treaty law, this doctrine may now be a matter of *jus cogens*—part of a "newly emerged general norm of nondiscrimination which seeks to forbid all generic differentiations among people . . . for reasons irrelevant to individual capabilities and contribution"[6] so that its omission would not prejudice the resolution of controversies arising under Article 2.

A distinct problem is, however, that Article 2(2) (a) is quick to provide that "[n]o State shall be compelled to grant preferential treatment to foreign investment"—the Calvo Doctrine reincarnate—and without "even . . . a genuflection" to "the natural corollary of nondiscrimination," as pointed out by Brower and Tepe.[7] Indeed, given that Article 2(2) (c), by referring only to "foreign property," implicitly authorizes a state to exempt its own nationals from wealth deprivation measures, and that it would have all compensation controversies arising out of foreign-wealth deprivations "settled under the domestic law of the nationalizing State"—the Calvo Doctrine reborn again—the genuflection looks to be in the opposite direction. Additionally, despite the repeated deference in the NIEO Charter to such principles as "common interest and co-operation," "equal rights," "equity," "respect for human rights and fundamental freedoms," and "social justice," other provisions that do invoke the language of nondiscrimination do so, similarly, not to guard against but to widen governmental power in order to give priority to what will aid the less-developed countries (LDC's). A more direct challenge to the doctrine of alien nondiscrimination as traditionally conceived in the context of foreign-wealth deprivation (at least outside Latin America) is thus hard to imagine.

Considering the historical inspiration and principal authorship of the NIEO Charter, this manifestly one-sided approach is of course not difficult to fathom. However, it does raise a complex of difficult questions that beg for objective analysis. Without attempting any definitive answers here— answers that only an extended and much needed dissertation can supply— let us consider briefly what some of these might be.

Take the "simplest" case first. Putting aside qualifying treaty commitments (which would appear guaranteed by chapter I of the NIEO Charter), it seems proper to conclude, as did Gillian White over a decade ago, that "[t]here is as yet no rule of international law which provides that a State is guilty of illegal discrimination if it nationalises alien proper in a field where there are no national interests capable of being affected."[8] The concept of discrimination meaning or implying choice, this conclusion is logical. More importantly, it is wise. In Baade's words:

> [N]ationalizations in many underdeveloped countries with few major
> natural resources tend to be discriminatory by the mere force of

circumstances, because the natural resource that is nationalized is exclusively in the control of enterprises belonging to one foreign power, frequently, though not necessarily, the former colonial power. . . . If it is urged that even such discriminations are to be proscribed, the purpose of the asserted rule becomes clear. It is not envisaged as an enumeration of the conditions of the legality of nationalizations, but [as] an attempt to insulate one of the most important areas of international investment from nationalization completely. It is, in other words, an attempt to substitute the restrictions of international law for the restraints previously imposed by colonialism and gunboat diplomacy.[9]

In a world that can ill afford losing anyone's respect for the rule of law, these opinions are prudent.

Yet troublesome questions arise even in this simplest ("no national interests") case. For example, what if more than one alien interest is capable of being affected? In the absence of indigenous targets, are deprivation-prone elites free to discriminate among resident aliens willy-nilly? Or what if a "nationalization" or "expropriation" of one or more alien interests is done in whole or in part for reasons of retaliation or reprisal? Leaving aside the desirability or propriety of infusing the alien nondiscrimination doctrine with the concepts of retaliation and reprisal, are past trends opposing such actions, along with carefully nurtured principles of proportionality, to be disregarded because only alien interests are at hand? Of course, these questions tend toward the rhetorical as posed, suggesting negative answers. However, recast to call up complementary issues of fact and policy—*i.e.,* are *all* discriminations among and between aliens unlawful? are all retaliatory deprivations against aliens impermissible?—they recommend extreme caution.

The same can be said of these and related questions in the more heterogeneous context where there are also national interests capable of being affected. For example, in the initial matter of determining who among existent national and alien proprietors shall be subjected to deprivation, is it lawful or unlawful to single out an alien interest on any one or more of the following (illustrative) grounds:

> (1) that, as an actual or perceived agent of a foreign power or as an unwanted reminder of colonial or imperialistic association, the alien interest inhibits true foreign policy independence?

> (2) that, as part of a politically sensitive sector or because of certain business practices, it frustrates given social, economic, or environmental values and policies of the domestic order?

> (3) that, in contrast to competing national or alien interests to whom the host government might be obligated, it cannot lay claim to express or implied contractual promises not to deprive? or

> (4) that, concession agreement or not, it monopolizes, otherwise dominates, or disproportionately exploits a particular resource or field?

Similarly, as regards the eventual matter of determining which of the targeted national or alien interests shall be entitled to what compensation (if any), do not one or all of these and possibly other kinds of discriminations have some appropriately differentiating role to play? My point is this: whatever the disabilities of the NIEO Charter in general, and of Article 2 in particular, it is difficult to accept categorically the following conclusions reached by White some years ago:

> (1) that "[m]easures which are aimed exclusively at alien-owned property in a field where there are also national interests constitute illegal discrimination";

> (2) that "[m]easures which are general in scope but which single out . . [alien] property . . . for unfavourable treatment (usually in the matter of payment of compensation) constitute a breach of the [alien nondiscrimination] rule unless there is justification for such treatment in treaty provisions."[10]

These conclusions, I submit, are too facile. Additionally, they risk a questionable ethnocentricity. In Tom Farer's words:

> Latin American governments and scholars [have] consistently urged the view that international law require[s] nothing more than the equality of treatment for indigenous and foreign investors. Yet, although they [have] pulled all the right buttons on the international legal console and pedaled vigorously, they might as well have been silent for all the effect they [have] had on the views expounded in Western universities and chancelleries or, for that matter, on the gunboats and marines dispatched periodically to enforce the "law."[11]

Echoing Baade on the simplest ("no national interests") case, this expression, too, is prudent warning.

All of which suggests, as urged above, that there is substantial need for objective reappraisal of the doctrine of alien nondiscrimination as traditionally espoused. I hasten to add, though, that one must start from the oft neglected truism that discrimination is not per se unlawful or bad; indeed, no unqualified doctrine of nondiscrimination could be constituted part of customary international law without sacrificing important community values. McDougal, Lasswell, and Chen (concerned to banish all discriminations "irrelevant of individual capabilities and contribution"[12]) usefully counsel in this way: "whether a particular differentiation of aliens and nationals has a reasonable basis in the common interest of the larger community must . . . depend not only upon the value primarily at stake in the differentiation but also upon many particular, and varying, features of the context in which the differentiation is made."[13] Of course, to avoid tipping the balance too much in one direction, one should counsel further that the same holds true for any particular *non*differentiation of aliens and nationals also; nondifferentiations, too, if they are to have "a reasonable basis in the common interest," must be seen to depend upon the complexities of fact and policy to which the Yale scholars refer. Yet, regrettably, these counsels tend to fall on deaf ears. Many of the NIEO Charter's enthusiasts (quick to bypass the doctrine of alien nondiscrimination in quest of largely unrestricted "self-determination"), as well as many of its opponents (slow to concede any system change lest access to resources and profit margins be reduced), often choose to ignore these complexities and consequently render the attendant ambiguities moot.

However, for all that one may appeal for heightened fact/policy sensitivity on all sides, there is at least one aspect of the doctrine of alien nondiscrimination that *in principle* should not be open to debate. Actually, it is central to heightened fact/policy sensitivity, the diacritical skein that winds through all the questions raised so far. I refer to the concept of arbitrariness, praised by Orrego Vicuña as a "profound moral judgment about what is just and unjust."[14] Whether the question is to determine which alien interest shall be subjected to deprivation, or to decide who shall receive what compensation therefor (if any), or to evaluate the procedures for reaching these determinations and decisions (this last issue being one we associate with "denial of justice" claims), it cannot—must not—be answered arbitrarily (*i.e.,* capriciously or without reasons sanctioned by the common interest of an increasingly interdependent and interpenetrating world community). To be sure, left unrefined, the concept of arbitrariness does not augment legal certainty. As Cornelius Murphy has observed, "Arbitrariness is not a self-evident norm from which, through a process of deduction, one can make judgments about specific controversies."[15] What is just and fair (*i.e.,* nonarbitrary) discrimination is a question that is capable of final solution only by reference to the discrete fact/policy context (a point well understood by American constitutional lawyers even as they invoke the so-called strict scrutiny, intermediate scrutiny, and rational basis tests to prove or disprove a "compelling State interest," a "substantial State interest," or "administrative convenience" in race, sex, and alienage discrimination cases). And, even then, given that people (decision makers) unconsciously arrange what they secretly desire, it is a matter of interpretation. For example, the two lower United States courts in *Banco Nacional de Cuba v. Sabbotino* held the 1960 Cuban takeovers of North American sugar interests to be unlawfully "discriminatory"[16] notwithstanding their having been undertaken in retaliation for what Cuba avowedly considered, not without some justification, acts of illegal economic aggression. To quote Murphy again, "An impartial tribunal, taking that circumstance into consideration, [might] have reached a different conclusion "[17]

Nevertheless, considering the many authoritative human rights formulations and practices that have followed upon the UN Charter and the Universal Declaration of Human Rights (let alone the noble aspirations these expressions represent), it seems correct—nay necessary—to conclude that *foreign-wealth deprivation decisions* (substantive and procedural) taken solely for reasons of racial, religious, cultural, ethnic or nationality aversion or preference should and do constitute unlawful discriminations for being arbitrary. Indeed, if there is any basis, in the context of foreign-wealth deprivation, for maintaining that the doctrine of alien nondiscrimination has achieved *jus cogens* stature, it is in this realm of "simple human respect," of such general acceptance as to challenge even the most zealous advocate of the NIEO Charter.

On the other hand, given the yet fragile state of the global human rights system, and taking into account the NIEO Charter's understandable (but, I submit, myopic) rejection of the principle of diplomatic protection (as most vividly seen in Article 2), even a modest gesture in opposition to arbitrary discrimination would have been salutary. The point is not, per the "minimum standard of international justice," that aliens always should be treated *prima facie* more favorably than nationals regarding who shall be deprived or compensated for what (nor, indeed, per the "equal treatment standard," that aliens always should be treated no more favorably than nationals). The point is, rather, that no one, not even depriving state nationals, should be deprived of her or his wealth arbitrarily—that is, without some reasonable justification in terms of, say, per United States constitutional law for example, a "compelling State interest," a "substantial State interest," or even mere "administrative convenience." Incorporating the Calvo Doctrine without qualification, and hence disregarding the potential capriciousness of *all* domestic systems (including so-called civilized ones), Article 2 grossly underestimates the importance of this value and thereby does unwitting disservice even to the Third World interests it was intended to help. The history of exploitation prompting its formulation and adoption is perfectly clear; but generalized southern suspicion of the North is no less dysfunctional than generalized Northern ethnocentrism vis-à-vis the South. In Richard Lillich's words:

> [W]hile it is true that "the ideas of justice and fair dealing incorporated in the accepted norms of conduct for European nations were carried over into the wider sphere of the international society of the nineteenth century," there is no need to apologize for attempting to establish a universal consensus behind justice and fair dealing.[18]

Article 2 and the Principle of Compensation

We come now to subparagraph 2(c) of Article 2 and its seeming repudiation of the principle of compensation as an international regulatory norm in the foreign-wealth deprivation context. To appreciate its full import, it should be seen against General Assembly Resolution 1803 (XVII) on Permanent Sovereignty over Natural Resources, adopted in 1962.

In cases of "nationalization, expropriation or requisitioning," the 1962 resolution provided, "the owner *shall* be paid appropriate compensation, in accordance with the rules in force in the State taking such measures in the exercise of its sovereignty *and in accordance with international law.*" For the next decade at least, this formulation was regarded generally, among developed and developing nations alike, as a reasonably accurate reflection of customary international law. Article 2(2) (c), however, reflecting growing Third World dissent from the international compensation principle at least as articulated by the liberal West, does not follow suit. While also providing for "appropriate compensation" upon the deprivation of foreign wealth, it does so by way of a predatory "should," and subject only to the "relevant laws and regulations and all circumstances that the [depriving] State considers pertinent," *i.e.,* without any express reference to international law standards and procedures, not even by implication through cross-reference to Resolution 1803 (XVII). Indeed, because it mandates as well that all compensation controversies "*shall* be settled under the domestic law of the nationalizing State and by its tribunals" (except insofar as the concerned parties might "freely and mutually" choose otherwise), its intent is to renounce international law (or its relevance) in this realm. Concededly, the preparatory history of Article 2(2) (c) leaves room to contend that this negative interpretation is unwarranted. Citing the remarks of the Chairman of the UNCTAD working group charged with drafting the NIEO Charter (Ambassador Jorge Castañeda), upon the occasion of the Draft Charter's submission to the Second Committee of the General Assembly, former Judge Jiménez de Aréchaga maintains that the drafters intended only to avoid the inference, per the industrial West, that "appropriate compensation . . . in accordance with international law" necessarily means, specifically, "prompt, adequate, and effective compensation." Concededly, too, there may be no need to reiterate the applicability of international law in every diplomatic instrument because, as some say, international law applies *ipso jure* to all state acts; and besides, a reiteration requirement might foster the notion that international law is irrelevant in the absence of its explicit mention. Nevertheless, because the preparatory history leading up to the article's adoption (including its final debate in the 29th session of the General Assembly) renders the issue ambiguous at best, because some key postadoption developments tend to corroborate a nationalistic or self-determinist bias, and because, over time, the "full permanent sovereignty" principle has been used by its most vigorous exponents to legitimize the refusal of states to submit foreign-wealth deprivation disputes to international law standards and procedures, the repudiation of the principle of compensation as an *international* regulatory norm seems a reasonable conclusion.

Indeed, recalling that Article 2 affords little or no protection against potentially capricious legal regimes and therefore potentially arbitrary discriminations, one might even say that Article 2(2) (c) actually repudiates the notion of compensation itself. Lillich edges close to this judgment in his historical review of the substantive erosion of Resolution 1803 (XVII).[19] The matter is, I think, ambiguous. Article 2(2) (c) does provide for "appropriate compensation" (albeit in terms of the precatory "should" rather than the mandatory "shall"). In fact, it invokes this language in the face of two immediately preceding and related General Assembly formulations that spoke, first, in terms of "*possible* compensation"[20] and, second, without any reference to compensation whatsoever.[21] On the other hand, what good is a promise, especially a discretionary one, when there is not the slightest gesture against the potential for arbitrary discrimination? No doubt a great deal in many instances. Such must have been the view, it seems, of some of the industrialized Nordic countries which, at the sixth Special Session, evinced a generally favorable regard for the then proposed NIEO Charter (in contrast to the United States, the United Kingdom, the Federal Republic of Germany, and Japan). However, as once suggested by Mr. Justice Holmes, a right without an effective remedy may be no right at all.

In any event, assuming our interpretation is correct, we have in Article 2(2) (c) what looks to be no minor challenge to the international law principle of compensation as traditionally—even recently—conceived, and it is to this challenge that I now turn. As stated above, there are two key issues that seem most in need of attention, one of law (*lex lata*) and one of policy (*de lege ferenda*).

An Issue of Law

In ascending order of persuasiveness, there are at least four complementary arguments in support of the proposition that Article 2(2) (c) is an authoritative statement of existing international law, each derived from a perception about the NIEO Charter as a whole:

> *first,* per former President Echeverría of Mexico, that the Charter was intended to place its articulated principles on "a firm legal footing";

> *second,* that its provisions are framed by such weighty preambular imagery—e.g., "*The General Assembly . . . Solemnly adopts* the present Charter . . ."—as to at least imply binding legal effect;

> *third,* that the Charter, even though a General Assembly resolution, is no ordinary resolution and hence is more prescriptive than recommendatory; and

> *fourth,* that the Charter, having won the overwhelming endorsement of the UN membership (*i.e.,* by a vote of 120-6-10), reflects mature legal concepts and expectations that go beyond pious expressions of morality.

None of these arguments, singly or in combination, is entirely convincing.

To begin with, mere good intentions and weighty imagery are not alone sufficient to make law, let alone terminate long-standing and still significantly accepted legal norms. The point is elementary. Moreover, as considerably documented in the award on the merits in the international arbitration between Texaco Overseas Petroleum Company and California Asiatic Oil Company, on the one hand, and the Government of the Libyan Arab Republic, on the other, the *travaux préparatoires* and debates leading up to the Charter's adoption show that few of the UN members seriously believed they were creating law in the binding or codificatory sense (high hopes and rhetorical flourishes notwithstanding).

The third and fourth arguments are not so easily handled. Despite its "legislative history," the NIEO Charter is no ordinary General Assembly resolution (else why the profound feelings stirred?) and it did receive a large majority vote. One of course can point to the conventional wisdom that General Assembly resolutions have only recommendatory force. Also, it can be shown that, in addition to the many votes cast against particular provisions, the Charter in general, and Article 2 in particular, received the negative votes and abstentions of a very powerful segment of the global economic community, without whose support no amount of wishful thinking can do much good (or at least not for those provisions which aroused vigorous dissent or as between those members who disagreed fundamentally). It probably is correct to conclude, in fact, that these debating points, along with certain postadoption practices to be noted hereinafter, are, on final analysis, decisive. After all, law is no mere body of rules accompanied by convictions of "obligation" or "duty." It is, rather, "a process of decision taken in accordance with formal authority *and supported by effective control,* with the matter of control (or sanction), when not confined to the official threat or use of force, commonly being reduced . . . to what Professor McDougal has called 'expectations about reciprocal claim and mutual tolerance.'"[22] Nevertheless, it is too extreme (if not utterly incorrect) to say, as one critic of the NIEO Charter has done, that "General Assembly Resolutions do not *in any way* have the force of law."[23] One need but consider, for obvious example, how the Universal Declaration of Human Rights (or, more precisely, some of its irreducible minimal has come to be widely regarded as having more than hortatory value.

In the first place, the NIEO Charter was in fact adopted by a very large margin (albeit, as noted, without unanimous and important endorsement). Second, it is replete with the language of legal obligation, reflecting the General Assembly's original, even if compromised, intention "to establish or improve norms of universal application for the development of international economic relations on a just and equitable basis." Third, it is one of the most vigorous and important demonstrations of a long Third World effort to bring about radical changes in the international economic order, dating back to the Afro-Asian Conference at Bandung in 1955 and underscored at numerous conferences and intergovernmental negotiating sessions since that seminal meeting. Finally, reflecting perhaps the juridical cogency of these and similar factors, the Charter and especially certain of its provisions, such as Article 2(2) (c), clearly have generated strong resistance in the "no legal effect" Northern/Western school, which accurately perceives a major parry and thrust to its long-standing dominance of the global economic system—a curious response for proponents of the view that the Charter has only recommendatory import.

In other words, if we contemplate the truism that the venerable "legal question/political question" distinction invariably produces results that can be rationalized only by knowing the relevant identifications, expectations, and demands of the decision maker involved, it is not enough to indulge in normatively ambiguous classification and terminology, which tends more to obfuscate than to clarify. What is needed is frank recognition that, as Lewis Carroll's Humpty Dumpty would tell us, a "charter," "declaration," or "resolution" will be called "binding" or "recommendatory" depending largely upon one's policy preferences, qualified by processes of "reciprocal claim and mutual tolerance," and that therefore it is the actual practice of states and other actors (and the policy reasons underlying that practice) that finally determines whether the NIEO Charter in general, and Article 2(2) (c) in particular, have "binding," "recommendatory," or no effect whatsoever.

Looking, then, to the most recent available evidence of state practice in the foreign-wealth deprivation field, one finds that in the great majority of cases the depriving countries ultimately have granted compensation in an amount and form not inconsistent with the "partial" compensation and valuation standards prevalent since World War II, and often with express reference to international law.[24] Admittedly, much of this evidence stems from North Americans (including myself), some of it predates the creation and adoption of the NIEO Charter, and only a minor share reveals what has been done to resolve "indirect," "constructive," or "creeping" expropriation controversies. Nevertheless, the basic compensation pattern is clear. Furthermore, in each of the reported cases since the NIEO Charter, all of them "expropriation" or "nationalization" cases, the respondent countries have been ones that voted *for* the adoption of the Charter.

All of this argues for the proposition that the principle of compensation as an *international* regulatory norm is yet alive, even if under attack. From a jurisprudential point of view, it matters not at all that the individual settlements, lump sum agreements, and arbitral awards that make this finding possible have resulted, more or less, from what the legal positivists would call "extralegal" expediencies. As the late Professor (recently Judge) Baxter once wrote, specifically with reference to lump sum agreement making, "[i]f one were to seek absolute equality of bargaining power and the complete absence of inducements or pressures, very few settlements of international disputes or arrangements of matters of mutual concern could be taken as evidence of customary international law."[25]

Thus, for all of the above reasons, it is necessary to conclude that Article 2(2) (c) is not at present an authoritative statement of existing international law, *i.e., not lex lata.* Bearing in mind, however, that the law never has been chiseled in granite, one always must be sensitive to changing circumstances, especially at this revolutionary time when, according to a growing number of people, the world is undergoing a historical shift comparable at least to the transition from feudalism to the modern state system. States that do not accept either the legitimacy or the content of existing law will continue to make the point that the Charter and, in particular, Article 2(2) (c) reflect a new standard of international law; and over time they may gain support for this position, especially if the North does not respond swiftly and adequately to the South's increasingly urgent and entirely understandable developmental appeal. In short, even though the NIEO Charter itself may be perceived as almost a "dead letter" juridically, Article 2(2) (c) may be the start of a fresh practice whose impact on the law, although currently without immediate binding force, could be substantial in the future.

An Issue of Policy

This essay began with a parable from Franz Kafka to stress the point that, over the years, the preponderance of the peoples of the Third World have gotten little or no real opportunity to participate in, and benefit from, the existing global economic order. This leads one to ask, irrespective of all that has been said so far, whether the LDC's, now acutely alert to this "distributive injustice" (albeit too frequently without reference to their own internal orders), are not absolutely correct in insisting upon drastic system (including normative) change. One can legitimately wonder whether there is any real possibility of eliminating or substantially reducing global inequities as long as we continue to think and act according to the dictates of the present world order.

Now whether this line of questioning is appropriate to NIEO Charter Article 2(2) (c) is a matter over which reasonable minds can differ. Farer, for example, has observed that the issue of compensation, at least when standing alone, probably is only "marginally relevant" to the redistribution of the global product.[26] And as Richard Lillich and I have documented in great detail, the Article 2(2) (c) challenge to international law actually seldom arises because the vast majority of compensation claims for the loss of foreign-owned wealth—an estimated 95 percent since World War II—are settled through the negotiation of international lump sum agreements. Still, if only as a symbol of the Third World's demand for radical change, Article

2(2) (c) should be considered in these lights. At the very least, such questioning impels one back to the basics of justificatory policy, something that seldom occurs when one stands more on the dominant than on the unfavored side of a legal tradition. If the international law principle of compensation cannot meet the test of the contemporary (and future) common interest, then surely, and especially if it actually contributes to the problem of global poverty, it ought to give way to one that does.

On what basis, then, might the international law principle of compensation be justified, if at all? Certainly not, one would suppose, on those Western conceptions of *laissez-faire* justice which inspired it and which, in later years, especially during the 19th century, made "the inviolability of private property" (and the correlative "duty" to make reparation for damage done thereto) a *sine qua non* of international square dealing. In our ideologically cloven world, such a rationale would be untenable. For any international law principle to survive, it must advance the common interests not of a limited ideology but of the wider (global) community it purports to serve.

Of course, the "common interest of the world community" is something that is easier to talk about than it is to apply, especially in particular cases. Nevertheless, in a world aspiring to greater "distributive justice" for *all* peoples (no less highly generalized an abstraction), it is appropriate—indeed essential—to insist that the principle of compensation be made to serve "a world public order of human dignity" or, as Myres McDougal puts it, "a world public order in which values are shaped and shared more by persuasion than by coercion, and which seeks to promote the greatest production and widest possible sharing, without discriminations irrelevant of merit, of all values among all human beings."[27] That is, if it is to avoid desuetude, the international law principle of compensation must find validation in the degree to which it actually promotes a world economy that holds out, if not the assurance of complete security and total abundance, at least the prospect of minimum order and basic well-being for all. Only if it assists in the achievement of a peaceful, equitable, productive and, one should add, ecologically sensitive balance among competing legitimate demands can or should the principle be vindicated. Then, being identified more with the interests of the world community as a whole than with the interests of any particular group or groups, it would require neither sponsor nor justification.

The probable Third World response is, however, that it is Article 2(2) (c), which is centrally concerned with the negative developmental impact of direct foreign investment (DFI) by transnational corporations, not the international law principle of compensation, that is most likely to advance the world economy of human dignity to which I have just alluded. Starting from the realistic Kafkaesque perception that "[u]nfortunately, there are very few examples in history of the rich surrendering their power willingly or peacefully [to the poor]," as the former Director of the Policy Planning and Program Review Department of the World Bank has put it,[28] the argument would have at least three interdependent strands:

> (1) By allowing for greater autonomy among host societies, Article 2(2) (c) would give effective meaning to the principle of "full permanent sovereignty." As a consequence, it would eliminate vestiges of colonialism and other inequities in global economic relations, permit greater control over harmful DFI as represented especially by transnational corporations, and thereby afford greater freedom of choice among alternative paths to development (including, if desired, so-called dissociative strategies of development).
>
> (2) Whatever the alarms sounded by the capital-exporting world (raised more as scare tactics, it would be argued, than as matters of deep conviction), the principles and procedures of Article 2(2) (c) would not deter DFI measurably. In fact, they would encourage such investment because they would help instil greater host-country self-respect, which in turn enables precisely those stable political climates that make for foreign investment security.
>
> (3) By requiring foreign-wealth deprivation controversies to be settled according to the law and through the tribunals of the depriving state, Article 2(2) (c) would facilitate compensation decisions consistent with the depriving state's capacity (or incapacity) to pay. The consequence of such a risk allocation approach to compensatory decisions—involving a judgment that foreign investors (especially transnational corporations) are generally better situated to bear the costs of "nationalization" and other forms of deprivation—would be to promote global wealth redistribution and thereby facilitate the meeting of basic human needs.

These and like arguments, I suggest, must not be taken lightly. They reflect both a profound (and by no means wholly unwarranted) belief that the present global order systematically discriminates against the interests of the poor, and an equally profound (and by no means wholly unwarranted) conviction that there is no way to reverse this state of affairs except by challenging head-on the criteria, rules, and procedures by which that order, in particular its economic parts, has operated heretofore. Concededly, for persons historically more on the giving than on the receiving end of economic (and political) decision, this injunction does not transform easily into changed behavior. Nonetheless, it is essential not to forget, in the words of former UN Under-Secretary-General for Economic and Social Affairs Philippe de Seynes, that "the historical circumstances of decolonization, memories of exploitation and the persistence of unequal bargaining powers have created the atmosphere in which foreign investment is now being judged."[29]

On the other hand, as de Seynes simultaneously observes (albeit in special contextual terms), one also dare not forget the "inescapable fact that non-renewable resources acquire value largely through international markets and [that] they can be exploited only through the most complex technological and logistic operations."[30] De Seynes's implicit message is, I think, that most countries, including those of the Third World, need private foreign capital and know-how to effect full employment and raise standards of living. At any rate, while it is difficult to construct *general* assessments in this connection (as shall be seen in a moment), the thesis seems by and large accurate.

In the first place, "petrodollars" and foreign aid programs notwithstanding, there simply are not now (for military, political, and other reasons) sufficient public funds to meet the needs of economic development on a global scale; and, in any event, such funds typically are "tied" in ways that the LDC's often and legitimately find onerous. More importantly, however, public assistance does not commonly bring with it the sustained research and development, managerial/technical skills, and access to foreign markets and credit institutions that in many respects are critical to development and that typically we associate with DFI, especially on the part of multinational corporations.

The same can generally be said, secondly, of such DFI alternatives as "know-how" or "management" contracts, "licensing" agreements, and "turn-key" operations. Furthermore, while certainly not to be discouraged, these "nonequity" alternatives are not without their own problems in terms of (social) cost and harmonious government-business relations.

Finally, even countries pledged to achieving their developmental goals strictly or mainly through "self-help" or "self-reliant" strategies, avowedly to "dissociate" themselves from too great a dependence on foreign entrepreneurship and industrial modes of development, ordinarily cannot and do not foreclose foreign enterprise altogether. As Jimoh Omo-Fadaka has written, "Self-reliance does not mean that countries will not need or accept international assistance for their development. Obviously, they will need and seek foreign capital for particular projects. They would welcome such capital and assistance whether from private corporations or from government—provided these catalyze their development."[31]

In sum, irrespective of the utility of such conventional distinctions as "capitalism" and "socialism," there is considerable evidence that at this stage in history the achievement of a world economy of human dignity requires at least some kinds of DFI. Indeed, it is this fact, in combination with the premium now being placed on the principle of "full sovereignty," which underlies, in Oscar Schachter's words, "the ambivalence in the attitudes and legislation of many of the developing countries."[32]

Yet, it is one thing to say that the LDC's need DFI (or at least certain kinds of DFI) and quite another to say that, in turn, this need compels the international law principle of compensation. Indeed, it is precisely this mental leap that is rejected by much of the Third World. Accordingly, it behooves one to look more closely, even if only briefly, at the three major counterarguments given.

1. The Antidomination/Proequity Argument. The contention is widespread in the developing world (and assisted by Marxist and New Left writings on the international economy) that DFI, at least as practiced by the transnational corporations commanding the field, is generally detrimental to Third World development, hence not to be encouraged, and therefore beyond the reach of the international law principle of compensation. This thesis derives from one or both of at least two distinct perceptions about transnational corporations: first, that these firms, capable of circumventing national policies and regulations, are prone to coercive, fraudulent, or otherwise dubious practices which subvert the local political order; and second, that these enterprises perpetuate an inequitable international division of labor, encourage dependency technologies more appropriate to the "metropole" than to the "periphery," and disregard the crux of development as the satisfaction of basic human needs. In the Northern/Western world, where history has favored private property rights more than the social interest, these perceptions have been given regrettably short shrift.

Yet there is substantial basis for the argument, even if, as happens to be true, it often is espoused by elitist Third World spokesmen. Past disclosures of bribery, duress, and "covert operations" on the part of transnational corporations and their "home" countries amply justify the first perception noted; and there are rich and growing data to the effect that multinational enterprise (past and present) is not as economically virtuous as its proponents claim, that in fact it tends to inflict major harm upon host (particularly developing) societies, at least from a needs-oriented point of view. The multinational corporations, planned on a planetary scale and at economic levels rivaled only by a few nation-states, can be shown in many instances to be oblivious to the interests of the poor countries. Operating in extremely oligopolistic markets, intent upon global profit maximization, and generally committed to GNP-growth models of development, they are arranged more to reinforce than to repeal what Dieter Senghass has called the "structurally crippled" condition of most Third World economies.[33] "Were [these companies] genuinely multinational and representational in their ownership and policies, and more broadly oriented to meeting human needs rather than increasing stockholder profits," write John and Magda McHale, "they could be considered as a useful and cohesive force in an economically and politically fragmented world."[34] Unfortunately, however, or so the McHales conclude, "this is not the case."[35] Market incentives do not by themselves generate much concern on the part of commercially motivated foreign investors to attend to LDC needs.

Understandably, therefore, the Third World search is on for new ways and means to deal with DFI. Still, I believe one may legitimately question the desirability of abandoning the international law principle of compensation in this particular connection. Not that it should not be required to account for abusive and societally detrimental practices attributable to DFI when applied in the important postdeprivation process of valuation. To the contrary, this accounting can and should be pressed fully. Yet, do we not risk unwanted, possibly inequitable, results when, as Article 2(2) (c) of the NIEO Charter seems to do, we abandon the principle altogether?

Consider, for example, the truism that DFI is comprised neither entirely of multinational enterprise nor entirely of unsavory or harmful business activity. To be sure, the owners or managers of private foreign capital and technology are not engaged in charitable works. Writes Harlan Cleveland: "Generating and fulfilling effective demand, not meeting basic human needs, [has been] the criterion of business judgment. The 'bottom line,' not the 'bottom billion,' [has been] the central focus of public policy."[36] Nevertheless, in our "more or less"—not "either-or"—world, many foreign investors do try to act the "corporate good citizen." Moreover, economic cost-benefit analyses of the impact of DFI upon Third World development, including some analyses of transnational corporate activity, reveal that private profit can be consistent with social objectives (*e.g.,* in certain technology transfers, manpower training, and local subcontracting). These observations and findings, although necessarily qualified by the principal interests and world views of the analysts involved (corporate management, labor/trade union, home country, host country, or other), naturally complicate the Third World argument and consequently present economic crosscurrents not easily maneuvered by lawyers. But the legal policy question remains nonetheless: is it equitable (desirable), especially in the absence of safeguards against arbitrary discrimination, to withhold from essentially responsible foreign investors an international assurance, even a minimal one, of an "appropriate" or "fair" return in the event of a publicly inspired wealth deprivation? Regarding the private enterprise that has yet to make an investment and that presumably is "on notice," an "assumption of risk" argument may suffice as an answer. It clearly is a dubious rejoinder, however, for the enterprise that already is in place and that may well have gotten there on the basis of an official invitation or other representation made earlier (a point one hopes is not lost on those LDC's which sooner or later will expand their own trade and investments to neighboring and more distant countries).

Also to be considered is the consequence of a domesticated compensation principle upon claimants and controversies not associated with major foreign enterprise: for example, upon minor foreign entrepreneurs and individual property owners (or upon alien personal injury and other nonwealth claims). One possible answer is that Article 2(2) (c) is not meant to affect other than major DFI. Another is that most—perhaps all—of these variables are covered by international human rights prescriptions and customary "denial of justice" principles. Were Article 2(2) (c) an authoritative statement of international law, an alert advocate surely would so argue. The interpretative enterprise being the highly subjective phenomenon that it is, however, the fact remains that Article 2(2) (c), which is silent in these respects, is potentially capable of corrosive effect beyond the major DFI context. Moreover, despite recent campaigns from Washington and elsewhere, the accelerating march of authoritarianism worldwide hardly warrants unqualified optimism about human rights and "denial of justice" protections. To be sure, many societies North and South will be undeterred in assuring protection to individual foreign nationals who are in some way deprived at the hands of local authorities. Indeed, many will do so irrespective of any sense of international legal obligation. Nevertheless, by virtue of its understandable preoccupation with the developmental impact of transnational corporations and other major foreign enterprise, Article 2(2)(c) overlooks the interest of individuals from throughout international society (including from the developing world) in not being asked to shoulder disproportionately painful burdens compared to all the rest.

In sum, as regards the antidomination/proequity argument, Article 2(2).(c) appears to overreach. By withholding the compensation issue from international law standards and procedures, and in a manner that fails to safeguard against arbitrary decision, it invites inequities of its own— inequities that ultimately can work to the disadvantage of the long-term interests of the LDC's themselves. Granted, one can insist that the historic plight of the Third World is so gross an inequity as to justify incurring all or most other inequities. However, this value choice seems unnecessary when it comes to the compensation issue in the *prescriptive* as distinct from *applicative* context. My point is not that there should not be strenuous efforts to eliminate imperious and otherwise "inappropriate" foreign investment modes and practices, even serious consideration of fundamental kinds of system change. What is questioned is whether rejection of the international law principle of compensation is the best way to achieve this objective. Better suited to the task, it would seem, are multilateral codes of conduct and grievance machinery, perfected regulatory legislation at the national level, preinvestment "screening" arrangements and agreements, joint ventures, "unpackaging" and "phase-out" programs, and the like. Such new and improved methods of regulation and accountability, I believe, are less apt to risk inequitable or otherwise unwanted results because, in contrast to Article 2(2) (c), they favor discrete assessments that are alert to the infinite complexity of particular cases and national economies. Indeed, as G. K. Helleiner suggests, lately increased experimentation along these lines may well account for a recent precipitous decline in formal "nationalization" and "expropriation" disputes involving U.S. firms abroad.[37] At any rate, given the growing North/South consensus on international regimes capable of promoting greater accountability,[38] not to mention the attention given to remedial national regulation measures in Article 2(2)(b) of the NIEO Charter itself, these alternative approaches seem more likely to win universal endorsement and therefore more useful resolutions to the problems of Third World underdevelopment.

2. The Nondeterrence Argument. The contention that withdrawal of the international principle of compensation—of an internationally pledged "appropriate" return—would *not* deter DFI measurably is one that for obvious reasons is strongly resisted in the Northern/Western world (at least officially). However, it is a thesis that deserves greater deference than ordinarily it receives. The so-called promotional pacemaker, for example, who typically starts new LDC ventures (especially in the manufacturing sector where often there is little or no indigenous entrepreneurial experience), only to withdraw once the enterprise is under way, is unlikely to be easily dissuaded. Often the same can be said, too, of resource-dependent enterprises which, despite alternative sources or synthetic substitutes, may find themselves so "locked in" as to make minimal compensation assurances virtually meaningless; or, indeed, of any (at least large-scale) foreign investor who, by demonstrating reasonably strict or even general adherence to host country priorities and policies, stands to reduce the risk of uncompensated deprivation and therefore the probability of being deterred by the absence of compensation promises. Also, as surely no pedant's footnotes need substantiate, insurance schemes, pricing mechanisms, tax write-offs, and various bookkeeping devices, while not without cost to corporate shareholders and customers, make it possible for many foreign investors to spread or otherwise offset potential losses in ways that make the risk of uncompensated deprivation a less significant factor in foreign investment decision making than is commonly believed.

Still, even if as only one of the many risks and uncertainties of foreign investment, there is no blinking the fact that a heightened potential for uncompensated deprivations, as implied by Article 2(2) (c), would have a chilling effect upon DFI. Without a minimal assurance against major loss— "at least a short-range assurance of an adequate return . . . and recovery"[39]— small foreign investors, for example, who do not have the flexibility of the multinational corporations, would likely as not be deterred. In fact, although the evidence is mixed, there is reason to believe that the "chill factor" would extend even to the multinationals, and to national and international aid, trade, and lending institutions as well. Controlled as the latter are by governments that favor stable and understandable (to them) business environments, a hardening on their part can also be reasonably expected.

True, it can be said that Article 2(2) (c) does not repudiate the notion of compensation itself, that it appears only to remove it from international jurisdiction. This argument is in no way helped, however, by the failure of the NIEO Charter to assure against arbitrary discrimination, a truly sorry omission that always must be recalled when contemplating Article 2(2) (c). Also, it can be said that the capacity of the LDC's to achieve their objectives through collective action (as most conspicuously illustrated by some of the recent successes of the OPEC countries) can serve as an effective countervailing force to the threat of withheld foreign capital and know-how. However, there is evidence that the early optimism surrounding "commodity power" has receded; and, in any event, the policy is fraught with complexities that are not easily controlled no matter how earnest the desire. Finally, it can be argued that by emphasizing (1) private technology purchases and public technology transfers, and (2) "dissociative" or "self-reliant" strategies of development, dependence on DFI can be sharply reduced, and with it the need for concern about the issue of deterrence. This last rebuttal cannot be lightly dismissed. Yet it is, I believe, too extreme in underestimating, first, the "smoother, more automatic, and sometimes even (socially) cheaper access to technology" that is afforded by multinational firm (in contrast to "licensees or one-shot, arm's length purchasers of 'shelf' technology");[40] second, the potentiality of new "appropriate technologies" through smaller (but more vulnerable) DFI; and third (and more generally), the fact of an increasingly *interpenetrating,* if not always truly *interdependent,* world.

Thus, Article 2(2) (c) again appears to overreach. By elevating the principle of "full permanent sovereignty" to heights equivalent to those of earlier monarchical times, it does unwitting disservice to precisely that constituency it was designed to help; it risks losing those great reservoirs of *beneficial* private (and public) foreign capital and know-how which must be tapped (although unequivocally reoriented to meet basic needs) if genuine distributive justice is to be achieved. It is not denied that a repudiation of the international law principle of compensation would produce adjustments that over time would establish new stabilities of expectation and behavior. But in the meanwhile, forgetting for the moment the reconstructed interventionist predilections of some Northern constituencies, what would be the cost/benefit ratio?

3. The Wealth Redistribution Argument. One positive response to the foregoing question is, as noted earlier, that the possibilities for redistributing the global product would be that much more enhanced. By requiring foreign-wealth deprivation controversies to be settled according to domestic law principles and procedures, Article 2(2) (c). it can be argued, would facilitate compensation decisions consistent with a depriving state's capacity (or incapacity) to pay and thereby help reduce glaring economic inequities.

There is, I think, larger merit to this contention than Northerners (especially Americans) ordinarily are inclined to give it, at least when it is limited to the short run. Among other things, we blanch at "deep pocket" theories of risk allocation that presume foreign investors (especially the multinational corporations) to be relatively well situated to shoulder the costs of "nationalization" and other forms of wealth redistribution. Perhaps out of some blind allegiance to outworn shibboleths that posture any socialist experiment as the work of the devil, or perhaps because of some anthropomorphic conception of business enterprise that resists explaining why collectivities should not be treated differently than individuals, we tend to discount the variety of schemes, pricing mechanisms, tax write-offs, and other risk-spreading devices that, though costly, make such burdens at least bearable.

Nevertheless, my sense is that Article 2(2) (c) overreaches yet again. In the first place, although saying so is to risk charges of paternalism, it is by no means clear that a general acceptance of Article 2(2) (c) would lead to true distributive justice. The Third World elitism that infuses much of the NIEO debate and the authoritarianism that now is rising throughout the South afford scant assurance that basic human needs would actually be met (a point that alone might justify international jurisdiction over the compensation issue, especially if the West were to give to "economic, social and cultural rights" the same prominence it now gives to "civil and political rights"). Second, there is, as seen, the possibility that a domestication of the principle of compensation would deter needed beneficial foreign capital and technology, particularly in the absence of assurances against arbitrary discrimination. While exaggerated in the North, this potential cost should not be minimized. Finally, there are systemic complexities that, although often neglected by deprivation-prone governments, nonetheless complicate the process of wealth redistribution in ways that are not always quickly evident. As David Apter has observed,

> what might be called the "Algerian solution" of extensive nationalization is not so easily accomplished. Enclaves can easily be taken over and, if not run by the government, handed over to a consortium. But where MNC domination affects an entire sector, such as large-scale fabrication plants, or petrochemicals, the problem is that the efficiency of the operation, the profits of the firm, are a function of an international network of pricing, tax rebates, labor agreements abroad, and so forth. To nationalize the part of the organization operating in a particular country is not to nationalize the network. Hence, unless the multinational sector consists of subsidiaries in which there is virtually no connection to the productive and financial facilities of the rest of the firm, the Algerian solution is very awkward, leading to inefficiencies, bureaucracy, and a different set of social overhead costs. Dependency, then, is built into intermediate modernization. Control cannot simply be a function of nationalization or any stock-in-trade solutions. No one can nationalize the metropolitan impact, the world market, the pricing and transfer policies.[41]

Of course, lawyers untrained in economics (and who therefore bring no obvious comparative advantage to the Third World's wealth redistribution argument) must be wary to avoid quick judgments in this realm, especially since even the economists can be found to disagree.[42] On balance, however, it is fair to say that, while certainly to be taken more seriously than it has been, the argument exaggerates the redistributive potential. Article 2(2) (c) looks to be the wrong tool for the right job.

* * * *

Thus, although not to minimize in any way the need to make the global wealth process work for the many instead of the few, one must conclude that Article 2(2) (c) should not be recommended as *de lege ferenda.* For all the reasons noted, it would tend more to retard than to promote a world economy of human dignity. Deprecating the wisdom of long experience that a minimum of security and fair dealing is required to ensure economic progress and reward, it plays too lightly with the fundamental truth of our time: the increasing interpenetration and interdependence of peoples and problems, and the consequent emergence of a planetary culture whose survival and development depend not on confrontation but on cooperation. Utilizing the essentially conservative principle of "full permanent sovereignty" as a weapon of socioeconomic change (only to challenge, by way of double irony, an essentially radical principle that was fired in the crucible of royal encroachment and despotism), Article 2(2) (c) places the interests of the host state above all other interests, thereby fosters precisely that competitive nationalism which is at the root of North-South inequities, and consequently risks further contributing to the Third World's economic malaise.

Even so, if we recall the Kafka parable quoted at the outset and face up to the crippled state of the LDC's as a consequence mainly of the asymmetrical structures that the "metropole" has visited upon the "periphery" since the beginning of colonialism (rather than of some "backward" inability to generate investment capital), it is difficult to escape a profound unease over the conclusions reached so far. It is hard not to sympathize with the "man from the country" who seeks a flexible and highly decentralized system to ensure that his economic and other priorities will be met.

In the first place, as suggested earlier, there is mounting evidence that LDC links to the industrialized world, through aid, trade, investment, and migration (not least at the hands of the multinational corporations), not only have failed to improve the lot of the world's poor, but actually have worked to their "de-development." Summarizes M.I.T. economist Jagdish Bhagwati:

> [T]here is the doctrine of "malign neglect" which views the impact of . . . links between the rich and the poor nations as primarily detrimental to the latter group. In the apt description of Osvaldo Sunkel, integration of the developing countries in the international economy leads to their domestic disintegration. This doctrine also supports the economic notion, used extensively by the Swedish economists Knut Wicksell and Gunnar Myrdal, of growing disequilibrium and exploding sequences, rather than the classical notions of equilibrium. Thus, multinational corporations disrupt domestic salary structures by introducing islands of high-income jobs that cause exorbitant wage demands by others seeking to keep up with the

Joneses in the multinationals. International trade leads to the perpetuation of the role of developing countries as producers of primary, unsophisticated products that relegate them to a secondary and inferior position in the international division of labor. Furthermore, in the classic Prebisch thesis, the terms of trade of the primary-product-exporting developing countries have declined and will continue to do so, conferring gains on the developed and inflicting losses on the developing countries. The brain drain to the developed countries deprives the developing countries of scarce skills and the talents that make economic progress possible. The attractions of Western standards of living make domestic setting of priorities and raising of savings difficult if not impossible.[43]

Second, the postdeprivation application of the international law principle of ("appropriate") compensation historically has not displayed much concern for the extent to which, as *one* measure of valuation, the deprived foreign investor has contributed to the local social interest or not, least of all the interest of meeting basic human needs. The language of "excess profits" has entered the valuation vocabulary in recent years, to be sure; but the language of "prompt, adequate, and effective" nevertheless prevails as the central rallying cry, with "book value" as the *cri du coeur.* Finally, but by no means least importantly, there is an indelicate paternalism attached to any thesis that argues, in essence, that the LDC's do not know what is good for themselves. The point speaks for itself.

Still, Article 2(2) (c) does not ensure against arbitrary discrimination. To invoke the Kafka parable one last time, it does not ensure that, once in control, the "man from the country" will not himself become a despised "doorkeeper." This is, I think, *the* fundamental difficulty with Article 2(2) (c), the main reason why it should be rejected.

Suppose, however, that Article 2(2) (c) were to be revised so as to prohibit arbitrary discrimination, and explicitly *as a matter of international legal concern.* What then? Could we not *then* endorse, as appears to be true of Article 2(2) (c), a "domesticated" principle of compensation? More provocatively, if we could point to an express *international* prohibition against arbitrary discrimination, *and assume that the LDCS seeking juridical dissociation would be fully cognizant of the risks of withdrawn capital and know-how,* why not leave the matter of compensation to the local authorities?

I confess no absolute certainty on this issue. Clearly, it is no answer to say that such a revision would be merely an exercise in "anticolonialist" or "antiimperialist" sentimentality. Major changes obviously would be wrought, including the possibility (probability?) of an "equal treatment" rather than "minimum international standard" application of the compensation principle. Nor is it an answer that under such revised circumstances the LDC's would be more likely than other countries to evade their nondiscrimination obligations. A more vivid assertion of ethnocentric hubris would be hard to imagine. Yet it is an answer, surely, that the economically and militarily powerful North (not to mention newly arrived powers in the developing world) might manipulate the revision to the detriment of the LDC's. However uncertain the notion of "appropriate compensation," the concept of "arbitrary discrimination" (with a lesser history of case-by-case refinement) is vaguer still, and thus more susceptible of interpretative abuse. Either because of a perception (real or otherwise) of an LDC evasion of nondiscrimination obligations or because large economic or political interests might be at stake, it regrettably is not difficult to conceive of a compensation or other foreign-wealth deprivation controversy generating rapid-fire charges of "arbitrary discrimination" for the purpose of justifying a unilateral intervention of some coercive sort. And therein lies a basis for genuine concern.

True, some Third World spokesmen might claim (contrary to what I contend above) that these abusive risks are reason enough to disregard the NIEO Charter's failure to warrant against arbitrary discrimination in the first place. But this would be to turn the argument on its head. The point is not to renounce language that, even if imperfect, is serviceable as a check on potentially abusive LDC power. The point is to encourage arrangements, including the establishment of international tribunals or equivalent resolutive mechanisms, that can reduce conflict and promote cooperation beneficial to all.

Nevertheless, real dangers lurk. Despite the lessons supposedly learned from Vietnam, it is too facile and risky to indulge the popular cliché (or an economic coercion equivalent) that "the days of gunboat diplomacy are over." To be sure, it always can be insisted that the dangers are worth risking. Stability—often a euphemism for maintaining the status quo—is not and cannot be the optimal requirement of the international or any other system *all the time*. In this instance, however, even if we admit to the LDC straitjacket, is it really necessary to tempt serious harm? Is the international law principle of compensation necessarily inconsistent with the principle of "full permanent sovereignty"?

My sense is that there is a promising middle way. Rather than scrap the international law principle of ("appropriate") compensation altogether, and consequently invite potentially explosive inequities and harm damaging to *everyone's* self-interest (at least over the long run), international lawyers should undertake to redefine or reform it, and in a way that will force no major compromise upon the principle of "full permanent sovereignty" *as responsibly conceived*. They should accommodate it to the basic human needs and second-order values (as appropriate) for which "full permanent sovereignty" should be presumed to stand.

Of course, this route is not easy to follow. It requires serious psychological and political as well as economic adjustments, both North and South. Also, it requires enlightened commitment by all concerned policy analysts—especially the economists and lawyers—to fashion "scientific" indicators and formulas that can tell us where private profit ends and social responsibility begins. Yet, if the more broadly intended models of development strategy worked out by the Argentine Bariloche Foundation and the American Overseas Development Council are any indication, it can be done. More importantly, it must be done. In addition to giving objective meaning to the concept of "appropriate compensation" by admitting into the balance of relevant considerations such potential (and two-way) evils as "duress" and "fraud," this compromissary option would help catch the urgent structural problems of North-South economic relations that in the context of foreign-wealth deprivation have so far escaped adequate international attention (and consequently produced more confrontation than conciliation). It is of course to the credit of the UN Commission on Transnational Corporations that this option is on its agenda for the formulation of a transnational corporate "code of conduct." Yet the option merits far wider attention still. As stated in the RIO ("Reshaping the International Order") Report to the Club of Rome, coordinated by Nobel Laureate Jan Tinbergen, there is a pressing need

> for new development strategies— national and international—defined and designed, not merely to meet the criterion of private or state profitability, but rather to give priority to the expressions and satisfaction of fundamental human values. Society as a whole must accept the responsibility for guaranteeing a minimum level for all its citizens and aim at equality in human relations. . . .[44]

The essence of the above argument is, of course, that the international law principle of compensation should be treated more as a presumption than as an inflexible rule; that the test of its legitimacy should be the extent to which it actually promotes the common interest of a world economy of human dignity; and that on these terms it seems neither an impossible nor an onerous norm for developed and developing countries to accept. Indeed, unless it is because the logical extension of this preferred view is that the burden of policy proof should rest upon the depriving state whenever the compensation question is handled by its domestic tribunals, or that it should rest upon the injured foreign investor whenever the issue may be decided by its home jurisdiction, it is difficult to see why anyone should refuse to do so. A concomitant approach, I concede, is the active development of interparty preinvestment arrangements at the national level and decisionmaking mechanisms on the international plane that can more easily forestall and handle foreign-wealth deprivation disputes in an equitable and impartial manner, a key concern of the UN Commission on Transnational Corporations mentioned above. But to acknowledge this approach is less a concession than it is a suggestion about where in this special realm the North-South dialogue should be bending much of its energies.

Conclusion: Summary and Postscript

In the preceding pages, I have considered how, from a world order policy perspective, one ought to greet the failure of Article 2 of the Charter of Economic Rights and Duties of States to provide for or otherwise honor the international law public purpose doctrine, the doctrine of alien nondiscrimination, and the principle of compensation, as traditionally understood and applied in the foreign-wealth deprivation context. By way of conclusion, it is useful to reiterate the principal judgments reached.

(1) The failure of Article 2 to provide for the so-called public purpose doctrine is no cause for alarm. The doctrine never has been sanctioned as a "rule" of international law whose violation *independently* engages international responsibility. Its omission, therefore, is entirely consistent with state practice.

(2) The failure of Article 2 to provide for the doctrine of alien nondiscrimination is explained by, and therefore must be seen against, a historical backdrop of imperialistic and ethnocentric application. This backdrop not having been adequately perceived or appreciated by Northern/Western analysts over the years, the doctrine is therefore much in need of fundamental review and reappraisal. However, the failure of Article 2 to ensure against *arbitrary* discrimination is an egregious omission that should not be tolerated.

(3) The apparent repudiation by Article 2(2) (c) of the international law principle of ("appropriate") compensation should be recognized neither as *lex lata* nor as *de lege ferenda*. It cannot be recognized as *lex lata* because it was not expected to have "binding" legal effect, because a large segment of the international economic community opposed its adoption, and because it has not been confirmed in post-adoption practice. Moreover, it should not be recognized as *de lege ferenda* because, on final analysis, it would work to the overall detriment of the developing world (in large part because of its failure to protect against arbitrary discrimination) and thereby inhibit the achievement of a world economy of human dignity. However, to ensure at least minimal sensitivity to the *problématique* of universal well-being, the international law principle of ("appropriate") compensation should be made to accommodate to the principle of "full permanent sovereignty" as responsibly defined. In its application, it should be infused with basic human needs considerations; it should be treated more as a rebuttable presumption than as an inflexible rule.

These judgments, I recognize, are not likely to be received enthusiastically by all who are concerned about the interrelation of direct foreign investment and territorial sovereignty. I suffer no illusion that they will be viewed as anything other than a "sellout" among certain capital-exporting constituencies or, conversely, as anything other than a liberal apology for the capitalist status quo among certain elements in the developing world. Identifying with the common interest of the world as a whole and consequently deferring to no particular special interest—least of all the "Inherent Rights Group" and the "Hard Socialist Group" in Thomas Bergin's "imaginary debate"[45]—they challenge both the old and the proposed new order of things. This middle course seems appropriate, however. The great challenge lies less in "proving" the rightness or wrongness of the competing special claims (and values) involved, but in formulating, clarifying, and applying policies that will simultaneously satisfy developmental goals and attract beneficial private capital and technology. Such is the essence, in any event, of what is involved in much of the Law of State Responsibility (and International Claims) generally: the accommodation, in creative and humane fashion, of the exclusive interest of each nation in achieving economic freedom and well-being, on the one hand, and of the exclusive interest of the foreign investor in being assured at least a minimum of security and cooperation, on the other. It is hoped that what has been said here will move that process of accommodation a bit further than has been done heretofore.

Notes

1. F. Kafka, Parables and Paradoxes 61 (Schocken paperback ed. 1961).

2. Mazrui, *Panel Discussion on the New International Economic Order,* in The New International Economic Order: the North-South Debate 173, 374 (J. Bhagwati, ed. 1977).

3. Voting against the NIEO Charter, in significant part because of Article 2, were Belgium, Denmark, the Federal Republic of Germany, Luxembourg, the United Kingdom, and the United States. Abstaining were Austria, Canada, France, Ireland, Israel, Italy, Japan, the Netherlands, Norway, and Spain. The U.S. vote against the Charter was in accordance with American Bar Association Resolution No. 301, adopted at the Association's annual meeting in August 1974, and *reproduced in* 9 Int'l Law. 405 (1975).

4. Although the requirement that the taking of an alien's property be for a public purpose—or be based on reasons of public necessity or public utility—is frequently mentioned in international adjudications and the works of text writers, there is little authority in international law establishing any useful criteria by which a state's own determination of public purpose can be questioned. There appear to be few, if any, cases in which a taking has been held unlawful under international law on the sole and specific ground that it was not for a public purpose.

Restatement (Second) of Foreign Relations Law of the United States § 185, comment b, at 553 (1965).

5. Baade, "Permanent Sovereignty over Natural Wealth and Resources," in *Essays on Expropriations* (R. Miller and R. Stanger, eds. 1967), p. 23.

6. M. McDougal, H. Lasswell, and L. Chan, *Human Rights and World Public Order: The Basic Policies of an International Law of Human Dignity* (1980), p. 738.

7. Brower & Tepe, *The Charter of Economic Rights and Duties of States: A Reflection or Rejection of International Law?,* 9 Int'l Law. 295, 306 (1975).

8. G. White, *Nationalisation of Foreign Property* (1961), p. 144.

9. Baade, *supra* note 5, at 24–25.

10. G. White, *supra* note 8, at 144.

11. Farer, *The United States and the Third World: A Basis for Accommodation,* 54 Foreign Aff. 79, 84 (1975).

12. *Supra* note 6, at 738.

13. *Id.* at 758 n.82.

14. Orrego Vicuna, *Some International Law Problems Posed by the Nationalization of the Copper Industry by Chile,* 67 AJIL 711, 715 (1973).

15. Murphy, *Limitations Upon the Power of a State to Determine the Amount of Compensation Payable to an Alien Upon Nationalization,* in 3 The Valuation of Nationalized Property in International Law 49, 59 (1975).

16. Banco Nacional de Cuba v. Sabbatino, 307 F.2d 845 (2d Cir. 1962), affirming a district court decision holding the Cuban actions to be unlawfully discriminatory, 193 F.Supp. 375 (S.D.N.Y. 1961). The United States Supreme Court reversed these decisions in 376 U.S. 398 (1964). For criticism of these two lower court decisions, see Dawson & Weston, *supra* note 12, at 84–96.

17. Murphy, *supra* note 15, at 62.

18. Lillich, *Forcible Self-Help by States to Protect Human Rights,* 53 Iowa L. Rev. 325, 327–28 (1967).

19. *See* Lillich, *supra* note 18, at 190: "Resolution 1803 (XVII) . . . still affords the best opportunity for an eventual consensus on the thorny compensation question. It can no longer be assumed, however, that developing as well as developed States still consider it reflective of customary international law" (footnote omitted). *Compare with* Murphy, note 15 *supra*.

20. GA Res. 3171 (XXVIII) on Permanent Sovereignty over Natural Resources, 28 UN GAOR, Supp. (No. 30) 52, UN Doc. A/9030 (1974), *reprinted in* 13 ILM 238 (1974).

21. Declaration on the Establishment of a New International Economic Order, GA Res. 3201 (S-VI), UN GAOR, 6th Spec. Sess., Supp. 1, UN Doc. A/9559/ *reprinted in* 68 AJIL 798 (1974), 13 ILM 715 (1974), adopted without vote on May 1, 1974, with reservations by the Federal Republic of Germany, France, Japan, the United Kingdom, and the United States.

22. R. Lillich and B. Weston, *International Claims: Their Settlement by Lump Sum Agreements* (1975), p. 15.

23. Haight, "The New International Economic Order and the Charter of Economic Rights and Duties of States," 9 *International Lawyer* (1975), p. 597.

24. For a summary of compensation and valuation standards prevalent since World War II, see 1 R. Lillich & B. Weston, *supra* note 22, at 207–56.

25. Baxter, *Treaties and Custom,* 129 Recueil des Cours 25, 89 (1970 I).

26. Farer, *supra* note 11, at 84.

27. McDougal, *Perspectives for an International Law of Human Dignity,* in M. McDougal & Associates, Studies in World Public Order 987 (1960).

28. M. ul Haq, The Third World and the International Economic Order 10 (Overseas Development Council Development Paper No. 22, 1976).

29. De Seynes, Statement on the United nations Study of Multinational Corporations to the Southwestern Legal Foundation, International and Comparative Law Center, Symposium on Private Investments Abroad, Dallas, Texas, June 13, 1974, UN Doc. OPI/CESI NOTE/254, at 3 (1974).

30. *Id.* at 4.

31. Omo-Fadaka, "Development: The Third Way," *Alternatives* (1975), p. 47.

32. O. Schachter, *Sharing the World's Resources* (1977), p. 126.

33. Senghass, *If You Can't Keep Up With the Rich . . . Keep Away,* Development Forum, May 1977, at 3.

34. J. McHale & M. McHale, Basic Human Needs: A Framework for Action 194 (Report to the UN Environment Programme, April 1978).

35. *Ibid.*

36. Cleveland, *Toward an International Poverty Line,* in J. McHale & McHale, *supra* note 34, at 3.

37. Helleiner, *supra* note 98, at 297. Helleiner cites the following two studies of the Bureau of Intelligence and Research of the US Department of State: Nationalization, Expropriation, and Other Takings of United States and Certain Foreign Property Since 1960 (1971); Disputes Involving US Foreign Direct Investment: July 1, 1971 Through July 31, 1973 (1974).

38. *See, e.g.,* The Impact of Multinational Corporations, note 103 *supra. See also* Ball, *Proposal for an International Charter,* in Global Companies 167 (G. Ball ed. 1975); E. Rostow, *The Need for a Treaty,* in *id.* at 156.

39. O. Schachter, *supra* note 32, at 125.

40. Helleiner, "International Technology Issues: Southern Needs And Northern Responses," in *the New International Economic Order: The North-South Debate* (J. Bhagwati, ed. 1977), pp. 297–298.

41. Apter, *Charters, Cartels, and Multinations—Some Colonial and Imperial Questions,* in The Multinational Corporation and Social Change, (1976), pp. 1 and 24.

42. *See, e.g.,* Garnick, *"The Appeal of Confiscation" Reconsidered: A Gaming Approach to Foreign Economic Policy,* 11 Econ. Dev. & Cultural Change 353 (1963), a reply to Bronfenbrenner. *See also* Bronfenbrenner's reply to Garnick: *Second Thoughts on Confiscation,* 11 Econ. Dev. & Cultural Change 367 (1963).

43. Bhagwati, *Introduction,* in The New International Economic Order, *supra* note 40, at 1, 2–3.

44. J. Tinbergen, et al., Reshaping the International Order—A Report to the Club on Rome 63 (1976).

45. *See* Bergin, *The Compensation Rule: An Imaginary Debate,* in 2 The Valuation of Nationalized Property, at 3.

PART 4

The Future of
International Law

25

The Future of International Law

Louis Henkin

Systemic Change and Changed Law

The international system is substantially changed from what it was a half-century ago. Sixty states have become near-200, most of them new states. All states are equal and independent in principle. For a quarter-century they grouped in three "worlds," two of them defined by ideology, the third by non-alignment—by a spirit of "a plague on both your worlds" and by bonds of common colonial history, resentment, poverty. Towards the end of the twentieth century, that configuration of three worlds has vanished: there is no Second World, therefore no Third World. But surely we are not one world. The political system is fluid and its configuration difficult to describe and to characterize; surely, it is too early for confident prognostications as to what will emerge.

The international system remains a system of states but it includes important inter-state organizations—political, economic, social—that are more than the sum of the states that comprise them, that have a life and character of their own and pervade and impose on the system of states, transmuting its character. The system will continue to take account also of other actors of substantial independence and importance, multinational companies which cannot be cabined within the borders of any one state or even of several states combined.

Changes in the system have been accompanied by changes in the character of statehood. States continue to value their independence, autonomy and impermeability, but state borders are now more readily permeable in fact, which has diluted the importance of the veil of statehood. States can

Louis Henkin, "The Future of International Law," in *International Law: Politics and Values,* 1995, The Hague: Martinus Nijhoff Publishers. Reprinted with kind permission from Kluwer Law International and the author.

control physical penetration, as by overflight in their airspace, but they cannot easily prevent communication or exclude information, they cannot prevent inspection by satellite from outer space, and national frontiers can do little to keep out or combat a growing number of environmental threats whose dimensions transcend those borders: depletion of stratospheric ozone, acid rain, disposal of hazardous wastes, nuclear and large industrial accidents, loss of biological diversity, global warming, deforestation, desertification—a list that continues to lengthen with greater understanding of the biosphere.

Some states are now present within other states not merely through diplomatic missions but by hosts of other official bodies, state instrumentalities, state-owned corporations and assorted agencies or agents, engaged in a myriad of activities. Therefore we have seen some erosion of the concept of state sovereignty and of some of its earlier implications, such as state sovereign immunity. The international system has accepted a fundamental permeation of state societies as a result of the International Human Rights Movement that is an essence of the contemporary *Zeitgeist:* how a state treats its own inhabitants is now of international concern and a staple of international politics and law.

Changes in the system and in the significances of statehood have brought change in the sources of law. The principle of consent is essentially intact but it has been softened. Custom is now made by new forms of practice, as in the law of human rights. Without unanimity and without agreed theoretical justification, international law has developed the concept of *jus cogens* and has given it some content, for example, the "higher law" prohibiting the use of force, genocide, apartheid. Now customary law does not merely result from long practice that has become custom, but is also made purposefully and quickly. The making of customary law now reflects pressures for acquiescence through the uses of consensus (especially in the United Nations General Assembly).

Withal, the inter-state system remains conservative in matters of law: law is still not easy to make or to change. Yet there has been some new law and some change in old law. In ways that exemplify the politics of lawmaking in a system of states, vast areas once largely extraneous to a system of territorial states, effectively *res nullius* or *res communis,* have now been significantly integrated into the system. Commonage has been redefined as "the common heritage of mankind." The commonage of the seas has been reduced by coastal state expansion; in the seas beyond national jurisdiction, commitment to common heritage has inspired a major international creation providing for new inter-state institutions, inter-state enterprise, and some revenue sharing, though the new regime for mining the deep sea-bed has not yet come into effect and there is reason to doubt that it will be realized in important measure. The commonage now includes outer space, and some would add the polar regions and, in a related sense, the global environment.

International law continues to reflect the system's commitment to values of state independence and autonomy. The law of the United Nations Charter against inter-state force and other forcible intervention is firm and has been reaffirmed by the International Court of Justice in the *Nicaragua* case,[1] though the law against intervention in internal wars has perhaps been modified to permit counter-intervention. The liberal system of states has produced impressive co-operative arrangements, notably through the United Nations and its specialized agencies (including the World Bank and the International Monetary Fund) as well as GATT, and analogous regional bodies; but co-operation has left intact the basic free-market system which much of the world considers inequitable. Commitment to welfare principles is still weak and the international welfare system is primitive at most. But a major expansion of the domain of law, the international system's concern for how a state treats its own inhabitants, is now the subject of an impressive corpus of human rights law.

There has been change also in the forces and forms of inducements to comply. A growing network of arbitration is now intrinsic to international trade. Radical increase in dispute settlement arrangements made possible new law that would otherwise be too soft to be acceptable, as in the 1982 Convention on the Law of the Sea. For the law on human rights, political bodies (e.g., in the United Nations) and special "machinery" established by treaty to induce compliance are supplemented by non-governmental organizations that seek to mobilize outrage and shame to terminate and deter gross violations.

International law has become more modern by slowly shedding some of its conceptualism and its mythology in response to the needs of the international system, of individual states and of human beings. The law of state jurisdiction to prescribe has responded to the needs of complex inter-state corporate arrangements and multi-state economic transactions, modifying strict categories by criteria of reasonableness. Some erosion in the conception of state sovereignty has washed away some previous assumptions about sovereign immunity.

Politics and Law in the Years Ahead

The last decade of the Twentieth Century has brought important change to the political system and a promise of more. Half a century ago the system organized itself for collective action—to maintain international peace and security, to enhance economic and social cooperation among states, to promote human rights, human welfare, human dignity. For forty years collective action for peace and security was virtually immobilized by bi-polarity in the system, by ideological cold war between nuclear super powers, by an underdeveloped and unaligned Third World.

The demise of Communism, the disintegration of the Soviet empire, and the fragmentation of the Soviet Union changed the world order fundamentally. Immediately, dramatically, importantly, it revived the Security Council, inspired in it an activist mood, and committed it to an activist mode. The Security Council acted, almost as originally intended, to defeat aggression and restore international peace in the Persian Gulf. It took a broad view of the demands of international peace and security to support humanitarian intervention by various means (including economic sanctions) in the former Yugoslavia, Haiti, Libya and Cambodia, and by a measure of military intervention to bring food and order in Somalia.

The reactivation of the Security Council holds important promise, as well as major problems, for the international system at the turn of the century. The Council's new vitality, indeed its successes and opportunities, have compelled attention to the adequacy and legitimacy of its composition for the 21st Century—how many members; how many permanent members (if any), and which; the acceptability and reach of the veto. New responsibilities have revived consideration of the need or desirability of U.N. forces pursuant to Article 43 of the Charter, and how to provide other resources to support the larger role of the Secretary General in the new United Nations. The new activism of the Security Council has raised legal issues as to the scope of its authority and whether its determinations, recommendations and decisions are subject to review by the U.N. General Assembly, or by the International Court of Justice, in any or some circumstances.

The revival of collective action for international peace and security has coincided with (and perhaps inspired) recognition of the need of collective action, or more effective collective action, to meet other international concerns—economic recession in the developed world and chronic depression and underdevelopment in the large "Third World"; the regulation of international trade and finance; the threat to the environment—national, international, global. New institutions and new dispositions will bring new law for the new century.

Despite revolution in East and Central Europe, and the resulting changed world order, one ought not anticipate radical change in the law in the decades ahead. The inter-state system will be long with us and therefore inter-state politics and inter-state (international) law. There is no reason to expect change in the basic assumptions of statehood and of a state system, no prospect of significant attenuation of state values of autonomy and independence of states and of impermeability of their territory and society. But the international political system is no longer characterized by intense bipolarism and we have moved into a field of more fluid political forces.

By some measures, the United States is the only super-Power, but others may claim super-Power status by virtue of other indicia, and all are exploring hesitatingly, uncertainly, their place and their posture. The former U.S.S.R. now fragmented and in financial difficulties, in search of internal stability and new international roles, is not to be discounted. The Third

World will still have the solidarity forged by a common colonial history and common problems of underdevelopment, and its numbers will count, but the significance of being "Third," unaligned, will lessen, and perhaps too its political weight and influence. The system, I expect, will be characterized by divisions that are pragmatic rather than ideological, economic rather than political, and even the common gross distinction between developed and less-developed states will blur and we will recognize a fluid spectrum of degrees of development as some state economies flourish and others falter.

The new array of forces in the system will surely have effect on the content of international law and on compliance with that law. The former U.S.S.R. is not a super-Power, but cooperation rather than confrontation between it and the United States promises new law and better compliance from both of them and in the system at large. Surely, global cold war will not be the obstacle to the development of new law and institutions, for peace and security, human rights, the environment, or to the use and growth and modernization of the International Court of Justice. No other state—China—or groups of states will succeed to the U.S.S.R. role, though China may continue norms and institutions—in human rights, in collective economic-social action, in Security Council intervention. Japan and Germany are prominent candidates for leadership, India may reemerge, Indonesia, Korea, Singapore loom as possible models if not leaders. Much may depend on the United States which, some fear, may decline leadership and drift into international inactivity or even isolationism. Europe is in disarray, the movement of the European Economic Community towards greater unity has slowed, its institutions for political action in cooperation with the United States have been languishing for want of leadership, initiative, and a clear mission.

Values and Law

The international system, one may anticipate, will continue to evolve its accommodation between traditional state values and a growing concerns for human values. Since states are not likely to wither away, the values they represent will surely not be neglected. State autonomy remains a powerful value, but the distinction between state and human values will be blurred in so far as state values and human values continue to converge. The right of a state "to be let alone" subsumes the rights of its inhabitants to be let alone, to maintain their traditions and culture, as well as their ways of life. The national interest of every state now includes prominently its need (and obligation) to develop its abilities to respect and ensure civil and political rights and to achieve progressively the full realization of the economic, social and cultural rights of its inhabitants. The difficulty will be—as it has been—to continue to refine and adjust the international and the domestic, the state values and the human values, and—within each state—the individual right and the public good. The need is to promote in every state a culture of respect for individual freedom, autonomy and other human rights, and to overcome cultural resistances such as those reflecting commitment to gender inequalities and to disrespect for outsiders.

One can state with substantial confidence that systemic attention to human values will continue to increase. Egregious violations of human rights will continue to command world attention and machinery for inducing compliance will continue to evolve. Additional conventions will come into effect—as has that on the Rights of the Child, and some day perhaps one on the elimination of religious intolerance. The customary law of human rights will grow slowly. Despite past frustrations, the idea of a United Nations High Commissioner for Human Rights has been realized, but the power of the office may prove to be less than human rights champions have hoped. . . . Regional machinery will grow even stronger in Europe (attracting also some Eastern neighbours) and in Latin America. It will evolve in Africa, and will burgeon in parts of Asia and in the Arab world. (If hopes for peace in the Middle East, are realized, they will bring also stronger commitment to human rights and sharply reduce the causes of violation.) The politicization of human rights in the universal organizations, notably in the United Nations, can be contained and should not prevent greater activism in support of human rights, especially as regards egregious, "consistent patterns of gross violations."

The World Conference on Human Rights (June 1993, Vienna) revealed a movement, led by China and others, to dilute international standards in the name of cultural diversity and to mobilize resistance to international scrutiny under the banner of state "sovereignty." The attempt did not succeed at Vienna, but it promises battles during the years ahead in the United Nations and in other political fora. Particularly disturbing to human values has been the appearance of sympathy for a new "model," represented by a few countries that have apparently achieved economic success based on private enterprise, but accompanied by political repression. The United States and the West will doubtless resist such tendencies—ironic consequences of the end of Communism—and Japan may also lend its important influence against them.

The problem of refugees will continue to plague the international system. It is hopeless (and many would say undesirable) to expect a right of free movement and free entry into any country; it is even too much to expect a widely recognized right of asylum. But the principle of *non-refoulement* recognized in the Convention on the Status of Refugees may have become customary law and may apply also to persons who do not satisfy the Convention's special definition of refugee; the principle may yet be extended beyond persons already in a state's territory, to require admission of some refugees in some circumstances. In all, the problem cannot abide neglect: home states will be pressed to help alleviate causes of refugee flow, and other states will be pressed to accept quotas for admission to their territory, or for financial contribution to resettlement elsewhere. The human rights of refugees "in orbit"—in transit or in countries of first haven—have to be developed.

The resistances of the state system will be strong, and shifting values will continue to be in tension in efforts to address world poverty, perhaps the most troubling issue on the international agenda—and therefore also on the international law agenda—for the decades ahead.

A Law Agenda for the Turn of the Century

It would seem reasonable for the political system to address the change in world order by reexamining developments in international law during the Cold War with a view to overcoming the obstacles and eliminating other baneful influences of ideological conflict. There is little evidence of any disposition to do so: in the unorganized (or hardly organized) state system, it is difficult enough to make law in response to pressing, particular needs.

Speculation about change in international law during the decades ahead might consider an agenda under three headings:

- pending business: the conclusion of ongoing efforts and pursuit of present trends;
- the world agenda: common problems crying to be addressed;
- the divided agenda: the problems that seem urgent to some states but on which the world is divided and the international system therefore resistant.

Pending Business

In the decades ahead, one can expect, states will strive to complete the recent agenda, to resolve remaining issues and fill lacunae. Specifically, briefly:

The law of the sea has desperately needed to be restabilized on the basis hammered out during 20 years; it might be stabilized as customary law but it was preferable by far to bring into effect the 1982 Convention with the modifications necessary to overcome powerful resistance (especially by the United States). In July 1994 the stumbling block to universal agreement—the provisions of the 1982 Convention on the Law of the Sea on mining the sea-bed beyond national jurisdiction—was apparently removed by some accommodation, because mining appeared not to be economically interesting for decades ahead and political passions engendered by those issues had abated, both in the United States and in the Third World. With the obstacle to wide, general ratification removed, the law of the sea should achieve stability and discourage additional derogations from freedom and commonage.

Even if the 1982 Convention comes into effect for states generally, experience in the exclusive economic zones of various coastal states may bring some further erosion of the freedom of the seas. States pursuing navigation (including military navigation) will resist interference with freedom to navigate in the exclusive economic zones, but freedom of research there (and in territorial seas) has been languishing. One may hope for success for the efforts to restore and strengthen the tradition of freedom of such research, through cooperation in research and through transfer of technology and data. Even more threatening is the prospect of new claims by coastal states, such as Chile's claim, advanced in 1993, to an interest in a "presential sea"[2] (*mar presencial*)—high seas claimed to be of "special interest" to a coastal state. Chile claimed that its "presential sea" was intended to protect the economic dimensions of its EEZ and its territorial sea, and to promote its economic development generally; Chile claimed that it would be entitled to participate in and observe activities by other states in that sea. Such claims have met strong resistance. One may hope that general ratification of the 1982 Convention will prevent such further threats to the commonage.

Pending (or continuing) business of another kind will have to be addressed and at least receive greater clarification. Some of it is of major importance: the law on the use of force needs to be attended to. With the end of the Cold War and less pressure for Big Power interventions and counter-interventions, some clarification in that law, and some answers to questions not answered in the *Nicaragua* case, become more likely.[3] When the United Nations succeeded in reversing the Iraqi invasion of Kuwait, the law of the Charter was enforced and the Security Council revived, became activist, and expanded its authority. In Somalia, in the former Yugoslavia, in Cambodia (against the Khmer Rouge), against Libya (over the Lockerbie affair), in Haiti, the Council's actions have raised issues as to the meaning and scope of "threat to international peace and security," as to whether there are limits on Security Council determinations, decisions and actions, and whether the International Court of Justice or the General Assembly might have a voice in setting such limits. In the former Yugoslavia, hostilities and ethnic cleansing raised issues aggravated by uncertainties as to statehood and state borders, and long dormant questions in the law of state succession. These events gave sharp relevance to questions as to the permissibility of humanitarian intervention by individual states, by groups (such as the members of NATO or the Conference on Security and Cooperation in Europe), or by the United Nations. Terrible events in the former Yugoslavia also gave relevance to issues under the Geneva Convention and the Nuremburg principles on crimes against humanity, and the law and procedures governing war-crimes.

The end of the Cold War and growing cooperation between the United States and the states of the former U.S.S.R. should help reaffirm the original values and the original interpretation of the law of the Charter. Might it also help mobilize the force of law for the battle against terrorism, which is destructive of both state and human values, and which every state publicly condemns but which a few states continue to promote or condone? Can there be new law, and general agreement to enforce existing law, to bring the few states responsible for or tolerant of terrorism into the network of prevention, deterrence and punishment?

Law is not only for major disorders. For the student of international law, there is need for clearer law if not new law for resolving conflicts in the exercise of jurisdiction. Some conflicts will be accommodated by agreement, some by acquiescence in what other states initiate. The principle of "reasonableness"—by that or some other name—is, I believe, irresistible. It is also time for the multinational corporation to be brought out from the primitive framework of concepts of territoriality and nationality. Nationality is a concept that has meaning and vitality for state relations to individual human beings, but its origins in state "sovereignty" render it suspect and in need of some rethinking; it will have to be replaced, modified, or adapted to state relations to companies with multiple centres and innumerable inter-corporate relationships. The same multi-corporate relationships may suggest different results for different purposes. An "international companies law" seems unlikely, but guidelines and codes of behaviour are developing and need clarification and codification. The concept of territoriality will have to be adapted when it is to be applied to integrated activities in a world economy which disregards state lines, or to drug conspiracies that flout laws of several states and even involve state governments.

There are other problems that await solution or resolution: I suggest a brief agenda which is only a sampling. The law of the moon and outer space is far from resolved. Does outer space need to be defined, and what should be its definition? Claims of equatorial states to the Geostationary Orbit may yet be revived and will need to be addressed. Disputes in the polar regions have been shelved, not resolved, and they may not long remain quiescent if the pursuit of mineral wealth there becomes economically interesting. With increasing pragmatism, some of the harsh lines of dualism may be further blurred: more states will incorporate customary law and treaties; more states will re-examine the place of international law in the hierarchy of national jurisprudence. Is it time, perhaps, to seek co-ordination and harmonization?

And—in a random sampling—there is need for clarification of the law on national execution of arbitral awards. The role of equity and equitable principles has seen new life as a result of the need to delimit zones in the sea. The dispute over the measure of compensation for nationalization of foreign properties is quiescent but may flare again. The law of remedies needs development, including the definition and formalization of permissible self-help.

The World Agenda

I have mentioned major issues on the common world agenda that need further resolution or clarification—the law of the sea; intervention and counterintervention; terrorism, etc. Other international problems need new law, or additional law, or renewed commitment to existing law. Some world problems are not attended to in the study of international law but ought to be.

Arms Control

The control of armaments is on every state's agenda but it stands higher with some states than with others, and there are differences amongst states as to which arms of which states should be regulated, by what means, on what terms. The super-Powers had negotiated strategic arms limitations and limits on troops and conventional weapons in Europe, and delicate complex negotiations concluded successor agreements with the states that succeeded the U.S.S.R. Such negotiations are hardly the concern of international lawyers generally, but agreements that emerge are law, most-important law, that affect our lives as human beings, as citizens and as lawyers. Like other arms control agreements in the past, new agreements may include novel undertakings, establish novel machinery to verify and induce compliance, and raise novel issues of interpretation.

The super-Powers were united in their desire to prevent nuclear proliferation but in the past their different predilections, their rivalries and their competitive relations with other countries prevented them from effective co-operation to prevent new members from joining "the nuclear club." What new forms of co-operation, among which states, need now to be designed to prevent or deter proliferation? Other Powers that have nuclear or other advanced technology to export doubtless do not wish to see it put to military uses, but they seem to be more sanguine about the danger, or perhaps less hopeful that it can be prevented; they do not wish to disturb friendly relations with states eager to buy, or to sacrifice a highly lucrative export market and a continuing participation in major technological development. Armaments, both nuclear and conventional, have become a hallmark of prestige and influence, a key investment of buyers, a major industry for sellers. For too many countries, armaments are a political lever in the region and a bulwark against domestic change. The dismemberment of the U.S.S.R. and of Yugoslavia has led to extended hostilities that have inspired an urgent quest for weapons, and ready sources of supply, open or clandestine. Can, will, the system produce necessary law to control these dangers? Will it help particular states in the difficult task of confining their military to the barracks so as to secure constitutional government?

The World Environment

The world environment has suffered deterioration as a result of human activities for centuries, perhaps since history began; deterioration has accelerated with industrialization, modernization and radical technological advance. In recent years deterioration has reached frightening proportions.

Contrary to some impressions there is substantial international law on the environment and it continues to grow at an accelerating pace.[4] That law includes:

- agreements against pollution of the commonage of the seas;
- conventions for the protection of the atmosphere, ozone layer and global climate;
- obligations relating to trade in endangered species and the protection of the world's natural and genetic resources;
- norms governing the transboundary movement of hazardous wastes and for protection against nuclear and other transboundary accidents;
- agreements that require attention, in the planning process, to activities within a state that are likely to cause significant adverse transboundary impact;
- obligations of all states under customary international law to refrain from emitting pollution materials, to observe generally accepted international rules and standards, to warn other states, to cooperate in prevention and cleaning up, to compensate for injury.

The environment achieved a place on the international agenda at Stockholm in 1972 and international bodies have addressed it in small quiet ways, but mobilized effort languished and deterioration continued to outstrip agreed remedies. Scientists have continued to proclaim ever more ominous warnings but scientific uncertainty has sometimes made agreement on causes and solutions difficult. Agreement is also made difficult by attempts to assign liability for damage and to apportion remedial costs. The international system, however, appears to be moving from an often ineffective liability/remedial approach to environmental problem-solving to a more preventive approach; it is more effective to prevent pollution or resource degradation because damages are often irreversible, or reversible only at unacceptable costs.

The "Earth Summit" held in Rio in 1992 (UNCED) was a significant incremental step in the evolution of international environmental law. It signalled that "sustainable development" had achieved a place on the environmental agenda and endorsed democratic environmental decision-making as a fundamental premise of sustainability. At the same time, UNCED did not introduce a "New International Ecological Order" as some had hoped. The normative content of some of the UNCED instruments were disappointing and differences between developed and developing states curtailed significant progress on some critical issues, including financing of global environmental protection measures, transfer of technology, and control of natural resources.

As the Rio Conference reemphasized, the international law of the environment has to move far beyond where it is, to face issues beyond those of transborder pollution, marine pollution, weather modification, contamination of outer space, polar areas and common water resources. The international system has to address the environment in its relationship to development, to trade, to human rights, with which international law is familiar, as well as traditionally "domestic" problems—population growth, depletion of the ozone layer, deforestation, desertification, the preservation of biological diversity. At Rio the needs were recognized but the obstacles to agreement starkly revealed, principally—in few words—the conflicting claims of development and environment and how the costs and other burdens resulting from environmental control shall be distributed.

The world environment provides an urgent law agenda for the international system. We must hope that states will act on that agenda wisely and in time.

Other matters, perhaps of lesser moment, remain unregulated, or inadequately regulated, because, in a system that essentially can legislate only unanimously and with the consent of the regulated, there are conflicts in values, in judgment, or in perceived national interest. Some problems seem so intractable that even states that are most vulnerable to present disorders do not care—or dare—to suggest regulation. Surely, for example, those states that have large oil resources and have in the past exploited their monopoly for great gain (or have used the monopoly as a political weapon), will not agree to economic law regulating cartels or concerted economic boycott. Other states that occasionally dream of emulating the oil states by exploiting their control of other scarce resources will also resist such law, if only from Third World solidarity, at least until they come to see acute danger to themselves from the availability of such economic weapons.

The Divided Agenda

I have suggested items on a common agenda; there are also quests for new law on which the world is divided. In large part that division derives from different degrees of satisfaction and dissatisfaction with the present system by developed and less developed states, particularly with its commitment to liberal, free-market economic principles.

Law Agenda of Developed States

The developed Western states remain reasonably content with the present system and its law, a system based on state autonomy and the need for state consent. a liberal system with a free-market economy. Especially since they remain a small minority in the system, developed states protect their autonomy by refusing to accept majority rule in bodies that are to have power, for example, the United Nations Security Council, and by refusing to grant authority to bodies that operate by majority, for example, the United Nations General Assembly.[5]

They protect their authority by seeking law that would reinforce the international system as they have known it and its values of stability and order. Those values, they insist, are not theirs alone but, perhaps because they have more to lose, developed states are more strongly committed to pursuing them.

Terrorism. Developed states have sought to reinforce traditional law holding states responsible for acts of terrorism originating in their territory; they have sought universal agreements of co-operation against aerial and related forms of terrorism.[6] But while all governments recognize their own vulnerability to terrorism, and almost all join in decrying it, international law to deal with it effectively has been slow in coming. Every cause which different terrorist groups claim to represent has evoked some governmental support or condonation; in particular, some governments continue to resist outlawing those who terrorize under the banner of "self-determination," "people's liberation," or other slogans of a "new political order." The conventions designed to protect aviation have been adhered to by many states but a fully effective international law against such terrorism would require agreement by virtually all states to prevent potential hijackers or saboteurs from preparing and arming for their venture, to deny them haven, to punish them severely or extradite them to states that will do so. Terrorists have in fact been justified in their confidence that they would find some country to harbour them. (In the past, some libertarian countries, too, have been reluctant to agree to law that would require them to deny asylum to a refugee who hijacks a plane to escape tyranny.)

Pollution Control.   Environmental protection is on the world agenda, a common need not a parochial one, but developed states have been more eager than poorer countries to reverse the tides of pollution and restore and maintain the world ecology and environment. Even the developed world, however, has been far from united in this effort, for its own commitments are uneven and its interests divided. Maritime states, for example, have resisted measures to defend against, or clean up, "oil spills," measures which coastal states in particular have sought; few states champion the general interest against pollution of the high seas. Developed states have pressed for universal standards to defend against air pollution, and less-developed states have been required to include environmental protection measures in projects for which they sought financing from the World Bank. But developing states continue to resist stringent environmental controls as an obstacle to rapid, less-expensive development and a luxury which, they say, developed states can now afford only after centuries of perpetrating environmental degradation.

The Open Market.   The developed states wish to improve the economic system they have had. They seek to maintain substantial autonomy and *laissez-faire* in trade and finance, in a substantially free market, calibrated by co-operative mechanisms like the International Monetary Fund, GATT and similar institutions in which the developed states have a dominant say and maintain their essential autonomy. The developed states have also continued to insist on the integrity of the properties and investments of their nationals in other countries. They are prepared to consider increasing their aid to poorer countries if others—including the former Communist Powers and the "Third World rich"—will also do their share, but they insist that foreign aid is voluntary, and they resist any attempt to impose a legal obligation upon them to extend such aid. They have finally recognized the debt problem, an impossible burden for the poor states and painful too for the lending rich, and they are pressing for alleviating measures, but within the voluntary, market system.

Social Problems.   The Western world has sought universal co-operation for population control. Third World states have resisted external programmes to that end, and coercive conditions on foreign assistance, as improper interference in their internal affairs. Some societies also have religious and other cultural objections to population control; some purport to see in such programmes racism and even genocide, and an effort by the developed world to deny the Third World the population they need for development and security.

The Western world has sought universal attacks on other social problems—the remnants of slavery, slave trade and forced labour, the oppression of women and children, illiteracy. Some in the Third World have closed their eyes to some of these ills (even to abiding slavery). Some poor states have been prepared to receive aid to alleviate these and other social problems, but they resist strict scrutiny or other strings even by international bodies (such as ILO, WHO, UNESCO). The developed world has also sought law to assure freedom of international communication, whether through audio-visual or print media, and cultural exchange. The Third World has sometimes seen these efforts as forms of cultural imperialism, and some states have asserted the need to protect their cultural heritage from foreign cultural corruption.

Third World Agenda

The Third World law agenda is the agenda of the poor majority of states. As a majority with a significant measure of solidarity, its members have sought to create new institutions in which majorities rule (an end they pursued during negotiations at the Conference on the Law of the Sea). and to increase the powers of existing institutions in which majorities rule, such as the United Nations General Assembly. In those efforts they have met the firm resistance of powerful states, rooted in the traditions of the system, in the principles of state autonomy and the need for state consent. And even poorer states, generally part of the majority, have been reluctant to accept principles of community rule and derogations from their autonomy.

New states joined—willingly, eagerly—a system with established traditions and laws. At one time, the new states and their fellows in the Third World asserted a right to re-examine international law and the international legal system and to take full part in its codification, development or modification. In essentials, new states were bound by what they found; in essentials, they favoured what they found.

The Third World has in fact left important marks on contemporary international law. It has put political self-determination as well as sovereignty over natural resources ("economic self-determination") at the head of both the International Covenant on Civil and Political Rights and the International Covenant on Economic, Social and Cultural Rights, over objections that these were not rights of individuals and therefore did not belong in either Covenant. The Third World made the Convention on the

Elimination of All Forms of Racial Discrimination perhaps the strongest human rights convention and has influenced many states to adhere to it. The Third World can properly claim credit for the demise of apartheid and the establishment of majority rule in South Africa. The Third World has reasserted the favoured norm of small Powers—non-intervention in internal affairs—and has had it enshrined in new declarations and treaties.

Even when the developing states have had less than full success in their efforts to reshape the law, they have not left it unaffected. Though international law continues to require just compensation for nationalized foreign properties, capital importing states have succeeded in reshaping the facts if not the law of investment: capital exporters now hesitate to rely on that law, and prefer to address the issues of nationalization by special agreements. Similarly, Third World states have not succeeded in building strong international legal defences against the power of multinational enterprises but they are finding comfort in what they can do by national legislation, co-operative arrangements and United Nations guidelines.

The principal item on the Third World agenda continues to be development, primarily economic development, and escape from the law of the market. Developing states have sought relief from existing debts and carrying charges and better terms for new debts; they want grants instead of loans. They have sought new trade and aid patterns—higher prices for their raw materials, lower prices for fuel and for the industrial products they must buy, and access to sophisticated technology on favourable terms. They have sought these by law, as of right and without strings, not by grace or charity of developed state, not under Western tutelage and scrutiny. By new international arrangements and agreements based on "welfare principles" rather than free-market *laissez-faire,* the majority has hoped to satisfy basic human needs for their people, narrow the gulf between rich and poor states, accelerate economic modernization for all, and bring the fruits of science and technology everywhere. That has been the significance of the demand for a new international economic order.

The New Economic Order is not likely to come soon and it has nearly disappeared from Third World rhetoric, but a new economic order is continually in process, an order made up of discrete steps, some small, some larger—some preferences in trade, some debt relief, some financial assistance—within the present liberal free-market system.

The two agendas I have described reflect different perspectives and different needs—wants—by different states in a system of states. In a system committed to autonomy and consent, new law is not easy to make. Failure of agreement on matters where values are not commonly shared— notably those governing the economy—prevents agreement also on matters of common interest on the world agenda—the world environment, arms control. Compromise, accommodation, will doubtless come on some matters, not soon on others.

Conclusion

The international system is not in perfect health and its law reflects the system's weaknesses. The hopes of 1945 for a peaceful world are frayed and the law on the use of force is in some disarray. The interdependence of states demands international ecological and economic regulation but there has been insufficient success in achieving it. Technological advance continues to aggravate inequalities, but there is no law and there are no legal institutions to make the economic system more just and efficient, to reduce gross inequalities, or even to create a minimal "welfare system" that would assure the basic human needs of all five billion inhabitants of the earth. Some new important law can be anticipated. One can expect some firm agreement on the law of the sea. One can hope for an emergence of political forces that would result in a universal law against terrorism.

There is little basis for expecting radical change in the law generally: one cannot predict the unpredictable. State values which are intrinsic to the state system will not be easily sacrificed. States will remain reluctant to give up their autonomy and their right to withhold consent to international regulation. The system shows no signs of moving to community.

Only one subject still on the distant horizon perhaps warrants bold speculation. Increasingly we are being warned of looming environmental catastrophe. Might urgent necessity move the international system to develop an authentic conception of "commonage" in the global environment and reflect that conception in law?

A concept of commonage, and a law of commonage, have long been with us. For centuries a system of states defined by territory accepted a commonage beyond their territories, the commonage of the seas. As technology brought additional "extraterritorial" spaces into the ken of human activity, principles of commonage were extended to the extraterritorial air space, then to the moon, planets, and outer space. Conceptions of commonage have burgeoned also in the polar regions of the earth. The idea of commonage brought some law of commonage. Under international law, extraterritorial commonage has been everybody's or nobody's. In the seas, commonage came to mean "the common heritage of mankind" though to date without final, universal agreement as to what that entails.

But increasingly we are beginning to recognize a different commonage, a common heritage not in the earth's resources but in the earth itself, in the global environment and in its preservation for future generations. That commonage is not extraterritorial, or not only extraterritorial; it is within as well as without state territory; it is affected by what states do and do not do both inside their territories and beyond them. Might global danger require a new conception of commonage, one that supports international regulation that is not only extraterritorial, one that cannot wait on universal enlightenment to bring universal consent to what may be essential? The international system has accepted regulation that penetrates and permeates societies for the human values of human rights; might it have to accept even more intrusive regulation, more intrusive enforcement, and radical forms of international financing, for human survival?

A basic international order is in place, reflecting established customary law, confirmed and extended by contemporary multi-lateral treaties and by a network of bilateral arrangements. A remarkable international human rights law is in place representing an irreversible commitment to human values and *pro tanto* erosion of state values. For the rest, the mythology of sovereignty and the commitment to state autonomy and impermeability are still major obstacles to making needed law and to effective enforcement of some law that has been made, for example, in human rights. The international system—and the rules and the politics of law-making—favour state autonomy, *laissez-faire*. That leaves many needs of the system and of individual countries unmet. There is urgent need for some new law, an instrument of politics, and there can be no effective law if politics does not will it. There is urgent need for better enforcement machinery, but there can be no such machinery if politics does not will it. Political will to make and induce compliance with law requires general agreement, which requires a will by some—the rich, the mighty, the wise, the brave—to lead, and by all—including the many poor—to join and help.

Notes

1. *Military and Paramilitary Activities in and Against Nicaragua* case *(Nicaragua* v. *United States), ICJ* (1986), p. 14 (Merits).

2. Chile's claim to a presential sea would cover more than 19,967,000 kilometers (8 million square miles) of high seas.

3. One must hope that the United States invasion of Panama in December 1989 and attempts to justify the action will not engender new uncertainties in the law.

4. Indeed some suggest that it is time to slow the rate of negotiating international environmental agreements and to concentrate on effectively implementing those already concluded.

5. For example, developed states joined in some sanctions against the Republic of South Africa but did so only voluntarily, by consent, to the extent they deemed it expedient; they did not consent to end all trade or to impose other sanctions that might have proved expensive to those who imposed them.

6. An attempt to conclude a general convention on terrorism has not yet succeeded. See. e.g., Measures to Prevent International Terrorism, GA Res. 44/29 (1989). Despite efforts by some states, the resolution did not call for a conference to define terrorism.

Index

About the Book

This anthology presents classic and contemporary essays covering such enduring subjects of international law as treaties and international courts, as well as the newly developing areas of the environment, human rights, and war crimes.

Reflecting the fact that national leaders increasingly must balance considerations of domestic politics with a sensitivity to international legal concerns, the collection includes theoretical and policy perspectives encompassing political as well as legal and philosophical frameworks. Designed to appeal to audiences in both law and political science, the readings distinguish between the elements of international law that function as an "operating system" to mediate disputes among specific nations and those that work as a normative, prescriptive device to resolve problems of concern to the broader global community.

Charlotte Ku is executive vice president and executive director of the American Society of International Law. **Paul F. Diehl** is professor of political science at the University of Illinois at Urbana-Champaign.